THE COLONIAL RECORDS OF NORTH CAROLINA

[Second Series]

Volume I	*North Carolina Charters and Constitutions, 1578–1698*, edited by Mattie Erma Edwards Parker
Volume II	*North Carolina Higher-Court Records, 1670–1696*, edited by Mattie Erma Edwards Parker
Volume III	*North Carolina Higher-Court Records, 1697–1701*, edited by Mattie Erma Edwards Parker
Volume IV	*North Carolina Higher-Court Records, 1702–1708*, edited by William S. Price Jr.
Volume V	*North Carolina Higher-Court Records, 1709–1723*, edited by William S. Price Jr.
Volume VI	*North Carolina Higher-Court Records, 1724–1730*, edited by Robert J. Cain
Volume VII	*Records of the Executive Council, 1664–1734*, edited by Robert J. Cain
Volume VIII	*Records of the Executive Council, 1735–1754*, edited by Robert J. Cain
Volume IX	*Records of the Executive Council, 1755–1775*, edited by Robert J. Cain
Volume X	*The Church of England in North Carolina: Documents, 1699–1741*, edited by Robert J. Cain
Volume XI	*The Church of England in North Carolina: Documents, 1742–1763*, edited by Robert J. Cain and Jan-Michael Poff

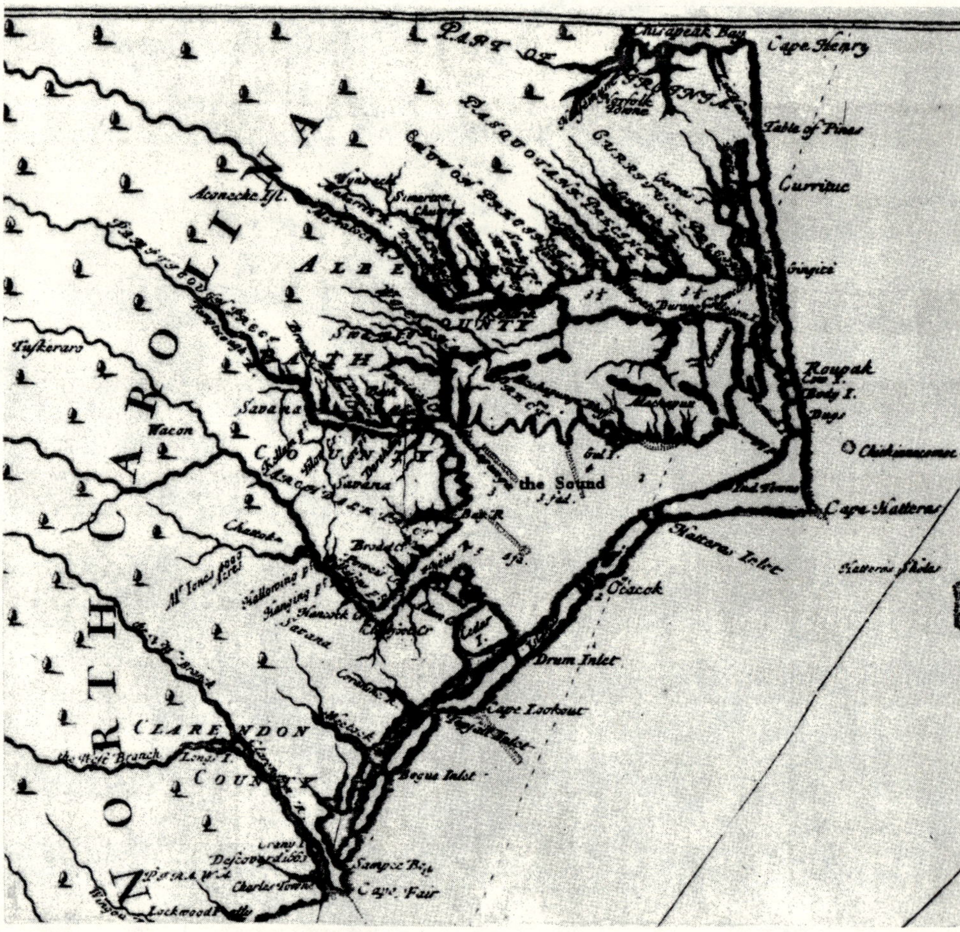

Section of a Map of Carolina by John Lawson, 1709

THE COLONIAL RECORDS OF NORTH CAROLINA
[Second Series]

VOLUME IV

NORTH CAROLINA HIGHER-COURT RECORDS 1702-1708

WILLIAM S. PRICE, JR., *Editor*

Assisted by RUTH CLOW LANGSTON AND DONNA HOLMES GOSWICK

DEPARTMENT OF CULTURAL RESOURCES
DIVISION OF ARCHIVES AND HISTORY
RALEIGH, NORTH CAROLINA
1974

Reprinted, 2008

Library of Congress Catalog Card Number 74-620060
ISBN 978-0-86526-025-2

Printed by Theo Davis Printing

Acknowledgment is hereby made to Dr. Jerry C. Cashion for the gracious donation of funds to assist in reprinting this volume.

Table of Contents

Illustrations

Preface

Persons using this volume of *The Colonial Records of North Carolina* will notice some changes in format from the three previous volumes which have appeared in the series. Henceforth, volumes will be numbered and the series will be called *The Colonial Records of North Carolina* [Second Series] in order to distinguish it from the ten volume series of the same title issued from 1886 to 1890, under the editorship of William L. Saunders.

The Advisory Editorial Board for this series has not met since December, 1965, and will no longer be listed in the front matter of subsequent volumes. Its members: John Alden, Lester J. Cappon, Lambert Davis, W. Edwin Hemphill, Cecil Johnson, Hugh T. Lefler, William S. Powell, David Stick, and Robert H. Woody performed major services in the early days of the series. They suggested priorities for publication, the form which letterpress volumes should take, archival agencies to be searched for potentially relevant material, and countless other items based on their own experiences in historical research, editing, and publishing. The Colonial Records Project owes a great debt of gratitude to these men and takes this occasion to express a portion of it.

At the close of August, 1971, Mrs. Mattie Erma Edwards Parker retired from a decade of service as editor of the Colonial Records Project. Those persons who have used her three earlier volumes in this series know the precision of her work and the meticulousness of her scholarship. What they cannot know is the thoroughness with which she presided over the inventory of nearly a half million manuscripts relating to colonial North Carolina, located primarily within the state, but also scattered to such diverse places as Texas, Michigan, and California. I have tried to adhere to the editorial standards set by Mrs. Parker in the three previous volumes. In fact, much of the initial organization of this volume was done before she retired. Some minor changes in procedure have been made between publication of the earlier volumes and the present one; they are explained in the "Editorial Method" section of the introduction which follows.

The staff of the Colonial Records Project wishes to express its warm thanks to Mrs. Memory F. Mitchell, chief, Historical Publications Section of the North Carolina Division of Archives and History. Her encouragement and technical skill have been most helpful. In addition, Mrs. Mitchell is a licensed attorney and her answers to certain legal questions growing out of the material have solved a number of dilemmas.

The editor acknowledges with gratitude the advice of Dr. William H. Willis of the Department of Classical Studies at Duke University in expanding certain Latin abbreviations. Dr. Herbert R. Paschal of East Carolina University, Mr. William S. Powell of the University of North Carolina at Chapel Hill, and Mrs. Mattie Erma Edwards Parker have read most of the introductory matter to this volume. Their useful criticisms have saved me from some careless errors; what errors may remain are solely mine. My mentor and friend, Dr. R. D. Higginbotham of the University of North Carolina at Chapel Hill, has helped me in ways too numerous to list.

Much of the routine but essential work of the Colonial Records Project has been facilitated by excellent liaison with Mr. C. F. W. Coker, former chief, Archives and Records Section, and Mr. Paul P. Hoffman, head, Archives Branch, and their fine staff. Dr. H. G. Jones, state historian and director of the Division of Archives and History, has shown consistent understanding and a steady appreciation of the Colonial Records Project.

Finally, I wish to thank my brother, Reynolds, who knows the reasons why. My wife, Pia, and my daughters, Marie Elizabeth and Katherine, have been patient with the peculiarities of a historical editor. But most of all, they have been nice to go home to at the end of the day.

January 19, 1974 William S. Price, Jr.

Introduction to the Volume

THE DOCUMENTS IN THIS VOLUME

This volume contains records of the higher courts of the North Carolina colony for the period beginning January 1, 1702, and ending December 31, 1708. With a few exceptions, all of the documents were transcribed from manuscripts held by the North Carolina Office of Archives and History, Raleigh. The exceptions are microfilm copies of documents made at the Chowan County Courthouse, Edenton, in 1941. Apparently, those documents no longer exist in manuscript form. The microfilm was made by the Genealogical Society of Utah, and a copy of it is at the Office of Archives and History, Raleigh. Although in previous volumes in this series, it was necessary to resort frequently to the microfilm, fewer documents were lost for the period after 1701 than for earlier years. All Chowan County Courthouse records of the colonial period were transferred to Raleigh in the fall of 1961.

In volume III of this series, *North Carolina Higher-Court Records, 1697-1701,* all of the General Court dockets, minutes, and recorded papers were contained in a single bound folio volume of manuscripts designated CCR 102 at the Office of Archives and History. Such a situation does not exist in the present volume. Dockets, minutes, and recorded papers, where available, have been taken from various locations as the variety of shelf numbers preceding these entries indicates. In some instances it has been necessary to use rough notes (called scratch minutes) taken by the clerk of court where no finished minutes were available. Where finished minutes do exist, no scratch minutes have been printed even though they are available in some instances. No General Court dockets are extant for the years 1707 and 1708, with the exception of one which appears within the minutes for July, 1708. Likewise, no minutes (nor any other papers) occur for the October, 1708, General Court; those fragmentary pieces of the March, 1708, session are too mutilated to transcribe. Chancery records are very sparse throughout the period. Two explanations for the disrupted state of the records for 1702 through 1708 seem likely. Beginning in 1704, North Carolina underwent a period of extreme disruption beginning with the Anglican-dissenter struggle, followed by the Cary Rebellion, and closing with the Tuscarora War, which ended early in 1715.[1] These

[1] For a discussion of these events, see pp. xxiv-xxx, below.

troubles, coupled with the lack of either a fixed courthouse or a capitol, could explain the absence of many records and the paucity of others.[2] In addition, the manuscript collection called CCR 102 contains the following notation: "Memorandum it appears that All the Records of the Court from March 1707 to March [1711] which Includes the time wherein Mr. Moseley presided in the Generall Court is all taken out and destroyed."[3] As readers of this volume can see, Moseley may have indeed destroyed some of the records from 1707 to 1711, but he certainly did not annihilate all of them.

Papers of the governor and council clearly relating to matters in executive session are not included in this volume. Such documents are sometimes filed in archival collections of court materials, since many of them are phrased in judicial language and since the clerk of the General Court in this period was usually clerk of the council also. Collections CCR 187 and CCR 192 in Raleigh contain many council papers in addition to higher-court records. This material is comprised primarily of petitions concerning road repairs, initial land surveys or corrections to earlier ones, and Indian affairs.

With the possible exceptions of land grants and wills, existing court records contain the fullest account of the North Carolina colony prior to about 1715 when council and assembly records begin to appear with some regularity; governor's papers remain scarce throughout the proprietary period. Therefore, as was the policy in volumes II and III of this series, virtually every extant record which applies to this volume has been printed.[4] Undoubtedly, this leads to a sense of repetition for anyone who might wish to read through this book; but the Advisory Editorial Board believed that because so little was known about the

---

[2] Conditions under which these records were kept in proprietary North Carolina are treated in H. G. Jones, *For History's Sake: The Preservation and Publication of North Carolina History, 1663-1903* (Chapel Hill: University of North Carolina Press, 1966), 3-23, hereinafter cited as Jones, *For History's Sake*. In addition, there are no dockets, minutes, or recorded papers of higher courts for the years 1709 through 1710. There are dated file papers for those two years, primarily in CCR 139 and CCR 191, addressed to both the General Court and the Court of Chancery. However, these file papers, when viewed alone without the supporting dockets and minutes, do not prove that higher courts sat during 1709 through 1710. In all likelihood, if higher courts met at all in the two year period, they did so without the usual regularity.

[3] Jones, *For History's Sake*, 18, contains a transcription of this memorandum which renders the latter year as 1715. The staff of the Colonial Records Project, however, reads it as 1711; and considering the abundance of higher-court records after 1710, such a reading seems correct. From March, 1711, through the final proprietary court session in July, 1730, there is (with the exception of four sessions) an unbroken record of General Court minutes. The editor has not been able to identify the author of the memorandum in CCR 102, but the handwriting is definitely an eighteenth century script.

[4] Documents which cannot be ascribed definitely to higher courts have been omitted from this volume as have a few manuscripts which very nearly duplicate others.

first half century of permanently settled North Carolina, every available document should be published. This editor, as did Mrs. Parker before him, agrees with the recommendation of the board and has followed it.

THE NORTH CAROLINA COLONY, 1702-1708

A recent authority has estimated that the white and black population of North Carolina in 1700 was 10,720; by 1710 the figure had grown to 15,120. Since 1665 the Lords Proprietors had authorized a grant of fifty acres to every person who brought a slave above the age of fourteen into the colony. While Reverend John Urmston in 1709 rated the percentage of Negroes in North Carolina at one sixth of the whites, a more recent estimate of black population cites only 415 Negroes in 1700 increasing to 900 a decade later. In addition to the white and black population, about 5,000 Indians dwelt on the colony's coastal plain; roughly 80 percent of these were members of the Tuscarora tribe.[1]

North Carolina colonists resided in two loosely defined settlements along the rivers and streams emptying into the Albemarle and Pamlico sounds. The more northern and older of the two settlements consisted of four precincts which had been established by 1668 as parts of the County of Albemarle. Although Albemarle County ceased to be recognized as a governmental unit in 1689, the term continued to be applied to the area composed of the four precincts of Chowan, Currituck, Pasquotank, and Perquimans well into the eighteenth century.[2] Since 1670 these precincts had been authorized to elect five representatives each to the lower house of assembly. Beginning in 1696 when writs of election were issued to precincts other than those in Albemarle, such units were allowed only two assemblymen apiece and, in rare cases, three. The resulting inequity in representation, which favored the Albemarle region above any other, would cause a political upheaval in the colony

[1] United States Bureau of the Census, *Historical Statistics of the United States, Colonial Times to 1957* (Washington: Government Printing Office, 1961), 756; John Spencer Bassett, *Slavery and Servitude in the Colony of North Carolina* (Baltimore: Johns Hopkins Press [Fourteenth Series, Volumes IV-V of the *Johns Hopkins University Studies in Historical and Political Science*], 1896), 17, 19; Mattie Erma Edwards Parker (ed.), *North Carolina Higher-Court Records, 1697-1701,* [Volume III] of *The Colonial Records of North Carolina* [Second Series], edited by Mattie Erma Edwards Parker and William S. Price, Jr. (Raleigh: Office of Archives and History [projected multivolume series, 1963—]), xii, hereinafter cited as Parker, *Higher-Court Records,* III. For the uncertainties involved in estimating colonial populations, see Wesley Frank Craven, *The Colonies in Transition, 1660-1713* (New York: Harper and Row, 1968), 15-16, 350-351, hereinafter cited as Craven, *Colonies in Transition.*

[2] Parker, *Higher-Court Records,* III, xii-xiii; David Leroy Corbitt, *The Formation of the North Carolina Counties, 1663-1943* (Raleigh: State Department of Archives and History, Revised Edition, 1969), xxiii, hereinafter cited as Corbitt, *Formation of North Carolina Counties.*

during the middle of the eighteenth century.[3] The County of Bath was formed in 1696 and nine years later had become sufficiently populous to be divided into three precincts: Archdale, Pamptecough, and Wickham. At some time prior to 1712, the names of these precincts were changed respectively to Craven, Beaufort, and Hyde. About 1705 a small group of Huguenots from Virginia settled in Bath County. As the county grew, communities sprang up along the south shore of the Pamlico River. On March 8, 1705/6, one of these settlements was incorporated as the township of Bath by the General Assembly. Among the town's first commissioners was John Lawson, explorer and author of *A New Voyage to Carolina*, who may have engineered the drive for incorporation.[4]

Long before the representation controversy over the disproportionately large Albemarle delegation in the assembly, there was hostility between the newer precincts of Bath and the older ones to the North. The two regions were separated by forty miles of dense, uninhabited wilderness. Overland transportation between Albemarle and Bath was virtually nonexistent, and waterborne traffic was irregular at best.[5] Inhabitants of the Albemarle region dominated the major provincial offices, and the unofficial seat of government during the years 1702 through 1708 was a settlement at Little River on the border between Pasquotank and Perquimans precincts. Finally, the commerce of the Albemarle precincts revolved around trade through Virginia and the Atlantic; the Bath precincts tended to look westward and southward to an Indian trade.

The religious composition of North Carolina was varied. Since 1669 the Fundamental Constitutions had promised a high degree of toleration in the colony. Freemen were required merely to acknowledge God's existence as well as the need for public and solemn worship. Any seven persons of like beliefs could form a church, and officials could take oaths of office by affirmation rather than by swearing. Subsequent

---

[3] Lawrence F. London, "The Representation Controversy in Colonial North Carolina," *North Carolina Historical Review*, XI (October, 1934), 264.

[4] Samuel A'Court Ashe, *History of North Carolina, 1584-1925* (Greensboro and Raleigh: Charles L. Van Noppen and Edwards and Broughton, 2 volumes, 1925), I, 161, hereinafter cited as Ashe, *History of North Carolina;* Herbert R. Paschal, Jr., *A History of Colonial Bath* (Raleigh: Edwards and Broughton Company, 1955), 5-7, hereinafter cited as Paschal, *Colonial Bath*; Petitions made by inhabitants of Wickham and Archdale precincts requesting that vestries and county courts be established in their boundaries are contained in Albemarle County Papers, 1678-1714, Volume II, CR 2.002, State Archives, Office of Archives and History, Raleigh, hereinafter cited as CR 2.002.

[5] William L. Saunders (ed.), *The Colonial Records of North Carolina* (Raleigh: State of North Carolina, 10 volumes, 1886-1890), I, 600-603, hereinafter cited as Saunders, *Colonial Records;* Parker, *Higher-Court Records*, III, xii-xiii.

revisions to the Fundamental Constitutions in 1682 and 1698 provided that the legislature should build churches and maintain clergy of the Church of England from public funds, while still tolerating dissenters. Despite the change, the Fundamental Constitutions promised a greater degree of religious toleration than existed in most American colonies.[6]

In reality, most inhabitants of North Carolina had no formal religious affiliation. The largest group of dissenters in the province was the Society of Friends, whose members were called Quakers. Two Anglican missionaries writing in 1708 and 1709 respectively estimated the percentage of Quakers in the colony at between one seventh and one tenth of the whole population. Members of the sect held many important posts in the courts and administrative offices of the province. In 1704 one observer wrote that Quakers controlled the lower house of assembly.[7] While Friends resided throughout the colony, they were most heavily concentrated in Perquimans Precinct. They also were quite numerous in Pasquotank Precinct, but whether they constituted a majority there is unknown.[8] That so many Quakers lived in North Carolina was the result of conversion rather than immigration. The first preacher of any denomination known to have visited the province was William Edmundson, a Friend, who traveled throughout Albemarle in May, 1672. He was followed in October by the famous Quaker leader, George Fox, who spent eighteen days in North Carolina gathering large numbers of converts through his inspired preaching. During the next two decades, several Quaker missionaries entered the colony where their message was received enthusiastically by a population

[6] Mattie Erma Edwards Parker (ed.), *North Carolina Charters and Constitutions, 1578-1698*, [Volume I] of *The Colonial Records of North Carolina* [Second Series], edited by Mattie Erma Edwards Parker and William S. Price, Jr. (Raleigh: Office of Archives and History [projected multivolume series, 1963—]), 148-150, 227-230, 238-239, hereinafter cited as Parker, *Charters and Constitutions;* M. Eugene Sirmans, *Colonial South Carolina: A Political History, 1663-1763* (Chapel Hill: University of North Carolina Press, 1966), 14-15, hereinafter cited as Sirmans, *Colonial South Carolina.* One historian contends that from the earliest days of Carolina the Lords Proprietors were just as committed to establishing the Church of England in their provinces as they were to religious toleration. See R. D. W. Connor, *The Colonial and Revolutionary Periods, 1584-1783,* Volume I of *History of North Carolina,* by R. D. W. Connor, William K. Boyd, J. G. de Roulhac Hamilton, and others (Chicago and New York: Lewis Publishing Company, 6 volumes, 1919), 85, hereinafter cited as Connor, *The Colonial and Revolutionary Periods.*

[7] Saunders, *Colonial Records,* I, 600-603, 686-687, 708-715.

[8] Saunders, *Colonial Records,* I, 689; Hugh Talmage Lefler and Albert Ray Newsome, *North Carolina: The History of a Southern State* (Chapel Hill: University of North Carolina Press, Revised Edition, 1963), 53, hereinafter cited as Lefler and Newsome, *North Carolina.*

without any Anglican minister.[9] Certainly, the zenith of Quakerism in North Carolina occurred in 1694 when John Archdale, a convert of Fox and a proprietor, was made governor. Although he spent most of his time in South Carolina, Archdale personally chose a deputy governor for Albemarle and exempted all Friends from militia duty. By 1700 there were at least three weekly Quaker meetings in the colony: two in Perquimans and one in Pasquotank precincts.[10]

Another dissenting sect in the colony was a group which John Blair, an Anglican missionary in 1704, characterized as "something like Presbyterians."[11] Whether or not Blair was referring to polity or theology in his characterization is unknown. At any rate, the group was not an organized denomination. In cooperation with the Quakers, the sect had formed enough of a political bloc to preserve religious toleration in Albemarle for many years.[12]

Among organized denominations in North Carolina in 1702, adherents of the Church of England were few, but they probably outnumbered the dissenters. When a missionary of the Society for the Propagation of the Gospel (SPG) first entered the colony in 1704, he called vestries together in every precinct. At least three precincts each built a small church and established glebes. They also hired a lay reader whom they paid to conduct two weekly services. Most Anglicans resided in Chowan and Currituck precincts.[13]Regardless of their numerical strength, Church of England men were among the leading figures of the colony, and most of the Lords Proprietors were also Anglicans. By 1700 the four major resident political figures, who were among the wealthiest men in the province, were Anglicans: Samuel Swann, Thomas Pollock, Henderson Walker, and William Glover.[14]

---

[9] Connor, *The Colonial and Revolutionary Periods,* I, 85-86; Rufus M. Jones, *Quakers in the American Colonies* (New York: Russell and Russell, Incorporated, Second Edition, 1962), 285-286, hereinafter cited as Jones, *Quakers in the Colonies;* Francis C. Anscombe, *I Have Called You Friends: The Story of Quakerism in North Carolina* (Boston: Christopher Publishing House, 1959), 59-61, hereinafter cited as Anscombe, *I Have Called You Friends.*

[10] Connor, *The Colonial and Revolutionary Periods,* I, 86; Jones, *Quakers in the Colonies,* 307-308; Stephen B. Weeks, *Religious Development in the Province of North Carolina* (Baltimore: Johns Hopkins Press [Tenth Series, Volume V of the *Johns Hopkins University Studies in Historical and Political Science*], 1892), 33, hereinafter cited as Weeks, *Religious Development in North Carolina.* For an explanation of Quaker beliefs (including prohibitions against swearing oaths and bearing arms) as well as the structure of their meetings, see Anscombe, *I Have Called You Friends,* 35-55.

[11] Saunders, *Colonial Records,* I, 602.

[12] Ashe, *History of North Carolina,* I, 156-159.

[13] Saunders, *Colonial Records,* I, 600-603; Lefler and Newsome, *North Carolina,* 53; Ashe, *History of North Carolina,* I, 159.

[14] Ashe, *History of North Carolina,* I, 151.

When Henderson Walker became chief executive of the colony in 1699, he maneuvered to improve the position of the Church of England. At the urging of the Lords Proprietors, the Vestry Act of 1701 was enacted under his guidance. It provided for the organization of vestries in every precinct, erection of churches, and maintenance of the clergy through a poll tax. The bill had passed by a narrow margin; but two years later the Lords Proprietors disallowed it, not because of its intolerance, but for its inadequate maintenance of the clergy.[15] Despite this reversal, Walker and his fellow Anglicans were encouraged to press on in behalf of their church by the elevation of John Grenville, Baron Granville, to the senior position among the Lords Proprietors in 1701. Granville was a zealous Anglican and much of the subsequent treatment of dissenters in North Carolina and South Carolina was due to his policies and appointments.[16] At this critical juncture in 1701, the Church of England established the Society for the Propagation of the Gospel in Foreign Parts to provide Anglican missionaries to the colonies. Within three years, North Carolina had received an Anglican minister from the society and a large donation of religious books from SPG founder, Thomas Bray.[17]

The quality of life in North Carolina from 1702 through 1708 was crude and provincial. An examination of John Lawson's map of the colony first published in 1709 reveals the nearly complete absence of towns—the one exception being Bath, in which Lawson had a personal interest.[18]Although it ranked as the largest settlement in the province, Bath had only fifty to sixty inhabitants in 1708.[19]

Agriculture was the basis of the North Carolina economy. Several varieties of crops were grown, but the major export commodities were tobacco and corn. Hogs comprised the vast majority of livestock and

---

[15] Weeks, *Religious Development in North Carolina*, 34; Connor, *The Colonial and Revolutionary Periods*, I, 88.

[16] Sirmans, *Colonial South Carolina*, 76-77; William S. Powell, *The Proprietors of Carolina* (Raleigh: Carolina Charter Tercentenary Commission, 1963), 62.

[17] Sirmans, *Colonial South Carolina*, 77; Thomas Bray to unidentified correspondent, undated, Colonial Court Records, Jury Papers, 1676-1760, CCR 188, State Archives, hereinafter cited as CCR 188; Stephen B. Weeks, *Libraries and Literature in North Carolina in the Eighteenth Century* (Washington: Government Printing Office, 1896), 178-179.

[18] For a description of the Lawson map and a catalog of its various copies, see William P. Cumming, *The Southeast in Early Maps* (Chapel Hill: University of North Carolina Press, 1962), 178-179. The coastal portion of the map is reproduced as the frontispiece to this volume.

[19] Harry Roy Merrens, *Colonial North Carolina in the Eighteenth Century: A Study in Historical Geography* (Chapel Hill: University of North Carolina Press, 1964), 154, hereinafter cited as Merrens, *Colonial North Carolina*.

were sometimes driven to Virginia for sale, but much pork and lard were shipped directly from the colony.[20] Peas and beans of several kinds were grown on most farms as a supplement to the farmer's own diet and were sometimes exported. While statistics on the export of tobacco and corn were not kept in early eighteenth century North Carolina, these commodities played a part in both the coastal and transatlantic trade.[21] Overland commerce between Albemarle and Virginia was limited by the lack of good roads. One experienced traveler in 1704 said that the roads in North Carolina were the worst he had seen anywhere. They were often marred by large holes or blocked by fallen trees and branches. Most traffic within the colony as well as outside of it was waterborne, and canoes, small sailing craft, and rowboats were abundant.[22]

Any freeholder in the province could vote in assembly elections. Although no property qualification for the franchise was stated in the Fundamental Constitutions, most freeholders possessed at least fifty acres because of the headright system.[23] Clearly, some planters in the colony, such as Thomas Pollock and Samuel Swann, were men of great wealth. However, their incomes and property would not seem impressive by modern standards, since only £150 a year could support a comfortable existence.[24]

The closing years of the seventeenth century had been tranquil in contrast to the two decades of turmoil preceding them. Reorganization of the government, authorized by the Lords Proprietors in 1691, had produced harmonious results in North Carolina by 1700. Although deputy governors were appointed by the governor in Charleston (then called Charles Town), they needed the consent of at least three resident councillors for most important actions.[25] These councillors, each of

[20] John Lawson, *A New Voyage to Carolina*, edited by Hugh Talmage Lefler (Chapel Hill: University of North Carolina Press, 1967), 80-82, 88, 94, hereinafter cited as Lawson, *New Voyage;* Shipping invoices, February 3 and 8, 1703/4, May 2, 1704, Treasurers' and Comptrollers' Papers, Ports, Port Roanoke, Customs House Papers, 1682-1760, State Archives, Raleigh, hereinafter cited as Roanoke Customs House Papers.

[21] Merrens, *Colonial North Carolina*, 110-111, 120-121; Among the commodities listed for export in records of the period, aside from those mentioned above, are pitch, tar, feathers, barrel staves, wheat, snake root, and bee's wax. See Roanoke Customs House Papers, July 7, 1703, October 20, 1703, February 8, 1703/4.

[22] Saunders, *Colonial Records*, I, 600-603; F. W. Clonts, "Travel and Transportation in Colonial North Carolina," *North Carolina Historical Review*, III (January, 1926), 16-35.

[23] Parker, *Charters and Constitutions*, I, 145.

[24] Michael Garibaldi Hall, *Edward Randolph and the American Colonies, 1676-1703* (Chapel Hill: University of North Carolina Press, 1960), 219, hereinafter cited as Hall, *Randolph and the Colonies*.

[25] Parker, *Higher-Court Records*, III, xi-xiii, xx.

whom was a deputy of one of the Lords Proprietors (and thus sometimes were referred to as lords deputies), made their homes and livings in the colony. To a large degree, they provided a permanence to government and possessed a knowledge of internal affairs unavailable to a novice dispatched from Charleston. In the absence of a deputy governor, the president of the council, chosen by a vote of his peers, would serve as chief executive. During 1702 through 1708, two chief executives of North Carolina were deputy governors, Robert Daniel and Thomas Cary; while three were presidents of the council, Henderson Walker, William Glover, and Thomas Cary during his second term. In the event of a vacancy on the council, the chief executive and three councillors could appoint someone to the seat and swear him in as a proprietor's deputy until the will of the Lords Proprietors was known.[26]

The air of stability which characterized the years after 1695 still permeated North Carolina in 1702, but it was soon to be dissipated. Underneath the outward tranquility, there was an anxiety linked to events as disparate as a war in Europe and tense confrontations within the colony's own precincts. Queen Anne's War, known as the War of the Spanish Succession in Europe, opened in 1702. During that year, the price of tobacco in London stood at a healthy 83 shillings per hundredweight. However, as the conflict spread to the shipping lanes of the Atlantic, colonial planters faced a critical shortage in their means of overseas transport. Provincial surpluses began to accumulate. Shipping costs from the Chesapeake region to England doubled, and once the freight reached Britain, it could not easily be exported to the continent. Thus, from 1703 until the close of the war in 1713, a depression gripped the Chesapeake colonies.[27] In addition to this tension, there was some anxiety among Albemarle settlers about the growth of Bath County. Assemblymen from Bath about 1705 petitioned Governor Daniel and the council for more favorable treatment than they had received in the past. They stressed their rapid expansion, while com-

[26] Parker, *Higher-Court Records,* III, xx; Herbert R. Paschal, Jr., "Proprietary North Carolina: A Study in Colonial Government" (unpublished doctoral dissertation, University of North Carolina, Chapel Hill, 1961), 233-242, hereinafter cited as Paschal, "Proprietary North Carolina." An undated document of about 1708 naming Edward Moseley as Lord Granville's deputy on the council illustrates the ability of the chief executive and council to appoint as a proprietor's agent a man whose views conflicted with those of his superior. Moseley at the time was allied with the dissenters—a position thoroughly out of step with Granville's views. See Council deputation, undated, Colonial Court Records, Miscellaneous Papers, 1677-1775, CCR 192, State Archives, Raleigh, hereinafter cited as CCR 192.

[27] Craven, *Colonies in Transition,* 301-303; Lewis Cecil Gray, *History of Agriculture in the Southeastern United States to 1860* (Washington: Carnegie Institution, 2 volumes, 1933), I, 268-269.

plaining about the lack of higher courts in their region and the burden of a quitrent rate which was greater than that in Albemarle.[28] It seems clear that the younger precincts to the south were beginning to demand a more equitable role in the administration of the colony.

Because most settlements bordered on wilderness areas, colonists in North Carolina lived in constant dread of Indian attacks. While there was no major uprising between 1702 and 1708, several tribes conducted raids on white plantations; and on at least two occasions, settlers attacked Indian towns.[29] Residents in Bath County lived in close proximity to the powerful Tuscaroras, and they carefully assured the red men that they intended no harm. During 1704 several leading citizens of Bath asked the deputy governor and council to send an emissary to the Tuscaroras with pledges of peace on behalf of the whole province.[30] Clearly, these colonists feared provoking the hostility of such a mighty tribe and such a large potential source of wealth.

Although there were depressed tobacco prices resulting from Queen Anne's War, part of the commerce of North Carolina grew during 1702 through 1708. In spite of difficulties with some of the coastal tribes, trade increased with the Indians for furs, particularly deerskins, and to a lesser degree, wildcat, muskrat, beaver, otter, bear, fox, wolf, and raccoon pelts. This Indian trade offered huge potential profits. Much of the famous Byrd family's wealth in Virginia was based on such traffic. In South Carolina, colonists participating in the Indian trade were viewed as cheaters and swindlers by many white settlers; nonetheless, some sizable fortunes were made.[31] Writing from North Carolina in 1703, Christopher Gale, who had recently come to the colony from England, told his father of the profits to be made in the Indian trade. Cheap cloth, hats, axes, and nails could be exchanged for valuable furs with the local tribesmen. In a short time, a man could accumulate a comfortable living in a place where English money had roughly three

---

[28] House of Burgesses to Deputy Governor Daniel and council, undated, CCR 192.

[29] Deposition on Indian raid, October 20, 1703, CCR 192; Report by Henderson Walker on Indian raid, May 14, 1701, CCR 192; John Lawson to unidentified correspondent, June 23, 1701, CCR 192; Militia commission for campaign against the Keeahwee Indians signed by Robert Daniel, undated, Albemarle County Papers, 1678-1714, Volume I, CR 2.001, State Archives, hereinafter cited as CR 2.001; William Powell to Captain William Barrow, October 20, 1704, CR 2.001.

[30] Petition to governor and council, February 29, 1703/4, CCR 192.

[31] Elizabeth Donnan, "Eighteenth Century Merchants: Micajah Perry,"*Journal of Economic and Business History,* IV (January, 1931), 72-73, hereinafter cited as Donnan, "Micajah Perry;" Sirmans, *Colonial South Carolina,* 72-73.

times as much buying power as it possessed in the mother country.[32] Many Indian traders resided in Bath County, and leading residents such as John Lawson had sizable interests in the traffic.[33]

The Indian trade attracted English investment capital to North Carolina. One name which occurs frequently in higher-court litigations during 1702 through 1708 is that of Micajah Perry, a London merchant who headed the firm of Perry and Lane. Perry had interests in tobacco and furs which extended into New York, Pennsylvania, Maryland, Virginia, and the Carolinas. His influence with the Board of Trade had enabled him to place William Byrd on the Virginia royal council and had encouraged him to try for at least two other appointments to that body.[34] Perhaps Perry had become interested in North Carolina through his acquaintance with Phillip Ludwell, a former governor of the province who was living in Virginia. At any rate, during 1702 through 1708, the New Pennsylvania Company, of which Perry was a director, was extremely active in the North Carolina Indian trade.[35]

Another Englishman with interests in the growing commerce of the colony was Robert Quary, also connected with the New Pennsylvania Company. A judge of the Pennsylvania Vice-Admiralty Court and member of the SPG, Quary had once resided in South Carolina but left in 1693 following a close liaison with the anti-proprietary faction there.[36] After March, 1702, he took over leadership of the attack on proprietary colonies from Edward Randolph, whom he succeeded as surveyor general of customs in North America. A vigorous supporter of charter resumption (a plan to bring all proprietary colonies under control of the crown), Quary became friendly with Micajah Perry, who was also a resumptionist. Part of the battle over charter resumption was related to the question of who would regulate the lucrative trans-Appalachian Indian trade almost completely dominated by South

[32] Christopher Gale to his father [Miles Gale], August 5, 1703, transcript from the Stowe Manuscripts, British Museum, London, in English Records, State Archives. A significant portion of this letter is printed in Walter Clark (ed.), *The State Records of North Carolina* (Winston and Goldsboro: State of North Carolina, 16 volumes, numbered XI-XXVI, 1895-1906), XXII, 732-735. In addition to several errors in transcription, Clark incorrectly attributes the letter to William Gale.

[33] Parker, *Higher-Court Records,* III, xiv; Pp. 245-246, below.

[34] Donnan, "Micajah Perry," 72-84; Richard L. Morton, *Colonial Virginia* (Chapel Hill: University of North Carolina Press, 2 volumes, 1960), I, 414.

[35] Pp. 348-350, 417-419, below. Most General Court actions in the March-May 1706 session involved the New Pennsylvania Company. Micajah Perry signed a petition to the House of Lords in March, 1705, protesting oppression of dissenters in Carolina as disruptive of trade. See Saunders, *Colonial Records,* I, 634-640.

[36] I. K. Steele, "The Board of Trade, the Quakers, and Resumption of Colonial Charters, 1699-1702," *William and Mary Quarterly,* Third Series, XXIII (October, 1966), 598, 601; Sirmans, *Colonial South Carolina,* 52-53.

Carolina merchants—a question of great interest to Perry.[37]

While the Indian trade in North Carolina never approached the scale of that in its sister colony, the traffic was much greater than some historians have thought. Although North Carolina had no discernible role in the trans-Appalachian trade, there was a sizable commerce with tribes inside the province.[38] Articles circulated in the Indian trade and values of pelts received were itemized in several court documents from 1702 through 1708, and many varieties of furs were shipped out of the colony in the period.[39]

North Carolina engaged in commerce with many colonies involving agricultural commodities, raw goods, and manufactured items. By 1704 the province was collecting export duties on deer, bear, beaver, otter, and wildcat skins as well as raw beef and cowhide. Import duties were charged on rum.[40] These levies applied to waterborne trade which was the chief means of transport for goods entering and leaving the province. However, there was some overland trade between Virginia and Albemarle, chiefly in livestock. So many North Carolina farmers carried their tobacco into Virginia for shipping elsewhere that in 1702 the legislature of that colony reenacted an earlier prohibition of the traffic.[41]

Although a seven-to eight-foot depth at Currituck and Roanoke prevented all but small vessels from entering Albemarle Sound, fifteen to thirty ton coasting craft could navigate the hazards easily. A large proportion of these ships came from Massachusetts, but from 1687 to 1689 only 3 percent of the vessels licensed for trade by that colony were bound for North Carolina. However, much of the province's commerce

[37] Hall, *Randolph and the Colonies,* 217; Parker, *Higher-Court Records,* III, xxx. To what extent the New Pennsylvania Company was involved in the machinations is unclear. Perhaps documents in other colonies might clarify the matter.

[38] Verner W. Crane, *The Southern Frontier, 1670-1732* (Ann Arbor: University of Michigan Press, 1929), 157-158; Donnan, "Micajah Perry," 83. Donnan clearly had not examined any higher-court records when she wrote of Perry: "In his relations with Carolina, he seems never to have engaged in trade."

[39] Pp. 260-263, 419-421, below; Shipping invoices, October 20, 1703, May 2, 1704, August 25, 1704, Roanoke Customs House Papers. Types of furs shipped included deer, muskrat, fox, wildcat, beaver, otter, bear, and raccoon skins.

[40] Legislative act, undated [in Thomas Snoden's hand], CR 2.002.

[41] Parker, *Higher-Court Records,* III, xix; Curtis P. Nettels, *The Money Supply of the American Colonies before 1720* (Madison: University of Wisconsin Press, 1934), 112-113, hereinafter cited as Nettels, *Money Supply of the Colonies.*

was conducted by unlicensed craft. Numerous coves and the treacherous Outer Banks offered refuge to pirates and illegal traders; in fact, Virginians referred to Albemarle as "Rogue's Harbor."[42] In 1701 only eight ships departed from Boston for North Carolina; before the decade ended Boston was licensing twenty-nine vessels a year for Albemarle. These craft carried corn, pork, hides, and tobacco to both old and New England. North Carolina also exported corn, pork, and tobacco to the Leeward Islands, chiefly in New England bottoms.[43]

Several leading figures in North Carolina owned their own ships built in Massachusetts. Thomas Pollock, John Porter, William Wilkison, and John Tooke, all of whom appear in the documents in this volume, possessed one or more of such vessels. Pollock's brigantines were quite active in the Caribbean trade often bringing him molasses, rum, and sugar.[44] Newcomers to the colony such as Christopher Gale and John Lawson seem to have turned to the Indian trade rather than more traditional commerce in their quest for wealth. On the other hand, Edward Moseley, who entered the province about 1704, engaged in the same activities which had proved fruitful for planter-merchants like Thomas Pollock and John Porter.

In the case of Gale, Lawson, and Moseley, all of whom entered the colony around 1702 and would be important political figures before 1708, service in a provincial office marked their rise to wealth and power. During 1702 through 1708, Christopher Gale was attorney general and a justice of the General Court; John Lawson was deputy surveyor of Bath County;[45] Edward Moseley was a councillor and speaker of the assembly. In addition, Gale and Moseley expedited their climbs to power by marriages to wealthy, well-placed widows. Gale married the widow of a former chief executive, Thomas Harvey; Moseley, of a former chief executive, Henderson Walker.[46] The infusion

---

[42] Robert Earle Moody, "Massachusetts Trade with Carolina, 1686-1709," *North Carolina Historical Review*, XX (January, 1943), 44-45, hereinafter cited as Moody, "Massachusetts Trade with Carolina."

[43] Moody, "Massachusetts Trade with Carolina," 45; Nettels, *Money Supply of the Colonies*, 113.

[44] Moody, "Massachusetts Trade with Carolina," 47-53.

[45] In Lawson, *New Voyage*, xviii, there is a note stating that John Lawson became surveyor of North Carolina in 1709 but no mention of his earlier office in Bath County. As deputy surveyor of Bath, Lawson did a great deal of his land grant work personally. See pp. 444-446, below and the petition of Furnifold Green to president and council, undated, CR 2.002. For a copy of Lawson's commission as surveyor of Bath County, see Surveyor's commission, undated [in Thomas Snoden's hand], Colonial Court Records, General Court Papers, 1717-1754, CCR 140, State Archives.

[46] Moseley's marriage bond hints at the wealth he was acquiring through this match. See pp. 202-203, below.

of ambitious young men into the economic and social life of the colony would be a factor in the gathering upheaval culminating in the Cary Rebellion.

ANTECEDENTS OF THE CARY REBELLION

The chronological span of the Cary Rebellion is difficult to define precisely. Cary's enemies said that the period of his illegal rule began on July 24, 1708, and lasted until January 22, 1710/11, when the last of his major allies was removed from office. The armed confrontation between the forces of Cary and those of Edward Hyde, who had become chief executive early in 1711, occurred during May through July, 1711. However, this instance was not the first in which Cary's supporters had taken up arms. During the spring of 1708, there was some violence between allies of Cary and those of William Glover, president of the council.[1] When the Tuscarora War opened in the autumn of 1711, it seemed to many colonists that one set of hostilities had blended into another. Some people claimed that defeated Cary supporters had urged the Indians to attack.[2] Regardless of what the exact dates of the Cary Rebellion were, it clearly had its origins in the years 1702 through 1708.

A leading causal factor in the rebellion was the struggle between Anglicans and dissenters in the Carolinas. With the elevation of Lord Granville as palatine (chief among the Lords Proprietors) in 1701, intolerant policies flourished. In North Carolina, Henderson Walker engineered the Vestry Act of 1701 while Robert Daniel, as a member of the South Carolina council, successfully opposed the election of a dissenter as president of that body.[3] However, not until the appointment of Sir Nathaniel Johnson to the governorship of Carolina in March, 1703 (he would reside in Charleston and send a deputy to North Carolina), would dissenters feel persistently threatened. A professional soldier and a devout Anglican, Sir Nathaniel had been governor of the Leeward Islands before entering South Carolina in 1689. During his tenure in the islands, he had sought to exclude dissenters from political office. As governor in Charleston, Johnson immediately set about establishing the Church of England in the colony. In April, 1704, he called an emergency session of the South Carolina assembly and hurried through a bill which excluded dissenters from that body. This purged lower house then passed a measure establishing the Church of England in the province. In London, the Lords Proprietors

[1] Saunders, *Colonial Records,* I, 708-715, 760-772, 793, 803-804.

[2] E. Lawrence Lee, *Indian Wars in North Carolina, 1663-1763* (Raleigh: Carolina Charter Tercentenary Commission, 1963), 21.

[3] Sirmans, *Colonial South Carolina,* 76.

upheld the two acts by a vote of four to two with Granville casting three of the votes in favor—his own and two proxies. An agent employed by South Carolina dissenters then appealed to the House of Lords for disallowance of the measures. Gaining the support of the SPG, which felt that the acts granted the state too much power over the church, the agent convinced the peers to oppose the laws. In March, 1706, Queen Anne instructed the Lords Proprietors to disallow both measures.[4]

In the meantime, Johnson proceeded to further his goals elsewhere by sending his ally, Robert Daniel, as deputy governor to North Carolina in July, 1703. A zealous Anglican, Daniel had immigrated to South Carolina from Barbados in the 1690s. In addition to membership on the proprietary council, he had commanded the South Carolina militia in 1700. Known to Granville, Daniel could be counted on to press the Anglican cause in North Carolina.[5] Because Daniel was a landgrave and thus part of the provincial nobility established by the Fundamental Constitutions, the North Carolina council looked upon his appointment with great enthusiasm. The councillors also were impressed by his prominence in Charleston.[6]

Shortly after his arrival in Albemarle, Daniel set about gathering Anglican supporters into his administration. He succeeded in placing a prominent local Church of England leader, Thomas Pollock, in the council.[7] Other lords deputies included Henderson Walker, Samuel Swann, and William Glover, who were among the most important Anglicans in the province. Thus fortified, the deputy governor began to move against dissenters. Daniel probably realized that he could not establish the Church of England in North Carolina until he had excluded from the assembly all dissenters who, along with tolerant Anglicans, formed a majority in the lower house. Early in 1704 the instrument which he needed for such a purge arrived in the form of an oath of allegiance to Queen Anne and the Protestant succession. Daniel required that all members of the government swear to the oath; he would not allow affirmations as had been done in the past. Since Quakers were prohibited from swearing by their religious creed, they were barred from the assembly which met late in 1704. That body then passed a vestry act requiring public support for erection of Anglican churches as well as a measure barring from places of trust anyone who

---

[4] Sirmans, *Colonial South Carolina*, 80, 87-88.

[5] Sirmans, *Colonial South Carolina*, 29, 85; Weeks, *Religious Development in North Carolina*, 41.

[6] North Carolina Council to Governor Nathaniel Johnson, undated, CCR 188.

[7] Councillor's commission, 1703, CR 2.001.

had not sworn the oath of allegiance.[8]

The Quakers soon began seeking firmer alliances with other dissenters and with Anglicans who disliked Daniel's methods and the increased taxation necessary to implement church establishment. Gathering support throughout the colony, the dissenters petitioned Sir Nathaniel Johnson early in 1705 to remove Daniel from office. Locked in his own struggle with non-Anglicans in South Carolina, Johnson agreed and sent Thomas Cary to North Carolina as deputy governor on March 21, 1704/5.[9] Dissenters were pleased initially with the appointment, because Cary was related by marriage to John Archdale, the Quaker proprietor.[10] However, Cary had also enjoyed a close friendship with Governor Johnson. When Sir Nathaniel had been commissioned governor of Carolina in June, 1702, Cary had been one of two men posting the £2,000 bond required of Johnson by the Lords Proprietors. Identified as a merchant, he also posted the same bond for the new governor of the Bahamas. Cary was obviously a man of some wealth.[11]

When he arrived in North Carolina, Cary found Anglicans in most places of power. What instructions he possessed from Johnson or what his own religious convictions were are unknown, but the deputy governor cast his lot with the Anglicans. Although the law requiring oaths of allegiance was still on the statute books, dissenters had assumed that Cary would not enforce it. However, when the General Court met on

[8] Connor, *The Colonial and Revolutionary Periods,* I, 90-91; Lefler and Newsome, *North Carolina,* 54-55; Paschal, "Proprietary North Carolina," 292-296. An order by Daniel and the council requiring the freeholders of Pasquotank Precinct to elect four new burgesses because of refusals by Caleb Bundy, Jeremiah Symonds, Augustine Scarborough, and John Hawkins to take oaths of allegiance is reprinted in J. R. B. Hathaway (ed.), *North Carolina Historical and Genealogical Register,* III (January, 1903), 136, hereinafter cited as Hathaway, *Historical and Genealogical Register.* Hawkins had declined to take an oath as justice of the General Court in October, 1702, but he was not barred from the bench because of it. See p. 41, below. Because of large gaps in primary source materials relating to this period, it has been necessary to use secondary materials to fill in some details. However, Connor, and especially Ashe, must be used with caution for events surrounding the Cary Rebellion.

[9] Executive proclamation, March 21, 1704/5, CR 2.001; Connor, *The Colonial and Revolutionary Periods,* I, 91; Ashe, *History of North Carolina,* I, 159-160.

[10] Jones, *Quakers in the Colonies,* 352n. George Stevenson of the North Carolina Office of Archives and History has written an unpublished paper on the Cary Rebellion providing much genealogical data on Cary, Moseley, and other leading figures of the uprising. While Jones claims that Cary was Archdale's son-in-law, Mr. Stevenson contends that he was Archdale's stepson.

[11] Minute books of the Carolina proprietors, June 18, 1702, July 3, 1702, microfilm copy of Colonial Office 5/289, British Public Record Office, London, in Colonial Records Project, State Archives, hereinafter cited as C. O. 5/289 film. Cary possessed several merchant vessels in Charleston.

March 27, the oath act was read and put into execution.[12] At the General Assembly meeting in November, 1705, Quaker members were again required to take oaths; they refused and were excluded. Then Cary and his allies passed a law which voided the election of anyone found guilty of promoting his own candidacy. This loosely defined bill gave the majority faction in the lower house the power to exclude any undesirable member and was designed to be used against troublesome non-Quakers (who had no religious convictions, against oath swearing).[13]

The dissenters and some disgruntled Anglicans now decided to send an agent to England to plead for relief. In October, 1706, their chosen representative, John Porter, left Albemarle for London. A prominent merchant, General Court justice, and former speaker of the lower house, Porter almost certainly was not a Quaker and, in fact, may have been an Anglican.[14] Although he did not take the oaths of office with his fellow justices at the October-November, 1705, session of the General Court, he had taken them in March, 1705.[15] In England, Porter received the support of the Quaker proprietor, John Archdale, who persuaded the Lords Proprietors to issue orders to Porter suspending Sir Nathaniel Johnson's authority over North Carolina, removing Cary as deputy governor, naming five new councillors, and authorizing the council to elect a chief executive.[16]

Returning to Albemarle in October, 1707, Porter found William Glover and the council presiding over the government because Cary had left for a visit to South Carolina. This arrangement appeared satisfactory to Porter, who called the new lords deputies together and

---

[12] P. 144, below.

[13] Ashe, *History of North Carolina*, I, 160; Connor, *The Colonial and Revolutionary Periods*, I, 92; Saunders, *Colonial Records*, I, 708-715.

[14] Both Jones, *Quakers in the Colonies*, 352n, and Weeks, *Religious Development in North Carolina*, 51, say that Porter probably was not a Quaker. CCR 191 contains an intriguing set of depositions concerning a physical attack by Thomas Cary on John Porter. The documents are undated and belong to an unidentified lower court. They have been printed (with several errors in transcription) in Hathaway, *Historical and Genealogical Register*, III (April, 1903), 224-226. It is likely that the abovementioned confrontation occurred prior to Porter's trip to England in October, 1706.

[15] Pp. 149, 198, below. For an undated oath supporting the Protestant succession which Porter signed, see Hathaway, *Historical and Genealogical Register*, I (April, 1900), 267. Caution must be used in researching Porter's career, since there appear to have been at least three individuals named John Porter residing in North Carolina during the early eighteenth century.

[16] Connor, *The Colonial and Revolutionary Periods*, I, 92; Saunders, *Colonial Records*, I, 708-715. Lord Granville died on December 3, 1707. It is possible that his deteriorating physical condition during 1707 facilitated Archdale's efforts.

nominated Glover as president of the council.[17] Glover was elected, but the vote was illegal since Porter's instructions required that Cary and the former councillors be present for the voting. Porter knew exactly what he was doing, however, and would later use the illegality of the election to force Glover out of office.[18]

On November 3, 1707, Glover convened the General Assembly at John Hecklefield's house at Little River. Joining him in the upper house as lords deputies were Porter, Foster, Newby, Hawkins, and Thomas Cary, recently returned from South Carolina. After requesting that the lower house send its list of members to him, the president proposed dissolution of the assembly without any further business. Cary objected, but the following day Glover and the rest of the council dissolved the General Assembly.[19] Although he had been required to convene the assembly in compliance with the biennial act which specified that a legislative session be held every two years, Glover apparently did not want Cary to use the gathering as a forum.

At some point between the close of the assembly in November, 1707, and the summer of 1708, Glover turned on the dissenters. Apparently, he decided to revive the oath of office and force the Quaker councillors to take it. Seeing the turn of events, Thomas Cary moved to join with Porter and the dissenters in the hope of regaining the chief executive's office. After receiving assurances of toleration from Cary, Porter moved decisively. Late in the summer of 1708, he called together both Cary's old councillors and the new ones, as he was originally supposed to have done in October, 1707, and announced that Glover's election as president had been illegal. Glover, joined by Thomas Pollock, protested vigorously and armed violence broke out between the two factions.[20] Soon though, both sides agreed to let the General Assembly determine the validity of their rival claims. Cary and Glover each issued separate writs of election to every precinct which then proceeded to elect two sets of burgesses—one pledged to Cary and one, to Glover. Cary men predominated in Bath County and Perquimans and Pasquotank precincts; Glover men controlled Currituck Precinct,

---

[17] A proclamation signed by Glover and the new councillors shortly after the election reveals that Porter, Francis Foster, Gabriel Newby, and John Hawkins were part of the executive branch of government. Newby and Hawkins were definitely Quakers; Foster may have been. See Executive proclamation, undated, CCR 192.

[18] Saunders, *Colonial Records,* I, 708-715; Connor, *The Colonial and Revolutionary Periods,* I, 92-93.

[19] Journal of the Upper House of Assembly, November 3-4, 1707, CR 2.001.

[20] Connor, *The Colonial and Revolutionary Periods,* I, 93; Ashe, *History of North Carolina,* I, 164-165; Saunders, *Colonial Records,* I, 688, 708-715. The tensions surrounding these events are illustrated in the minutes of the July, 1708, General Court. See pp. 402-406, below.

and Chowan was almost evenly divided.[21] In Chowan Precinct, a participant in the events, Thomas Pollock, described the voting there. Daniel Hallsey read Glover's writ at the polling place; then Robert Fendall read Cary's. As the poll proceeded, ninety-four freemen voted for the five assemblymen pledged to Glover; sixty-five, for Cary's burgesses. Both sets of delegates were authorized to attend the General Assembly on October 11, 1708, where only one of them would be seated by a vote of the whole lower house.[22] In the critical maneuvering for control of the October assembly, Cary forces scored an early, ultimately decisive victory. Edward Moseley, an Anglican vestryman, was chosen speaker of the house. Despite his religious affiliation, he was a Cary supporter. Through Moseley's careful management, Cary delegates were seated from every precinct except Currituck. Upstairs at John Hecklefield's house, where this assembly was meeting, Cary and his council occupied one room while Glover and his council sat in another. When news of the Cary victory in the lower house arrived, Glover departed. He hastened to Virginia where he wrote a letter to the assembly claiming that his flight was necessary because Cary had threatened to kill him. He further stated:

> [I] doe offer my Self as the Queen's Prisoner [to] be Sent in chains if the matter so require to the [governor] Generall of Carolina And thence to her Majesties [*torn*] courts att Westminster, Provided that the Said Collonel Cary and mr. John Porter who have been the chief instruments of thes unhappy troubles will be obleidged with good Security in the Sume of two thousand Pound personally to appeare and Persecute me.[23]

Of course, Glover did not receive a sympathetic hearing from the assembly; nor did he really think that he would, since he had addressed the letter: "To the gentlement mett and Pretending themselves to be the house of Burgesses."[24] The General Assembly nullified the test oaths, and the council officially elected Cary president. Despite its support of Cary, this assembly was not his pawn. Its members demanded and received an inspection of Porter's instructions from the Lords Pro-

[21] Lefler and Newsome, *North Carolina,* 54-55; Connor, *The Colonial and Revolutionary Periods,* I, 93; Ashe, *History of North Carolina,* I, 166-167.

[22] Thomas Pollock to unidentifed correspondent, October, 1708, the Pollock Letter Book, 1708-1761, PC 31.2, State Archives, hereinafter cited as PC 31.2.

[23] William Glover to the North Carolina Burgesses, undated, quoted in Thomas Pollock to unidentified correspondent, October, 1708, PC 31.2; Connor *The Colonial and Revolutionary Periods,* I, 94-95.

[24] William Glover to the North Carolina Burgesses, undated, quoted in Thomas Pollock to unidentified correspondent, October, 1708, PC 31.2.

prietors. They also forced Cary to look into a recent murder in the colony which he had not previously investigated. After passing twelve rather routine acts, Cary and the council prorogued the assembly on October 27, 1708.[25]

As chief executive, Cary replaced some local officers of suspect loyalty with dissenters, but such actions were rare. With the council, he proceeded to liberalize land grant policy in the hope of promoting immigration. Most significantly, Cary rewarded his supporters in Bath County by lowering the quitrent rate there.[26] However, the chief executive continued to have trouble with the lower house. When the assembly convened in November, 1709, Cary had elevated Edward Moseley to the council. Without Moseley's firm guidance, the burgesses got bogged down in procedural arguments and accomplished little.[27]

The Lords Proprietors were slow to intervene in the situation in North Carolina. In December, 1708, they appointed Edward Tynte to be governor of Carolina and instructed him to make Edward Hyde deputy governor of North Carolina.[28] Arriving in the colony early in 1711, Hyde had no legal claim on the deputy governorship because Tynte had died before commissioning him. However, he was warmly received in Albemarle, and his position as a distant kinsman of the queen was so impressive that the council elected Hyde to the presidency. He called a General Assembly for March, 1711, where he recommended harsh legislation against dissenters and the arrest of Cary and Porter. From his home in Bath, Cary rallied his supporters to resist, and the armed conflict known as the Cary Rebellion began.[29]

---

[25] Journal of the Upper House of Assembly, October 11-27, 1708, CR 2.001. A portion of this journal has been printed in Hathaway, *Historical and Genealogical Register*, I (April, 1900), 304, but the date is given incorrectly as October 11, 1709.

[26] Ashe, *History of North Carolina*, I, 167-168; Thomas Cary to John Porter, February 9, 1708/9, CCR 188.

[27] Journal of the Upper House of Assembly, November 7-19, 1709, CR 2.001.

[28] Minute books of the Carolina proprietors, December 9, 1708, C. O. 5/289 film; Ashe, *History of North Carolina*, I, 167-168.

[29] Connor, *The Colonial and Revolutionary Periods*, I, 97-98; Saunders, *Colonial Records*, I, xxvii-xxix.

NORTH CAROLINA HIGHER COURTS, 1702-1708

The third volume of this series, *North Carolina Higher-Court Records, 1697-1701* (1971), contains an extremely detailed introductory essay on higher courts.[1] The author discusses composition of the courts, judicial and administrative procedures, jurisdiction, relations between precinct and higher courts, conduct of trials, court personnel, and the evolution of legal concepts. This writer shall not attempt to reiterate the points made in that extensive treatment. Rather, he shall concentrate on areas in which some of the procedures and concepts discussed in volume III underwent changes, however slight.

During the years 1702 through 1708, the following courts exercised jurisdiction over the entire North Carolina colony: the General Court, which tried cases at law; the Court of Chancery, which heard suits in equity; the Court of Admiralty, which had jurisdiction over maritime matters; and a series of special courts of uncertain function which met irregularly. Five lower courts existed—one each in the four precincts of Albemarle County and one in Bath County. In December, 1705, Bath County was divided into three precincts, each having its own lower court by 1708.[2]

As it has been in earlier years and would continue to be throughout the proprietary period, the General Court remained the busiest of the higher courts. Actions involving less than twenty shillings were not cognizable in this court, but in other matters it seems to have had concurrent jurisdiction with the precinct courts. The practice of naming seven justices to the General Court, begun in March, 1700, ended by March, 1701. The earlier procedure of appointing six justices which had started in 1697 was followed (with one known exception) from 1702 through 1708. Three of the four extant commissions for justices during the period name six men, at least two of whom were councillors. These two councillors were always among the three justices of the quorum. Throughout the years covered in this volume, a quorum consisted of three justices, one of whom had to be a justice of the quorum.[3] The commission for the March, 1708, session of the General Court named only four justices; two were justices of the quorum (one of these two was definitely a councillor). By July, 1708, the court returned to the pattern of six justices.[4]

---

[1] Parker, *Higher-Court Records*, III, xxxviii-lx.

[2] Paschal, *Colonial Bath*, 5; Paul M. McCain, *The County Court in North Carolina before 1750* (Durham: Duke University Press, 1954), 13-14. Functions of the precinct courts are treated in Parker, *Higher-Court Records*, III, xxxviii-xl.

[3] Pp. 28-29, 177-178, 399, 414, below. It is probable that all three justices of the quorum were councillors, but this writer has only been able to identify two positively in each instance.

[4] Pp. 399, 414, below.

Meeting three times a year, in March, July, and October, the General Court convened in a private home in Perquimans Precinct during 1702 through 1708. The chief officers of the court were the provost marshal, the clerk, and the attorney general, as they had been in earlier years.[5] Grand jurors continued to be sworn when there were criminal charges, and petit jurors were summoned for all courts. In an effort to equalize the burden placed on Perquimans Precinct in supplying jurors, the General Court justices in October, 1704, ordered the marshals of the three adjacent precincts to provide six men apiece "to appear upon A Jury att Every Generall Court in this Province."[6] During the same session, the court also ruled that every plea in a personal action must be submitted in writing. Oral pleas had been permitted in such actions in previous years.[7] Despite the new rule, written pleas did not proliferate after October, 1704. In fact, a ruling of the October, 1707, General Court shows that oral pleading may have continued, although the reference to pleading in this instance could be nontechnical. The court said "that if any person in pleading shall Interupt another whilst he is pleading [*he*] shall pay ten Shillings to the use of the Lords proprietors."[8]

The General Court further tightened its procedures when it ruled in July, 1706, that no actions would be postponed because of failure of the principals to appear on time. Henceforth, cases would be heard in the order in which they occurred on the docket. The court also said that "all Issues Shalbe made up the Court Day in the Morning before the Court Sitts and that there Shalbe Twelve Actions for Each Day of the Court and all Writts Shalbe returnable att a Day certaine and notice given to the Defendant in the Copy of the Declaration of the Day." Continuing problems with jurors caused the General Court to rule in October, 1706, that petit and grand jurors who failed to appear when summoned would be fined ten and twenty shillings respectively.[9]

As it had been since 1697, the form of action most often used in the General Court from 1702 through 1708 was *trespass on the case,* usually called *case*. The action of *debt* continued to be the second most frequently used form. Despite the availability and use of debt, detinue, trover and conversion, trespass, and other specialized forms of action, most suits which appear to have fitted one or more of these forms were brought in case.[10]

[5] Parker, *Higher-Court Records,* III, xli-xliii. A courthouse built for the General Court was destroyed by fire at the close of 1701.

[6] P. 131, below.

[7] P. 125, below; Parker, *Higher-Court Records,* III, xlv.

[8] P. 383, below.

[9] Pp. 273, 309, below.

[10] Various forms of action as well as the means of satisfying them are treated in Parker, *Higher-Court Records,* III, xlvi-l.

The attorney general continued to prosecute criminal cases in the name of the crown rather than in the proprietors' names. Jury trials were available on request and followed a plea of *not guilty*. For those persons convicted, punishments varied, but none seemed particularly severe. During 1702 through 1708, no one was sentenced to death, and most people were merely put under bond for good behavior for a certain period.[11] In one of the most violent crimes of the period, punishment was circumvented. When Thomas Dereham was convicted of manslaughter in the July, 1702, General Court for beating a man to death with a cat of nine tails, he claimed *benefit of clergy* and was thus "Savd by his Book" from severe punishment. Dereham then was sentenced to be branded on his left thumb with the letter *M* but succeeded in getting that judgment suspended until the trial could be reviewed in England.[12]

Confusion about whether North Carolina courts were courts of the crown or of the proprietors continued through 1708. Especially after 1704 the number of writs issued in the proprietors' names increased. The source of this confusion does not appear to have arisen from any known instruction from either the proprietors or the crown. Perplexing though the problem may be for the present day scholar, it does not seem to have hindered court business.[13]

Most cases tried in the General Court were brought under its original jurisdiction, but some appeals were heard from precinct courts. The higher court continued to share some administrative functions with the lower courts such as probate of wills and proof of landrights, but these duties decreased after 1702, indicating that such matters were being handled increasingly on the precinct level. As in previous years, the General Court appears to have had final jurisdiction on matters of law. Sometimes its judgment was stayed until a case had been heard in the Court of Chancery, but appeal was based on failure of the common law to provide a remedy rather than on error by the General Court.[14]

The Court of Chancery was composed of the deputy governor (from 1702 through 1708, the governor of Carolina resided in Charleston) and the proprietors' deputies (councillors). When no deputy governor

---

[11] Parker, *Higher-Court Records*, III, l-li, treats criminal action in detail.

[12] Pp. 33-34, below. For a discussion of benefit of clergy, see Theodore F. T. Plucknett, *A Concise History of the Common Law* (Boston: Little, Brown, and Company, Fifth Edition, 1956), 439-441, hereinafter cited as Plucknett, *The Common Law*.

[13] It is worth noting that Tobias Knight, who was clerk of the General Court after 1704, was also secretary of the colony and had probably been commissioned directly by the proprietors. His predecessor as clerk of the court, Thomas Snoden, held his post by virtue of a commission issued by Samuel Swann, who was secretary before Knight.

[14] Parker, *Higher-Court Records*, III, li-lii.

was in the colony, the president of the council presided. As a court of equity, chancery operated under procedures and principles which enabled parties to find relief not obtainable in courts of law. For instance, a fraudulent transfer of property which a common law court might have to regard as legal could be nullified in a court of equity. The Court of Chancery considered the parties concerned as well as the issues and procedures to which a court of law was bound.[15]

In North Carolina, the Court of Chancery sometimes heard appeals directly from the precinct courts which had not passed through the General Court.[16] Such a hearing could result in a reversal of the earlier judgment by the court of law, but this action did not mean that chancery was higher than the General Court. Rather, it supplemented the work of the law court by doing what it could not do. Terminology in equity courts differed from that in courts of law. For example, a complainant was an *orator* or *petitioner* rather than a *plaintiff*.[17]

Few records of the Court of Chancery survive for the period 1698 to 1711. Prior to 1698, the records of the General Court and chancery were kept together, since the governor and council composed both bodies. In the thirteen years down to 1711, few records relating to the executive, legislative, and judicial functions of the council have survived. Those documents which are available indicate that the Court of Chancery did continue to meet on a somewhat irregular basis.[18]

The confusion which had surrounded admiralty cases in 1698 was not greatly clarified in the years covered in this volume. During 1698 a case which was properly meant for a vice-admiralty court had been tried in the Palatine's Court. At the core of this problem was a constitutional argument between Virginia and North Carolina over whether or not a vice-admiralty court in the former colony had jurisdiction extending to the latter.[19] The question was still unresolved when a North Carolina Court of Admiralty convened at Little River on October 3, 1704. A justice and three judges sat on the bench; three of these four men were justices of the General Court, and the fourth, William Barcliffe, would become a justice during the March-May, 1706, General Court.[20] Other officers of the General Court served at the trial:

---

[15] Plucknett, *The Common Law*, 673-674, 681.

[16] P. 430, below; Parker, *Higher-Court Records*, III, lii.

[17] Pp. 429, 431, below. For details on functions and procedures of the Court of Chancery, see Parker, *Higher-Court Records*, III, lii-liii.

[18] Parker, *Higher-Court Records*, III, liii.

[19] Parker, *Higher-Court Records*, III, lv-lvii.

[20] Although the name of the fourth justice is rendered as *Bartlett* in the Court of Admiralty minutes, the person being referred to is almost certainly *Barcliffe*, sometimes rendered *Barclift*.

Christopher Gale was attorney general; John Hecklefield, the provost marshal, was "Marshal of the Admiralty;" and the minutes were written in the hand of Thomas Snoden, clerk of the General Court.[21] No other records of a vice-admiralty court exist through 1708 and what business, if any, there was for such a body may have been dealt with by the chief executive and council.[22]

Only one document of the Palatine's Court (composed of the governor and council) appears in this volume, and it is the final proprietary manuscript which can be assigned to that court.[23] Apparently, the reorganization of government which was completed in 1697, after suspension of the Fundamental Constitutions in 1691, had decreased the need for the Palatine's Court.[24] Previous functions of the Palatine's Court undoubtedly were absorbed by the other higher courts and the council sitting in a judicial capacity.

The same reorganization which had phased out the Palatine's Court also gradually erased the Grand Court. Originally held by the Grand Council (composed of the governor and proprietors' deputies), the functions of the Grand Court were absorbed primarily by the General Court.[25] After 1706 higher-court documents were no longer addressed to the Grand Court.[26]

Clearly, not every possible judical gap could be filled by the reorganization of government completed in 1697.[27] Situations requiring the attention of a higher court would arise when it was inconvenient

[21] Pp. 467-468, below.

[22] Hathaway, *Historical and Genealogical Register*, I (October, 1900), 611-612, contains an oath signed by John Porter and Thomas Symons on April 3, 1705, to serve as justices of the Court of Admiralty. The document no longer exists having been lost sometime between its transcription in 1900 and the microfilming of Chowan County records in 1941. Of course, the document in no way proves that an admiralty court met in 1705—only that one might have. One authority believes that no ordinary admiralty case from North Carolina was ever tried in a Virginia court, see Carl W. Ubbelohde, Jr., "The Vice-Admiralty Court of Royal North Carolina, 1729-1759," *North Carolina Historical Review*, XXXI (October, 1954), 520. For a discussion of admiralty jurisdiction, see Erwin C. Surrency, "The Courts in the American Colonies," *American Journal of Legal History*, XI (July and October, 1967), 356, hereinafter cited as Surrency, "Courts in the Colonies."

[23] P. 469, below. Hathaway, *Historical and Genealogical Register*, III (April, 1903), 228-229, contains a document dated September 12, 1717, in which Governor Charles Eden and the council change the site for a General Assembly meeting based on previous authorization in an undated legislative enactment designating the Palatine's Court to so act.

[24] Parker, *Higher-Court Records*, III, liv. Although there was a revision of the Fundamental Constitutions in 1698, it never appears to have been put into effect.

[25] Parker, *Higher-Court Records*, III, xx-xxi.

[26] Pp. 469-473, below.

[27] The adjustments required of the governor and council during reorganization are discussed in Paschal, "Proprietary North Carolina," 241-242, 245-246.

to call a special session of a court, or when some question about proper jurisdiction would be raised. For these reasons and because they were authorized by the proprietors to perform judicial functions, the governor and council would sometimes sit as a court other than chancery.[28] Throughout the proprietary and royal periods in North Carolina, the council would continue to perform certain functions as a court of law.[29]

EDITORIAL METHOD

The method utilized in transcribing documents for this volume is based on rules for the "expanded method" in Oscar Handlin and others, *Harvard Guide to American History* (Cambridge: Belknap Press of Harvard University Press, 1960) and on the style sheet prepared for *American Legal Records* by the Littleton-Griswold Committee of the American Historical Association. Most abbreviations and contractions have been expanded. Those retained include all proper names, dates, titles, amounts of money, and abbreviations in use today, as set forth in *Webster's Seventh New Collegiate Dictionary* (Springfield: G. and C. Merriam Company, 1970) and Henry Campbell Black, *Black's Law Dictionary, Fourth Edition* (St. Paul: West Publishing Company, 1951). If more than one expanded form fitted the context, abbreviations were retained as written. In that gray area where one must distinguish between abbreviations, contractions, or misspellings on the part of the contemporary scribe, no expansion has been made where the literal meaning is clear. It is hoped that this procedure will enhance the original flavor of the documents. Various symbols indicating *pounds, shillings,* and *pence* are rendered as £, *s.*, and *d.*

Spelling in the manuscripts has been followed with the exception of expansions, substitution of *th* for the symbol indicating the archaic letter *thorn,* and substitution of modern usage with respect to *i, j, u,* and *v.* Interpolation of *sic* has been restricted primarily to pointing out discrepancies in dates, monetary calculations, and where an improperly used word might alter the meaning of the text. A few obvious slips of the pen have been silently corrected.

Capitalization in the manuscript has been followed with some exceptions. Each heading, paragraph, or notation is begun with a capital regardless of its form in the manuscript. The first word following a period ending a sentence or other passage is capitalized. If a proper name is not capitalized in the manuscript, it is not capitalized in this volume unless it meets one of the above criteria.

Very limited modification has been made in *punctuation.* Periods

[28] Pp. 473-477, below.

[29] Surrency, "Courts in the Colonies," 253, 268; Leonard Woods Labaree, *Royal Government in America* (New Haven: Yale University Press, 1930), 408-409.

follow paragraphs and entries which require them as well as all retained abbreviations. Commas have been placed in lists of names changed from vertical to horizontal form. In a few cases, the editor has deleted extremely erratic punctuation, such as colons or dashes after every few words.

Square brackets enclose material supplied editorially. Inferred readings of missing and partially missing passages are printed in roman type. The remaining supplied material is in italics. Included are case headings for groups of file papers, the shelf numbers of containers of documents, dates for certain undated documents, and such interpolations as *torn*, *illegible*, and *endorsed*. In italicized case headings, however, roman type is used for the abbreviation of *versus*. Proper names in these case headings are rendered according to their preferred spelling in the index.

Angle brackets enclose material which occurs in the manuscript but has been moved from one position to another. Such material includes case headings, jury lists, and notations moved into the text from the margin. It also includes page numbers, supplied by a contemporary hand, which have been moved into the text. Transposed material is in italics except that roman type is used for the manuscript page numbers and for the word versus or its equivalent in case headings.

Centered *shelf numbers* of the respective containers precede the text of all file papers. The absence of a shelf number elsewhere indicates that the document appears on the manuscript page with the preceding document or is on a page immediately following and bound with that one.

Footnotes in the text have been held to a minimum. They are used to include material of inconsistent or unusual placement in the manuscript, to point out significant words which were lined through in the text, to suggest possible readings to certain words and abbreviations, and to explain the inclusion of scratch minutes to fill out some areas where finished minutes are not available. It is hoped that the extensive cross-referencing in the index will compensate in part for the paucity of footnotes. As in previous volumes in this series, it is assumed that the reader will have access to such standard reference works as *The Oxford English Dictionary* and *Black's Law Dictionary*.

Selection of documents for this volume has followed identification procedures set for earlier volumes in the series. Dated court documents were sorted and indexed; lists of justices, clerks, marshals, and deputies were compiled for each court session; frequent reference was made to the biographical data and the index to inventory reports in the files of the Colonial Records Project. All of this information was then used to identify the undated papers which comprise about 35 percent of the file papers in this volume. Some manuscripts could not definitely be assigned to a specific court session but, because of internal evidence, fell within the years 1702 through 1708. They are included in the appropriate chapters in sections headed, *Date Undetermined*.

The documents are divided into three groups which are treated as chapters. The first, and by far the largest, chapter consists of records of the General Court. The second consists of the limited number of Court of Chancery records which have survived. In the final chapter are documents from miscellaneous higher courts presided over either by the justices of the General Court or the governor and the council.

In the first two chapters, documents have been arranged according to the term of court to which they are related. Such groups are presented chronologically on the basis of the date the court sat. Documents for a given term appear in the following order, if all types are available: dockets, minutes, papers recorded by order of court, and file papers. Recorded papers are printed in the same sequence in which they were written down by the clerk of court. File papers in suits and prosecutions for a given term are grouped according to case; those groups are arranged alphabetically according to the name of the plaintiff. Case headings have been arbitrary with regard to term of court, for in cases continued through several terms, the time when certain papers were introduced often cannot be determined precisely. Undated file papers in cases which were referred from one court session to another are printed in the first session in which they are docketed. This procedure is being followed since many of the cases are continued to sessions beyond 1708. By referring to the index, the reader can gather all of the references to a particular case in this volume. Some papers, apparently related to suits withdrawn, have been placed with those of a given term on the basis of dates in the documents despite absence of references to such cases in the dockets or minutes. File papers in cases for a given term are followed by miscellaneous papers, such as petitions to prove landrights. All file papers are printed in *smaller type* than that used for other documents.

In arranging documents in the third chapter, four major groupings have been utilized in the following order: Court of Admiralty; Special Courts (Grand Court, Palatine's Court, and Special Courts); Council in a Judicial Capacity (not Chancery); and Notes to Clerks of Court. Within these four groupings, documents are arranged in the same order followed in the first two chapters. However, they are not supplied with case headings.

Some of the cases in this volume relate to actions commenced in the two preceding volumes in this series. The reader is referred to the excellent indexes in volumes II and III if he wishes to trace cases originating prior to 1702.

Dates in manuscripts have not been altered. They appear, of course, in old style (according to the Julian Calendar). Page 93 of the *Harvard Guide to American History* contains a table for converting old style dates to new style.

ABBREVIATIONS USED IN SHELF REFERENCES FOR DOCUMENTS

CCR Colonial Court Records, State Archives, Office of Archives and History, Raleigh

CR County Records, State Archives, Office of Archives and History, Raleigh

Mf Microfilm Collection, State Archives, Office of Archives and History, Raleigh

SS Secretary of State Papers, State Archives, Office of Archives and History, Raleigh

Records of the General Court

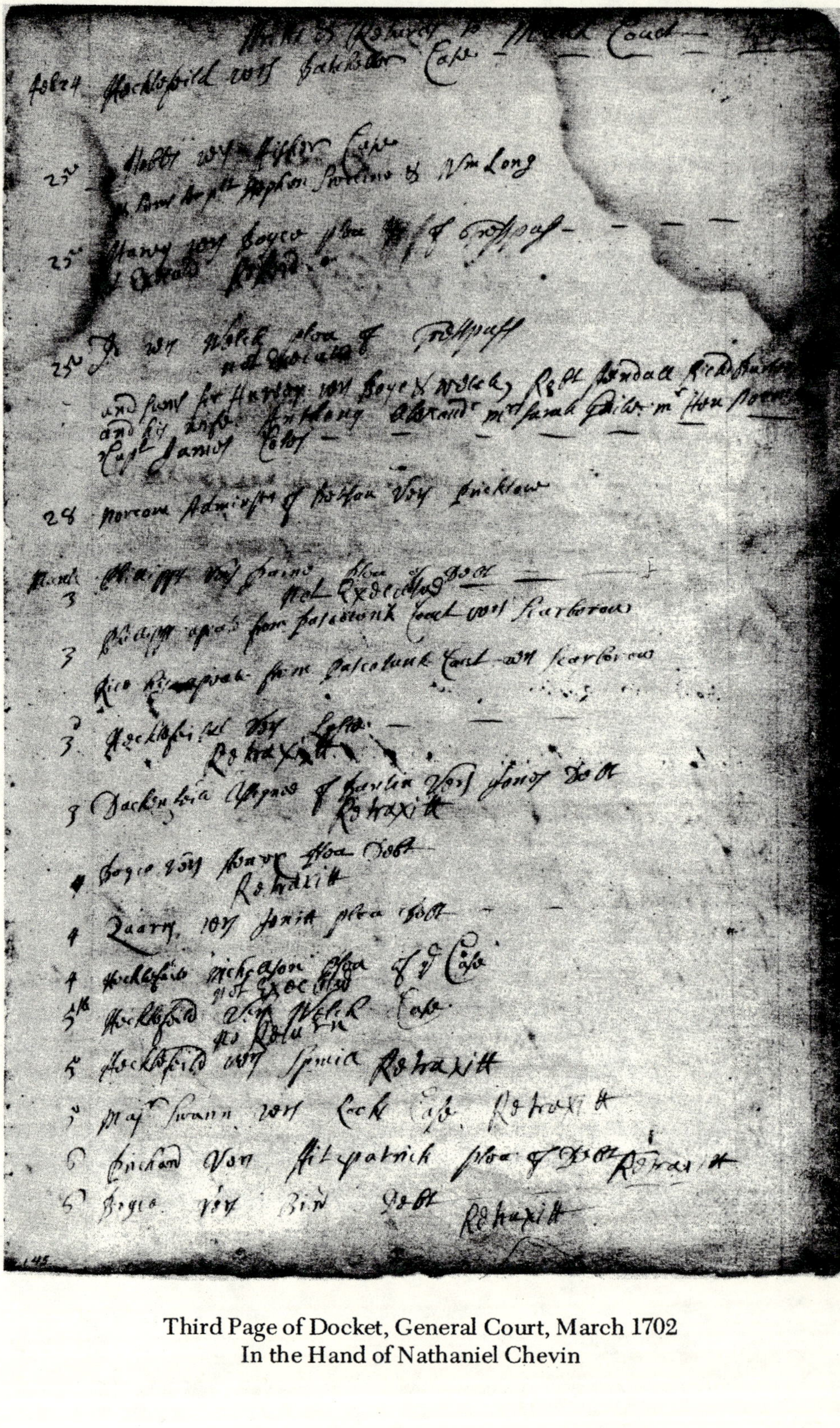

Third Page of Docket, General Court, March 1702
In the Hand of Nathaniel Chevin

Records of the General Court

[*CCR 102*]

<144> Refferences to March Court

Prichard versus Moline Order versus Marshall.

Mcgregory and Wife versus Mayo.

2 apeals from Pascotank.

Writts and Returns to March Court

9br 12 The Honorable Major Saml. Swan attorney of Colonel Ludwell versus Powell in a plea of Debt. Retraxitt.

William Glover Esqr. Versus Powell plea of the Case. Returned Executed and Retraxitt.

Ditto Jno. Bird versus Jonathan Bateman Plea of the Case. Returned Executed and Retraxitt.

Ditto Mr. Wm. Duckenfeild versus Bottomly Plea Debt. Retraxitt.

Doctor Jno. Hecklefeild Administrator of Pordige versus Steel plea Debt. Not Executed.

24 Wattson Versus Burnett. Returned Executed.

Cuttlett versus Williams. Returned Executed.

28th Barnsfeild versus Holford plea Debt. Returned.

Idem versus Idem plea Case.

Mr. Fra. Foster Takes Execution against Jno. Holford for Debt 11 17 01 with Costs. 00 19 10.

Janry. 16 Mr. Jno. Porter versus Fewox plea Defamation. And summons for plaintiff Mr. Duckenfeild Cuthbert Phelps and wife. Jno. Clearest Jno. Lewis Humphry Legg Mr. Jno. Tucker.

Dito Idem versus Idem Plea Debt and summons for plaintiff Cornel Fitzpatrick and Tho. Arnold.

Idem assignee of Humphrey Legg versus Fuox Plea of Case. And summons for the plaintiff Geo. Chambers.

<144*a*>[1] Janry. 17th Benington Versus Frayley Plea Debt.

Idem versus Griffin plea of the Case.

Idem versus Andiver Case.

27 Colonel Pollock versus Holmes Case. Retraxitt. 23 12 05.

Idem versus Evins Case. 04 07 03.

29 Boyce versus Harvey Defamation.

29 Chevin versus Laker Case. Retraxitt.

29 Anderson Versus Averitt. Plea Debt. Returned Executed and Retraxitt.

Jan. 26th Major Swann versus Williams Debt and Retraxitt.

Feb. 12 Boyd versus Lysle Case. Retraxitt.

[1]6 Duckenfeilds writt scire facias versus Prichard and wife administrators of Henly. Returned Executed.

16 Dereham versus Truwhitt Debt for 7=18=00.

Feb. 18 Adams Assignee of Copeland versus West Debt 840 pounds tobacco. No Return.

19 Richard Plater Esqr. Attorney General versus Capt. Tho. Blount Case. Returned Executed. Retraxitt.

23th Godfrey Spruill assignee of Pope Versus Duckenfeild Debt. Returned Executed.

24 Falkconer Versus Evins Case.

Idem versus Flowers Case.

Idem versus Rooks Case.

<145> Feb. 24 Hecklefeild Versus Batchellor Case.

25 Hobbs versus Fisher Case. And summons for plaintiff Stephen Swaine and Wm. Long.

25 Harvey versus Boyce plea of Tresspass. Returned Executed. Reffered.

25 Idem versus Welch plea of Tresspass. Not Executed. And summons for Harvey versus Boyc and Welch, Robt. Fendall Richd. Burtenshall and his wife: Anthony Alexander Mrs. Sarah Gaile: Mr. Hen. Norman Capt. James Coles.

---

[1] Pages 144*a*, 145 and 145*a* of the manuscript are headed, "Writts and Returns to March Court."

28 Norcom Administrator of Betson Versus Pricklove.

March 3 Phillipps Versus Paine plea of Debt. Not Executed.

3 Phillipps apeale from Pascotank Court versus Scarborow.

Rice his apeale from Pascotank Court versus Scarborow.

3d Hecklefeild Versus Lysle. Retraxitt.

3 Duckenfeild Assignee of Buntin Versus Jones Debt. Retraxitt.

4 Boyce Versus Fewox Plea Debt. Retraxitt.

4 Quarry versus Jenitt plea Debt.

4 Hecklefeild Nichollson Plea of the Case. Not Executed.

5th Hecklefeild Versus Welch Case. No Return.

5 Hecklefeild versus Spruill. Retraxitt.

5 Major Swann versus Rooks Case. Retraxitt.

6 Prichard Versus Fitzpatrick plea of Debt. Retraxitt.

6 Boyce Versus Bird Debt. Retraxitt.

<145*a*> March 5 [*sic*] Patrick Keneday Versus Fugate Case. Retraxitt.

6 Fugate Versus Keneday Case. Retraxitt.

6 Luten versus Russell and Abington Plea of Debt.

10 Chevin versus Clark plea of the Case.

14 Porter Attorney of Smith Attorney of Hambleton etc. Versus Pollock and Hunt Case.

14 Porter Information versus Hougton for perjury. And summons for Informer Argill Simonds Humphrey Legg Richard Davenport John Foster and Gabriell Nuby.

Relph versus Rawlison plea Case. Retraxitt.

Russell versus Palin plea Case. Retraxitt.

[*CCR 102*]

<145*a*> Att a Generall Court Holden for the Province of North Carolina att the house of Doctor Jno. Hecklefeild in Little River the 31 of March 1702 Being Present The Honorable Wm. Glover Richard Plater: Tho. Symond Esqrs.

The Courts Comission is published and the Honorable Wm.

Glover and Richd. Plater Esqrs. takes the Oaths by Law appoynted before the Honorable president And Thomas Symonds Esqr. Doth on the Penallty of Perjury before The Honorable President Subscribe to the said Oaths by Law apoynted.

Upon the petition of Capt. Thomas Luten provost Marshall Ordered that Doctor Jno. Hecklefeild Administrator of Mr. Geo. Pordage pay to Capt. Thomas Luten the sum of three pounds five shillings one peny.

The Marshall being Comanded to arest the body of Mr. Edward Mayo to Answer the sute of Mr. Hugh Mcgregory to the Last Court in October And the Defendant not apearing Order past against the marshall <146> That he have the body of the said Mayo att this Court alias Judgment to be Confirmed against the marshall And the said Hugh Mcgregory by Mr. Danl. Phillipps his attorney Craves that the sute may be Dismist. Ordered that the action be Dismist and the plaintiff pay Costs alias Execution.

Mr. Daniel Phillipps Comes to prosecute his apeale from the precinct Court of pascotank upon an Atteachment against Augustine Scarborow upon the goods and Chattells of Walter Reedall for the sum of 27 shillings per account And the said Scarborrow Comes and for plea saith that he hath not in his hands of the goods and Chattells of the said Reedall more than two Iron potts one Chest and two bushells of Beanes and makes oath to the said plea.

Ordered that Augustine Scarborow Deliver to Daniell Phillips the aforesaid goods and Chattells Viz. 2 Iron potts one Chest and two Bushells of Beanes alias Execution.

Daniell Rice Comes to prosecute his apeale from the precinct Court of pascotank upon an atteachment against the goods and Chattell of Walter Reedall in the hands of Augustine Scarborow And the said Scarborrow haveing upon his Oath Declared that he hath not of the goods and Chattells of the said Reddall in his hands save only the two Iron potts and one Chest and two Bushells of Beanes the apealant asks no further.

The Marshall was Comanded to arest the body of Jno. Burnett att the sute of Jno. Wattson in a Plea of the Case And the plaintiff Came Nott. Ordered that the action be Dismist and the Plaintiff pay Costs alias Execution.

The Marshall was Comanded to arest the body of Edward Williams att the sute of Thos. Cutlett in a Plea of the Case and the plaintiff Came not. Ordered that the action be Dismist and the plaintiff pay Costs alias Execution.

William Barnsfeild Comes by Mr. Daniel Phillips his attorney to prosecute his sute against Jno. Holford in a Plea of Debt for the sum of one pound foureteen shillings and six pence And the Defendant Came not. Ordered that the marshall have the body of Jno. Holford on the first Day of the next Generall Court the Last Tuseday in July Alias Judgment to be Confirmed against the marshall.

William Barnsfeild by Mr. Daniel Phillips his attorney Comes to prosecute his sute against Jno. Holford in a Plea of the Case and Declares for five pound by acount And the Defendant Came nott. Ordered that the marshall have here the body of Jno. Holford att the next Generall Court alias Judgment to be Confirmed against the Marshall.

<146*a*> The marshall was Comanded to arest the body of Wm. Frayly att the sute of Cornelious Benington in a plea of Debt and the plaintiff Came not. Ordered that the sute be Dismist and the plaintiff pay Costs alias Execution.

The marshall was Comanded to arest the body of Jno. Griffin att the sute of Cornelious Benington in a Plea of the Case and the plaintiff Came not. Ordered that the action be Dismist and the plaintiff pay Costs alias Execution.

The Marshall was Comanded to Arest the body of Tom Andiver att the sute of Cornel. Benington in a Plea of the Case and the plaintiff Came nott. Ordered that the sute be Dismist and the plaintiff pay Costs Alias Execution.

Colonel Wm. Wilkison produces a Warrant of Attorney from Colonel Thomas Pollock and prays itt may be Recorded. Ordered the Warrant of attorney be Recorded.

Colonel Thomas Pollock by Colonel Wm. Wilkison his attorney Comes to prosecute his sute against Thomas Evins in a Plea of the Case and Declares for 4=17=4 per the ballance of acounts And the Defendant Came not And the plaintiff by Colonel Wm. Wilkison etc. proves part of the acount by the Receite And oath thereunto of Daniell Deane Viz. These perticulars two gallons of Rum three gallons of Malasses three paire of shoos two pound of sugar one halfe Round file And the Defendant Came not. Ordered that the marshall have here the body of Tho. Evins att the next Generall Court the Last Tuseday in July next alias Judgment to be Confirmed against the Marshall.

Adjourned till to morrow Morning 9 a Clock.

Aprill the first Court meets Present utt supra as allso Major Samuel Swann And Jno. Hawkins Esqr. who hearing the Comission Published Do Solemnly take the oath by Law apoynted.

Uppon the Petition of Capt. Thomas Relfe Executor of Tho. White Deceased shewing that he hath paid as farr as he hath Assetts of the Estate aforesaid and prayes a quietus est and to be Discharged And he bringing no Accounts pertaineing to the Estate Ordered That the petitioner shall produce a faire acount of the said Estate and what he has Disburst to the next Generall Court in July next.

Mr. Jno. Porter Comes to prosecute his sute against James Fewox in a plea of Debt for five pounds in Pork and produces a Bill for the same And the Defendant Comes and owns the Bill But sayes that he has paid part <147>[2] of the Bill and produces a Receite for the sum of Eleven shilling and foure pence halfpeny. Ordered that James Fewox pay to Mr. Jno. Porter the sum of foure pound Eight shillings seaven pence halfpeny with Costs of sute in pork alias Execution.

Mr. Jno. Porter Assignee of Humphry Legg Comes to prosecute his sute against James Fewox in a Plea of the Case and Declares for the sum of [*blank*] upon a Penall Bond And the Defendant Comes and Defends the sute and for plea saith that Upon a speciallty an Action of Debt Lies and not an action of the Case And the Court opinion is agreeable to the Defendants plea And Prays a nonsute on the said Action. Ordered that a Nonsute be granted to the Defendant and the plaintiff pay Costs.

The Marshall being Comanded to arest the body of James Fewox att the sute of Mr. Jno. Porter in a Plea of Defamation and the plaintiff not apearing to prosecute Ordered that the sute be Dismist and the plaintiff pay Costs alias Execution.

Adjourned for two hours.

One a Clock the Court meets present Wm. Glover Richd. Plater Thomas Symonds Jno. Hawkins Esqrs.

Mathew Prichard etc. Comes to prosecute his sute against Robt. Moline by order against the marshall from the Last Court and the Defendant by Elinor his Wife Comes and sayes that sattisfaction they have allready made and the plaintiff prays Judgment for Costs of sute and Asks no further. Ordered that Robt. Moline pay Costs Alias Execution.

An Indenture between Henry Lisle and Mr. Wm. Duckenfeild was acknowledged per the said Lysle and prays itt may be Recorded. Ordered itt be Recorded.

Mr. Jno. Benitt Came to prosecute his apeale from the precinct Court of Curatuck upon an action brought by him against Mr. Benj. Tull. And the process Copy of the Judgment of the precinct Court not apearing Ordered that the apeale be Dismist and the said Benitt pay Costs.

[2] Page 147 of the manuscript is headed, "April first Generall Court."

<147*a*>[3] A Letter of Attorney from Tho. Symonds Esqr. Attorney to Winthorp and Midlecott merchants of New England was acknowledged to Mr. Jno. Porter By Tho. Simond Esqr. Mr. Jno. Porter attorney etc. and James Took Executor etc. By mutuall Consent joyns Issue and the plaintiff Complaines for severall Bills acounts and Chattells belonging to the [Administrators] Winthorp and Midleton merchants of Boston and the Defendant James Took Comes and Conffesses. Ordered that James Took Deliver unto Mr. Jno. Porter Attorney etc. all Bill accounts and papers belonging to Winthorp Midlecott and Company which is in his hands.

The marshall was Comanded to arest the body of Chris Bailes att the sute of Richard Berry in a Plea of the Case And the plaintiff apeared not to prosecute. Ordered the sute be Dismist and the plaintiff pay Costs alias Execution.

A Writt of scire facias brought by Wm. Duckenfeild Esqr. etc. Administrator of Slaugtor Deceased upon a former Judgment of the Generall Court and produces the Copy of the said Judgment from the Record against Mathew Prachard and Sarah his Wife Administrators of Patrick Henly and the said Prichard and his Wife Comes and For plea saith they have not assetts in theire hands and the Complainant per Rich. Plater Esqr. his attorney prays the said Judgment may be [Revived]. Ordered that Mathew Prichard and Sarah his Wife Administrators of Henly Deceased pay to Wm. Duckenfeild Esqr. etc. the sum of [*blank*] with Costs of sute alias Execution.

Upon the Petition of Doctor Godfrey Spruill Ordered that James Fewox pay to the petitioner for his travell and Attendance five shillings and ten pence with Costs alias Execution.

The marshall was Comanded to arest the body of Levie Truwhitt att the sute of Mr. Tho. Deerham in a Plea of Debt and the plaintiff Came not to prosecute. Ordered that the sute be Dismist and the plaintiff pay Costs alias Execution.

<148> The Marshall was Comanded to Arest the body of Saml. West att the sute of Mathew Adams Assiggne of Copeland and the plaintiff Came not to prosecute. Ordered that the action be Dismist and the plaintiff pay Costs alias Execution.

On Petition of Wm. Hardee Ordered that James Fuox pay to the said petitioner the sum of seaven shillings and six pence for his travell and Attendance this Court.

Grand Jury sworne Viz. Dr. Godfrey Spruill Jno. Billitt Augustine Scarborow Rich. Madren Fra. Hendrick Jno. Daviss Danl. Rice Jno. Jones Edw. Winder David Prichard Wm. Winberry Jno. Huften

[3] Pages 147*a* and 148*a* of the manuscript are headed, "Generall Court Aprill the 2d."

Henry Sawyer Wm. Bartlett Na. Grey Wm. Stevens James McDaniel.

The Court Adjourned till to morrow morning 9 a Clock.

Thursday Aprill 2d 1702 Court meets. Present utt supra.

The Marshall being Comanded to arest the body of Tho. Evins att the sute of Jno. Falcoer in a Plea of the Case and the plaintiff not apearing to prosecute Ordered that the sute be Dismist and the plaintiff pay Costs alias Execution.

The Marshall was Comanded to arest the body of Jno. Flowers att the sute of Jno. Falconer in a Plea of the Case and the plaintiff Came not to prosecute. Ordered that the action be Dismist and the plaintiff pay Costs Alias Execution.

The Marshall was Comanded to Arest the body of Mary Rooks att the sute of Jno. Falconer in a Plea of the Case and the plaintiff not apearing to prosecute Ordered that the sute be Dismist and the plaintiff pay Costs alias Execution.

The Humble petition of Tho. Palmer as [mariing] the Administratrix of Jno. Riggins Deceased shewing that he hath paide Debts out of the Estate to the full sum of the Inventory and prayes a quietus est And The Honorable Court Request Mr. Tho. Boyd and Mr. Gabriel Nuby Newly to Auditt the said acounts and mak Report thereof to this Court And they Report to the Court that he hath paid beyond the Extent of the apraisement. Ordered that Tho. Palmer Be Dismist from the said Estate.

And then the Court Adjourned till one a Clock in the afternoon.

And then the Court Meets [present] utt supra.

Upon the Complaint of Richard Plater Esqr. <148*a*> Shewing that Thos. Twiddy maliciously hath abused the Complainant. Ordered that the marshall take the said Twiddy in to Custody and Comitt him to the stocks there to sitt one hour.

A Conveyance of a Tract of Land was acknowledged by Wm. Godfrey to Thomas Bartlett and Sarah his Wife Came and Relinquishes all her title of Dower to the same.

Dr. Godfrey Spruill Acknowledges a Deed of Gift of a tract of Land Lying in Scoperlung to Jno. Stewart And James Fewox Attorney to Mrs. Johanah Spruill Comes and Relinques her title of Dower to the same and proves his Letter of Attorney by the oathes of Roger Snell and Wm. Hardee.

A tract of Land was Acknowledged by Jno. Bayly to Jno. Daviss and Elinor Wife of the said Jno. Bayly Comes and Relinques all her title of Dower to the same.

And then the Court Adjourned till to Morrow Morning 8 a Clock.

Fryday Aprill the 3d Court Meets. Present the Honorable Wm. Glover Esqr. Tho. Symonds Jno. Hawkin Esqrs.

The Juriors for our Sovereigne Lord the king Do present That Abraham Hobbs of the Precinct of Pequimons not haveing the feare of god before his Eyes did on or about the 18 or 19th of day of November Last past in the precinct of Pequimons feloniously with force and arms Kill and beare away one hogg of the Value of Eighteen shillings properly belonging to the Honorable President Contrary to the pease of our sovereigne Lord the king his Crowne and Dignity and against the statutes in that Case made and provided. And the said Abraham Hobbs being Areigned Pleads not Guilty and Casts himself upon god and the Countrey and Rich. Plater Esqr. Attorney Generall who prosecutes on his Majesties behalf Likewise And the Marshall for the tryall thereof hath Empaneled Mr. Jno. Blount Mr. Wm. Long Mr. Brian Fitzpatrick Mr. Rich. Davenport Mr. Jno. Foster: Mr. Robt. Fendell Mr. Saml. Parsons Mr. Tho. Boyd: Mr. Argill Symonds <149> Mr. Wm. Simpson: Mr. Wm. Barrow: Mr. Nich. Tylor who allso Came and to give a true Verdict in the premisses being sworne upon the Holy Evangelist say he is guilty and he humbly praying Transportation Ordered that he be Banisht out of the Government for Ever.

Upon the Petition of Wm. Voss Ordered that the marshall take into Costody the body of William Powell and him to hold Untill he give bond with good security for his good behaviour in the sum of fifty pounds.

The Marshall being Comanded to arest the body of Mr. Wm. Boyce att the sute of Mr. Thomas Harvey in a Plea of Tresspas and the Defendant Comes and prayes the matter may be Referred till the first Day of the next Generall Court for and that his Cheife Evidence Viz. Mrs. Juliana Laker by Reason of Lameness is Disabled from being att this Court which he proves by the Oath of Mr. Laurence Mague. Ordered that the action be Refered till the first day of the Next Generall Court.

Upon the Petition of Mr. Cornelious Jones Shewing that the Estate of Mr. Geo. Pordage stands Indebted to the petitioner in the sum of one pound Eighteen shillings and Nine pence which he proved by his oath Doctor Jno. Hecklefeild being present Ordered that Doctor Jno. Hecklefeild Administrator of the goods and Chattells of George pordage pay to the petitioner the sum of one pound Eighteen shillings with Costs alias Execution.

Mr. Jno. Porter Came on the 3d Day of the Generall Court and gives the Court here to understand and be Informed That Thomas Houghton of the precinct of Pequimons is Guilty of Willfull perjury for and that the said Houghton being Called to give in upon oath before the Honorable President whither he did not before the Bieniall Assembly here Colonel William Wilkison in his own house Publish or Read a Certaine Wrighting which was Called an agreivance In which was Conteined seditious and libellous matters against the goverment <149*a*>[4] he Replied upon his oath he heard no such paper and that he had no agreivance but what he had from Gabriel Nuby And notwithstanding the Informer saith he is able to prove by Evidence that the said Houghton had such a paper and the said Houghton being brought and Charged with the said Information saith he is not guilty and thereupon Casts himself upon the Countrey and the Attorney Generall Likewise and the Marshall is Comanded to Cause to come twelve good and Lawfull men of the vicinage and who etc. By whom etc. and there Came Mr. Jno. Blount Mr. Wm. Long: Mr. Cornelious Jones: Mr. Robt. Fendall: Mr. Benj. Tull Mr. Wm. Reed: Mr. Wm. Barrow: Mr. Nich. Tylor: Mr. Fra. Foster: Mr. Henry Norman: Mr. Saml. Paine Mr. Tho. Boyd who Impanelled and sworn upon the Holy Evangelist say he is not Guilty. Ordered that the Information be Dismist and Informer pay Costs Alias.

Upon the Petition of Robt. Murry Ordered that Thomas Norcom Administrator of the goods and Chattells of Fra. Betson Deceased pay to the Petitioner the sum of one pound seaventeen shillings when he shall have Assetts in his hands being Due to the said Murry by acount proved in the precinct Court of Pequimons.

Doctor Godfrey Spruill Assignee of Mrs. Ann Pope Executrix of Mr. Richard Pope Comes to prosecute his sute against Mr. Wm. Duckenfeild in a Plea of Debt for the sum of ten pound five shillings in skins And the Defendant Came not. Ordered that the Marshall have the body of Mr. Wm. Duckenfeild att the first day of the next Generall Court alias Judgment to be Confirmed against the Marshall.

Upon Petition of James Ward Ordered that Tho. Norcom Administrator to the goods and Chattells of Francis Bettson pay to the petitioner the sum of one pound nineteen shillings when he shall have Assetts with Costs of sute alias Execution.

<150> Thomas Norcom Administrator of the goods and Chattells of Francis Betson Deceased Comes to prosecute his sute against Jno. Pricklove in a Plea of Detinue and Declares for severall goods and moneys in the hands of the Defendant belonging to the Estate of the said Betson Deceased which he unjustly Deteines And the said

[4] Page 149a of the manuscript is headed, "Generall Court Aprill the 3d 1702."

Pricklove Comes and Defends the sute and for plea saith that any of the goods or Chattells of the said Betson in his hand he Doth not Deteine But that what goods or moneys are in his hands belonging to the said Estate he hath by order of the precinct Court of Pequimons And produces a Copy thereof from the Record and thereupon he Casts himself upon the Countrey and the Plaintiff Likewise And the Marshall is Comanded to Cause to Come Twelve good and Lawfull men of the Vicinage And who etc. By whome etc. and there Came Jno. Blount Benj. Tull: Robt. Fendall: Cornel. Jones: Argill Symonds Henry Norman: Jno. Relfe: Wm. Jackson Samuel Paine: Wm. Simpson Archibald Holmes who Empanelled and sworne upon the Holy Evangelist say We find no Cause of action. Ordered that the sute be Dismist and the plaintiff pay Costs alias Execution.

Information being made to this Honorable Court by Jno. Neale Thomas Spencer Patrick Mackcoone upon theire oaths of sundry Impudent Imperious and Abominable Expression Uttered by William Powell against The Government and members of this Honorable Court. Ordered that he be punished by Receiveing twenty stripes on his bare back Well Laid on Duereing the Courts sitting And allso in Consideration of his Wicked and Turbulent spiritt towards his majesties subjects and Neighbours on the Sand banks it is further ordered that his uncertaine Entries by him made be Voyd. And that he pay Costs alias Execution.

Itt being Represented to this Court by the Honorable President that great Complaints hath been made by Jonathan Bateman that Samuell Paine (who was apoynted to Receive the tenths of Oyl for the Honorable Presidents use) Did unjustly seize upon the said Batemans Oyle The said Bateman and Samuel Paine Apearing before the Honorable Court the said Samuell Paine by the oaths of Jno. Neale Thomas Spencer and Patrick Mackcoon <150*a*> makes it Evidently apeare that any Oyl belonging to the said Bateman he hath not seized but what was Lawfull for him to do in behalf of the Honorable President for his Tenths.

Upon the Petition of Robt. Fendall Ordered that Tho. Harvey Pay to the petitioner for his travell and atendance the sum of Eight shillings and foure pence with Costs alias Execution.

Capt. Tho. Luten Comes to Prosecute his sute against Daniell Russell and Mr. Tho. Abington in a Plea of Debt and Daniel And Declares for the sum of two pound thirteen shillings and nine pence And Daniell Phillips attorney of Russell and Abbington Comes and Confesses Judgment. Ordered That Daniell Phillips pay to Capt. Tho. Luten the sum of 2:13:9 with Costs alias Execution in behalf of Abington and Russell.

Mr. Jno. Porter Attorney of John Smith attorney of Hambleton fogo and paterson Comes to prosecute his sute against Colonel Tho. Pollock and Capt. Jno. Hunt Executors of Adam Gambell Deceased and the Defendant not appearing

Ordered [the Honorable] President in Barr to the said action as being Attorney to Jno. Gambell attorney to James Gambell Legatiee Comes and saith [that] the plaintiffs theire action ought not to have for and that the said Smith hath not Power by his Letter of Procuration to Constitute any attorney under him and produces the Comision of attorney from Hambleton fogo and paterson, which appearing Ordered That the action be Dismist and the plaintiff pay Costs alias Execution.

[*Signed:*]
W. Glover, Thomas Symons, Jno. Hawkins.

RECORDED BY ORDER OF COURT

[*CCR 102*]

<151>[5] This Indenture made the First day of Aprill Anno domini 1702 Between Henry Lisle of North Carolina on the one part Labourer And William Duckenfeild of the said province Esqr. on the other part wittnesseth that the said Henry Lisle (For and in Consideration of the Full and Just sum of Forty two pounds Whearof the said Henry Lisle standeth now Indepted to the said Willm. Duckenfeild) hath granted Bargined sold Assigned and sett over unto the said Wm. Duckenfeild his Executors Administrators or Assigns All that one plantation: lyeing att Reckahock Together with All Cattle Hogs Houshold goods upon the said plantation and allsoe all Estate Reall or personall whearof the said Henry Lisle standeth now posessed within the above said provenc and allso one great Conoo with all Appurtences Theirto belonging To Have and to hold the a Bovesaid plantation Cattle Hogs Houshold stuff Conoo and all other the premises unto the said Wm. Duckenfeild his Executors administrators and Assigns from the date of these presents Forever and the said Henry Lisle doth from himselfe his Heires Executors Administrators and Assigns covonant promise agre and grant to and with the said Wm. Duckenfeild his heirs Executors Administrators shall seale and acknoledge all other act and acts thing and things which shall be by said Wm. Duckenfield requiered for the truth security of the said dept In witnesse where of the partys to these

[5] Page 151 of the manuscript is headed, "Recorded by Order."

prests to the parts of the Indenture Interchengeble have sett to there hands and seals the day and yeare first above written.

Sigillat etc. delivrnce Henry Lisle Sigillum
Presentra C. Gale
Wm. Chilton

FILE PAPERS IN SUITS AND PROSECUTIONS

[*Anderson* v. *Averitt*]

[*CCR 148*]

North Carolina Ss. To the provost Marshall or Depty

These are in his majesties name to Will and require you to arest the body of Tho. Averitt and him to hold so that he may apear att the next Generall Court the Last Tuseday in March next att the house of Dr. John Hecklefeild in Little River on the 2d Day of the Court to Answer the plaint of Jno. Andrson in a plea of Debt and have there this writt.

Janry. 27th 1701/2 N. Chevin Clk. Curiae

[*Endorsed:*]
Executed februry the 6 1701/2 by me Thos. Luten provost marshall

[*Boyce* v. *Bird*]

[*CCR 148*]

North Carolina Ss. To the Provost Marshall or Depty

These are in his Majties name to Will and Require you to arest the body of Jno. Bird and him to hold so that he may apear att the next Generall Court to be holden for this Government the Last Tuseday in this Instant March att the house of Doctor Jno. Hecklefeild in Little River to Answer the plaint of Mr. Wm. Boyce merchant in Plea of Debt and have there this writt. Dated att the secretaries Office March the 4th 1701/2.

N. Chevin, Clericus Curiae

[*Endorsed:*]
Boyes versus Byrd
This Rit was Executed march the [4] 1701/2 by me Daniell Philipes deputy marshall

[*Chevin* v. *Frayly*]

[*CCR 139*]

[*Torn*] Carolina Ss. To the Provost Marshall or Depty

[*Torn*] are in her Majesties Name to Will and Require you to [*torn*] the body of Wm. Frayly and him to hold so that he may apeare att the next Generall Court to be holden for thes province [*torn*] last Tusday in March next att the house of Capt. John Hecklefeild in Little River on the Second Day of the Court to answer the plaint of Nath. Chevin in a Plea of the Case [*torn*] have there this Writt. Datd Feb. 17th 1702.

N. Chevin Clk.

[*Chevin* v. *Laker*]

[*CCR 191*]

To the Generall Court

Nath. Chevin is plaintiff Versus Mrs. Juliana Laker Defendant in the Plea of the Case and Complaines that the Defendant stands Indebted to the plaintiff in the sum of two pound six shillings and ten pence per account (as by wayes and means Convenient he is Ready to make apeare) And which to Render she Doth Refuse to the Plaintiffs Damage five pounds for which he brings his action and prays Judgment for the same with Costs and shall Pray etc.

Copia Vera Na. Chevin Clk.

[*Endorsed:*]
Chevin versus Laker

[*CCR 148*]

[North] Carolina Ss. To the Provost Marshall or Depty

[These] are in his Majties Name to Will and require you to arest the body [of] Juliana Laker and her to hold so that she may apeare att the [next] Generall Court the Last Tuseday in march next att the house of Dr. [John] Hecklefeild in Little River to Answer the plaint of Nath. Chevin in a plea [of the] Case and have there this writt. Dated Janry. 27 1701/2.

N. Chevin Clk.

[*Endorsed:*]
Executed by me Peter Grey deputy Marshall

[*Crown* v. *Blount*]

[*CCR 148*]

North Carolina Ss. To the provost Marshall or Depty

These are in his Majesties name to Will and Require you to arest the body of Capt. Tho. Blount and him to hold so that he may apeare att the next Generall Court to be holden for this province the Last Tuseday in March att the house of Dr. Jno. Hecklefeild in Little River on the 3d Day of the Court to answer the plaint of Richard Plater Esqr. Attorney General in a plea of the Case and have there this writt. Dated Febry. the 18 1701/2.

N. Chevin, Clk.

[*Endorsed:*]
[*Illegible*] Copy of this writ with the decleration Left att the house of the defendant by me Thos. Luten provost marshall

[*Crown* v. *Ellitt*]

[*CCR 139*]

[*Torn*]

The Jurors for our Soveraigne Lord the king Do present That Thomas Ellitt of the Precinct of Pascotank in province aforesaid not haveing the feare of god before his Eyes did about the Last of November Last or the first of Decembr. feloniously Kill and leave away one Cow Belonging to mr. Cornelious Jones of the Same place of a pied Couler Against the peace of our Soveraigne Lord the King his Crowne and Dignity and Contrary to the Statutes in that Case made and provided And prays that the Penalty of the Statute may be Inflicted upon him as the Law in that Case Directs.
Aprill the 2d 1702
We the Jurers doe find bill of Vera

[*Torn*]
Mr. Jno. Relf
Mrs. Mary Willson

[*Dereham* v. *Truewhitt*]

[*CCR 191*]

North Carolina Ss. To the 2d Day of the Generall Court

Mr. Tho. Dearham is plaintiff versus Levie Truwhitt Defendant in a plea of Debt and Complains [that the] Defendant stands Justly Indebted and owing to the plaintiff in the sum of 7=18=0 (as by his bill in [court] produced may apeare) and which to Render he Doth refuse to the plaintiffs Damage 16 pounds sterling for which he brings his action and prays Judgment for the same [with] Costs and shall pray etc.

Copia Vera N. Chevin, Clericus Curiae

[*Endorsed:*]
Dereham versus Truwhitt

[*Duckenfield and wife, administrators* v. *Henley, administrator*]

[*CCR 185*]

No. Carolina Ss. To the Provost marshall or Depty

Whereas att a Generall Court holden for this Government Oct. the 11th

1697 Mr. Wm. Duckenfeild and Susanah his Wife Administrators of the goods and Chattells of Thos. Slaughter Obtained a Judgment by Due and Legall Process against Patrick Henly Administrator of the Goods and Chattles of Tho. Clancy Deceased for the Sum of twelve pounds Sterling with Costs of Sute alias Execution. And the Said Judgment being not yet Satisfied These are therefore by Vertue of the aforesaid Order to will and require you to Summons Mr. Mathew Prichard and Sarah his Wife Administrators of the Goods and Chattells of Patr. Henly to Appeare att the Next Generall Court to be held att the house of Doctor Jno. Hecklefeild in Little River the Last Tuseday in March next on the 2d Day of the Court to Shew Cause why Execution Should not go forth Upon the Said Order hereof fayl not Dated Feb. 18 1701/2.

N. Chevin Clk.

[*Harvey* v. *Fisher*]

[*CCR 148*]

No. Carolina Ss. To the provost Marshall or Depty

These are in his Majties name to Will and Require you to arest the body [*torn*] Fisher and him to hold so that he may apeare att the next Generall [Court to] be holden for this Government the Last Tuseday in march next [at the] house of Doctor Jno. Hecklefeild in Little River to Answer the plaint [of] Thomas Harvey in a Plea of the Case and have there this writt. Dated Febry. the 24th 1701/2.

N. Chevin, [Clericus Curiae]

[*Endorsed:*]
Executed the 18 of March by Me Peter Grey deputy Marshall

[*Harvey* v. *Welch*]

[*CCR 140*]

To the 3d Day of the Generall Court

Tho. Harvey of the Precinct of Pequimons is plaintiff Versus Thomas Welch Defendant in a Plea of the Case for Tresspass and Setteth forth Thatt on or a bout the 6th Day of July 1701 the Defendant Came to the habitation of the plaintiff in the precinct of pequimons And then and there did unjustly Uncover and Demollish the house of the plaintiff And the Same Layd open, The plaintiff being att thatt time from home by Reasone Whereof the plaintiff Lost out of his house the Value of one hundred pounds in money and goods which is to the plaintiffs Damage Att Least three hundred pounds Sterling for which he brings his action and prayes Judgment for the Same with Costs of Sute and Shall pray etc.

Copia Vera N. Chevin Clericus Curiae

[*Hecklefield* v. *Nicholson*]

[*CCR 191*]

To the Honorable Generall Court first Day

Capt. Jno. Hecklefeild is plaintiff Versus William Nicholson Defendant in a Plea of the Case and Says that the Defendant Stands Indebted and owing to the plaintiff in the Sum of 2:11: per account (as by wayes and meanes Convenient he is Ready to prove) And which to Render the Defendant Doth Refuse to the plaintiffs Damage five pounds for which he brings his Action and prays Judgment for the Same with Costs and Shall Pray etc.

Copia Verea Na. Chevin Clericus Curiae

[*Hecklefield, administrator* v. *Spruill*]

[*CCR 184*]

To the 4th Day of the Generall Court

Doctor Jno. Hecklefeild Administrator of the Goods and Chattels of George Pordage is plaintiff versus Mr. Godfrey Spruill Defendant in a Plea of Debt and Complains that the Defendant Stands Indebted to the plaintiff (qualified as aforsaid) in the Sum of Eleven pound Eleven Shillings and Six pence as by Bill under his hand beareing Date 9br. the 10th 1698 may apeare which to Render he Dose Refuse to the plaintiffs Damiage thirty pounds for which he brings an action and prays Judgment for the Same with Costs and Shall pray etc.

Copia vera Na. Chevin Clericus Curiae

[*Endorsed:*]
Hecklefeild versus Spruill

[*CCR 184*]

No. Carolina Ss. To the Provost Marshall or Depty

These are in his Majtis name to Will and require you to arest the Body of Mr. Godfrey Spruill and him to hold so that he may apear att the next Generall Court the Last Tusday of this Instant Month att the house of Doctor Jno. Hecklefeild in Little River to Answer the Plaint of Doctor Jno. Hecklefeild Administrator to George Prodige Deceased in a Plea of Debt and have there this Writt.

Dated March the 6th 1701/2 N. Chevin Clk.

[*Endorsed:*]
Executed the 16 of March by Me Peter Grey deputy Marshall

[*Hecklefield and wife* v. *Welch*]

[*CCR 191*]

To the 3d day of the Generall Court

Doctor Jno. Hecklefeild And Eliz. his Wife is plaintiff versus James Welch Defendant in a Plea of the Case and shews that the Defendant stands Indebted and owing to the plaintiffs in the sum of twenty five shillings per account (as by wayes and means Convenient they are Ready to make apear) and which to Render he Doth Refuse to the plaintiffs Damage fifty shillings for which they have brought theire action and prayes judgment for the same with Costs and shall Pray etc.

Copia Vera N. Chevin Clericus Curiae

[*Endorsed:*]
Jo. Hecklefeld versus Welch

[*McGregory and wife, administrators* v. *Mayo*]

[*CCR 183*]

N. Carolina SS. To the Generall Court

Hugh McGregor and Africca his wife Administrators of the goods and Chattells of Mrs. Em Mayo deceased Late wife of Edward Mayo versus the said Edward Mayo defendant in a plea of detinue Complaines that wheras at the death of the Said Em Mayo Remained and yett Remaineth in the hands of the Said Edward Mayo one Negroe man properly belonging to the Said Em Mayo Seperat from the Estate of the Said Edward Mayo as by wayes and meanes Convenient the plantife is Ready to make Apear the Said Edward Mayo the premises very well knowing and Said purpose the plantife to defraude the said Negroe doth detaine and to Render to the plantife doth Refuse though often demanded to the plantifes damage the Summe of Eightie pounds starling for which they have brought their Suit and prayes Judgment for the Same with Cost and shall pray.

Hugh MacGregor

[*Endorsed:*]
Mcgregory and Wife versus Mayo
[*Illegible*] Marshall
Hu maggregary adversely Rasion [*sic*]

[*CCR 183*]

No. Carolina ss. Generall Court Oct. 29th 1701

Present the Justices

Hugh Macgregory and Affrica his Wife Administrator and Administratrix of Em Mayo Late Wife of Edw. Mayo Deceased Comes to prosecute theire

Sute against Edw. Mayo in a Plea of Detinue and the Defendant Came not. And the plaintiff by Mr. Danl. Phillips theire Attorney prayes Order against the Marshall.

Ordered that the Marshall have the body of Edw. Mayo att the Next Generall Court the Last Tuseday in March Next Alias Judgment to be Confirmed against the Marshall.

Copia Vera N. Chevin Clericus Curiae

[*Pollock* v. *Evans*]

[*CCR 191*]

Generall Court 2d Day

The Honorable Colonel Tho. Pollock is plaintiff Versus Tho. Evins Defendant in a Plea of the Case and sayes that the said Evins stands Justly Indebted and owing to the plaintiff in the sum of 4=17:3 per account (as by Wayes and means Convenient he is Ready to make apeare) and which to Render he Doth Refuse to the plaintiffs Damage 8=00=00 [for] which he brings his action and prays Judgment for the same with Costs and shall pray etc.

Copia Vera N. Chevin Clk. Court

[*Endorsed:*]
Pollock versus Evins

[*Pollock and Hunt, executors,* v. *Walker, attorney of Gambell*]

[*CR 2.002*]

The Replication of Hendrson Walker Esqr. To Colonel Tho. Pollock and Capt. Jno. Hunt

The Replication of Hendrson Walker Esqr. Attorney of Jno. Gambell Attorney of James Gambell of Glasscow in Scottland to Colonel Tho. Pollock [*torn*] Capt. Jno. Hunt Executors of the Last Will and Testament of Adam Gambell late of this Goverment Shews That as to the first Reason this honoble Court [*torn*] given a Months time since the Last Court fo[*torn*] Said Defendants.

As to the 2d The Complainant saith that Mr. Porter never Qualifyed as a Lawfull Attorney [*torn*] Smith whereby to bring any pretended action [*torn*] Defendants for that the said Smith had never noe [*torn*] soe to doe.

And the Complainant humbly shewes that about this [*torn*] 3 yeare the said Smith Came in here Qualafyed [*torn*] Attorney to Hambleton Paterson and fogo and the said Executors Ought according to equity [*torn*] good Conscyence have paid the testators debts if a [*torn*] was due and not to make a pretence of a [*torn*] to keep the Complainant from his Just Legacy that the Said [*torn*] have had the estate of the Complainant 7 yeares [*torn*] hands and will keep the same Longer if not Releived by this honorable [*torn*].

That as to any [*illegible*] as long as they are [*torn*] the Executor may keep the same in their [*illegible*] your Complainant prays the Executors may be Compelled [*torn*] answer according to the Bill and he shall pray.

[*CCR 181*]

Colonel Tho. Pollock Executor of Mr. Adam Gambell Cr.

To Summons and deponents evidence for probate Gamb. Will	00:04:00
To petition order and Copy for appraisers	00:03:00
To probate copy and [record] Will	00:10:00
To 2 Summons and depositions to prove Gambels agreement	00:04:00
To petition order and record	00:05:00
To petition order and Copy for answer	00:03:00
To order record returne of Gambel Account	00:01:00
To record Inventory and deposition	00:07:00
To record 3 accts. debt and Credit and 3 auditts [*blank*]	

[*Porter* v. *Fewox*]

[*CCR 191*]

North Carolina To the Honorable the Generall Court

John Porter Declares against James Fewox in an action of Deffamation Case and setts forth that the said James Fewox hath for a Considerable time made it his Buisnesse through this whole [Government] with apremeditated mallice in a most Vile manner to scandalisse and bespatter the name and reputation of this Complainant having Declared to divers persons that the said Porter was a Roage and that hee would Indite him for such a person and that hee was [Soe] proved and that it was proved that this Complainants Books and accounts was all false and in perticuler the said Fewox made it his Buisness to goe to severall persons Indebted to the Complainant and did Examine them whether they had past their bills to this Complainant and when they owned they had and that it was their just Dew to pay it hee swore they were fools and that if they had not past their bills hee would have Discharged them for six pence or sum such small matter and when hee was by the same persons reproved alleaging to him god forbid that they should goe to deprive mee of my Just right Fewox replied god Dam: him hee was a cheating roage and soe proved and that any persons that had to refuse to pay their accountts dew and that this Complainant Could not recover them with severall other most scurrilous Expressions: to others alleaging that this Complainant has unjustly cut his half Bushell thereby to make it Lesse then necesare and that hee saw it soe Cutt with a multitude of other such like mallicious reports; and more Especially one or a bout the Eight day of August Last past neare ronoake Inlett where this Complainant with his wife and famaly was one board a Vessell then wholy hired and one of the service of this Complainant where hee was a bout his Lawfull Imployment the said Fewox Coming to the side there with out any Just provocation fell out a busing him Calling this Complainant roage sun of a bich [*illegible*] Roage and that hee stayed in Virginia a long as hee Could and that now hee had stayed heare as Long as hee Could and Cheated Every body hee was going to pencillvania to turn Quaker but hee would bee at the Charge to print booty and send after him theather what a roage hee had bin all his Life time allso Called this Complainants wife (who gave him not one word neither first nor Last) all the Damned whores and biches that his foule mouth Could Expresse; and the said fewox allso having made all or the most part of the befor going scandalous reports not only to the Inhabitants of this Government but to strangers Inhabitants of a Country where a great part of this Complainants Conserns and Merchandise lies and hath soe for severall years: the which reports being uttered to persons alltogether strangers and Unacquainted with this Complainant hee appeales to the Concience of all Conciencious and Considerate persons what prejudice it is to all men and in particuler to such whose Livelihood depends in a great part one their trade and Commerce in the world as it is well Knowne to the Country mine dus and hath dun Ever sence I Came into this place being now tenn years sence, and allso having strong motives to beleve that the said Fewox is in Couraged and prompt one by Colonel Wilkeson a person as it appears from his owne mouth who hath bourne an Implacable mallice [*torn*] to this Complainant for divers years though with out Cause: by which meanes the same report is likely to take the Deeper Impression in the minds of [sum] persons who is not soe acquainted with the said Wilkisons wicked practises as others are who have bin acquainted with him and his actions of a Long time.

The premesses Considered this complainant saith that the before said abuses and scandalls is designed and tends to noe Lesse then which noe person is able to support him selfe and famaly in the world in any Fation and allso: leads to the starving of a mans famaly and paste that in ages to Come the which ought by all Cristian men to bee tenderly Considered the Law of god and man forbiding it with out Just and Lawfull Cause; by all which this Complainant saith hee is by the said James Fewox Damnified in his reputation and trade to the Vallue at Least of two hundred pounds sterlen hath therfore brought this action of Defamation before this Honorable Court against the said James Fewox for the said sum of two hundred pounds sterlen humbly Craving Judgment for the same with Costs and hee shall pray etc.

[*Endorsed:*]
Porter versus Fuox
Evidence: Mr. Duckenfield: Cutbert Philps and wife: John Steward: John Lewen Humphry Legg and Mr. Tucker the master of Colonel Wilkisons sloop.

[*Porter, assignee* v. *Fewox*]

[*CCR 148*]

North Carolina ss. To the Honorable the Generall Court

John Porter assignne of Humphry Legge declares against James Fewox in an action of the Case and Sayes as assignnee aforesaid that the Said Fewox Stands Indebted to him as by a Peanall bond under hand and Seale of the said

James Fewox will appear past to the said Humphry Legge bearing date the 27th day of June 1700 for the payment and delevry of one hundred forty and fower bushells of merchantable well drest Indian Corne to bee delivred at the uper dwelling house of John Porter in Chowan and to bee upon all Demands after the 10th Day of March next after the aforesaid Date the Condition of which bond is that the said Fewox Shall pay Seventy two bushells of Corn in manner and according to him befor Sett forth: the which having bin often demanded and hee refusing to performe it according to the Conditions; this Complanant therefore Saith the whole bond before Specified is become dew and: Therfore prays Judgment of this Honorable Court for the Same against the Said James Fewox and that hee pay Costs and Damages. And he Shall pray etc.

N. Chevin Clericus Curiae

To prove this deccluration Sumons George Chambers

[*Endorsed:*]
Porter versus Fewox

[*Porter, attorney of Smith, attorney* v. *Pollock and Hunt, executors*]

[*CCR 181*]

No. Carolina Ss. To the provost Marshall or Depty

These are in his Majesties name to Will and Require you to arest the body of Colonel Tho. Pollock and Capt. Jno. Hunt Executors of [*torn*] Last Will and Testament of Adam Gambell Deceased and them [*torn*] so that they may apeare on the 3d Day of the next Generall Court to Answer the plainte of Mr. Jno. Porter Attorney to Jno. Smith Attorney to Mr. Robt. Hambleton Mr. Jno. Fogo Mr. Alexander Peterson Merchants of London in a Plea of the [*torn*] and have there this writt Dated March 17 1701.

N. Chevin Clk.

[*Endorsed:*]
Porter versus pollock
This writ was Executed marh. the 24 1701/2 by me Thos. Luten Provost [*torn*]

[*Prichard* v. *Fitzpatrick*]

[*CCR 148*]

North Carolina ss. To the honorable the Generall Court

Matthew prichard is plaintiff against Bryant Fitzpatrick Defendant in a plea of Debt Complaines that the Defendant stands justly indebted to the plaintiff in the full summ of Twenty one pounds Nine shillings Currant money of North Carolina by Bill as by wayes and Meanes Convenient the plaintiff is ready to make appear Which said summ of Twenty One pounds Nine shilling the

Defendant hath not rendred to the plaintiff tho' often thereunto requested but still doth refuse to render to the plaintiffs Damage Fifty pounds sterling and therefore he brings his sute and prays Judgment for the same with Costs of sute and shall pray etc.
Entred 11th Feabry. 1701

[*Endorsed:*]
Prichard versus Fitzpatrick

[*CCR 148*]

No. Carolina: Ss. To the Provost Marshall or Depty

These are in the Name of his Excellency the palatine and Lords proprietors to require you to arrest the Body of Bryan Fitzpatrick and him in safe Custody hold soe that he appear att the next Generall Cort to be holden for the Government aforesaid att the house of Mr. John Hecklefield in Little River to Answer the Complaint of Matthew prichard in a plea of Debt and have there this Writt. Dated the Eleaventh Day of Feabry. Anno Domini 1701.

N. Chevin Clericus Curiae

[*Endorsed:*]
Executed by Leaveing a Copye of the Ritt and declaration

[*Quary* v. *Evans*]

[*CCR 148*]

No. Carolina: Ss. To the Provost Marshall or Deputy

These are in his Majties Name to Will and require you to arest the body of Thomas Evins [*blank*] and him to hold so that he may apeare att the next Generall Court to be holden for this Province the Last Tuseday in March next att the house of Doctor Jno. Hecklefeild in Little River To Answer the plaint of Colonel Robert quarey in a Plea of the Case the 3 day of the Corte and have there this writt. Date febry. the 24th 1701/2.

N. Chevin Clericus Curiae

[*Endorsed:*]
Nonestadneses [*sic*]

[*Quary* v. *Jennitt*]

[*CCR 191*]

To the 3d Day of the Generall Court

Colonel Robt. Quarry is plaintiff versus Jno. Jennitt Defendant in a plea of Debt and Setteth forth that the Defendant stands Indebted to the plaintiff in the sume By Bill under his hand etc. and in the sume of 11 Barills of Tarr and which to Render he Doth refuse to the plaintiffs Damage ten pounds for which he brings his action and prays Judgment for the same with Costs and shall Pray etc.

Copia N. Chevin Clk.

[*Endorsed:*]
Quarry versus Jennitt

[*Swann* v. *Rooks*]

[*Mf. Reel C.024.30024*]

To the 3d Day of the Generall Court

The Honorable Major Saml. Swann is plaintiff versus Mary Rooks Defendant in a plea of the Case and Complains that the Defendant stands Indebted and owing to the plaintiff in the sum of 1=13=4 per account and which to Render she Doth Refuse to the plaintiffs Damage 3=10=00 for which he brings his action and prays Judgment for the same with Costs and shall Pray etc.

Copia Vera N. Chevin Clericus Curiae

[*Swann* v. *Williams*]

[*CCR 191*]

To the 2d Day of the General Court

The Honorable Major Samuel Swann is Plaintiff Versus Lewis Williams Defendant in a Plea of Debt and Complains that the Defendant stands Indebted and owing to the Plaintiff in the sum of five hundred Ninety two pounds of Pork (as by his Bill bearing Date Janry. 20th 1696/7 may apeare) and which to Render he Doth Refuse to the plaintiffs Damage six hundred pounds of Pork for which he brings his action and prayes Judgment for the Same with Costs and Shall pray etc.

Copia Vera N. Chevin Clk.

[*Endorsed:*]
Swann versus Williams

[*CCR 148*]

North Carolina Ss. To the Provost Marshall or Depty

These are in his Majties Name to Will and require you to arest the body of Lewis Williams and him to hold so that he may apear att the next Generall Court to be holden for this Province the Last Tuseday in March Next on the 2d Day of the Court att the house of Docter Jno. Hecklefeild in Little River to Answer the plaint of The Honorable Major Saml. Swann in a Plea of Debt and have there this Writt. Dated Janry: the 27th: 1701/2.

N. Chevin, Clk. Curiae

[*Endorsed:*]
This rit was Executed febry. the 21 1701/2 by me Thos. Luten provost marshall

[*Swann, attorney of Ludwell* v. *Powell*]

[*CCR 191*]

To the first Day of the Generall Court

The Honorable Saml. Swann Esqr. Attorney of Colonel Phillip Ludwell of Virginia is plaintiff versus Wm. Powell Defendant in a Plea of Debt and Declars that the said Powell stands Indebted and owing to the plaintiff (qualified as aforsaid) in the sum and quantity of six hundred and foureteen pounds of Pork (as by Bill under hand may apeare) and which to Rendr he Doth Refuse to the plaintiffs Damage seaven pounds sterling for which he brings his action and prayes Judgment for the same with Costs of sute.

Copia Vera N. Chevin Clk. Curiae

[*Endorsed:*]
Swann versus Powell

[*CCR 148*]

No. Carolina Ss. To the provost Marshall or Deputy

These are in his Majtis Name to will and Require you to arest the body of Wm. Powell and him to hold so that he may apeare att the next Generall Court to be held the Last Tusday in March Next to Answer the plaint of the Honorable Major Saml. Swann Attorney of Colonel Phillip Ludwell in a plea of Debt and have there this writt. Dated 9th Day of 9br 1701.

N. Chevin Clk.

[*Endorsed:*]
This rit was Executed nover. the 9 1701 by me Thos. Luten provost marshall

MISCELLANEOUS FILE PAPERS

[*Pordage, George, account*]

[*CCR 180*]

Mr. Geo. Pordige Dr.

To petition Order and Copy on Dobbs Effects	00:03:00
To prove Capt. Luttens Letter attorney	00:02:06
To ordr Apraisors and Copy	00:02:00
To Comission of Administration and Record	00:05:00
To Return Inventory and Record	00:03:06
To action writt Declareation etc. versus Tuke	00:05:00
To Calling Action and Entring plea	00:01:06
To Justices	00:02:06
	01:05:00

N. Chevin Clk.

[*Endorsed:*]
Mr. Geo. Pordige

[*Spruill, Tanner, letter of attorney*]

[*CCR 185*]

I the Subscriber doeth hearby Constitut apoynt and ordain James fewox in my Steede and in my nane to Relinquish my Right of Dower to three hundred Acers of Land Given by my husband Godfrey Spruill unto our Son in Law John Stuart and to Anritta his wife and their heires as witness my hand and Seall this 20th march 1701/2.

Signed and Sealed
in the presents of
Roger Snell
will Gurdy his Marke

Tanner Spruill

[*Justices' commission*]

[*CCR 192*]

North Carolina Ss. John Earle of Bath Palatine and the Rest of the true and Absolute Lords Proprietors of all Carolina Greeting To our Trusty and Well beloved Samuel Swann Esqr. William Glover Esqr. Richard Plater Esqr. Thomas Symonds John Hawkins Wm. Collins Esqrs.

We do hereby Commissionate and appoynt you and Every of you joyntly and Severally Dureing our pleasure Justices for this Goverment of North Carolina to keep or Cause to be kept his Majesties peace as allso all Laws and Ordinances made for the well Government of this province And we do hereby Authorize and Impower you or any three of you (whereof we will that one of you Samuel Swann Wm. Glover Richard Plater Esqrs. shall be one) to hold a Generall Court for this Government att the times hereafter Expresst that is to say to begin the Last Tuseday in the Moneth of July, the Last Tuseday in the Moneth of October the Last Tuesday in the Moneth of March, And the same to Adjourn from time to time and from place to place as you or any three of you (whereof we will that one of you Samuel Swann William Glover Richard Plater Esqrs. shall be one) shall think meet And in the said Court to hold pleas heare and Determine All and all Maner of Actions sutes and Causes whatsoever as Well Criminall as Civill Reale Mixt personall or of any other Kind or nature whatsoever, and in all such Causes to Award Judgment, and to Issue out all such Writts and process as to the Due Administration of Justice Doth belong, In all things proceeding acording to the Lawes and Ordinances of this Government and as Neare as Conveniently may be to the Lawes and Customes of England. And for as much as by Reason of the Dificulty of Passages And Extremity of Weather it may hapen that three or more of you Cannott apeare att the times above exprest We Do hereby further Authorize and Impower you or a [*torn*] of you in such Case being there present to Adjourn the Court to any time not exceeding ten Dayes an to the same place. And we Do hereby Comand the Provost Marshall to Cause to Come before you att the times before Exprest or any othertimes by You appoynted so many Good and Lawfull men of this

Government as shall be Necessary for the tryall of such Causes as Shall be brought before you.

Given under our hands and the seale of the Colony the 12th Day of November in the 13th Yeare of his Majesties Reigne 1701.

Wittness Our Trusty and Well beloved Henderson Walker Esqr. President of our Councill and Comander in Cheife of our said Province and the Rest of our Trusty and well beloved Councellors of State etc.

[*Signed*:]
Henderson Walker, Francis Tomes, Thomas Pollock, Richard Sanderson.

[*CCR 102*]

Writts and Returns to Generall Court in July 1702

Viz. Refferences

Colonel Tho. Pollock Versus Tho. Evins from Last Court by order versus Marshall.

Harvey Versus Boyce Referrd till first day of this Court.

Spruill Assignee of Pope Versus Duckenfeild Order versus Marshall.

Aprill 7th The Honorable Wm. Glover Versus Houghton Plea Case. Executed.

7 Hecklefeild versus Steele Plea. Return Executed. Retraxitt.

Idem Administrator Pordage versus Idem plea Debt. Retraxitt.

7 Voss versus Butler Attorney formerly of Manwarein Plea Case.

13 Jones and Deeds Merchants of London Versus Duckenfeild plea Debt. And summons for plaintiff Hen. Lisle and Retraxitt.

14 Stewart versus Jennitt Plea Debt. Not Executed.

June 4th Frayly Versus Handcock plea Debt.

2d Day

11 Fewox versus [Monteage] plea of the Case. Returnd not Executed.

11 Paine versus Cole.

11 Fewox versus Batchelor plea Debt. Not Executed.

11 Idem versus Idem plea Case. Not Executed.

16 Glover versus Lysle Case. Not Executed.

July: 6 Beray versus Bayley.

[*CCR 102*]

<152> July Court 28 1702

Att a Generall Court holden att the house of Doctor Jno. [*torn*] in Little River the 28th Day of July Anno Domini 1702. Present The Honorable Major Samuel Swann William Glover Richard Plater Esqrs.

The Court sitts and Adjourns till to morow Morning 8 a Clock.

July 28th [*sic*] Court meets and sitts present The Honorable Major Saml. Swann Tho. Symonds Rich. Plater Esqrs.

The Honorable Colonel Thos. Pollock Came to prosecute his sute against Tho. Evins in a Plea of the Case Referd from the Last Court by order against the marshall that he have the body of the said Evins att this Court Alias Judgment to be Confirmed against the Marshall and upon the Examining the accounts the Ballance Due to Colonel Tho. Pollock apears to be £4=2*s.*=4*d.* which he proves by his oath And the Defendant Came not to this Court. Orderd that Capt. Thos. Luten Provost Marshall make payment to Colonel Tho. Pollock of the sum of 4:2:4 with Costs of sute alias Execution.

And upon Petition of Capt. Thos. Luten Orderd that Ateachment be granted to the Petitioner against the goods and Chattells of Tho. Evins for the forementioned sum of 4=2=4 with Costs.

The Grand Jury are sworn and Charge given. Viz. Robt.Wallis: Saml. Davis: Wm. Lufman: Stephen Richardson Fra. Hendrick: Jno. Bishop Jno. Meads: Tho. Cooper: Wm. Jones: Robt. Temple Coten Robison: Jno. [Wheatley] Tho. Durantt: James Perisho: Peter pacill John Jones Arch. Holms Robt. Lowry.

Mr. Wm. Duckenfeild acknowledges a Conveyance for a tract of Land and Plantation Lying in Flatty Creek to Rich Ashworth.

A will of Wm. Ledford Deceased was Proved by the oaths of Doctor Godfrey Spruill and Canaan Simpson who Did both sweare that the Deceased Did give Directions for the giveing all the Remainder of his Estate to his Wife and was omitted by Doctor Spruill who writt the will.

Tho. Harvey Comes by Mr. Tho. Snoden and Mr. Jno. Williss his attorneys to prosecute his sute against Mr. Wm. Boyce By Refferrence from the Last Court in a Plea of tresspass and Complaines that the Defendant hath unjustly Demolished and Broken the Dwelling house of the Plaintiff and severall Injures hath Donne <152*a*> By means of which Laying open his house the plaintiff Lost one hundred pounds in money and goods for which be brings his action of Tresspass. And the Defendant by Colonel Wm. Willkison his Attorney denyess to the Declaration and thereupon Casts himself upon the Countrey and the aforesaid Snoden and Willis attorney for the plaintiffs Likewise and the Marshall is Comanded to Cause to Com 12 etc. and who etc. By whome etc. And there Came Godfrey Spruill: Saml. Paine James Carroon: Wm. Armor: Rich. Ashworth: Tho. Twiddee: Denis [McLendon] James Oats: Fra. Beasely: Tho. Gillam: James Thickpen: [Jenken] Williams who Empanelld and Sworn Upon theire Oaths say We find a Tresspass with one Shilling Damage. And after the Verdict the Defendant by Colonel Wm. Wilkison his attorney saith that the Defendant in the said action by a statute of Parliament ought to pay no more Costs than Damages and further saith that the plaintiff hath sumonsed severall persons with sute which are not able to give any Evidences and therefore prays that the Charge of such persons sumond may not be allowd. Orderd that the Defendant pay to the plaintiff the one shilling Damage given by the Jury and Costs of sute for three Evidences only in the action and the plaintiff to sattisfy what Evidence was sumoned more in the said sute with Costs alias Execution.

Archibald Holms Proves an Account Due to himself from the Estate of Mr. Charles Wright Deceased Mr. Wm. Boyce being present in Court for the sum of £3=10*s*.=6*d*.

Upon the Petition of Geo. Kinserly Orderd that Tho. Harvey pay to the Petitioner the sume of ten shillings for his attendance two Courts with Costs of sute alias.

Upon Petition of Mr. Henry Norman Orderd That Thos. Harvey pay to the Petitioner the sum of twenty one shillings and Eight pence for his travell and attendance att two Courts with Costs of sute alias Execution.

Doctor Godfrey Spruill Assignee of Mrs. Ann Pope Came to prosecute his sute against Mr. Wm. Duckenfeild and Declares for the sum of £10 1*s*:00 in skins and produces a Bill under the Hand and seale of the said Duckenfeild to Rich. Pope in his Life time Late Husband of the Assignee Ann Pope. And the Defendant Comes and for Plea saith that the plaintiff his action ought not to have for and that by the 12th act of assembly[6]

[*SS 310*]

[*Illegible*].

Nonsute or a Verdict found for the Defendant the plaintiff Shall

[6] The text of CCR 102 breaks off at this point. However, the minutes are continued in SS 310. What portion of the text, if any, has been lost is unknown. The minutes in SS 310 are finished minutes (the official set); they are written by Nathaniel Chevin, clerk of the General Court, and are signed by the justices of the court.

pay to Defendant 8/4 in the Generall Court and 4/2 in the precinct Court and [*torn*] barrd all further action in that Case till the nonsute be satisfied. And Saith that he hath had two nonsutes upon the said Bill allready in the Generall Court and therefore prays to be Dismist.

And the Honorable Court overules his Plea for and that in the Last Clause of that Act it is provided thatt all Executors or Administrators Shall not be Lyable to the Penallty of that act and the plantiff being Assignee of Ann Pope Executrix of Richard Pope

Ordered that Mr. Wm. Duckenfeild pay to Doctor Godfrey Spruell Assignee as aforesaid the Sum of ten pound five Shillings in Skins viz. Drest buck Skins att 2*s*. per pr. Drest Doe Skins att 18*d*. with Costs of Sute alias Execution.

Upon the Petition of Mr. Fra. Perrott

Order'd that Godfrey Spruill pay to the Petitionr the Sum of Eleven Shillings and 8*d*. for his travell and Attendance this Court with Costs.

The marshall was Comanded to arest the body of Tho. Houghton and the Defendant Came not.

Orderd that the marshall have the body of Tho. Houghton att the next Generall Court alias [*torn*].

The Marshall was Comanded to arest the body of Chris. Butler Late Attorney of Stephen Manwareing att the Sute of Wm. Voss and the Plaintiff Came not to Prosecute.

Ordered that the Sute be Dismist and the plaintiff pay Costs alias Execution.

Saml. Paine Came to Prosecute his sute against Capt. James Coles [*torn*] a Plea of the Case and the Defendant Came not and the Plaintiff is [Willing] that the action hang till the next Generall Court.

Upon Petition of James Thickpen

Orderd that Wm. Voss pay the Petitioner 8*s*./4*d*. for his Travell and Attendance att this Court with Costs.

Edward Berry Came to prosecute his Sute against Christopher Bailes in a Plea of the Case and Complaines of Several Disturbances and molestations offerd by the Defendant to the Plaintiff in the Hindring him in his Lawfull Survey and the Defendant by Tho. Norcom his attorney Comes and Demurrs to the Declaration and thereupon Casts himself upon the Countrey and the Plaintiff Likewise and the marshall is Comanded to Cause to Come twelve true and Law full men of the Vicinage and who etc. By whome [etc.] And there Came Fra. Foster Benj. Tull: Saml. Paine [*torn*] Armor Denniss McLendon James oats Jenkin Williams Fra. Beasly: Abraham Warren Jno. West Wm. Gascins Jno. Bird who Impannelld and Sworn

Upon theire Oaths Say we find for the Plaintiff with Costs of Sute.

Orderd that The plaintiff have the Land he Declars for and that The Surveyor Lay out the Same and the Defendant pay all Costs.

The Jurors for our Sovereigne Lady the Queen Do Present That Tho. Dereham Gentleman of the County of Bath have not the feare of God before his Eyes but being Led away by the Instigation of the Devill Did feloniously and of mallice prepensd att Severall times with Sevrall Weapons But more perticularly to Witt on or about the tenth day of Sept. Last past in the County of Bath aforsaid against the Peace of our Late Sovereigne Lord the King Did with force and Armes Assault the Body of Wm. Hudson then being in the Peace of god and the Lord the King and him the Said Wm. Hudson Did then and there with a Certain Weapon Comonly Called or Known by the Name of a Catt of Nine tayles Feloniously and malitiously Strike beat Wound and Kill That the aforsaid Wm. Hudson Afterwards to Witt on or about the 20th Day of Sept. Last past in the Countey of Bath aforsaid then and there by reason of the aforsaid Mortall Strokes and Wounds Did Depart this Life against the Peace etc. Who being areigned Pleads not Guilty and Casts himself upon god and the Countrey and Richd. Plater Esqr. Attorney Generall Likewise And the Marshall is Comanded that he Cause to Come twelve good and Lawfull men of the Vicinage and who etc. By whome etc. And there Came Mr. Fra. Foster Benj. Tull: Saml. Paine: Wm. Armor: Deniss McLendon: Jams Oats Jenkin Williams: Fra. Beasly: Abraham Warren: Jno. West Wm. Gascins: Jno. Bird And being Sworn Upon the Holy Evangelist to give true Verdict in the Premists Upon the Holy Evangelist Say

Wee find him Guilty of Man Slaughter And the said Dearham humbly Prays that Sentens may be suspended till to morrow.

And then the Court adjourns till to morrow morning 8 a Clock.

Fryday morning 8 a Clock Court Meets present Utt Supra. August the first.

A Conveyance of a tract of Land and plantation was acknowledged by John Huffton to Mr. Jno. Pariss.

Jno. Bayly and Elinor his wife acknowledges a Coveyance of a tract of Land and plantation to John Huffton.

Letters of Attorney from Rebeca Bird Wife of Jno. Bird was [*torn*] to Nath. Chevin was provd per the oaths of Mr. [*illegible*] Wheatley.

A Conveyance of a tract of Land and plantation in pequimons Precinct was Acknowledged by Jno. Bird and Nath. Chevin and Rebecca Bird Unto Mr. Tho. Harvey.

Upon Petition of Wm. Reed Praying that a tract of Land formerly in the occupation of Capt. Jno. Gibbs and [*illegible*] may be granted to the Petitionr and prays that the [Labour] thereon may be Apraised.

Orderd that it be granted to the Petitioner and that [*torn*] Baily James Cary and Edw. Jelfe apraise the Labour [*torn*] two of them.

A Deed of Conveyance and Release was Acknowledged by [*torn*] Duckenfeild Esqr. to Mr. John Ardrene.

Upon the Petition of Eliz. Stewart

Orderd that Mr. Wm. Boyce pay to the Petitioner the Sum [*torn*] Eight Shillings and four pence for her travell and Attendance [*torn*] Court.

Thomas Dereham haveing yesterday been Convicted [of] Manslaughter and Savd by his Book and Sentens Suspended

Ordered that the Said Thomas Dereham be Burnt in [*torn*] Brawne of the Left thumb with a hott Iron haveing the Letter M And Pay all Costs that Doth acrue.

And upon the Humble Petition of the Said Tho. Dereham [*torn*] Court in Clemency Doth Repreive the Said Sentence Untill [*torn*] Majesties Pleasure therein be farther known.

Upon Petition of Wm. Reed and James Cary

Orderd that Edward Berry Pay to Each of the Petitioners theire travell and attendance nine Shillings and two pence.

Upon Petition of James Cary

Ordered that Christopher Bayly pay to the Petitioner for his Travell and Attendance nine Shillings and two pence With Costs of Sute.

[*Signed*:]
Samuel Swann, W. Glover, thomas symons, Richard Plater.

FILE PAPERS IN SUITS AND PROSECUTIONS

[*Berry* v. *Bailes*]

[*CCR 187*]

To the Honorable Generall Court For The County of Albemarl in North Carrolina

Edward Berry of the Precinct of Corrotuck Plaintiff Complaines against Christopher Bailes of the Precinct aforesaid Defendant in a Plea of the Case That; that is to Say the Plaintiff hath lately Purchased of William Reede of the Precinct of Corrotuck in the Province of North Carrolina the Rights of an Entry of Land in the Precinct of Corrotuck and after Purchase made by the Plaintiff, the Plaintiff did within time Limitted by Law Imploy the Surveyor to lay out the said Land, and the Plaintiff theron was Disturbed and Ressisted by the Defendant who stoped the Plaintiffs Chaine Pretending Right to the said Land by Virtue of Labour thereon don which method of Labouring on Entred Land till a Survey of Rights be first had the Plaintiff Conceives to be Repugnant to an order of the Palatine Court, or otherwise the Plaintiff is Ready by Severell Evidences to prove the said Labor was by the Defendant don Some months after the Limitted date of the Entry, by which unjust disturbences and Stoppages of the Chainc thc Plaintiff is Damnified ten Pounds sterling therefore the Plaintiff hath brought his Action against the Defendant and Demands Judgment for the same with Cost and further prayes order for the surveying of his Land.

Edwd. Berry Signum

[*Endorsed:*]
Edwd. Berrys Declarition Versus Christopher Bailes
We of the Jury Find for the plaintiff with Cost of sute

[*Crown* v. *Dereham*]

[*CCR 182*]

North Carolina SS.

Know all men by these presents that We Thomas Dereham Joseph Rogers, and William Handcock all of the County of Bath in the province of North Carolina doe all, and every one of us bind our selves in the penalty of fifty pound a piece of lawful money of this province to William Brice Sherrif for the County aforesaid, for the true and personall Appearance [*torn*] Thomas Dereham att the next generall Court holden for this Province, and there to [*torn*] what shall be alleadgd against him by the Kings Attorney, or any others authorised to prosecute his Majties Suite on the behalf of William Hudson late deceased to which Obligation we above mention'd bind our Heirs Administrators, and Assigns this fifteenth day of Aprill Anno Domini 1702.

Sealed Signed and Delivered
in the presence of us
Levi Truewhitt
John Lawson

Tho. Dereham
Joseph Rogers His mark
William Handcock his marke

[*Fewox* v. *Batchelor*]

[*CCR 139*]

[*Torn*] Ss. To the Provest Marshall or depty

Thes are in their Maijtys name to will and Requier you to Arest the Body of Jno. Batcheler and him to hold so that he may a peare the next Generall Corte to be holden for this provence the Last Tusday in July Next att the house of doctor Jno. Hecklefeild in Litell Rever to answer the plaint of James

Fewox In a plea of dept and have their this writt dated June the 20th 1702.

Na. Chevin Clericus Curiae

[*Frayly* v. *Hancock*]

[*CCR 148*]

To the First day of the Generall Court

Wm. Frayly of the County of Bath is plaintiff Versus william handcock of the same place defendant In a plea of debt and Complains that the defendant stands Indebted and owing to the plaintiff one Inden Boy Named Tom Aged a Bought Eight years which the said handkock did promise to delevir as By his Note under his hand Baring date the 17th: of Aprill: 1702 may apeare But the same too delevir and Render to the plaintiff the defendant doth refuse to the plaintiffs Damadg Sixty pounds Sterling for [*torn*] he Brings his action and prays Judgment for the Same with Costs and Shall pray.

[*Endorsed*:]
Frayly Versus Handcock

[*Glover* v. *Houghton*]

[*CCR 191*]

To the first Day of the Generall Court

The Honorable Wm. Glover Esqr. is plaintiff versus Tho. Houghton Defendant in a Plea of the Case and Complains that the said Houghton stands Indebted to the Complainant by account for Sundry goods and Merchandizes to the Value of 54 shillings (as by wayes and meanes Convenient he is Ready to make appear) and which to render he doth Refuse to the plaintiffs Damage five pound ten shillings for which he brings his sute and prays Judgment for the same with Costs.

Copia Vera N. Chevin Clericus Curiae

[*Endorsed:*]
Glover versus Houghton

[*Harvey* v. *Boyce*]

[*CCR 191*]

To the 3d Day of the Generall Court

Thomas Harvey of the Precinct of Pequimons is plaintiff Versus Wm. Boyce Defendant in a Plea of the Case for Trespass and setteth forth, That on or about the 6th Day of July 1701 the Defendant aforesaid Came to the habitation of the plaintiff in the precinct of Pequimons and then and there Did unjustly uncover and Demollish the house of the plaintiff and the same Layd Open the plaintiff being then from home By reason Wherof the plaintiff Lost out of his house att the same time the Value of one hundred pounds in money and goods which is to the plaintiffs Damage att Least three hundrd pounds sterling for which he brings his action and prays Judgment for the same with Costs and shall pray etc.

Copia Vera N. Chevin Clericus Curiae

[*Endorsed:*]

Harvey versus Boyce

We find a tresspass with on Shilling Damage for the Plaintiff

[*CCR 148*]

North Carolina ss. To Mr. Tho. Snoden Attorney etc. and Mr. Jno. Williss

These are to authorize and appoint you to appear for me Tho. Harvey in an action of the Case for Trespasse Depending betwixt me the said Thomas Harvey plaintiff and William Boyce Defendant And him the said William Boyce to implead prosecute and the said Cause now Depending to bring to Judgment And This shall be yor sufficient warrant and I will pay you your fees Witnesse my hand this 28th day of July Anno Domini 1702.

Witnesse hereunto Thomas Harvye
Denis Macklendin

[*Swann, assignee* v. *Houghton*]

[*CCR 148*]

North Carolina Ss.

Att a Generall Court holden July 29th 1701/2 [*sic*]. Present the Justices.

The Honorable Major Samuel Swann Assignee of Jno. Anderson by Due and Legall process Obtaind a Judgment against Thomas Houghton for the sum of £3=6=8 Viz.

Ordered that Thomas Hougton pay to the Honorable Major Samuel Swann the sum of £3=6=8 with Costs of sute alias Execution.

These are therefor by Vertue of the aforesaid Order to Will and Require you to take into your Costody so much of the goods and Chattells of the said Thomas Hougton wheresoever to be found in this government as shall sattisfy the aforesaid Debt and Costs And the same you shall Deliver to the Honorable Major Samuel Swann after Lawfully Aprised and the overpluss if any be you shall Return to the said Hougton Hereof fayl not. Dated att the Secretarys office May the 4th 1701/2 [*sic*].

N. Chevin Clericus Curiae

Clerks Fees	
To action writt Declaration etc.	00:05:00
2 summons and [*illegible*] action	00:02:06
Entered Judgment Confest and order	00:02
Amercement and file bill	3
Execute Enter and Return	3
Bill Costs	6

Marshalls Fees	
To arest etc.	4:11
2 summons	1:08
Serve Execute	5
	11: 7

	00:16:00
	11: 7
	1: 7:07
Debt	3: 6: 8
Costs	1: 7: 7
Totall	4:14: 3

Errors Excepted Per N. Chevin Clk.

[*Endorsed:*]
Seased by virtue of this Excucution one Large Conew and prayesed

£ *s. d.*
3 15 0

Executed the 8 of June by Me Peter Grey deputy Marshall

[*CCR 148*]

June the 9th 1702

Then Execewted and Apraisd of the Estate of Thomas Hauton for the yuse of Major Samell Swan as followeth

	£ S. *D.*
By one Cannew	3:15:00
on writt [*illegible*] whither	[*blank*]
on blake Kame	1 4 0

The said praisers whom are Christofer Butler Jeames Fiser John Hare Samuell Heth Sworne before Capttain Jeames Cole.

[*Voss* v. *Butler*]

[*CCR 191*]

North Carolina Ss. To the first day of the Generall Court

William Voss is plaintiff Versus Christopher Butler Defendant As being formerly Attorney to Stephen Manwareing Late of this Province in plea of Case And setteth forth that the said Manwareing stood Indebted and owing to the Complainant in the sum of five pounds and Departed this Government without any sattisfaction thereof made and Constituted the said Butler his attorney who Did promiss [*torn*] pay to the Complainant the aforesaid sum and hath made the [*torn*] Debt [*illegible*] much in his account [*illegible*] with James Thickpen who is now attorney [*torn*] said Manwareing yett notwithstanding the same to Render and pay to the Complainant the said Butler Doth neglect and refuse to the plaintiffs Damage ten pounds sterling for which he brings his action and prays Judgment for the same with Costs and shall pray etc.

Copia Vera N. Chevin Clk Curiae

[*Endorsed:*]
Voss versus Butler

[*CCR 139*]

No. Carolina Ss. To the Provost Marshall or Deputy

These are in his majesties name to Will and Require you to Arest the Body of Christopher Buttler and him to hold so that he may appeare att the next Generall Court to be Holden att the house of Doctor Jno. Hecklefeild in Little River to Answer the plaint of William Voss in a Plea of the Case and have there this writt.

Dated Aprill the 8th 1702.

N. Chevin, Clk. Curiae

[*Endorsed:*]
Voss versus Buttler
Executed June the 18 per me Tho. Luten Provost marshall

MISCELLANEOUS FILE PAPERS

[*Fox, Mary, petition*]

[*CCR 180*]

To the Worshipfull Courte

The Humble Pittition of Mary Fox Widdow Sheweth Thatt Wheareas your Pittitioner purchaseing Land of Owing Daniell now Deseased before the acknowledgeing of the said Land in Courte and now after noe acknowledgement Can be firmely granted to yor Pittitioner the Exceketrix of the abovesaid Owing Daniell Came and Demanded of your Pittitioner parte of Pay for the Said Land which was Delivered to the Exceketor Tho. Jones one Cow and two two yeare old hefers which Promised if the Said Land Could not be acknowledged to Returne the Said Cattle again and your Pittitioner Shall humbly begg of your worshipfull Courte that you would be pleased To grant an order that my Catle may be retorned to the Same place wheare Received and your Pittitioner Shall in Deuty pray. Apll. the 6th 1702.

Mary Fox

Mary fox 640 acrs on Sulmon Creek on the back of mr. perrott

[*Endorsed:*]
Rowland Buckly

[*Huffton, Jno., recognizance*]

[*CCR 191*]

No. Carolina Ss.

Jno. Huffton Accknowledges towards our Soveraigne Lady the Queene the Sume of Twenty pounds to be Levyed upon his Lands and Tenements Goods and Chatles by way of Recognizance. The Condition of this Recognizance is Such that If the a bove Jno. Huffton doe and shall appeare at the next Generall Court to be holden at Capt. Jno. Hecklefields then and there to Answer all

Such matters and things as shall be objected against him Concerneing his Attempt of Authority and on the meane tyne Shall be of his Good beheviour.

[*Endorsed:*]
Jno. Hufftons Recognizance

[*SS 310*]

Refferrences from Last Court

Glover versus Houghton.

Paine Versus Coles.

Writts and Returns to October Court

[*Torn*] Glover Esqr. Consignee of Colonel Quarry and Company versus Lisle Case. [*Illegible*] a true Copy of Writt and Declaration Left att the Dwelling house of the Defendant.

Ashworth Versus Palmer Case. Returnd Executd.

Duckenfeild Esqr. Versus Evins Case. Returned Executed.

[*Illegible*] Versus Batchellor Debt. Returnd Executed and [*illegible*]. Retraxitt.

Phelps Versus Evins Case. Returd Executed. Retraxitt.

Tylor versus Banks Assalt and Battery. Retraxitt. Return and Composition made.

Idem versus Id. Case. Retraxitt. Returnd Retraxitt.

Frayly versus Hancock. Debt. Return Executd.

Burnsfeild versus Olford. Debt. Retraxitt.

Idem versus Id. Case. Returnd Executed. Retraxitt.

Rice versus Scarboro. Plea of the Case.

[*SS 310*]

Att a Generall Court holden att the House of Capt. Jno. [*torn*] in Little River October 27 1702 Being present The Honorable Samuel Swann Esqr. Thos. [*torn*] William Glover Esqr. Jno. Hawkins Esqr.

The Courts Comission is Published and By Vertue of a Dedimus From the Honorable President to the Honorable Major Samuel Swann and the Honorable Wm. Glover Esqr. Do Solemnly take the Oaths by [*torn*] Appoynted before the Honorable Samuel Swann Esqr. And also [*torn*] Honorable Samuell Swann Esqr. Do Take the aforsaid Oaths before [*torn*] Glover Esqr. And Mr. Jno. Hawkins being not [Free] Do subscribe to the aforsaid Oaths.

Adjournd till to Morrow Morning 9 a Clock.

Wednsday morning Oct. 28 1702

Court meets present Utt Supra.

Daniel Phillips presents a Lettr of Attorney from Samuel Davis by the oaths of Mr. Jno. Jenins and Barthol. Hewitt.

The Marshall Was Comanded to Arest the body of Capt. Coles att the Sute of Saml. Paine Refferd from Last Court [*torn*] and the plaintiff Came not to prosecute.

Orderd that the Action be Dismist and the plaintiff pay Costs.

Rich. Ashworth Came to prosecute his Sute against Jno. [*torn*] in a Plea of the Case and Complaines for one Canoo Lent to [*torn*] by the plaintiff which was Return Spoyld and Stavd, and the [*torn*] by Mr. Thos. Snoden his Attorney for pleas Saith that [*torn*] they Did Borrow But for Spoyling and Staveing the Same [*torn*] have not and there upon Casts himself Upon the Country [*torn*] plaintiff Likewise. And the Marshall is Comanded to Cause to Come twelve Lawfull men of the vicinage and By whome etc. and there Came Jno. Bird Walter Tanner [*torn*] Harriss: Richard Neat: Rich. Madren: Geo. Kinserly: James [*torn*] Mathew Winn: Augstin Scarborrow: Jer. Symonds: Christopher [*torn*] Bartholomew Hewitt Who Impaneld and Sworne Say [*torn*] find for the plaintiff thirty Shillings for the Cannoo and Damage with [*torn*].

Orderd that Jno. Palmer pay to Rich. Ashworth the Sum of [*torn*] for his Canoo and Damage with Costs of Sute alias Execution.

Wm. Duckenfeild Esqr. Came to prosecute his Sute against Thomas Evins [*torn*] Plea of the Case for [*blank*] and the Defendant Came [*torn*].

Ordered that the marshall have the body of Tho. Evins att the [*torn*] Generall Court Alias Judgment against the Marshall.

The Marshall was Comanded to Arest the body of [*torn*] and the plaintiff Came not to prosecute.

Orderd that the Action be Dismit and the plaintiff pay Costs alias Execution.

The Court Adjourn'd for two Hours.

12 a Clock Court meets Present ut Supra.

Daniel Rice Came to prosecute his sute against Augustine Scarborrow in a Plea of the Case And the Defendant By Mr. Tho. Snoden his Attorney for Plea Saith that the plaintiff his Action ought not to have for and that the Action is unduly Enterd they Receiveing the Copy Declaration Som Days before the Arrest which appearing

Orderd that the Action be Dismist and the plaintiff pay Costs alias [*blank*].

Upon the Petition of Rich. Clark

Orderd that Richard Ashworth pay to the Petitioner Eight shillings and 4*d*. with Costs alias Execution.

Upon the Petition of Wm. Waymouth

Orderd that Richd. Ashworth pay to the Petitioner Eight shillings and four pence with Costs for his travell and Attendance.

Upon the Petition of Wm. Waymouth

Orderd that Jno. Palmer pay to The petitionr the Sum of Eight Shillings and four pence for his travell and Attendance with Costs of Sute alias Execution.

Adjournd till 3 a Clock afternoon.

3 a Clock Court meets Present ut Supra.

Nathan Hall and Hannah his Wife Acknowledges Conveyance to Geo. Jordan.

Jno. Willowby Acknowledges Conveyance of a tract of Land and plantation to Jno. Anderson.

Wm. Hutchison Provd Rights to 700 Acers of Land by Importation Viz. Moses Whitaker twice Importd Franc. [*torn*] twice Importd Wm. Thomas twice Importd Jno. [*torn*] Tho. Cowlisle Jno. Gray Jno. Oliver Wm. Hutchson [*torn*] times Imported And Asignd to Nathanl. Chevin.

Simon Knight provd his Right to 100 Acers of Land by importation of Himself and Eliz. Knight.

Mr. Jos. Reading Provd his Rights to 250 Acers [*torn*] Land by Importation of Edw. Dickason [*torn*] Jno. Corerty Joseph [*torn*].

Jos. Chowne provs [*torn*] to 150 Acers of Land [*torn*] Importation of himself 3 times.

Mr. Tho. Babb provd his Right to one hundred [*torn*] of Land by Importation of himself twice.

Deborah Willowby Wife of Jno. Willowby [*torn*] Court and Relinqueshes her Right of Dower to [*torn*] of Land Sold by her husband to Jno. Anderson.

[*Signed:*]

Samuel Swann, W. Glover, Jno. Hawkins

FILE PAPERS IN SUITS AND PROSECUTIONS

[*Duckenfield* v. *Evans*]

[*CCR 191*]

No. Carolina Ss. To the first day of the Generall Court

Wm. Duckenfield Esqr. is plaintiff Versus tho. Evins defendant in a plea of the Case and Complains that the defendant Stands Indepted and owing to the plaintiff in the Sum of two pounds thirteen Shillings By Account as wayes and means Conveniant he is Ready to make a peare and which to Render he Doth Refuse to the plaintiff Damadg five pounds for which he Brings his Action and prays Judgment for the Sam with Costs etc. Shall pray.

[*Endorsed:*]
Duckenfld versus Evins

[*Fewox* v. *Batchelor*]

[*CCR 148*][7]

North Carolina Ss. To the Provost Marshall or Depty

These are in her Majty name to will and Require you to arest the body of Jno. Batchellor and him to hold so that he may apeare att the next Generall Court to be holden the Last Tuseday in Octobr. next att the house of Doctor Jno. Hecklefeild in Little River to Answer the plaint of James Fewox in a Plea of Debt and have there this writt Dated August the 4 [*torn*].

N. Chevin Clericus Curiae

North Carolina Ss. To the Provost Marshall or Depty

These are in her Majty name to Will and require you [to arest] the body of Jno. Batchellor and him to hold so that he may apear att the next Generall Court the Last Tuseday in Octobr. next att the house of Doctor Jno. Hecklefeild in Little River [to Answer] the plaint of James Fewox in a Plea of the Case and have [there] this writt Dated August 4th 1702.

N. Chevin Clericus Curiae

[*Endorsed:*]
Fewox versus Batchellor

[*Rice* v. *Scarborough*]

[*CCR 148*]

North Carolina ss. To the honorable the Generall Cort To the third Day

Daniel Rice is plaintiff against Augustine Scarbro Defendant in a plea of the Case Complaines that Whereas the plaintiff did on or about the Year One thousand Six Hundred Ninety and One purchass of the Defendant in the Dominion of Virginia Severall Goods and Chattles to the Vallue of Twenty pounds and Upwards and He in Some Short time after the Defendant absconding himself and departing out of that Goverment and comeing into this Severall of the Said Goods and Cattles were by due process of Law taken away from and recovered out of the plaintiffs Custody (to Witt) the Vallue thirteen pounds

[7] These writs for two separate actions against a single individual are written on the same piece of paper.

Three Shillings Sterling with Ninty Two pounds of Tobacco Costs on a Judgement on an Attachment out of Middlesex Cort the 2d of Jary. 1692 obteyned by Mr. John Smith and Five Shillings by an Attachment Under the Hand of Mr. John Cant with Twelve Shillings Costs obteyned by one Thomas Gardner and the plaintiff further Complaines that for the Obteyning of his Rights and Just due he has been att the Expence and Charge of Five pounds Sterling for his travell and Charges into the Dominion of Virginia on purpose to fortify himself for the Recovery of his just Right att which by Wayes and meanes Convenient the plaintiff is ready to make appear which Said Summ of Thirteen pounds and Three Shillings with Ninety Two pounds Costs and five Shillings with Twelve Shillings Costs and five pounds amounting in the whole to Nineteen pounds Sterling and ninety and Two pounds of Tobacco the Defendant hath not rendred to the plaintiff but Still doth refuse to render tho' often thereunto requested in this Goverment by the plaintiff to the plaintiffs Damage fifty pounds Sterling and thereupon he brings his Sute and prayes Judgment for the Same with Costs of Sute and Shall pray etc.

8ber 12th 1702 Copy N. Chevin Clk.

[*Endorsed:*]
Rice Versus Scarborow

[*CCR 148*]

North Carolina Ss. To the Provost Mashall or deputy

These are In the name of his Excellency the Cul.[8] and Lords proprietors to will require you to arest the body of Augustine Scharbrough: and him Safely to So that he may apeare at the Next: Generall Court to be held for this province the Last Tusday In October: at the Generall Court house In perquimons at the House of John: Hackenfield To Answer plaint of Daniell: Rice In a pleuf: the Case.

This being a true Copey deliverd by me Daniell: philops Deputy Marshall
Dated the 17th of Oct. 1702

[*Endorsed:*]
To all Christian people

MISCELLANEOUS FILE PAPERS

[*Chowne, Joseph, petition*]

[*CCR 140*]

To the Honorable Court

The Humble petition of Joseph Chowne shewing that he hath Rights Viz. Edw. Dickison Thos. Smith Joshua Evins Jno. Coverly Joseph Babb Jos.

[8] This abbreviation may stand for the Latin word *culmen*, which is a contraction of *columen*, meaning *summit, acme, chief.* In any event, the scribe is referring to the Palatine.

Chown 3 times transportation Jno. Ellis Ready to prove and Cravs Certificate and shall pray.

Joseph Chowne

[*Davis, Samuel, letter of attorney*]

[*CCR 192*]

Albemarle

To all Cristian people to whom this present shall Come know ye that I Samuel Davis of pascotank precinct have made Constituted ordained and appointed for me and in my Stead my wellbeloved friend Mr. Danel Phillips to be my true and Lawfull atturney for me and in my name to Escheat 970: acres of Land Lying and being on the Sowthwest Sid of pascotank River between the plantation of Mr. Wm. Collings and the Land of Tho. Rook in wittness wherof I have hereuto Set my hand and Seal this 21st day of october 1702.

Signed Sealed and Deliverd — Samuell Davis [*torn*]
In the presence of
John Jenens his marke
Barthemle Hewit his mark
John Billit

[*Hutchison, William, petition*]

[*CCR 187*]

To the Honorable Coart

The Humble Petition of Wm. Hutchison Shewing that he hath 14 Rights viz. Moses Whittaker twice Imported Fra. Elliss twice Imported Wan Thomas twice Imported: Jno. Lamlette Tho. Cowlisle Jno. Gray Jno. Oliver Wm. Hutchison 4 time Trasportd Read to pro and Cravs Cort and shall Pray etc.

Wm. Hutchison

[*Knight, Simon, petition*]

[*CCR 140*]

To the Honorable Generall Court

The Humble petition of Simon Knight praying to prove 2 Rights himself and Eliz. his Daughter and shall Pray.

I Do Declare in the presence of god and under the penallty of perjury Declare that the said Rights Do properly belong to me and that no Land has been taken up for the same by me nor maner of person to the best of my Knowledge.

Simon Knight

[*SS 310*]

Writts and Returns to March Court 1703

Refferences from Last Court

Duckenfeild versus Evins.

Oct. 30 Porter attorney Jones Versus Slade plea Debt and Summons for plaintiff Andiver Willson.

31 Bird versus Reed Plea Debt.

Idem Versus Id. Plea Case and Summons for plaintiff Tho. Abington.

9ber 6 Rice Versus Scarborow Plea Case. Retraxitt.

6 Winn Versus Jenins Plea Defamation. Return Executed.

6 Arderne Versus Monteague Executor of Collins Case.

Holmes versus Stewart Plea Case. Retraxitt.

[*Torn*].

Wilkison attorney of Huggen [declin] New York versus Delemare and Wife. Case. Return Executed.

Mathew Winn Versus Jno. Jenins plea Defamation. [*Torn*] for plaintiff Jno. Jones Margt. Mcbride Robt. Morgan: Jno. Anderson: Walter Taner. Return Executed.

Jones Merchant Virginia versus Goodridg Master Pink Adventure Case.

Idem versus Idem Case.

Idem versus Id. Detinue. Returnd Executd.

Idem versus Derham.

Capt. Goodridg versus Fred. Jones Plea Case. Returnd Executed.

Capt. Hecklefeild versus Fewox plea Case. Retraxitt.

Falconer versus Paine ple Case. Retraxitt.

Chevin versus Frayly Case.

Mr. Gale Versus Welch Plea Assault and Battery and Summons for plaintiff Mr. Robt. Fendall and Walter Tanner.

Idem versus Evin Plea Case. Return Executed.

[*Torn*] 3 Mr. Jno. Porter versus Butler Plea Defamation. Summons for plaintiff Capt. Luten and Danl. Deane. Returnd Executd.

Cradock versus Goodridg Case.

Simpson versus Simson Case. Returnd too Late to be Executed.

Falconer versus Norcom Case. Returnd too Late to be Executed.

Heckleffeild Atteachment Cobb.

[*CCR 103*]

Att a Generall Court Holden att the House of Jno. Heclefeild March the 29th 1703 Being present the Honorable Wm. Glover Thos. Symonds Rich. Plater William Collins Esqrs.

The Courts Comission being Published Mr. Rich. Plater and Mr. William Collins Do Solemly take the Oathes by Law appointed before the Honorable president.

Mary Rooks acknowledged a Conveyance of a tract of Land and plantation to Robt. Hosea.

A Letter of Attorney from Capt. Jno. Hecklefeild to Daniell Phillips was acknowledged per the Constituent.

And then the Court Adjournd till to Morrow Morning 7 a Clock.

Wednsday the 30th of March 1703 the Court Meets Present the Honorable Major Saml. Swann Wm. Glovr Tho. Simonds Rich. Plater Wm. Collins Esqrs.

Mr. Jno. Porter and Mr. Rich. Plater Do mutually Agree [*illegible*] in an action of Debt and the matter being Fully Debated

Orderd that Mr. Rich. Plater pay to Mr. Jno. Porter the Sum [*torn*] five pounds In Pork With Costs alias Execution.

Mr. Jno. Potter attorney of James Jones Comes to prosecute his [*torn*] against Henry Slade and the Defendant Came Nott.

Orderd that the Marshall have the body of Henry Slade att the Next Court holden for this province the Last Tusday in July Next alias Judgment to go against the Marshall.

Jno. Bird Comes by Thomas Snoden his attorney to prosecute his Sute against Wm. Reed In a Plea of Debt and the Said Reed Comes and prayes a Refferrence till Next Court and Shewing Sufficinet Reasons for the Same

Orderd that the action be Refferred to the first Day of the next Generall Court.

Mr. Jno. Bird Comes by Thomas Snoden his attorney to prosecute his Sute against Wm. Reed In a Plea of the Case and Says that the Said Reed Stands Indebted to the plaintiff in the Sum of 2 14 5 per account and the Said Reed Comes and prove payment Made by the Subscription of Augustine Scarborrow.

Orderd that the Sute be Dismist and the Plaintiff pay Costs.

Mathew Winn Comes by Thos. Snoden his attorney to prosecute his Sute against Mr. Jno. Jennins in a Plea of Defamation And the Defendant Comes and pleads Justification and prays a Refferrence till the Next Court.

Orderd that the action be Refferrd to the first Day of the Next Generall Court.

The Marshall Was Comanded to arest the body of Roger Monteague Executor of the Last Will and Testament of Rich. Collins Deceased and the plaintiff Came Nott to prosecute and the Defendant prays a Nonsute att the Sute of Mr. Jno. Arderne. Ordered that a Nonsute be granted to the Defendant.

Mr. Jno. Porter Comes to prosecute his Sute against Nich. Fillert and Declares for the Sum of 8..10:4 in Pork and the Defendant Comes and Confesses.

Orderd that Nich. Fillert pay to Mr. Jno. Porter the Sum of 8 10 4 In fresh pork With Costs of Sute alias Execution.

Collonell Wm. Wilkison attorney of Mr. Huggendeclin of New-york Comes to prosecute his Sute against Fra. Delemaire and An his Wife and the Defendant Came Not.

Orderd that the Marshall have the body of Fra. Delamere and Ann his Wife att the first Day of the Next Generall Court alias Judgment to be Confirmed against the Marshall.

Mathew Winn Comes per Tho. Snoden his attorney to prosecute his Sute against Jno. Jenins in a Plea of Defemation and the Defendant prays a Refference till Next Court which is Granted.

Upon the Petition of James Tooke

Orderd that Administration of the Estate of Jno. Took Deceased be Comitted to the petitioner and that Capt. Jeremiah Goodridg Capt. Nick. Jones and Mr. James Bridgham apraise the Same being first Sworne by the Honorable Saml. Swann Esqr.

A Letter of Attorney from Ralph Chapman to Tho. Boyd was provd per Oath of Wm. Glovr Esqr.

Capt. John Hunt acknowledges a Sale of a plantation to Thos. Boyd attorney of Ralph Chapman and Eliz. his Wife Relinquishes all her title of Dower to the Same.

Mr. Christopher Gale brings an account against the Estate of Jno. Harvey Esqr. and Colonel Wm. Wilkison Executor of Jno. Harvey Esqr. being present Saith not.

Orderd that Colonel Wm. Wilkison pay to Mr. Chris. Gale as he being Executor to Jno. Harvey the Sum of 3 19:11 with Costs.

A Will of Saml. Pricklove was proved by the Oath of Fra. Penrice and the Subscription of Jno. Anderson.

Geo. Harriss is sworn Deputy Marshall for pascotank precinct and takes the oath by Law apoynted.

Mr. Jno. Porter Comes to prosecute his Sute against Christopher Butler and Says he is Damnifid in his Credit and Reputation by the Said Butler in the Sum of £300 Sterling and the Marshall Makes Returne a true Copy of the Writt and Declaration Left at the Dwelling house of the plaintiff and the Defendant Came Not and the Court is of opinion that the Marshall Amend the Return of the writt and Return Non Est Inventus Which being Done the plaintiff prays that an Attachment may go forth against the goods and Chattells of the Defendant.

Orderd that the Marshall Atteach so much of the goods and Chattells Rights and Credit of the Said Butler as Will amount to the Sum [*torn*] for with Costs etc.

Mr. Chris. Gale Came to prosecute his Sute against tho. Evins in plea of the Case for the Sum of 2:13:2 ½ and proves the Same per Oath.

Orderd that tho. Evins pay to Mr. Chris. Gale the Sum of 2 13:2 ½ with Costs alias Execution.

Walter Craddock Comes to prosecute his Sute against Capt. Jeremiah Goodridg in a Plea of the Case for the Sum of 57: 14: per Account and the Defendant Saith not.

Orderd that the Marshall have the body of Capt. Jeremiah Goodridg att the Next Generall Court in July Next alias Judgment to be Confirmed against the Marshall.

Upon Petition of Dorothy Simpson

Orderd that Mr. Henry White Mr. Jno. Rapier Mr. James Davis Shall Lay out all the Lands wherof Wm. Simpson Deceased was possesst in his Life time and Shall Return to the petitioner the one third thereof to be to her as her Dower.

Mr. Wm. Glovr by his petition Shews that the Estate of Richd. Coll[*torn*] Stands Indebtd to him in the Sum of 7 18 5 and prays an Order for the Same and Roger Monteage being Present Saith not.

Orderd that Roger Monteague pay to the Honorable Wm. Glovr in the Sum of Seaven pound Eighteen Shillings and five pence with Costs of Sute alias Execution if Assets to be found.

Upon the Petition of Jno. Meads

Orderd that Tho. Symons pay unto the petitioner the Sum of five pounds as he being Executor of Charles Jones Deceased itt being for the Bringing up a Negro Boy.

Capt. Jeremiah Goodridg Came to prosecute his Sute against Mr.

Fredrick Jones In a Plea of the Case and the Defendant Saith Nott and Mr. Tho. Snoden attorney for the plaintiff prays Judgment against the Marshall. Ordr that the Marshall have the body of Mr. Peter Godfrey attorney of Fred. Jones att the next Court. <*Peter Godfrey attorney of Fred. Jones.*>

A Bill of Sale from Mr. Wm. Duckenfeild to Mr. Jno. Porter Was Acknowledged.

A Conveyance of a tract of Land etc. was Acknowledged by Mr. Wm. Duckenfeild to Richd. Ashworth.

[*Signed:*]
Samuel Swann, W. Glover, thomas symons, Richard Plater, Wm. Collings.

FILE PAPERS IN SUITS AND PROSECUTIONS

[*Arderne* v. *Monteague*]

[*CCR 180*]

To the first Day of the Generall Court

Mr. Jno. Arderrne is plaintiff versus Roger Monteague Executor of the Last Will and Testament of Rich. Collins Deceased Defendant In the Case and Complaines that the aforesaid Collins [*torn*] Contractd account with the plaintiff for the Sum of 3=18=3 (as by wayes and means Convenient he is Ready to make apeare) which to Render and pay the Said Collins in his life time Did not nor the Defendant as Executor but Refuses the Sume to the plaintiffs Damage Eight pounds for which he brings action and prays Judgment for Same with Costs and Shall pray.

Copia Vera N. Chevin Clericus Curiae

[*Endorsed:*]
Arderne Versus Monteague

[*Craddock* v. *Goodridge*]

[*CCR 191*]

To the Honorable the Generall Court

Walter Cradock Late Mate of the Late Pink Adventure Complains against Jeremiah Goodridg Late Master of the same in an Action upon the Case for that the said Jeremiah Goodridg Standeth Justly Indebted unto the plaintiff in the full and Just Sum of fifty seaven pounds and foureteen Shillings of Sterling money of England which by Wayes and meanes Convenient he the plaintiff is Ready to make apeare being the Consideration money Due to the plaintiff for Work Done by the plaintiff by the Space of Nineteen Moneths and Seaven Dayes att the Request of the Said Jeremiah Goodridg and by his Orders which aforsaid Sum of Money the Defendant hath refused and Doth as Yett Refuse to pay to the plaintiff tho to do the Same he hath by the Plaintiff been requested To the Plaintiffs Damage one hundred pounds Sterling money of England for which he brings this Action And Humbly Cravs Judgment of this Honorable Court for the Same With Costs of Sute And Shall pray etc.

Copia Tho. Snoden[9] Clericus Curiae

[*Endorsed:*]
Craddock versus Goodridg
February the 10th

[*CCR 148*]

North Carolina Ss. To the provost Marshall or Depty

These are in her Majesties name to will and Require you to arest the Body of Capt. Jeremiah Goodridge and him to hold so that he may appear att the next Generall Court to be holden the Last Tuseday in March next att the house of Capt. Jno. Hecklefeild in Little River To Answer the plaint of Walter Craddock in a Plea of the Case and have there this Writt.

Dated: Janry. 7th 1702/3

N. Chevin Clerk

[*Endorsed:*]
Janery The 24 1702
This Rit executed by me on Capt. Guterig John Foster debetty marshall

[*Crown* v. *Winn*]

[*CCR 188*]

North Carolina Ss.

The Jurors for our Sovereigne Lady the Queen Do present that Mathew Winn of the Precinct of Pascotank in the Province aforesaid not haveing the feare of god before his Eyes but being Led away by the Instigation of the Devill Did feloniously And of malice prepenced Att the house of mr. Jno. Jenins in the precinct and province aforesaid Viz. About the 15th Day of December [*torn*] falsly Swear upon the Holy Evangelist this Fals Oath Ocasioned as Followeth Viz. By Vertue of a Warrant from Under the hands of mr. Jno. Jenins for the Recovery of a Sow which belongd to An Indian and which was in the Possession of the Said Winn. And being Recevd by Vertue of the aforsaid Winn he was Asked by mr. Jenins for the Piggs that Came of the Sow he Answered upon Oath that he never Saw the Sow bring any Piggs nor never Saw any Pigs Suck the said Sow which Belongd to the Indian [*torn*] said Winn hath foresworne himself and is Perjurd against the Peace of our Sovereigne Lady the Queen her Crowne and Dignity and against the forme

[9] *Na. Chevin* written and lined out.

of the Statute in that Case made and Provided.

Plater Attorney
pro Domina Regina

[*Endorsed:*]
Indictment Versus Winn
Wee of the Jury finde Ignoramus

[*Falconer, consignee* v. *Paine*]

[*CCR 192*]

To the first day of the Generall Court

Jno. Falconer Consignee of Colonel Robt. Quarry and New pensylvania Company is plaintiff versus Samuel paine Defendant in a plea of the Case and Complaines that the Defendant Stands Indebted to the plaintiff in the Sum of 3 13=00 by his Assumption and promiss to pay the Same for the account of William Hartley (as by wayes and meanes Convenient he is Ready to make appeare) but the same to Rendr acording to his Assumption he Doth refuse to the plaintiffs Damage 7:6 for which he brings his action and prays Judgment for the Same with Costs and shall pray etc.

Copia vera N. Chevin Clk.

[*Endorsed:*]
Falconer versus Paine

[*Gale* v. *Evans*]

[*CCR 148*]

To Thomas Snoden Attorney etc.

These are to authorize and appoint you to appear for me Thomas Evens att the Suite of Mr. Christopher Gale in an action of accompts Depending betwixt the Said Christopher Gale plaintiff And the said Thomas Evans Defendant And to receive the Declaration against me att his Suite And there upon to confesse Judgment by non sum informatus nil Dicit or otherwise And in soe doing this Shall be your Sufficient warrant And I will pay you your Fees Witnesse my hand this 31th Day of March Anno Domini 1703.

Witnesse hereunto
N. Chevin
Thos. Luten

Tho. Evans

[*Hecklefield* v. *Fewox*]

[*CCR 191*]

To the 2d Day of the Generall Court

Capt. Jno. Hecklefeild is plaintiff Versus James Fewox Defendant in a Plea of the Case and Complaines that the Defendant hath Contracted account with the plaintiff to the Value of five pound Nine Shillings (as by Wayes and

Meanes Convenient he is Ready to make appeare) and which to Render he Doth refuse to the plaintiffs Damage ten pounds for which he brings his action and prays Judgment for the same with Costs and Shall Pray etc.

Copia Vera N. Chevin Clk.

[*Endorsed:*]
Hecklefield Versus Fewox

[*Jones* v. *Dereham*]

[*CCR 148*]

North Carolina Ss.

Mr. Fredk. Jones of James City County in Virginia alias Mr. Fred. Jones and Company Merchants in London [complain] against Thomas Dereham of Pamplico in the County of Bath in the Goverment of North Carolina in an Action of Debt [*illegible*] the Defendant Stands justly indebted to the Plantiff in the penalty of One Thousand pounds Sterling as by an Obligation under his hand Seal'd and delivered (here in Court ready to be produced) bearing Date the Sixth day of February 1701/2 for the Conditionall payment of Two hundred Forty Seven pounds Eight shillings and Threepence in Skinns and Furrs at a certain price therein mentiond, and Two hundred and Ten pounds Ten [*torn*] and Six pence in Country Commodities at a certain price therein likewise mentioned relation unto the Land[*torn*] being had more fully and at large doth and may appear the which summs of money as aforesaid the Defendant refuseth topay whereupon the plantiff brings this action and Craves judgement of [*torn*] Worshipfull Court with Cost of suit and shall pray etc.

February 10, 1702/3 Fred. Jones

[*Winn* v. *Jennings*]

[*CCR 191*]

To the first day of the Generall Court

Mathew Winn is plaintiff Versus Mr. Jno. Jenins Defendant in a Plea of Defamation And Complaines for and that Whereas the Plaintiff hath been of good Report And hath Ever Well behavd himself towards all her majesties Leige People and good neighbours amongst whome he hath Livd And hath Never been accused or taxed with any Unjust or unlawfull action but hath Ever by his Honest and Lawfull Endevears gotten his Livelihood [*illegible*] all places where he hath Lived, [*illegible*] Nevertheless the Defendant (the same Well Knowing) yett of meer Malice and Ill will Intending thereby to Abase and Lesson the Reputation And Creditt of the Plaintiff amongst all his good neighbors and to Render the plaintiff base and Ignominious the Defendant Did att the Last Generall Court held in October Last att the house of Capt. Jno. Hecklefeild before Divers Wittnesses then and there present Utter and pronounce these slanderous base and Scandalous Words Viz. Ile prove you (meaneing the plaintiff) [*illegible*] Ile prove you perjured before all the

Countrey And allso att the same time and place the Defendant [saeth] saide You (meaneing the plaintiff) are a hogstealeing Rogue and Ile prove you a hogstealer By which Malicious Fals Scandalous Words Spoken in so publick a Place and time the Plaintiff saith he is Damnified in his Reputation and Creditt in the sum of one hundred pounds sterling for which he brings his Action and Prayes Judgment for the Same With Costs and Shall Pray etc.

Copia Vera N. Chevin Clericus Curiae
[*Endorsed:*]
Winn versus Jenins North Carolina Ss.
Petti Jury
Cornel. Jones, Jno. Reed, [*Torn*], Jno. Winbery, [*Illegible*], Tho. Mercer, Jno. Jones, [*Torn*], Jno. Willowby, Jno. Dicks, [*Illegible*] Foster, James [*Illegible*], Simon Trumball, Wm. Lufman, Jno. Scarborow, Richd. Jeffer, Wm. Reed.
We of the Joure finds the Plente £2-10*s*.-0*d*. Damigs with Kost of Sute.
Jenins, Attorney, Huggindectyn

[*CCR 191*]

Tho. Barcock Aged 60 years or thereabuts being Deposed and sworn saith that a bout 3 a yeare ago he gave to tom Harriss an Indian a sow Shote and after he had had itt a Considerable time it Run from him and was Gott amongst Mathew Winns hoggs and the Indian Coming to me Desird me to go to Mathew Winns with him to gett the Shote being marked a Cropp Lefte Eare and 2 Slitts in the Cropp an over keel and under keell in the Right and Mathew Win Yeilded to Deliver the Shote to the Indians but never had it till Daniell Phillips Recoverd it by a Warrant from Jno. Jenins and Further saith not.

Thomas Barcock Signum

[*Endorsed:*]
Barcocks Deposition

[*CCR 103*]

To July Court From March Court Refferences and orders against the Marshall Videlicet

Porter atturney Jones Versus Slade. Order versus Marshall.

Bird versus Reed. Refferrd.

Winn Versus Jenins. 2 Actions. Refferd.

Wilkison Attorney Huggendeclin Versus Lemarr and Wife. Order versus Marshall.

Porter versus Battle. Non Est Inventus Returnd.

Cradock versus Goodridg. Order versus Marshall.

Goodridg Versus Jones. Order versus Marshall.

Chevin versus Frayly Case for 3:9:6 per account.

Fredrick Jones versus Jeremiah Goodridg Plea Case. Damage £1000.

Idem and Company versus Ditto plea Case. Damage £500. Non Est Inventus.

Wm. Duckenfeild Esqr. Versus Monteague Plea Case. No Returns.

Idem Versus Daw Plea Debt. No Returns.

<*May 6th 1703*>

Mr. Boyd atteact Dr. Swann.

Mr. Henry Baker Merchant of Virginia versus Early Plea Case.

Cobb etc. versus Fewox. Retraxitt.

Chapman versus Powell. Detinue. Return Executed.

Idem versus Sulicun. Case. Retraxitt.

Semmons versus Fitzpatrick. Not Executed.

Nuby versus Frayly Debt. Executed.

Platt Versus Martin. Retorn Executed.

Stanton Versus Bundy Tresspass on the Case. Return Executed.

Houghton Versus Norman. Return Executed.

Scarborow per Supersedias against Rice.

Griffin Supersedias against Jones.

Wm. Reed versus Benj. Tull Case.

[*CCR 103*]

North Carolina Ss. July Court

Att a Generall Court Holden att the house of Capt. Jno. Hecklefeild in Little River the 27th Day of July 1703 Present The Honorable Major Saml. Swann, William Glover, Thomas Symonds, Jno. Hawkins, Richd. Plater Esqrs. Justices.

The Court being Proclaimed Do adjourn till to morrow Morning 9 a Clock.

Wednesday morning 8 a Clock Court meets Present Utt Supra.
Major Swann absent.

The Marshall being Comanded to arest the body of Henry Slade att the Sute of Mr. Jno. Porter attorney of James Jones and the Plaintiff Came not to Prosecute.

Orderd that the Action be Dismist and the Plaintiff pay Costs.

Jno. Bird Comes to prosecute his Sute against Wm. Reed in a plea of Debt for 17:00-00 and the Defendant Comes and prayes Oyer of the Bill which being had he pleads account in Ban which being allowd there is found to be Due to the plaintiff 12=3:6.

Orderd that Wm. Reed pay to Mr. Jno. Bird the Sum of 12:3:6 with Costs of Sute alias Execution.

Mathew Winn Acknowledges a Conveyance of Land to Robt. Morgan.

The Grand Jury Sworn Mr. Jno. Bird Mr. Denniss Maclendon David Prichard Tho. Lewis Wm. Winbery Rowland Buckly Saml. Prichard James Prichard Rich. Mardren Rich. Stamp Thomas pendleton Phill. Talksey Daniell Rice James Fewox Rich. Jesper.

Mathew Winn Comes by Colonel Wm. Wilkison and Mr. Thomas Snoden his Attorneys to prosecute his Sute against John Jenins in a plea of Defamation for these Words You are a perjurd Rogue you are a Hogstealing Rogue and Ile prove it And the Defendant Comes and pleads Justification and brings Severall Evidences to prove it And the plaintiff by Colonel Wm. Wilkison his attorney Says that A person Can not be perjured Except in [*illegible*] a Court of Record And thereupon Casts himself upon the Country And the Defendant Likewise and the Marshall is Comanded to Cause to Com 12 etc. who etc. By whome etc. And there Came Cornel Jones Jno. Relfe Jno. Winbery [*torn*] mercer, Jno. Jones Jno. Willowby, Jno. Dicks James Foster Simon Trumball Wm. Lufman Jno. Scarborou Wm. Reed Who Impaneld and Sworn Say we find for the plaintiff two pound ten Shillings with Costs.

Orderd that Jno. Jenins pay to Mathew Winn two pound ten Shillings With Costs alias Execution.

And the Court Adjournd till to morrow Morning 8 a Clock.

Thursday Morning 8 a Clock the Court Meets.

Present Wm. Glover Esqr. Tho. Simonds Jno. Hawkins Richard Plater Esqr.

Upon the Petition of Wm. Glover Esqr. assignee of Colonel Robt. Quarry and Company praying Judgment against Chris. Butlers Estate [*illegible*] Colonel Wm. Wilkison being Present to Whome the Estate Was bound over.

Orderd that Colonel Wm. Wilkison pay unto Wm. Glover Esqr. the Sum of fifty three Shillings with Costs alias Execution.

Colonel Wm. Wilkison Attorney of Mr. Huggen Declan of New York Coms to prosecute his Sute against Mr. Fra. Delamare and Ann his Wife Executors of Rich. Pope Deceased and Declares for severall goods and merchandize Recd. by the Said Pope from the plaintiff in New York Amounting to the Sum of £144. And the Defendant Comes by Mr. Tho. Boyd theire Attorney and Denies the Declaration and Says the Said Goods they Nevr Recei'd And Colonel William Wilkison produces an Account under the hand of the Said Huggendeclin Attested by the Corporation and under the [Seal] of New York. And the Defendant Casts themselves upon the Country and the Plaintiff Moved that a Jury might be Empanelled one halfe of [*illegible*] for the Tryall of this Case And was Directd by the Court to sue out a Writt of Venire Spec[*torn*] for Such a Jury to the Next Court And he refused and prayes to Com to tryall. And the marshall is Requird to Cause to Com twelve etc. and who etc. By Whome etc. and there Came Cornelious Jones Jno. Relfe Jno. Winbery Tho. Mercer, who being Sworn and before any other of the Fellows had taken the oath Colonel Wm. Wilkison objected against the Jury as Insufficient and Departed the Court Then the Rest upon the Panell was Likewise Sworn Viz. (And the whole matter So farr as it Lay before the Court was given them in Charge) Jno. Jones Jno. Willowby Jno. Dick James Foster Simon Trumball Wm. Luffman Wm. Reed Daniell Phillips and upon the Holy Evengelist Say We of the Jury find for the Defendant with Costs of Sute.

Wm. Rayfeild provs his Rights to 200 Acres of Land by Importation of Wm. Rafeild Ann Patience and Wm. Rafeild.

The Marshall Was Comanded to arest the body of Chris. Butler att the Sute of Mr. Jno. Porter and the writt was Returnd to the Last Court Non Est Inventus And Now the Marshall Returns Mortuus Est.

Craddock Versus Goodridg Plea Case for the Sum of fifty seaven pound fourteen Shillings And the Defendant by Colonel Wilkison his attorney Says that the Declaration he had not in Due time and therefore prays to be Dismist and is Dismist.

A Letter attorney from Jer. Goodridg to Colonel Wilkison was proved per oath of James Coles.

Jeremiah Goodridg by Colonel Wm. Wilkison his attorney Comes to prosecute his Sute against Mr. Fredrick Jones Late of London in a Plea of the Case and Mr. Peter Godfrey attorney of the Said Jones Comes and Says that the Declaration in Due time he had not and prays to be Dismist.

Ordered that the Action be Dismist and the Plaintiff pay Costs.

Mathew Winn Comes per Colonel Wm. Wilkison and Mr. Tho Snoden his Attorneys to Prosecute his Sute against Mr. Jno. Jenins in a Plea of Defamation and Declares for Damage £200 and the Defendant Comes and puts them upon proof of the Declaration and Casts himself upon the Country and the plaintiff Likewise and the Marshall is Comaned etc. and who etc. By whome etc. and there Came Cornel Jones Jno. Relfe Jno. Winbery: Tho. Mercer Jno. Jones Jno. Willowby Jno. Dicks James Foster Symon Trumbell Wm. Luffman Wm. Reed Dan. Phillips who Empaneld and Sworne on the Holy Evangelist Say we find for the plaintiff one Shilling with Costs. Orderd Jno. Jenins pay to the plaintiff 1 Shilling Damage and 1 Shilling Costs.

Fredrick Jones and Company Comes per Mr. Peter Godfrey their Attorney to prosecute theire Sute against Jeremiah Goodridg in a Plea of the Case and the writt being Returnd Non Est Inventus the plaintiff prays Atteachment Orderd he have Atteachment.

Mr. Tho. Boyd haveing Ateacht the Estate of Tho. Swann of Roxberry for the Sum of £2 16*s*. And Mr. Rich. Plater Comes and Replevins the Atteachment.

Orderd that Mr. Rich. Plater pay to Mr. Tho. Boyd the Sum of two pound Sixteen Shilling with Costs alias Execution.

Collonel Henry Baker By the Honorable Saml. Swann Esqr. Comes to prosecute his Sute against Wm. Early in a plea of the Case for the Sum of £24 17:4 And the Defendant Comes and prays a Refferrence and by Joynt Consent it is Refferrd.

Ralph Chapman per Mr. Thos. Snoden his attorney Comes to prosecute his Sute against Wm. Powell in a Plea of Detinue and the Defendant Came not and the plaintiff prays Judgment against the Marshall.

Orderd that the Marshall have the body of Wm. Powell att the next Generall Court the Last Tuseday in October alias Judgment to be Confirmd against the Marshall.

The Marshall was Comanded to Arest the body of Wm. frayly att the Sute of Gabriel Nuby and Nuby Came not to prosecute.

Orderd that the action be Dismist and the Plaintiff pay Costs alias Execution.

Tho. Platt Came to prosecute his Sute against Joell Martin in a Plea of the Case for Breach of Covenant And the Defendant Came Not.

Ordered that the marshall have the body of Joell Martin att the next Court the Last Tuseday in Octo. alias Judgment to be Confirmd against the Marshall.

Richard Houghton by Tho. Snoden his attorney Comes to prosecute his Sute against Henry Norman for Severall things the

Consideration of an Indenture between them and the Defendant Comes and prays Oyer of the Indenture and that it may be proved which was Done.

Orderd that Henry Norman pay to the plaintiff one New Coat and briches Servicable and good one Handsaw one Drawing Knife one Round Share one [*illegible*] which shall be servicable To be Delivrd Imediatly with Costs alias Execution.

The Court Adjournd till to morrow morning 9 a Clock.

Friday Morning 9 Clock Court meets Present utt Supra.

On the Petition of Margt. Macbride

Orderd that Math. Winn pay to the petitioner for her travell and Attendance Ninteen Shillings and two pence with Costs alias Execution.

Isaack Gilford and Jos. Gilford being Bound over to this Court makes theire apeareance and pray to be Dischargd.

And they are Dismist paying Costs.

Upon Motion of Mr. Tho. Snoden

Orderd that a Will of Rich. Stiballs Shall be Recorded.

Wm. Reed Came to prosecute his Sute against Benj. Tull plea of Case and the Defendant Came not Ordered that the marshall have the body of Benj. Tull att the Next Court the last Tuseday in October next alias Judgment to pass against the Marshall.

Tho. Stanton versus Caleb Bundy Plea Case by agreement Refferrd to Next Court the Last Tuseday in Octobr.

[*Signed:*]

W. Glover, thomas symons, Richard Plater, Jno. hawkins.

RECORDED BY ORDER OF COURT

[*CCR 103*]

Know all men by these presents that I Henry Baker of Virginia Nominated Constituted Authorized and appoynted and in my stead and place Do put my Very good Friend Saml. Swann Esqr. in Carolina to be my true and Lawfull attorney Irevocably to Sue for Levie Recovr Receive Demand and take of Wm. Early of the Said Carolina the Sum of 24 17=4½ Or of any other person or persons Indebted to the Said Baker within the abovesaid Country. Giving and Granting unto my Said Attorney my full and whole powers and Lawfull Authority in the Execution of the Premisses to arest atteach Implead Imprisson and out of Prison againe to Deliver the Said Wm. Early his heires etc. Until they or Som of them Shall have Fully Sattisfied the Debt abovsaid and upon Receite thereof or of any

Part thereof acquittances or any other Lawfull Discharges in that behalf for me and in my Name to make Seale and Deliver And all other Act and Acts thing and things Device or Devices in the Law whatsoevr for me and in my Name to Do Conclude and finally to finish in full Large and ample a Maner as I may might or Could Do were I Said personally present Ratifiing allowing and Confirming all and whatsoever my Said Attorney Shall Legally Do or Cause to be Don herein. Given under my hand And Seale the 17th Day Apll. 1703.

Seld and Delivrd in presence of Hen. Baker Signum
Jno. Alstone
James Flemin his marke
Richl. Barfeild

FILE PAPERS IN SUITS AND PROSECUTIONS

[*Chevin* v. *Griffin*]

[*CCR 190*]

July Court 1703

Geo. Griffin is Debtor To N. Chevin Videlicet

To Supersedias selfe and [President]	10
To 6 Sumons Viz. Torkley Harison his wife Mcgregory Abbington Grey	6
Calling Cause Entering apearance	2
Order Recognizance and Dismising etc.	3*s*
	£ 1:1

N. Chevin
[*Endorsed:*]
Geo. Griffins Account

[*Houghton* v. *Norman*]

[*CCR 192*]

To the Honorable Generall Court 2d Day

Richard Houghton is plaintiff Versus Mr. Henry Norman Defendant in an action of the Case upon Breach of Covenant And setteth forth that the Defendant by Covenant and Indenture beareing Date the 21 Day of Sept. 1695 is thereby bound (for the Consideration of the Plaintiffs service to the Defendant the terme of seaven Years which the Plaintiff hath faithfully and Fully served) to Learne the Plaintiff the Coopers trade and to provide for him Cloathing Diet Washing and Lodging as allso to pay him one Maire of three yeare old And a sett of Coopers tools usefull for his Imploy allso two New sutes of aparill one of searge and the other of som good Wearing Cloth with hatts shoos and shiffts and stockins answerable (As by the said Indenture Relation thereunto being had will apeare) Yet the Defendant the Covenant and Agrement and Condition Nott Regarding the same to Fullfill and pay to the Plaintiff Doth wholy refuse whereby the Plaintiff saith is Damnified and hath Damage sustained to the Value of twenty pound sterling for which the Plaintiff Brings his Action And Humbly prays Judgment for the Condition of the Indenture with Damages and Costs of sute and shall Pray etc.

Copia Vera [N. Chevin]

[*Endorsed:*]
Houghton Versus Norman
And 1 Summons

[*CCR 192*]

This Indenture Maide the twenty First day of Septemr. In the yeare of our Lord god one Thousand Six Hundered ninety and Five betwene Thomas Houghton of yawpin Talor of the one part and Henery Norman of pequimons Cooper of the other part Now this Indenture Wittnesseth that the Said Thomas Houghton hath and hereby doth bind and obleag his Sonn Richard Houghton to Live and serve Henery Norman and Ann his now Wiffe For the Full Space and time of Saven Whole yeares From the day of the date hereof In all Mannor of Lawffull Imployment and to behave him Selfe as an Aprentize by the Law of England is Required For and In Considderation whereof the said Henery Norman doth hereby oblege himselfe his Exeequtors Administrators and assigneys to Larne him the said Richard the Coopers Tread and to Find him with Mate drinke wasshing and Lodging and Apparill Convenient to keep warme and to pay him one Mayre of three years ould of a good Stature at the Expyration of three years End And a sett off Coopers Tooles Useffull For this Compty And at the Expyration of the time to pay him two new Suits of Apperell one of Sarge and the other of Summe good Weareing Cloth with hats Shooes and shiffts and stockings Answerable And iff it soe Happen that Henery Norman and Ann his wiffe shall Happen to dye and depart this Liffe beffore the Expyreation of the said terme of Saven years that then the said Richard Houghton Shall bee absolutly Free From his Servitud In Wittness Whereof the partys to these presents have here Unto sett theyre hands and seales the day and yeare above Written.

Sined sealed and delivred
in the presents of us
Anthony Dawson
Stephen Manwaring
The marke of Thomas Clarke

Tho. Houghton
Henery Norman his marke
Richard Hoghton his marke

[*Endorsed:*]
Thomas Clark, Samell [*illegible*].

[*Nuby* v. *Frayly*]

[*CCR 191*]

North Carolina ss.

Gabriell Nuby is plaintiff against William Frilie Defendant in an action of Debt and Setteth forth that the Defendant by an obligation from under his hand and Seale oblidgd himselfe to pay or cause to be payd unto the plaintiff etc. the Just Summe of four hundred pounds of good well dress'd Porke and Merchantable upon Demand after the Tenth of December next ensuing the date of the Said Bill As by the Said Bill and the Date thereof relation being thereunto had doth and may more fully appear and refuseth payment tho' thereunto by the plaintiff Demanded To the plaintiffs Dammage five pounds Sterling For which he hath brought this action and humbly Craves Judgment of this Honorable Court for the Same with Costs of Suite And Shall pray etc.

Gabriell Nuby
Vera Copia Tho. Snoden Clericus Curiae

[*Endorsed:*]
Nuby versus Frilie
In Debt
Sur obligatory

[*Platt* v. *Martin*]

[*CCR 139*]

To the Generall Court the Last Tuesday in July 1703

Mr. Thomas Platt of Virginia is Plaintiff and attacheth the Body of Joell Martin Senior of Pamlicoe in the County of Bath in a Plea of the Case, and Complaines that he Contracted Bargained, and agreed; with the Joell Martin aforesaid Defendant, Some time in September last past, for the Passage of the Said Martin and his family (etc.) into Pamlicoe; for Sattisfaction whereof by agreement the Said Plantiff was to have four Pounds pade him by the Said Defendant, immediately after his arrival in the County of Bath (alias Pamlicoe) aforesaid and whereas the Plantiff haveing performed his part in the Transportation of the Defendant as per Bargaine, and haveing Demanded the Summ of four Pounds; the payment whereof the Defendant doth Refuse, which is unto the Plantiffs great Detriment and Dammage for which he here hath brought his action and Craves Judgment for the Same with Cost and Shall pray.
May the 21st: 1703

[*Endorsed:*]
Platt versus Martin
Order versus Marshall
Mr. Martin dickluration

[*Reed* v. *Tull*]

[*CCR 148*]

To the Honorable Generall Court of North Carrolina

William Reed Plantiff hath Brought his action of the Case on assumpsett against Benj. Tulle Defendant.

To Witt That That is to Say That Kath. Hobs Stood Justly Indebted unto the plantiff by Accountt the Sum of Four pounds Seaventeen shillings and Six pence and the said Kath. Hobs for the sum aforesaid and for other Consederations was willing to Serve the plantiff Two Years, the Defendant by fair promises perswaded the said Kath. Hobs to Leave the plantiff and to lieve with him, upon which the plantiff Demanded his Money, and the Defendant did assume and promiss to pay the plantiff what the said Kath. Hobs did owe him in laiving the plantiff upon which promiss the plantiff was Sattisfied which was in July and August in the year of our Lord God 1702 Since the plantiff hath Demanded of the Defendant the afore Said Sum of Four pounds Seaventeen Shillings and Six pence Knowing it was Justly due from the afore said Kath. Hobs, and the Defendant Refuses payment Therefore the Plantiff hath Brought his action and Demands Judgment of this Honorable Court against the Defendant for the aforesaid Sum of Four Pounds Seaventeen Shillings and Six pence with Costs etc.

[*Endorsed:*]
Reed versus Tull
Order versus Marshall
Wee of the Juore find for the platif one pound sevnteen shilling and 12 pence with the Coste

[*CCR 103*]

Referrences and Defaults from July Court to October Court

First Day

Colonel Baker versus Wm. Early. Reffered by Consent.

Stanton versus Bundy. Refferd etc.

Platt Versus Martin. Order Versus Marshall.

Reed Versus Tull. Order Versus Marshall.

Writts and Returns to October Court

Augst.	2	Semons Versus Fitzpatrick Plea Case. Executed.
	2	Craddock Versus Goodridg. Plea Case. Non est inventus.
	3	Capt. Hecklefeild Administrator Pordage versus Warren plea Case. Retraxit.
	3	Idem Versus Sanderson. Case. Executed.
	3	Idem Versus Phillips. Case. Executed.

3 Idem Versus Bishop. Case. Retraxit.

3 Idem Versus Nichollson Case. Executed.

3 Idem Versus Bray Case. Not Executed.

2d day

September 2 Captain Hecklefield Administrator of Pordage versus Warren. Plea Case. Executed.

4th Bishopp versus Phillipps. Plea Case. Executed.

5th Jones versus Goodridge in Case. No Declaration fil'd.

6th Goodridge etc. versus Jones etc. Plea Case. Executed.

29th Ward and Butler widdow versus Leigh in Covenant. Retraxit.

[*Torn*]ber 1 Pritchard versus Fitz=patrick Plea Case. Executed.

8th Nuby versus Frilie Plea Debt. Not Executed.

10th Wilson assignee etc. versus Jordan administrator etc. Plea Debt. Executed.

15th Clarke versus Leigh. Plea Debt.

[*CCR 103*] [10]

Att A Generall Court Holden att the House of Captain John Hecklefield in Litle River October the 26th 1703. Present The Honorable Wm. Glover, The Honorable John Porter, The Honorable Christopher Gale, The Honorable Thomas Symonds, The Honorable John Blunt, Esqrs.

The Courts Commission being published and the Members having taken the usuall Oaths and the Oath for the due discharging the office of Justices the Court Satt present ut Supra.

The Honorable Court adjourn'd till to Morrow Morning 7 Clock.

Accordingly on Wednesday Morning the Court meets present ut Supra Except Glover.

---

[10] There is no single complete set of minutes for this session of the General Court. The minutes offered here were gathered from three separate collections. Those taken from CCR 189 are scratch minutes (rough notes taken by the clerk from which he would write the finished minutes), and there is some duplication of information between them and the portion taken from CCR 102.

Collonell Henry Baker by the Honorable Major Samuel Swann his Attorney Comes to prosecute his Suite against Wm. Early Defendant in A plea of the Case and declares that the Defendant Stands Justly indebted to the plaintiff in the full and Just Summe of £24-17*s*.-4*d*. ½ And for plea the Defendant Sayth he is not indebted in the aforesaid Summe and objects against certaine of the Articles Exhibited in Court And itt appearing to the Honorable Court that the reall Summe of £20-13*s*.-9¼ is due from the Defendant to the plaintiff the Defendant Confesses Judgment for the Same.

Order'd that the Defendant pay to the plaintiff the aforesaid summe of £20-13*s*.-9*d*. ¼ with Cost of Suite alias Execution.

The Marshall being required to arest the body of Joell Martin to answer the Complaint of Thomas platt And the Defendant Came not And the Marshall not bringing the body of the Defendant

Order'd that Judgment be Confirm'd against the Marshall for the Summe of £4 according to the plaintiffs Declaration with Costs.

[*CCR 189*]

Upon petition of Capt. John [*illegible*] John Steward late of the province of N. Carolina deceased stands Indebted unto him one pound Six shillings and nine pence and Craved order against Godfrey Sprewell Administrator of the said John Steward Deceased and is denyed by the Court by reason the said Godfrey Sprewell being not Legally supeaned to make Defence therein.

Upon Petition of Capt. John Hecklefield shewing that John Lilly late of the province of North Carrolina [*torn*] stand Indebted unto him Twenty Shillings and [*torn*] order against Joseph Smith [Executor] the said John Lilly Deceased and it is denyed by the Court by reason the said Joseph Smith being not Legally supeaned to make Defence therein.

Bryan Fitzpatrick came into Court and acknowledged his deed of sale of six Hundred and fourty acres of land unto Ralph Chapman and the same ordered [to] be recorded.

Presentment is made to the Grand Jury that Susannah Evans of the precinct of Coratuck in the County of Albemarle [in] the province of North Carolina not having the fear of God before her Eyes but being led by the Instigation of the Devill did on or about the twenty fifth day of July last past the body of Deborah Bourshier being then in the peace of our soveraigne Lady the Queen Divelishly and Malitiously bewitch and by assistance of the Devill afflict with mortall paynes the body of the said Deborah Bourshier whereby the said Deborah Departed this life And alsoe did Diabolically and malitiously bewitch severall other of her Majesties Liege subjects against the peace of our said soveraigne Lady the Queen and against the forme of the statute in that Case made and provided And the Marshall is Comanded to come etc. And there Came Mr. Robt. Wallis James Farlow Wm. Early Francis Beasly James Ward John [Widby] John Wattkins [Zak] Keton Robt. Lowry William Simson William Luftman Hugh Prichard Cornelius Jones Richd. Stamp Richd. Mardson Cornelius Fitzpatrick who were Impananlled and [is] sworn saying wee of the Jury find no Bill and the person Ignoramus and it is ordered that the said Susanh. Evens be acquitted paying the Charges.

Presentment is made to the Grand Jury that Martha Richardson of the precinct of Corratuck of the County of Albemarl in the province of North Carolina [*torn*] having the fear of God before her Eyes but [being] [*torn*] On by the Intigation of the Divill did on [*torn*] the 20th day of July last past the Body of [William] Parker being in the peace of our Sovereign Lady the Queen Devillishly and Maliciously B[ewitch] and by asistance of the Devill afflict the Body [*torn*] said William Parker and also did Diabolically [and] maliciously Bewich severall other of her [*torn*] Leige subjects against the peace of [*torn*] sovereign Lady the Queen and against [*torn*] of the statute in that case made and provided [*torn*] the marshall is Commanded to come etc. and [*torn*] came Mr. Robt. Wallis James Farlow William Early Francis Beasly James Ward John [*torn*] John Wattkins Zachary Keeton Robt. Lowry [William] Simson William Luftman Hugh Prichard [Cornelius] Jones Richd. Stamp Richd. Madran Cornelius Fitzpatrick who were Impanelled and sworne saying wee of the Jury find no Bill and the person Ignoramus and it is ordered that the said Martha Richardson be acquitted paying the Charge.

Colonel Wm. Wilkinson comes into Court and acknowledges his Deed of sale of five Hundred and sixty Acres [*torn*] Mr. Edwd. Smethwick and the same ordered to be recorded.

Mr. Edwd. Smethwick and his wife Sarah comes in [*torn*] and acknowledges their Bill of sale of Five Hundred and sixty acres of Land unto Colonel William Wilkinson and the same ordered to be recorded.

[*CCR 102*]

<153> Upon petition of Capt. John Hecklefeild Doctor for [*illegible*] [*torn*] Orderd that Mr. Thomas Boyd Executor of the last will and [testament] of Archibald Burnett Deceased pay unto Capt. John Hecklefeild [*torn*] summe of [8]*s.* 3*d.* with Costs alias Execution.

Matthew Pritchard Comes to prosecute his suite against [Bryan] Fitzpatrick in a Plea of the Case and setts forth that the [Defendant] stands Justly Indebted to the plaintiff in Diverse summes of [Money] amounting in the whole to six pounds fifteen shillings and [*torn*] good Cowes and Calves and one yearling Heifer and the [Defendant] Comes and Confesses Judgment for the summe of six pounds and fifteen shillings and one good Cow and Calf Orderd that the Defendant pay unto the plaintiff the summe of six pounds fifteen shillings and one good Cow and Calf with Costs alias Execution.

Richd. Rose being bound over to his behaviour to be of good aberance to James Anderson makes his appearance and prayes to be dismist and no Processe being return'd he is Dismist paying Costs.

Bryan Fitzpatrick acknowledges a Deed of sale to Ralph Chapman.

Upon Petition of Mr. Thomas Boyd praying for [letter] of administration of the Estate of Francis West Deceased in his minority Ordered that the said Thomas Boyd bring an account of the said Francis West's Estate to the next Court.

Upon Petition of John Torkington praying to be admitted to prove five Rights is admitted and Proves five Rights to 250 acres of Land by the Importation of himselfe Martha his wife Wm. Torkington Anne Starke and Francis Starke.

Upon Petition of the Honorable John Porter Esqr. praying to be admitted to prove Nyneteen Rights is admitted and proves Rights to 950 acres of land by the Importation of himselfe his wife four Children and Thirteen Negroes.

Captain John Hecklefield by his Petition shewing that Wm. Boyce late of the Province of Maryland Deceased stands indebted unto the petitioner in the summe of five pounds tenne shillings and six pence and praying an Order against Joanna Tayler Executrix of the said Boyce Will is Denied the said Joa. Tayler not being legally summon'd [to] make Defence therein.

Captain John Hecklefield by his Petition shewing that John Stuart late of this Province Deceased stands indebted to him in one pound six shillings and Nyne pence and praying an Order for the same against Godfry Spruell Administrator of the said Stuart's Estate is Denyed [the] said Godfry Spruell being not legally summoned to make Defence herein.

Captain John Hecklefield by his Petition shewing that John Lilly late of this Province Deceased stands indebted to him in Twenty shillings and praying Order for the same against Joseph Smith Executor of the said Lillys last will and testament is Denyed the said Joseph Smith not being legally sumoned to make Defence therein.

<153*a*> [*Torn*] Fitzpatrick acknowledges a Deed of sale of six hundred and [*torn*] acres of Land to Ralph Chapman and the same ordered to be [*torn*].

Edward Smethwick and his wife Sarah acknowledge a Bill of [*torn*] five Hundred and sixty acres of Land unto Collonell Wm. Wilkinson [*torn*] same ordered to be Recorded.

[Colonel] Willm. Wilkinson acknowledges A Deed of sale of five hundred and sixty acres of Land unto Mr. Edward Smethwick and the same orderd to be recorded.

Upon Petition of the Honorable Wm. Glover Esqr. That Christopher Butler and Thomas Norcomb were Joyntly and severally bound to the petitioner in the summe of Twelve pounds Eleven shillings and tenne pence and of the same summe he sayes he hath received two pounds and seventeen shillings and the remainder of the aforesaid summe of £09-14*s*.-10*d*. for which he craves Judgment of the said Norcom for the same And the said Norcom Comes and Confesses Judgment. Orderd that Thomas Norcom pay unto the petitioner the summe of Nyne pounds fourteen shillings and tenne pence with Costs alias Execution.

Uppon Petition of John Evans shewing that the Estate of Thomas Bourshier deceased is Indebted to him and Diverse persons in this Government And that the said Estate is in Danger by a person unknown to be Conveyed away out of this Government. Orderd that the Provost Marshall take into his Custody the said Bourshiers Estate and the same to secure untill Disposd of by Due Course of Law.

Upon motion of Captain Richd. Sanderson Ordered that Wm. Reed pay unto Captain Richd. Sanderson 2*s*.-6*d*. for one Dayes Attendance as an Evidence for the said Reed with Costs alias Execution.

[*Signed:*]
W. Glover, John Porter, C. Gale, Thomas Symons.

RECORDED BY ORDER OF COURT

[*CCR 102*]

<154> Know all men by these presents That I John Cobb [*torn*] of London Gentleman doe hereby Constitute appoint Ordain [*torn*] and in and by these presents have Constituted appointed [*torn*] and made and in my place and stead put and placed my Trusty [*torn*] beloved Friend Hugh Campble of the Province of [North] Carolina Gentleman my true and Lawfull Attorney for me and [*torn*] Name and to my use to ask Demand Recover and receive of [*torn*] from all and all manner of person or persons within the [*torn*] of North Carolina aforesaid and alsoe of and from all and every person and

persons within the County of Princess Anne within [*torn*] Majesties Dominion of Virginia All and all manner of Goods and merchandizes porke Tobacco wheat Corne summe and summes of money whatsoever Due to me by Bill Bond writing or Account or by any other wayes whatsoever And the person or persons upon refusall or neglect of payment or Delivery of the same for any parte or parcell thereof to arrest Imprison to Implead and proceed to Judgment and Execution and in prison to Detain and Keepe untill satisfaction had and made for the same and every parte and parcell thereof and upon such satisfaction had and made the person or persons soe refusing or neglecting to make payment againe out of prison to release and Discharge and one or more acquittance or accquittances Release or Releases Discharge or Discharges for me and in my Name to make seale sign and Deliver for the same or any part or parcell thereof and one or more Attorney or Attorneys under him to make Constitute and appoint for the better Execution of the premisses and againe att pleasure to revoke hereby Ratifying Confirming and allowing all and whatsoever lawfull act or acts thing or things Device or Devices my said Attorney or Attorneys or any or either of them shall lawfully doe or cause to be done for the better Execution and obtaining the premisses. In Witnesse whereof I have hereunto sett my hand and seale the Twentieth Day of August 170[3] In the second yeare of the Reigne of her Majesties Queen Anne over England etc. Annoqe Domini 1703.

Signed Sealed and Delivered in the presence of
John Hunt
Richard Plater
Recorded per Order

John Cobb sigillum

<154*a*>[11] [*Torn*] hereby Constuded by me John Cobb in behalfe of [*torn*] and Company That if itt shall please God to Call by Death Hugh Campbelle my Attorney as within Mentioned That I doe hereby Constitute and appoint [one] James Tooke to act and Doe for me as fully and amply in all respects as if my former Attorney was alive or my selfe personally present Witnesse my hand and seale this 23d of August 1703.

Witnesse
John Hunt
Richard Plater

John Cobb sigillum

[11] Page 154*a* of the manuscript is headed, "Recorded per order."

FILE PAPERS IN SUITS AND PROSECUTIONS

[*Clarke* v. *Leigh*]

[*CCR 191*]

North Carolina ss. To the Honorable the Generall Court

Thomas Clarke is plaintiff against Daniell Leigh Defendant in an action of Debt and Setteth forth that the Defendant Standeth Justly Indebted to the plaintiff in the full and Just Summe of three pounds Sterling in the Vendable Commodityes of this Country as by A bill from under the Defendants hand and Delivered to the plaintiff relation being thereunto had doth and may more fully appear and refuses payment To the plaintiffs Dammage Six pounds Sterling for which he hath brought this action and humbly Craves Judgment of this Honorable Court for the Same with Costs of Suite and Shall pray etc.

Thomas Clarke

[*Endorsed:*]
Clarke versus Leigh
In Debt
Sur Obligatory

[*Crown* v. *Evans*]

[*CCR 102*]

The Jurors for our Soveraign Lady the Queen Present upon their Oaths that Susannah Evans of the precinct of Coratuck in the County of Albemarle in the aforesaid Province Not having the fear of God before her Eyes but being led by the Instigation of the Devill did on or about the twenty Fifth day of July last past the body of Deborah Bourchier being then in the peace of our Soveraigne Lady the Queen Devilishly and malitiously bewitch and by assistance of the Devill afflict with Mortall paines the body of the said Deborah Bourchier whereby the said Deborah departed this life and alsoe did diabolically and Malitiously bewitch Severall other of her Majesties Liege Subjects against the peace of our Said Soveraigne Lady the Queen and against the forme of the Statute in that Case made and provided etc.

Plater per Domina Regina

[*Endorsed:*]
We of the Jury find the Bills of Ignoramus

[*CCR 148*]

Corahtuck precinct august the 31t 1703

The Deposition of Tho. Boucher aged: 39: yeares or there aboutt sayeth that upon the: 24th: of July 1703 your Deponents Houshould (or fammaly) was Then in perfect helth Excepting one person which was Recovering out of his sallivation: the same day att Eve I your deponent Called one Tho. Walker a servant of yor Deponents to Come to meet: but he instantly Cryed out that his paines was soe Great that he Cold not Come Crying out of his belley and stummack and soe Continueth dissabled to this Day; the next morning it being the 25th of July: 1703 the aforesaid Walkers wife Came from John Evans his House and youre Deponent said to her I was very Glad that shee was Come that shee might nurse her husband; within one hower or two my wife was taken with a pain in her feet soe Exstreemly and sevearly that shee Cryed out: and acquainted me that her paine was in such sort that her feet Felt as if a thousand alls or nailes was Pearsing them and Could Have noe Ease but when her feet was put in hott water soe she Continued: 24: howers Then the paine seassed in her feet but shee was tormented in her bowels to the day of her death the which sickness Continued abought a month and many helpfull men and woman: indevered to give her Ease and helpe but all in vaine and it was observed that [*illegible*] shee was taken sick shee Cried owt of John Evans his wife still saying that shee was an Evall woman and that shee was sattisfied that she suffered Those great paines by her meanes and Ernestly desiered mee to have her Examined and serched for shee should sertainly Dy but it may serve to prevent her from Doing more Mischeif This she said with many more words Releating to the said Evans his wife ading that shee Coold not slumber but she thought of her before many persons present soe that in a bought a weake after shee was taken I Thomas Bowcher your Doponent was allso Taken with strainge and unuseual paines in my stomack and belley and Prevyiparts and am still afflicted to this day soe that I and my wife Could herdly Tell which Shoid Dy furst and Tho. Taylor and his wife and all the people of my famally ware soe bad that one Could not helpe another: sometime before my wife Dyed John Evans Came for me To meet his wife att Mr. Tho. vandermulens to appeare before Mr. Richd. Cominfort for she that was his wife was not willing to heare such Reports against her selfe I Readely went and there acquainted what obligation my wife had Laid one me to serch the matter more plaine John Evans and his wife Did abuse me and my wife and he Thretned me that he wold much bruse by body I acquainted him that I was sick he said that he did not beleive but that I was as well as he this is what is most pertinent and what I Can Remember the which I doe attest and sett my hand unto.

Tho. Bowcher

Copia Vera Test. Edwd. Tayler Clk. Court

This Deposition Sworen Too in open Court The 31st day of august 1703 Test. Edwd. Tayler Clk. Court

[*Endorsed:*]
The Deposition of Tho. Bowcher

[*CCR 192*]

To the honorable Generall Court

Jno. Eveans humbly Sheweth Wheras yor pettitioner having his Wife brought to this honorable Court as a Conficted Person: being Concerned with familier Spirits under the Notion of a Wich to yor pettitioners great Damage and Detriment yor pettitioner humbly prays that this honorable Court may bring the same to proofe and tryall Liveing so far a Distance and yor pettitioner As in Duty bound Shall pray.

[*CCR 192*]

North Carolina ss. To the Honorable the Generall Court

The Humble Petition of Susannah Evans Most humbley Sheweth That Tho. Bourchier hath put your petitioner to great Charge and trouble by Causing your petitioner to be Comitted for A Witch And your petitioner humbly prays your Honors will be pleased to grant an Attachment against the Said Bourchiers Estate and She Shall pray etc.

[*Goodridge* v. *Jones, et al.*]

[*CR 24.901.1*]

North Carolina Ss.

Jeremiah Goodridge of this Government of north Carolina late master or commander of the late pinke adventer of London Complaines in behalfe of himselfe and Company Against Mr. Freder. Jones and the rest of the owners of the said lat pink adventer in an Action of the Case setteth Fourth and Saith that the Said Mr. Fred. Jons and the rest of the owners of the Said late pink adventer standeth Justly indebted unto the plaintiff and company in the Sum of three hundred twenty four pound Eight Shillings and one farthing as by an acct. beareing Date the tenth of July in the year aforesaid 1702 made use in pequimins precinct which in the abovesaid Goverment at the Request of Mr. Thomas Jons who was agent or facter for and in behalfe of the defendant whose orders and Derections the plaintiff was to follow as by wayes and meanes he is ready to make appeare when thereto required the which Sum abovesaid the defendant refusseth to paye by which the plaintiff Saith he and the rest of the Company are Damnified the Sum of Sixe hundred fourty Eight pounds Sixtene Shillings and one halfepeny and therupon hee bringeth this Action and humblye Craves Judgment of This honorable Court for his Debt and damages with Costs and he Shall as In Duty bound pray.

To the Generall Court Sept. 26d 1703 Jeremai Goodridge

Mr. Snoden Sir bee so kind as to continue this or acep.

[*Endorsed:*]
Goodrige etc. v. Jones etc.
In Case

[*CCR 139*]

North Carolina Ss. To the Provost Marshall or Deputy

These are in her Majesties Name to will and require you to arrest the body of Frederick Jones etc. and him to hold Soe that he may appear the Second Day of the next Generall Court to be held for this province the last Tuesday in October next att the House of Captain John Hecklefeld in little River to answer the Complaint of Jeremiah Goodridge etc. in A Plea of the Case and have there this writt Dated the 6th day of September 1703.

Tho. Snoden Clericus Curiae

[*Hecklefield* v. *Boyd, executor*]

[*CCR 179*]

To the Honorable the Generall Court

The Humble petition of John Hecklefield Most humbly Sheweth That Archibd. Burnet deceased was indebted to your petitioner in the Summe of fifteen Shillings and that Mr. Tho. Boyd was appointed Executor of the last will and testament of the Said archibd. Burnett.

Wherefore yor said petitioner prayes that your Honors will be pleased to grant an Order that the Said Tho. Boyd may pay the aforesaid Summe to your petitioner and he as in duty bound Shall pray etc.

[*Endorsed:*]
Executed June the [*illegible*]

[*Hecklefield* v. *Phillips*]

[*CCR 191*]

To the Honorable Generall Court

Capt. Jno. Hecklefeild is plaintiff Versus Daniel Phillips Defendant in a Plea of the Case and setteth forth that the Defendant hath Contracted account with the plaintiff within three Years Last past to the Value of Eighteen pound ten Shillings and nine pence (as by Wayes and means Convenient he is Ready to make appeare) and which to Render he Doth Refuse to the plaintiffs Damage thirty seaven pounds Sterling for which he brings his Action and prays Judgment for the Same with Costs and shall Pray.

Copia Vera Na. Chevin Clk.

[*Endorsed:*]
Hecklefeild versus Phillips

[*CCR 148*]

North Carolina Ss. To the Provost Marshall or Deputy

These are in her Majty Name to will and require you to arest the body of Daniel Phillips and him to hold so that he may apeare the first Day of the next Generall Court to be Holden the Last Tuseday in October next att the house of Capt. Jno. Hecklefeild in Little River to answer the plaint of Capt. Jno.

Heckleffeild in a Plea of the Case and have there this writt take good bond.

Dated August 2d 1703 Nath. Chevin [Clerk]

[*Endorsed:*]
Executed 7br the 20 Per George Harris Dep. Marshall

[*CCR 148*]

At A Generall Court Held at the House of Capt. John Hecklefield for the Province of North Carolina this 27 day of October 1703
Present the Justices

Capt. John Hecklefield Plantif comes to prosecute his Suit against Danll. Phillips Defendant in a plea of the Case for the Sum of Eighteen Pound ten Shilling and nine pence and the Defendant not appearing the plantiff Craves an Order against the Marshall and the provost Marshall Craves an attachment against the Defendants Estate.

Ordered that the Marshall Attaches as much of the Defendants Estate as will answer and pay the aforesaid sum of Eighteen Pounds Tenn shilling and Nine pence with Cost and the Same to Secure and a returne of the Same to make to the next Court.

[*Hecklefield, administrator* v. *Warren*]

[*CCR 184*]

To the first Day of the Generall Court

Capt. Jno. Hecklefeild Adminstrator of the Goods and Chattells of George Pordage Deceased is plaintiff Versus Abraham Warren Defendant in a Plea of the Case And Sayes that the Defendant Stood Justly Indebted and owing to mr. George Pordage in his Lifetime the Sum of one pound Eight Shillings and ten pence by Account which Said Sum the Defendant Did never pay to the Said Pordage in his Life time And the Same to Render And pay to the Plaintiff (Qualified as aforsaid) the Defendant Doth Refuse Wherefore the plaintiff brings his Action and Prays Judgment for the Same With Costs and Shall pray etc.

Copia Vera Nath. Chevin Clericus Curiae

[*Endorsed:*]
Hecklefeild Administrator Pordage Versus Warren

[*CCR 139*]

North Carolina ss. To the provost Marshall or Deputy

These are in her Majesties Name to will and require you to arrest the body of Abraham Warren and him to hold Soe that he may appear att the next Generall Court the last tuesday in October next att the House of Captain John Hecklefield in Little River to answer the plaint of Captain John Hecklefield administrator to the Goods and Chattells of George Pordage deceased in A Plea of the Case and have there this writt Dated the 6th day of September 1703.

Tho. Snoden Clericus Curiae

[*Endorsed:*]
Executed the 7th day of 7ber by mee John Hecklefield

[*Hecklefield and wife* v. *Nicholson*]

[*CCR 191*]

To the 3d Day of the Generall Court

Doctor Jno. Hecklefeild and Eliz. his Wife is plaintiffs versus [*blank*] Nicholson Defendant in a plea of the Case and Complains that the Defendant stands Indebted and owing to the plaintiffs in the sum of 30*s.* per Account (as by wayes and means Convenient he is Ready to make apear) and which to Render he Doth refuse to the plaintiffs Damage three Score shillings for which they bring theire Action and prays Judgment for the same with Costs and shall Pray etc.

Copia Vera N. Chevin Clericus Curiae

[*Endorsed:*]
Jno. Hecklefeild versus Nichollson

[*Jones and Company* v. *Goodridge*]

[*CCR 148*]

North Carolina ss. To the Provost Marshall or Deputy

These are in her Majesties Name to will and require you to arrest the body of Jeremiah Goodridge and him to hold Soe that he may appear att the next Generall Court to be held [for] this Province the Last Tuesday in October next att the House of Captain John Hecklefield in Little River to answer the Complaint of Frederick Jones and Company in a Plea of the Case and have there this writt Dated 21 day of September Anno Domini 1703.

Testis Tho. Snoden Clericus Curiae

[*Endorsed:*]
Non est Inventus

[*Nuby* v. *Frayly*]

[*CCR 148*]

North Carolina ss. To the provost Marshall or Deputy

These are in her Maties Name to will and require you to arrest the body of William Frilie and him to hold soe that he may appear the Second day of the Generall Court to be held for this province the last Tuesday in October next att the House of Captain John Hecklefield in Little River to answer the Complaint of Gabriel Nuby in a Plea of Debt and have there this writt Dated October the 8th 1703.

Tho. Snoden Clericus Curiae

[*Prichard* v. *Fitzpatrick*]

[*CCR 148*]

North Carolina Ss. To The Honorable The General Cort

Matthew Pritchard is plaintiff against Bryan Fitz Patrick Defendant In a plea of the Case Complaines That the Defendant Stands justly indebted to the plaintiff in The Just Sume of Six pounds Eleven shillings Currant money of N. Carolina by Bill under his hand and seale dated the 1st day of Aprill 1702 and foure Shillings by account And the Plaintiff further Complaineth that the Defendant Stands further indebted to the plaintiff four good Cows and Calves and also on yearling heifer by his writeing under his hand and seal bareing Date This 1st day of Aprill 1702 as by ways and meanes Convenient The plaintiff is Ready to make apeare all which a Counts is The whole To the Sume of Six pounds fifteen shillings foure Good Cows and Calves and one yearling Heifer and which The Defendant hath not Rendred to the Plantiff but still doth refuse to render tho often thereunto requested To the Plaintiff's Damege Thirty pounds Sterling and Therefore he brings his sute and prays Judgment for the Seame with Costs of Sute And Shall pray.

[*CCR 148*]

North Carolina The Right Honourable John Granvile Palatine and The Rest of The Lords and Absolute Proprietors of The said province To The Marshall Send Greeting we Singluly Command you without any Delay to atack The Body off Bryan FitzPatrick Planter So as to have him personaly Apeare at The Next General Court to be holden at The House of Capt. Jno. Hacklefild on The Twenty Sixth day of This Instant october: 1703 To Answer The Complaint of Mathew Prichard In an acttion of The Case for Thirteen pounds Sixteen Shillings and Foure pence Wittness my and Seale This 2d day of octber 1703.

Samll. Norton Secretary

[*Endorsed:*]
Executed the 15th day of October by me Tho. Houghton Deputy Marshall

[*Reed* v. *Sanderson*]

[*CCR 139*]

North Carolina ss. To the provost Marshall or Deputy

These are in her Majesties Name to will and require you to Subpena Captain Richard Sanderson Junior Soe that he may appear the Third Day of the next Generall Court to be held for this province the last Tuesday in October next att the House of Captain John Hecklefield in Little River to answer the Bill of Complaint of William Reed And have there this writt Dated the 24th of September 1703.

Tho. Snoden Clericus Curiae

GENERAL COURT, OCTOBER 1703

[*Ward and Butler* v. *Leigh*]

[*CCR 179*]

North Carolina ss.

James Ward and Annaritta Butler widdow of the precinct of Chowan are plaintiffs against Daniell Leigh Defendant in A Plea of Covenant and Sett forth that the Defendant by A writing from under his hand bearing Date the 16th day of July 1703 did Covenant and grant to and with the plaintiffs upon the penalty of five pounds Sterling to doe his utmost Endeavour to teach the Said James Ward and Christopher Son of the Said Annaritta [*torn*] to read write and Cast Accompt to the end of the rule of Divesion as by the Said writing from under the Defendants hand relation being thereunto had doth appear Neverthelesse the Defendant his aforesaid Covenant and Contract to keep and performe hath hitherto refused and doth as yet refuse to the plaintiffs Damage £5 Sterling for which they have brought this action And humbly Crave Judgment of this Honorable Court for the Same with Costs and Shall pray etc.

Tho. Snoden Clericus Curiae

[*Endorsed:*]
Ward and Butler vs. Leigh
In Covenant
Ads. Dampnus £5

[*CCR 148*]

North Carolina ss. To the provost Marshall or Deputy

These are in her Majesties Name to will and require you to arrest the body of Daniell Leigh and him to hold Soe that he may appear att the next Generall Court held for this province att the House of Captain John Hecklefield in Little River the last Tuesday in October next to answer James Ward and Annaritta Butler in a [*torn*] of Covenant And have there this writt Dated the 29th day of September Anno Domini 1703.

Tho. Snoden Clericus Curiae

[*Endorsed:*]
Executed Sept. the 30 by me Jno. Byrd deputy Mershall

MISCELLANEOUS FILE PAPERS

[*Fitzpatrick, Bryan, deed of sale*]

[*CCR 187*]

To all Christian People to whom these presents Shall Come I Bryan Fitzpatrick of the precinct of Perquimons Send greet Greeting in our Lord god Everlasting now Know ye that I the above Said Fitzpatrick for divers good Causes and Considarations me herunto moving and more Espeacily for Competent Summ already Sattisfied Contented and pd. Doth Alinate barginn and

Sell and for Ever make Saile unto Ralph Chapman Senior of [*illegible*] one tract or parcell of Land lieing and being in the presinct above Said Containing Six hundred and forty acres being upon the South Side of Aligator Creek Called by the name of Calfe pasture begining at a pine Standing upon the river and So runing with Various Courses To have and to hold the Said Land with all profitts and privilidges and Appurtenances whatsoever without any Lett trouble or molestation whatsoever that Shall or may Acrew by me my heirs [*torn*] for Ever and further I the above Said Bryan Fitzpatrick Doth oblidge my Selfe my heirs Executors Administrators to [*torn*] and Defend the Said Saile from all persons that Shall or may lay any Claime title or [*torn*] therunto and for Assurance herof I oblidge my Self my heirs Executors Administrators in the penell Summ of twenty Six pound Sterling money of England in Wittness my hand and Seale this 28th Day of 8ber. 1703.

Signed Sealed and Delivered in presence of us — Bryan Fitzpatrick Signum

Danll. Leigh
Cornalius Jones Signum
Wm. Early

Acknowledged in Court the 28th day of October 1703.

Tho. Snoden Clericus Curiae

[*Endorsed:*]
Bryan Fitzpatrick
Deed Saile
Ralph Chapman

[*Paine, Samuel, deed of sale*]

[*CCR 187*]

Albemarle Ss. Aprill 3 1703

Know all men by thes presents that I Samuell paine of the abovesaid County do alienat bargain sell and doe by these presents Alienate bargain and sell from me my hiers executors administrators to Mr. Joseph Cook of pensilvania cooper to him his hiers executors administrators and assings for ever a certain tract of land lying and being in the presinct of pascotank bounding one the west side of flaty Creek so along the sound Joyning to John Bolmans line being survayed by the abovesaid Samll. paine which the draugh of the abovesaid land will evidently show containing eghty five acres with all rights privilliges and heriditements therto beloning with all woods wooland ground and clear grount therto belonging or apertaning being for a valuable consideration alredy in hand receved of the abovesaid Cooke with waranty from any person or persons that [*torn*] pretend any claim or clams from me or any person or persons what so ever in confirmation wherof I have heerto Set my hand and afixed my Seall day and year abovesaid.

Signed Seald and delivered
in presens of us
James Caron
Thomas Boyd
John dea his mark

Samll. Payen

Acknowledged the 27th day of Octobr from Samuel Payne to Mr. Tho. Boyd in behalfe of Joseph Cooke

[*torn*] Tho. Snoden Clericus Curiae

[*Endorsed:*]
Joseph Cook
Sale of land from paien

[*Smithwick, Edward, indenture*]

[*CCR 187*]

This Indenture made the 27th of 8br in the year of our Lord one thousand Seaven hundred and three By and between Mr. Edward Smethwick of the province of No. Carolina of the one part and Colonel Wm. Willkison of the Same province above Said Now Know Yee That I the above Said Edward Smethwick for divers good Causes and Considarations more herunto moving and more Espeacily for a Valuable Considaration already Sattisfied Contented and paid by and with the Consent of Sarah my Wife have Alinated bargined and Sold and for Ever made Saile unto Colonel Wm. Wilkison his heirs Executors Administrators or his or your Assignes for Ever one tract or parcell of Land lyeing and being in the County of Albemarle in the province of No. Carolina in the presinct of Chowan: Containing five hundred and Sixty Acres beginning at a red Oake Standing by the River and So bound by varius Courses according to patten. To have and to hold the Said tract of Land as above Said with all intents and porposes with all profitts and privilidges Appurtinances whatsoever to me my heirs Executors Administrators any ways belonging to Appertaining by me my heirs Executors Administrators And further I the abovesaid Smethwick Doth oblidge my selfe my heirs Executors Administrators to warrent and defend the Said Colonel Wm. Wilkison from all Letts trouble or molastation whatsoever from all person or persons that Shall or may lay any Claim title of Interest therunto as wittness my hand this Day [*torn*] of 8ber 1703.

[*Torn*]
[*Illegible*] Leigh
Thomas Blount

Edward Smithwick
Sarah Smithwick Signum

[*Endorsed:*]
Acknowledged in Court the 28th day of Octobr 1703. Tho. Snoden Clericus Curiae

[*Tarkinton, Jno., petition*]

To the honorable Generall Court

Jno. Tarkinton humbly Sheweth That your pettitioner humbly prays that he may be Admitted to prove five rights and your pettitioner as in duty bound Shall pray.

<*John Tarkington, Martha his wife, Wm. Tarkington, Anne Starke, Francis Starke.*>

[*CCR 139*]

Orders against the Marshall and References to March Court 1704

Hecklefield versus Phillips in Case. Attachment.

Goodridge versus Jones in Case. Order versus Marshall. Returnd Satisfaction made.

Bishopp versus Phillipps in Case. Attachment. Attached one Negro Woman.

Martin versus Platt. Supersedeas in Cancellaria.

Stanton versus Bundy in Trespasse. Retraxit.

Jones versus Payne in Case. Executed. Retraxit.

Hecklefield Attorney Jones versus Phillips in Case. Retraxit.

Norkam versus Butler vidua in Case. Retraxit.

Jones versus Goodridge in Case. Executed.

Anderson versus Mekins in Case. Non est inventus.

Pierce versus Burkett in Detinue. Executed.

Pierce versus Hartly in Case. Executed.

White versus FitzPatrick in Debt. Concordia.

Bell versus Hughes in Case. Non est inventus.

Bell versus Randall in Case. Non est inventus.

Bell versus Davis in Case. Executed.

Duckenfield versus Powell in Debt. Executed.

Duckenfield assignee of Powell versus Farrow in Debt. Non est inventus.

Duckenfield versus Montegue in Case. Executed.

Blount versus Chilton in Case. Mortuus est.

Anderson versus Beesley in Debt. Executed.

White versus Inkeson and Berry in Case. Retraxitt.

Porter versus Smith in Case. Retraxit.

Porter versus Smith Attachment. Satisfaction made.

Porter versus Ayres in Case. Non est Inventus.

Porter versus Ayres Attachment. Attached 510 pounds of Salted Porke A Skellitt and old Chest in Richd. Davenports hand.

Boswell versus Payne in Debt. Retraxit.

Mary Rookes versus Albertson in Trespasse. Retraxit.

Rookes versus Albertson in Trespasse. Retraxit.

Norkam Attorney of Burtenshall versus Burkett. Executed.

Banister versus Fitzpatrick in Debt. Retraxit.

Banister versus Hartly in Debt. Executed.

Hecklefield Administrator of Pordage versus Steel in Debt. Executed.

Anderson versus Fuawkes in Debt. Not Executed.

Cobb versus Evans in Debt. Executed.

Glover versus Evans in Case. Executed.

Griffin versus Jones in Case. Not Executed

Collings versus Smith in Case. Non est inventus.

Pettiver versus Pursell in Case. Retraxit.

Hecklefield and Uxor versus Godfrey in Case. Executed.

Craddocke versus Goodridge in Case. Executed.

Hosier against Kitchin in Case. Executed.

Snoden Assignee etc. versus Frilye in Debt. Concordia.

Norman and Uxor versus Gale and Uxor in Case. Retraxit.

Williams versus Eggerton in Case. Executed.

Keel versus Phillipps in Debt. Executed.

Spruel versus Evans in Debt. Executed.

Chevin versus Powell in Debt. Executed.

Jones versus Wayte in Case. Executed. Retraxit.

Coles versus Goodridge in Case. Executed.

Swann vidua administratrix versus Fuawkes in Debt. Not Executed.

Colonel Robt. Quary etc. versus Cockeram in Debt. Not Executed.

Benington versus Richd. Booth in Case. Retraxit.

Bennington versus Bradley in Case. Retraxit.

Captain Blunt and Uxor versus Worley in Assault and Battery. Executed.

Captain Blunt and Uxor versus Worley in Trespasse Sur Case. Executed.

Frilye versus Worley in Debt. Executed. Evidences James Blunt, Henry Lisle, Tho. Cooper for Defendant.

[*CCR 139*]

Att A Generall Court held att the House of Captain John Hecklefield in Little River the 28th Day of March Anno Domini 1704. Present The Honorable Wm. Glover Esqr., The Honorable John Porter Esqr., The Honorable Chr. Gale Esqr. Justices.

The new Laws Published as the Law Directs.

The Court Satt present ut Supra.

The marshall is required to bring forth the body of Mr. Frederick Jones to answer the Complaint of Jeremiah Goodridge and both partyes appear and referr'd by Consent till to Morrow.

And then the Court adjourns till 5 of Clock in the afternoon.

Att 5 of Clock in the afternoon the Court meets present ut Supra. And then adjourns till to morrow morning att 7 Clock.

On Wednesday Morning att 7 of Clock the Court meets present Mr. Symons instead of Mr. Glover.

John Burket Acknowledges A Tract of Land to Richd. Burtenshall and Orderd to be recorded.

An acknowledgment of an Assignment of A Tract of Land from Jacob Overman to Robert Cock his wife relinquishes her right of Dower in Court.

A Deed of Sale acknowledged in Court from Tho. Snoden to John Bateman.

Mr. Gale absent.

The Marshall is Comanded to bring forth the Body of Frederick Jones and Company etc. to answer the Complaint of Jeremiah Goodridge for that the Defendants Stand Justly Indebted to the plaintiffs in the full and Just Summe of Three Hundred Twenty and four pounds

Eight Shillings and one farthing as by an Account bearing Date the tenth Day of July in the year of our Lord 1702 etc. And for Plea the Defendant in behalfe of himselfe Comes and Saies that the aforesaid Jeremiah Goodridge to his writt and Declaration aforesaid ought not to be answered because he Saies that there is manifest variance betweene the writt and Declaration aforesaid and Diverse Incertainties therein And this he is ready to averr wherefore he prayes Judgment if the aforesaid Jeremiah Goodridge to his writt and Declaration aforesaid ought to be answered etc. And the plaintiff for Replication doe averr and Say that the Writt and Declaration fild by the plaintiff against the Defendants is good in Law And the Opinion of this Court is that there is variance betwixt the plaintiffs writt and Declaration.

Orderd that the action be dismiss'd and the plaintiff pay Costs.

Upon Petition of Frederick Jones praying lettres of Administration upon the Estate of Walter Craddock as greatest Creditor.

Orderd that the petitioner have letters of administration of the Said Craddocks Estate.

The Marshall is required to arrest the body of Wm. Powell to Answer the Complaint of Wm. Duckenfield Esqr. in A Plea of Debt for the Summe of One and Twenty pounds Nyne Shillings and Nyne pence And the plaintiff Came not Orderd that the action be dismissed and the plaintiff pay Costs.

The Marshall is required to arrest the body of Roger Montegue to answer the Complaint of Wm. Duckenfield Esqr. in a plea of the Case for Seven pounds by his Assumption and both partyes agreed referrd by Consent to the next Court.

The Marshall is required to arrest the body of Henry Hartly to answer the Complaint of Mr. John Banister in a plea of Debt for the Summe of four pounds and the Defendant Came not Orderd to be referr'd to the next Generall Court.

The Marshall is required to arrest the body of Tho. Evans to answer the Complaint of John Cobb for the Summe of four pounds And Mr. Richd. Plater by a Power of Attorney from Hugh Campbell Attorney of the plaintiff appeares for the plaintiff and the Defendant Comes and Confesses Judgment.

Orderd that Thomas Evans pay unto John Cobb the Summe of four pounds with Costs alias Execution.

<*Craddock* versus *Goodridge*>

The plaintiff by Captain James Coles his Attorney Complaines for fifty Seven pounds and fourteen Shillings and the Defendant Declaration not given in time.

Orderd that the action be dismissed and the plaintiff pay Costs.

Captain James Coles by his Motion to this Court Setts forth that he ought to Stand the lawfull Attorney of Walter Craddock late of this Government And that no person ought to have lettres of Administration of the Said Craddocks Estate before A Registry of the Death of the Said Craddock.

Ordered that no person have lettres of Administration of the Said Craddocks Estate till the Matter be further known.

<*Spruell* versus *Evans*>

The plaintiff by Richd. Plater his Attorney Declares against the Defendant for tenne pounds and both partyes being agreed Orderd to be referrd till the next Court.

<*Chevin* versus *Powell*>

The plaintiff Declares against the Defendant in Debt for fifty Shillings in Porke Merchantable and well Saved and well packt att 50*s*. per barell or good butt well Conditioned Beef well Saved att 25*s*. per Barrell and the Defendant Came not.

Orderd that the Marshall bring forth the body of the Said Wm. Powell to the next Court alias Judgment to be Confirmd against the Marshall.

<*Coles* versus *Goodridge*>

The plaintiff Declares against the Defendant for fifteen pounds eighteen Shillings and two pence in Case And the Defendant puts the plaintiff to the proof of his Declaration and puts himselfe upon the Country and the plaintiff likewise And the Marshall is required to cause to come twelve true and lawfull men etc. who neither etc. to whom etc. By whom etc. And there came Mr. Dennis Macclendon Mr. John Anderson Mr. Henry Bradly Mr. Richd. Burtenshall Mr. Willm. Willms. Mr. Jenkin Willms. Mr. Tho. Boswell Mr. John Dicks Mr. Henry Creech Mr. Roger Montegue Mr. Samuel Payne and Mr. Robert Hosier who Impanell'd and Sworne Say wee of the Jury find for the Defendant.

Orderd that the action be dismist and the plaintiff pay Costs.

<*Capt. Hecklefield and Uxor* versus *Godfrey*>

The plaintiffs Declare against the Defendant for that the Defendant is heir apparent to Eliz. Godfrey in her Minority late Deceased and that the Said Eliz. Godfrey in her life time was Indebted to the plaintiffs in the Summe of One Hundred Fifty and Six pounds and tenne pounds [*torn*] disburs'd and [*illegible*] more for funerall

Charges and for plea the Defendant Says he as heir is not Chargeable with the Debts of the Said Eliz. Godfrey in her Minority.

And the opinion of this Court is that an Heir is not Chargeable with the Debts of his Ancestors Except by Bill or Bond wherein the Heir is bound or by Record or Debts to the Queen.

Orderd that the action be dismist and the plaintiff pay Costs.

Upon petition of Jane Dean praying to be allowed for two dayes Coming and two dayes going as an Evidence for Captain Blunt versus John Worly

Orderd that Captain Tho. Blunt pay unto Jane Dean the Summe of Eleven Shillings and Eight pence with Costs alias Execution.

And then the Court Adjournd till to Morrow Morning 8 of Clock.

On Thursday Morning 8 of Clock the Court meets present ut Supra as alsoe Mr. Tho. Symonds.

<*Bishopp* versus *Phillipps*>

The plaintiff Declares against the Defendant in an action upon the Case for the Sume of Nyne pounds Thirteen Shillings and five pence And for plea the Defendant Sayth that the plaintiff hath not his action well brought itt appearing to the Court that the action was not well brought.

Ordered that the plaintiff be nonsuite and pay Costs.

<*Willm. Glover Esqr.* versus *Evans*>

The plaintiff Declares against the Defendant for four pounds And the Defendant Comes and Confesses Judgment for £3-17*s.*-7*d.*

Orderd that The Defendant pay to the plaintiff £3-17*s.*-7*d.* with Costs alias Execution.

<*Anderson* versus *Beesley*>

The plaintiff Declares against the Defendant for £2-15*s.*-3*d.* payable in Porke barrells And the Defendant Came not And the plaintiff Craves an order against the Marshall.

Orderd that the Marshall bring forth the body of Francis Beesley to the next Generall Court to answer the plaintiffs Complaint alias Judgment to be Confirm'd against the Marshall.

The Provost Marshall prayes an Attachment against the Estate of Francis Beesley which is Granted.

The Marshall Craves an Attachment against the Estate of Wm. Powell which is granted upon the Said Powells non appearance to answer the Complaint of Nath. Chevin.

<*Porter Esqr.* versus *Ayres*>

The Marshall is required to attach Soe much of the Estate of David Ayres as will Satisfye the plaintiff £4-5*s.* and the Marshall makes return Attach'd 510 pounds of Salted Porke A Skellet and old Chest And the plaintiff prayes the Attachment may be Continued till the next Generall Court which is granted.

<*Bannister* versus *Hartly*>

The plaintiff by Captain James Coles his Attorney Declares against the Defendant for four pounds Sterling And the Defendant Came not And the plaintiff prayes an Order against the Marshall.

Orderd that the Provost Marshall bring forth the body of Henry Hartly to the next Generall Court to answer the plaintiffs Complaint alias Judgment to be Confirm'd against the Marshall.

Whereas by Judgments past at pascotank Court against George Harris itt appeared Mr. Christopher Gale and Sarah his wife were Debtors to the Estate of the Honorable Thos. Harvey Deceased in the Summe of £41-10*s.*-6½ Itt appeares that the aforesaid Summe was payd and Satisfyd to the Testator in his life time Excepting the Summe of £16-00-04½.

And then the Court Adjourns till 3 of Clock in the Afternoon.

Att 3 of Clock in the afternoon the Court meets present ut Supra.

And then Adjourns till to Morrow Morning 7 of Clock.

Friday Morning 7 of Clock the Court meets present ut Supra.

Wm. Collings Esqr. Sworn Justice for this Government of North Carolina present.

A power of Attorney from Anne Caroon to John Hecklefield prov'd by the oths of Sam. Payne and Tho. Welch.

Anne Caroon by Captain John Hecklefield her Attorney relinquishes her right of Dower of A Tract of land Sold by James Caroon her husband unto George Elcott.

Upon Petition of Sam. Payne Shewing that by A Bond past from Thomas Boyd to Sam. Payne for the Summe of Six pounds for A tract of Land Conditionally That if the Said Boyd did not pay the Said Summe of Six pounds then the Said Land to returne to the Said payne and the Said Tho. Boyd Confesses Judgment.

Orderd the property of the Land be reversd to the Said payne according to the Condition of the Said Record.

Mr. Jeremiah Goodridg Summoned on her Majesties behalfe to give Evidence against James Coles Committed for Severall Outrages and abuses and Threatnings Contrary to the peace of our Soveraigne Lady the Queen and Came not.

Order'd that the Marshall take the Said Jeremiah Goodridge in to Custody till he give bond with Security to make answer for his Contempt herein att the next Generall Court.

Mr. Sam. Norton and Captain James Coles Comitted for Severall Outrages by them Commited against the peace of our Sovereigne Lady the Queen Upon their humble Submission are Dismist without Day.

A Deed of Sale acknowledged in Court from Sam. Payne to Tho. Boyd.

And then the Court Adjourns till the Court in Course.

[*Signed:*]
W. Glover, John Porter, C. Gale, thomas symons, Wm. Collings.

RECORDED BY ORDER OF COURT

[*CCR 103*]

I Jacob Overman Doe hereby assigne over all the Right Title and Interest of the within mentioned Tract of Land and premisses unto Robert Cock his Heires and Assignes for ever Witnesse my hand this Twenty Nynth Day of March Anno Domini 1704.

Witnesse hereunto Jacob Overman
Tho. Snoden

FILE PAPERS IN SUITS AND PROSECUTIONS

[*Bannister* v. *Hartly*]

[*CCR 148*]

North Carolina ss. To the Provost Marshall or Deputy

These are in the Name of his Excellency the Pallatine and rest of the true and absolute Lords and Proprietors to will and require you to arrest the body of Henery Hartly And him to hold Soe that he may appear att the next Generall Court to be held for this Province the last Tuesday in March next att the House of Captain John Hecklefield in Little River to answer the Complaint of Mr. John Bannister In A Plea of Debt and have there this writt Dated the 12th Day of Febr. Anno Domini 170[*blank*].

Tho. Snoden Clericus Curiae

[*Endorsed:*]
Executed March ye 2

[*Bell* v. *Davis*]

[*CCR 191*]

North Carolina ss. To the Honorable Generall Court etc.

Boaz Bell is plaintiff against William Davis Defendant in A plea of the

Case for breach of Covenant and Setteth forth and Declares that the Defendant Covenanted and Contracted with the plaintiff to goe to A certaine place called Corissaw[12] as Mariner in Company with the plaintiff Master of the Sloop Anne on board the Sloop Anne and back againe to this Province Nevertheless the Defendant his Covenant and Contract hath not performed whereby the plaintiff Sayth he is Dampnifyed Twenty pounds Sterling for which he hath brought this action And humbly Craves Judgment of this Honorable Court for the Same with Costs of Suite And he Shall pray etc.

Copia Tho. Snoden Clericus Curiae

[*Endorsed:*]
Bell versus Davis
In case
Sur breach of Covenant
Retraxit

[*Bell* v. *Hughes*]

[*CCR 148*]

North Carolina ss. To the Provost Marshall or Deputy

These are in the Name of his Excellency the Pallatine and rest of the true and absolute Lords and Proprietors to will and require you to arrest the body of Thomas Hughes and him to hold that he may appear att the next Generall Court to be held for this Province the last Tuesday in March next att the House of Captain John Hecklefield in Little River to answer the Complaint of Boaz Bell in A Plea of the Case and have there this writt Dated the 8th of December Anno Domini 1703.

Tho. Snoden Clericus Curiae

File A bill in Chancery Mary Rookes versus Esau Albertson and Sett forth in the bill the land not laps'd. Summon for plaintiff Richd. Bayly and Rebeccah his wife John Bayly Henry White John [Hufley] and John Anderson. Unity the wife of Robt. White and Richd. Melton.

[*Bell* v. *Randall*]

[*CCR 191*]

North Carolina ss. To the Honorable the Generall Court etc.

Boaz Bell is Plaintiff against Nicholas Randall Defendant in A Plea of the Case and Setteth forth that the Defendant for and in Consideration of the Summe of Three pounds per Month to be payd by the Plaintiff did Covenant and agree to and with the plaintiff to officiate as Mariner aboard the Sloop Anne in Company with the plaintiff Commander of the Said Sloop to A Certaine place

[12] Possibly Curaçao.

called Corrissaw[13] and back againe to this Province and was Entertaind by the plaintiff in his Service the Space of Nyne Dayes upon the aforesaid Contract Nevertheless the Defendant his Said Covenant and Agreement hath not performed nor kept whereby the plaintiff Sayth he is Dampnifyed One hundred pounds Sterling for which he hath brought this action and humbly Craves Judgment of this Honorable Court for the Same with Costs of Suite And he Shall pray etc.

Copia Tho. Snoden Clericus Curiae

[*Endorsed:*]
Bell v. Randall
In Case Sur Breach of Covenant

[*Benington* v. *Booth*]

[*CCR 140*]

North Carolinas To the honorable ginerall Cort

Cornelias Benington plaintif Vests Richard Booth Defendant in a plea of the Case and upon a sumsion Seteth forth that the Defendant Standeth owing and Justley in Depted Unto the plaintif the Sum of two pounds Nineteen Shillings and one peny to Be paid in wheat furs or Dearskins of the price Curant of this Cuntery Upon demand and which to render he Duth Refuse though often Demanded It Still Unpaid to the plaintfs damadg five pounds for which he Bringeth his Action and Craveth Judgment for his [dept] of this honorable Cort with Costs of Sute and Shall pray.

Cornelias Benington

[*Endorsed:*]
Beninton Vest Booth

[*Blount* v. *Chilton*]

[*CCR 191*]

North Carolina ss. To the Honorable Generall Court etc.

Thomas Blount is plaintiff against Wm. Chilton Defendant In a Plea of the Case and Setteth forth that the Defendant Stands Justly Indebted to the plaintiff in the full and Just Summe of Six pounds and tenne Shillings as by wayes and meanes Convenient the plaintiff is ready to make appear and refuses payment to the plaintiff Thirteen pounds Sterling for which he hath brought this action and humbly Craves Judgment of this Honorable Court for the Same with Costs of Suite And he Shall pray etc.

Tho. Blount

[*Endorsed:*]
Blount versus Chilton
In Case [*illegible*]
February the 2d

[13] Possibly Curaçao.

[*CCR 148*]

North Carolina ss. To the Provost Marshall or Deputy

These are in the Name of the Excellency the Palatine and rest of the true and absolute Lords and Proprietors to will and require you to arrest the body of William Chilton and him to hold Soe that he may appear att the next Generall Court to be held for this Province the last Tuesday in March next att the House of Captain John Hecklefield in Little River to answer the Complaint of Thomas Blount in A Plea of the Case and have there this writt Dated the 2d Day of February Anno Domini 1703/4.

Tho. Snoden Clericus Curiae

Take good bond being no Housekeeper

[*Endorsed:*]
Blount versus Chilton
Executed Febr. the 7th Per Jno. Hecklefield Provost Marshall

[*Boswell* v. *Paine*]

[*CCR 191*]

North Carolina ss. To the Honorable Generall Court etc.

Thomas Boswell is plaintiff against Samuel Payne Defendant in a Plea of Debt and Setteth forth that the Defendant Stands Justly Indebted to the plaintiff in the full and Just Summe of Thirty Shillings as by A writing Obligatory from under the Defendants hand and ready to be produc'd in Court relation being thereunto had doth and may more fully and att large appear and refuses payment whereby the plaintiff Sayth he is Dampnifyed Three pounds Sterling for which he hath brought this action and humbly Craves Judgment of this Honorable Court for the Same with Costs of Suite And he Shall pray etc.

Copia Tho. Snoden Clericus Curiae

[*Endorsed:*]
Boswell versus Payne
In Debt
Sur obligatory
Retraxit

[*Carlton* v. *Cuttlett*]

[*CCR 102*]

1703 Tho. Cuttlett Deceased Dr.		Per Contra Cr.	
	s. d.		*£ s. d.*
[To] Leveys pd. Mr. Cole: . .	: 3: 4	By Looking after my	
[To] pd. Richd. Beasly	: 5: 0	hoggs	1: 5:
[To] pd. Ezer Alberton	: 5: 0		Dt.- 10: 9: 4
[To] pd. Robt. Hosey	: 5: 0		
[To] pd. Mr. Kemball	:12: 0	Due to ballance	9: 4: 4
[To] two years diett washing and Lodg	5: 0: 0		

[To] my trouble in yor Sickness		:10: 0
[To] a Coffin		:10: 0
[To] a Sheat		: 8: 0
[To] diging the grave		: 1: 6
[To] funarall dinner	:1	:10: 0
[To] 3½ yds. ozinbrigs		: 7: 0
[To] 3 praiters		: 7: 6
[To] Justice		: 5: 0
totalle	10:	9: 4
Secretary Fees		:14: 6
	11:	3:10

Erroes Excepted
Per Arthur Carlton
Aprill Court 1704 provd in
Court by the oath of Arthur Carlton
N. Chevin Clk.

[*Chevin* v. *Powell*]

[*CCR 191*]

To the Honorable the Generall Court

Nath. Chevin is plaintiff Versus William Powell Defendant in a Plea of Debt and Saith that the Defendant Stands Indebted to the plaintiff in the Sum of 50 Shillings Sterling to be pd. in Pork merchantable well Saved and well packt att forty Shillings per Barrill or good fatt Well conditioned Beef well Saved att twenty five Shillings per Barrill to be paid att the plaintiffs Dwelling house in Mattacomack Creek (as by his Bill bearing Date the 23 Janry. 1701/2 may apeare) and the Same to Render the Defendant doth Refuse to the plaintiffs Damage five pounds Sterling for which he brings his action and prays Judgment for the Same with Costs and Shall pray etc.

Copia N. Chevin

[*Endorsed:*]
N. Chevin versus Powell
In Debt
Judgment Confered

[*Coles* v. *Goodridge*]

[*CCR 148*]

North Carolina ss. To the Honorable Generall Court etc.

Captain James Coles is plaintiff against Jeremiah Goodridge Defendant in a Plea of the Case and Setteth forth and declares That the Defendant Stands Justly Indebted to the plaintiff in the full and Just Summe of Fifteen pounds Eight Shillings and two pence as by wayes and meanes Convenient the plaintiff is ready to make appear and refuses payment whereby the plaintiff sayth he is Dampnifyed Thirty pounds sterling for which he hath brought this action and humbly Craves Judgment of this Honorable Court for the Same with Costs of Suite and he Shall pray etc.

Tho. Snoden Clericus Curiae

[*Endorsed*]
Coles versus Goodridge
In Case
Entred the 17th day of March 1703/4
We of the Jurey find for the defendent

[*Collins* v. *Smith*]

[*CCR 191*]

North Carolina ss. To the Honorable Generall Court etc.

Tho. Collings is plaintiff against [*illegible*] Smith Defendant In a plea of the Case and Setteth forth and Declares that the Defendant Stands Justly Indebted to the plaintiff In the full and Just Summe of four pounds payable to the plaintiff halfe in Silver Current and halfe [*torn*] porke as by wayes and meanes Convenient the [*torn*] ready to make appear and refuses payment whereby the [*torn*] Sayth he is Dampnifyed Eight pounds Sterling for which [*torn*] hath brought this action And humbly Craves Judgment of this Honorable Court for the Same with Costs of Suite And he Shall pray etc.

Tho. Snoden Clericus Curiae

[*Endorsed:*]
Collings versus Smith
In Case
March the 3d

[*Crown* v. *Norton and Coles*]

[*CCR 148*]

North Carolina ss. To the provost Marshall or Deputy

Whereas Mr. Samuel Norton and Mr. James Coles att the House of Capt. John Hecklefield on Tuesday the 28th Day of March have Comitted many Outrages abuses and Threatenings in the hearing and presence contrary to the peace of our Soveraigne Lady the Queen

These are therefore in the Name of his Excellency the palatine and the rest of the true and absolute Lords and Proprietors to will and require you to take and in your Safe Custody to keep them the said Samuel Norton and Capt. James Coles Gentleman untill they give bond with security to make their personall appearence On Friday the 31th of this Instant March before the Generall Court held etc. to answer Such matters as Shall be objected against them on her majesties behalf in the mean time to be of good abearence to all her Majesties Liege people Given under our hands and Seales this 28th Day of March Anno Domini 1704.

[*Endorsed:*]
Memorandum to Register the Births of Three Children for Cornelius which Patrick

[*Duckenfield* v. *Monteague*]

[*CCR 191*]

[*Illegible*] To the Honorable Generall Court etc.

[*Illegible*] Esqr. is plaintiff against Roger Montegue Defendant in A Plea of the Case [*illegible*] that the Defendant by his Assumption Stands Justly Indebted to the plaintiff in the full and Just Summe of Seven pounds as by wayes and means Convenient the plaintiff is ready to make appear Nevertheless the Defendant his Assumption not regarding the aforesaid Seven pounds hath not payd but the Same to the plaintiff doth refuse to pay whereby the plaintiff Sayth he hath Damage to the value of fourteen pounds Sterling for which he hath brought this action and humbly Craves Judgment of this Honorable Court for the Same with Costs of Suite And he Shall pray etc.

Tho. Snoden Clericus Curiae

[*Endorsed:*]
Duckinfield v. Montegue
In Case
February 11th

[*Duckenfield, assignee* v. *Farrow*]

[*CCR 191*]

North Carolina ss. To the Honorable Generall Court etc.

Wm. Duckenfield Esqr. Assignee of Wm. Powell is plaintiff against Francis Farrow Defendant in A Plea of Debt and Setteth forth that the Defendant Stands Justly indebted to the plaintiff Qualifyed as aforesaid in the full and Just Summe of Fiveteen pounds five Shillings and Six pence payable to the plaintiff Qualifyed as aforesaid in ventable Country Commodityes as by A writing obligatory from under the Defendants hand ready to be produc'd in Court relation being thereunto had doth and may more fully appear Neverthelesse the Defendant refuses payment whereby the plaintiff Sayeth he is Dampnifyed Thirty pounds and tenne Shillings Sterling for which he hath brought this action and humbly Craves Judgment of this Honorable Court for the Same with Costs of Suite And he Shall pray etc.

Tho. Snoden Clericus Curiae

[*Endorsed:*]
Duckenfield assignee versus Farrow
In Debt
Sur obligatory
February 11th 1703/4

[*CCR 148*]

North Carolina ss. To the Provost Marshall or [Deputy]

These are in the Name of his Excellency the Palatine [*torn*] the rest of the true and absolute Lords and Proprietors to [*torn*] require you to arrest the body of Francis Farrow and him to hold Soe that he may appear att the next

Generall Court to be held for this Province the [*torn*] Tuesday in March next att the House of Captain Hecklefield in Little River to answer the Complaint of Wm. Duckenfield Esqr. Assignee of Wm. Powell In A Plea of Debt and have there this writt Dated the 11 Day of February Anno Domini 1703/4. Take good bond.

Tho. Snoden Clerk

[*Endorsed:*]
Non Est Invent

[*Hecklefield and wife* v. *Godfrey*]

[*CCR 181*]

North Carolina ss. To the Honorable Generall Court etc.

Captain John Hecklefield and Elizabeth his wife are plaintiffs against Wm. Godfrey Defendant in A plea of the Case and Sett forth and Declare That the Defendant [is] Heir apparent to Eliz. Godfrey in her Minority late Deceased and that the Said Eliz. Godfrey in her life time was Indebted to the plaintiffs in the full and Just Sume of One Hundred Fifty and Six pounds for meat Drink Apparell and Education and tenne pounds Since the Death of the Said Eliz. Godfrey is Due to the plaintiffs out of the Said Elizabeth Godfreys Estate for funerall Charges Expended and disburs'd for the Said Eliz. Godfrey by the plaintiffs which Said Summes amount in the whole to One Hundred Sixty and Six pounds And the plaintiffs in fact Say that the [*torn*] Eliz. Godfrey in her life time not any part or parcell of the afforesaid Summe of money to the plaintiffs hath payd or Satisfyed nor the Defendant Qualifyed as aforesaid Since the Death of the Said Eliz. Godfrey the Sume to the plaintiffs hath payd tho' thereunto requested whereupon the plaintiffs [*torn*] brought this action and Crave Judgment of this Honorable Court for the [*torn*].

[*Endorsed:*]
Hecklefield and Uxor versus Godfrey
In Case

[*Jones* v. *Paine*]

[*CCR 140*]

North Carolina Ss. To the Honorable the Generall Court

Mr. Frederick Jones is Plaintiff against Samuel Payne Defendant in A Plea of the Case and Setteth forth that whereas by an Act of Assembly made in the yeare of our Lord God One Thousand Six Hundred Nynety and Nyne itt is Enacted that whosoever Shall Entertain or privately harbour any Runaways either white Servants or Negroes above One Night Shall for every Twenty four Houres afterwards pay Tenn Shillings to the Master of the Said Servant either white Servant or Negro and if the Master Shall Susteyine any Dammage above the Said Servants labour for the time of Such Concealment he Shall have his remedy att Law for Such Dammage over and above the Penalty hereby provided Nevertheless the Defendant the premisses well knowing and Contemning the Said Act of Assembly and the Authority thereof Did from the last Day of March in the year of our Lord 1702 unto the fifteenth Day of July then next ensuing Contrary to the Intent and Meaning of the Said Act of Assembly Entertaine and harbour One Henry Clarke the plaintiffs Servant whereby the plaintiff Sayth there is Due to him from the Defendant the Summe of £50 Sterling for the Defendants Entertaining the plaintiffs Said Servant and the plaintiff likewise Sayth that he is Damnifyed £20 Sterling which Said Summes amount in the whole to £70 Sterling for which he hath brought this action and humbly Craves Judgment of this Honorable Court for the Same with Costs of Suite and Shall pray etc.

[*Endorsed:*]
Jones versus Payne
In case
Ad Dampned £70 Sterling
9ber the 18th
Retraxit

[*Norcom* v. *Butler, executrix*]

[*CCR 179*]

North Carolina ss. To the Honorable the Generall Court

Thomas Norcom is Plaintiff against Annaritta Butler widdow Executrix of the last will and Testament of Christopher Butler Deceased Defendant in A Plea of the Case and Setteth forth that the plaintiff att the Speciall Instance and request of the Said Christopher in his life time and for the Said Christopher's own proper Matter and Debt being bound with the Said Christopher in his life time to the Honorable Wm. Glover Esquire for the payment of the Summe of £12 11*s.* 10*d.* And that att a Generall Court held for this Province the last Tuesday in October last the Said Wm. Glover Esquire Impleaded the plaintiff for the Summe of £9 14*s.* 10*d.* part of the Aforesaid Summe and Judgment for the Same And that the Defendant is Qualifyed to the Estate of the Said Christopher Butler Deceased [*torn*] refuses payment of the aforesaid Summe of £9 14*s.* 10*d.* tho by the plaintiff thereunto requested whereby the plaintiff Sayth he is Dampnifyed £19 Sterling for which he hath brought his Suite and humbly etc. And he Shall pray etc.

Tho. Snoden Clericus Curiae

[*Endorsed:*]
Norcom versus Butler widdow Executrix
In Case
30th October

[*Norcom, attorney of Burtenshall* v. *Burkett*]

[*CCR 191*]

North Carolina ss. To the Honorable Generall Court etc.

Thomas Norkam Attorney of Richd. Burtenshall is plaintiff against John

Burkett Defendant in A Plea of the Case and Setteth forth that in Covenant he the plaintiff had bought and purchased of the Defendant one Plantation Scituate lying and being on Pequimins River he the Defendant did assume and promise that he the Defendant the aforesaid Plantation purchased by the plaintiff as aforesaid to the plaintiff the next Ensuing Court would acknowledge Neverthelesse the Defendant his assumption not regarding the aforesaid Plantation to the plaintiff hath not as yett acknowledged but doth refuse to acknowledge the Same to the plaintiff To the plaintiffs Dammage Thirty pounds Sterling for which he hath brought this action and humbly Craves Judgment for the Same with Costs of Suite And he Shall pray etc.

Tho. Snoden Clericus Curiae

[*Endorsed:*]
Norkam Attorney Burtenshall versus Burkett
In Case
Summons Roger Snell, Jenkin Williams per plaintiff.
Retraxit

[*Norman and wife* v. *Gale and wife*]

[*CCR 192*]

North Carolina ss. To the Honorable Generall Court etc.

Henry Norman and Anne his wife are plaintiffs against Christopher Gale Esqr. and Sarah his wife Defendants In A plea of the Case upon Defamation and Sett forth and Declare That whereas the plaintiffs have att all times well behaved themselves and been of good repute amongst all her Majesties Liege people and never were Suspected or Conscious of Witch Craft which the Defendant Sarah well knowing yett of mere malice minding and Intending to lessen the Creditt and reputation of the plaintiffs and thereby Intending to bring the plaintiff Anne under the penalty of the Statute in Such Cases made and provided in the Month of February last past att the House of Cornelius Lerry late Deceased and within this Government in the audience and hearing of Divers of her Majesties Liege people did utter and pronounce these false Scandalous and Malitious words of and to the plaintiff Anne to witt you (meaning the plaintiff Anne) are a witch and Ile prove itt By which false Scandalous and Malitious words the plaintiffs in their Name fame and reputation Say they are Dampnifyd Two hundred pounds Sterling for which they have brought this action and humbly Crave Judgment of this Honorable Court for the Same with Costs of Sute And they Shall pray etc.

Copia Testis Tho. Snoden Clericus Curiae

[*Endorsed:*]
Norman and Uxor versus Gale and Uxor
In Case
Sur Defamation

[*CCR 148*]

North Carolina ss. To the Provost Marshall or Deputy

These are in the Name of his Excellency the Palatine and the rest of the

true and absolute Lords and Proprietors to will and require you to arrest the Bodyes of Christopher Gale Esquire and Sarah his wife and them to hold Soe that they appear att the next Generall Court to be held for this Province the last Tuesday in March next att House of Captain John Hecklefield in Little River to answer the Complaint of Henry Norman and Anne his wife In a Plea of the Case upon Defamation And have there this writt Dated the 28th Day of February Anno Domini 1703/4.

Tho. Snoden Clerk Court

[*Endorsed:*]
Executed March the 11th 1703/4 Per Tho. Welsh Deputy Marshall
Retraxit 18th

[*Peterson, attorney of Perry and Company* v. *Holmes*]

[*CCR 192*]

North Carolina Ss. To the honorable Generall Court etc.

Thomas Peterson Attorney to Micajah Perry and New Pensilvania Company is plaintiff against Thomas Holmes Defendant in a plea of Debt and Sayes that the Defendant by one writeing Obligatory under his proper hand and Seale beareing Date the third day of January 1704 Stands Justly Indebted to the plaintiff Quallifyed as aforesaid in the full and Just Summe of Three pounds Ten Shillings and four pence Sterling to be paid good Sound Merchantable porke or Corne upon Demand as in and by the Said writeing Obligatory here into Court brought and ready to be produced relation being thereunto had doth and may appeare which Said Sume of three pounds Tenn Shillings and four pence the Defendant hath not rendred to the plaintiff tho' often thereunto requested but the Same doth Still refuse to render to the plaintiffs Damage Seaven pounds and Eight pence Sterling and thereupon he brings his Suite and prayes Judgement for the Same with Costs of Suite and Shall pray etc.

T. Knight Secretary

[*Endorsed:*]
Copia Narratio
Peterson Attorney etc. versus Holmes
Entered Feb. 12th: 1705/6

[*CCR 192*]

No. Carolina Ss. To the Provost Marshall or his Deputy

. These are in her Majestyes name to will and require you to Arrest the body of Thoms. Holmes and him Safely hold Soe that he may be and appeare at the next Generall Court to be holden at the house of Captain John Hecklefield in Litle river on the last Tuesday in March next then and there to Answer the plaint of Tho. Peterson Attorney to Micajah Perry and New pensilvania Company in a plea of Debt and have there this writt Dated at the Secretarys Office this 16th day of February Anno Domini 1705/6.

Testis T. Knight Secretary

[*Endorsed:*]
Breve
Peterson versus Holmes
Non est inventus

[*CCR 192*]

North Carolina Ss: To the provost Marshall or his Deputy

These are in her Matyes name to will and require you to Sumons John Falconer and Tho. Holmes personally to be and [*torn*] at the next Generall Court to be holden at the house of Captain Jno. Hecklefield in Litle river on the last Tuesday in March next then and [*torn*] give Evidence in a Cause there Depending between Tho. Peterson [*torn*] New Pensilvania Company plaintiff and Tho. Holmes defendant on [*torn*] the plaintiff and have there this Summons Dated at the Secretarys Office 26th day of Feb: Anno Domini 1705/6.

Testis T. Knight Secretary

[*Endorsed:*]
Summons for Jno. Falconer and Tho. Holmes
Sumoned
Executed

[*CCR 188*]

This Bill bindeth me Thomas Holmes my Heirs Executtors Administrators or Assignes to Pay or Cause to be pd. unto Mr. Thomas Peterson his Assignes or Order the full and Just Sume of Three Pounds ten shillings and four pence Sterling to be pd. In good Sound Merchandable porke or Corne upon demand Ass Wittnesse my Hand and Seale this third day of Janry. 1704.

Testes Tho. Holmes <*Signum*>
Jno. Falconar
Tho. Holmes <*Signum*>

[*Endorsed:*]
Thomas Holmes bill for 3-10-4

[*Pierce* v. *Hartly*]

[*CCR 191*]

North Carolina ss. To the Honorable Generall Court

Joseph Pierce is plaintiff against Wm. Hartly Defendant in A plea of the Case and Setteth forth that the Defendant Stands Justly Indebted to the plaintiff in the full and Just Quantity of Two Hundred Weight of Merchantable Neat Porke as by wayes and meanes Convenient the plaintiff is ready to make appear and refuses payment whereby the plaintiff Sayth he is Dampnifyed

Fifty Shillings Sterling for which he hath brought this action and humbly Craves Judgment of this Honorable Court for the Same with Costs of Suite and he Shall pray etc.

Tho. Snoden Clericus Curiae

[*Endorsed:*]
Pierce versus Hartly
In Case
Entred the 8th of January
Retraxit

[*Porter* v. *Ayres*]

[*CCR 191*]

North Carolina ss. To the Honorable the Generall Court

Mr. John Porter is Plaintiff against David Ayres Defendant in A Plea of the Case and Setteth forth that the Defendant Standeth Justly Indebted unto the plaintiff in the full Summe of four Pounds and five Shillings in good Merchantable Neat fresh Pork (as by wayes and Meanes Convenient the Plaintiff is ready to make appear) and refuses payment to the Plaintiffs Dammage Eight Pounds and tenne Shillings for which he hath brought this action and humbly Craves Judgment of this Court for the Same with Costs of Suite And Shall pray etc.

John Porter

Copia Tho. Snoden Clericus Curiae
[*Endorsed:*]
Porter versus Ayres
In Case
Sur acct.

[*CCR 148*]

North Carolina ss. To the Provost Marshall or Deputy

These are in the Name of his Excellency the Pallatine and rest of the true and absolute Lords and Proprietors to will and require you to arrest the Body of David Ayres and him to hold Soe that he may appear att the next Generall Court to be held for this Province the last Tuesday in March next att the House of Captain John Hecklefield in Little River to answer the Complaint of Mr. John Porter in a Plea of the Case and have there this writt Dated this 2d Day of December Anno Domini 1703.

Tho. Snoden Clericus Curiae

[*Quary and Company* v. *Cockeram*]

[*CCR 192*]

North Carolina ss. To the Honorable Generall Court etc.

The Honorable Colonel Robt. Quary and New Pensylvania Company are plaintiffs against Hannah Cockeram Defendant In A Plea of Debt and Sett forth and Declare That the Defendant Stands Justly Indebted to the plaintiffs In the full and Just Sume of Six and Twenty pounds fourteen Shillings and two pence (As by a writing obligatory from under these Defendants hand and Seale ready to be produc'd in Court relation being thereunto had doth and may more fully and att Large appear) and refuses payment whereby the plaintiffs Say They are Dampnifyed Fifty and three pounds Sterling for which they have brought this action And Crave Judgment for the Same with Costs of Suite And they Shall pray etc.

Tho. Snoden Clericus Curiae

[*Endorsed:*]
Colonel [*illegible*] v. Hannah Cockeram
In debt
Sur obligatory
Entred February the 24

[*Stanton* v. *Bundy*]

[*CCR 191*]

To the 2d Day of the Generall Court

Thos. Stanton is plaintiff Versus Caleb Bundy Defendant in a Plea of tresspass on the Case for thatt the Defendant hath Unjustly stoped and molested the surveyor in the Lawfull survey of a tract of Land Lying in the precinct of Pascotank and Justly belonging to the Plaintiff whereby the Plaintiff saith he is Damnified and hath sustained Damage therby to the Value of ten pounds sterling for which the plaintiff brings his Action and prays Judgment for the same With Costs of sute and that he may proceed in his Lawfull survey and shall pray etc.

N. Chevin Clk.

[*Endorsed:*]
Stanton versus Bundy
Ressent to Oct. Court
Referrd till the afternoon
9ber the [9th]
We of the Jurie find no cauesse of action

[*CCR 191*]

The deposition of Robt. Keell aged about twintie three years as followeth pursuant to ane order of the honorble governor and councell to survay a tract of land upon ane old pattent for Tho. Stanton we began at a stump which was The place conclud upon by those apoynted by the forsaid power being the very place wher my father in law and my self began to survay befor runing acording to the courses of the old patent agreeing in a reasonable maner what the former survay and including the very place wher we were stopt befor by Caleb Bundy being the truth acording to the best of my knowledge and further saieth not.

Robt. Keell

[*White, assignee* v. *Fitzpatrick*]

[*CCR 191*]

[North Carolina ss.] To the Honorable [*torn*]

[Vincent] White Assignee of John [*torn*] against Bryan Fitzpatrick Defendant in A [*torn*] Defendant and Setteth forth that the Defendant Stands Justly indebted to the plaintiff Qualifyed as [*torn*] in the full and Just Summe of Fifty Shillings payable in Merchantable fresh Beef or porke as by [*torn*] writing Obligatory from under the Defendants [*torn*] appear and refuses payment whereby the [*torn*] sayth he is Dampnifyed five pounds Sterling for which hath brought this action and herein Craves Judgment of the Honorable Court for the Same with Costs of Suite and he Shall [pray].

Tho. Snoden [Clerk]

[*Endorsed:*]
White assignee versus Fitz Patrick
In Debt Sur [*illegible*]
Entred the 8th of January

[*CCR 148*]

North Carolina ss. To the Provost Marshall or Depty

These are in the Name of his Excellency the Palatine and rest of the true and absolute Lords and Proprietors to will and require you to arrest the body of Bryan FitzPatrick and him to hold Soe that he may appear att the next Generall Court to be held for this Province the last Tuesday in March next att the House of Captain John Hecklefield in little River to answer the Complaint of Vincent White Assignee of John Mead in a Plea of Debt And have there this writt Dated the 8th of January Anno Domini 1703/4.

Tho. Snoden Clericus Curiae

[*Endorsed:*]
Summons for the plaintiff John Hawkins, Francis Penrice, John Mead
[Executed] Feb. the 9th Per Jno. Hecklefield Provst Marshall

[*White* v. *Inkeson and Berry*]

[*CCR 191*]

North Carolina ss. To the Honorable Generall Court etc.

William White is plaintiff against Anne Inkeson and Edwd. Berry Defendants in A plea of the Case upon Defamation and Setteth forth and Complaines that whereas that plaintiff hath Ever been of good report and hath ever well behaved himselfe towards all her Majesties Liege People and good Neighbours amongst whom he hath lived And hath never been accused or taxed with any unjust or unlawfull Action but hath ever by his honest and lawfull Endeavours gotten his lively hood [*torn*] places where he hath lived Neverthelesse the Defendants the Same well knowing Yett of Meer Malice and ill will Intending thereby to abate and lessen the Reputation and Creditt of the plaintiff amongst all his good

Neighbours and to render the plaintiff base and Ignominious the Defendants the [*blank*] Day of [*blank*] last past Charged the plaintiff with Stealing A Cow of the Defendants and Searched the plaintiffs House for the Same And further the plaintiff Sayth that the Defendant [*illegible*] att the plaintiffs House on the Said [*blank*] Day of [*blank*] last past before Divers Witnesses then and there present did utter and pronounce these base and Scandalous Words Ile make will White (meaneing the plaintiff) find her meaning the aforesaid Cow By which malitious false and Scandalous words the plaintiff Sayth he is Dampnifyed in his Reputation and Creditt in the Summe of one hundred pounds Sterling for which he brings this action and prayes Judgment for the Same with Costs of Suite And he Shall pray etc.

Tho. Snoden Clericus Curiae

[*Endorsed:*]
White versus Inkeson and Berry
In Defamation
January the 27th
Summoned per plaintiff John Hare, Saml. Herst, John Long.

[*CCR 103*]

References and Orders against the Marshall from March Court 1704 to July Court following.

Duckenfield Esqr. versus Montegue in Case. Concordia.

Spruell versus Evans in Debt. Concordia.

Chevin versus Powell order versus Marshall. Dismist.

Anderson versus Beesley Attachment. Satisfaction made.

Banister versus Hartly Order versus Marshall. Retraxit.

Porter versus Ayres Attachment. Continued.

Writts and returnes to July Court 1704

Hecklefield versus Bishopp in Case. Retraxit.

Frilye versus Johnson in Case.

Goodridge versus Jones in Case. Retraxit.

Jones versus Goodridge in Case.

Jones versus Goodridge in Case.

Brice versus Platt in Case. Concordia.

Duckenfield Esqr. versus Powell in Debt.

Duckenfield Esqr. assignee Powell versus Farrow in Debt.

Steel versus Berry in Debt. Retraxit.

Anderson versus Fuawkes in Debt. Concordia.

Jones versus Butler in Debt. Retraxit.

Evans Assignee Hecklefield versus Fuawkes in Debt. Concordia.

Evans versus Phelps in Detinue. Dismist.

Evans versus Fare in Case. Dismist.

Pison versus Bird in Case. Retraxit.

Griffin versus Jones in Case. Retraxit.

Coles and Uxor versus Clack in Case. Retraxit.

Swan vidua Administratrix etc. versus Fuawkes in Debt. Executed.

Anderson versus Mekins in Case. Executed.

Chevin versus Bishopp in Case. Executed.

Wilkison versus Barrow in Trover. Executed.

Blount versus Moon in Case. In Custody Marshall.

Anderson Assignee etc. versus Carlton Administrator etc. in Debt. Concordia.

Perishoe versus Thigpen in Case. Executed.

[*CCR 103*]

<4> Att A Generall Court held att the House of Captain John Hecklefield in Little River the 25th Day of July 1704. Present The Honorable Willm. Glover, John Porter, Chr. Gale, Tho. Symonds, Esqrs. Justices.

The Marshall was required to arrest the Body of Richd. Johnson to answer the Complaint of Willm. Frilye in A Plea of the Case for Eight pounds and one Shilling and the plaintiff Came not.

Orderd That the action be dismist and the plaintiff pay Costs.

The Marshall was required to arrest the Body of Cuthbert Phelps to answer the Complaint of Thomas Evans in A Plea of Detinue for one Cow and Yearling And the plaintiff Came not.

Ordered That the action be dismist and the plaintiff pay Costs.

The Marshall was required to arrest the Body of Obadiah Fare to answer the Complaint of Thomas Evans in A plea of the Case for Thirty five Shillings And the plaintiff Came not.

Orderd that the action be dismist and the plaintiff pay Costs.

And then the Court Adjournd till to Morrow Morning 8 of

Clock. On Wednesday Morning att 8 of Clock the Court Meets present ut Supra.

A power of Attorney from Edward Phelps to Mr. Godfrey Spruell was prov'd by the Oaths of Anthony Alexander and John Hassold.

A Deed of Sale acknowledged in Court from Godfrey Spruell Attorney of Edward Phelps to Cuthbert Phelps.

<4*a*> A Power of Attorney from John Jennett to Godfrey Spruell was prov'd by the Oaths of Anthony Alexander and John Hassold.

A Deed of Sale acknowledged in Court from Godfrey Spruell Attorney of John Jennett to James Fuawkes.

An Assignment of A Deed of Sale acknowledged in Court from James Fuawkes and Anne his wife to John Hassold.

A Will of Cornelius Lerry prov'd by the oaths of James Fuawkes and Anne his wife and the Subscription of Henry Goring.

Upon Motion of Richd. Lerry one of the Executors of the last will and Testament of Cornelius Lerry Deceased Orderd that the Estate of the Said Cornelius Lerry be appraised by Mr. Caleb Caleway Mr. John Barrow Mr. John Stepney Captain James Coles and Mr. Archibald Holmes or any Three of them and that an Inventory of the Same be Exhibited to the next Generall Court and that Christopher Gale Esqr. Swear the Apprisors.

<Mr. Gale absent>

The Marshall was required to arrest the Body of Cornelius Jones to answer the Complaint of George Griffin in A Plea of the Case upon Defamation and the Defendant Came not And the plaintiff prayes an Order against the Marshall.

Orderd that the Marshall bring forth the Body of Cornelius Jones to the next Generall Court to answer the Said Griffins Complaint alias Judgment to be Confirm'd against the Marshall.

Upon Petition of Andrew Wilson praying allowance for Tenne Dayes Attendance as an Evidence in A Matter Depending between Mr. John Porter plaintiff and Henry Slade Defendant.

<5> Orderd that Mr. John Porter pay unto Andrew Wilson allowance Orderd by Law for five Dayes Attendance and four Dayes Coming and going as an Evidence for the Said Mr. John Porter with Costs.

Upon Petition of Thomas Abington

Orderd that George Griffin pay unto Thomas Abington the Summe of four Shillings and two pence for his Attendance as an Evidence in A Matter Depending between the Said Griffin plaintiff and Cornelius Jones Defendant with Costs.

And then the Court adjourns for one Hour And after one Hour the Court Meets present ut Supra.

Mary Swann widdow Administratrix of the Estate of Samuel Swann Junior Deceased Comes by Major Samuel Swann her Attorney to prosecute her Suite against James Fuawkes in A Plea of Debt for four pounds Seven Shillings and Seven pence Due and payable in good Sound Sweet well Conditioned Porke att or upon the Tenth Day of December next Ensuinge the date of A Bill past from the Defendant to the Said Samuel Swann Junior in his life time And the Defendant Comes and Confesses Judgment for the Same.

Orderd that James Fuawkes pay unto Mary Swann Widdow Administratrix etc. the Summe of Four pounds Seven Shillings and Seven pence in good Sound Sweet well Conditioned Porke as alsoe five Shillings and tenne pence to Obadiah Fare Summoned as Evidence in behalfe of the plaintiff with Costs of Suite alias Execution.

An Assignment of A Deed of Sale acknowledged in Court from Andrew Wilson to John Bateman Attorney of Jonathan Bateman and Orderd to be recorded.

A Deed of Sale acknowledged in Court from Elizabeth Dear to Andrew wilson.

<*5a*> A Bill of Sale from William Powell to William Duckenfield Esqr. was prov'd by the Oath of Henry Hartley.

A Bill from Francis Farrow to William Powell was prov'd by the oath of Willm. Reed.

An assignment of A Bill from William Powell to Willm. Duckenfield Esqr. was prov'd by the oath of Henry Hartly.

The Marshall was Commanded to arrest the Body of John Bishopp to answer the Complaint of Nathaniel Chevin in A Plea of the Case for Tenne pounds Sixteen Shillings and tenne pence And both partyes agreed referrd by Consent to the next Generall Court.

I Elizabeth Lowe Doe Sincerely Declare in the presence of God and on the penalty of perjury That I Saw John Archdale Sign and Seal A Power of Attorney to Emanuel Low and That Joshua Kent and Mary Danson Sign'd as Evidences to the Same. Elizabeth Low.

A Power of Attorney from John Archdale Esqr. to Emanuel Low was prov'd in Court by the Subscription of Elizabeth Lowe and Orderd to be recorded.

A Power of Attorney from Willm. Barrow to Peter Godfrey was prov'd by Major Samuel Swann.

The Marshall was required to arrest the Body of Willm. Barrow to answer the Complaint of Colonel Willm. Wilkison in A Plea of

Trover and Conversion And both partyes agreed referr'd by Consent to the next Generall Court.

A Deed of Sale from John Hollford to Colonel Willm. Wilkison was provd by the oaths of Thomas Blount and James Blount and alsoe that A Piece of Eight was Delivered by the Said John Hollford to the Said Colonel Wilkison in parte [*illegible*] hime in possession of the Same.

<6> The Marshall was required to arest the Body of James Thigpen to answer the Complaint of James Perishoe in A Plea of the Case And the Defendant praying A Reference

Ordered that A Reference be granted to the next Generall Court.

And then the Court Adjourns till to Morrow Morning att 7 of Clock.

On Thursday Morning att 8 of Clock the Court Meets present ut Supra.

The Honorable Samuel Swann Esqr. by Chr. Gale Esqr. her Majesties Attorney Generall informs this Court That John Pettiver hath arrived in to the Port of Roanoake with A Shallop Called the Thomas and Mary Burthen about two Tun loaden with Sundry Goods and Merchandizes and the Same hath unloaden and putt on Shoar without making any Entry of his Said vessell and Goods in this Port or producing any Cocquette permitt or Hearing from any of her Majesties Officers of the Customes in virginia from whence he last Came and without any Register of the Said vessell Contrary to the Lawes and Statutes in those Cases made and Provided and prayes Condemnation of the Said Shallopp and all her apparell and Furniture And that the Said Shallopp etc. may be appraised according to Law.

Orderd That the Said Shallopp etc. be forfeited according to Law he the Said Pettiver appearing in Court and Confessing Judgment And that She be appraised by Willm. Bartlett John Browne and Joseph Ming or any two of them And that returne of the Said appraisment be made to this Court And that the Said Shallopp etc. be dispos'd of as the Law in Such Cases directs.

A Power of Attorney from John Budd of Philadelphia to Mr. Samuel Norton of Carolina was provd by the oaths of John Browne and Thomas Welch and order'd to be recorded.

A Power of Attorney from Robert Milain of New York Tayler to John Hecklefield of Carolina was prov'd by the oaths of John Browne and Thomas Welch.

<6*a*> An Assignment of A Pattent acknowledged from Colonel William Wilkison to Samuel Pricklove and his Heires for ever and Orderd to be Recorded.

Upon Petition of James Fuawkes Shewing that by an Order of Court past the 26th Day of October 1703 the Provost Marshall was orderd to take the Estate of Thomas Bouchier Deceased in to his possession till otherwise Orderd by Due Course of Law And Shews that the Said Bouchiers' Estate was Indebted to him in the Summe of Seventeen pounds Six Shillings And that by vertue of the aforesaid Order Willm. Bray Deputy Marshall of Coratuck Seiz'd the Said Bouchiers Estate and the Same hath Confiscated and dispos'd of Contrary to Law And Prayes That the Said Bray may make his appearance att the next Generall Court to render A Just and true acct. of the Said Bouchiers Estate And for plea the Said Bray Sayes that Administration hath been Granted of the Said Estate and by vertue thereof itt hath been taken out of his hands of which he has assum'd to render an account the next Court.

Orderd That Willm. Bray make his appearance att the next Generall Court to be held for this Province to answer the Said Fuawkes's Complaint.

An Assignment of A Deed of Sale acknowledged from James Thigpen Attorney of Stephen Manwaring to John Anderson and Orderd to be recorded.

An Assignment of A Pattent acknowledged from John Anderson to James Laten.

A Bill of Sale from Willm. Powell to Willm. Duckenfield Esqr. was prov'd by the Oath of George Chambers.

A Bill from Francis Farrow to Willm. Duckenfield Esqr. was prov'd by the oath of George Chambers.

<7> By A Continuance from the last Court [*torn*] was required to Attach Soe much of the Estate of David Ayres as willpay and Satisfye the Honorable John Porter Esqr. the Summe of Four pounds and five Shillings And the plaintiff praying A Continuance of the Same till the next Generall Court

Orderd that the Attachment be Continued till the next Generall Court.

A Deed of Sale acknowledged from Francis Johnson to John Ainsley and Order'd to be recorded.

Whereas itt appeares to this Court That James Cesarson an Infant Stranger was putt into the hands of Willm. Gascoigne in order to Send him home to his Father And the Said Gascoigne's Widdow failing therein Orderd That he be discharg'd from all Service to the Said Gascoigne.

The Marshall is required to arrest the Body of Thomas Mekins to answer the Complaint of John Anderson in A Plea of the Case for Three pounds in fresh Porke And Captain John Hecklefield assumes in behalfe of the Defendant to pay the Said Summe of Three pounds with Costs.

Upon Petition of George Chambers

Orderd That Willm. Duckenfield Esqr. pay unto the Petitioner Twenty Shillings and Tenne pence for his Attendance as an Evidence in behalfe of the Said William Duckenfield Esqr. against Willm. Powell and likewise against Francis Farrow with Costs alias Execution.

And then the Court Adjourns till 3 of Clock in the afternoon.

Att 3 of Clock in the afternoon the Court Meets present ut Supra. <*7a*> John Blunt Esqr. Comes to prosecute his Suite against John Moon in A Plea of the Case for Eight pounds five Shillings and tenne pence And for Plea the Defendant putts the plaintiff to the proofe of his Declaration and Casts himselfe upon the Country and the plaintiff likewise And the Marshall is Commanded to Cause to Come Twelve true and lawfull men of the Vicinage Who neither etc. To whom etc. By whom etc. And there Came Mr. Henry Creech Mr. Robt. Morgan Mr. Abraham Warren Mr. Tho. Norcum Mr. Willm. Williams Mr. David Blake Mr. George Kingerley Mr. Francis Penrice Mr. Anthony Alexander Mr. Obadiah Fare Mr. Willm. Steel and Mr. Andrew Wilson who Impanell'd and Sworn Say wee of the Jury find for the plaintiff four pounds two Shillings and Eleven pence with Costs And the plaintiff allowes That twelve Shillings Shall be deducted out of the Said Order Orderd that John Moon pay unto John Blunt Esqr. Three pounds Tenne Shillings and Eleven pence with Costs alias Execution.

Henretta Butler produces an Account wherein the Estate of Christopher Butler is Dr. and Cr. and proves the Same by her oath.

And then the Court Adjourns till to Morrow Morning att 7 of Clock.

On Friday Morning 7 of Clock the Court meets present ut Supra Except Thomas Symonds Esqr.

And then the Court Adjourns till twelve of Clock.

Att 12 of Clock the Court meets present ut Supra And then Adjourns to the next Court in Course.

[*Signed:*]
W. Glover, John Porter, C. Gale.

RECORDED BY ORDER OF COURT

[*CCR 103*]

Recorded by Order

Know all men by these presents That I Edward Phelps Doe hereby Constitute appoint and Ordain my Trusty and wellbeloved Friend Godfrey Spruell to be my lawfull Attorney for me and in my behalfe to acknowlegee the abovementioned Bill of Sale for One Hundred Fifty and one Acres of Land to my Brother Cuthbert Phelps this next Generall Court As witnesse my hand and Seale this 24th of July 1704.

Testis E Sigillum
Antho. Alexander [*his mark*]
John Hasall [*his mark*]
Anne Fuox [*her mark*]

I William Wilkison of the precinct of Chowan in the Province of North Carolina for diverse Consideration me hereunto movinge Have Assigned and Sett Over And doe by these presents for me my Heires Executors Administrators and Assignes Assigne and Sett over unto Samuel Pricklove his Heires and Assignes for ever all my Right Title and Interest of the within mentioned Pattent To and for the only Sole proper use and behoofe of the Said Samuel Pricklove his Heires and Assignes for evermore Witnesse my hand this One and Twentieth Day of June Anno Domini 1704.

Witnesse hereunto Wm. Wilkison
Tho. Snoden
Tho. Luten

June the 21th 1704

Then this Assignment was Assign'd and Acknowledged by Collonell Willm. Wilkison And Orderd to be recorded.
Before me Robt. Daniell

Know all men by these presents That I James Thickpen of the precinct of Pequimins in the County of Albemarle lawfull and absolute Attorney of Stephen Manwaring for the more Sure and certaine Conveyance Suremaking and Confirmation of the Land within bargained and Sold or mentioned or Intended to be hereby bargained and Sold doe by these presents Grant bargaine and Sell Assigne and Sett over all my Right Title Interest property Claime and Demand whatsoever unto the Said James Laiton within mentioned his Heires and Assignes for ever according to the true Intent and meaning of the within mentioned Bargaine and Sale In witnesse whereof I have hereunto Sett my hand and Seale the Second Day of July 1704.

James Thickpen Signum

The word James being Interlind before Seal'd
Sealed and Delivered
In presence of
Tho. Snoden
John Anderson
Tho. Bossel his marke

Acknowledged in Court the 27th Day of July 1704.

Tho. Snoden Clericus Curiae

North Carolina

Know all men by these presents That I John Guinitt of this Province doe hereby Constitute appoint and Ordain my friend Godfrey Spruell to be my true and lawfull Attorney for me and in my behalfe to acknowledge a Deed of Sale for Three Hundred and Fifty acres of Land Granted by Deed of Sale to James Fuox and by him Sold and assigned to John Hassale this Court Witnesse my hand this 24th July 1704.

Testes Signum John Jennett
Antho: Alexander
Anne Fewox
John Hassold his marke

Prov'd in Court the 26th Day of July 1704.

Tho. Snoden Clericus Curiae

North Carolina ss. Recorded by Order

To all Christian people to whom these presents Shall Come I John Jennett and Dorothy his wife Sends Greetinge know yee that I John Jennett with the free and voluntary Consent of Dorothy my now wife for A valuable Consideration to us in hand payd and Secured to be payd by James Fuox where[*torn*] and wherewith we doe acknowledge our Selves fully Satisfyed Contented and payd have therefore bargained and Sold And doe by these presents for us our Heires Executors Administrators or assignes Sell alien make over and for ever Confirm unto the aforesaid Fuox his Heires or Assignes for ever all that our Right of A Plantation and labour and Tract of land Scituate lying and being in the precinct of Chowan in

Scoperlong River on the west Side against the Biteron Islands Containing Three Hundred and Fifty acres as by Entry may appear to have and to hold the Said Plantation and Tract of land free and Clear of all and all manner of Claimes and incumbrances of all and all manner of person or persons Claiming by from or under me or by my Order or procurement together with all labour and Improvements thereupon with all Housing fencing Timber and Timber Trees thereupon Standing lying growing to be to the proper use and behoof of the Said Fuox his Heires Executors Administrators or Assignes from henceforth and for ever and doe oblidge my Selfe to acknowledge the Same in Some Court of Record in this Government when thereunto reasonably required and to the true performance of the abovesaid premisses in every Article and Clause as is above exprest I bind me my Heires Executors administrators in the penall Summe of Twenty pounds Sterling In witnesse whereof we have hereunto Sett our hands and Seales this the 18th Day of March 1701/2 In the 13th year of the Raigne of our Soveraigne Lord Willm. the Third King of England Scotland and Ireland Rex fidei Defender.

Sign'd Seald and Delivered
in the presence of
Roger Snell
John Snell his marke

John Jennett [Seal]
Dorothy Jennett [Seal]

North Carolina Chowan Precinct

Know all men by these presents That I James Fuox of the Province and precinct aforesaid doe by these presents make over Infeoffe assigne and Confirme unto John Hassell his Heires or assignes for ever from me my Heires or assignes this within Deed of Sale with waranty from the Claime of any person or persons that Shall or may lay Claime thereunto lawfully from by or under me assent Consent or procurement In Testimony whereof I have hereunto Sett my hand and Seal the 16th Day of May Anno 1704.

Signed Seald and Delivred
in the presence of us
John Anderson
Seth Phelps

James Fuox Signum

Recorded by Order

Know all men by these presents That I Elizabeth Dear of the precinct of Chowan in this County of Albermarle doe by these presents Grant bargaine Sell Assigne and Sett over for A valuable Consideration in hand received all my Right Title interest property

Claime and Demand whatsoever unto A certaine Tract or plantation of Land Containing one Hundred and Fifty one acres Scituate on the South Side of Albemarle River in the precinct aforesaid bounding on William Ludford on the East John Jennett on the West and the Said Albemarle River on the North unto Andrew Wilson of the precinct aforesaid his Heires and Assignes for ever with all Houses Edifices buildings Orchards Gardens Woods Underwoods pastures feedings and appurtences whatsoever unto the Same belonginge or appertaininge To have and to hold the Said Plantation or Tract or parcell of land of one Hundred and Fifty one acres the Said Andrew Wilson his Heires and Assignes for ever To the use of the Said Andrew Wilson his Heires and Assignes for ever I hereby warranting the Sale thereof from me my Heires Executors and Administrators against all manner of persons whatsoever lawfully Claiming by from or under me my Heires Executors and Administrators In Witnesse whereof I have hereunto Sett my hand and Seale this Five and Twentyeth Day of July Annoque Domini 1704.

Sealed and Delivered   Eliz. Dear   her marke
in presence of
James Coles
P. Godfrey

Recorded by Order

Know all men by these presents That I Andrew Wilson of the precinct of Pequimins for a Valuable Consideration to me in hand payd by Jonathan Bateman of the precinct aforesaid The Receipt whereof is hereby acknowledged and thereof doe accquitt and discharge the Said Jonathan Bateman Have by these presents Granted bargained and Sold And doe by these presents grant bargaine and Sell unto the Said Jonathan Bateman all my Right Title Interest property Claime and Demand unto one Hundred and Fifty acers of land within mentioned to be Sold or therein intended or proposed to be bargained and Sold with the appurtenances therein Contained I hereby warranting the Sale thereof from me my Heires Executors and Administrators against all persons whatsoever In witnesse whereof I have hereunto Sett my hand and Seale this Six and Twentyeth Day of July Annogue Domini 1704.

Sealed and Delivered   Andrew Wilson   his marke
in presence of
James Coles
P. Godfrey

Know all men by these presents That I Francis Johnson of Scuppernung in the precinct of Pequimins for A valuable Consideration in hand received of John Ainsley of the precinct aforesaid have granted bargained and Sold and by these presents grant bargaine and Sell unto the Said John Ainsley all my Right Title interest property Claime and demand whatsoever unto a certain Tract of Land Containing one Hundred and Nynety one acres of Land Scitutate and lying on the East Side of Scuppernung River in the precinct aforesaid adjoyning to the South Side of Canaan Symsons Land with all Houses Edifices buildings orchards gardens with the appurtenances thereunto belonginge unto the Said John Ainsley his Heires and Assignes for ever To have and to hold the Said Tract of one Hundred and Nynety one acres of Land unto the Said John Ainsley his Heires and Assignes for ever hereby warranting the Sale of the Said Land against all persons whatsoever from me my Heires Executors and Administrators unto the Said John Ainsley his Heires and assignes for ever In Witnesse whereof I have hereunto Sett my hand and Seale this five and Twentyeth day of July Annoge Domini 1704.

Seald and Deliverd in presence of Francis Johnson Signum

Obadiah Fare Signum
James Fuox Signum

FILE PAPERS IN SUITS AND PROSECUTIONS

[*Anderson* v. *Fewox*]

[*CCR 191*]

North Carolina ss. To the Honorable Generall Court etc.

John Anderson is plaintiff against James Fuawks Defendant In a plea of Debt and Setteth forth and Declares that the Defendant Stands Justly Indebted to the plaintiff in the full and Just Summe of Three and Thirty Shillings and four pence payable to the plaintiff in Country pay (As by a writing obligatory from under the [*torn*] and ready to be produc'd in Court relation being thereunto had doth and may more fully and att large appear) yett the Defendant refuses payment whereby the plaintiff Sayth he is Dampnifyed Three pounds Sterling for which he hath brought this action And humbly Craves Judgment of this Honorable Court for the Same with Costs of Suite and he Shall pray etc.

Tho. Snoden Clericus Curiae

[*Endorsed:*]
Anderson versus Fuawks
In Debt
February 25th

[*Anderson, assignee* v. *Carlton, administrator*]

[*CCR 180*]

North Carolina ss. To the Honorable Generall Court

John Anderson Assignee of Dennis Mcclendon is plaintiff [*torn*] Arthur Carlton administrator in his own wrong of the Estate of Thomas Cuttlett Deceased in A plea of Debt and Setteth forth and Declares That the aforesaid Thomas Cutlett in his lifetime became bound unto the aforesaid Dennis Macclendon in the Summe of Fifty Shillings payable to [*torn*] Said Dennis Macclendon in Porke as by a writing obligatory relation beinge thereunto had doth and may more fully [*torn*] bind the aforesaid Dennis Macclendon by an Indorsment [*torn*] abovesaid writing Obligatory Qualifyed the plaintiff to [*torn*] aforesaid Summe of Fifty Shillings And the plaintiff in fact Sayth that the aforesaid Thomas Cuttlett the Said Summe of Fifty Shillings in his life time to the Said Dennis Mcclenden hath not payd nor to the plaintiff Qualifyed as aforesaid And the plaintiff further Complaines that the Defendant hath [*torn*] himselfe of and disposed of the Estate of the [*torn*] Cutlett Deceased without being thereto legally Qualifyed [*torn*] the aforesaid Summe of Fifty Shillings refuses to pay [*torn*] plaintiff Qualifyed as aforesaid tho' thereunto he hath been requested wherefore the plaintiff Sayth he is Dampnifyed five pounds Sterling for which he hath brought this action and humbly Craves Judgment of this Honorable Court for the Same with Costs of Suite And he Shall [*torn*].

Tho. Snoden Clk.

[*Endorsed:*]
[*Illegible*] Assignee versus Carlton Administrator etc.
In Debt
Entered the 24th June 1704

[*CCR 180*]

North Carolina ss. To the Provost Marshall or Deputy

These are in the Name of his Excellency the Palatine and the rest of the true and absolute Lords and Proprietors to will and require you to arrest the Body of Arthur Carlton Administrator in his own wrong of the Estate of Thomas Cutlett Deceased and him to hold Soe that he make his personall appearence att the next Generall Court to be held for this Province the last Tuesday in July next at the House of Captain John Hecklefield in Little River to answer the Complaint of John Anderson Assignee of Dennis Macclendon in A plea of Debt And have there this writt Dated the 24th Day of June Anno Domini 1704.

Take good Bond   Tho. Snoden Clericus Curiae

[*Endorsed:*]
Executed June the 26th

[*Blount* v. *Moon*]

[*CCR* 148]

North Carolina ss. To the Honorable Generall Court etc.

John Blunt Esqr. is plaintiff against John Moon Defendant in A plea of the Case and Setteth forth and Declares That the Defendant Stands Justly Indebted to the plaintiff in the full and Just Summe of Eight pounds five Shillings and tenne pence as by wayes and meanes Convenient the plaintiff is ready to make appear and refuses payment whereby the plaintiff Sayth he is Dampnifyed Sixteen pounds Sterling for which he hath brought this action and humbly Craves Judgment of this Honorable Court for the Same with Costs of Suite And he Shall pray etc.

Tho. Snoden Clericus Curiae

[*Endorsed:*]
Blunt Esqr. versus Moon
In Case
Entred 28th June 1704

[*Duckenfield, assignee* v. *Farrow*]

[*CCR* 148]

North Carolina ss. To the Provost Marshall or Deputy

These are in the Name of his Excellency the Pallatine and rest of the true and absolute Lords and Proprietors to will and require you to arrest the body of Francis Farrow And him to hold Soe that he may appear att the next Generall Court to be held for this Province the last Tuesday in July next att the House of Captain John Hecklefield in little River to answer the Complaint of Wm. Duckenfield Esqr. assignee of Wm. Powell In a Plea of Debt And have there this writt Dated the Third Day of Aprill Anno Domini 1704. Take bond.

Tho. Snoden Clericus Curiae

[*Endorsed:*]
Non est Inventus
John Moon Dr. to Captain Hecklefield

	£ s. d.
To writs and amercement	0— 7—6
To Sumons 4 Evidence	0— 4—0
To 20 Dayes Imprisonment	1— 0—0
	1—11—6

[*Evans* v. *Fair*]

[*CCR* 148]

North Carolina ss. To the Honorable Generall Court etc.

Thomas Evans is plaintiff against Obadiah Fare Defendant in A Plea of the

Case and Setteth forth and Declares that the Defendant Stands Justly Indebted [to the] Plaintiff in the full and Just Summe of Thirty and five shillings (as by Wayes and meanes Convenient the plaintiff is ready to make appeare) [*illegible*] payment whereby the plaintiff Sayth he is Dampnifyed Three [*illegible*] Sterling for which he hath brought this action and humbly [*illegible*] Judgment of this Honorable Court for the Same with Costs and he Shall pray etc.

Tho. Snoden Clericus Curiae

[*Endorsed:*]
Evans versus Fare
In Case
Entred 1st June 1704

[*Frayly* v. *Johnson*]

[*CCR 148*]

North Carolina ss. To the Honorable Generall Court

Willm. Freyley is plaintiff against Richd. Johnson Defendant in A Plea of the Case and Complaines that the Defendant Stands Justly indebted unto the plaintiff in the full and Just Summe of Eight pounds and one Shilling as by wayes and means Convenient the plaintiff is ready to make appear Neverthe-less the Defendant refuses payment of the Summe aforesaid to the [plaintiffs] Dammage Sixteen pounds Sterling Wherefore the plaintiff hath brought this action and humbly Craves Judgment of this Honorable Court for the aforesaid Debt and Dammages [*torn*] Costs of Suite And he shall pray etc.

Tho. Snoden Clericus Curiae

[*Goodridge* v. *Jones*]

[*CCR 148*]

North Carolina ss. To the provost Marshall or Deputy

These are in the Name of his Excellency the Pallatine and rest of the true and absolute Lords and Proprietors to will and require you to arrest the body of Frederick Jones and him to hold soe that he may appear att the next Generall Court to be held for this Province the last Tuesday in July next att the House of Captain John Hecklefield in little River to answer the Complaint of Jeremiah Goodridge In a plea of the Case for 104 [*illegible*] and have there this writt Dated the 29th Day of March Anno Domini 1704. Take good bond.

Tho. Snoden Clericus Curiae

[*Endorsed:*]
Writt
Executed March the 29th 1704

[*Hayman* v. *Holmes*]

[*CCR 148*]

North Carolina ss. To the Provost Marshall or Deputy

These are in the Name of his Excellency the Palatine and the rest of the true and absolute Lords and Proprietors to will and require you to Subpoena Archibald Holmes to make his personall appearance on the Third Day of the next Generall Court to be held for this Province the last Tuesday of this instant July att the House of Captain John Hecklefield in Little River to Answer the Complaint of Henry Hayman And have there this Subpoena Dated the 24th Day of July Anno Domini 1704.

Tho. Snoden Clericus Curiae

[*Endorsed:*]
By vertue hereof you are to appear on thursday next at my house
John Hecklefield Provost Marshall

To Archibald Holmes
July the 25th 1704

[*Hecklefield* v. *Bishop*]

[*CCR 191*]

To the Honorable the Generall Cort

Capt. Jno. Hecklefield is plaintiff Versus Jno. Bishop Defendant in a plea of the Case and Saith that the defendant Being Inployed by the plaintiff as his Reacevir or Collecter and had Depts put into his hands which he Recived for the plaintiff to the Valew of twelve pounds Eighteen Shillings and Refuseth to Render acount of the Same which Is to the plaintiffs damadge twenty five pounds Sterling for which he Bringeth his action and prayes Judgment for the Same with Costs of Sute And Shall pray.

[*Endorsed:*]
Hecklefield versus Bishop

[*Jones* v. *Butler, executrix*]

[*CCR 179*]

North Carolina ss. To the provost Marshall or Deputy

These are in the Name of his Excellency the Palatine and the rest of [*torn*] true and absolute Lords and Proprietors to will and require you to arrest the Body of Heneritta Butler Widdow Executrix of the [*torn*] will and Testament of Christopher Butler Deceased And her [*torn*] that She make her personall appearence att the [*torn*] Court to be held for this Province the last [*torn*] July next att the House of Captain John Hecklefield in [*torn*] River to answer the Complaint of Frederick Jones in A [*torn*] of Debt and have there this writt Dated the first Day of May Anno Domini 1704.

Take good Bond. Tho. Snoden Clk.

[*Endorsed:*]
Executed [*illegible*]

[*Jordan* v. *Pritchard*]

[*CCR 148*]

North Carolina ss. To the Provost Marshall or Deputy

These are in the Name of his Excellency the Palatine and rest of the true and absolute Lords and Proprietors to will and require you to Subpoena David Pritchard to make his personall appearance on the Third Day of the next Generall Court to be held for this Province the last Tuesday of this Instant July att the House of Captain John Hecklefield in Little River to make answer to A Bill of Complaint Exhibited against him by Joseph Jordan Complainant And have there this Subpoena Dated this 1[3] Day of July Anno Domini 1704.

Tho. Snoden Clericus Curiae

[*Endorsed:*]
Subpoena
Jordan versus Pritchard

[*Perishoe* v. *Thickpen, attorney of Manwaring*]

[*CCR 148*]

North Carolina ss. To the Honorable Generall Court etc.

James Perishoe is plaintiff against James Thigpen Attorney of Stephen Manwaring Defendant in a plea of the Case and Setteth forth and declares that the said Stephen Manwaring in to a certaine Tract of Land of the plaintiff's Scituate lying and being in Pequimins in this Province Containing Two Hundred and Forty acres with force and armes hath Entred and unlawfully possessed himselfe of the Same and the [defendant] Qualifyed as aforesaid the Same doth hold and to the plaintiff to render doth refuse To the plaintiff's grievous Dammage for which he hath brought this action and humbly Craves an Order for the Same with Dammages and Costs of Suite And he Shall pray etc.

Tho. Snoden Clericus Curiae

[*Endorsed:*]
Perishoe versus Thigpen Attorney etc.
Retraxit
In Case
Entred 8th July 1704

[*CCR 148*]

North Carolina ss. To the Provost Marshall or Deputy

These are in the Name of his Excellency the Palatine and the rest of the true and absolute Lords and Proprietors to will and require you to arrest the body of James Thigpen Attorney of Stephen Manwaring and him to hold Soe that he may appeare att the next Generall Court to be held for this Province the last Tuesday of this Instant July att the House of Captain John Hecklefield in little River to answer the Complaint of James Perishoe in A plea of the Case And have there this writt Dated the 8th day of July Anno Domini 1704.

Tho. Snoden Clericus Curiae

[*Endorsed:*]
Executed

[*Porter* v. *Slade*]

[*CCR 191*]

To the Honorable Generall Court

Andrew Wilson humbly Sheweth Wheras yor pettitioner haveing given his Attendance [*torn*] this honorable Court in a Diffirence depending between Mr. Jno. Porter as plantiffe and Mr. Henr. Slade Deffendant Tenn Days: Eight here at Court and two Comeing and goeing perfore yor pettitioner humbly Craves and order for the same as the Law allows and he shall pray.

[*Swann, administratrix* v. *Fewox*]

[*CCR 139*]

[*Torn*] Carolina ss. To the Honorable Generall Court

[*Torn*] Administratrix of Samuell Swann Junior is plaintiff [*torn*] Fuawkes Defendant in A plea of Debt and Setteth forth and Sayes that the Defendant Stood Justly Indebted to the Said Samuel Swann Junior in his life time in the full and Just Summe of Four pounds Eleven Shillings and Seven pence payable in good Sound Sweet Well Conditioned porke att or upon the Tenth Day of December next ensuinge the Date of A certaine writing obligatory ready to be produc'd in Court Sign'd and Delivred by the Defendant to the Said Samuell Swann Junior in his life time as by the Said writing obligatory relation being thereunto had doth and may more fully appear And the plaintiff in [Cort] Sayth that the Defendant the aforesaid Summe to the Said Samuel Swann Junior in his life time hath not payd and the Same to the plaintiff Qualifyed as aforesaid hath not payd but the Same doth refuse to pay to the plaintiffs Dammage [*torn*] pounds Sterling for which she hath brought this action and [*torn*]

Craves Judgment of this Honorable Court for the Same [*torn*] of Suite and She Shall pray etc.

Tho. Snoden Clericus Curiae

[*Endorsed:*]
[*Torn*] versus Fuawkes
In Debt Sur [*torn*]
Entred June 1t 1704

[*Wilkison* v. *Barrow*]

[*CCR 148*]

North Carolina ss. To the Honorable Generall Court etc.

Wm. Wilkinson is plaintiff against Wm. Barrow Defendant in A Plea of Trover and Conversion and Setteth forth and Declares That by A Deed of Sale bearing Date the Twenty Eighth Day of October in the year of our Lord Seventeene Hundred and one the plaintiff for and in Consideration of the Summe of Thirteen pound Sterling Currant money of England in hand payd unto John Allford of this Province purchased of the Said John Allford Three Cowes and Calves and was in full and ample possession of the Same as by the said Deed of Sale ready to be produc'd in Court relation being thereunto had doth and may more fully appear Neverthelesse the Defendant the premisses well knowing by vertue of processe issued out of the Court for the County of Bath to the Marshall Directed in or about the Month of February in the yeare of our Lord 1701/2 Seized of the aforesaid Three Cowes and Calves the proper Estate of the plaintiff and the Same Converted to his own use and behoofe and the Same to render to the plaintiff hath hitherto refused and doth as yett refuse tho' to doe the Same by the plaintiff he hath been requested whereby the plaintiff Sayth he is Dampnifyed Twelve pounds Sterling for which he hath brought this action and Craves Judgment of this Court for the Same with Costs of Suite And he Shall pray etc.

Tho. Snoden Clericus Curiae

[*Endorsed:*]
Wilkinson versus Barrow
In Trover and Conversion
Entred June 21th 1704

MISCELLANEOUS FILE PAPERS

[*Archdale, John, letter of attorney*]

[*CCR 192*]

[*Torn*] virginia and for Carolina

Know all men by these presents That I John Archdale doe hereby Constitute and Appoint my Son in Lawe Emanuel Lowe to be my true and lawfull Attorney And in Case of Death his Executors Executrix for me and in my Name to receive all Debts Dues and Demands whatsoever and to give full Discharges for the Same and to Call to Acct. for all Stocks of Cattle upon all my plantations in North Carolina [*torn*] Doe and Execute all other matters in my Stead which an Attorney may or ought lawfully to Doe witnesse my hand and Seale this 26th of the Month Called July Seventeen Hundred and Three and in the Second year of the Reigne of Queen Anne.

John Archdale

Wittnesses being first Stampt
Joshua Kent
Elizabeth Lowe
Mary Danson
Proved in Court the 26th Day of July 1704
Recorded the 4th day of August

Thos. Snoden Clericus Curiae

[*Duckenfield, William, letter of attorney*]

[*CCR 192*]

Carolina

Know all men by these presents that I William Duckenfeild Esqr. of Chowan precinct out of the Speecall trust and Confidence which I ripose in the fidellitie wisdome prudence and Circumspection of my trusty and well beloved frend and Kinsman John Ardrene have made ordaind Constituted and in my place and Stead put and deputed and by these presents do make ordain Constitute and in my place and Stead put and depute him the Said John Arderne my true and Lawfull Atturney, for me and in my name and to my use, to Ask demand Sue for and recover Leavy and recive all Such Sum and Sums of money Bonds Bills Executions Reckonings both debts Accompts and demands whatsomever which are any ways due and oweing unto the Said William Duckenfeild of and from any manner of person or persons whatsomever within the Said Province or elsewhere and to Sue Implead prosecute Imprison Arbitrate Compound or Aquitt as the nature of the Cause Shall require it And the Same So Recived or recouvred discharges releises or Aquittances, either in Law or equitie in my name to make Seal and deliver In all things to Act and do According to the nature of the cause, In as full larg and ample manner and form to all Intents and purposes, As if I myselfe were personally present at the doing thereof, Giving allso and by these presents Granting to my Said Attorney my full power and Authoritie to Constitute and depute one or more Attourneys and him as he Shall think fitt so the due Execution hereof if need require And Lastly I do hereby Warrant and will hereafter forever defend Whatsomever my Said Attourney Shall Legally do as cause to bee done in the premisses, As Wittnesse my hand and Seal this 12th Apll. in the year 1704.

Sighnd and Delivred In presence of

William Duckenfeild

Henry Lysle
[*Illegible*] Cooke
[*Illegible*] Snoden
Francis Tomes

This Day Came before me Wm. Duckenfield Esqr. and Sign'd and Delivred the above Power of Attorney to Mr. John Arderne Witnesse my hand this Twelfth Day of Aprill Anno Domini 1704.

Richd. Sanderson Senior

[*Endorsed:*]
Letter of Atturney

[*Gale, Christopher, commission*]

[*CCR 139*]

North Carolina ss. The Honorable Landgrave Robert Daniell Esqr. Lieuetenant Generall vice Admirall and Deputy Governor etc.
To the Honorable Christopher Gale Esqr.

I out of the Confidence I have in the prudence Wisdome and Integrity of you Christopher Gale Doe hereby Constitute and appoint you the Said Christopher Gale her Majesties Attorney Generall and Procurator for and in the behalfe of the Palatine and rest of the Lords Proprietors of this Province Impowering and requiring you in and upon her Majesties behalfe to Implead and prosecute all and every or any person or persons whatsoever that Shall att any time or times hereafter be Comitted upon breach of any of the penall Lawes and Statutes and Sentence and Execution to urge for in her Said Majesties behalfe against all and every or any Such person or persons lawfully Convict by Judgment of Twelve etc. to Fine or Such Corporall paines or punishment as the Nature of the offence and the Law in Such Case requires You are hereby likewise authorized and required in and upon the behalfe of his Excellency the Palatine and Lords Proprietors of this Government to Implead and prosecute all and every or any person or persons whatsoever for the Forfeiture of all Bonds fines and Recognisances past and Due by Such person or persons to the Said Palatine and Lords Proprietors within this Government And the Same to dispose of for the Said Palatine and Lords Proprietors use as by me you Shall be directed And to act and Doe all and every other matter and thing that to an Attorney Generall belongeth or may Lawfully be required And this Commission to Continue during my pleasure Given under my hand and Seale this Fourth Day of Aprill Anno Domini 1704.

[*Phelps, Edward, deed of sale*]

[*CCR 187*]

North Carolina

Know all men by these presents that I Edward Phelps of the Province aforsaid for a valuable consideration do hearby Sell make over [*torn*] and confirme all my Right title and Interest of a tract [*torn*] parcell of Land containing on hundred fifty and on Acers [*torn*] Land Latly in the possesion of my father Cuthbert [Phelps] Deceased Lying and being on the Soath Syde of Albamarle River about a mile distant from the Land bounding [*torn*] the

Land now in possesion of John Jennit together with all wood waters Earable Ground Houses fenceing orchards and all other Emunities and hereditaments thereunto belonging unto my brother Cuthbert Phelps his heires or asignes forever warenting the aforesaid premises from me my heires executors or administrators or from any other person or persons [*torn*] the Same by any act of myne my heirs [*torn*] or by our privity or procurement in witness whearof I have hearunto Sett my hand and Seale the 24th [*torn*] 1704 for a valuable Conseration.

Enterlin'd befor Signing

Signed Sealed and delivered
In presence of
Godfr. Spruill
Signum Anthon. Alexander
John Hassall

Edw. E. Phelps

[*Endorsed:*]
Acknowledged in Court the 26th Day of July 1704.
Tho. Snoden Clericus Curiae

[*CCR 103*]

References etc. from July Court to October Court 1704

Wilkison versus Barrow in Trover.

Chevin versus Bishopp in Case. Retraxit.

Perishoe versus Thigpen in Case. Retraxit.

Porter Esqr. versus Ayres Attachment. Continued.

Alexander versus Mekins Junior in Case.

Pettiver versus Falconar in Case. Concordia.

Peterson Assignee etc. versus Cockeram in Debt.

Pollock Esqr. versus Mountfort in Case. In Custody.

Pollock and Henderson versus Mountfort in Case. In Custody.

Porter versus Brice in Case. Concordia.

Glover Esqr. versus Brice in Case. Concordia.

Bateman versus Batchelor in Debt. Executed.

Swann Esqr. versus Mercer in trespasse Sur Case. Executed.

Duckenfield Esqr. versus Farrow in Debt. Retraxit.

Jones versus Coles in Case. Executed.

Coles versus Jones in Case. Executed.

Cock versus Steel in Covenant.

Snoden versus Tarkington in Case. Executed.

Payne versus Pierce in Case. Executed.

Swann Esqr. versus Truewhitt in Debt. Executed.

Wilkison versus Brice in Debt.

Wilkison versus Brice in Case.

Wilkison versus Fuawkes in Debt. Retraxit.

Wilkison versus 3 Houghtons in Debt. Executed.

Wilkison versus Raphell in Debt. Not Executed.

Wilkison versus Wm. Hartly in Debt. Not Executed.

Wilkison versus 2 Hartlyes in Debt. Not Executed.

Wilkison versus 2 Phelps in Case. Not Executed.

Hecklefield versus Williams in Case. Non est Inventus.

Ayres versus Williams in Debt. Retraxit.

Holmes versus Truewhitt Attachment. Concordia.

Snoden versus Fuawkes Attachment. Retraxit.

Macclendon and Uxor versus Warren in trespasse Sur Case. Executed.

Keel versus Wallis in trespasse Sur Case. Executed.

Brown versus Markham Senior in Case. Retraxit.

Hecklefield versus Williams Attachement. Concordia.

Anderson versus Williams Attachment. Concordia.

[*CCR 103*]

<12> Att A Generall Court held att the House of Captain John Hecklefield on Tuesday the 31th Day of October 1704 And then Adjournd till to Morrow Morning 8 of Clock.

On Wednesday Morning att 8 of Clock the Court meet present The Honorable Willm. Glover, Chr. Gale, Tho. Symonds, John Blount Esqrs. Justices.

By A Reference from the last Court Collonel Wm. Wilkison Comes to prosecute his Suite against Captain Willm. Barrow in A plea of Trover and Conversion for Three Cowes and Calves And the Defendant by Peter Godfrey his Attorney Comes and for Plea Sayth that by vertue of processe Issued out of the Court for the County of Bath to the Marshall Directed in or about the Month of February In the

Year of our Lord 1701/2 he was not Seized of Three Cowes and Calves the proper Estate of the plaintiff and the Same Converted to his own use and behoofe as is Sett forth by the plaintiff in his Declaration upon which he Casts him Selfe upon the Country And the plaintiff likewise And the Marshall was required to Cause to Come twelve true and lawfull men etc. To whom etc. Who neither etc. By whom the matter may be found And there Came Mr. Archibald Holmes Mr. Willm. Benbury Mr. Willm. Charlton Mr. Thomas Hoskins Mr. Edward Standen Mr. Dennis Macclendon Mr. Roger Snell Mr. Abraham Warren Mr. Garrett Pursell Mr. John Hawkins Mr. Thomas Barcock and Mr. Richd. Madron who Impanelld and Sworn Say wee of the Jury doe find for the plaintiff Three Cowes and Calves with Costs and Twelve Shillings Dammage.

Orderd That Captain Willm. Barrow pay unto Collonel Willm. Wilkison three Cowes and Calves with Costs and Twelve Shillings Dammage alias Execution.

<12*a*> A Power of Attorney from Jonathan Bateman to John Bateman was prov'd by the Oath of Thomas Mercer.

Orderd that Every plea Shall be Given in writing in every personall action Comenc'd to this Court.

Jonathan Bateman Comes by John Bateman his attorney to prosecute his Suite against Richd. Batchelor in A Plea of Debt for Two pounds Tenne Shillings And the Defendant by Levi Truewhitt his Attorney Comes and Defends the force and Injury of the Said action and for plea Sayth that the plaintiff his action ought not to have for that his Declaration is altogether uncertaine both as to the Day Month and Year when the Said Bill was Contracted and in what County itt was payable as well alsoe the Degree and Mistery of the plaintiff and Defendant ought by Law to be in the Said writt and Declaration all which is not in the least Mentioned Wherefore he humbly Craves A Non Suite etc.

And the Opinion of this Court is That for the Uncertainty of the Declaration A Nonsuite be Granted.

Upon Petition of Captain John Hecklefield against Hugh Campbell and Affrica his wife Executrix of the last Will and Testament of Hugh McGregor Deceased praying to prove an Account against the Estate of the Said Hugh MacGregor Deceased and is admitted.

Captain John Hecklefield produces an account against the Estate of Hugh MacGregor Deceased for the Summe of Two pounds Three Shillings and Eight pence ½ and proves the Same by his Oath.

Upon Motion of Collonel Wm. Wilkison praying that allowance may be Granted to James Blount for Six Dayes Coming and

Going and Three Dayes Attendance as Evidence for Collonel Wm. Wilkison against Captain Wm. Barrow.

<13> Orderd That allowance be Granted unto the Said James Blount according to Act of Assembly.

Upon Motion of Collonel Wm. Wilkison praying allowance may be Granted to Levi Truewhitt Evidence for the Said Wilkison against Captain Wm. Barrow

Orderd That Collonel Wm. Wilkison pay unto Levi Truewhitt for his attendance as Evidence Two Shillings and Six pence with Costs alias Execution.

Upon Petition of Thomas Blount

Orderd That Collonel Wm. Wilkison pay unto the Petitioner allowance for his Attendance as Evidence for the Said Collonel Wilkison against Captain Wm. Barrow for Four Dayes Coming and Going and Three Dayes Attendance as per Act of Assembly alias Execution.

The Honorable Saml. Swann by Mr. Wm. Swann his Attorney Comes to prosecute his Suite against Thomas Mercer in A plea of Trespass upon the Case and Setteth forth and Declares That the Defendant in the precinct of Pequimins and in this Province with force and Arms in and upon A Certaine Plantation the Rightfull Inheritance and proper Estate of the plaintiff hath wrongfully Entred and the Same from the plaintiff doth wrongfully Detaine and withhold to the plaintiffs Dammage Two Hundred pounds Sterling And for Plea the Defendant in proper person Sayth That the plaintiff hath not Right to the Plantation Specifyed in the plaintiffs Declaration.

T M

And the Matter heard and Debated.

Itt is the Opinion of this Honorable Court That the plaintiff be possessed of the plantation Specifyed in the plaintiffs Declaration.

<13*a*> Ordered That the Provost Marshall putt the plaintiff in possession of the aforesaid Plantation And That the Defendant pay Costs alias Execution.

And in Barr of the Said Order The Defendant humbly prayes That all further proceedings may be Stopt till A hearing of the premisses be had in the Honorable Court of Chancery And prayes an Injunction in Chancery which is Granted.

Richd. Davenport and John Davenport by their humble petition Shew That being bound by Recognisance to keep the peace with Archibald Holmes and all her Majesties Liege people Appear and are Discharg'd from the Same.

Mr. Frederick Jones by Mr. Peter Godfrey his Attorney Comes to prosecute his Suite against Captain James Coles in A Plea of the Case for the Summe of Fifteen pounds Eighteen Shillings and two pence And the Defendant Craves A Reference And by Consent the Matter is referr'd to the next Generall Court.

Captain James Coles Comes to prosecute his Suite against Mr. Frederick Jones in A Plea of the Case for the Summe of Fifteen pounds Eighteen Shillings and two pence And the Defendant by Mr. Peter Godfrey his Attorney prayes A Reference to the next Generall Court And by Consent of both partyes referr'd to the next Generall Court.

John Coles made Oath to A Deposition and Orderd to be Recorded.

A Deposition of Jeremiah Goodridge Sworne to before the Honorable Saml. Swann Esqr. was presented to the Court and Orderd to be recorded.

<14> Thomas Snoden Comes to prosecute his Suite against John Tarkington in A Plea of the Case for Twenty Four Shillings And the Defendant Came not.

Orderd That the Provost Marshall have the Body of the Said John Tarkington to the next Generall Court to answer the Said Thomas Snoden's Complaint alias Judgment to be Confirmd against the Marshall.

Collonel Thomas Pollock Comes to prosecute his Suite against Henry Mountfort in A Plea of the Case and Complaines That the Defendant as Master of the Brigantine Martha bound for Boston in New England had taken in his Charge aboard the Said Vessell Sometime in July last Two Hundred Forty and Four Barrells of Porke Some Skinnes Furrs Tanned Leather and other Goods of the plaintiffs as appeares by Bills of Lading under his hand here in Court which aforesaid Goods the Defendant acknowledged to have received in good Order and well Conditioned and assumed and oblidged himselfe Safely to Deliver the Goods abovementioned att Boston in New England And alsoe being in the plaintiffs Imploy and under his pay as Master of his Brigantine was oblidged Carefully to look after and Safe from Dammage to keep whatever the plaintiff putt on board Notwithstanding which by the Defendants want of Care Sufficient and necessary in Discharging his Duty of A Master within the Sound and Rivers of this Province hath not only Dampnifyed and Spoiled most of the Goods aforesaid but hath alsoe hindred the Vessell from proceeding her Said Voyage A Considerable time to the plaintiffs great Charge and Trouble and Four Hundred pounds Dammages.

And the Defendant Stands Mute and answers not <14*a*> And

the plaintiff by Mr. Thomas Boyd his Attorney prayes That Judgment may be Entred upon A Nihill Dicit Which is Granted.

Thomas Pollock Esqr. and David Henderson Come to prosecute their Suite against Henry Mountfort Mariner in an action of the Case and Declare That the Defendant as Master of the Brigantine Martha bound for Boston in New England had taken in his Charge aboard the Said vessell Two Thousand Six Hundred and Nynety Dressed Dear Skinns with A Considerable Number of Furrs of the plaintiffs which he acknowledged himselfe to have received in good Order and well Conditioned and assumed and oblidged himselfe to deliver up the Same in like good Order and well Conditioned as appears by Bills of Lading here in Court produc'd Notwithstanding which by the Defendants want of Such Sufficient and necessary Care as A Master of a Vessell ought to have he hath Dampnifyed and lost A great part of the Goods To the plaintiffs Dammage Three Hundred pounds And the Defendant Stands Mute and Answers not And the plaintiff by Mr. Thomas Boyd his Attorney prayes That Judgment may be Entred upon a Nihil Dicit which is Granted.

The Marshall was required to arrest the Body of John Pierce to answer the Complaint of Samll. Payne in A Plea of the Case for Seven pounds Four Shillings and two pence And the plaintiff Came not And the Defendant by Mr. Richard Plater his Attorney prayes A Nonsuite against the plaintiff.

Orderd That A Nonsuit be Granted And that the plaintiff pay Costs alias Execution.

<15> A Power of Attorney from John Pierce to Mr. Richd. Plater was prov'd by the Honorable Willm. Glover Esqr. and Orderd to be Recorded.

Collonel Willm. Wilkison Comes to prosecute his Suite Against Thomas Willm. and Richd. Houghton in A Plea of Debt for Thirty one pounds five Shillings and Three pence by Bill And Thomas Houghton one of the Defendants Comes and Confesses Orderd That Thomas Houghton pay unto Collonel Willm. Wilkison One and Thirty pounds five Shillings and Three pence with Costs alias Execution.

Dennis Macclendon and Deborah his wife Executrix of the last Will and Testament of Nathaniel Sutton Deceased Come to prosecute their Suite against Abraham Warren Defendant in A Plea of Trespass upon the Case And Sett forth and Declare that the Defendant in the precinct of Pequimins in this Province with force and Arms into A certaine plantation the proper Estate and Rightfull Inheritance of the plaintiffs hath wrongfully Entred and the Same from the plaintiffs doth wrongfully withhold To the plaintiffs

Dammage Two Hundred pounds Sterling And prayes that the Defendant may be removed and the plaintiffs restored to their proper Right And the Defendant by Thomas Norcomb his Attorney for plea Sayth That he hath not Entred with force and Arms in to the plantation Specifyed in the plaintiffs Declaration but in to the Same hath Entred lawfully and the Same doth hold as Guardian to Richd. Sutton Orphan of George Sutton Deceased and putts himselfe upon the Country and the plaintiff likewise And the Marshall was required to Cause to Come <15*a*> Twelve true and lawfull men of the Vicinage To whom etc. Who neither etc. By whom etc. And there Came Mr. Archibald Holmes Mr. Willm. Benbury Mr. Thomas Hoskins Mr. Edward Standen Mr. Roger Snell Mr. Garrett Pursell Mr. John Hawkins Mr. John Yelverton Mr. Richd. Madron Mr. John Bellitt Mr. Richd. Davenport and Mr. John Davenport who Impanelld and Sworn Say wee of the Jury find for the plaintiff with Costs and twelve pence Damage.

Orderd That A Writt be directed to the Provost Marshall to putt the plaintiffs in possession of the plantation And that Abraham Warren pay Costs and Twelve pence Dammage alias Execution.

Upon Petition of Cornelius Benington praying allowance for Four Dayes Coming and going and Two Dayes Attendance as Evidence for Collonel Thomas Pollock against Henry Mountfort.

Orderd That Collonel Thomas Pollock pay unto Cornelius Benington allowance for Four dayes Coming and going and Two dayes Attendance as per act of assembly with Costs alias Execution.

And then the Court Adjourns till to Morrow Morning 7 of Clock.

On Thursday Morning Seven of Clock the Court Meets present ut Supra.

By An Attachment from March Court the Marshall was required to attach Soe much of the Estate of David Ayres wherever to be found in this Government as will pay and Satisfye the Honorable John Porter Esqr. (by A Continuance hanging two Courts att the plaintiffs request) the full Summe of Four pounds and five Shillings And the plaintiff Came not.

Orderd That the Matter be dismist and the plaintiff pay Costs alias Execution.

<16> Robt. Keel by Mr. Thomas Boyd his Attorney Comes to prosecute his Suite against Robert Wallis Defendant in A Plea of Trespasse upon the Case and Complaines That the Defendant in the precinct of Pascotank in this Province with force and Arms in to A certaine plantation the proper Estate and rightfull Inheritance of the plaintiff hath wrongfully Entred and the Same from the plain-

tiff doth wrongfully withhold and Detaine To the plaintiffs Dammage Two hundred pounds Sterling And prayes That the Defendant may be removed and the plaintiff restored to his proper Right And the Defendant by Mr. John Lawson his Attorney Comes and Defends the force and Injury when etc. and Sayth he hath not Entred in to the Rightfull Inheritance of the plaintiff nor the Same from the plaintiff doth withhold in manner and forme as the plaintiff hath alledged in his Declaration and putts himselfe upon the Country and the plaintiff likewise And the Marshall was Commanded to Cause to Come Twelve true and lawfull men etc. To whom etc. who neither etc. By whom etc. And there Came Mr. Archibald Holmes, Mr. William Benbury Mr. Thomas Hoskins Mr. Edward Standen Mr. Caleb Caleway Mr. Thomas Dereham Mr. Levi Truewhitt Mr. Roger Snell Mr. Garrett Pursill Mr. John Yelverton Mr. Richard Madron and Mr. Caleb Bundy who Impanell'd and Sworn Say wee of the Jury find for the Defendant.

Orderd That the action be dismist And the plaintiff pay Costs alias Execution.

<16*a*> Simon Trumbull in Custody of the Marshall and Orderd att the Complaint of Anne his wife to make his personall appearance on the Second Day of the Generall Court to make answer for making an assault and Sorely beatinge and abusing and Maiming Anne his Said Wife Appears and the Matter Debated before this Honorable Court And the Said Simon behaving himselfe insolently before the Honorable Willm. Glover Esqr. att the time of his Commitment and likewise behaving himselfe insolently before the Court.

Orderd That the Marshall take into his Custody the Body of the Said Simon Trumbull and him Safe keep till he Shall give bond with good and Sufficient Security for his good behaviour towards Anne his wife and be of good abearance to all her Majesties Liege people to the next Generall Court And that Anne his wife be Sommoned to make her personall appearance att the next Generall Court.

Orderd That Mary Rooks be Subpoenaed to the next Generall Court to give Evidence in behalfe of the Queen against Simon Trumbull.

Robt. Cock Committed for making an assault upon Mrs. Elizabeth Hecklefield and Orderd to appear att this Court to answer the Same Came not but made an Escape from the Marshall.

Orderd That the Provost Marshall or Deputy take into his Custody the Body of the Said Robt. Cock Soe that he make his appearance att the next Generall Court to answer the aforesaid Complaint.

Upon Petition of James Perishoe Shewing that he bought formerly of Stephen Manwaring late of this Government A parcell of land <17> being in Estimation Two Hundred acres by A Bill of Sale ready to be producd in Court might appear being in Consideration of A Deed of Sale in Exchange of a Plantation and Tract of Land belonginge to the Said Stephen Manwaring And that the Petitioner hath but Seventy Seven acres and prayes to be possess'd of Two Hundred Acres the Quantity purchased.

Orderd That James Thigpen Attorney of Stephen Manwaring lay out for the Petitioner Two Hundred acres of land lying in Pequimins as Conveniently as Can be not Injuring the Plantation call'd the Long Reach.

Upon Petition of Willm. Charlton praying allowance as Evidence for Anthony Alexander against Thomas Mekins

Orderd That Anthony Alexander pay unto Willm. Charlton for Three Dayes Coming and going and Three Dayes Attendance as is ascertained by Act of Assembly with Costs alias Execution.

Upon Petition of Willm. Branch praying allowance as Evidence for Anthony Alexander against Thomas Mekins

Orderd That Anthony Alexander pay unto Willm. Branch for Three Dayes Coming and going and Three Dayes Attendance as is ascertained by Act of Assembly with Costs alias Execution.

A Power of Attorney from Ralph Chapman to Thomas Boyd was prov'd by the Oaths of Thomas Snoden and John Arderne Esqr. and Orderd to be recorded.

<17*a*> Orderd That every Marshall of the Three Adjacent precincts Summons Six Men to appear upon A Jury att Every Generall Court in this Province.

Upon Petition of Zachariah Keeton and Marrying the widdow of Zachary Jackson Deceased and being Guardian in the Right of his wife of Lucy the Sole Daughter and Heiresse of the Said Zachary Jackson prayes A Division of the Land and plantation granted to Zachary and David Jackson by Willm. Jackson their Father according to the tenour of the will of Willm. Jackson Senior Deceased.

Orderd That Mr. Henry White Mr. John Davis Mr. Robt. Lowry Mr. James Davis Mr. Jeremiah Symonds and Mr. James Tooke or any Four of them make A Division of the Land and Plantation aforesaid according to the Tenour of the will of Willm. Jackson Senior Deceased.

[*Signed:*]
W. Glover, C. Gale, John Blounte.

RECORDED BY ORDER OF COURT

[*CCR 103*]

Know all men by these presents That I Ralph Chapman of Rhode Island in America Ship Carpenter for diverse good Causes and Considerations me hereunto movinge Have Constituted Ordained appointed and in my Stead and place putt And doe by these presents Constitute Ordaine appoint and in my Stead and place putt my Trusty and well beloved Friend Thomas Boyd of the Province of North Carolina Cooper my true lawfull and absolute Attorney for me and in my Name to grant lett Sell or dispose of all my lands and Plantations whatsoever Scituate Lying and being in the Province aforesaid with full power to Sell dispose of and Convert to his own use and behoofe all or any parte or parcell of Stocke of Cattle or Hoggs properly belonginge to me the Constituent in the Province aforesaid And further to accomplish transact and doe all and every other lawfull and reasonable act and Acts thing and things in as full large and ample manner to all Intents and purposes as if I my Selfe was there personally present to doe the Same although the matter herein Comprized wanted more Speciall authority Ratifying holding firm and allowing whatever my Said attorney Shall for me and in my Name act and Doe in the premisses In witnesse whereof I have hereunto Sett my hand and Seale this 25th Day of August Anno Domini 1704.

Signed Sealed and Delivered in the presence of
John Arderne
Tho. Snoden

Ralph Chapman Sigillum

Recorded by Order

FILE PAPERS IN SUITS AND PROSECUTIONS

[*Alexander* v. *Mekins*]

[*CCR 148*]

North Carolina ss. To the Honorable Generall Court etc.

Anthony Alexander is plaintiff against Thomas Mekins Junior Defendant In A plea of the Case and Setteth forth and Declares that the Defendant in the yeare of our Lord God 1703 being Intrusted with one Shallopp the proper Estate of the plaintiff did in Albermarle Sound in the precinct of Chowan and in this Province Suffer the aforesaid Shallopp through Carelessnesse and Negligence to be Stav'd Sink and Suffer Shipwrack To the plaintiffs Dammage Tenne pounds Sterling for which he hath brought this action and humbly

Craves Judgment of this Honorable Court for the Same with Costs of Suite And he Shall pray etc.

Tho. Snoden Clericus Curiae

[*Endorsed:*]
Alexander versus Mekins Junior
In Case
Entred 1st 7ber

[*Ayres* v. *Williams*]

[*CCR 191*]

North Carolina ss. To the Honorable Generall Court etc.

Thomas Ayres is plaintiff against Wm. Willms. Defendant in A Plea of Debt and Setteth forth and Declares that the Defendant Stands Justly Indebted to the plaintiff in the full and Just Summe of Tenne pounds Seven Shillings and Six pence payable to the plaintiff in manner and forme as by A Bill from under the Defendants hand ready to be produc'd in Court relation being thereunto had doth and may more fully and att Large appear And the plaintiff further Sayth that the Defendant designs to depart out of this Province and refuses to make payment of the Summe aforesaid or give Security to the plaintiff for the Same wherefore the plaintiff hath brought this action And humbly Craves Judgment of this Honorable Court for the Summe aforesaid or that the Defendant may give Security for the Same with Costs of Suite And he Shall pray etc.

Tho. Snoden Clericus Curiae

[*Endorsed:*]
Ayres versus Williams
In Debt Sur obligatory
Entred 11th 8ber 1704

[*Bateman* v. *Batchelor*]

[*CCR 191*]

North Carolina ss. To the Honorable Generall Court etc.

Jonathan Bateman is plaintiff against Richd. Batchelor Defendant in A Plea of Debt and Setteth forth and Declares that the Defendant Stands Justly Indebted to the plaintiff in the full and Just Sume of Two pounds tenne Shillings as by A Bill from under the Defendants hand ready to be produc'd in Court relation being thereunto had doth and may more fully and att large appear and refuses payment whereby the plaintiff Sayth he is Dampnifyed Two pounds Sterling for which he hath brought this action and humbly Craves Judgment of this Honorable Court for the Same with Costs of Suite And he Shall pray etc.

Tho. Snoden Clericus Curiae

[*Endorsed:*]
Bateman versus Batchelor
In Debt

[*Browne* v. *Markham*]

[*CCR 148*]

N. Carolina Ss. To the Honorable Generall Court

Jno. Browne is plaintiff and complaines against Anthony Markham Senior Defendant in a plea of the case and setteth forth that the Defendant stands justly indebted to the Plaintiff in the full and just summe of three pounds (payable in porke according to the usuall price of this country) which by waies and means convenient the plaintiff is ready to make appear which haveing often demanded the Defendant refuses payment of the same which is to the plaintiff's Damage six pounds for which he brings this action and craves judgement of this Honorable Court for the Same with Costs of sute and shall pray etc. Dated this 21 of 8br 1704.

Copia Testis John Browne

[*Endorsed:*]
Browne versus Markham Senior
Case
Narratio
Entred the 21 8br

[*CCR 139*]

North Carolina ss. To the Provost Marshall or Deputy

These are in the Name of his Excellency the Palatine and rest of the true and absolute Lords and Proprietors to will and require you to Arrest the body of Anthony Markham Senior And him to hold Soe that he make his personall appearance att the next Generall Court to be held for this Province the last [*torn*] in October next att the House of Captain John Hecklefield in Little River to Answer the Complaint of John Browne In A plea of the Case And have there this writt Dated the 25th Day or August Anno Domini 1704.

Tho. Snoden Clericus Curiae

[*Endorsed:*]
Brown versus Markham
Executed the 21 8ber 1704
Narratio
Augt. the 29th 1704

I hereby impower you to Execute the within writt in the precinct of Chowan. John Hecklefield Provost Marshall
To Mr. John Foster Deputy Marshall

[*Coles* v. *Jones*]

[*CCR 148*]

North Carolina ss. To the Honorable Generall Court etc.

Captain James Coles is plaintiff against Frederick Jones Defendant in A

Plea of the Case and Complaines That the Defendant Stands Justly Indebted unto the plaintiff in the full and Just Summe of Fifteen pounds Eighteen shillings and two pence (as by wayes and meanes Convenient the plaintiff is ready to make appear) and refuses payment whereby the plaintiff Sayth he is Dampnifyed Thirty pounds Sterling [*torn*]efore the plaintiff hath brought this action and humbly Craves Judgment of this Honorable Court for the Same with Costs of Suite And he Shall pray etc.

Tho. Snoden Clericus Curiac

[*Endorsed:*]
Coles versus Jones
In Case
Entred Augt. 20th 1704
Referrd
Retraxit

[*Crown* v. *Trumball*]

[*CCR 148*]

N. Carolina Ss. To Capt. Jno. Hecklefield provost Marshall

I send you herewith the body of Simon Trumball brought before me upon the complaint of Anne his wife for making an assault upon her the said Anne and her sorely beating abusing and maiming which he confesseth and threatneth to repeat the like usage to her again, These are therefore to require and comand you him to receive into your Custody and safely to keep till he shall become bound with good security to appear the second day of the next generall Court to answer the same and in the meantime to be of good behaviour towards our soveraigne Lady the Queen and all her liege people especially towards the said Ann his wife and this shall be your sufficient warrant Given under my hand and seal the 11 of 8ber 1704.

W. Glover

[*Endorsed:*]
To Mr. Francis Penrise
You are hereby in the Queens name required to deliver Simon Trumball now in your Custody with this present precept to the Provost Marshall. Given under my hand the 11 of 8br 1704.

W. Glover

[*Hecklefield* v. *Williams*]

[*CCR 191*]

North Carolina ss. To the Honorable Generall Court etc.

Captain John Hecklefield is plaintiff against Willm. Williams Defendant in A Plea of the Case and Setteth forth and Declares that the Defendant Stands Justly Indebted to the plaintiff in the full and Just Summe of five pounds tenne Shillings and three pence payable to the plaintiff in Porke as by wayes and meanes Convenient the plaintiff is ready to make appear and refuses payment whereby the plaintiff Sayth he is Dampnifyed Tenne pounds Sterling for which he hath brought this action and humbly Craves Judgment of this Honorable Court for the Same with Costs of Suite And he Shall pray etc.

Tho. Snoden Clericus Curiae

[*Endorsed:*]
Hecklefield versus Williams
In Case
Entred 7th October

[*Jones* v. *Coles*]

[*CCR 191*]

North Carolina Ss. To the Honorable Generall Court etc.

Mr. Fred. Jones Merchant of Virginia Complains against Captain James Coles of the precinct of Pequimmins in the Proprietorshipp of North Carolina in a Plea upon the Case For that the Defendant Standeth Justly Indebted unto the Plantiff in the full and Just Summe of fifteen pounds eighteen Shillings and two pence as by ways and meanes convenient the Plantiff is ready to make appear the which Said Summe the Defendant refuseth to pay to the dammadge of the Plantiff the Summe of thirty one pounds Sixteen Shillings and four pence Sterling whereupon he bringeth this Action and craves Judgment of this Honorable Court for his debt dammages and Cost and Shall pray etc.

Fred. Jones

[*Endorsed:*]
Jones versus Coles
Retraxit
Referrd

[*Keele* v. *Wallis*]

[*CCR 191*]

North Carolina ss. To the Honorable Generall Court etc.

Robert Keel is plaintiff against Robert Wallis Defendant In A Plea of Trespasse upon the Case and Complaines that the Defendant in the precinct of Pascotank in this Province with force and armes into A Certaine Plantation the Proper Estate and rightfull Inheritance of the Plaintiff hath wrongfully Entred And the Same from the plaintiff doth wrongfully withhold and detaine whereby the plaintiff Sayth he is Dampnifyed Two Hundred pounds Sterling for which he hath brought this action And prays that the Defendant may be removed And the plaintiff restored to his Proper Right with Judgment for Costs And he Shall pray etc.

Copia Tho. Snoden Clericus Curiae

[*Endorsed:*]
Keel versus Wallis
Trespasse Sur Case
Narratio
Wee of the Jury find for the Defendant

[*Macclendon and wife, executrix* v. *Warren*]

[*CCR* 185]

North Carolina ss. To the Honorable Generall Court etc.

Dennis Macclendon and Deborah his wife Executrix of the last will and Testament of Nathaniel Sutton Deceased are plaintiffs against Abraham Warren Defendant in A Plea of Trespasse upon the Case and Sett forth and Declare that the Defendant in the precinct of Pequimins in this Province with force and armes into A certaine plantation the proper Estate and rightfull Inheritance of the plaintiffs hath wrongfully Entred and the Same from the plaintiffs doth wrongfully with hold to the plaintiffs Damage Two Hundred pounds Sterling wherefore the plaintiffs have brought this action and humbly pray that the Defendant may be removed and they restored to their proper right with Judgment for Damages and Costs of Suite And they Shall pray etc.

Tho. Snoden Clericus Curiae

[*Endorsed:*]
Macclendon and Uxor Executrix versus Warren
In trespasse Sur Case
Narratio
Entred 16th 8ber 1704
Wee of Juriey finde four the plentive with Cost and twelve pens damage

[*Parker* v. *Lane*]

[*CCR* 148]

No. Carolina Ss. To the provost Marshall of the County of Bath or Deputy

These are in her Matyes name to will and require you to Arrest the body of Dutton Lane and him Safely hold Soe that he be and appear at the next Generall Court to be holden at the house of Capt. Jno. Hecklefields in Litle river on the last Tuesday in this Instant Octob. then and there to answer the Plaint of Geo. Parker in a plea of the Case and have there this writt Dated at the Secretarys office this 14th day of Octob. Anno Domini 1704.

Testis T. Knight Secretary

[*Endorsed:*]
Parker versus Lane
In Case

[*Pettiver* v. *Falconer*]

[*CCR* 191]

North Carolina ss. To the Honorable Generall Court The First Day

John Pettiver is plaintiff against John Falconar Defendant In A plea of the Case and Setteth forth and Declares That the Defendant Stands Justly Indebted to the plaintiff one Good Cow and Calf [*torn*] the Value of One pound Seventeen Shillings and Six pence and twelve Shillings and Six pence payable to the plaintiff in Country Commodityes as by wayes and meanes Convenient the plaintiff is ready to make appear all which the Defendant refuses to pay tho' by the plaintiff requested Whereupon the plaintiff Sayth he is Dampnifyed Five pounds Sterling for which he hath brought this action and humbly Craves Judgment of this Honorable Court for the Same with Costs of Suite And he Shall pray etc.

Tho. Snoden Clericus Curiae

[*Endorsed:*]
Pettiver versus Falconar
In Case
Entred Augt. 25th

[*Pollock* v. *Mountfort*]

[*CCR 191*]

North Carolina ss. To the Honorable etc.

To the 1t Day of the Generall Court

Thomas Pollock complains against Henrey Mountfort Mariner in ane actione of the case and declares That wheras the said Defendant as Master of the Brigantene; [*torn*] bound for Boston in new England had taken in his charge aboard the said vessell some tyme in July Last two hundred fortie and four Barells of Pork some skins, furrs tanned Leather and other goods of the Plantiffs as appears by Bills of Lading under his hand heer in court produced which forsaid [*torn*] the Defendant acknouledged to have Receaved in good order and well conditioned and assummed and oblidged himself to safly [*torn*] deliver the goods above mentioned at Boston in new England and also being in the said Plantifs imploy and under his pay as master of his Brigantene was oblidged carefully to Look after and safe from damage to keep what ever the plantiffe put one board. Notwithstanding which by the Defendants want of Sufficient and necessary care in Discharging his Dutis of a master within the sound and rivers of this Province hath not only Damnyfyed and Spoyled Most of the goods aforsaid but hath also hindred the vessell from proceiding the said voyadge a considerable tyme and put the plantiffe unto very considerable trouble and charges to the plantifs [Damage] 400 pounds for whitch he brings his action and humbly craves judgment of this honorable court and for the same and for his costs and humbly pray as in duty Bound [*illegible*].

[*Pollock and Henderson* v. *Mountfort*]

[*CCR 139*]

North Carolina ss. To the Provost Marshall or Deputy

These are in the Name of his Excellency the Palatine and the rest of the

true and absolute Lords and Proprietors to will and require you to arrest the Body of Henry Montford And him to hold Soe that he make his personall Apperance att the next Generall Court to be held for this Province the Last Tuesday in October next att the House of Captain John Hecklefield in Little River to answer the Complaint of Collonel Thomas Pollock and David Henderson in A plea of the Case To the plaintiffs Dammage Three Hundred pounds And have there this writt Dated the 17th Day of August Anno Domini 1704.

Take good bond Tho. Snoden Clericus Curiae

[*Endorsed:*]
Pollock and Henderson versus Montfort
In Case
Exsecuted August the 19th 1704 by me Jno. Byrd Deputy Marshall

[*Swann* v. *Mercer*]

[*CCR 140*]

North Carolina ss. To the Honorable Generall Court etc.

The Honorable Samuel Swann Esqr. is plaintiff against Thomas Mercer Defendant in A plea of Trespasse upon the Case and Setteth forth and Declares that the Defendant in the precinct of Pequimins and in this Province with force and armes in and upon A certaine plantation the rightfull Inheritance and proper Estate of [*torn*] plaintiff hath wrongfully Entred and the Same from the plaintiff doth wrongfully detaine and withhold to the plaintiffs Dammage [*torn*] Hundred pounds Sterling wherefore he hath brought this Suite And humbly Craves an Order for the Same with his Damages and Costs of Suite And he Shall pray etc.

Tho. Snoden Clericus Curiae

[*Endorsed:*]
Swann Esqr. versus Mercer
In Trespasse Sur Case
Entred the 23d 7ber

[*CCR 192*]

I doe authorize and Impower my beloved Sonn William Swann to appeare on my behalfe at the Next Genneral Court In an Action there depending between me as plaintiff against Thomas Mercer Defendant and also In one other action depending In the Said Court between me as plaintiff against Levy Truewhitt defendant wittness my hand this 30th day of October 1704.

Samuel Swann

Allow'd of and orderd to be recorded Testis Tho. Snoden Clericus Curiae

[*Swann* v. *Truewhitt*]

[*CCR 191*]

North Carolina ss. To the Honorable Generall Court etc.

Honorable Samuel Swann Esqr. is plaintiff against Levi Truewhitt

Defendant In A Plea [*torn*] Debt and Setteth forth and Declares that the Defendant Stands Justly indebted to the plaintiff in the full and Just Summe of Eight pounds as [*torn*] meanes Convenient the plaintiff is ready to make appear and refuses payment whereby the plaintiff Sayth he is Dampnifyed Sixteen pounds Sterling for which he hath brought this action and humbly Craves Judgment [*torn*] this Honorable Court for the Same with Costs of Suite And he Shall pray etc.

Tho. Snoden Clericus Curiae

[*Endorsed:*]
Swann Esqr. versus Truewhitt
In Debt
Entered 4th Octobr.

[*Wilkison* v. *Hartly*]

[*CCR 191*]

North Carolina ss. To the Honorable Generall Court etc.

William Wilkison is plaintiff against Willm. Hartly Defendant in A Plea of Debt and Setteth forth and Declares That the Defendant Stands Justly Indebted to the plaintiff in the full and Just Summe of Seven pounds one Shilling and Eight pence as by A Bill from under the Defendants hand and Seale ready to be produc'd in Court relation being thereunto had doth and may more fully and att large appear Neverthelesse the Defendant refuses payment of the Summe aforesaid wherefore the plaintiff hath brought this action and humbly Craves Judgment of this Honorable Court for the Same with Costs of Suite And he Shall pray etc.

Tho. Snoden Clericus Curiae

[*Endorsed:*]
Wilkison versus Hartly
In Debt Sur obligatory
Entred the 10th 8ber

[*Wilkison* v. *Hartlys*]

[*CCR 191*]

North Carolina ss. To the Honorable Generall Court etc.

Willm. Wilkison is plaintiff against Henry and Wm. Hartly Defendants in A Plea of Debt and Setteth forth and Declares That the Defendants oblidgd themselves in the penall Summe of Six and Twenty pounds [*blank*] with Condition under [*illegible*] for the payment of Thirteen pounds Eight Shillings and tenne pence in good Neat Clean Drest Merchantable fresh porke as by a Bond from under the Defendants hands and Seales ready to be produc'd in Court relation being thereunto had doth and may more fully and att large appear Neverthelesse the plaintiff in fact Sayth that the Defendants refuse payment of the aforesaid Summe payable in manner and forme aforesaid wherefore he hath brought this action and humbly Craves Judgment of this

Honorable Court for the Same with Costs of Suite And he Shall pray etc.

Tho. Snoden Clericus Curiae

[*Endorsed:*]
Wilkison versus 2 Hartlyes
In Debt Sur obligatory
Entred 10th 8ber 1704

[*CCR 148*]

North Carolina ss. To the Provost Marshall or Deputy

These are in the Name of his Excellency the Palatine and the rest of the true and absolute Lords and Proprietors to will and require you to arrest the Bodyes of Henry and Willm. Hartly and them to hold Soe that they make their personall appearance att [*torn*] next Generall Court to be held for this Province the [*torn*] Tuesday of this Instant October att the House of Captain John Hecklefield in Little River to answer the Complaint of Willm. Wilkison in A Plea of Debt And have there this writt Dated the 10th Day of October Anno Domini 1704. Take good bond.

Tho. Snoden Clericus Curiae

[*Endorsed:*]
To Jno. Foster to execute per order of John Hecklefield Provost Marshall
Breve
Wilkison versus 2 Hartleys
In Debt
Evidence, John Reevely, James Dennis
This Return not Executed by me John foster debetey marshall

[*Wilkison* v. *Houghtons*]

[*CCR 191*]

North Carolina ss. To the Honorable Generall Court

Wm. Wilkison is plaintiff against Thomas, Willm. and Richd. Houghton Defendants in A Plea of Debt and Setteth forth and declares that the Defendants Stand Joyntly and Severally Indebted to [*torn*] plaintiff in the full and Just Summe of one and Thirty pounds five Shillings and three pence as by A Bill from under the Defendants hands and Seales ready to be produc'd in Court relation being thereunto had doth and may more fully and att large appear Neverthelesse the Defendants and every of them refuse payment of the Summe aforesaid to the plaintiff wherefore he hath brought this action and humbly Craves Judgment of this Honorable Court for the Same with Costs of Suite And he Shall pray etc.

Tho. Snoden Clericus Curiae

[*Endorsed:*]
Wilkison versus Houghtons
In Debt
Entred 10th 8ber

[*CCR 148*]

North Carolina ss. To the Provost Marshall or Deputy

These are in the Name of his Excellency the Palatine [*torn*] the true and absolute Lords and Proprietors to will and require [*torn*] the Bodyes of Thomas, William and Richard Houghton [*torn*] to hold Soe that they make their personall appearance [*torn*] next Generall Court to be held for this Province the [*torn*] of this instant October att the House of Captain John [*torn*] in Little River to answer the Complaint of Willm. Wi[*torn*] plea of Debt And have there this writt Dated [*torn*] of October Anno Domini 1704. Take good bond.

Tho. [*torn*]

[*Endorsed:*]
Breve
Wilkison versus 3 Houghtons
This Retorned Executed by me John foster debety marshall

[*Wilkison* v. *Phelps*]

[*CCR 148*]

North Carolina ss. To the Provost Marshall or Deputy

These are in the Name of his Excellency the Palatine and the rest of the true and absolute Lords and Proprietors to will and require you to arrest the Body of Bartholomew Phelps And him to hold Soe that he make his personall Appearance att the next Generall Court to be held for this Province the last Tuesday of this Instant October att the House of Captain John Hecklefield in Little River to answer the Complaint of Willm. Wilkison in A Plea of the Case and have there this writt Dated the 10th Day of October Anno Domini 1704. Take good Bond.

Tho. Snoden Clericus Curiae

[*Endorsed:*]
Breve
Wilkison versus Phelps
This not Executed by me John foster debuty mashall

[*Wilkison* v. *Raphell*]

[*CCR 191*]

North Carolina ss. To the Honorable Generall Court etc.

Wm. Wilkison is plaintiff against Wm. Raphell Defendant in A Plea of Debt and Setteth forth and Declares That the Defendant Stands Justly Indebted to the plaintiff in the full and Just Summe of Nyne pounds Tenne Shillings and three pence as by A Bill from under the Defendants hand and Seale ready to be produc'd in Court relation being thereunto had doth and may more fully and att large appear Nevertheless the Defendant refused payment of the Summe aforesaid wherefore the plaintiff hath brought this action and humbly Craves Judgment of this Honorable Court for the Same with Costs of Suite And he Shall pray etc.

Tho. Snoden Clericus Curiae

[*Endorsed:*]
Wilkison versus Raphell
In Debt
Entred 10th 8ber

[*CCR 189*]

References etc. from October Court to March Court 1705

Jones versus Coles in Case. Retraxit.

Coles versus Jones in Case. Retraxit.

Snoden versus Tarkington Order versus Marshall. Satisfaction made.

Coles versus Stimson in Case. Godfrey versus Browne Attachment £9.

Wilkison versus Brice in Debt. Payne versus Perce Attachment.

Wilkison versus Barrow in Case.

Pettiver versus Davis in Debt. Executed.

Godfrey versus Cretchington in Case. Retraxit.

Peterson Assignee etc. versus Falconar [*illegible*]. Retraxit.

Peterson and Company etc. versus Houghton in debt. Non est inventus.

Wilson versus Ruckman in Debt. Retraxit.

Friley versus Brice in Debt. Executed.

Friley versus Lakar in Case. Executed.

Friley versus Long in Debt. Executed.

Falconar versus Berry in Case. Executed. Retraxit.

Friley versus Berry in Debt. Executed.

Falconar versus Lisle [in] Case. Executed.

Glover Esqr. versus Lisle in Debt. Executed.

Glover Esqr. versus Wm. Sawyer in Case. Executed.

Glover Esqr. versus John Sawyer [*illegible*]. Retraxit.

Glover Esqr. versus Conden in Case. Retraxit.

Glover Esqr. versus Hosea in Case. Executed.

Glover Esqr. versus Leflear in Case. Retraxit.

Glover Esqr. versus Neal in Case. Executed.

Peterson Assignee etc. versus Williams in Debt. Retraxit.

Blake versus Walker Widdow [in] Trover and [Conversion]. Executed.

Treuwhitt versus Watson in Debt.

[Smith] versus Swann in Debt. Executed.

Smith versus Swann in Case. Executed.

Hecklefield versus Pettiver in Debt. Executed.

Hecklefield versus Pettiver in Case. Executed.

Boyd versus Crowe in Debt.

[Stone] versus Evans in Case. Sur Defamation.

Friley versus Adams [*illegible*] in Trover and Conversion.

Plater versus Evans in Case. Noe Declaration filed. Executed.

Norton Assignee etc. versus Low in Debt. Executed.

Norton Assignee etc. versus Low in Debt. Executed.

Snoden versus Brethwaite in Debt. Retraxit.

[Hunt] versus Bunting etc. in [Cancellaria].

[*Illegible*] versus Low Bill in [Cancellaria].

[*Illegible*] versus Swann Bill in [Cancellaria].

Peterson Assignee etc. versus Duckenfield [*illegible*] in Case Debt. Executed.

[*CCR 103*]

<18*a*> Att A Generall Court held att the House of Captain John Hecklefield in Little River the 27th Day of March 1705 present The Honorable Willm. Glover, Chr. Gale, Wm. Collings, John Blount Esqrs. Justices.

The Act Entituled an Act Qualifying members of the House of Burgesses and all persons of office and Trust within this Government was read and Orderd to be putt in Execution.

The Honorable Wm. Glover Chr. Gale Wm. Collings and John Blount Esqrs. Severally take and Subscribe to the Oaths appointed by Law.

Thomas Snoden Clerk of this Court takes and Subscribes to the Oath appointed by Law.

A Power of Attorney from Madam Anne Walker to the Honorable Saml. Swann Esqr. was prov'd by the Oaths of Robt. Fendall and Thomas Snoden and Orderd to be recorded.

A Conditionall Deed of Sale from Ralph Chapman to Mr. Thomas Boyd prov'd by the Oaths of the Honorable John Arderne Esqr. and Thomas Snoden and Orderd to be recorded.

A Power of Attorney from Saml. Norton to Tho. Snoden prov'd by the Oath of Captain John Hecklefield.

A Lease of A Plantation from John Evans to Willm. Parker acknowledged in Court and Orderd to be recorded.

<19> Upon Petition of Thomas Boyd and Winifred his wife relict of John West Deceased praying Lettres of Administration on the Estate of Francis West an Infant Son of the Said John West and Winifred

Itt is the Opinion of this Court That the Said Winifred is nearest of Kin to the Deceased and that thereby the Right of Administration belongs to the Petitioner And That Certificate thereof be made to the Governor and Councill.

Upon Petition of Benjamin West praying to be Admitted to Chuse his Guardian is admitted and Chuses Thomas Boyd his Guardian.

And then the Court adjourns till to morrow morning 8 of Clock.

On Wednesday morning 8 of Clock the Court meets present ut Supra.

A Deed of Sale from Danl. Phillipps to the Honorable Willm. Glover Esqr. acknowledged in Court and orderd to be recorded.

Captain John Heckleﬁeld and Elizabeth his wife by Chr. Gale Esqr. her Majesties Attorney Generall desire this Honorable Court to understand and be inform'd That Robt. Cock of this Province not havinge the fear of God before his Eyes but being led away by the instigation of the Devill on or about the Month of September last past with force and Armes in and upon the Body of the Said Elizabeth Heckleﬁeld being then in the peace of our Soveraigne Lady the Queen an assault did make and her the Said Elizabeth Sorely beat and abuse and other Injuryes to her done against the peace of our Said Soveraigne Lady the Queen etc. And the Said Robt. Comes and Confesses the Information.

Orderd That the Said Robt. Cock give bond with Security for his good abearance towards all her Majesties Liege people and make his appearance att the next Generall Court.

And the Said Robt. Cock assumes on his own behalfe in the

Summe of Ten pounds and Robt. Hosea assumes on behalfe of the Said Robt. Cock in the Summe of Five <19*a*> pounds to her Majestie That the Said Robt. Cock Shall be of good Abearance to all her Majesties Liege people [*torn*] likewise make his personall appearance att the next Generall Court.

John Pettiver Comes to prosecute his Suite against Willm. Davis in A Plea of Debt for Six pounds Nyne Shillings Eight pence by Bill payable upon Demand And the Defendant Comes and Confesses.

Orderd That Willm. Davis pay unto John Pettiver the Summe of Six pounds Nyne Shillings and Eight pence with Costs alias Execution.

Willm. Freyley Comes to prosecute his Suite against Willm. Brice and Declares for Seven pounds Seventeen Shillings and Six pence And the Defendant Comes and Sayes that the writt was Issued out late and that he the Defendant had not time to Summons Evidences to prove the ballance of the aforesaid Summe alledg'd in the plaintiffs Declaration and prayes A Reference to the next Generall Court which is granted for the aforesaid reasons they being made appear to the Court.

A Power of Attorney from Richd. Smith to Captain John Heckle-field prov'd by the Oath of Thomas Snoden.

Willm. Brice Comes to this Court and Sayth he is Justly indebted unto Collonel Willm. Wilkison in the Summe of Eighteen pounds tenne Shillings and Six pence one half payable in Drest Buck Skinns att the rate of Two Shillings per Skinn and the other half payable in Drest Doe Skinns att Eighteen pence per Skinn and Confesses Judgment for the Same.

Orderd That Willm. Brice pay unto Collonel Willm. Wilkison Eighteen pounds Ten Shillings and Six pence the one half in Drest Buck Skinns att Two Shillings per Skinn and the other half in Drest Doe Skinns att Eighteen pence per Skinn alias Execution.

Richd. Smith by Captain John Hecklefield his Attorney Comes to prosecute his Suite against Willm. Swann in A Plea of Debt for Five and Twenty pounds payable to the plaintiff in Albemarle County in Country Commodityes [*torn*] Creditt to liking And for plea the Defendant Sayes That <20> the Debt Sued for is payd by the plaintiffs Order as per Reciept here ready to be produc'd will appear And for Tryall thereof does refer himselfe to the Country And the plaintiff likewise And the Marshall was required to Cause to Come twelve true and lawfull men of the vicinage etc. To whom etc. who neither etc. By whom the Matter may be found And there Came Mr. Willm. Reed Mr. Danl. Phillipps Mr. Roger Middleton Mr. Robt. Keel Mr. Joseph Wicker Mr. Richd. Thorpe Mr. Walter

Tanner Mr. Francis Penrice Mr. Richd. Rose Mr. John Norcum Mr. Saml. Herst and Mr. Saml. Payne who Impanelled [*torn*] Sworn Say wee of the Jury doe find for the Defendant.

Orderd That the action be dismist and the plaintiff pay Costs alias Execution.

Upon Petition of Willm. Thorpe prayinge allowance as Evidence for Richd. Smith versus Willm. Swann

Orderd That Richd. Smith pay unto Willm. Thorpe allowance for two dayes Coming and two dayes going and two Dayes Attendance as per Act of Assembly with Costs alias Execution.

Upon Petition of Joseph Wicker being Sumon'd as Evidence for Richd. Smith versus Willm. Swann

Orderd That Richd. Smith pay unto Joseph Wicker allowance for two dayes Coming and two dayes going and two Dayes Attendance as per Act of Assembly with Costs alias Execution.

Richd. Smith by Captain John Hecklefield his Attorney Comes to prosecute his suite against Willm. Swann in A Plea of the Case and Complaines That the Defendant Stands Justly indebted unto the plaintiff one pound Ten Shillings And for Plea the Defendant Sayth he is not indebted unto the plaintiff in the Summe of One pound Tenn Shillings in manner and forme as the plaintiff hath alledg'd in his Declaration but Sayth he hath well and truly payd the Same And upon Motion of the Said Captain John Hecklefield That the Defendant Should make Oath to his account pleaded in ballance of the aforesaid Summe Specifyed in the plaintiffs Declaration And the Defendant proving the Same by his Oath.

<20*a*> Orderd That the action be dismist and the plaintiff pay Costs alias Execution.

Upon the Petition of Widdow Trumbull

Orderd That the Estate of Simon Trumbull late Deceased be apprised by Willm. Stephens Willm. Barcliffe John Jones and Thomas Boyd or any Three of them and that an Inventory thereof be given in to the next Generall Court.

Pensylvania Company by Thomas Peterson their Attorney Come to prosecute their Suite against Thomas Houghton And Declare for the Summe of Ten pounds one Shilling and three pence by Bill And the Defendant Comes and Confesses.

Orderd That Thomas Houghton pay unto Pensylvania Company the Summe of Ten pounds one Shilling and Three pence with Costs alias Execution.

Thomas Peterson assignee of Collonel Robt. Quary and Pensylvania Company Comes to prosecute his Suite against Willm. Duckenfield Esqr. in A Plea of Debt for Sixty one pounds Nyneteen Shillings and Three pence half peny payable to the plaintiff Qualifyed as aforesaid in manner and forme following videlicet Good drest Buck Skinns att two Shillings per Skinn Good Drest Doe Skinns att one Shilling Six pence per Skinn Good Drest Otter Skinns att Four Shillings per Skinn Beaver att Three Shillings per pound Racoon Skinns att Six pence per Skinn Fox and Catt att one Shilling per Skinn And the Defendant by the Honorable John Arderne his Attorney Comes and Sayes That the Defendant by reason of Sicknesse is incapacitated to Attend this Court and prayes A Reference to the next Generall Court which is Denyed And the plaintiff prayes an Order against the Marshall which is Granted.

Upon Petition of Captain John Hecklefield

Orderd That an Attachment be Granted against the Estate of Willm. Duckenfield Esqr.

Mr. Peter Godfrey in behalfe of Mr. Frederick Jones proves an account against Captain James Coles for the Summe of Fifteen pounds Eighteen Shillings and two pence And prays the Same may be recorded.

Orderd that the Same be accordingly recorded.

<21> Upon Petition of Saml. Payne praying to prove Nyne Rights is Admitted and proves the Same by his Oath videlicet Saml. Payne John Day Paul Wakefield [*torn*] McBride Truman McBride Hugh Clarke John [*torn*] James Oughay and one Negroe.

Captain James Coles Comes to prosecute his Suite against John Stimson in A Plea of the Case for Two pounds two Shillings in Porke And the Defendant Came not And the plaintiff prayes an Order against the Marshall.

Orderd That the Provost Marshall bring forth the Body of the Said John Stimson to the next Generall Court to answer the aforesaid Complaint alias Judgment to be Confirmd against the Marshall.

Upon Petition of Captain John Hecklefield

Orderd That an Attachment be Granted against the estate of John Stimson.

Willm. Freyley Comes to prosecute his Suite against James Long in A Plea of Debt and Declares for A Cow and Calfe to be delivered att the Defendants Pen by Bill And the Defendant Came not And the plaintiff prayes an Order against the Marshall.

Orderd That the Provost Marshall bring forth the Body of the Said James Long to the next Generall Court to answer the aforesaid Complaint alias Judgment to be Confirmd against the Marshall.

Upon Petition of Captain John Hecklefield

Orderd That an Attachment be granted against the Estate of James Long.

Upon Petition of Mr. Thomas Blount praying allowance for attendance as Evidence for Willm. Freyley against James Long

Orderd That Willm. Freyley pay unto Mr. Thomas Blount allowance videlicet for two dayes Coming and two Dayes Going and One Day Attendance as per Act of Assembly with Costs alias Execution.

Upon Petition of Richd. Rose

<21*a*> Orderd That Willm. Freyley pay unto Richd. Rose [*torn*] Summe videlicet for two dayes Coming and two Dayes going and one Day Attendance as per Act of Assembly with Costs alias Execution.

And then the Court Adjournd till to Morrow Morning 8 of Clock.

Thursday Morning 8 of Clock the Court meets present ut Supra as alsoe the Honorable John Porter Esqr. A Member of this Court.

The Honorable John Porter Esqr. takes and Subscribes to the Oath appointed by Law.

Upon Petition of John Pettiver praying to prove Eleven Rights is Admitted and proves these following Rights by his Oath videlicet John Pettiver Willm. Davis Edward Clarke Danl. Dyer Judith Clack Mary Downe Negroe Peter Indyan John Indyan Tom Negroe Naunce Indyan Jenney.

Willm. Freyley Comes to prosecute his Suite against Edward Berry in A Plea of Debt for Eight pounds payable in fresh porke by Bill And the Defendant Comes and Confesses Judgment.

Orderd That Edwd. Berrey pay unto Willm. Freyley the Summe of Eight pounds in fresh Porke with Costs alias Execution. And in Barr of all further proceedings the Defendant prays Stay of Execution till A further hearing of the premisses be had in the Honorable Court of Chancery which is granted.

The Marshall was Commanded to arrest the Body of Captain Willm. Barrow to answer the Complaint of Collonel Willm. Wilkison in A Plea of the Case for Three pounds Eighteen Shillings and Eleven pence And the plaintiff Came not.

Orderd That the action be dismist and the plaintiff pay Costs alias Execution.

Upon An Attachment Issued out by Mr. Peter Godfrey against the Estate of John Browne The Marshall makes [*illegible*] Attach'd Four pounds in the hands of David [*illegible*] Six pounds in the hands of Willm. Sawyer and[14]

---

[14] The manuscript breaks off at this point. There are no other copies of minutes available for this session of the General Court.

FILE PAPERS IN SUITS AND PROSECUTIONS

[*Blake* v. *Walker, executrix*]

[*CCR 186*]

North Carolina ss. To the Honorable Generall Court etc.

David Blake is plaintiff against Anne Walker Widdow Executrix of the last Will and Testament of Henderson Walker Esqr. Deceased Defendant in A Plea of Trover and Conversion and Complaines that the Said Henderson Walker Esqr. in his life time videlicet in the year of our Lord God 1698 Seized and possessed himselfe of one Negroe Man named Tony of the Value of Fifty pounds the proper Estate of the plaintiff and the Same detained and Converted to his own proper use and behoofe And the plaintiff Sayth that neither the aforesaid Henderson Walker Esqr. in his life time nor the Defendant Since the death of the Said Henderson Walker Esqr. the aforesaid Negroe to the plaintiff have rendred but the Same to render have and doe Still refuse to the plaintiffs Dammage One Hundred pounds Sterling Wherefore the plaintiff hath brought this Suite and Craves Judgment of this Honorable Court for the aforesaid Negroe with Dammages and Costs of Suite And he Shall pray etc.

Tho. Snoden Clericus Curiae

[*Endorsed:*]
Blake versus Walker vidua Executrix etc.
Narratio in Trover and Conversion
Entred 21th Feby. 1704/5

[*Boyd, executor* v. *Crosse*]

[*CCR 179*]

North Carolina ss. To the Honorable Generall Court etc.

Thomas Boyd Executor of the last will and Testament of Archibald Burnett Deceased is plaintiff against James Crosse Defendant in A Plea of Debt and Complaines that the Defendant Stood Indebted unto the Said Archibald Burnett in his life time in the full and Just Summe of Four pounds payable to the Said Archibald Burnett in Country Commodityes or in Sowing work Conveniently in Pascotank or little River As by A Bill from under the Defendants hand bearing Date the 27th of Novembr. 1702 ready to be produc'd in Court relation being thereunto had doth and may more fully and att large appear Neverthelesse the Defendant refuses payment of the aforesaid Summe to the plaintiff Qualifyed as aforesaid To the plaintiffs Dammage Eight pounds Sterling wherefore the plaintiff hath brought this action and humbly Craves

Judgment of this Honorable Court for the Same with Costs of Suite And he Shall pray etc.

Copia — Tho. Snoden Clericus Curiae

[*Endorsed:*]
Boyd Executor etc. versus Crosse
Narratio in Debt Sur obligatory
Entred 28th Feby. 1704/5
Wee of the Jury find for the Defendant

[*CCR 148*]

North Carolina ss. To the Provost Marshall or Deputy

These are in the Name of his Excellency the Palatine and the rest of the true and absolute Lords and Proprietors to will and require you to Sumons Edward Tayler to make his personall appearance att the next Generall Court to be held for this Province the last Tuesday in March next att the House of Captain John Hecklefield in Little River to give Evidence between Thomas Boyd plaintiff and James Crosse Defendant in A plea of Debt And have there this Sumons Dated the 28th Day of February Anno Domini 1704/5.

Tho. Snoden Clericus Curiae

[*Endorsed:*]
Executed

[*CCR 188*]

N. Carolina

Know all men by these presents that I James Cross am justly indebted unto Archd. Burnet in the full Summ of four pounds to be paid conveniently in pascotank or litle River in Countrey commodities or in Sowing work 2 or 3 Months after the date hereof To which Said payment well and truly to be made I bind me my heirs executors to him his heirs or assigns as witnes my hand and Seall this 27 Novm. Anno 1702.

James Cross

Signed Sealed and Delivered
In presence of us
Edward Tayler
Robert Swain his marke

[*Endorsed:*]
Bill
James Cross
£4

[*Coles* v. *Stimson*]

[*CCR 191*]

North Carolina To the Honorable Generall Court etc.

Captain James Coles is plaintiff against John Stimson Defendant In A plea of the Case and Setteth forth and Declares That the Defendant Stands Justly Indebted to the plaintiff in the full and Just Summe of Two pounds and two Shillings payable to the plaintiff in fresh Porke As by wayes and meanes Convenient the plaintiff is ready to make appear Which Said Summe the Defendant refuses to pay to the plaintiffs Dammage Four pounds Sterling for which he hath brought this action And humbly Craves Judgment for the Same with Costs of Suite And he Shall pray etc.

Tho. Snoden Clericus Curiae

[*Endorsed:*]
Captain Coles versus Stimson
Narratio in Case
Entred Xber 25th 1704
Order versus Marshal
Excuted by me Wm. Bray

[*Crown* v. *Cock*]

[*CCR 191*]

North Carolina To the Honorable Generall Court

Capt. John Hecklefield and Elizabeth his wife of this Province by Chr. Gale her Majesties Attorney Generall etc. desireth this Honorable Court to understand and be inform'd That Robt. Cock of this province not haveing the [*torn*] of God before his Eyes but being led away by the Instigation of the Devill on or about the Month of September [*torn*] past with force and Armes in and upon the Body of the Said Elizabeth Hecklefield [*torn*] then in the peace of our Soveraigne Lady the Queen an assault did make and her the Said Elizabeth Sorely beat and abuse and other Injuryes unto her done against the peace of our Soveraigne Lady the Queen etc.

Gale per Domina Regina

[*Endorsed:*]
Evidences for the Queen
Captain John Hecklefield, Eliz. Hecklefield, Mary Rookes
Plea Guilty

[*Crown* v. *Jordan*]

[*CCR 191*]

North Carolina ss. To the Honorable Generall Court

Captain John Hecklefield High Sherriffe of this Province by Chr. Gale her Majesties Attorney Generall etc. desireth this Honorable Court to understand and be informd That whereas by an Act made in the Third yeare of the Raigne of Edwd. the First over England etc. Entituled an Act (all men Shall be ready to pursue felons) itt is provided that all Generally be ready and apparrelled att the Commandments and Summons of Sherriffes and att the Cry of the Country to Sue and arrest Felons (when any Need is) as well within

Franchise as without and they that will not Soe doe and thereof be attainted Shall make A Grievous Fine to the King as by the Said Act relation being thereunto had more fully and att large will appear Notwithstanding which act Joseph Jordan of the Precinct of Pascotank in this Province the validity of the Said Act not regarding but Contemning the Same and the Authority thereof Sometime in the Month of February last past att Pascotank aforesaid tho' often Commanded and Summoned thereto by the Informant High Sherriffe aforesaid One John Moor alias Ralph Smith alias Silvester Matthews as A Felon did Suffer to Escape Contrary to the forme of the Statute aforesaid and in Contempt of her Majestie her Crown and Dignity.

Gale per Domina Regina

[*Crown* v. *Stone*]

[*CCR 148*]

North Carolina ss. To the Provost Marshall or Deputy

Whereas John Evans Came before me and made Complaint upon Oath that he hath been robbed by Phillip Stone of this Province of A Bill of Eighteen pounds payable from the Said Phillip Stone to the Said John Evans against the peace of our Soveraigne Lady the Queen.

These are in her Majesties Name to will and require you to take into Custody the Said Phillip Stone And him Safly to keep till he Shall become bound with good Security for his appearance att the next Generall Court to be held for this Province the last Tuesday in March next att the House of Captain John Hecklefield to answer what shall be objected against him on her Majesties behalf and for his good abearance towards our Said Soveraigne Lady the Queen and all her liege people in the mean time And this Shall be your Sufficient Warrant. Given under my hand the 2d Day of November 1704.

[*CCR 148*]

Know all men by these presents that wee John Evans of the Province of North Carolina Planter and John Hunt of the Same Planter Doe acknowledge our Selves to owe and Stand Indebted unto his Excellency the Palatine and the Lords Proprietors of the Province aforesaid in the full and Just Summe of Twenty pounds of good and Current money of England to the which payment well and truly to be made Wee bind our Selves and either of us Joyntly and Severally our Heires Executors Administrators and Assignes firmly by these presents Sealed with our Seales Dated the 2d Day of November 1704.

The Condition of the abovewritten obligation is Such That if the above bound John Evans Doe and Shall make his personall appearance att the next Generall Court to be held for this Province the last Tuesday of March next att the House of Captain John Hecklefield in Little River and then [and] there prosecute Phillip Stone for Robbery Comitted [by the] said Stone Against the Said John Evans. That then the above written obligation to be void and of none effecte or else to be and remain in full force power and vertue.

Seal'd Sign'd and Delived
in the presence of
Tho. Snoden
John Hecklefield

John Evans his marke
John Huntt

[*CCR 188*]

North Carolina ss.

The Jurors for our Soveraigne Lady the Queen present upon their Oaths That Philip Stone of the precinct of Coratuck in this Province not having the fear of God before his Eyes but being led away by the Instigation of the Devill did Sometime in October last past violently and forcibly assault the Body of John Evans being in the peace of our Soveraigne Lady the Queen and feloniously Rob Steal and take away from the Said John Evans one Bill of Value of Eighteen pounds the proper Goods and Chattells of the proper Goods and Chattells of the Said John Evans and payable from the Said Philip Stone to the Said John Evans Contrary to the peace of our Said Soveraigne Lady the Queen and against the forme of the Statutes in that Case made and Provided.

Gale per Domina Regina

[*Endorsed:*]
Billa Vera
John Evans, Wm. Britnor, Senior, Wm. Barken, [*illegible*], Johannah Parker, hd. sweare, Margarett Barret, hd. [*illegible*]

Evidences for our Soveraigne Lady the Queen against Stone
Wm. Swan, Wm. Floyd

[*Duckenfield* v. *Fee*]

[*CCR 148*]

North Carolina Ss. To the Honorable Generall Court etc.

Willm. Duckenfield Esquire is plaintiff against Danll. Fee defendant in a plea of Debt and Says that the defendant Stands Justly Indebted unto the plaintiff in the full and Just Summe of Eight pounds Six Shillings in Good fresh Merchantable porke To be paid upon demand as in and by one Certaine writeing obligatory Under the proper hand and Seale of the defendant beareing date the 12th December 1702 here in to Court brought and ready to be produced relation being thereunto had doth and may appeare which Said Summe of Eight pounds Six Shillings the Defendant hath not rendred to the plaintiff tho often thereunto requested but the Same doth Still refuse to render to the plaintiffs Damage Sixteen pounds twelve Shillings Sterling and thereupon he brings his Suite and prayes Judgement for the Same with Costs of Suite and Shall pray etc.

Tobs. Knight Secretary

[*Endorsed:*]
Narratio
Duckenfield Esqr. versus Fee
In Debt
Entered Nov. 22d 1704

[*Evans* v. *Stone*]

[*CCR 191*]

[The deposition of] Samuel Shakesper being [*torn*] years old or there abouts being sworn saith that he the said Samuel Shakesper Came down the bay a Long with Phillip Ston and that thay Came away in the night for the said Ston pretend that he was afraid of Cornel Certia and the said Ston was [indebted] to Shakespear and when the said Shaksper did ask the said Ston to pay him the said Ston sed that he wood pay him With the pint of his sord and this was at Ston fathers and Stons father Chid him and wase going to strik him and Ston swor that he would kill his father if he did and that he brought William [*illegible*] Lid aLoung with him to the brige in norfolk County John Hall and Thomas Cheerwood shode a bill of twelve pound and shode it to Cornel Wilson and the said Shakesper under stud that thay Gave Cornel Wilson order to a Rest Ston but Ston Lift his bot and wint into Corotuk and got other men to transport [hir] for him and further saith not; Samuel Shaksper sworn in a defunice depending between John Evens and Phillip Ston in North Carolina before me.

James Wilson Juner

[*Endorsed:*]
W[*torn*]n
Jo[*torn*]icker

[*CCR 148*]

To the Honorable Landgrave Robert Daniell Esqr. Lt. Generall Viz. admirall and deputy Governor and Councill of N. Carrolina

The petetion of John Evins humbly sheweth That Phillip Stone since Robbing your pettetioner of the bond formerly Complained of doth perforce deteyn a house and [*torn*] hundred and sixty Eight Acres of Land to the same [belonging] Least from your pettetioner to the said Stone at the Rent of forty shillings for the terme and time of one whole year, which Leas Expired and Ended the 15th day of January Last past as the Leas here Ready to produce which to your Honors more at Large apear, and at the Expiration of which time your pettetioner In company with two of his neighbors did in a civill and Modest maner demand the Line[*torn*] his house and plantation with the Rent then due butt was per the said Stone obstina[tely] denied boath on pretence your pettetioner owed him ten pounds pretended to have been per him [*torn*] Stone paid in Mr. Wintworths store as a fine or Compensation of five years Rent [*torn*] for the a Forsaid Land and premises, which sum of ten pounds your pettetioner owns to have received from the said Stone in maner as afforsaid and for a Consideration of a Lease dated [the] 11th day of october 1703 which Leas was per the said Stone Rendered back In January [*torn*] to your pettetioner Who Readily Remitted and paid back the [*torn*] afforsaid sume of ten pound to the said Stone in the afforsaid store before the signing of the Letter [*torn*] for the one year Last past as per the Account under the Bookeepers hand your pettetioner is Ready to make appear, all which your pettetioner Repeated to the said Stone without other sattisfaction then to hear him swear in a profaine and wicked maner without provocation that he would kill and Murther your pettetioner or any other person as should disturb his quiett posesion, per which arbitary Unjust demand of tenn pound made per the said Stone, your pettetioner [*torn*] Conceives to have been a design to [Extort] the Ballance of Accounts it being near [*illegible*] due on the Bond forcably taken as per your pettetioners Account will appear, and som time after [*torn*] denyed your pettetioner per advice of som persons of Corrotuck finding the house voyd and dores oppen took possesion of the same, and the said Stone at Wintworths store on hearing therof with often Repeated oaths swore the death of your pettetioner as soon as he should gett to the house and William Bray then In company [with] the said Stone at the afforsaid store came Imediatly on horsback to the house your pettetioner had posesed and the said Stone coming after afoot and the said bray with an ax forced and split open the dore without any precept or warrant for his so doing and seized your pettetioner and turned him out [*torn*] and ordered your pettetioner Instantly away or he would Lay him in Irons on which threat [*torn*] pettetioner went away Leaving him the said Bray at the house, and soon after my departure Phillip Stone came with a great batt or staff an without notice given struck Wm. [*torn*] and Cripled his arme [*torn*] by his own words would [*torn*] done him further damage if his [*torn*] had not broak, after which he run into the house cen[*torn*] or took [*torn*]den gun which your pettetioner while he had possesion of the house had taken the pins out fearing if he forcable Enter[*torn*] might make some Ill [*torn*] and snaped the said gun at the Body of Johanah parker and [finding] him selfe disapoynted [*torn*] his guns firing he beat hur with the Butt end to that [degree] as Confined hur abedd for severall days, and afterward Inquired for your Pettetioner Exspresing [*torn*]ble for his departure swearing he was Resolved to have Killed him if possiable he [*torn*]ld and the next day at [court] did publicquely in a grevious maner beat and by words [abuse] your pettetioner and continues yet to threaten your pettetioner and often publicquely swears he was never so greived as at his not Killing your pettetioner and his guns not firing at the woman and is Commonly observed and Known to walk with a gun or staff, all which has per your pettetioner and seaverall others been complained of to the Shreife whose prisoner he is without any Redress the Shreif Contrary to the order of the Honorable Richd. Sanderson Esquire and for Reason to your pettetioner unknown seems Rather to Indulge then Restreyn his arbitrary abusfull actions, the said Stone doth also affirm that he hath Entred a [cavett] for the Escheat of the Land he now forcably holds, which Land your pettetioner first heild per Right of dower as Marring the Widdow and Relict of Richd. Harris deceased who was the first patentee, and since hath been [per John] bennitt Extended fo[*torn*]t as the only proper Estat of the said Harris In Right of which Extent [*torn*] pettetioner hath also purchased [for] the sume of seaventeen pound as by Receipt will apear, do therfor Humbly move your and beg your Honor would stop the Curr[*torn*] of his unjust proceeding against your pettetioners Land, and also beg he may be [*torn*] Secured and Confined then yett he hath or Reduced to a more [*torn*] civell behaviour as your pettetioner may without fear or danger fo[*torn*] his Lawfull Impliments and your pettetioner as In duty bond shall Ever pray etc.

[*Falconer* v. *Berry*]

[*CCR 148*]

North Carolina ss. To the Provost Marshall or Deputy

These are in the Name of his Excellency the Palatine and the rest of the true and absolute Lords and Proprietors to will and require you to arrest the Body of Edward Berry And him to hold Soe that he make his personall appearance at the next Generall Court to be held for this Province [*torn*] last Tuesday in March next att the House of Captain John Hecklefield in Little River to answer the Complaint of John Falconar in A Plea of the Case And have there this writt Dated the 10th Day of February Anno Domini 1704/5. Take good bond.

Tho. Snoden Clericus Curiae

[*Endorsed:*]
Breve
Falconar versus Berry
This Ritt Executed on berry for falconar by me John foster debettey marshall

[*Falconer, consignee* v. *Lisle*]

[*CCR 192*]

North Carolina ss. To the Honorable Generall Court etc.

John Falconer Consignee of Colonel Robt. Quary and Pensylvania Company is plaintiff against Henry Lisle Defendant in A Plea of the Case and Complaines that the Defendant Stands Justly Indebted unto the plaintiff Qualifyed as aforesaid in the full and Just Summe of Seven pounds Thirteen Shillings and four pence as by wayes and Meanes Convenient the plaintiff is ready to make appear Nevertheless the Defendant refuses payment of the Summe aforesaid To the plaintiffs Dammage Fourteen pounds Sterling

Wherefore the plaintiff hath brought this action and humbly Craves Judgment of this Honorable Court for the aforesaid Debts and Dammages with Costs of Suite And he Shall pray etc.

Copia Tho. Snoden Clericus Curiae

[*Endorsed:*]
Falconar etc. versus Lisle
In Case
Entred 12th Feby.

[*Frayly* v. *Adams*]

[*CCR 191*]

North Carolina ss. To the Honorable Generall Court etc.

William Friley is plaintiff against Matthew Adams Junior Defendant In A Plea of Trover and Conversion and Complaines that the Defendant Detaines and keeps back from the plaintiff one Cow and Calf the proper Estate of the plaintiff And the Same hath Converted to his own proper use and behoofe and refuses to render the Same to the plaintiff tho' thereunto requested wherefore the plaintiff hath brought this action and humbly Craves Judgment of this Honorable Court for the Same with Costs of Suite And he Shall pray etc.

Tho. Snoden Clericus Curiae

[*Endorsed:*]
Friley versus Adams Junior
In Trover and Conversion
Entred the 28th Feby.

[*CCR 148*]

North Carolina ss. To the Provost Marshall or Deputy

These are in the Name of his Excellency the Palatine and the rest of the true and absolute Lords and Proprietors to will and require you to arrest the Body of Matthew Adams Junior And him to hold Soe that he make his personall appearance att the next Generall Court to be held for this Province the last Tuesday in March next att the House of Captain John Hecklefield in Little River to answer the Complaint of William Friley in A Plea of Trover and Conversion And have there this writt Dated the 28th Day of February Anno Domini 1704/5. Take good bond.

Tho. Snoden Clericus Curiae

[*Endorsed:*]
Non inventus

[*Frayly* v. *Berry*]

[*CCR 139*]

North Carolina ss. To the Provost Marshall or Deputy

These are in the Name of his Excellency the Palatine and the rest of the

true and absolute Lords and Proprietors to will and require you to Summons John Hare Samuel Hearst and Elizabeth Oats widdow Severally to make their personal Appearance att the next Generall Court to be held [*torn*] this Province the last Tuesday of this Instant [*torn*] att the House of Captain John Hecklefield in Little River to Give Evidence between William Friley plaintiff and Edward Berry Defendant on behalfe of the Defendant And have there this Summons Dated the 3d Day of March Anno Domini 1704/5.

Tho. Snoden Clericus Curiae

[*Endorsed:*]
This Summons Executed by me John foster debutey marshall

[*Frayly* v. *Laker*]

[*CCR 148*]

North Carolina ss. To the Provost Marshall or Deputy

These are in the Name of his Excellency the Palatine and the rest of the true and absolute Lords and Proprietors to will and require you to arrest the Body of Juliana Lakar and her hold Soe that She make her personall appearance att the next Generall Court to be held for this Province the Last Tuesday in March next att the House of Captain John Hecklefield in Little River to answer the Complaint of William Freyley in A plea of the Case And have there this writt Dated the 10th Day of February Anno Domini 1704/5. Take good bond.

Tho. Snoden Clericus Curiae

[*Endorsed:*]
Breve
Freyley versus Lakar
This Ritt returned by leaveing a Copey of ritt and declaration by me John foster debetey marshll

[*Glover, consignee* v. *Conden*]

[*CCR 192*]

North Carolina ss. To the Honorable Generall Court etc.

Willm. Glover Esqr. Consignee of Colonel Robt. Quary and Pensylvania Company is plaintiff against John Conden Defendant in A Plea of the Case and Complaines that the Defendant Stands Justly Indebted to the plaintiff Qualifyed as aforesaid in the full and Just Summe of four pounds Sixteen Shillings and Nyne pence for Severall Goods Wares and Merchandizes Which aforesaid Summe is payable to the plaintiff in fresh porke as by wayes and Meanes Convenient the plaintiff is ready to make appear Nevertheless the Defendant refuses payment of the aforesaid Summe payable in the Specie aforesaid To the plaintiffs Dammage Eight pounds Sterling Wherefore the plaintiff hath brought this action and Craves Judgment of this Honorable Court for the Same with Costs of Suite And he Shall pray etc.

Tho. Snoden   Clericus Curiae

[*Endorsed:*]
Glover Esqr. etc. versus Conden
In Case
Entred 12 Feby.

[*CCR 148*]

North Carolina ss.   To the Provost Marshall or Deputy

These are in the Name of his Excellency the Palatine and the rest of the true and absolute Lords and Proprietors to will and require you to arrest the Body of John Conden And him to hold Soe that he make his personall appearance att the next Generall Court to be held for this Province the last Tuesday in March next att the House of Captain John Hecklefield in Little River to answer the Complaint of William Glover Esquire Consignee of Colonel Robt. Quary and Pensylvania Company in A Plea of the Case And have there this writt Dated the 12th Day of February Anno Domini 1704/5. Take good bond.

Tho. Snoden   Clericus Curiae

[*Endorsed:*]
Breve
Glover Esquire etc. versus Conden
Excequeted

[*Glover, consignee* v. *Hosea*]

[*CCR 192*]

North Carolina ss.   To the Honorable Generall Court etc.

Willm. Glover Esqr. Consignee of Colonel Robt. Quary and Pensylvania Company is plaintiff versus Robert Hosea Defendant in A Plea of the Case and Complaines that the Defendant Stands Justly Indebted unto the plaintiff Qualifyed as aforesaid in the full and Just Summe of Two pounds Eight Shillings and three pence in fresh porke Which aforesaid Summe the Defendant assumd to pay to the plaintiff for and upon the Account and behalfe of Mary Rooks of this Province Neverthelesse the Defendant his assumption not regarding but minding to Defraud and Deceive the plaintiff of the Summe aforesaid The Same to the plaintiff hath not payd To the plaintiffs Dammage Four pounds Sterling Wherefore the plaintiff hath brought this action and Craves Judgment of this action and Craves Judgment of this Honorable Court for the aforesaid Debt and Dammages with Costs of Suite And he Shall pray etc.

Tho. Snoden   Clericus Curiae

[*Endorsed:*]
Glover Esqr. etc. versus Hosea
Narratio in Case
Entred 12th Feby.

[*Glover, consignee* v. *Leflear*]

[*CCR* 192]

North Carolina ss. To the Honorable Generall Court etc.

Willm. Glover Esqr. Consignee of Colonel Robt. Quarry and Pensilvania Company is plaintiff against Alexander Leflear Defendant in A Plea of the Case and Complaines that the Defendant Stands Justly Indebted to the plaintiff Qualifyed as aforesaid in the full and Just Summe of Four pounds Eleven Shillings and Seven pence for Severall Goods Wares and Merchandizes Which aforesaid Sume this Defendant assum'd to pay to the plaintiff in fresh porke att Such place as the plaintiff Should appoint And the plaintiff in fact Sayth that he the plaintiff hath from time to time appointed the House of John Jennings in Pascotank the Place for paying as aforesaid Neverthelesse the Defendant his assumption not regarding but minding to defraud and deceive the plaintiff [*torn*] as aforesaid of the aforesaid Summe payable in manner aforesaid The Same to the plaintiff Qualifyed as aforesaid hath not payd To the plaintiffs Damage Nyne pounds Sterling Wherefore the plaintiff hath brought this Action and Craves Judgment of this Honorable Court for Same with Costs of Suite And he Shall pray etc.

Tho. Snoden Clericus Curiae

[*Endorsed:*]
Glover Esqr. etc. versus Leflear
Narratio in Case
Entred 12th Feby.

[*Glover, consignee* v. *Lisle*]

[*CCR* 192]

North Carolina ss. To the Honorable Generall Court etc.

Willm. Glover Esqr. Consignee of Colonel Robt. Quary and [*torn*] is plaintiff against Henry Lisle Defendant in A Plea of Debt and Complains [*torn*] Defendant Stands Justly indebted to the plaintiff Qualifyed as [*torn*] full and Just Summe of Thirty Eight pounds three Shillings and [*torn*] Severall Goods Wares and Merchandizes Sold and Deliver'd [*torn*] to the Defendant as by wayes and Meanes Convenient the [*torn*] make appear Neverthelesse the Defendant refuses payment of [*torn*] Wherefore the plaintiff hath brought this action And humbly [*torn*] Judgment of this Honorable Court for the Same with Costs of Suite [*torn*] pray etc.

Tho. Snoden [*torn*]

[*Endorsed:*]
Glover etc. versus Lisle
Narratio in Debt
Entred 12 Feby.

[*CCR* 139]

North Carolina ss. To the Provost Marshall or Deputy

These are in the Name of his Excellency the Palatine and the rest of the true and absolute Lords and Proprietors to will and require you to arrest the Body of Henry Lisle and him to hold Soe that he make his personall appearance att the next Generall Court to be held for this Province the last Tuesday in March next att the House of Captain John Hecklefield in Little River to answer the Complaint of William Glover Esqr. Consignee of Collnell Robt. Quary and Pensylvania Company in A Plea of Debt And have there this writt Dated the 12th Day of February Anno Domini 1704/5. Take good bond.

Tho. Snoden Clericus Curiae

[*Endorsed:*]
Breve
Glover Esqr. etc. versus Lisle

[*Glover, consignee* v. *Neal*]

[*CCR* 192]

North Carolina ss. To the Honorable Generall Court etc.

Willm. Glover Esqr. Consignee of Colonel Robt. Quary and Pensylvania Company is plaintiff against John Neal Defendant in A Plea of the Case and Complaines that the Defendant Stands Justly Indebted unto the plaintiff Qualifyed as aforesaid In the full and Just Summe of Eight pounds Seventeen Shillings and Eleven pence for goods wares Merchandizes and Creditt which aforesaid Summe was Contracted to be payd in fresh Porke Oil Whale bone or Dear Skinns att the Dwelling House of the plaintiff in Little River as by wayes and meanes Convenient the plaintiff is ready to make appear Neverthelesse the Defendant the aforesaid Summe payable in maner and Specie aforesaid hath not payd to the plaintiffs Dammage Sixteen pounds Sterling Wherefore the plaintiff hath brought this action and Craves Judgment of this Honorable Court for the aforesaid Debt and Dammages with Costs of Suite And he Shall pray etc.

Tho. Snoden Clericus Curiae

[*Endorsed:*]
Glover etc. versus Neal
In Case
Entred 12th Feby.

[*Glover, consignee* v. *Sawyer*]

[*CCR* 192]

North Carolina ss. To the Honorable Generall Court etc.

William Glover Esqr. Consignee of Colonel Robt. Quary and Pensylvania Company is plaintiff against John Sawyer Defendant in A Plea of the Case and Complaines that the Defendant Stands Justly Indebted unto the plaintiff

Qualifyed as aforesaid in the full and Just Summe of Thirteen pounds Seventeen Shillings and Eight pence farthing for Goods Creditt and Merchandizes which aforesaid Sume the Defendant assum'd to pay to the plaintiff in fresh porke att Such place as the plaintiff Should appoint And the plaintiff in fact Sayth That he the plaintiff hath from time to time appointed the House of John Jennings in Pascotank the place for payment as aforesaid Neverthelesse the Defendant his assumption not regarding but minding to defraud and deceive the plaintiff Qualifyed as aforesaid of the aforesaid Summe payable in manner aforesaid The Same to the plaintiff Qualifyed as aforesaid hath not payd To the plaintiffs Dammage Twenty Eight pounds Sterling Wherefore the plaintiff hath brought this action and Craves Judgment of this Honorable Court for the aforesaid Debt and Damages with Costs of Suite And he Shall pray etc.

Tho. Snoden Clericus Curiae

[*Endorsed:*]
Glover etc. versus John Sawyer
Narratio in Case
Entred 12th Feby.

[*CCR 192*]

North Carolina ss. To the Provost Marshall or Deputy

These are in the Name of his Excellency the Palatine and the rest of the true and absolute Lords and Proprietors to will and require you to arrest the Body of John Sawyer And him to hold Soe that he make his personall appearance att the next Generall Court to be held for this Province the last Tuesday in March next att the House of Captain John Hecklefield in Little River to answer the Complaint of William Glover Esqr. Consignee of Colonel Robt. Quary and Pensylvania Company in A Plea of the Case And have there this Writt Dated the 12th Day of February Anno Domini 1704/5.

Take good bond. Tho. Snoden Clericus Curiae
[*Endorsed:*]
Breve
Glover Esqr. etc. versus John Sawyer

[*Glover, consignee* v. *Sawyer*]

[*CCR 191*]

North Carolina ss. To the Honorable Generall Court etc.

Willm. Glover Esqr. Consignee of Colonel Robt. Quary and Pensylvania Company is plaintiff against Willm. Sawyer Defendant in A Plea of the Case and Complaines that the Defendant Stands Justly Indebted unto the plaintiff Qualifyed as aforesaid in the full and Just Summe of Twenty one pounds Sixteen Shillings and Eleven pence for Severall Goods Creditt and Merchandize Which aforesaid Summe the Defendant assum'd to pay to the plaintiff in fresh porke att Such place as the plaintiff Should appoint And the plaintiff in fact Sayth That he the plaintiff hath from time to time appointed the House of John Jennings in Pascotank the place for payment as aforesaid Nevertheless the Defendant his Assumption not regarding but minding to defraud the plaintiff Qualifyed as aforesaid of the aforesaid Summe payable in manner aforesaid The Same to the plaintiff Qualifyed as aforesaid hath not payd To the plaintiffs Dammage Forty pounds Sterling wherefore the plaintiff hath brought this action and Craves Judgment of this Honorable Court for the aforesaid Debt and Dammages with Costs of Suite And he Shall pray etc.

Tho. Snoden Clericus Curiae

[*Endorsed:*]
Glover etc. versus Wm. Sawyer
Narratio in Case
Entred 12th Feby.

[*Godfrey* v. *Browne*]

[*CCR 191*]

The Humble Petition of Peter Godfrey Sheweth That whereas one Jno. Browne late of the precinct of passpotanke did on or about sometime in the month of Xber last past clandestinely depart this Country and Stood at the Same time Indted unto your hounors petitioner the full and Just Summe of tenne pounds fifteene shillings and three pence halfe penny and the Said Browne haveing Sundry debts due in this Country yor hounors petitioner haveing caused Sundry Attachments to be issued out prayes An order for the Said debt and Cost and your petitioner Shall as in duty bound pray.

[*Godfrey* v. *Cretchington*]

[*CCR 191*]

North Carolina ss. To the Honorable Generall Court etc.

Peter Godfrey of the Province aforesaid merchant is plaintiff against Saml. Cretchington of the Same planter Defendant in A plea of the Case and Complaines that the Defendant Stands Justly indebted to the plaintiff in the full and Just Summe of four pounds [*illegible*] Shillings and three pence half peny parte hereof payable to the [*torn*] in good Sound Merchantable Porke and the remainder [*torn*] Shoes att 4*s*. per pair att the now dwelling house of the plaintiff which aforesaid Summe payable as aforesaid the Defendant refuses to pay To the plaintiffs Dammage Eight pounds Sterling Wherefore the plaintiff hath brought this action And humbly Craves Judgment of this Honorable Court for this Debt and Damages with Costs of Suite And he Shall pray etc.

Tho. Snoden Clericus Curiae

[*Endorsed:*]
Godfrey versus Cretchington
Entred 12th Jany. 1704/5

[*Hecklefield* v. *Pettiver*]

[*CCR 148*]

North Carolina ss. To the Honorable Generall Court etc.

Captain John Hecklefield is plaintiff against John Pettiver Defendant in A Plea of the Case and Complaines that the Defendant Stands Justly Indebted unto the plaintiff in the full and Just Summe of Fifteen pounds Sixteen Shillings and Three pence halfpeny as by wayes and meanes Convenient the plaintiff is ready to make appear Nevertheless the Defendant refuses payment of the aforesaid Summe tho' by the plaintiff thereunto requested To the plaintiffs Dammage Thirty pounds Sterling Wherefore the plaintiff hath brought this action and humbly Craves Judgment of this Honorable Court for the aforesaid Debt and Dammages with Costs of Suite And he Shall pray etc.

Tho. Snoden Clericus Curiae

[*Endorsed:*]
Hecklefield versus Pettiver
In Case
Entred 28th Feby. 1704/5

[*CCR 190*]

Mr. Pettiver is Dr. March 1704

	£ s. d.
Aprill the 24th	
To Expenses	01:02:00
To one Gallon Molesses	00:04:00
To 7 barrells of corn	02:18:04
July 19th and 20th	
To Expenses	00:11:09
25 to Do. at Court	03:12:10½
To pd. Mr. Swann	00:15:00
Augt. the 13	
To Expenses	00:07:04½
To Arresting Mr. Falconer etc.	00:07:06
To Do. Garrett Purcell	00:07:06
To 123 daies maintenance of his servant, as per order of Court sent to me at 12*d.* per day as by act of Assembly allowd to the Marshall	06:03:00
	16:09:04

Errors Excepted per John Hecklefield

[*Endorsed:*]
Wee of the Jury find that [*illegible*] is Due to the plaintiff £14=19*s.*=4*d.*
With Cost

[*Keele* v. *Phillips*]

[*CCR 148*]

North Carolina ss. To the Honorable Generall Court etc.

Robert Keel is plaintiff against Daniel Phillips Defendant In A Plea of Debt and Setteth forth and Declares that the Defendant to witt on the Last Day of August In the year of our Lord 1702 for A Consideration [*torn*]ed of the plaintiff became bound to the plaintiff in the Summe of [*torn*]ty pounds Current pay of this Country Conditionally that [*torn*] Defendant Should proceed in Law and use Such meanes as by Law is required to the best of his Endeavour for the recovering of A Tract of Land remaining In A Pattent Exprest and [*torn*] [would] in A Certaine writing Obligatory Signd Seald and Delivered by the Defendant to the plaintiff And ready to be produced in Court As by the said writing Obligatory and the Condition thereunder Indors'd relation being thereunto had doth and may more fully appear Neverthelesse the Defendant hath not performed the Condition aforesaid whereby the plaintiff Sayth that the aforesaid Fifty pounds is Justly Due and owing from the Defendant to the plaintiff for which he hath brought this action And humbly Craves Judgment of this Honorable Court for the Same with Costs of Suite And he Shall pray etc.

Tho. Snoden Clericus Curiae

[*Endorsed:*]
[*Torn*] versus Phillips
In Debt
February 25 1704/5
Retraxit

[*Norton, assignee* v. *Low, attorney of Low*]

[*CCR 148*]

North Carolina ss. To the Honorable Generall Court etc.

Saml. Norton Gentleman assignee of Captain John Hecklefield is plaintiff against Anne Low attorney of Emanuel Low Defendant in a Plea of Debt and Complaines That the Defendant Qualifyed as aforesaid Stands Justly indebted unto the plaintiff Qualifyed as aforesaid in the full and Just Summe of Three pounds as by wayes and meanes Convenient the plaintiff is ready to make Neverthelesse the Defendant Qualifyed as aforesaid refuses payment of the aforesaid Summe to the plaintiff Qualifyed as aforesaid To the plaintiff's Dammage Six pounds Sterling Wherefore the plaintiff hath brought this action And humbly Craves Judgment of this Honorable Court for the aforesaid Debt and Damages with Costs of Suite And he Shall pray etc.

Tho. Snoden Clericus Curiae

[*Endorsed:*]
Norton etc. versus Low etc.
Entred 26th Februy. 1704/5

[*Norton, assignee* v. *Low, attorney of Low*]

[*CCR 148*]

North Carolina ss. To the Honorable Generall Court etc.

Saml. Norton Gentleman assignee of Jacob Litten is plaintiff against Anne Low Attorney of Emanuel Low in A Plea of Debt and Complaines That the Defendant Qualifyed as aforesaid Stands Justly indebted unto the plaintiff in the full and Just Summe of Tenne pounds Fifteen Shillings as by wayes and meanes Convenient the plaintiff is ready to make appear Neverthelesse the Defendant Qualifyed as aforesaid refuses to pay to the plaintiff Qualifyed as aforesaid the aforesaid Summe To the plaintiffs Dammage Twenty pounds Sterling wherefore the plaintiff hath brought this action and humbly Craves Judgment of this Honorable Court for the aforesaid Debt and Dammages with Costs of Suite And he Shall pray etc.

Tho. Snoden Clericus Curiae

[*Endorsed:*]
Norton etc. versus Low etc.
Narratio in Debt
Entred 26th Feby. 1704/5

[*Paine* v. *Pierce*]

[*CCR 140*]

North Carolina ss. To the Honorable Generall Court etc.

Saml. Payne is plaintiff against John Pierce Defendant in A plea of the Case and Setteth forth and Declares that the Defendant Stands Justly Indebted to the plaintiff in the full and Just Sume of Seven pounds four Shillings and two pence as by wayes and meanes Convenient the plaintiff is ready to make appear and refuses payment whereby the plaintiff Sayth [*torn*] is Dampnifyed Fourteen pounds Sterling for which he hath brought this action and humbly Craves Judgment of this Honorable Court for the Same with Costs of Suite And he Shall pray etc.

Tho. Snoden Clericus Curiae

[*Endorsed:*]
Payne versus Pierce
In Case
Narratio
Entred 3d October

[*Pensylvania Company* v. *Falconer*]

[*CCR 192*]

North Carolina ss. To the Honorable Generall Court

Pensylvania Company are plaintiffs against John Falconar Defendant In A

Plea of the Case and Complain and Declare that the Defendant Stands Justly Indebted to the plaintiffs in the full and just Summe of Two Hundred Thirty Seven pounds Eight Shillings and Eleven pence as by wayes and meanes Convenient the plaintiffs are ready to make appear Nevertheless the Defendant refuses payment of the Summe aforesaid wherefore the plaintiffs have brought this action And humbly Crave Judgment of this Honorable Court for the Same with Costs of Suite And they Shall pray etc.

Tho. Snoden Clericus Curiae

[*Endorsed:*]
Pen. Company versus Falconar
In Case
Entred Jany. 18th 1704/5

[*CCR 192*]

North Carolina ss. To the Provost Marshall or Deputy

These are in the Name of his Excellency the Palatine and the rest of the true and absolute Lords and Proprietors to will and require you to arrest the Body of John Falconar and him to hold Soe that he make his personall appearance att the next Generall Court to be held for this province the last Tuesday in March next att the House of Captain John Hecklefield in Little River to answer the Complaint of Pensylvania Company in A Plea of the Case And have there this writt Dated the 18th Day of January Anno Domini 1704/5. Take good Bond.

Tho. Snoden Clericus Curiae

[*Endorsed:*]
Breve
Pensylva. Company versus Falconar
In Case
To Jno. Foster to Execute per order of John Hecklefield Provost Marshall
Not Executed by a not from Capt. hackellfield by me John foster debetty marshall

[*CCR 192*]

1704

John Falconar to Micajah Perry and New Pensylvania Company:
Account Current

Dr.

1699	To Sundry goods sold	£ 4:04:08
1700	To do.	£362:19:00½
	To do.	£207:14:10½
1701	To do.	£ 15:14:01
	To nt. proceed of Rum sold	£ 31:12:06

To nt. proceed of mallosses sold	£ 5:14:00
To nt. proceed of Sugar sold	£ 2:10:00
To 1 pr. of hand screws	£ 2:00:00
To a great Cannoe sold Richd. Davenport	£ 22:00:00
To Colonel Robert Quarry account	£ 88:10:06
	£742:19:08

Cr.

Per Sundry returns mades as per Invoyce	£177:17:02
Per Sundry disbursments on Sloop Roanoke	£ 3:11:08
Per do. on the Sloop Tryall	£ 14:07:06
Per Proffitt and Sale	£ 18:13:06
Per 600 pounds of tobacco delivered to Wm. Glover	£ 3:00:00
Per Sundry charges as per account	£163:14:06
Per do. charg'd in Storedge	£ 9:07:00
Per Sundry debts assign'd Nicholas Tyler	£120:05:05
Per A list of debts delivered to Josiah Rolfe	£232:02:11
	£742:19:08

Apll. 4th 1704

This day made up the above account with John Falconar and doe hereby acknowledge to have received full Satisfaction of the above account (provided that the said Falconar doth prove that the list of debts above mention'd deliver'd to Josiah Rolfe be the true and proper debts of the said Perry and Company and at this time due) being in full of all accounts and demands to this day between the said Falconar and Micajah Perry and New Pensylvania Company.

per me Jos. Rolfe Attorney for said Company

[*Endorsed:*]
A [*illegible*] From the Pensylvania Company per Mr. Jos. Rolfe attorney

[*Pensylvania Company* v. *Houghton*]

[*CCR* 192]

North Carolina ss. To the Honorable Generall Court

Pensylvania Company are plaintiffs against Thomas Houghton Defendant In A Plea of Debt and Complain and Declare that the Defendant Stands Justly indebted to the plaintiffs in the full and Just Summe of Tenne pounds one Shilling and Three pence as by A Bond from under the Defendants hand bearing Date the 9th Day of January 1702/3 and ready to be produc'd in Court relation being thereunto had doth and may more fully appear Neverthelesse the Defendant refuses payment of the Summe aforesaid Wherefore the plaintiffs have brought this action and humbly Crave Judgment of this Honorable Court for the Same with Costs of Suite And they Shall pray etc.

Tho. Snoden Clericus Curiae

[*Endorsed:*]
Pensylva. Company versus Houghton
Narratio in Debt
Entred 18th Jany. 1704/5
Judgment Confest

[*Pettiver* v. *Davis*]

[*CCR 148*]

North Carolina ss. To the Honorable Generall Court etc.

John Pettiver is plaintiff against Willm. Davis Defendant in A Plea of Debt and Complaines and Declares That by A writing obligatory from under the Defendant's hand bearing Date the Twelfth Day of October in the year of our Lord God 1702 ready to be produced in Court he the Defendant Stands Justly indebted to the plaintiff in the full and Just Sume of Six pounds Nyne Shillings and Eight pence Sterling payable to the plaintiff upon Demand as by the said writing obligatory relation being thereunto had doth and may more fully appear And the plaintiff in fact Sayth that the Defendant the aforesaid Summe hath not payd but the Same to pay doth altogether refuse To the plaintiff's Dammage Twelve pounds Sterling Wherefore the plaintiff hath brought this action And humbly prayes Judgment of this Honorable Court for the aforesaid Debt and Dammages with Costs of Suite And he Shall pray etc.

Tho. Snoden Clericus Curiae

[*Endorsed:*]
Pettiver versus Davis
Narratio Debt Sur obligatory
Entred 20th Jany. 1704/5
Judgment Confest

[*Porter* v. *Truewhitt and Dereham*]

[*CCR 148*]

North Carolina Ss. To the provost Marshall or his Deputy

These are in her Matyes name to will and require you to Arrest the bodys of Levy Trewhitt and Thos. Dereham and them Safely hold Soe that they may be and appeare at the next Generall Court to be holden at the house of Captain John Hecklefield in Little river on the last Tuesday in March next then and there to Answer the plaint of John Porter Esqr. in a plea of Debt and have there this writt Dated at the Secretarys Office this 24th day of January Anno Domini 1704.

Testis T. Knight Secretary

[*Endorsed:*]
Breve
Porter versus Trewhitt and Dereham
Executed per me Edward pitts Deputy marshall

[*Smith* v. *Swann*]

[*CCR 148*]

North Carolina ss. To the Honorable Generall Court etc.

Richd. Smith is plaintiff against William Swann Defendant in A Plea of Debt and Complaines That the Defendant Stands Justly Indebted unto the plaintiff in the full and Just Summe of Five and Twenty pounds payable to the plaintiff in Albemarle County in Country Commodityes or Creditt to liking as by A writing obligatory from under the Defendants hand bearing Date the 4th Day of September 1703 and ready to be produc'd in Court relation being thereunto had doth and may more fully and att Large appear Neverthelesse the Defendant refuses payment of the aforesaid Summe according to the Tennor of the aforesaid writing obligatory To the plaintiffs Dammage Fifty pounds Sterling wherefore the plaintiff hath brought this action and humbly Craves Judgment of this Honorable Court for the Same with Costs of Suite And he Shall pray etc.

Tho. Snoden Clericus Curiae

[*Endorsed:*]
Smith versus Swann
In Debt
Entred 28th [*illegible*] 1704/5
Wee of the Jury Find For the Defendant

[*CCR 148*]

North Carolina ss. To the Provost Marshall or Deputy

These are in the Name of his Excellency the Palatine and the rest of the true and absolute Lords and Proprietors to will and require you to Summons Joseph Wicker Samuel Slade and Richard Thorpe Severally to make their personall appearance att the next Generall Court to be held for this Province the last Tuesday in March next att the House of Captain John Hecklefield in Little River to give Evidence between Richard Smith plaintiff and William Swann Defendant in A Plea of Debt on behalfe of the plaintiff And have there this Summons Dated the 28th Day of February Anno Domini 1704/5.

Tho. Snoden Clericus Curiae

[*Stone* v. *Evans*]

[*CCR 148*]

North Carolina ss. To the Honorable Generall Court etc.

Philip Stone is plaintiff against John Evans Defendant in A Plea of the Case upon Defamation and Complaines that whereas the plaintiff hath alwaies been of good fame and Creditt both in Virginia as elsewhere the plaintiff hath lived and never was esteemed Conscious of Felony or Robery but hath alwayes honestly behaved himselfe towards his Neighbors and all her Majesties Liege people with whom he hath had Comerce or Conversation which the Defendant well knowing but Envying the happy Condition of the plaintiff on or about the 31th Day of October last past att the House of Captain John Hecklefield within this Province before the Honorable Robt. Daniel Esquire Deputy Governor of the province aforesaid and Severall others of her Majesties Liege people did utter and Declare these false Malitious and Scandalous Words of and concerning the plaintiff videlicet Phillip Stone meaning the plaintiff robbed me meaning the Defendant of A Bill of Eighteen pounds payable from the said Stone meaning the plaintiff to me meaning the Defendant By meanes of which false malitious and Scandalous Words the plaintiff was immediately taken in to Custody and not only in Danger of losing his good Name reputation and Estate but alsoe of his life as by A Statute in Such Cases is made and Provided wherefore the plaintiff Saith he is Dampnifyed Two Hundred pounds Sterling whereupon he hath brought this action and humbly Craves Judgment of this Honorable Court for the Same with Costs of Suite And he Shall pray etc.

Tho. Snoden Clericus Curiae

[*Endorsed:*]
Stone versus Evans
In Defamation
Entred the [*blank*] Day Feby. 1704/5
Wee of the Jury find for the Defendant

[*CCR 148*]

North Carolina ss. To the Provost Marshall [*torn*]

These are in the Name of his Excellency the [Palatine] and the rest of the true and absolute Lords and Proprietors to will and require you to arrest the Body of John Evans and him to hold Soe that he make his personall appearance att the next Generall Court to be held for this Province the last Tuesday in March next att the House of Captain John Hecklefield in Little River to Answer the Complaint of Phillip Stone in A Plea of the Case upon Defamation And have there this writt Dated the 10th Day of February Anno Domini 1704/5.

Tho. Snoden Clericus Curiae

[*Endorsed:*]
Stone versus Evans
Breve
Executed

GENERAL COURT, MARCH 1705

[*Truewhitt* v. *Watson*]

[*CCR 148*]

North Carolina ss. To the Honorable Generall Court

Levi Truewhitt is plaintiff against John Watson Defendant in A plea of Debt and Complaines that the Defendant Stands Justly indebted unto the plaintiff in the full and Just Summe of Seven pounds payable to the plaintiff part in work and the other part in Country Comodityes As by A writing obligatory from under the Defendants hand ready to be produc'd in Court relation being thereunto had doth and may more fully and att Large appear Neverthelesse the Defendant refuses payment of the aforesaid Summe according to the Tennor of the aforesaid writing obligatory To the plaintiffs Dammage Fourteen pounds Sterling wherefore the plaintiff hath brought this action and humbly Craves Judgment of this Honorable Court for the aforesaid Debt and Dammages with Costs of Suite And he Shall pray etc.

Tho. Snoden Clericus Curiae

[*Endorsed:*]
Truewhitt versus Watson
In Debt Sur obligatory
Entred 25th Feby. 1704/5

[*CCR 148*]

North Carolina ss. To the Provost Marshall or Deputy

These are in the Name of his Excellency the Palatine and the rest of the true and absolute Lords and Proprietors to will and require you to arrest the Body of John Watson And him to hold Soe that he make his personall appearance att the next Generall Court to be held for this Province the last Tuesday in March next att the House of Captain John Hecklefield in Little River to answer the Complaint of Levi Truewhitt in A Plea of debt And have there this writt Dated the 26th Day of February Anno Domini 1704/5. Take good bond.

Tho. Snoden Clericus Curiae

[*Endorsed:*]
Non inventus

[*Wilkison* v. *Barrow*]

[*CCR 148*]

North Carolina ss. To the Honorable Generall Court etc.

Colonel Willm. Wilkison is plaintiff against Captain Willm. Barrow Defendant in A Plea of the Case and Complaines and Declares That the Defendant Stands Justly Indebted to the plaintiff in the full and Just Summe of Three pounds Eighteen Shillings and Eleven pence payable to the plaintiff in Drest Buckskins and Doeskins as per Act of Assembly which the plaintiff is ready to make appear Neverthelesse the Defendant refuses payment of the Summe aforesaid payable to the plaintiff in manner as is aforesaid To the plaintiffs Damage Six pounds Sterling wherefore the plaintiff hath brought this action And humbly Craves Judgment of this Honorable Court for the Same with Costs of suite And he Shall pray etc.

Tho. Snoden Clericus Curiae

[*Endorsed:*]
Wilkison versus Barrow
Narratio in Case
Entred Jany. 15th 1704/5
Dismist

[*Wilkison* v. *Brice*]

[*CCR 191*]

North Carolina ss. To the Honorable Generall Court etc.

Willm. Wilkison is plaintiff against Willm. Brice Defendant In A plea upon the Case and Setteth forth and Declares That the Defendant Stands Justly Indebted to the plaintiff in the full and Just Summe of Two pounds Thirteen Shillings and five pence payable to the plaintiff in Pork and Seven Large Drest Doe Skinns as by wayes and Meanes Convenient the plaintiff is ready to make appear All which to pay the Defendant refuses whereby the plaintiff Sayth he is Dampnifyed Six pounds Sterling wherefore he hath brought this action and humbly Craves Judgment of this Honorable Court for the Same with Costs of Suite And he Shall pray etc.

Tho. Snoden Clericus Curiae

[*Endorsed:*]
Wilkison versus Brice
In Case
Entred the 10 8ber

MISCELLANEOUS FILE PAPERS

[*Evans, John, indenture*]

[*CCR 187*]

This Indenture Made This 8th Day of Janry. Anno Domini 1704/5 and in the Third year of the Reign of our Soveraign Lady Ann of England Scotland france and Ireland Queen etc. Between John Evans of the precinct of Corahtuck in the County of Albemarle and in the province of North Carrolina (the Lawfull attorney of Mary Harress) of the one Parte and William Parker of the precinct County and province aforesaid of the other parte Wittnesseth That the Said John Evans for the Consideration of Seventeen Pounds Sterling money of England in hand Paid unto him the Said John Evans by the Said William Parker at and before the Ensealing and Delivery of these presents, the receipt where of he the Said John Evans Doth hereby acknowledge and there of and of Every part and percell there of Doth hereby also Clearly acqit and discharg the Said William Parker his Heirs and Assigns: and for Divers other good Causses and Considerations him the Said John Evans there unto Moving, hath Demised, granted, bargained, and to farme letten, and by these presents hath bargained and Sould unto the Said William Parker his Executors Administrators and Assignes one Plantation and Tract of Land Containing Two Hundred and Sixty Eight Acers Situate Lying and being in the precinct County and province afore Said To Have And To Hold the Said Two hundred Sixty and Eight Acers with Houses out houses Wood and under Woods Water and Water Courses with the pastures Orchards fruit Tres Nusseriary gardens, with all the Comodyties Hereditaments and Appurtenances there unto belonging or in any waies appurtaining Unto him the Said William Parker his Executors Administrators and assignes from the Day of the Date hereof untel the full End and terme of ninty nine yeares from thence next Ensuing and fully to be Computed Compleat and Ended yeilding and paying therefore yearly and Every year During the Said Term, unto the Said John Evans his Heirs Executors Administrators or assignes one tenth Day of April one Capen if it be Lawfully Demanded and it is here by Concluded and agreed by and between the Said parties to these presents and the Said John Evans doth for Himselfe his Heirs Executors Administrators and assignes Covenant, Promise and agree To and with the Said William Parker his Executors Administrators and Assigns that it Shall and may be Lawfull to and for the Said William Parker his Heirs Executors Administrators and Assigns, quietly and peaceable to have hold occupy, possess and Enjoy all and Singuler the Said Two Hundred Sixty and Eight Acers (which Said Land is bounded by and with A Ligne of Marked trees one Each Side and Joyning to Richard Cominforts Land) with the premisses, with their and Every of their Appurtenances from time to time and at all times hereafter During the Said Term without the Lawfull let and interruption of him the Said John Evans his Heirs Executors Administrators or Assigns or of Any other person or persons whatsoever, Lawfully claiming from by or under them or Either of them and also freed and Discharged of and from all and all manner of former Bargains, Sales Gifts Grants Judgment Executions and other Charges of incumbrances Whatsoever, had, made, done or Suffered by them, or Either of them provided alwayes and it is nevertheless agreed and Concluded by and between the Parties aforesaid to these presents, and it is the true Entent and meaning thereof, that if the Said John Evans his Heirs Executors or administrators Shall Well and Truly pay or Cause to be paid Unto the Said William Parker his Executors Administrators and Assigns the full and Entire Sum of Seventeen pound Good and Lawfull Money of England at or before the tenth Day of June next Ensuing the Date of these presents and the Same to be Delivered at the Said William Parkers Dweling house in the precinct County and province afore Said That then this present Indenture, Demise, and Grant, and Every Clause and Article therein Contained, Shall cease, Determine, be voyd, and of none Efect; any thing in these presents Contained to the Contrary therof, in any wise notwithstanding other wise to Remaine in full forse power and vertue in Witness Where of I have hereunto Set my hand and fixt my Seale the Day and year first above written.

Signed Seald and Delivered
In the presents of
Richd. Sanderson
Edwd. Tuyler
Thomas Taylor

The mark of John Evans

[*Endorsed:*]
Acknowledged in Court the 27th Day of March 1705 and Orderd to be recorded Tho. Snoden Clericus Curiae

[*Piner, Edward, et al., summons*]

[*CCR 148*]

This is to will and Requierer you Mr. Willm. [brea] to sommans in her maggist nem Edward piner Jams Crose Andrew Consall to make ther porsene-bell appearens at the neaxt generall Courtt faill nott as you shall answer to the Contrary This: 14: in her maggist behalf This 15 day of March 1704/5.

To Mr. William brea
Sop shirie to Exsequet and
macke Retourn

Richard Sanderson

[*Endorsed:*]
March the 17 1704/5 by uarty of a [comiean] dyrected Same by Colonel Jon hacelfield Theare impower you John Wallis to Execut this Sapene one the with in menshoned parsons faill not as you will anser the Contrary given under my hand Wm. Bray

[*Walker, Ann, letter of attorney*]

[*CR 24.901.1*]

Know All Men by these presents that I Ann Walker widow and Executrix of the Honorable Henderson Walker Esqr. deceased have made ordained, and deputed, and In my Stead and place by these presents Constituted my Loveing Brother Samuel Swann of the precinct of Pequimins my true and Lawfull attorney for me and In my Name, and to my use and behoofe to Aske, Demand, Recover, and Recieve all and all manner and Singular Debts, duties, Summ and Sums of money porke or Corne or any other Commodities, goods, wares, or Merchandize, as are or Shall be due or oweing unto me the Said Ann Walker In Quality aforsaid or any otherwise from any person or persons whatsoever Inhabiting In the province of North Carolina, giving and by these presents granting unto my Said Atturney full power and Authority for me and In my Name qualified as aforsaid, or any otherwise, and to my onely use and behoofe, to Sue, Arrest, Implead, and prosecute to Judgment and Imprison any of my debtors aforsaid and at his pleasure Such person or persons out of prison to deliver, and upon Reciept of any Summ or Summs of Money Porke, Corne, or other Commodities, goods, wares, or merchandize to my use to be Recieved of any of the persons aforsaid acquittance or acquittances, or other Lawfull discharge or discharges for the Same for me and In my Name to give, and also for me and In my Name to Appeare, answer and Defend In any Court of this province, In any Cause, Action, Suite or debate whatsoever that Shall or may be brought against me In quality aforsaid or any otherwise by any person or persons whatsoever and all and Every other thing and things which Shall be needfull to be donn the Same to doe as fully to all Intents and purposes as I myselfe might do if I were there personally present holding for firme and Stable whatsoever my Said Atturney Shall Lawfully do or Cause to be donn by these presents Sealed with my Seale dated at Pequimins In North Carolina the 21th day of October 1704.

Sign'd Seal'd and Delivred and the word Walker interlin'd before Seald in the presence of
Tho. Snoden
Robert Fendall

Ann Walker her marke

[*Endorsed:*]
Madam Walkers Letter of Atturney to: S: S:
A Power of Attorney from Madam Anne Walker to the Honorable Saml. Swann Esqr. provd in Court and Orderd to be recorded March the 27th 1705.

Tho. Snoden Clericus Curiae

Recorded the 5th of Aprill 1705 by Tho. Snoden Clericus Curiae

[*Justices' commission*]

[*CCR 192*]

North Carolina Ss. The Honorable Thomas Cary Esqr. Lieutenant Generall Vice Admirall and Deputy Governor And the rest of our trusty and well beloved Councellors of State Greeting

To our trusty and well beloved William Glover John Porter Christopher Gale William Collins John Blount Hugh Campbell Esqrs.

Wee being well assured of your Prudence Loyalty and Integrity doe hereby Comissionate and appoint you Jointly and Severally dureing our pleasure Justices for this Government of North Carolina to Keep or Cause to be Kept her Majesties peace as also all Lawes and ordinances made for the well Government of this Province and wee doe hereby authorize and Impower you or any three of you (whereof wee will that one of you Willm. Glover John Porter or Christopher Gale Shall be one) to hold a Generall Court for this Government at the times hereafter Expressed that is to Say Last Tusday in the Monthes of July October and March And the Same to adjourne from time and from place to place as you or any three of you (where of wee will that one of you Wm. Glover Jno. Porter and Christopher Gale Esqrs. Shall be one) shall thinke meet And in the Said Court to hold pleas heare and determine all and all manner of Actions Suites and Causes whatsoever as well Criminall as Civill reale mixt personall or any other Kind or Nature whatsoever And in all Such Causes to award Judgement and to Issue out all Such writts and processe as to the due administration of Justice doe belong In all things proceeding according to the Lawes and ordinances of this Government and as neare as Conveniently may be to the Lawes and Customes of England and for as much as by reason of the dificulty of passages and Extremity of weather itt may happen that three or more of you Cannot appeare at the tyme above Expresst wee doe hereby further authorize and Impower you or any of you in Such Case being present to adjourne the Court for any tyme not Exceeding tenn dayes unto the Same place and wee doe hereby Comand the provost Marshall to Cause to Come before you at the Tymes Exprest above or any other tymes by you appointed soe many good and Lawfull men of this Government as shall be necessary for the tryall of Such Causes as shall be brought before you.

Given under our hands and Seale of the Collony the thirty first day of March in the fourth yeare of the Raigne of our Soveraigne Lady Anne Queen of England etc. Anno Domini 1705.

[*Signed:*]
Thomas Cary, Samuel Swann, John Arderne, Rich. Sanderson, [*torn*]

[*CCR 189*]

Docquett of Actions to July Court 1705

Referrences etc. from March Court 1705 to July Court following

1. Freyley versus Brice in Debt. Referred.
2. Hecklefeild versus Pettiver Executor per 14:19:4.
3. Godfrey versus White Attorney.
4. Pettiver versus Davis Executor per 6:9:8. Non est Inventus.
5. Peterson Consignee etc. versus Duckenfeild.
6. Freyley versus Long Attorney. Returned Executed. Satisfaction made.
7. Glover versus Neale Attorney. Satisfaction Made.
8. Freyley versus Laker Attorney. Executed. Satisfaction made.
9. Swann widdow versus Fewox Executor. Satisfaction made.

Writts and returnes to July Court 1705

10. Freyley versus Johnson in Case. Executed.
11. Bray Attorney etc. versus Burtenshall in Debt. Executed. Satisfaction made.

12. Albertson versus Norton in Debt.

13. West Guardian etc. versus Pison. Trespass Super Casu. Executed.

14. Wilkinson versus Olliver in Case. Executed.

15. Colonel Daniell versus Norton in Debt. Returned.

16. Penrice versus Norton in Case. Returned.

17. Wilson Attorney etc. versus White in Debt. Non est Inventus.

18. Stone versus Evans in Case. Executed.

19. Tooks versus Holmes in Debt.

20. Low versus Reed in Case.

21. Jordan versus Reed in Debt. Discontinued.

22. Glover Esqr. Consignee etc. versus Banks in Case. Not Executed.

23. Idem versus Pritchard Executor etc. in Case. Executed.

24. Idem versus Cooper in Case. Not Executed.

25. Idem versus French in Case. Executed.

26. Idem versus Freyley in Case. Executed.

27. Idem versus Fewox in Case. Executed.

28. Idem versus Flowers in Case. Executed.

29. Idem versus Grey in Case. Executed.

30. Idem versus Harris in Case. Executed.

31. Idem versus Hall in Case. Executed.

32. Idem versus Hartly in Case. Executed.

33. Idem versus Jennett in Case. Executed. Returned.

34. Idem versus Johnson in Case. Executed. Returned.

35. Idem versus Lang in Case. Executed.

36. Idem versus Luerton in Case. Executed.

37. Idem versus Luffman in Case. Executed.

38. Idem versus Nash in Case.

39. Idem versus Newby in Case. Executed.

40. Idem versus Phillipp et viz. in Case. Executed.

41. Idem versus Pritchard in Case. Executed.

42. Idem versus Simson in Case. Executed.
43. Idem versus Twiddy in Case. Executed.
44. Idem versus Phelps in Case. Executed.
45. Spruell versus Phelps in Case. Executed.
46. Houghton versus Clarke in Case. Executed.
47. Lile versus Chevin Case.
48. Stone versus Floyd in Debt. Executed. Judgment Confessed.
49. Idem versus eundem in Case. Executed.
50. Idem versus Parker in Case. Executed.
51. Boyd Attorney etc. versus Anderson in Debt.
52. Knight versus Scarbrough in Case. Executed.

[*Endorsed:*]
Dockett to July Court
1705

[*CCR 104*]

<314> Att a Generall Court Held at the House of Capt. Jno. Hecklefeild in Little River on Tuseday the 31st day of July Anno Domini 1705. Present the Honorable William Glover, John Porter, John Blount Esquires Justices.

This Court Adjourned till to Morrow Morneing Eight of Clock.

Wednesday Morneing 8 of Clock this Court Meets present ut supra.

The Comission of the peace was read and the abovesaid Justices severally tooke and subscribed the Oathes by Law appointed.

Mr. Thomas Snoden produced a Deed of sale from him the said Snoden to Obadiah Benjamin Gumbleton for a Tract of Land Conteyneing three hundred Acres of Land be the same more or less and acknowledged the same to be his proper Act and Deed in open Court.

William Houghton and Saml. Herst Proved upon their Oathes in Open Court a power of Attorney from Constant Snoden to Mr. Tho. Snoden and the same was ordered to be recorded.

Upon Petition of Mary Anne Doughton shewing that she has served her Indented tyme with Mr. Jno. Pettiver her Master and prayes to be dismissed from her said servitude and it appeareing to this Court that the said pettiver was not sumoned to shew Cause to the Contrary. Ordered that the Marshall doe sumons the said pettiver personally to appeare here on fryday next to answare the said Complaint.

James Fewox personally appeared and acknowledged a Deed of sale to William Hardie of part of a Tract of Land Conteyneing by Estimation One hundred Acres or thereabouts.

Wm. Hardie and Edie his wife personally appeared and in open Court Acknowledged an Assignement of a Pattent of Two hundred and Twenty Acres of Land lyeing in Chowan precinct to Jno. Tarkinton.

<315> John Jones and Elizabeth his wife personally appeared and acknowledged an Assignement of a pattent for two hundred Acres of Land to the Honorable Colonel Thomas Cary Esqr.

William Fryly Comes to prosecute his suite against Juliana Laker in an Action of the Case and Complaines that the Defendant stands Justly Indebted to the plaintiff in the full and Just summe of seaven pounds Eight shillings and six pence and the Defendant Comes and sayes that she Cannot pleade to the said Action she not haveing a Copy of the Declaration Delivered to her and thereupon Craves a Non suite which is Granted.

William Fryley Comes to Prosecute his suite against Richd. Johnson in a plea of the Case and Complaines that the Defendant stands Justly Indebted to the plaintiff in the full and Just sume of Eight pounds and one shilling as by wayes and meanes Convenient the plaintiff is ready to make appeare, And the Defendant Came not and the plaintiff prayes an Attachment against the Defendants Estate which is Granted.

John West Guardian of Lewis Alexander and Emanuell Knight Orphans of Lewis Alexander Knight Deceased Comes by Mr. Tho. Boyd his Attorney to prosecute his suite against Edwd. Daniell Pison in a plea of Trespass on the Case and Complaines that the Defendant into one plantation His Lawfull and rightfull Inherritance of the plaintiff Quallifyed as aforesaid scituate lyeing and being in the precinct of Pequimins within the Jurisdiction of this Court with force and Armes hath Entered and the same from the plaintiff quallify as aforesaid doth deteyne and withold and other Injuryes to him done to the plaintiffs Damage foure pounds Sterling which the plaintiff is ready to Averr and the Defendant by James Cole his Attorney Comes and sayes that he the Defendant into one plantation the Lawfull and rightfull Inherritance of the plaintiff Quallifyed as aforesaid scituate lyeing and being in the precinct of pequimans within the Jurisdiction of this Court with force and Armes hath not Entered in manner and forme as the plaintiff has aleadged in his Declaration but saith he the Defendant by Virtue of an order of

Court held for the precinct of pequimins beareing <316> Date the 13th day of July 1703 and hath peaceably Enjoyed not without Mollestation from that tyme till now and humbly prays this Action to be dismissed with Costs etc. And by Consent of both partyes the matter being referred to the Court. Ordered that a Writt of [*blank*].

Then this Court Adjourned till to Morrow Morning 8 of Clock.

Thursday Morne 8 of Clock this Court meets present ut supra.

Archibald Holmes personally appeared and proved a power of Attorney from Henry Warren and Eliz. his wife to Thomas Norcum by his Corporall Oath.

Thomas Norcum personally Came and appeared and acknowledged a Deed of sale from Henry Warren and Eliz. his wife to James Minge.

Isaacc Wilson and Tymothy Clare personally appeared and upon their solemn Affirmation proved a Bond of the penalty of thirty pounds from John White to Mr. Peter Godfrey.

Phillipp Stone Comes to prosecute his suite against Jno. Evans in a plea of the Case and Complaines that the Defendant stands Justly Indebted to the plaintiff in the full summe of Eighty Nine pounds fourteen shillings by Account as by wayes and meanes Convenient the plaintiff is ready to make appeare. And the Defendant Came not and the plaintiff prayes an order against the Marshall which is Granted. And Capt. John Hecklefeild provost Marshall Comes and prayes an Attachment against the said Evan's Estate which is Granted.

Thomas Houghton Comes to prosecute his suite against Thomas Clarke in a plea of the Case and Complaines that the Defendant stands Indebted to the plaintiff in the full summe of seaven pounds and Eleaven pence by Account as by wayes and meanes Convenient the plaintiff is ready to make appeare And the Defendant Came not and the plaintiff prayes an Order against the Marshall which is Granted. And Capt. Jno. Hecklefeild provost Marshall Comes and prayes an Attachment against the said Clarke's Estate which is Granted.

<317> Landgrave Robert Daniell Esqr. by Mr. Thomas Snoden his Attorney Comes to prosecute his suite against Capt. Nicholas Thomas Jones in a plea of the Case and Complaines that the Defendant stands Indebted to the plaintiff in the summe of One hundred and Eighteen pounds and fifteen shillings. And Capt. Jno. Hecklefeild Attorney to the Defendant Comes and prayes the matter may be referred to the next Court and the plaintiff Agrees thereto whereupon It is ordered that the matter be referred to the next Court accordingly.

Tobias Knight Esqr. Secretary of this Province Comes to prosecute his suite against Augustine Scarbrough in a plea of the Case and Complaines that the Defendant on the seaventeenth day of July at the now dwelling house of Joseph Peggs in the precinct of pascotanck and within the Jurisdiction of this Court designeing and Evely Intending to take away the Good name Fame Creditt and reputation of the plaintiff did in the Heareing of divers of her Majestyes Leidge people pronounce utter and declare these false scandelous and Mallitious words (viz.) thou (meaneing the plaintiff) art a vaggabond a runagate and a rascall and divers other scandelous false and Malitious to and of the plaintiff did utter and declare to the plaintiffs Damage five hundred pounds sterling and prayes Judgement for the same etc. And the Defendant Comes and pleads Non Culpabilis and of this he put himselfe upon the Country and the plaintiff likewise And the Marshall was Comanded to Cause to Come twelve true and Lawfull men etc. to whom etc. who neither etc. by whome etc. and there Came Mr. Will. Long Mr. Jno. Norcum Mr. Will. Fryley Mr. Jno. Jennett Mr. Edwd. James Mr. Lewis Williams Mr. William Jones Mr. Frans. Henrick Mr. Arch. Holmes Mr. James McDaniell Mr. Robert Hosea and Mr. Saml. Hearse who being Impannelled and Swoarne say Wee of the Jury find for the plaintiff with Costs and five shillings Damages. Ordered that the said Augustine Scarborough doe pay unto the said Tobias Knight the said sume of five shillings with Costs alias Execution.

Then this Court adjourned till five of Clock in the afternoon.

Five of Clock in the afternoon this Court meets present ut supra.

<318> Mr. Emanuell Low Attorney to the Honorable John Archdale Esqr. Comes to prosecute his suite against William Reed in a plea of the Case and Complaines that whereas the Defendant did sometyme in the Month of October or November in the yeare One thousand six hundred Ninety and five take to Farme of Rent of Daniell Akehurst Esqr. Deceased then Agent for and Entrusted by the said Jno. Archdale for the letting to farme severall Plantations in the precinct of Pascotank a Certaine Plantation and Lands therunto belonging scituate on Newbegun Creeke in the precinct of pascotanke aforesaid under the yearely Rent of three hundred weight of Fresh porke and the Defendant hath either by himselfe or his Tenant quietly and peaseably occupyed and Enjoyed the said Plantation and Lands for the full tyme and terme of Nine yeares Ended in the Month of October or November last past for which said Nine yeares Rent soe ended there became due to the plaintiff Quallyfyed as aforesaid the Quantity of One thousand seaven hundred weight

of fresh Porke as by wayes and meanes Convenient the plaintiff is ready to make appeare and prays Judgement etc. And for plea the Defendant in proper person Comes and Defends the force and Injury where etc. and sayth that he the Defendant is not Indebted unto the plaintiff in the full and Just sume of One thousand seaven hundred pounds of fresh porke in maner and forme as the plaintiff hath specfyed in his Declaration and of this he puts himselfe upon the Country And the Marshall was Comanded to Cause to Come twelve true and Lawfull Men etc. to whom etc. who neither etc. by whom etc. and there Came Mr. Willm. Long Mr. Jno. Norcum Mr. Willm. Fryly Mr. Jno. Jennett Mr. Edwd. James Mr. Lewis Williams Mr. Willm. Jones Mr. Francis Henrick Mr. Arch. Holmes Mr. James McDaniell Mr. Robert Hosea and Mr. Saml. Hearse who being Impannelled and swoarne say wee of the Jury find for the the Defendant. Ordered that the suite be Dismissed and the plaintiff pay Costs alias Execution.

Then this Court Adjourned till to morrow morning 8 of Clock.

Fryday Morne 8 of Clock this Court Meets present ut Supra.

Willm. Duckenfeild Esqr. personally Came and in open Court acknowledged a Deed of Sale of Divers Goods and Chattles to the Honorable Jno. Arderne Esqr.

<319> Phillipp Stone Comes to prosecute his Suite against Wm. Parker in a plea of the Case and Complaines that the Defendant stands Indebted to the plaintiff in the full summe of Eight pounds Eighteen shillings by account. And the Defendant Came not And the plaintiff prayes an Order against the Marshall which is granted And Capt. Jno. Hecklefeild Comes and prayes an Attachment against the said Parkers Estate which is Granted.

Anne Trumball widdow personally appeared and proved an Inventory of the Estate of Symon Trumball her late husband upon Oath.

Isaac Wilson Attorney to Mr. Peter Godfrey Comes and prayes an Attachment against the Estate of Jno. White for thirty pounds Due by Bond to the said Peter Godfrey which is Granted.

Upon Petition of Tymothy Clare praying to be allowed for his travall and Attendance being Sumoned as an Evidence by Isaac Wilson Attorney to Mr. Peter Godfrey against Jno. White Ordered that Isaac Wilson pay the said Tymothy Cleare five Shillings and tenn pence for such his Travell and Attendance with Costs alias Execution.

Then this Court Adjourned till tomorrow morneing 8 of Clock.

Saturday Morne 8 of Clock this Court meets present ut supra.

In Pursuance of an order of this Instant Court Mr. John Pettiver Comes and by his Pettition showeth that he doth not deteyne Mary Anne Doughton a servant by any Indenture as she hath sett forth in her petition but that Shee being in Prison in Virginia was sold to him the said Pettiver for her prison Fees but noe such sale appeareing to this Honorable Court Ordered that the said Mary Anne Doughton be sett free from any farther servitude to the said pettiver accordingly and that he the said pettiver pay her her Costs herein.

Ordered that Dr. Godfrey Spruell with whome Mary Anne Doughton Compleated her servitude doe pay her the Corne and Clothes as by Law is Due to her for her servitude aforesaid.

<320> Phillipp Stone Comes to prosecute his suite Against William Floyd in a plea of Debt and Complaines that the Defendant stands Justly Indebted to the plaintiff in the full and Just summe of three pounds and thirteen shillings sterling by Bill and the Defendant Comes and Confesses. Ordered the said William Floyd pay unto the said Phillipp Stone the said Summe of three pounds thirteen shillings sterling with Costs alias Execution.

Mr. Edwd. Moseley Comes and in open Court acknowledged a Bond of the penalty of One thousand pounds from him the Said Moseley to the Honorable Saml. Swann Esqr. and Mr. John Lillington and the honorable Swan Esqr. prayes the same may be recorded which is Granted.

Upon a matter of reference from the last Court Isaac Wilson Attorney to Peter Godfrey Comes and prayes Judgement against Jno. Browne for six pounds which Money was returned to be in the hand of Willm. Sawyer but it appeareing to this Court by writeing obligatory under the proper hand of the said John Browne with other witnesses that there is but Twenty shillings in the hands of the said Sawyer that is due to the said Browne. Ordered that the said Sawyer pay unto the said Wilson Attorney etc. the said summe of Twenty shillings with Costs alias Execution.

Upon Petition of Mr. Thomas Peterson shewing that Symon Trumball Deceased in his lifetyme became Indebted to the petitioner in the sume of forty one pounds two shillings and Eight pence as by a Certaine writeing Obligatory under his hand and seale beareing Date the 21st day of Augt. Anno 1704 here into Court brought and ready to be produced to your Honors relation being thereunto had doth and may appear and prayes Judgement for the same with Costs etc. And Anne Trumball Administratrix of the said Symon Trumbal Comes and by her petition shows that the said summ in the said petersons petition prayed for is dew as is demanded but humbly sayes <321> shee has not Assetts in her hands sufficient wholy to satisfy the same and prays that Judgement may not be given against her for more than the said Assetts amounts unto. Ordered that the said Anne Trumball doe pay to the said Peterson as farr as the Assetts in her hands will Extend unto with Costs alias Execution.

Then this Court Adjourned till 6 of Clock.

Att 6 of Clock this Court meets present ut Supra.

Ordered that Mary Anne Doughton pay unto Wm. Houghton five shillings his own travell and horse in Sumoneing of Mr. John Pettiver on an Extraordinary occasion.

[*Signed:*]
W. Glover, John Porter Senior, John Blount.

FILE PAPERS IN SUITS AND PROSECUTIONS

[*Daniell* v. *Jones*]

[*CCR 140*]

North Carolina Ss. To the Honorable the Generall Court

Landgrave Robt. Daniell Esqr. is plaintiff against Capt. Nicholas Thomas Jones Defendant in a plea of the Case and Complaines that the defendant Stands Indebted to the plaintiff in the full Summe of One hundred and Eighteen pounds and fifteen Shillings for divers Goods and Comodityes delivered by the plaintiff or his order to the defendant or his order as by a bill of Loading under the proper hand of the defendant and here ready to be produced to this Honorable Court relation being thereunto had doth and may appeare Nevertheless the defendant refuseth to redeliver or render an account of the Same or pay the aforesaid vallue to the plaintiffs Damage Two hundred Thirty Seaven pounds Ten Shillings Sterling and thereupon he brings his Suite and prays Judgement for the Same with Costs of Suite and Shall pray etc.

Tobs. Knight Secretary

[*Endorsed:*]
Daniell versus Jones
Entred 2d: Sept. 17 [*torn*]

[*CCR 192*]

Gentlemen

I have an action depending this Generall Court against Nicholas Thomas Jones I hereby Constitute Thomas Snoden my Attorney in that Case And pray that he may be admitted as Such And you will oblidge.

To the Honorable Members
of the General Court These

Yours
Robt. Daniell

[*Frayly* v. *Johnson*]

[*CCR 191*]

North Carolina [*torn*] To the Honorable Generall Court etc.

Wm. Frilye is plaintiff against Richd. Johnson Defendant in A plea of the Case and Setteth forth and Declares That the Defendant Stands Justly Indebted to the plaintiff in the full and Just Summe of Eight pounds and one Shilling as by wayes and meanes Convenient the plaintiff is ready to make appear and refuses payment whereby the plaintiff Sayth he is Dampnifyed Sixteen pounds Sterling for which he hath brought [*torn*] action and humbly Craves Judgment of this Honorable Court for [*torn*] with Costs of Suite And he Shall pray etc.

Tho. Snoden Clericus Curiae

[*Endorsed:*]
Frilye versus Johnson
In Case
Entred the 10th May

[*CCR 148*]

North Carolina ss. To the Provost Marshall or Deputy

These are in the Name of his Excellency the Palatine and the rest of the true and absolute Lords and Proprietors to will and require you to arrest the Body of Richd. Johnson and him to hold Soe that he make his personall appearance att the next Generall Court to be held for this Province the last Tuesday in July next att the House of Captain John Hecklefield in Little River to answer the Complaint of Willm. Freyley in A Plea of the Case And have there this writt Dated the 30th Day of Aprill Anno [Domini] 1705. Take good bond.

Tho. Snoden Clericus Curiae

[*Endorsed:*]
Freyley versus Johnson
Breve
To Mr. David Blake to Execute per order of John Hecklefield Provost Marshall
Executed by me the 2 day of July 1705

[*Glover, consignee* v. *Banks*]

[*CCR 192*]

North Carolina Ss. To the Honorable the Generall Court

William Glover Esqr. Consignee of Colonel Robert Quary and New pensilvania Company is plaintiff against James Banks Defendant in a plea of the Case and Complaines that the Defendant Stands Justly Indebted to the plaintiff Quallifyed as aforesaid in the Summe of One pounds Twelve Shillings and Six pence in fresh porke by account for Sundry Goods Creditts and Merchandizes Delivered by the plaintiff or his order to the Defendant or his order as by wayes and meanes Convenient the plaintiff is ready to make appear which Said Summe of One pound Twelve Shillings and Six pence the Defendant hath not rendred to the plaintiff tho' often thereunto requested but Still doth refuse to render to the plaintiffs Damage three pounds five Shillings Sterling and there upon he brings his Suite and prayes Judgement for the Same with Costs of Suite and Shall pray etc.

Tobs. Knight Secretary

[*Endorsed:*]
Glover versus Bank
Narratio

[*CCR* 192]

No. Carolina Ss. To the Provost Marshall or his Deputy

These are in the name of his Excellency the Palatine and rest of the true and absolute Lords and [*torn*] of this province to will and require you to Arrest the body of James Banks and [*torn*] hold Soe that he may appeare att the Next Generall Court to be holden for this [*torn*] at the house of Capt. John Heckle-feild on Litle river the las Tuesday in July next Ensueing then and there to Answare the plaint of Willm. Glover Esqr. Consignee [*torn*] Colonel Robert Quarry and New pensilvania Company in a plea of the Case and have this writt Dated at the Secretarys Office the 23d of June Anno Domini 1705.

Testis Tobs. Knight Secretary

[*Endorsed:*]
Glover versus Banks
Breve
Not executed

[*Glover, consignee* v. *Cooper*]

[*CCR* 192]

North Carolina Ss. To the Honorable the Generall Court

William Glover Esqr. Consignee of Colonel Robert Quary and New pensil-vania Company is plaintiff against George Cooper Defendant in a plea of the Case and Complaines that the Defendant Stands Justly Indebted to the plaintiff quallifyed as aforesaid in the full Summe of Two pound four Shillings and Eight pence in fresh porke by account for Divers Goods Credits and Merchan-dize Delivered by the plaintiff or his order to the Defendant or his order as by wayes and meanes Convenient the plaintiff is ready to make appeare which Said Summe of Two pounds four Shillings and Eight pence the Defendant hath not rendred to the plaintiff tho' often thereunto requested but the Same doth Still refuse to render to the plaintiffs Damage five pounds Sterling and thereupon he brings his Suite and prayes Judgment for the Same with Costs of Suite and Shall pray etc.

Tobs. Knight Secretary

[*Endorsed:*]
Glover versus Cooper
Narratio

[*CCR* 192]

No. Carolina Ss. To the Provost Marshall or his Deputy

These are in the name of his Excellency the Palatine and rest of the true and absolute Lords and Proprietors of this Province to will and require you to Arrest the body of George Cooper and him Safely hold Soe that he may appeare at the next Generall Court to be holden for this province at the house of Capt. John Hecklefeild on litle River the last Tuesday in July next Ensueing then and there to Answer the plaint of Wm. Glover Esqr. Consignee of Colonel Robert Quarry and new pensillvania Company in a plea of the Case and have there this writt Dated at the Secretarys Office the 23d day of June Anno Domini 1705.

Testis Tobs. Knight Secretary

[*Endorsed:*]
Glover versus Cooper
Breve
Not executed

[*Glover, consignee* v. *Fewox*]

[*CCR* 192]

North Carolina Ss. To the Honorable the Generall Court

William Glover Esqr. Consignee of Colonel Robt. Quary and new pensilvania Company is plaintiff against James Fewox Defendant in a plea of the Case and Complaines that the Defendant Stands Justly Indebted to the plaintiff quallifyed as aforesaid in the full Summe of Nine pounds Nine Shillings and two pence in fresh porke by account for divers Goods Credits and Merchandize delivered by the plaintiff or his order to the Defendant or his order as by wayes and meanes Convenient the plaintiff is ready to make appeare which Said Sume of Nine pound Nine Shillings and two pence the Defendant hath not rendred to the plaintiff tho' often thereunto requested but the Same doth Still refuse to render to the plaintiffs Damage Twenty pounds Sterling and thereupon he brings his Suite and prayes Judgement for the Same with Costs of Suite and Shall pray etc.

Tobs. Knight Secretary

[*Endorsed:*]
Glover etc. versus Fewox
Narratio

[*CCR 192*]

[*Torn*] Carolina Ss. To the Provost Marshall or his Deputy

These are in the name of his Excellency the Palatine and rest of the true and absolute Lords and proprietors of this province to will and require you to Arrest the body of James Fewox and him Safely hold Soe that he may appeare at the next Generall Court to be holden for this province at the house [*torn*] Capt. John Hecklefield in Litle River the last Tuesday in July next Ensueing then and there to Answare the plaint of Willm. Glover Esqr. Consignee of Colonel Robert Quary and New pensilvania Company in a plea of the Case and have ther this writt Dated at the Secretarys Office the 23d Day of July Anno Domini 1705.

Testis Tobs. Knight Secretary

[*Endorsed:*]
Executed
[*torn*] Fewox
Breve

[*Glover, consignee* v. *French*]

[*CCR 192*]

North Carolina Ss. To the Honorable the Generall Court

William Glover Esqr. Consignee of Colonel Robert Quary and New pensilvania Company is plaintiff against Richard French Defendant in a plea of the Case and Complaines that the Defendant Stands Justly Indebted to the plaintiff Quallifyed as aforesaid in the full Summe of five pounds Thirteen Shillings in fresh porke by account for Divers Goods Credits and Merchandizes Delivered by the plaintiff or his order to the Defendant or his order as by wayes and meanes Convenient the plaintiff is ready to make appear which Said Summe of five pounds Thirteen Shillings the Defendant hath not renderd to the plaintiff tho often thereunto requested but the Same doth Still refuse to render to the plaintiffs Damage Twelve pounds Sterling and thereupon he brings his Suite and prayes Judgement for the Same with Costs of Suite and Shall pray etc.

Tobs. Knight Secretary

[*Endorsed:*]
Glover versus French
Narratio

[*CCR 192*]

No. Carolina Ss. To the Provost Marshall or Deputy

These are in the name of his Excellency the Palatine and rest of the true and absolute Lords and proprietors to will and require you to Arrest the body of Richard French and him Safely hold Soe that he may appeare at the next Generall Court to be holden for this province at the house of Capt. John Hecklefield on Litle river the last Tuesday in July next Ensueing then and there to Answer the plaint of Wm. Glover Esqr. Consignee of Colonel Robt. Quarry and New pensilvania Company in a plea of the Case and have there this writt Dated at the Secretarys Office the 23d day of June Anno Domini 1705.

Testis Tobs. Knight Secretary

[*Endorsed:*]
Glover versus French
Breve
Excuted the 14 day of July

[*Glover, consignee* v. *Luerton*]

[*CCR* 192]

No. Carolina Ss. To the Honorable the Generall Court

Willm. Glover Esqr. Consignee of Colonel Robert Quary and New pensilvania Company is plaintiff against Jno. Luerton defendant in a plea of the Case and Complaines that the Defendant Stands Justly Indebted to the plaintiff quallifyed as aforesaid in the full Summe of three pounds thirteen Shillings and Nine pence in fresh porke by Account for Divers Goods Credits and Merchandizes Delivered by the plaintiff or his order to the Defendant or his order as by wayes and meanes Convenient the plaintiff is ready to make appeare which Said Summe of three pounds thirteen Shillings and nine pence the Defendant hath not rendred to the plaintiff tho' often thereunto requested but the Same doth Still refuse to render to the plaintiffs Damage Eight pounds Sterling and thereupon he brings his Suite and prayes Judgement for the Same with Costs of Suite and Shall pray etc.

Tobs. Knight Secretary

[*Endorsed:*]
Glover versus Luerton
Narratio

[*CCR* 192]

North Carolina Ss. To the provost Marshall or his Deputy

These are in the Name of his Excellcy the Palatine and rest of the true and absolute Lords and proprietors of this province to will and require you to Arrest the body of Jno. Luerton and him Safely hold Soe that he may appeare at the next Generall Court to be holden for the Said Province at the house of Capt. John Hecklefeild in Litle river on the last Tuesday in July next Ensueing then and there to Answare the plaint of Willm. Glover Esqr. Consignee of Colonel Robert Quary and New pensilvania Company in a plea of the Case and have there this Writt Dated at the Secretary's Office the 23d day of June Anno Domini 1705.

Testis Tobs. Knight Secretary

[*Endorsed:*]
Glover versus Luerton
Breve
Executed

[*Glover, consignee* v. *Nash*]

[*CCR 192*]

North Carolina Ss. To the Honorable the Generall Court

William Glover Esqr. Consignee of Colonel Robert Quary and New pensilvania Company is plaintiff against Jno. Nash Defendant in a plea of the Case and Complaines that the Defendant Stands Justly Indebted to the plaintiff qualifyed as aforesaid in the full Summe of two pounds Eight Shillings and Nine pence in fresh porke by account for Divers Goods Credits and Merchandizes Delivered by the plaintiff or his order to the Defendant or his order as by wayes and meanes Convenient the plaintiff is ready to make appeare which Said Summe of two pounds Eight Shillings and Nine pence the Defendant hath not rendred to the plaintiff tho' often thereunto requested but the Same doth Still refuse to render to the plaintiffs Damage five pounds Sterling and thereupon he brings his Suite and prayes Judgement for the Summe with Costs of Suite and Shall pray etc.

Tobs. Knight Secretary

[*Endorsed:*]
Glover versus Nash
Narratio

[*Glover, consignee* v. *Pritchard*]

[*CCR 192*]

No. Carolina Ss. To the Honorable the Generall Court

William Glover Esqr. Consignee of Colonel Robert Quary and New Pensilvania Company is plaintiff against Samll. Pritchard defendant in a plea of the Case and Complaines that the defendant Stands Justly Indebted to the plaintiff quallifyed as aforesaid in the full Sume of three pounds Nine Shillings and ten pence in fresh porke by account of Divers Goods Credits and Merchandizes Delivered by the plaintiff or his order to the Defendant or his order as by wayes and meanes Convenient the plaintiff is ready to make appeare which Said Summe of thre pounds Nine Shillings and tenn pence the Defendant hath not rendred to the plaintiff tho' often thereunto requested but the Same doth Still refuse to render to the plaintiffs Damage Seaven pounds Sterling and thereupon he brings his Suite and prays Judgement for the Same with Costs of Suite and Shall pray etc.

Tobs. Knight Secretary

[*Endorsed:*]
Glover versus Pritchard
Narratio

[*CCR 148*]

No. Carolina Ss. To the Provost Marshall or his Depty

These are in the name of his Excellency the Palatine and rest of the true and absolute Lords and Proprietors of this Province to will and require you to Arrest the body of Samll. Pritchard and him Safely hold Soe that he may appeare at the next Generall Court to be holden for this Province at the house of Capt. Jno. Hecklefield in litle river on the last Tuesday in July next Ensueing then and there to Answare the Plaint of Wm. Glover Esqr. Consignee of Colonel Robert Quary and new Pensilvania Company in a Plea of the Case and have there this Writt Dated at the Office the 23d day of June Anno Domini 1705.

Testis Tobs. Knight Secretary

[*Endorsed:*]
Breve
Glover versus Pritchard

[*Peterson, attorney of Pensylvania Company* v. *Trumball, administratrix*]

[*CCR 186*]

No. Carolina Ss. To the Honorable the Generall Court

The Humble Petition of Mr. Thomas Peterson Agent to the Pensilvania Company humbly Complaineing Sheweth That Symon Trumball deceased did in his Life tyme become Justly Indebted unto your petitioner in the full and Just Summe of forty one pounds two Shillings and Eight pence by a Certaine writeing obligatory under his hand and Seale beareing Date the Twenty first day of Augt. Anno 1704 hereinto Court brought and ready to be produced to your Honors relation being thereunto had doth and may and that the Said Symon Trumball in his life tyme never paid the Same to your petitioner nor Anne Trumball (his Administratrix) Since his Decease Wherefore Your petitioner humbly prayes your honors to take the Same into your honors Serious Consideration and Give your petitioner Judgement for the aforesaid Sume of forty One pounds two Shillings and Eight pence with Costs and your petitioner as in Duty Bound Shall pray etc.

[*Endorsed:*]
Petersons Petition

[*CCR 186*]

To the Honorable Generall Court etc.

The Humble petition of Thomas Peterson Sheweth That Simon Trumbull late of this Government Stood Indebted unto your Petitioner in the full and Just Summe of Forty one pounds By Bill from under his hand ready to be produc'd in Court And That Anne Trumball widdow and relict of the Said Simon is Qualifyed to the Said Simon's Estate having obtaind Commission of Administration upon the Same And prayes an Order for the Same And he Shall pray etc.

Tho. Peterson

To the Honorable Generall Court etc.

The petition of Anne Trumbull Widdow humbly Sheweth That She hath obtain'd Commission of Administration uppon the Estate of her Deceased husband Simon Trumbull late of this Government and humbly prayes an Order for appraisment of the Same And that your Honors will be pleasd to appoint apprisors of the Same And She Shall pray etc.

[*CCR 186*]

North Carolina Ss. To the honorable Generall Court

The humble petition of Anne Trumball Administratrix of Symon Trumball deceased Sheweth That The Said Sume in Mr. Petersons Petition pray'd for is due as is demanded But your petitioner humbly Says She has not Assetts in her hands Sufficient wholy to Satisfy the Same Wherefore humbly prays your honors Consideration therein and that Judgement may not pass for more then the Said Assetts amounts unto and Shall pray etc.

[*Endorsed:*]
Trumballs Petition

[*Peterson, attorney of Perry and Company* v. *Kingsly*]

[*CCR 139*]

[*Torn*] Carolina Ss.

Whereas George Kingsly is departed out of this Government and have left no Attorney to Answer for him according to Law

To the provost Marshall or his Deputy

These are therefore in her Majestyes name to will and require you to Attach Soe much of the Estate of the Said Geo. Kingsly wherever to be found in this Government as will pay and Satisfy Thomas Peterson Attorney of Micajah Perry and New Pensilvania Company the Sume of Tenn pounds Twelve Shillings and Six pence with Costs and the Same in Safe Custody Keep untill otherwise ordered by due Course of Law and make returne of your proceedings herein to the next Generall Court Dated at the Secretarys Office this 25th day of May Anno Domini 1705.

Testis T. Knight Secretary

[*Endorsed:*]
John Meads

[*Stone* v. *Evans*]

[*CCR 148*]

North Carolina Ss. To the Honorable the Generall Cort

Phillip Stone is plaintiff against John Evans Defendant in a plea of the Case Complaines that the Defendant Stands justly indebted to the plaintiff in the full Sume of Eighty Nine pounds Fourteen shillings by account as by wayes and meanes Convenient the plaintiff is ready to make appear which Said Sume of Eighty Nine pounds fourteen Shillings the Defendant hath not rendred to the plaintiff tho' often thereunto requested but Still doth refuse to render to the plaintiffs Damage One Hundred Seaventy Nine pounds Eight Shillings Sterling and therefore he brings his Sute and prayes Judgment for the Same with Costs of Sute And shall pray etc.

May: 14th: 1705 Tobs. Knight Secretary

[*Endorsed:*]
[Stone] versus Evans
Case

[*CCR 148*]

North Carolina Ss. To the Provost Marshall or Deputy

These are in the name of his Excellency the Palatine and the rest of the true and absolute Lords and Proprietors to require you to arrest the Body of John Evans and him in Safe Custody hold Soe that he may appear att the next Generall Cort to be holden for this Goverment the last Tuesday in July att the house of Captain John Hecklefield in Little River to answer the plaint of Phillipp Stone in a Plea of the Case and have there this Writt Dated the 14th of May 1705.

Testes Tobs. Knight Secretary

[*Endorsed:*]
Stone versus Evans
July [*illegible*] Excuted [*illegible*] me Wm. Bray deputy marshall

[*Stone* v. *Floyd*]

[*CCR 148*]

North Carolina Ss. To the honorable the Generall Court

Phillipp Stone is plaintiff against William Floyd Defendant in a plea of Debt and Says that the Defendant stands Justly Indebted to the plaintiff in the Just Summe of three pounds thirteen Shillings Sterling Money to be paid in the precinct of Coratuck upon demand as in and by One writeing Obligatory under the hand and Seale of the Said William Floyd beareing Date the 12th day of December Anno Domini 1704 and now ready to be produced in Court relation being thereunto had doth and may more fully and at large appeare which Said Summe of three pounds thirteen Shillings Sterling Money as aforesaid the Defendant hath not rendred to the plaintiff tho often thereunto requested but the Same doth Still refuse to render to the plaintiffs Damage Seaven pounds Six Shillings Sterling and thereupon he brings his Suite and prays Judgment for the Same with Costs of Suite and Shall pray etc.

Testis Tobs. Knight Secretary

[*Endorsed:*]
Narratio
Stone versus Floyd
In Debt

[*CCR 148*]

North Carolina Ss. To the provost Marshall or his Depty

These are in the name of his Excellency the pallatine and rest of the true and absolute Lords and proprietors to will and require you to Arrest the body of Willm. Floyd and him Safely hold Soe that he may appeare at the next Generall Court to be holden for his Province at the house of Capt. Jno. Hecklefield in Litle River on the last Tuesday in this Instant July then and there to Answer the plaintiff Phillip Stone in a plea of Debt and have there this writt Dated at the Office the 16th day of July Anno Domini 1705.

Testis Tobs. Knight Secretary

[*Endorsed:*]
Breve
Stone versus Floyd
In Debt
Excuted by me Wm. Bray July the 22:1705

[*CCR 189*]

Docquett of [March] to October Court 1705

References from March Court 1705 to October Court following

1. Stone versus Floyd in Debt. Executed.
2. Idem versus Parker in Case. Attachment.
3. Idem versus Evans in Case. Attachment.
4. Fryly versus Johnson in Case. Attachment.
5. Wilson Attorney etc. versus White in Debt. Attachment Executed.
6. Stoughton versus Clarke in Case. Attachment Executed.
7. Glover Consignee etc. versus Pritchard in Case. Continued.
8. Idem versus Phillips and etc. in Case.
9. Idem versus Nash in Case.
10. Idem versus Fewox in Case.
11. Idem versus French in Case.
12. Idem versus Cooper in Case.
13. Idem versus Pritchard Executor etc. in Case.
14. Idem versus Bankes in Case.
15. Idem versus Luerton in Case.
16. Wilkinson versus Houghton.

Writts and returnes to October Court 1705

17. Hecklefield versus Lehay in Case. Noe return.
18. Peterson Attorney etc. versus Barr in Debt. Executed.
19. Idem versus Smyth in Debt. Executed.
20. Idem versus Eundem in Debt. Executed.
21. Daniell versus Jones in Case. Executed. Retraxit.
22. Swann [*illegible*] versus Skiner in Debt.
23. Idem versus Pargiter in Debt.
24. Idem versus Snell in Debt. Executed.
25. Idem versus Fewox in Debt. Executed.
26. Idem versus Phelps in Debt. Not Executed.
27. Idem versus Spruell in Debt. Executed.
28. Hecklefield versus Wilson in Debt. Not Executed.
29. Hunt versus Bunting in Case. Executed.
30. Porter versus Powell in Debt. Executed.
31. Idem versus Fewox in Debt. Executed.
32. Idem and Company versus Grills in Case. Executed.
33. Gale versus Jordan in Case. Executed.
34. Giles versus Rayfield in Case. Not Executed.
35. Tewhitt versus Watson in Case.
36. Idem versus Eundem in Debt.
37. Hawkins versus Jones in Debt. Executed.
38. Wilkinson versus Devenport in Debt. Executed.
39. Idem versus Hearse in Debt. Executed.

[*CCR 104*]

<327> North Carolina Ss.

Att a generall Court holden for this Province at the house of Capt. Jno. Hecklefield in Litle river on Tuesday the 30th day of October Anno Domini 1705. Present the Honorable Christo. Gale, Will. Collins Esquires Justices.

This Court Adjournes till to Morrow Morneing 8 of Clock.

Wednesday Morneing 8: of Clock this Court meets present ut Supra with the Honorable Jno. Porter Esqr.

Then the Comission of the peace was read and the above written Christopher Gale and Will. Collings Esquires Severally take and Subscribe to the Oathes by Law appointed and the Oath for Executeing the office of a Justice of peace.

Ordered that for the future at every adjournment a perticuler Account be Entered in the Journall of the Severall Justices then present And that every Morneing when the Court first Sitts the last days Journall and proceedings be read over before the Court.

By an Attachment from the last Court between Isaac Willson Attorney of Peter Godfry plaintiff and John White defendant the said Isaac Willson Comes by Capt. Jno. Hecklefield his Attorney and prays Appraisors may be appointed to appraise the Goods following (videlicet) one Cow one Yeareling one Steere three yeares old one Heyfer of the Same with Advantage which is returned by the Marshall to be the proper Estate of the Said White and by the said Marshall Attached And the Court appoints Saml. Parsons Andrew Reed and Jno. Bateman or any two of them to Appraise the abovesaid Goods and Chattles and make report of their proceedings therein to the next Generall Court.

Then this Court adjournes till two of Clock in the after noone.

Att 2 of Clock this Court meets and adjournes till to Morrow Morne Seaven of Clock.

Thursday Morneing 7 of Clock the Court meets present The Honorable Jno. Porter Christopher Gale and Wm. Collings Esquires Justices.

<328> The Honorable Saml. Swann Esqr. Comes to prosecute his Suite against Jno. Snell defendant in a plea of Debt and Complaines for four pounds two Shillings and Eight pence to be paid in Good Merchantable Tarr at the plaintiffs owne Landing at the rate of Eleven Shillings per Barrell and the Defendant Comes and Confesses.

Ordered that the said Jno. Snell pay unto the Said Saml. Swann the Said Sume of four pounds two Shillings and Eight pence with Costs alias Execution.

The Honorable Saml. Swann Esquire Comes to prosecute his Suite against James Fewox Defendant in a plea of Debt and Complaines for the full quantity of Nine Barrells of Good Merchantable Tarr to be paid and Delivered at the plaintiffs owne Landing and the Defendant Comes and Confesses. Ordered that the Said James

Fewox pay and Deliver unto the Said Saml. Swann the Said quantity of Nine Barrells of Tarr with Costs alias Execution.

The Honorable Saml. Swann Esqr. Comes to prosecute his Suite against Godfrey Spruell defendant in a plea of Debt and Complaines for Seaven pounds Nineteen Shillings and Eleaven pence to be paid in Good Merchantable Tarr at the plaintiffs owne Landing at the rate of Eleaven Shillings per Barrell and the Defendant Comes not and the plaintiff prays an order against the Marshall which is Granted.

And Capt. Jno. Hecklefield provost Marshall Comes by Geo. Harris and prayes an Attachment against the Said Spruells Estate which is Granted.

Then this Court adjourned till 10 of Clock.

Att 10 of Clock the Court meets present ut Supra with the Honorable Jno. Blount Esqr.

The Honorable Wm. Glover Esqr. Consignee of Colonel Robert Quarry and New Pensilvania Company Comes to prosecute his Suite against Danll. Phillipps and Joan his wife defendants in a plea of the Case and Complaines for Seaven pounds Eight Shillings and the Said Danll. Phillips appeares and Confesses.

Ordered that the Said Daniell Phillipps and his wife or one of them pay unto the Said Wm. Glover the Said Sume of Seaven pound Eight Shillings with Costs alias Execution.

<329> The Honorable Wm. Glover Esqr. Consignee of Colonel Robert Quary and New Pensilvania Company Comes to prosecute his Suite against David Pritchard Executor etc. of Eliasco Buckley deceased Administrator etc. of Rowland Buckley deceased defendant in a plea of the Case and Complaines for Eight pounds two Shillings and Seaven pence in fresh porke for divers Goods Credits and Merchandizes delivered by the plaintiff or his order to the Defendant or his order and the Defendant Comes not and the plaintiff prayes an order against the Marshall which is Granted. And the Provost Marshall Comes and prays an Attachment against the Said Pritchards Estate which is Granted.

William Glover Esqr. Consignee of Colonel Robert Quarry and New Pennsilvania Company Comes to Prosecute his Suite against Jno. Lureton in a plea of the Case and Complaines for Three pounds thirteen Shillings and Nine pence in fresh porke by Account for Divers Goods Credits and Merchandizes delivered by the plaintiff or his order to the Defendant or his order. And the Defendant appeares not and the plaintiff prays an order against the Marshall which is Granted. And the Provost Marshall prays an Attachment against the Estate of the Said Lureton which is Granted.

John Porter Esqr. Comes to prosecute his Suite against James Fewox Defendant in a plea of Debt and Complaines for One hundred forty and four Bushells of Good Sound well dressed Merchantable Indyan Corne And the Defendant Comes and pleads Non est factum And the plaintiff for want of his Evidences to prove the bond prays a referrence to the next Court which is Granted.

Jno. Porter Esqr. Comes to prosecute his Suite against Wm. Powell defendant in a plea of Debt and Complaines for twelve pounds Six Shillings to be paid in Merchantable Drest Buck and Doe Skins the Buck at two Shillings per Skin and the Doe Skins at Eighteen pence per Skin and the Defendant appeares not and the plaintiff prayes an order against the Marshall which is Granted. And the Provost Marshall Comes and prayes an Attachment against the Said Powells Estate which is Granted.

<330> Jno. Porter Esqr. and Company Comes to prosecute their Suite against Richd. Grills defendant in a plea of the Case and Complaines for Twenty Six pounds by Account and the Defendant appeares nott and the plaintiff prays an order against the Marshall which is Granted. And the Provost Marshall Comes and prays an Attachment against the Said Grills's Estate which is Granted.

Jno. Snell Comes and in open Court acknowledged an Assignement of a Patent for a Tract of Land Conteyneing five hundred and Tenn Acres Lyeing In pequimons precinct to John Dicks.

Thomas Peterson Attorney to Micajah Perry and New Pensilvania Company Comes to prosecute his Suite against Robt. Barr of the County of Bath Defendant in a plea of Debt and Complaines for Twenty Eight pounds fifteen Shillings by Bill Dated 15th September 1704 And the Defendant appeares not and the plaintiff prays an order against the Marshall which is Granted. And the Provost Marshall Comes and prayes an Attachment against the Estate of the Said Barr which is Granted.

Tho. Peterson Attorney of Micajah Perry and New Pensilvania Company Comes to Prosecute his Suite against Richd. Smyth of the County of Bath Defendant and Complaines for Ninety four pounds one Shilling and three pence to be paid in Good fresh Merchantable Porke And the Defendant appeares Not and the plaintiff prays an order Against the Marshall which is Granted. And the Provost Marshall Comes and prays an Attachment against the Said Smyths Estate which is Granted.

Thomas Peterson Attorney of Micajah Perry and New Pensilvania Company Comes to prosecute his Suite against Richd. Smyth of the County of Bath Defendant in a plea of Debt and Complaines for One pound Eight Shillings And Six pence in Good Sound Merchantable fresh Pork And the Defendant appeares not and the Plaintiff prays an order against the Marshall which is Granted. And the Provost Marshall Comes and prays an Attachment against the Said Smyths Estate which is Granted.

Then this Court adjournes till three of Clock.

Att 3 of Clock this Court meets and Adjournes till fryday Morneing 10 of Clock.

Fryday Morne 10 of Clock this Court Meets present The Honorable Wm. Glover Chris. Gale Jno. Blount and Wm. Collings Esquires <331> Absent Chris. Gale Esqr.

John Bunting was Sumoned to Answer to Capt. John Hunt in a plea of the Case and the Plaintiff Came not Ordered that the Suite be dismissed and the plaintiff pay Costs alias Execution.

Obadiah Benjamin Gumbleton Came and in open Court acknowledged an Assignment of a pattent for a Certaine Tract of Land Lyeing at Allegator to Jno. Arnell.

Upon Petition of Ephrahim Lureton praying to be allowed for his Travell and Attendance as an Evidence between Jno. Porter Esqr. plaintiff and William Powell Defendant Ordered that he be allowed for four days Comeing and goeing and two dayes Attendance According to Act of Assembly.

Thomas Collins Eliz. Collins and Purnia Collins Came and in open Court acknowledged a Deed of Sale of a Certaine Tract of Land at the head of Lyllyes Creeke Conteyneing One hundred and thirty Acres to Will. White.

Cornelius FitzPatrick Came and in Open Court acknowledged a Deed of Sale of a Tract of Land called Allegator Point to Thomas Holloway.

Cornelius Fitz:Patrick Comes and in open Court acknowledged a Deed of Sale of a Tract of Land Conteyneing two Hundred Acres at Stumpy Point to Andrew Wilson.

Capt. Thos. Blount Comes and Prayes to be Allowed for his Travell and Attendance being Sumoned by James Fewox as an Evidence between Said Fewox and Jno. Porter Esqr. Ordered that the Said Capt. Blount for four dayes Comeing and Goeing and three dayes Attendance according to Act of Assembly.

Absent Mr. Porter.

Upon Information of Thomas Snoden Esqr. her Matyes Attorney Generall Shewing that he received Information from Jno. Porter Esqr. against Willm. Brice of this Province for Contemp of Authority for not Executeing a Warrant according to the tenour of the Same and prayes that the Said Brice may be taken in to the Custody of the Marshall untill he shall become bound with Good Security to Answer the Said Contempt. Ordered that the Said Brice be taken into Custody of the Marshall untill he become bound with Security <332> as aforesaid and that Jno. Burras and William Barrow be Sumonsed to appeare as Evidences on the penalty of ten pounds.

[*Signed:*]
W. Glover, John Porter, C. Gale.

RECORDED BY ORDER OF COURT

[*CCR 104*]

<323> No. Carolina Ss.

Know all men by these presents that I Edwd. Moseley Gentleman am held and firmely bound unto the Honorable Samll. Swan Esqr. and Mr. Jno. Lillington in the full and Just Summe of One thousand pounds to be paid to the Said Samll. Swann or Jno. Lillington or either of them their or either of their Heyres Executors Administrators or Assignes to which payment well and truely to be made I bind my Selfe my Heyres Executors and Administrators firmely by these presents Sealed with my Seale and Dated the fourth day of Augt. Anno Domini 1705.

Whereas the above bound Edwd. Moseley is by the Grace of God to Mary Madam Anne Walker widdow and in Consideration of the Estate the Said Walker may bring to the above bound Edwd. Mosely and he not haveing any Land or Tenements whereupon to Setle a Joynture to Said Walker. Therefore The Condition of this Obligation is Such That if the above bound Anne Walker Should happen to Survive the Said Edwd. Moseley that then he the Said Edwd. Moseley in his last Will and Testament shall leave unto her in Money Plate Jewells Slaves or household Stuff the full Summe of five hundred pounds without any Manner of Charge Limitation or Incumbrance whatsoever And also that the above bound Edwd. Moseley shall att any tyme dureing the Said Marriage permitt the Said Anne to make and putt her last will and Testament in writeing and therein to give and Bequeath unto any person or persons whatsoever any Summe or Summes not Exceeding five hundred pounds and Shall permitt and Suffer the Executors nominated in Said will to prove the Same And Shall well and truely pay unto any person or persons whatsoever all Such Summe and Summes of Money as the Said Anne in her will shall give and Devise provided the Same doe not Exceed five hundred pounds Then this Obligation to be void and of none Effect or else to remaine in full force and virtue.

Edward Moseley

<324> Sealed and Delivered
in the presence of
John Arderne
Thomas Blount
Tobs. Knight

Recorded the 23d day of Octob. 1705 by order Per Tobs. Knight Secretary

Know all men by these presents That I Constant Snoden for divers good Causes and Considerations me hereunto moveing Have Voluntarily freely and without Compultion thereto made Constituted ordeyned and appointed And doe by these presents make Constitute ordeyne and appoint my loveing husband Thomas Snoden my true and Lawfull Attorney for me and in my name to relinquish all my right of Dower of in and to a Tract of Land Scituate Lyeing and Beeing at Allegator in the Province of North Carolina the Said Tract of Land being Sold by my Said Husband unto Obadiah Benjamin Grumbleton ratifyeing holding firme and allowing whatever my Said Attorney Shall for me and in my name Act and doe in the premisses Witness my hand and Seale this 31st: day of July Anno Domini 1705.

Signed Sealed and Delivered — Constant Snoden her mark Seal
in the presence of
William Houghton his marke
Samll. Horst his marke

Recorded the 23d day of Octob. 1705 by order Per Tobs. Knight Secretary

<325> Albemarle County

Know all men by these presents that I Henry Warren with Eliz. my wife do Constitute and ordaine Thomas Norcum of the Same County to Act and doe for us and in our name and Stead to make over a Tract of Land Containeing One hundred and Twenty three acres upon the Sound Side between Henry Normans and Mr. James Mings as Witness our Hands and Seales.

Testis — Henry Warren his marke Seal
May the 2d 1705 — Eliz. Warren her marke Seal
Archibold Holmes
George Beck
William Egerton his marke

Recorded the 20d day of October 1705 by order Per Tobs. Knight Secretary

Know all Men by these presents That I Wm. Duckenfield of Salmon Creeke in the precinct of Chowan Esqr. as well for and in Consideration of Severall Summes of Money Layd out paid and Expended for me and many great Services for me done and performed by Jno. Arderne as also for and in Consideration of that naturall Love and Effection that I beare to the Said Jno. Arderne as being my Kinsman as also for divers other good Causes and Considerations mee hereunto Especially moveing Have Give to Granted Bargained and Sold And by these presents Doe Give Grant Bargaine and Sell unto the Said Jno. Arderne twenty thre Negro Indyan and Mallotta Slaves named and described as followeth (videlicet) Sambo Bess Kate Totty Virginia Mall Hannah old Hanah Nany Tony Nany Peggy Squire Roetty Cheshire Squire Mustapha Robbin Nat Jack Tom Ned and Sukee and all and Singulering Goods Cattle Chattles whatsoever as well reall as personall of what Kind vallue or Quallity the Same are or be whether moveable or Imoveable dead or liveing and in what place or places the Same shall or may be found as well in my owne Custody and possession as in the hands Custody or possession of any other person or persons whatsoever To have and to hold all and Singuler the Negro Indyan and Mallotta Slaves and all other the Goods Cattle and Chattles together with their Appurtenances unto the Said Jno. Arderne his Heyres Executors Administrators and Assignes to his and their owne proper use <326> and behoofe for ever and that Freely Quietly and peaceably and Entirely without any Contradiction Claime disturbance or Hindrance of any person whatsoever and without any account to me or any other whom soever to be madee [*illegible*]ared or here after to be rendered Soe that neither I the Said Wm. Duckenfield or any other for me or in my name any right Title Interest or Demand of or for the Said Negro Indyan and Malotta Slaves Goods Cattle and Chattles real or personall moveable or Immoveable dead or liveing or any part or parcell thereof ought to Exact Challenge Clayme or demand at any tyme hereafter but from all Actions right title Claime demand possession and Interest thereof shall be wholy barrd and Excluded by force of these presents and I the Said will Duckenfield my Heyres Executors and Administrators all and Singuler the Negro Indyan and Mallotta Slaves Goods Cattle and Chattles aforesaid to the said Jno. Arderne his Executors and Administrators against all people will warrant and forever do [Send] by these presents of which Negro Indyan and Mallotta Slaves Goods Cattle and Chattles of the aforesaid Will. Duckenfield have put the Said Jno. Arderne in full and peaceable possession by a Giveing and delivering of an Indyan Boy Called Natt which I gave and delivered at the Ensealeing and delivery of these presents In Witness whereof I have hereunto Set my hand and Seale this 2d day of Augt. In the Fourth yeare of the raigne of our Soveraigne Lady Anne by the Grace of God of England Scotland France and Ireland Queen defender of the Faith etc. Anno Domini 1705.

Sealed and delivered in the presence of
Tho. Abington
T. Knight
Tho. Houghton

Will. Duckenfield Seal

Memo. that the day and yeare above written the above named Wm. Duckenfield did put the above named Jno. Arderne in quiet and peaceable possession of all and Singuler the premissied Goods and Chattles above mentioned by the delivery of the above said Indyan boy Natt in the name of the whole and for the whole in the presente of
T. Knight
Tho. Abington

Recorded the 23d day of Octo. 1705 by order T. Knight Secretary

FILE PAPERS IN SUITS AND PROSECUTIONS

[*Daniell* v. *Jones*]

[*CCR 139*]

North Carolina Ss. To the provost Marshall or his Deputy

These are in her Majestyes name to will and require you to Arrest the body of Captain Nicholas Thomas Jones and him Safely hold Soe that he may appeare at the next Generall Court to be holden for this Government at the house of Captain John Hecklefield in Litle river on the [*torn*] Tuesday in October next Ensueing then and there to Answer the plaint of Landgrave Robert Daniell Esqr. in a plea of the Case and have there this writt Dated at the Secretarys office the 3d day of September Anno Domini 1705.

Testis Tobs. Knight Secretary

[*Endorsed:*]
Daniell versus Jones
Executed
Retraxit

[*Gale* v. *Jordan*]

[*CCR 148*]

North Carolina Ss. To the honorable the Generall Court

Christopher Gale Esqr. is plaintiff against Joseph Jordan defendant in a plea of the Case and Complaines that the Defendant Stands Justly Indebted to the plaintiff in the full and Just Sume of Two pounds Tenn Shillings due to the plaintiff by Account as being Attorney Generall and prosecuteing an Information against the Defendant in her Majestyes behalfe as by wayes and meanes Convenient the plaintiff is ready to make appeare which Said Summe of Two pounds Tenn Shillings the defendant hath not rendred to the plaintiff tho' often thereunto requested but the Same doth Still refuse to render to the plaintiffs Damage five pounds Sterling and thereupon he brings his Suite and prays Judgement for the Same with Costs of Suite and Shall pray etc.

Tobs. Knight Secretary

[*Endorsed:*]
Narratio
Gale Ar. versus Jordan
In Case
Entered October 5th 1705

[*CCR 148*]

North Carolina Ss. To the provost Marshall or his Deputy

These are in her Matyes name to will and require you to Arrest the body of Joseph Jordan and him Safely hold Soe that he may be and appeare at the next Generall Court to be holden for this Province at the house of Captain Jno. Hecklefield in Litle river on the Last Tuesday in this Instant October then and there to Answare the plaint of Christopher Gale Esqr. in a plea of the Case and have there this writt Dated at the Secretarys Office this 5th day of October Anno Domini 1705.

Testis Tobs. Knight Secretary

[*Endorsed:*]
Breve
Gale, Ar. versus Jordan
In Case
Executed by [me] George Harris Deputy marshall

[*Giles* v. *Rayfield*]

[*CCR 148*]

North Carolina Ss. To the honorable the Generall Court

Cornelius Giles is plaintiff against William Rafeild defendant in a ple of the Case and Complaines the Defendant Stands Indebted to the plaintiff in the full summe of One pound Thirteen Shillings by Account as by wayes and meanes Convenient the plaintiff is ready to make appeare which Said Summe of One pounds Thirteen Shillings the Defendant hath not rendred to the plaintiff tho' often thereunto requested but the Same doth Still refuse to render to the plaintiffs Damage three pounds Six Shillings Sterling and thereupon he brings his Suite and prayes Judgement for the Same with Costs of Suite and Shall pray etc.

Tobs. Knight Secretary

[*Endorsed:*]
Narratio
Giles versus Rafeild
In Case
Entered Octob. 5th: 1705

[*CCR 148*]

North Carolina Ss. To the provost Marshall or his Deputy

These are in her Matyes name to will and require you to Arrest the body of William Rafeild and him Safely hold Soe that he may be and appeare at the next Generall Court to be holden at the house of Captain Jno. Hecklefield in Litle river on the last Tuesday in this Instant October then and there to Answare the plaint of Cornelius Giles in a plea of the Case and have there this writt Dated at the Secretarys Office this 5th day of October Anno Domini 1705.

Testis Tobs. Knight Secretary

[*Endorsed:*]
Breve
Giles versus Rafeild
In Case
This Came but to hand the 23 day of ocktober

[*Glover, consignee* v. *Phillips and wife*]

[*CCR 192*]

North Carolina Ss. To the Honorable the Generall Court

Willm. Glover Esqr. Consignee of Colonel Robert Quary and New pensilvania Company is plaintiff against Danll. Phillipps and Joan his wife defendants in a plea of the Case and Complaines that the Defendants or one of them Stands Justly Indebted to the plaintiff qualifyed as aforesaid in the full Summe of Seaven pounds Eight Shillings in fresh porke by Account for divers Goods Credits and Merchandizes Delivered by the plaintiff or his order to the Defendants or one of them their or one of their order as by wayes and meanes Convenient the plaintiff is ready to make appeare which Said Summe of Seaven pounds Eight Shillings the Defendants nor either of them have not rendred to the plaintiff tho' often thereunto requested but the Same Doe Still refuse to render to the plaintiffs Damage fifteen pounds Sterling and thereupon he brings his Suite and prayes Judgement for the Same with Costs of Suite and Shall pray etc.

Tobs. Knight Secretary

[*Endorsed:*]
Glover versus Phillips and uxor eius
Narratio

[*CCR 192*]

No. Carolina Ss. To the provost Marshall or his Deputy

These are in the name of his Excellcy the Palatine and rest of the true and absolute Lords and Proprietors of this Province to will and require you to Arrest the body of Danll. Phillipps and Joan his wife and them Safely hold Soe that they may appeare at the next Generall Court to be holden for the Said province at the house of Captain Jno. Hecklefield in Litle river on the last Tuesday in July next Ensueing and then and there Answer the plaint of Wm. Glover Esqr. Consignee of Colonel Robert Quary and new pensilvania Company in a plea of the Case and have there this Writt Dated at the Secretarys Office the 23d day of July 17[*torn*].

Testis Tobs. Knight Secretary

[*Endorsed:*]
Glover versus Phillipps and uxor eius
Breve
Executed by me George Harris debety mashall

[*Hawkins* v. *Jones*]

[*CCR 139*]

North Carolina Ss. To the Provost Marshall or his Deputy

These are in her Majestyes name to will and require you to Arrest the body of John Jones and him Safely hold Soe that he may be and appeare at the next Generall Court to be holden at the house of Captain Jno. Hecklefield in Litle River on the last Tuesday in this Instant October then and there to Answer the plaint of John Hawkins in a plea of Debt and have there this writt dated at the Secretarys office this 10th day of October Anno Domini 1705.

Testis Tobs. Knight Secretary

[*Endorsed:*]
Hawkins versus Jones
In Debt
Executed

[*CCR 148*]

North Carolina Ss. To the provost Marshall or his Deputy

These are in her Matyes name to will and require you to Summons Thomas

Abington and Thomas Symons personally to be and appeare at the next Generall Court to be holden at the house of Captain Jno. Hecklefield in Litle river on the Last Tuesday in this Instant October then and there to give Evidence in a Cause there depending between Jno. Hawkins plaintiff and Jno. Jones defendant on behalfe of the plaintiff and have there this Sumons Dated at the Secretarys office this 12th day of October Anno Domini 1705.

Testis Tobs. Knight Secretary

[*Endorsed:*]
Sumons for Tho. Abington and Tho. Symons
Summon'd
Executed

[*Hecklefield* v. *Lehay*]

[*CCR 191*]

No. Carolina Ss. To the honorable the Generall Court etc.

Captain Jno. Hecklefeild is plaintiff against Ralph Lehay defendant in a plea of the Case and Complaines that the Defendant Stands indebted to the plaintiff in the full Summe of two pounds Eighteen Shillings and Seaven pence by account as by wayes and meanes Convenient the plaintiff is ready to make appear which said Summe of two pounds Eighteen Shillings and Seaven pence the defendant hath not rendred to the plaintiff tho' often thereunto requested but the Same doth Still refuse to render to the plaintiffs Damage Six pounds Sterling and thereupon he brings his Suite and prayes Judgement for the Same with Costs of Suite and Shall pray etc.

Tobs. Knight Secretary

[*Endorsed:*]
Narratio
Hecklefeild versus Lehay
In Case
Entred Augt. 6th:

[*Hecklefield* v. *Wilson*]

[*CCR 140*]

North Carolina Ss. To the Honorable the Generall Court

Capt. John Hecklefeild is plaintiff against Andrew Wilson Defendant in a plea of Debt and Says that the Defendant Stands Justly Indebted unto the plaintiff in the full and Just Summe of three pounds Twelve Shillings in Good Sound Merchantable fresh pork as by ways and meanes Convenient the plaintiff is ready to make appeare which Said Summe of Three pounds Twelve Shillings in the Comodity aforesaid the Defendant hath not rendred to the plaintiff tho' often thereunto requested but the Same doth Still refuse to render to the plaintiffs Damage Seaven pounds four Shillings Sterling and thereupon he brings his Suite and prayes Judgement for the Same with Costs of Suite and Shall pray etc.

Vera Copia Testis Tobs. Knight Secretary

[*Endorsed:*]
[*Illegible*] versus Wilson
In Debt

Capt. I Ded the best of my [*illegible*] for to Sarve it but by verey bad wether I could not git [over] from Scoper nung before the hard norwesters but if you plese to alter the Date I will Sarve it to the next Cort.

[*Hunt, assignee* v. *Bunting*]

[*CCR 185*]

North Carolina Ss. To the provost Marshall or his Deputy

These are in her Majestyes name to will and require you to Arrest the Body of John Buntin and him Safely hold Soe that he may be and personally appeare at the next Generall Court to be holden at the house of Captain John Heckle-feild in Litle river the last Tuesday in October next then and there to Answar the plaint of Captain Jno. Hunt Assignee of Hugh Campbill Attorney of Captain John Godwin Executor of Colonel John Leare Executor of Anne his wife Executrix of Seth Southwell Esqr. deceased in a plea of the Case and have there this writt Dated the 3 [*illegible*] day of September Anno Domini 1705.

Testis Tobs. Knight Secretary

[*Endorsed:*]
Hunt versus Bunting
Executed

[*Peterson, attorney of Perry and Company* v. *Barr*]

[*CCR 192*]

North Carolina Ss. To the Honorable the Generall Court

Thomas Peterson Attorney of Micajah Perry and New Pensilvania Company is plaintiff against Robert Barr of the County of Bath Defendant in a plea of Debt and Complaines that the Defendant Stands Justly Indebted unto the plaintiff quallyfyed as aforesaid in the full and Just Summe of Twenty Eight pounds and Sixteen Shillings per Bill Dated 16th Sept. 1704 as by the same bill here into Court brought and ready to be produced relation being thereunto had doth and may more fully and at large appeare which Said Sume of Twenty Eight pounds and Sixteen Shillings the Defendant hath not rendred to the plaintiff tho' often thereunto requested but the Same doth Still refuse to render to the plaintiffs Damage fifty Seaven pounds Twelve Shillings

Sterling and thereupon he brings his Suite and prayes Judgement for the Same with Costs of Suite and Shall pray etc.

Tobs. Knight Secretary

[*Endorsed:*]
Narratio
Peterson versus Barr
In Debt
Entred 8th Augt. 1705
Attach'd a parcell of black Cattell and one Great Canew per Edwd. Pitts

[*CCR 192*]

North Carolina Ss. To the Provost Marshall or his Deputy

These are in her Majestyes name to will and require you to Arrest the body of Robert Barr and him Safely hold Soe that he may appeare at the next Generall Court to be holden for this Government at the house of Captain Jno. Hecklefeild in Litle river on the last Tuseday in October next then and there to Answer the plaint of Thomas Peterson Attorney of Micajah Page and New Pensilvania Company in a plea of Debt and have there this writt Dated at the Secretarys Office this 8th day of Augt. Anno Domini 1705.

Testis Tobs. Knight Secretary

[*Endorsed:*]
Breve
Peterson versus Barr
In Debt
Executed

[*Peterson, attorney of Perry and Company* v. *Smith*]

[*CCR 192*]

North Carolina Ss. To the Honorable the Generall Court

Thomas Peterson Attorney of Micajah Perry and New Pensilvania Company is plaintiff against Richd. Smyth of the County of Bath Defendant in a plea of Debt and Complaines that the Defendant Stands Justly Indebted unto the plaintiff qualifyed as aforesaid in the full and Just Summe of One pound Eight Shillings and Six pence in Good Sound Merchantable fresh pork as in and by One writeing Obligatory beareing Date 12th day of Septr. 1704 and ready to be produced to this Honorable Court relation being thereunto had doth and may more fully and at large appeare which Said Summe of One pound Eight Shillings and Six pence the Defendant hath not rendred to the plaintiff tho' often thereunto requested but the Same doth Still refuse to render to the plaintiffs Damage two pounds Seaventeen Shillings Sterling and thereupon he brings his Suite and prayes Judgement for the Sum with Costs of Suite and Shall pray etc.

Tobs. Knight Secretary

[*Endorsed:*]
Narratio
Peterson versus Smyth
In Debt
Entred Augt. 8:1705

[*CCR 192*]

North Carolina Ss. To the Honorable the Generall Court

Thomas Peterson Attorney of Micajah Perry and New Pensilvania Company is plaintiff against Richard Smyth of the County of Bath Defendant in a plea of Debt and Complaines that the Defendant Stands Justly Indebted to the plaintiff Quallifyed as aforesaid in the full and Just Summe Ninety four pounds one Shilling and three pence to be paid in Good fresh Merchantable porke as in and by one writeing Obligatory beareing Date the 16th day of September 1704 and ready to be produced to this Honorable Court relation being thereunto had Doth and may more fully and at large appeare which Said Summe of Ninety four pounds One Shilling and three pence the Defendant hath not rendred to the plaintiff tho' often thereunto requested but the Same Doth Still refuse to render to the plaintiffs Damage One hundred Eighty Eight pounds two Shillings and Six pence and thereupon he brings his Suite and prayes Judgement for the Same with Costs of Suite and Shall pray etc.

Tobs. Knight Secretary

[*Endorsed:*]
Narratio
Peterson versus Smyth
In Debt
Entred 8th Augt. 1705

[*CCR 192*]

North Carolina Ss. To the provost Marshall or his Deputy

These are in her Majestyes name to will and require you to Arrest the body of Richard Smyth and him in Safe Custody hold Soe that he may appeare at the next Generall Court to be holden for the Government at the house of Captain John Hecklefeild in Litle River on the last Tuesday in October next then and there to Answer the plaint of Thomas Peterson Attorney of Micajah Perry and New Pensilvania Company in a plea of Debt and have there this writt Dated at the Secretarys Office the 8th day of Augt. Anno Domini 1705.

Testis Tobias Knight Secretary

[*Endorsed:*]
Breve
Peterson versus Smyth
In Debt
Executed

[*CCR 188*]

This Bill bindeth me Richard Smith of The Precinct of Bath In the Province of North Carrolina Planter, me, my heirs, Administrators, Executors or Asigns, To pay Unto Thomas Peterson, or his Order, on the Proper account of the New Pensilvania Company the full and Just Summ of Ninety four pounds, one Shilling and Three *d.* In good fresh Merchantble Pork and to be Deliver'd at any Good Landing for Either County to the Likeing of the Said Peterson, on or before the first day in Febry. next Ensueing the date hereof as Wittness my hand This 16th: Sept: 1704 In Pamptico.

Testis Richd. Smith
Nicholas Tylor
John frafin
Joseph Ming

[*Endorsed:*]
Richd. Smith
94.1.3

[*Porter* v. *Fewox*]

[*CCR 148*]

North Carolina Ss. To the Honorable the Generall Court

John Porter Esqr. is plaintiff against James Fewox Defendant in a plea of Debt and Complaines that whereas the Defendant by one writeing obligatory under his proper hand and Seale beareing date the 27th day of June 1700 did become bounden unto Humphry Legg his Heyres or order in the penalty of the full and Just Sume of One hundred forty and four busshells of Good Sound well drest Merchantble Indian Corne to be delivered at the upper dwelling house of the plaintiff in the precinct of Chowan and to be upon all demands after the tenth of March next Ensueing the aforesaid Date which Said writeing was and is by the aforesaid Humphry Legg assigned over to the plaintiff as in and by the Said writeing here into Court brought and ready to be produced relation being thereunto had it doth and may more fully and at large appeare Nevertheless the Defendant the aforesaid quantity of one hundred forty and four bushells of Indian Corne [or] any part thereof hath not paid and Delivered to the plaintiff tho' often thereunto requested but the Same [doth] Still refuse to pay or Deliver to the plaintiffs Damage twenty four pounds Sterling and thereupon he brings his Suite and prayes Judgement for the Same with Costs of Suite and Shall pray etc.

Tobs. Knight Secretary

[*Endorsed:*]
Narratio
Porter versus Fewox
In Debt
Entered Sept. 28:1705

[*CCR 148*]

North Carolina Ss. To the provost Marshall or his Deputy

These are in her Majestyes name to will and require you to Arrest the body of James Fewox and him Safely hold Soe that he may appeare at the next Generall Court to be holden at the House of Captain John Hecklefeild in Litle river on the last Tuesday in October next then and there to Answare the plaint of John Porter Esqr. in a plea of Debt and have there this writt Dated at the Secretarys office the 28th day of Sept. Anno Domini 1705.

Testis Tobs. Knight Secretary

[*Endorsed:*]
Breve
Porter versus Fewox
In Debt
Executed by me Daniel Hallsey Deputy marshal

[*Porter* v. *Powell*]

[*CCR 148*]

North Carolina ss. To the Honorable the Generall Court

John Porter is plaintiff against William Powell defendant in a plea of debt and Saith That the Defendant Stands Justly Indebted to the plaintiff in the sume of twelve pounds Six Shillings mony to be paid in merchantable Drest Buck and Doe skins the Buck at two Shillings per Skin and Does skins at Eighteen pence per Skin to be Delivered at the said Porters house in Chowan as by bill Under the hand and seal of the Defendant bearing date the 14th day Seper. 1701 will more at Large appear [the which] Sum in Specie aforesaid the Defendant refuses to render to the plaintiff though often demanded to the plaintiffs Damage twenty fore pounds Sterling mony the plaintiff therfore brings this action before this Honorable Court Craving judgment against the Defendant for the aforesaid Sum according to his bill aforesaid with his Just Damages and Costs of sute and he Shall pray etc.

John Porter

Evidence for the plaintiff Mr. Arderne and Epraim Lueton
[*Endorsed:*]
[Porter] versus Powell

[*CCR 148*]

North Carolina Ss. To the provost Marshall or his Deputy

These are in her Matyes name to will and require you to Arrest the body of William Powell and him Safely hold Soe that he may appeare at the next Generall Court to be holden at the house of Captain John Hecklefeild in Litle river on the last Tuesday in October next then and there to Answare the plaint of John Porter Esqr. in a plea of Debt and have there this writt Dated at the Secretarys Office the 10th day of Sept. Anno Domini 1705.

Testis Tobs. Knight Secretary

[*Endorsed:*]
Porter versus Powell
Executed

[*Porter and Company* v. *Grills*]

[*CCR 148*]

North Carolina Ss. To the Honorable the Generall Court

John Porter Esqr. and Company are plaintiffs against Richd. Grills Defendant in a plea of the Case and Complaines that the Defendant Stands Justly Indebted to the Complainants in the full Summe of twenty Six pounds by Account as by wayes and meanes Convenient the plaintiffs are ready to make appeare which said Summe of twenty Six pounds the Defendant hath not rendred to the plaintiffs or either of them tho often thereunto requested but the Same doth Still refuse to render to the plaintiffs Damage fifty two pounds Sterling and thereupon they bring this Suite and prayes Judgement for the Same with Costs of Suite and Shall pray etc.

Tobs. Knight Secretary

[*Endorsed:*]
Narratio
Porter and Company versus Grills
In Case
Entered Sep. 28th: 1704

[*CCR 148*]

North Carolina Ss. To the Provost Marshall or his Deputy

These are in her Majestyes name to will and require you to Arrest the body of Richard Grills and him Safeley hold Soe that he may be and appeare at the next Generall Court to be holden at the house of Captain John Hecklefeild in Litle river on the Last Tuesday in October next then and there to Answare the plaint of John Porter Esqr. and Company in a plea of the Case and have there this writt Dated at the Secretarys Office this [28th] day of Sept. Anno Domini 1705.

Testis Tobs. Knight Secretary

[*Endorsed:*]
Breve
Porter and Company versus Grills
In Case
Exegueted by me Danil Hallsey Deputy marshall

[*Swann* v. *Fewox*]

[*CCR 148*]

[*Torn*] Carolina Ss. To the honorable the Generall Court

Honorable Samll. Swann Esqr. is plaintiff against James Fewox Defendant in a plea of Debt and Says [the] Defendant Stands Justly Indebted to the plaintiff in full and Just Summe or Quantity of Nine [*torn*] of Good Merchantable Tarr to be paid and Delivered at the plaintiffs owne Landing [*illegible*] Certaine writeing under the proper hand of the Defendant Dated the first day [*illegible*] 1705 and now ready to be produced relation being thereunto had doth and may fully and at large appeare which Said Quantity of Nine barrells of Tarr the Defendant [hath] not paid nor Delivered to the plaintiff tho' often thereunto requested but the Same [doth] still refuse to pay or deliver to the plaintiffs Damage tenn pounds Sterling and thereupon he [*torn*] his Suite and prayes Judgement for the Same with Costs of Suite and Shall pray etc.

Tobs. Knight Secretary

[*Endorsed:*]
Swann versus Fewox
In Debt
Entered Sept. 29th: 1705

[*CCR 148*]

[*Torn*] Carolina Ss. To the provost Marshall or his Deputy

[These] are in her Matyes name to will and require you to Arrest the body of James Fewox and [him] Safely hold Soe that he may appeare at the next Generall Court to be holden at the [house] of Capt. Jno. Hecklefield in Litle river on the last Tuesday in October next then [and] there to Answare the plaint of The Honorable Samll. Swan Esqr. in a plea of Debt and have [there] this writt Dated at the Secretarys Office this 29th day of Sept. Anno Domini 1705.

Testis Tobs. Knight Secretary

[*Endorsed:*]
[*Torn*] versus Fewox
Excequeted by me Danl. Hallsey Debety marshall

[*CCR 188*]

This bill bindeth me James fewox my heirs Executors and administrators to pay unto Samuel Swann his Executors and assignes the Just quantity of nine barrells of good Merchantable Tarr to be pd. at the Said Swanns Landing In Pequimins River at or before the 15th day of July next Insueing wittness my hand this first day of May 1705.

James fewox <*Signe*>

Testis <*Sign*> James fewox
Obaah. Benjm. Gumbleton

[*Endorsed:*]
Ja. fewoxes [Account] 9 barrels tarr

[*CCR 148*]

[*Torn*] To the honorable the Generall Court

Samll. Swann Esqr. is plaintiff against Wm. Pargiter Defendant in a plea of Debt and Sayes that [*torn*] is Justly Indebted to the plaintiff in the full and Just Summe of Two pounds [*torn*] and four pence halfe peny to be paid in Tarr as by wayes and [*torn*] Convenient the plaintiff is ready to make appeare which Said Summe of [*torn*] Seaven Shillings and four pence halfe peny in the Comodity aforesaid [*torn*] hath not rendred to the plaintiff tho' often thereunto requested but the Same [*torn*] refuse to render to the plaintiffs Damage four pounds fourteen Shillings [*torn*] Sterling and thereupon he brings his Suite and prayes Judgement for the [same with] Costs of Suite and Shall pray etc.

Tobs. Knight Secretary

[*Endorsed:*]
Entered Sept. 29th:1705

[*Swann* v. *Phelps*]

[*CCR 148*]

North Carolina Ss. To the Honorable the Generall Court

The Honorable Samll. Swan Esqr. is plaintiff against Frances Phelps widdow defendant in a plea of Debt and Sayes that the Defendant Stands Justly Indebted to the plaintiff in the full and Just Summe of Seaven pounds Six Shillings and Tenn pence to be paid in Good Merchantable Tarr at the [plaintiffs] owne Landing at the rate of Eleaven Shillings per Barrell as by wayes and meanes Convenient the plaintiff is ready to make appeare which Said Summe of Seaven pounds Six Shillings and Tenn pence in the Comodity aforesaid the Defendant hath not rendred to [the] plaintiff tho' often thereunto requested but the Same doth Still refuse to render to the [*torn*] Damage fourteen pounds thirteen Shillings and Eight pence and thereupon he brings Suite and prayes Judgement for the Same with Costs of Suite and Shall pray etc.

Tobs. Knight Secretary

[*Endorsed:*]
Swann Esqr. versus Phelps widdow
In debt
Entered Sept. 29th:1705

[*CCR 148*]

North Carolina Ss. To the provost Marshall or his Deputy

These are in her Majestyes name to will and require you to Arrest the body of Phelps widdow and her Safely hold Soe that Shee may be and appeare at the Generall Court to be holden at the house of Captain John Hecklefeild in Litle river the Last Tuesday in October next then and there to Answare the plaintiff Honorable Samll. Swann Esqr. in a plea of Debt and have there this Writt at the Secretarys Office the 29th day of Sept. Anno Domini 1705.

Testis Tobs. Knight Secretary

[*Endorsed:*]
Breve
Swan Esqr. versus Phelps widdow
In Debt
Not sarved by Extremely whether

[*Swann* v. *Snell*]

[*CCR 148*]

North Carolina Ss. To the honorable the Generall Court

The Honorable Samll. Swann Esqr. is plaintiff against John Snell defendant in a plea of Debt and Sayes that the Defendant Stands Justly Indebted to the plaintiff in the full and Just Summe of four pounds [*torn*] and Eight pence to be paid in Good Merchantable Tarr at the plaintiffs owne Landing [*torn*] of Eleaven Shillings per Barrel as by wayes and meanes Convenient the Plaintiff is [ready] to make appeare which Said Summe of four pounds Six Shillings and Eight pence [*torn*] the Comodity aforesaid the Defendant hath not rendred to the plaintiff tho' often thereunto requested but the Same doth Still refuse to render to the plaintiffs Damage Eight pounds thirteen Shillings and four pence Sterling and thereupon he brings his Suite and prayes Judgement for the Same with Costs of Suite and Shall pray etc.

Tobs. Knight Secretary

[*Endorsed:*]
Swann Esqr. versus Snell
In [debt]
Entered Sept. 29th 1705

[*CCR 148*]

North Carolina Ss. To the provost Marshall or his Deputy

These are in her Majestyes name to will and require you to Arrest the body of John Snell and him safely hold Soe that he may appeare at the next Generall Court to be holden at the house of Capt. Jno. Hecklefeild in Litle river on the last Tuesday in October next then and there to answare the plaint of the Honorable Samll. Swann Esqr. in a plea of Debt and have there this writt Dated at the Secretarys Office the 29th day of Sept. Anno Domini 1705.

Testis Tobs. Knight Secretary

[*Endorsed:*]
[*Illegible*] versus Snell
Exesqued by me Daniel Hallsey Deputy marshal

[*Swann* v. *Spruill*]

[*CCR 148*]

North Carolina Ss. To the Honorable the Generall Court

The Honorable Samll. Swann Esqr. is plaintiff against Godfrey Spruell Defendant in a plea of Debt and Sayes that the Defendant Stands Justly Indebted to the plaintiff in the full and Just Summe of Seaven pounds Nineteen Shillings and Eleaven pence to be paid in Good Merchantable Tarr at the plaintiffs owne Landing at the rate of Eleaven Shillings per Barrell as by wayes and meanes Convenient the plaintiff is ready to make appeare which Said Summe of Seaven pounds Nineteen Shilling and Eleaven pence in the Comodity aforesaid the Defendant hath not rendered to the plaintiff tho' often thereunto requested but the Same doth Still refuse to render to the plaintiffs Damage Fifteen pounds Nineteen Shillings and tenn pence Sterling Whereupon he brings his Suite and prayes Judgement for the Same with Costs of Suite and Shall pray etc.

Tobs. Knight Secretary

[*Endorsed:*]
Narratio
Swann Esqr. versus Spruell
In Debt
Entered Sept. 29th 1705

[*CCR 148*]

North Carolina Ss. To the provost Marshall or his Deputy

These are in her Majestyes name to will and require you to Arrest the body of Godfrey Spruell and him Safely hold Soe that he may appeare at the next Generall Court to be holden at the house of Captain John Hecklefeild in Litle river on the last Tuesday in October next then and there to Answare the plaint of the Honorable Samll. Swann Esqr. in a plea of Debt and have there this writt Dated at the Secretarys Office this 29th day of September Anno Domini 1705.

Testis Tobs. Knight Secretary

[*Endorsed:*]
Breve
Swann Esqr. versus Spruell
[*Illegible*] Daniel Hallsey Debtey marshall ocktober [*illegible*] 1705

[*Truewhitt* v. *Watson*]

[*CCR 148*]

North Carolina Ss. To the Honorable the Generall Court

Levy Truewhitt is plaintiff against Jno. Watson Defendant in a plea of Debt and Sayes that Whereas the Defendant In and by one Certaine writeing

Obligatory under the proper hand of the Defendant beareing Date the 28th day of Augt. 1704 did oblidge himselfe unto Mr. Thomas Dereham to fall Maule and Cutt off Two thousand riders or Rayles between the Date of the Said writeing and Christmas day then next Ensueing for the Said Mr. Thomas Dereham at his the Said Derehams plantation or any other place of Conveniency that he pleases, which Said writeing has and is Since Assigned over by the Said Dereham to the plaintiff as in and by the Said writeing obligatory relation being thereunto had doth and may More fully and at Large appear Nevertheless the Defendant the Said Labour for the plaintiff hath not done tho' often thereunto requested but the Same doth Still refuse to doe Contrary to his obligation aforesaid to the plaintiffs Damage Seaven pounds Tenn Shillings Sterling and thereupon he brings his Suite and prayes Judgement for the Same with Costs of Suite and Shall pray etc.

Tobs. Knight Secretary

[*Endorsed:*]
Narratio
Truewhitt versus Watson
In Debt
Entered Octobr. 5th: 1705

[*Wilkison* v. *Davenports*]

[*CCR 148*]

North Carolina Ss. To the Honorable the Generall Court

William Wilkinson Esqr. is plaintiff against Richard Devenport and Jno. Devenport defendants in a plea of Debt and Sayes that the Defendants or one of them Stands Justly Indebted unto the [*illegible*] Summe of thirteen pounds Six Shillings and Six pence as in and by one Certaine writeing obligatory under the proper hands and Seales of the Defendants beareing Date the twelfth day of December 1702 and now ready to be produced relation being thereunto had doth and may more fully and at large appeare which Said Sume of thirteen pounds Six Shillings and Six pence the Defendants nor either of them have not rendred to the plaintiff tho' often thereunto requested but the Same doth Still refuse to render to the plaintiffs Damage Twenty Six pounds thirteen Shillings Sterling and thereupon he brings his Suite and prayes Judgement for the Same with Costs of Suite and Shall pray etc.

Tobs. Knight Secretary

[*Endorsed:*]
Narratio
Wilkinson versus Devenport
In Debt
Entered October 15th: 1705

[*CCR 148*]

North Carolina Ss. To the provost Marshall or his Deputy

These are in her Majestyes name to will and require you to Arrest the body of Richard Devonport and Jno. Devonport and them Safely hold Soe that they may appeare at the next Generall Court to be holden at the house of Captain Jno. Hecklefield in Litle river on the last Tuesday in this Instant October then and there to Answare the plaint of Willm. Wilkinson Esqr. in a plea of Debt and have there this writt Dated at the Secretarys office this 15th day of October Anno Domini 1705.

Testis Tobs. Knight Secretary

[*Endorsed:*]
Breve
Wilkinson versus Devenport
Executed

[*Wilkison* v. *Hears*]

[*CCR 148*]

North Carolina Ss. To the honorable the Generall Court

Willm. Wilkinson Esqr. is plaintiff against Samll. Hears defendant in a plea of Debt and Sayes that the Defendant Stands Justly Indebted to the plaintiff in the full and Just Summe of Seaven pounds two Shillings and four pence as in and by one Certaine writeing obligatory under the proper hand and Seale of the Defendant beareing date the Seaventeenth day of September 1703 and now ready to be produced relation being thereunto had doth and may more fully and at Large appeare which Said Sume of Seaven pounds two Shillings and four pence the Defendant hath not rendred to the plaintiff tho' often thereunto required but the Same doth Still refuse to render to the plaintiffs Damage fourteen pounds four Shillings and Eight pence and thereupon he brings his Suite and prayes Judgement for the Same with Costs of Suite and Shall pray etc.

Tobs. Knight Secretary

[*Endorsed:*]
Narratio
Wilkinson versus Hears
In Debt
Entered Octob. 15th: 1705

[*CCR 148*]

North Carolina Ss. To the provost Marshall or his Deputy

These are in her Majestyes name to will and require you to Arrest the body of Samll. Hears and him Safely hold Soe that he may appeare at the next Generall Court to be holden for this Province at the house of Captain Jno. Hecklefield in Litle river on the last Tuesday in this Instant October then and there to Answare the plaint of William Wilkinson Esqr. in a plea of Debt and have there this writt Dated at the Secretarys Office this 15th day of October Anno Domini 1705.

Testis Tobs. Knight Secretary

[*Endorsed:*]
Breve
Wilkinson versus Hears
In Debt
Executed

[*Wilson, attorney of Godfrey* v. *White*]

[*CCR 148*]

North Carolina Ss.

Att a Generall Court holden at the house of Capt. Jno. Hecklefield in Litle river on Tuesday the 30th day of October Anno Domini 1705. Present the Honorable the Justices.

By an Attachment from the last Court between Isaac Wilson Attorney of Peter Godfrey plaintiff and John White Defendant The Said Isaac Willson Comes by Captain Jno. Hecklefield [his] Attorney and prays Appraisors may be appointed to appraise the Goods [*illegible*] (videlicet) one Cow and one Yearling One Steere three yeares Old One Heifer [*torn*] the Same with advantage which is returned by the Marshall to be the [*illegible*] Estate of the Said White and by the Marshall Attached and the Court [*illegible*] Samll. Parsons Andrew Reed and Jno. Bateman or any two of them [to] appraise the abovesaid Goods and Chattles and make report of their proceedings therein to the next Generall Court.

Vera Copia Testis T. Knight Secretary

[*CCR 189*]

Docquett of Acctions to March Court 1706

Referrences and Attachments from October Court last

1. Glover Consignee etc. versus Pritchard in Case Referred.
2. Idem versus Nash in Case.
3. Idem versus Fewox in Case.
4. Idem versus French in Case.
5. Idem versus Cooper in Case.
6. Idem versus Banks in Case.
7. Swann Esqr. versus Spruell in Debt. Attachment Executed. Dismissed.
8. Glover versus Pritchard Executor etc. in Case. Attachment.

9. Idem versus Luerton in Case. Attachment Executed.

10. Porter versus Fewox in Debt. Referred.

11. Porter versus Powell in Debt. Attachment.

12. Idem and Company versus Grills in Case. Attachment.

13. Peterson Attorney etc. versus Barr in Debt. Attachment returned. Executed. Retraxit.

14. Idem versus Smyth in Debt. Attachment returned. Executed.

15. Idem versus Eundem in Debt. Attachment returned. Executed.

Writts and returnes to March Court

1. Boyd versus Paine. Attachment withdrawne.
2. Porter versus Payne. Attachment non pros.
3. Duckenfeild Esqr. versus Fee in Debt.
4. Idem versus Farrow in Debt. Return Executed.
5. Idem versus Molines in Debt.
6. Idem versus Smyth in Debt.
7. Idem versus Monteague in Debt. Return Executed.
8. Hecklefield versus Ward in Case.
9. Keel versus Scarbro in trespass Super Casu. Return Executed.
10. Porter versus Smyth et al. in Debt. Return Executed.
11. Idem versus Trewhitt et al. in Debt. Return Executed.
12. Idem versus Dereham in Debt. Return Executed.
13. Hawkeins versus Cross in Debt.
14. Peterson Attorney etc. versus Fryly in Debt. Executed.
15. Idem versus Eundem in Debt. Executed.
16. Idem versus Hewett in Debt. Return Executed.
17. Idem versus Daniell in Debt. Return Executed.
18. Idem versus Holmes in Debt. Return Non Est Inventus.
19. Idem versus Davis in Debt. Return Executed.
20. Idem versus Peggs in Debt. Return Executed.
21. Idem versus Eundem in Debt. Return Executed.
22. Idem versus Towers in Debt. Not Executed.

23. Idem versus Miller in Debt. Return Executed.

24. Idem versus Meads in Debt. Return Executed. Non pros.

25. Idem versus Eundem in Debt. Return Executed. Non pros.

26. Idem versus Rice in Debt. Return Executed. Non pros.

27. Idem versus Pettiver in Case. Return Executed.

28. Idem versus Andiver in Case. Return Executed.

29. Penrice versus Norton in Case. Retraxit. Non [*torn*].

30. Feillett versus Tull in Case. Return Executed.

31. Feillett versus Jenings in Case. Return Executed.

32. Feillett versus Sawyer in Case. Return Executed.

33. Idem versus Jenings in Case. Return Executed.

34. Tooke Executor etc. versus Bell in Debt.

35. Snoden versus Wallis in Case. Return Executed.

36. Gale Esqr. versus Lawson in Case. Return Executed. Retraxit.

37. Hecklefeild versus Vandermulen et al. in Case. Executed. Withdrawne.

38. Idem Attorney etc. versus Slade in Case.

39. Aires versus Stepvens in Debt. Return Executed. Retraxit.

40. Idem versus Eggerton in Debt. Not Executed.

41. Cary versus Phillips. Attachment. Return nulla Bona.

42. Idem versus Brownell. Attachment. Return Executed.

[*Endorsed:*]

Docquett to March Court

1706

[*CCR 104*]

<336> No. Carolina Ss.

Att a Generall Court holden at the house of Captain Jno. Hecklefield in Little river on Tuesday the 26th day of March Anno Domini 1706.

Present The Honorable Willm. Glover, Jno. Porter, Christo. Gale Esqrs. Justices.

Mr. Samll. Norton personally appeared and upon his Oath proved a Deed of Sale of a Tract of Land on the North Side of Pamptecough river from Nicho. Thomas Jones to Landgrave Robert Daniell Esqr.

Upon Motion of Thos. Houghton Senior being Comitted by James Cole Esqr. one of her Majestyes Justices of the peace for the precinct of pequimons as an Accessary in Stealeing of a Bull of the Goods and Chattles of Jno. Hopkins and prayes he may be dismissed upon Good Bayle for his appeareance the next Court.

Ordered that the provost Marshall Dismiss the Said Houghton out of Custody and take Good Bayle for his appeareance att his Tryall att the tyme the Court shall be adjourned to.

Then this Court adjourned till the first Tuseday in May next.

Tuesday the 7th day of May 1706 this Court Mett and adjourned till to morrow morne 8 of Clocke.

Wednesday Morne 8 of Clocke this Court Mett. Present The Honorable Willm. Glover, Jno. Porter, Christo. Gale Esqrs. Justices.

Mr. Thos. Boyd Presented a Comission from the honorable Thos. Cary Esqr. Deputy Governor etc. thereby appointing him provost Marshall of this Government which was read allowed of and ordered to be recorded. Then the said Boyd tooke and Subscribed the Severall othes by Law appointed to be taken in order for his Quallification.

Then the Severall Acts made the Last Assembly was openly read and published.

Then the Grand Jury was Swoarne.

Upon the Petition of Willm. Brice being Sumoned to appeare here to Answer a Contempt for not Serveing a Justice of the peaces Warrant to him directed and prayed to be Dismissed and the said Brice in all humble manner Submiting him Selfe to this Court asking pardon for Such his offence <337> Ordered that the said Brice be accquitted from the said Contempt paying Costs.

Then this Court adjourned till tomorrow morne 9 of Clock.

Thursday Morne 9 of Clocke this Court mett present ut Supra.

Jno. Shaw James Beesly and Rachell Baker personally appeared and upon their Oathes in Open Court proved the last Will and Testament of Colonel Wm. Wilkison Deceased.

A power of Attorney from Arthur Lunn to Thos. Snoden was proved.

Dr. James Feillett Comes to prosecute his Suite against Benj. Tull in a plea of the Case and Complaines for two pounds and the Defendant Came not and the plaintiff prayes an order against the Marshall which is Granted. And Mr. Thos. Boyd provost Marshall

Comes and prayes an Attachment against the Estate of the Said Tull which is Granted.

Thos. Barcliffe personally appeared and acknowledged a Deed of Sale of a peice of Land to Thos. Phelps.

Dr. James Feillett Comes to prosecute his Suite against Wm. Jenings in a plea of the Case and Complaines that the Defendant Stands Indebted to the plaintiff in the summe of four pounds Ten Shillings for Medicines Phissick vissitts and Attendance administred and done to and upon the Said Defendant Afflicted with the Country desease as by Agreement with the said Defendant and wayes and meanes Convenient the plaintiff is ready to make appeare etc. to the plaintiffs Damage Nine pounds Sterling and thereupon he brings his Suite etc. And the Defendant in proper person Comes and defends the force and Injury when etc. and for plea Saith that the plaintiff did an agreement make to and with the Defendant that he the plaintiff would make an absolute Cure of the distemper the Defendant was afflicted with and saith that the aforesaid agreement he the plaintiff hath not performed and this he is ready to Averr And of this he puts him Selfe upon the Country and the plaintiff in like manner. Whereupon the Marshall was Comanded to Cause to Come Twelve etc. to whome etc. who neither etc. by whome etc. and there Came Mr. Rob. Wallis Mr. Rob. Harrison Mr. Danll. Rice Mr. Thos. Collins Mr. Richd. Horton Mr. Thos. Barcliffe Mr. Jno. Stepney Mr. Rob. Keele Mr. Richd. Smyth Mr. James Beard Mr. Wm. White Mr. Jno. Sawyer, Who being Swoarne and Impannelled Say. Wee of the Jury find for the Defendant. Ordered that the suite be dismissed and the plaintiff pay Costs alias Execution.

<338> Then this Court adjourned for halfe an hour and mett againe.

Thomas Peterson Attorney to Daniell Zachary Comes to prosecute his Suite against Jno. Pettiver in a Plea of the Case and Complaines for twenty Seaven pounds Twelve Shillings and Ten pence And the Defendant by Thos. Snoden his Attorney Comes and by Consent of both partyes. It is ordered that the Same be referred to the next Generall Court.

Thos. Peterson Attorney to Micajah Perry and New Pensilvania Company Comes to Prosecute his Suite against Thos. Holmes in a plea of Debt and Declares for the Summe of three pounds ten Shillings and four pence Sterling And there being a Non est Inventus returned by the Marshall the plaintiff prayes an Attachment against the Defendants Estate Which is Granted.

Then this Court Adjourned till Four of Clock and at 4 of Clock mett againe.

An Indictment was found and presented by the Grand Jury against Thomas Houghton Junior in the following words (videlicet) The Jurors of our Soveraigne Lady the Queene upon their Oathes doe present that Thos. Houghton Junior of the precinct of pequimons in the aforesaid province not haveing the Grace of God before his Eyes but being led away by the Instigation of the Devill on or about the 26th day of Feb. last past in the precinct of pequimons and in this province did feloniously Kill Steal and beare away one three yeare old Bull of the vallue of Twelve Shillings and Six pence the proper Goods and Chattles of Jno. Hopkins of the precinct and province aforesaid against the peace of our Soveraigne Lady the Queene her Crowne and Dignity and Contrary to the forme of the Statute in Such Cases made and provided. Upon which Indictment the said Houghton was Arraigned and on his Arraignement pleaded not Guilty and thereupon put himselfe upon his Country who being Swoarne and Impannelled Say that the prisoner is not Guilty. Ordered that Thos. Houghton Senior and Thos. Houghton Junior doe remaine in Custody of the Marshall untill they shall pay their Fees and find Good Security for their Good Behaviour and That Thos. Houghton Senior doe make his personall appeareance at the next <339> Generall Court to Answer to Such things as by her Majestyes Attorney Generall shall be alleadged against him.

Then this Court adjourned till to Morrow Morne 9 of Clock.

Fryday Morne 9 of Clock this Court mett present ut Supra.

Robt. Keele Comes by Mr. Tho. Snoden and Mr. Edward Bonwick his Attorneys to prosecute his Suite against Augustin Scarbrough in a plea of Trespass on the Case. And the Defendant Comes in proper person and prayes a refferrence to the next Court and that he wants Councell and the Court haveing duely Considered the whole matter Ordered that the matter be referred to the next Generall Court accordingly.

James Feillett Dr. Medicine Comes to prosecute his Suite against Henry Sawyer Defendant in a plea of the Case and Complaines that the Defendant Stands Justly Indebted to the plaintiff in the full and Just Summe of Five pounds the one halfe in porke the other halfe in Corne for Medicines Phissick Vissits and Attendance administred and Done to and upon the said Defendants Daughter in Cureing her of the Country Dissease as by Agreement and wayes and meanes Convenient the plaintiff is ready to make appeare Nevertheless the Defendant the Said Summe of Five pounds to the plaintiff hath not rendred etc. to the plaintiffs Damage Ten pounds Sterling and thereupon Comenced this Suite etc. And the Defendant Comes in proper person and defends the force and Injury when etc. and for plea Saith that he the plaintiff an Agreement did make to and with the Defendant that he the plaintiff would Cure the Defendants Daughter of the Country Distemper in maner and forme as in the plaintiffs Declaration is alledged And likewise Saith that he the plaintiff the aforesaid Agreement hath not performed And this he is ready to Averr and of this he puts himselfe upon the Country. And the plaintiff likewise Whereupon the Marshall was Comanded to Cause to Come twelve etc. to whome etc. who neither etc. by whome etc. and there Came Mr. Robert Wallis Mr. Rob. Harrison Mr. Daniell Rice Mr. Tho. Collins Mr. Rich. Horton Mr. Tho. Barcliffe Mr. Jno. Stepney Mr. Rob. Keele Mr. James Beard Mr. Wm. White Mr. Tho. Arnold Mr. John Winbury who being Swoarne and Impannelled Say. Wee of the Jury find for the Defendant Ordered that the Suite be dismissed and the plaintiff pay Costs Alias Execution.

<340> James Feillett Dr. Medicine Comes to prosecute his Suite against Jno. Jenings Defendant in a Plea of the Case and Complaines that the Defendant Stands Indebted to the plaintiff in the Summe of Twenty one pounds five Shillings by Account for Divers Medicines Phissick Dressings and Attendings administred to and upon the Defendants Daughter Dorathy (at the Speciall Instance and request of the Defendant) as by wayes and meanes Convenient the plaintiff is ready to make appeare Nevertheless the Defendant the said Summe of Twenty one pounds Five Shillings the Defendant hath not rendred to the plaintiff etc. to the plaintiffs Damage Forty two pounds tenn Shillings Sterling and thereupon he brings his Suite etc. And the Defendant Comes by Thomas Snoden his Attorney and Defends the force and Injury when etc. And for plea Saith that he the Defendant hath well and truely paid and Satisfyed unto the plaintiff the full and Just Summe of Four pounds and Ten Shillings for Medicines Phissick Dressing and Attending administred to and upon the Defendants Daughter in mannor as in the plaintiffs Declaration is Exprest And further the defendant to the plaintiff is not Indebted And this he is ready to Averr and of this he Putts himselfe upon the Country and the plaintiff likewise. Whereupon the Marshall was Comanded to Cause to Come twelve etc. to whome etc. who neither etc. by whome etc. and there Came Mr. Robert Wallis Mr. Rob. Harrison Mr. Daniell Rice Mr. Tho. Collins Mr. Rich. Horton Mr. Tho. Barcliffe Mr. Jno. Stepney Mr. Robert Keel Mr. James Beard Mr. Wm. White Mr. Tho. Arnold Mr. Jno. Winbury who being Swoarne and Impannelld Say Wee of the

Jury find for the plaintiff Fifty Shillings besides the defendants Account allow'd.

Ordered that the Defendant pay unto the plaintiff the Said Summe of fifty Shillings besides the defendants Account of four pounds ten Shillings with Costs alias Execution.

Presentment is made by the Grand Jury that the Road upon the Sound Side from Mr. Gales and Mr. Minges. And the Pamplecough Roads And also the Road in Pascotanke that begins at Thomas Cartwrights and soe up to Hugh Pritchards wants repaireing. Ordered that the Severall overseers of the aforesaid roads be Sumoned to the next Generall Court to Shew Cause why the said Roads are not repaired accordingly.

Henry Norman Surveyor of the Highwayes between Mr. Gales and Mr. Mings appeared and upon his Submission and promise that the said Roads Should be [Amended] Ordered that he be dismissed.

<341> Thomas Snoden comes in proper person to prosecute his Sute against Robert Wallis Defendant in a plea of the Case and complaines that the Defendant Stands justly indebted to the plaintiff in the full and just Summe of Two pounds in Cureant Silver or Gold Money which the Defendant did assume to pay unto the plaintiff in Manner aforesaid etc. And the said Robert Wallis in his proper person comes and Defends the force and injury when etc. and Saith that he did not assume as the plaintiff in his Declaration hath falsely Sett Suggested and of this he putts himself upon the Country and the plaintiff likewise And the Marshall was Comanded to cause to come twelve etc. by whom etc. and who etc. and there came Mr. John Stepney Mr. Robert Harrison Mr Daniel Rice, Mr. Thomas Collings Mr. Richd. Horton Mr. Thomas Bacliff Mr. Robert Keel Mr. Richard Smith Mr. William White Mr. John Sawyer Mr. Thomas Arnold Mr. John Windbury who Sworne and Impannelled Say We find for the plaintiff. Ordered that the Defendant pay unto the plaintiff the Said Summe of Fourty Shillings as aforesaid with Costs alias Execution.

Upon petition of Thomas Collings Ordered that the Said Thomas Collings have Letters of Administration of the Estate of Alice Collings his Mother Deceased.

Upon petition of Thomas Collings Ordered that Mr. Wm. Steevens Thomas Mercer John Bateman and Joshua Calloway or any Three of them Inventory and appraise the Estate of Alice Collings Deceased being first Sworne before a Majestrate.

Thomas Houghton Senior in the Summe of Twenty pounds and

Richd. Smith and Wm. Houghton in Ten pounds a peece acknowledges to Stand indebted to our Soveraigne Lady the Queen which said Severall summes to be leavyed upon their Goods and Chattles Lands and Tenements etc. Upon Condition that the said Thomas Houghton Senior Shalbe of his good behaviour towards her Majestie and all her Leige people and make his appearance att the next Generall Court.

Thomas Houghton Senior in the Summe of Twenty pounds Richd. Smith and William Houghton in the Summ of Ten pounds a peece accknowledges to Stand indebted to our Soveraigne Lady the Queen which Said Severall Summs to be levyed upon their Land and Tenements etc. Upon Condition that Thomas Houghton Junior Shalbe of his good <342> behaviour towards her Majesties and all other her leige people for one Year and a Day.

Then this Court adjourned 'till too morrow morne 9 of the Clock.

Saterday Morne 9 of the Clock. This Court mett. Present the Honorable Wm. Glover, John porter, Christo. Gale, Francis De La Mare, Wm. Barcliffe Esqrs. Justices.

A new Comission of the peace was read and the above-named Justices tooke the Severall Oaths by Law appointed.

The honorable William Glover Esqr. Consignee of Colonel Robert Quary and New pensilvania Company comes to prosecute his Sute against David pritchard Executror etc. of Elanor Buckley Administratrix etc. of Rowland Buckley Defendant in a plea of the Case and Complaines that the Defendant in the Qualification aforesaid Stands justly indebted to the plaintiff Qualifyed as aforesaid in the Full Summ of Eight pounds Two Shillings and Seven pence in fresh porke by Account for divers goods Creditts and Merchandizes Delivered by the plaintiff or his Order to the aforesaid Rowland Buckley or his order as etc. And the Defendant comes and Confesses.

Ordered that the Said David pritchard pay unto the Said Wm. Glover Eight pounds Two Shillings and Seven pence in Fresh porke with Costs alias Execution.

John porter Esqr. comes to prosecute his sute against Wm. powell Defendant in a plea of Debt upon a Judgment obteyned against the Marshall the last Court and Declares that the Defendant stands justly indebted to the plaintiff in the summ of Twelve pounds six shillings money to be paid in Merchantable Buck and Doe skins the Buck att Two shillings per skin and Doe skins att Eighteen pence per skin to be Delivered att the said porters house in Chowan as by Bill under the hand and seal of the Defendant bearing Date the 14th Day September 1704: will more att large appear and the plaintiff then came not upon which a Judgment went against the Marshall and the plaintiff prayes that the former Judgment obteyened against the Marshall may be Confirmed.

Ordered that Captain Jno. Hecklefeild late Marshall doe pay unto the said Jno. porter the summ of Twelve pounds six shillings according to specialty with Costs alias Execution.

<343> John porter Esqr. and Company comes to prosecute their Sutes against Richd. Grills Defendant upon a Judgment obteyned against the Marshall the last Court and Declares that the Defendant Stands justly to the plaintiff in the full sum of Twenty Six pounds by account etc. and the Defendant came not and the plaintiff prays Confirmation of the aforesaid Judgment against the Marshall and Captain John Hecklefeild late provost Marshall comes and Defends the force and Injury when etc. and saith that Judgment against him for the summ exprest in the plaintiffs Declaration ought not to be Confirmed for he Saith That after a Writt obteyned against Richard Grills for the aforesaid Summ he the plaintiff Discourseing with the Defendant concerning the Estate of the said Richd. Grills did Declare and Utter to the Defendant these words (videlicet) he (meaning the said Richd. Grills) has Enough I'le take all and pay all and this the said John Hecklefield is ready to averr and of this he putts himself upon the Country And the plaintiffs comes and Demurrs to the Defendants plea and Saith that the same is not sufficient in Law to hinder Confirmation of Judgment admitting the pretended assumsit were true which that plea denyes because the words in the Defendants plea implyes a Generall Assumsit which ought not to hinder the plaintiffs former Judgment being Confirmed because the Defendant has his Remedy att Comon Law upon an Action brought on the same against the plaintiff and further saith that the said Defendants plea ought not to be allowed in Barr etc. because the pretended assumsit tho' false is alleaged to be in his own single Capacity and the Action now Depending is in Company and the Defendant joynes in the Demurrer And the Court haveing Duely weighed and Considered the whole matter Ordered that the said Captain John Hecklefield pay unto the said John porter and Company Twenty Six pounds according to Specialty with Costs alias Execution.

Thomas peterson Attorney of Micajah perry and new pensilvania Company comes to prosecute his Sute from a Continuance from the last Court against Richard Smith Defendant in a plea of Debt and Complaines that the Defendant stands justly indebted to the plaintiff qualifyed as aforesaid in the full and just Summ of Ninety four pounds one shilling and three pence to be paid in good fresh Merchantable porke as in and by one writeing obligatory beareing Date the 16th Day of September 1704 And the Defendant came and by consent of both parties Ordered that the whole matter be referred to the next Generall Court.

Thomas peterson Attorney of Micajah perry and new pensilvania Company comes to prosecute his Sute from a Continuance from the <344> last Court against Richard Smith Defendant in a plea of Debt and Complanes that the Defendant Stands justly indebted unto the plaintiff Qualifyed as aforesaid in the full and just Summ of One pound Eight shillings and six pence in good Sound Merchantable Fresh porke by one writeing Obligatory bearing Date the 12th Day of September 1704 and the Defendant comes and confesses.

Ordered that the said Richard Smith pay unto the said Thomas peterson the Summ of One pound Eight Shillings and Six pence according to Specialty with Costs alias Execution.

Thomas peterson Attorney of Micajah perry and new pensilvannia Company comes to prosecute his Sute against Thomas Andever Defendant in a plea of the Case and Declares for the Summ of Three pounds Six shillings and Eleaven pence half penny in fresh porke by Account for Divers Goods etc. And John Arderne Esqr. Attorney to Wm. Duckenfield Esqr. comes and on behalf of the said Duckenfield assumes the payment of the said Money with Costs and prayes that the Sute may be dismissed.

Ordered that the Sute be dismissed accordingly.

Ordered that the Sute between Saml. Swann Esqr. and Doctor Godfrey Spruel be dismissed upon non appeareance of Either party.

William Duckenfield Esqr. assignee of Wm. powell comes by John Arderne Esqr. his Attorney to prosecute his sute against Francis Farrow Defendant in a plea of Debt and Declares for Fifteen pounds Five Shillings and Six pence by a writeing obligatory and the Defendant came not and the plaintiff prayes an Attachment against the Defendants Estate which is granted.

Wm. Duckenfield Esqr. by John Arderne Esqr. his Attorney comes to prosecute his Sute against Roger Monteagne Defendant in a plea of Debt and Declares for Thirty Seaven Shillings and Six pence one by bill and the Defendant came not and the plaintiff prayes an Attachment against the Defendants Estate which is granted.

John porter Esqr. comes to prosecute his Sute against Richard Smith and Wm. Hancock Defendants in a plea of Debt and Declares that the Defendants or either of them Stands joyntly and Severally Stands justly indebted to the plaintiff in the full and just Summ of One Hundred and Forty pounds Seven Shillings and Eleven pence by a Writeing Obligatory bearing Date the 26 Day of Feabruary Anno 1703/4 etc. and the Defendant Smith Comes and Confesses. Ordered that the said Smith pay to the said porter One hundred and forety pounds Seven Shillings and Eleven pence according to Specialty with Costs alias Execution.

<345> And the Defendant Handcock came not and the plaintiff prayes an Attachment against his Estate which is granted.

John West personally appeared and accknowledged an Assignement of a patent of Thomas Boyd.

Wm. Godfrey and Captain John Hecklefield personally appeared and interchangeably acknowledged a Lease for life of Three Hundred Acres of Land being the plantation whereon the said Hecklefield now lives.

John porter Esqr. comes to prosecute his Sute against Thomas Dereham Defendant in a plea of Debt and Declares for the Summ of Foarteen pounds and Eight pence half penny by writeing Obligatory beareing Date the 18th Day of Aprill 1705 etc. and the Defendant Came not and the plaintiff prayes an Order against the late Marshall and Captain John Hecklefield late Marshall comes and prayes an Attachment against the Said Derehams Estate which is granted.

John porter Esqr. comes to prosecute his Sute against Levi Trewhitt and Thomas Dereham and Declares that the Defendants or Either of them Stands justly indebted to the plaintiff in the full Summ of Eleven pounds Eleven Shillings and Three pence by a Writeing Obligatory beareing Date the 18th Day of Aprill 1705 etc. and the Defendants came not and the plaintiff prayes an Order against the late Marshall which is granted and Captain John Hecklefield provost Marshall comes and prayes an Attachment against the Defendants Estates which is granted.

Upon Issue Joyned the last Court John porter Esqr. comes to prosecute his Sute against James Fuox and Declares for One hundred foarty and four Bushels of good Sound Merchantable Indyan Corne etc. and the Defendant came not and the plaintiff prayes Judgment by nihil dicit which is granted.

Ordered that the Said Fewox pay unto the Said porter One Hundred Fourty and four Bushels of Indyan Corne according to Specialty with Costs alias Execution.

John McKeel comes and upon his Oath upon the holy Evangelist proved an Account of Two pounds Two Shillings and Three pence due in Ballance upon the Estate of Mr. Richard plater Deceased. Ordered that Mr. Anthony Hatch Administrator with the Will annext to the Said Mr. plater pay unto the Said John McKeel the Same Summe of Two pounds Two Shillings and Three pence alias Execution.

Then this Court adjourned 'till the next Generall Court.

[*Signed:*]
W. Glover, <346> C. Gale, francis DeLaMare, William Barclift.

RECORDED BY ORDER OF COURT

[*CCR 104*]

No. Carolina Ss.

The Honorable Thos. Cary Esqr. Lieutenant Generall Vice Admiral and Deputy Governor.

To: Thomas Boyd

I out of trust and Confidence I have in the Loyalty abillity prudence and Integrity of you Thos. Boyd doe hereby Commissionate and appoint you provost Marshall of this Government of No. Carolina hereby Impowering you to Execute all writts warrants or other orders to you directed from me or any Court of record or Majestrate within this Government and to Act Execute and performe whatsoever to the Office of a provost Marshall doth belong in as full and large a maner to all intents and purposses as by the Lawes of this Government is appointed as also to demand and receive all Fees and profitts to the Said Office belonging and to Constitute and make Soe many deputyes for the better performance hereof as you shall See Convenient and all her Matyes Subjects in this Government are hereby required to be aideing and Assisting to you in the Execution hereof this Comission to Continue dureing my pleasure Given under my hand and Seale at Armes the 14th day of Aprill in the fifth yeare of her Majestyes Raigne Anno Domini 1706.

Thomas Cary

Recorded 1st day of June 1706 per T. Knight Secretary

FILE PAPERS IN SUITS AND PROSECUTIONS

[*Ayres* v. *Eggerton*]

[*CCR 191*]

No. Carolina Ss. To the Honorable Generall Court etc.

Thomas Aires is plaintiff against patrick Eggerton Defendant in a plea of debt and Sayes that the Defendant Stands Justly Indebted to the plaintiff in the full and Just Summe of Four pounds as in and by one Certaine writeing Obligatory under the proper hand of the Defendant here into Court brought and ready to be produced relation being thereunto had doth and may more fully and at large appeare which Said Summe of Four pounds the Defendant hath not rendred to the plaintiff tho' often thereunto requested but the Same doth Still refuse to render to the plaintiffs Damage Eight pounds Sterling and thereupon he brings his Suite and prayes Judgement for the Same with Costs of Suite and shall pray etc.

T. Knight Secretary

[*Endorsed:*]
Narratio
Aires versus Eggerton
In Debt
Entered March 11th 1705/6

[*CCR 148*]

North Carolina Ss. To the provost Marshall or his Deputy

These are in her Majestyes name to will and require you to arrest the body of Patrick Eggerton and him Safely hold Soe that he may be and appeare at the next Generall Court to be holden at the house of Captain Jno. Hecklefield in Litle river on the last Tuesday in this Instant March then and there to Answer the plaint of Thomas Aires in a plea of Debt and have there this writt Dated at the Secretarys Office this 11th day of March Anno Domini 1705/6.

Testis T. Knight Secretary

[*Endorsed:*]
Breve
Aires versus Eggerton
In Debt

[*Ayres* v. *Stevens*]

[*CCR 148*]

North Carolina Ss. To the honorable the Generall Court etc.

Thomas Aires is plaintiff against William Steevens Defendant in a plea of Debt and Sayes that the Defendant Stands Justly Indebted to the plaintiff in the full and Just Summe of Twenty Nine pounds as in and by one Certaine writeing obligatory under the proper hand and Seale of the Defendant here into Court brought and ready to be produced relation being thereunto had doth and may more fully and at large appeare which Said Sume of Twenty nine pounds the Defendant hath not rendred to the plaintiff tho' often thereunto requested but the Same doth Still refuse to render to the plaintiffs Damage Fifty Eight pounds Sterling and thereupon he brings his Suite and prayes

Judgment For the Same with Costs of Suite and shall pray etc.

T. Knight Secretary

[*Endorsed:*]
Narratio
Aires versus Steevens
In Debt
Entered March 11th: 1705/6

[*CCR 148*]

No. Carolina Ss. To the provost Marshall or his Deputy

These are in her Majestyes name to will and require you to Arrest the body of Willm. Stevens and him Safely hold Soe that he may be and appeare at the next Generall Court to be holden at the house of Captain John Heckle-field in Litle river on the last Tuesday in this Instant March then and there to Answer the plaint of Thos. Aires in a plea of Debt and have there this writt Dated at the Secretarys Office this 11th day of March Anno Domini 1705/6.

Testis T. Knight Secretary

[*Endorsed:*]
Breve
Aires versus Stevens
In Debt
Executed per Geo. Harris

[*Boyd* v. *Paine*]

[*CCR 148*]

Whereas Samll. Paine is departed out of this Government and have not Left any Attorney to Answare for him according to Law, being Indebted to Thomas Boyd Esqr. in the Sume of two pounds Seaven Shillings and two pence

North Carolina Ss. To the provost Marshall or his Deputy

These are therefor in her Majestyes name to will and require you to Attach Soe much of the Estate of the Said Samll. Paine where ever to be found in this Government as will pay and Satisfy the Said Thos. Boyd the Said Sume of two pounds Seaven Shillings and Two pence with Costs and the Same Safe in Custody Keep untill otherwise ordered by due Course of Law and make returne of your proceedings herein to the next Generall Court Dated at the Secretarys office the 30th day of October Anno Domini 1705.

Testis Tobs. Knight Secretary

[*Endorsed:*]
Attachment
Boyd versus Paine
For 2:7:2
Made up

[*Cary* v. *Phillips*]

[*CCR 148*]

No. Carolina Ss. To the Provost Marshall or his Deputy

Whereas Danll. Phillipps is gone out of this Country and have left noe Attorney to Answer for him according to Law and is Indebted to the honorable Colonel Thos. Cary Esqr. in the Sume of Five pounds Tene Shillings

These are therefore in her Majestyes name to will and require you to Attach Soe much of the Estate of the Said Phillipps wherever to be found in this Government as will pay and Satisfy the Said Thos. Cary the Said Sume of Five pounds Ten Shillings with Costs and the Same in Safe Custody Keepe untill otherwise ordered by due Course of Law and make returne of your proceedings herein to the next Generall Court Dated at the Secretarys Office the 22d day of January Anno Domini 1705/6.

Tobs. Knight Secretary

[*Endorsed:*]
Attachment
Phillips ads. The Honorable Colonel Cary
Nulla bona

[*Cary, attorney of Collins* v. *Brownell*]

[*CCR 148*]

North Carolina Ss. To the provost Marshall or his Deputy

These are in her Majestyes name to will and require you to Attach Soe much of the Estate of Geo. Brownell wherever to be found in this Government as will pay and Satisfy The Honorable Colonel Thos. Cary Esqr. Attorney to John Collins of South Carolina the Sume of forty pounds with Costs and the Same in Safe Custody Keep untill otherwise ordered by due Course of Law and make returne of your proceedings herein to the next Generall Court Dated at the Secretarys office this 23d day of January Anno Domini 1705/6.

Testis T. Knight Secretary

[*Endorsed:*]
Attachment
Geo. Brownell ads. Cary Attorney etc.
16 barrells of Pork and 60 barrells Tarr Attachment in the hands of Far. Green per me Edwd. Pitts Deputy Marshall
Execute per me Edward Pitts Deputy marshall

[*Crown* v. *Brice*]

[*CCR 148*]

North Carolina Ss. To the provost Marshall or his Deputy

These are in her Majestyes name will and require You to take the body of

Wm. Brice and him in Safe Custody hold untill he Shall become bounden with Good and Sufficient Security to Answer a Contempt of Authoritty in not Executeing a Warrant to him directed according to the Tenour of the Same at the next Generall Court here of fayle not as also to make returne of this precept to the next Generall Court Dated at the Secretarys office this 8th day of Janry. Anno Domini 1705.

Tobs. Knight Secretary

[*Endorsed:*]
This Executed per me Edwd. Pitts

[*Crown* v. *Houghtons*]

[*CCR 148*]

Know all Men by these presents that I Thomas Houghton Senior of the province of North Carolina planter doe hereby [Set] Asigne and Set over all my estate Reall and personall that I now Stand possessed of unto Capt. John Heckelfield his Executors Administrators and Assignes and all my Right Title and Interest therein this twenty Sixt day of March 1706.

The Condition of this Obligation is such, that if the above Said Thomas Houghton and Thomas Houghton Son of the Said Tho. Houghton Shall each of them personally Appearre at the dwelling House of the Said Capt. John Heckelfeild in littel River on the first Tuesday in May next, and there to abide the Sentence of the Generall Court then to be held; Then this Obligation Shall be Void and of None effect, otherwise to Stand in full force and Vertue.

Sealed and delivered in the presence of
Testis John Bishop
Wm. Houghton his mark

Tho. Houghton

[*Duckenfield* v. *Farrow*]

[*CCR 148*]

No. Carolina Ss. To the Honorable Generall Court etc.

Wm. Duckenfield Esqr. is plaintiff against Fran. Farow defendant in a plea of Debt and Says that Whereas the Defendant by one writeing Obligatory under the proper hand of the Defendant beareing Date the Eighteenth day of November 1699 did become oblidged to pay or Cause to be paid unto Wm. Powell his Heyres or Assignes the full and Just Summe of fifteen pounds five Shillings and Six pence to be paid in any ventable Country Comodityes to be paid the 10th day of November 1700 this bill is to be paid in two yeares day of payment Which Said Bill was and is Assigned over by the Said Wm. Powell to the plaintiff as in and by the said writeing obligatory here in to Court brought and ready to be produced relation being thereunto had doth and may more fully and at large appeare Nevertheless the defendant the Said Sume of fifteen pounds five Shillings and Six pence hath not rendred to the plaintiff tho' often thereunto requested but the Same doth Still refuse to render to the plaintiffs Damage thirty pounds and Eleaven Shillings Sterling and thereupon he brings his Suite and prayes Judgement for the Same with Costs of Suite and Shall pray etc.

Tobs. Knight Secretary

[*Endorsed:*]
Narratio
Duckenfield Ar. versus Farrow
In Debt
Entered Nov. 22d: 1705

[*CCR 148*]

No.Carolina Ss. To the provost Marshall or his Deputy

These are in her Matyes name to will and require you to Arrest the body of Fran. Farrow and him Safely hold Soe that he may be and appeare at the next Generall Court to be holden at the house of Captain John Heckle-field in Litle river on the Last tuesday in March next then and there to Answare the plaint of William Duckenfeild Esqr. in a plea of Debt and have there this writt Dated at the Secretarys Office this 22d day of Novber. Anno Domini 1705.

Testis Tobs. Knight Secretary

[*Endorsed:*]
Breve
Duckenfield versus Farrow
Execute per me Edward Pitts Deputy marshall

[*Duckenfield* v. *Mellynes*]

[*CCR 148*]

No. Carolina Ss. To the honorable Generall Court etc.

Wm. Duckenfield Esqr. is plaintiff against Robt. Mellynes defendant in a plea of debt and Says that the Defendant Stands Justly Indebted to the plaintiff in the full and Just Sume of Forty one Shillings and Eight pence to be paid upon demand in Some Merchantable Comody as in and by one Certaine writeing obligatory under the proper hand of the defendant beareing date the 18th day october 1704 and here into Court brought and ready to be produced relation being thereunto had doth and may more fully and at large appeare which Said Sume of forty one Shillings and Eight pence the defendant hath not rendred unto the plaintiff tho' often thereunto requested but the Same doth Still refuse to render to the plaintiffs Damage four pounds three Shillings

Sterling and four pence and thereupon he brings his Suite and prays Judgement for the Same with Costs of Suite and Shall pray etc.

Tobs. Knight Secretary

[*Endorsed:*]
Narratio
Duckenfild Esqr. versus Mellynes
In Debt
Entered Nov. 22d: 1705

[*Duckenfield* v. *Monteague*]

[*CCR 148*]

No. Carolina Ss. To the honorable Generall Court etc.

Wm. Duckenfield Esqr. is plaintiff against Roger Mounteaug defendant in a plea of Debt and Says that the Defendant Stands Justly Indebted to the plaintiff in the full and Just Sume of thirty Seaven Shillings and Six pence to be paid upon demand in Good Merchantable doable Matts at two Shillings and Six pence per Matt as in and by one Certaine writeing Obligatory under the proper hand of the Defendant beareing date the 24th Septembr. 1704 and here into Court brought and ready to be produced relation being thereunto had doth and may appeare which Said Summe of thirty Seaven Shillings and Six pence in maner as aforesaid the defendant hath not rendred to the plaintiff tho often thereunto requested but the Same doth still refuse to render to the plaintiffs Damage two pounds fifteen Shillings Sterling and thereupon he brings his Suite and prayes Judgement for the Same with Costs of Suite and Shall pray etc.

Tobs. Knight Secretary

[*Endorsed:*]
Narratio
Duckenfield Esqr. versus Mounteaug
In Debt
Entered Nov. 22d: 1705

[*CCR 148*]

North Carolina Ss. To the Provost Marshall or his Deputy

These are in her Majestyes name to will and require you to arrest the body of Roger Mounteaug and him Safely hold Soe that he may be and appeare at the next Generall Court to be holden at the house of Captain John Hecklefield in Little River on the last Tuesday in March next then and there to Answer the plaint of William Duckenfield Esqr. in a plea of Debt and have there this Writt Dated at the Secretary Office this 22 Day of Novembr. Anno Domini 1705.

[*Endorsed:*]
Duckenfield versus Mounteaug
Executed
Execute per me Edward pitts Deputy Marshall

[*Duckenfield* v. *Smith*]

[*CCR 148*]

North Carolina Ss. To the honorable Generall Court etc.

Willm. Duckenfield Esqr. is plaintiff against Richard Smyth defendant in a plea of Debt and Says that the defendant Stands Justly Indebted to the plaintiff in the full and Just Summe of One Pounds Seaven Shillings and Six pence in some vendable Comodytys as likewise thirty [Six] Matt as in and by one Certaine writeing obligatory under the proper hand of the Defendant beareing Date the thirteenth october 1704 and here into Court brought and now ready to be produced relation being thereunto had doth and may appeare which Said Sume of One pound Seaven Shillings and Six pence Nor the aforesaid quanty of thirty Matts the defendant hath not rendred unto the plaintiff tho often thereunto requested but the Same doth Still refuse to render to the plaintiffs Damage Twelve pounds Sterling and thereupon he brings his Suite and prays Judgement for the Same with Costs of Suite and Shall pray etc.

Tobs. Knight Secretary

[*Endorsed.*]
Narratio
Duckenfield Esqr. versus Smyth
In Debt
Entered Nov. 22d 1705

[*Feillett* v. *Jennings*]

[*CCR 148*]

No. Carolina Ss. To the Honorable the Generall Court etc.

James Feillett Dr. Medicine is Plaintiff against John Jenings Defendant in a Plea of the Case and Complaines that the Defendant Stands Indebted to the Plaintiff in the full and Just Summe of Twenty one pounds five Shillings by Account for divers Medicines Phissick Dressings and Attendings Administred to and upon the Defendants Daughter Dorathy (at the Speciall Instance and request of the Defendant) as by wayes and meanes Convenient the Plaintiff is ready to make appeare Nevertheless the Defendant the Said Summe of Twenty one pounds five Shillings to the Plaintiff hath not rendered tho' often thereunto requested but the Same doth Still refuse to render to the Plaintiffs Damage Forty two pounds tenn Shillings Sterling and thereupon he brings his Suite and Prayes Judgement for the Same with Costs of Suite and Shall Pray etc.

T. Knight Secretary

[*Endorsed:*]
Narratio
Feilett versus Jennings
In Case
Entred Feb. 25th: 1705/6

[*CCR 148*]

Jennings ads. Feillett

And the Defendant Comes by Thomas Snoden his Attorney and Defends the Force and Injury when etc. And for Plea Saith That he the Defendant hath well and truly payd and Satisfyed unto the plaintiff the full and Just Summe of Four pounds and Tenn Shillings for Medicines Physick Dressing and Attending administred to and upon the Defendants Daughter in manner as in the plaintiffs Declaration is Expresst and further the Defendant to the plaintiff is not Indebted And this he is ready to averr And of this he putts himselfe upon the Country.

John Jennings

[*Endorsed:*]
Jennings ads. Feillett
Plaint

[*CCR 148*]

May the 30th: 1705

Taken in hand John Jenning Daughter Dorothey afflicted with malignous Sores and cachoetes [ulcers] in her right arme and Legg to the number of about thirty or fourthy, two in her arme to the bigness of 8 or 9 inches in Square, one in her legg about one foot Squarre the rest of less bigness; the said Dorothey having been afflicted maney years ago of the countrey disease with contractura in the tree great articles of her arme and her Knee, with an entire deperdition of use and motion of those parts; moreover attended with considerably athrophy, Cakexia and Jeteritia; unto whom I have in the name of God administred and applied both inward and outward Medicines, being Employed by her father; and Keept under my Cure the Said Dorothey Jenning with dayly dressing and attending, as much as it was possible, Sometimes twice a day with bathing fomenting, Phagedenicq waters, Compound ointments, Chymicall and Galenical remedies, Salves and ointments and powders untill the 29th of August fallowing; in which time I brought the Said Dorothey's Arme to the last period of its cure; and I had performed with the Almighty blessing the cure of her, had not She by her unruliness, and unwillingness to follow my prescriptions, and to take inward Medicine, Stopt, and hindered the entire cure of her disease.

The Medicines

Imprimis

Dose i of panace hystoricq, and Cakecticg	00-05-0
Pound i of Phagedenicq Water for her sores	01-00-0
Dose i of Specificq against the countrey disease	00-05-0
Dose i of the Same	00-05-0
Pound i of Phaged water	01-00-0

Unguentunt Phagedenicq pound iii 03-00-0
Unguentunt resolution for malignous sores pound vi 03-00-0
Sarcoticq powders 01-00-0
Ung. apostolorum and deminio....................................01-10-0
Ung. incarning pound vi 03-00-0
Sarcoticq powders and resolutif Salts 01-00-0
Dressing, trouble and attending 06-00-0

Summa 21-05-0

J. Feillet Doctor Medicine

[*Endorsed:*]
John Jennings his accountt 21-05-0
J. Feillett plaintif
We of the Jurey find for the plantif fiftey Shillins besides the fendants Acount Alowed

[*CCR 190*]

May the 2th 1705

Doctor James fillet is Debtor

To him selfe his wife and his Child A Seven weeks diat washen and Lagen ....00=15=00
To: 3 bushells of corne at ....00=05=00
To: pastren for his Horse ....00=05=00
By Mr. Mackbrid ....00=03=00
To: 2: pounds of beas wax at ....00=02=00

04=10=00

Erors Excepted per John Jenings

[*Feillett* v. *Jennings*]

[*CCR 148*]

No. Carolina Ss. To the Honorable Generall Court etc.

James Feilett Dr. Medicine is plaintiff against Wm. Jenings Defendant in a plea of the Case and Complains that the Defendant Stands Justly Indebted unto the plaintiff in the full and Just Sume of four pounds Tenn Shillings for Medicines Phissik vissitts and Attendance administred and done to and upon the said Defendant aflicted with the Country disease as by agreement with the said Defendant and ways and means Convenient the plaintiff is ready to make appeare Nevertheless the Defendant the Said Sume of four pounds Tenn Shillings to the plaintiff hath not rendred tho' often thereunto requested but the Same doth Still refuse to render to the plaintiffs Damage

Nine pounds Sterling and thereupon he brings his Suite and prayes Judgement for the Same with Costs of Suite and Shall pray etc.

T. Knight Secretary

[*Endorsed:*]
Feilett versus Jenings
In Case
Entered Feb. 24th 1704/6 [*sic*]
We of the Jury find for the defendant

[*CCR 148*]

No. Carolina Ss. To the provost Marshall or his Deputy

These are in her Majestyes name to will and require You to Arrest the body of Wm. Jennings and him Safely hold Soe that he be and appeare at the next Generall Court to be holden at the house of Captain John Hecklefield in Litle river on the last Tuesday in March next then and there to Answer the plaint of [James] Feilett Dr. Medicine in a plea of the Case and have there this writt Dated at the Secretarys Office this 25th day of Febry. Anno Domini 1705/6.

Testis T. Knight Secretary

[*Endorsed:*]
Breve
Feilett versus Jenings
In Case
Executed by me George Harris debety mashall

[*CCR 148*]

Jennings ads. Feillett

And the Defendant in proper person Comes and Defends the force and Injury when etc. And for plea Saith that the plaintiff did an Agreement make to and with the Defendant That he the plaintiff would make an absolute Cure of the Distemper the Defendant was afflicted with and Saith That the aforesaid agreement he the plaintiff hath not performed And this he is ready to Averr And of this he putts himselfe upon the Country.

[*Illegible*] Willm. Jennings

[*Feillett* v. *Tull*]

[*CCR 148*]

No. Carolina Ss. To the Honorable the Generall Court etc.

James Feilett Dr. Medicine is plaintiff against Benjamin Tull Defendant in a plea of the Case and Complaines that the Defendant Stands Justly Indebted to the plaintiff in the full and Just Summe of two pounds which Said Summe of two pounds the Defendant Did Assume to pay unto the plaintiff for Divers Medicines and Phissick Administred to Martin Dennitt as by wayes and meanes Convenient the plaintiff is ready to make appeare Nevertheless the Defendant the Said Sume of two pounds to the plaintiff hath not rendred tho' often thereunto requested but the Same doth Still refuse to render to the plaintiffs Damage Four pounds Sterling and thereupon he brings his Suite and prayes Judgement for the Same with Costs of Suite and Shall pray etc.

T. Knight Secretary

[*Endorsed:*]
Narratio
Feilett versus Tull
In Case
Entered Feb. 25th: 1705/6

[*CCR 148*]

No. Carolina Ss. To the Provost Marshall or his Deputy

These are in her Majestyes name to will and require You to Arrest the body of Benjamin Tull and him Safely hold Soe that he may be and appeare at the next Generall Court to be holden at the house of Captain Jno. Hecklefield in Litle river on the last Tuesday in March next then and there to Answer the plaint of Dr. James Feilett in a ple of the Case and have there this writ Dated at the Secretarys office this 25th day of Febry. Anno Domini 1705/6.

Testis T. Knight Secretary

[*Endorsed:*]
Breve
Feilett versus Tull
In Case
Excuted by me Wm. Bray Deputy Marshall

[*Gale* v. *Lawson*]

[*CCR 148*]

No. Carolina Ss. To the honorable the Generall Court etc.

Christo. Gale Esqr. is plaintiff against Jno. Lawson defendant in a plea of the Case and Complaines that the Defendant Stands Indebted to the plaintiff in the full and Just Summe of Three hundred thirty three pounds Eight Shillings by account to be paid in Drest Buck Skinns at two Shillings per Skinn and drest Doe Skinns at Eighteen pence per Skin as by wayes and meanes Convenient the plaintiff is ready to make appeare which Said Sume of Three hundred thirty three Pounds Eight Shillings the Defendant hath not rendred to the plaintiff tho' often thereunto requested but the Same doth Still refuse to render to the plaintiffs Damage Six hundred Sixty Six pounds Sixteen

Shillings Sterling and thereupon he brings his Suite and prayes Judgement for the Same with Costs of Suite and shall pray etc.

T. Knight Secretary

[*Endorsed:*]
Narratio
Gale Esquire versus Lawson
In Case
Entered March 6th: 1705/6

[*CCR 148*]

No. Carolina Ss. To the provost Marshall or his Deputy

These are in her Majestyes name to will and require you to Arrest the body of John Lawson and him Safely hold Soe that he be and appeare at the next Generall Court to be holden at the house of Captain Jno. Hecklefield in Litle river on the last Tuesday in this Instant March then and there to Answer the plaint of Christo. Gale Esqr. in a ple of the Case and have there this writt Dated at the Secretarys Office this [6] th day of March Anno Domini 1705/6.

Testis T. Knight Secretary

[*Endorsed:*]
Breve
Gale Esqr. versus Lawson
Executed

[*Glover, consignee* v. *Luerton*]

[*CCR 192*]

North Carolina Ss. To the Provost Marshall or his Deputy

These are in her Majestyes name to will and require you to Attach Soe much of the Estate of Jno. Luerton wherever to be found in this Government as will pay and Satisfy the Honorable William Glover Esqr. Consignee of Colonel Robert Quarry and New pensilvania Company the Sume of three pounds thirteen Shillings and Nine pence and the Same in Safe Custody Keep untill otherwise ordered by due Course of Law and make returne of your proceedings therein to the next Generall Court Dated at the Secretarys Office this 8th: day of Janry. Anno Domini 1705.

Tobs. Knight Secretary

[*Endorsed:*]
Attachment versus Luerton ad sectam Glover
Atached 3 Cows and Calefs mardk with a fleurer de Leuce In the Left halefe meune In the Rite Ruing at [Cachock] by me Daniel Hallsey Deputy marshall

[*Hecklefield, attorney of Mellen* v. *Slade*]

[*CCR 148*]

No. Carolina Ss. To the honorable Generall Court etc.

Captain Jno. Hecklefeild Attorney of Robert Mellen is plaintiff against Henry Slade Defendant in a plea of the Case and Complaines that the Defendant Stands Indebted to the plaintiff quallifyed as aforesaid in the full and Just Sume of Ten pounds Two Shillings by Account as by wayes and meanes Convenient the plaintiff is ready to make appeare Nevertheless the defendant the Said Summe of Ten pounds two Shillings to the plaintiff quallifyed as aforesaid hath not rendred tho' often thereunto requested but the Same doth Still refuse to render to the plaintiffs Damage quallifyed as aforesaid the Sume of Twenty one pounds Sterling and thereupon he brings his Suite and prays Judgement for the Same with Costs of Suite and shall pray.

T. Knight Secretary

[*Endorsed:*]
Narratio
Hecklefeild Attorney etc. versus Slade
In Case
Entered March 9th: 1705/6

[*Hecklefield* v. *Vandermulen and Bray, attorneys of Wentworth and Company*]

[*CCR 148*]

No. Carolina Ss. To the honorable Generall Court etc.

Captain Jno. Hecklefield is plaintiff against Thomas Vandermulen and Wm. Bray Attorneys of Ebenezer Wentworth and Company Defendants in a plea of the Case and Complains that the Defendants quallifyed as aforesaid Stands Indebted to the plaintiff in the full Sume of Four pounds Eighteen Shillings and two pence halfe penny by account as by wayes and meanes Convenient the plaintiff is ready to make appeare which said Sume of four pounds Eighteen Shillings and two pence halfe peny the Defendants nor either of them hath rendred to the plaintiff tho' often thereunto requested but the Same doth Still refuse to render to the plaintiffs Damage Tenn pounds Sterling and thereupon he brings his Suite and prayes Judgement for the Same with Costs of Suite and Shall pray etc.

T. Knight Secretary

[*Endorsed:*]
Narratio
Hecklefield versus Vandermulen and Bray Attorneys etc.
In Case
Entered March 9th: 1705/6

[*CCR 148*]

No. Carolina Ss. To the provost Marshall or his Deputy

These are in her Majestyes name to will and require you to Arrest the bodys of Thomas Vandermulen and Wm. Bray Attorneys of Ebenezar Wentworth and Company and them Safely hold Soe that they be and appeare at the next Generall Court to be holden at the house of Captain Jno. Hecklefield in Litle river on the last Tuesday in this Instant March then and there to Answer the plaint of Captain Jno. Hecklefeild in a plea of the Case and have there this writt Dated at the Secretarys Office this 9th day of March Anno Domini 1705/6.

Testis T. Knight Secretary

[*Endorsed:*]
Breve
Hecklefield versus Vandermulen and Bray Attorneys etc.
This Ritt with Drad Wintworth will pay

[*Hecklefield* v. *Ward*]

[*CCR 148*]

N. Carolina Ss. To the Honourable Generall Court

Jno. Hecklefield is plaintiff against James Ward Defendant in a plea of the case and Setteth forth that the Defendant stands Justly indebted to the plaintiff in the full and just summe of One pound eight shillings and four pence halfe penny, payable in manner and forme following viz. the summe of twelve shillings and four pence halfe penny in pork at the usuall price of this Country, and the summe of sixteen shillings in good butter at six pence per pound, which said summe haveing often demanded the Defendant refuses to pay in manner abovesaid to the plaintiffs Damage two pounds sixteen shillings and nine pence wherefore he brings his action and craves judgement of this Honourable Court for the same with costs of sute and shall pray etc. Dated the 6th day of Novembr. 1705.

John Hecklefield

[*Endorsed:*]
Narratio
Hecklefield versus Ward
Fyled November 6th 1705
Satisfied

[*Keele* v. *Scarbrough*]

[*CCR 187*]

No. Carolina Ss. To the honorable Generall Court etc.

Robert Keel is plaintiff against Augustin Scarbrough planter defendant in a plea of Trespass on the Case and Complaines that the Defendant in the precinct of Paspotanck and within the Jurisdiction of this Court with force and Armes etc. into and upon a Certeyne plantation and Tract of Land Scituate lying and being in the aforesaid precinct the proper Estate and rightfull Inherritance of the plaintiff and whereon the Defendant now resides hath wrongfully Entered and the Same from the plaintiff doth wrongfully withhold and deteyne To the plaintiffs Damage Two hundred pounds Sterling and thereupon he brings his Suite and prayes that the Defendant may be removed and the plaintiff restored to his proper right and shall pray etc.

T. Knight Secretary

[*Endorsed:*]
Narratio
Keel versus Scarbro'
Trespass Super Casu
Referred
Wee of the Juriors find for the Defendant with Costes of Suite

[*CCR 148*]

North Carolina Ss. To the provost Marshall or his Deputy

These are in her Majestyes name to will and require you to Arrest the body of Augustine Scarborough and him Safely hold Soe that he may be and appeare at the next Generall Court to be holden at the house of Captain John Hecklefield in Litle river on the last Tuesday in March next then and there to Answer the plaint of Robt. Keele in a plea of Trespass on the Case and have there this writt Dated at the Secretarys Office this 1th day of Febry. Anno Domini 1705/6.

Testis T. Knight Secretary

[*Endorsed:*]
[*Torn*]
Thes Writte Executed by me Geo. Harris

[*CCR 148*]

North Carolina Ss. To the provst Marshall or his Depty

These are in her Matyes Name to will and require you to Sumons Hannah the wife of Garrard Cowen personally to be and appeare at the next Generall Court to be holden at the hous of Capt. Jno. Hecklefield in Litle River on the last Tusday in March next then and there to give Evidence in a Cause there Depending betwen Robert Keel plaintiff and Austin. Scarbro' defendant on behalfe of the plaintiff and have there this Sumons Dated at the Secretarys Office this 26th day of Feb. Anno Domini 1705/6.

Testis T. Knight Secretary

[*Endorsed:*]
Sumons for Hannah Cowen
Sarved

[*CCR 148*]

No. Carolina Ss. To the Provost Marshall or his Deputy

These are in her Majestyes name to will and require you to Sumons Dorathy Jenings personally to be and appeare at the next Generall Court to be holden at the house of Captain Jno. Hecklefield in Litle river on the last Tuesday in this Instant March then and there to give Evidence in Cause there depending between Robt. Keel plaintiff and Austin. Scarbro' defendant on behalfe of the Defendant and have there this Sumons Dated at the Secretarys office this 23d day of March Anno Domini 1705/6.

Testis T. Knight Secretary

[*Endorsed:*]
Executed John Mead
John Jenins

[*CCR 187*]

No. Carolina Scilicet To the honorable generall Court etc.

Robert Keel plaintiff against Augustine Scarbrough defendant and the said Augustine Scarbrough by James Melvin his Attorney comes and defends the force and injury when etc. and defieth Judgment of the declaration of him the said Robert the plaintiff and Saith that the same ought to abate for that he the said Robert in the preface of his declaration Setteth forth Robert Keel is plaintiff against Augustine Scarbrough planter defendant in a plea Trespass on the case, and in So declaring the said plaintiff hath mistaken his action and further he the said Robt. saith with force and arms etc. into and upon a certaine plantation and Tract of Land Scituate Lying and being in the aforesaid precinct but does not Set forth the day month yeare when this entry was made by the defendant as by Law he ought to have done nor doth he the said plaintiff set forth how he doth intitle himselfe to the said plantation and all this the said Augustine is ready to verifye, whereupon he demands Judgment of the declaration that the Same may abate, with costs.

James Melvin pro defendente

[*CCR 187*]

<*Keell* versus *Scarborough*>

And the plaintiffs by Tho. Snoden and Edwd. Bonwick his Attorneys for Answer Demurr in Law to the Insufficient Demurrer Exhibited by the Defendant to the Action Comenc'd against him by this plaintiff And Say that the aforesaid pretended Demurrer of the Defendants is not Sufficient or Valid in Law to Debarr the plaintiffs action for that the Same is uncertaine void of Substance and forme and that in the Same is Contained Double plea and this he is ready to Aver And pray Judgment ut primo [*illegible*] in the plaintiffs Declaration with Costs etc.

Tho. Snoden and Edwd. Bonwicke per querens

And the said defendant by James Melvin his attorney comes and saith that the plea of the defendant and the matter therein contained is certain and not double and thereof he demands Judgment.

James Melvin pro defendente

[*Penrice* v. *Norton*]

[*CCR 148*]

North Carolina Ss. To the honorable Generall Court etc.

Thomas Penrice is plaintiff against Samll. Norton Defendant in a plea of the Case and Complaines that the Defendant Stands Justly Indebted to the plaintiff in the full and Just Summe of three pounds Tenn Shillings by Account as by wayes and meanes Convenient the plaintiff is ready to make appeare which Said Sume of three pounds Tenn Shillings the Defendant hath not rendred to the plaintiff tho' often thereunto requested but the Same doth Still refuse to render to the plaintiffs Damage Seaven pounds Sterling and thereupon he brings his Suite and prays Judgement for the Same with Costs of Suite and Shall pray etc.

T. Knight Secretary

[*Endorsed:*]
Narratio
Penrice versus Norton
In Case
Entered Feb. 12th: 1705/6

[*Peterson, attorney of Perry and Company* v. *Andiver*]

[*CCR 192*]

North Carolina Ss. To the Honorable Generall Court etc.

Thomas Peterson Attorney to Micajah Perry and New Pensilvania Company is plaintiff against Thomas Andiver Defendant in a plea of the Case and Complaines that the Defendant Stands Indebted to the plaintiff quallifyed as aforesaid in the full and Just Summe of three pounds Six Shillings and Eleaven pence halfe peny in fresh porke by Account for divers Goods wares and Merchandizes as by wayes and meanes Convenient the plaintiff is ready to make appeare which Said Sume of three pounds Six Shillings and Eleven pence halfe peny the Defendant hath not rendred to the plaintiff tho' often thereunto requested but the Same doth Still refuse to render to the plaintiffs Damage Seaven pounds Sterling and thereupon he brings his Suite and prayes Judgement for the Same with Costs of Suite and Shall pray etc.

T. Knight Secretary

[*Endorsed:*]
Narratio
Peterson Attorney etc. versus Andiver
In Case
Entered Feb. 26th 1705/6

[*Peterson, attorney of Perry and Company* v. *Barr*]

[*CCR 192*]

North Carolina Ss. To the Provost Marshall or his Deputy

These are in her Majestyes name to will and require you to Attach Soe

much of the Estate of Robert Barr wherever to be found in this Government as will pay and Satisfy Thomas Peterson Attorney to Micajah Perry and New Pensilvania Company the Sume of Twenty Eight pounds fifteen Shillings with Costs and the Same in Safe Custody keep untill otherwise ordered by due Course of Law and make returne of your proceedings therein to the next Generall Court Dated at the Secretarys Office this 8th day of Janry. Anno Domini 1705/6.

Tobs. Knight Secretary

[*Endorsed:*]
Attachment versus Barr ad sectam Peterson
Executed Jan. 14th Edward Pitts deputy marshall

[*Peterson, attorney of Perry and Company* v. *Davis*]

[*CCR 148*]

[North] Carolina Ss. To the honorable Generall Court etc.

[*Torn*] Peterson Attorney to Micajah Perry and New Pensilvania Company [plaintiff] against Samll. Davis Defendant in a plea of Debt and Sayes that the Defendant by one writeing obligatory under his proper hand beareing Date the 9th day of December 1704 Stands Justly Indebted to the plaintiff quallifyed as aforesaid in the full and Just Summe of Six pounds two Shillings and three pence in Merchantable Fresh porke and to deliver it at Mr. John Jenings Landing pascotanke river as in and by the Said writeing obligatory here into Court brought and ready to be produced relation being thereunto had doth and may more fully and at large appeare which Said Sume of Six pounds two Shillings and three pence the Defendant hath not render'd unto the plaintiff tho' often thereunto requested but the Same doth Still refuse to render to the plaintiffs Damage twelve pounds four Shillings and Six pence Sterling and thereupon he brings his Suite and prayes Judgement for the Same with Costs of Suite and shall pray etc.

T. Knight Secretary

[*Endorsed:*]
Narratio
Peterson Attorney etc. versus Davis
In Debt
Entered Feb. 12th: 1705/6

[*CCR 148*]

North Carolina Ss. To the provost Marshall or his Deputy

These are in her Majestyes name to will and require you to Arrest the body of Samuell Davis and him Safely hold Soe that he may be and appeare at the next Generall Court to be holden at the house of Captain John Hecklefield in Litle river on the last Tuesday in March next then and there to Answer the plaint of Tho. Peterson Attorney of Micajah Perry and New pensilvania

Company in a plea of [*illegible*] and have there this writt Dated at the Secretarys office this [16] day of February Anno Domini 1705.

Testis T. Knight Secretary

[*Endorsed:*]
Breve
Peterson Attorney versus Davis
This Ritt Executed by me George Harris

[*Peterson, attorney of Perry and Company* v. *Frayly*]

[*CCR 192*]

North Carolina Ss. To the Honorable Generall Court etc.

Thomas Peterson Attorney to Micajah Perry and New Pensilvania Company is plaintiff against Wm. Frayly Defendant in a Plea of Debt and Sayes that the Defendant by one writeing obligatory under his Proper hand beareing Date the 30th day of March 1705: Stands Justly Indebted unto the plaintiff Quallifyed as aforesaid in the full and Just Summe of three pounds two Shillings and a halfe penny to be paid in porke or Corne Convenient to a Landing as in and by the Said writeing obligatory relation being thereunto had doth and may more fully and at large appeare which Said Summe of three pounds two Shillings and a halfe penny the Defendant hath not rendred to the plaintiff tho' often thereunto requested but the Same doth Still refuse to render to the plaintiffs Six pounds four Shillings and a penny Sterling and thereupon he brings his Suite and prayes Judgement for the Same with Costs of Suite and Shall pray etc.

T. Knight Secretary

[*Endorsed:*]
Narratio
Peterson Attorney etc. versus Fraly
Entered Feb. 12th 1705/6

[*CCR 148*]

North Carolina Ss. To the honorable Generall Court etc.

Thomas Peterson Attorney to Micajah Perry and New Pensilvania Company is plaintiff against Wm. Fryly defendant in a plea of Debt and Sayes that the Defendant by one writeing Obligatory under his proper hand beareing Date the 29th of July 1705 Stands Justly Indebted to the plaintiff quallifyed as aforesaid in the full and Just Summe of thirty five Shillings and Seaven pence halfe penny in Fresh porke to be paid at W. Glovers house as in and by the Said writeing obligatory relation being thereunto had doth and may [*torn*] at Large appeare which Said Summe of thirty [*torn*] and Seaven pence halfe peny the Defendant hath not [rendered unto] the plaintiff tho' often thereunto requested but the Same [doth] refuse to render to the plaintiffs Damage three pound Eleven shillings and three pence Sterling and therupon he brings his Suite and prayes Judgement for the Same with Costs of Suite and Shall pray etc.

T. Knight Secretary

[*Endorsed:*]
Narratio
Peterson Attorney etc. versus Fryly
In Debt
Entered Feb. [*torn*] 1705/6

[*CCR 192*]

North Carolina Ss. To the provost Marshall or his Deputy

These are in her Majestyes name to will and require you to Arrest the body of William Fryly and him Safely hold Soe that he may be and appeare at the next Generall Court to be holden at the house of Captain John Hecklefeild in Litle river on the last Tuesday in March next then and there to Answer the plaint of Tho. Peterson Attorney of Micajah perry and New pensilvania Company in a plea of Debt and have this writt Dated at the Secretarys Office this 16th day of Febry. Anno Domini 1705.

Testis T. Knight Secretary

[*Endorsed:*]
Breve
Peterson etc. versus Fryly
Executed by me Daniel Halsey Deputy marshall

[*Peterson, attorney of Perry and Company* v. *Hewett*]

[*CCR 192*]

North Carolina Ss. To the honorable Generall Court etc.

Thomas Peterson Attorney to Micajah Perry and New Pensilvania Company is Plaintiff against Bartholomew Hewett Defendant in a plea of Debt and Sayes that the Defendant by one writeing obligatory under his proper hand and Seale beareing Date the 8th of Janry. 1704 Stands Justly Indebted to the plaintiff quallifyed as aforesaid in the full and Just Sume of Nine pounds Seaventeen Shillings and Seaven pence halfe penny in fresh porke to be paid at Mr. John Jenings Landing in Pascotanke as in and by the Said writeing here into Court brought and ready to be produced relation being thereunto had doth and may more fully and at large appeare which Said Summe of Nine pounds Seaventeen Shillings and Seaven pence halfe peny the Defendant hath not rendred to the Plaintiff tho' often thereunto requested but the Same doth Still refuse to render to the plaintiffs Damage Nineteen pounds fifteen Shillings and three pence Sterling and thereupon he brings his Suite and prays Judgement for the Same with Costs of Suite and Shall pray etc.

T. Knight Secretary

[*Endorsed:*]
Narratio

Peterson Attorney etc. versus Hewett
In Debt
Entered Feb. 12th: 1705/6

[*CCR 188*]

This bill bindeth me Bartholomew Hewit of Pascotanck my heires Executors and Administrators to pay unto Mr. Tho. Peterson for the use of the Pensilvania Company or their assignes the Summ of nine pound Seaventeen Shillings and 7*d.* halfepeny in fresh porke at Mr. Jno. Jenings landing in pascotanck Witnesse my hand and Seal the 5th of Janry. 1704/5.

Thomas Sawyer <*Signum*> Bartholomew Hewit
W. Glover

[*Endorsed:*]
Bar. Hewit
9 17 7 ½

[*Peterson, attorney of Perry and Company* v. *Holmes*]

[*CCR 148*]

No. Carolina Ss. To the provost Marshall or his Deputy

These are in her Matyes name to will and require you to Attach Soe much of the Estate of Tho. Holmes wherever to be found in this Government as will pay and Satisfy Tho. Peterson Attorney of Micajah Perry and new Pensilvania Company The Sume of Three pounds Ten Shillings and four pence Sterling with Costs and the Same in Safe Custody Keep untill otherwise ordered by due Course of Law and make returne of your proceedings herein to the next Generall Court Dated at the Secretarys Office this 25th day of May Anno Domini 1706.

Testis T. Knight Secretary

[*Endorsement:*]
Attachment against Tho. Holmes ads. Peterson
Executed by me Daniel Halsey Debety marshall

[*Peterson, attorney of Perry and Company* v. *Meads*]

[*CCR 192*]

No. Carolina Ss. To the honorable the Generall Court etc.

Thos. Peterson Attorney to Micajah perry and New pensilvania Company is plaintiff against Jno. Meads defendant in a plea of Debt and Sayes that the defendant by one writeing obligatory under his proper hand and Seal beareing Date the 22d December 1704 Stands Justly Indebted to the plaintiff quallifyed as aforesaid in the full and Just Summe of Six pounds five Shillings to be paid in good fresh porke and delivered at the Landing of Mr. Wm. Glover in Litle river as in and by the said writeing obligatory here into Court brought and ready to be produced relation being thereunto had doth and may more fully and at large appeare which said Summe of Six pounds five shillings the

Defendant hath not rendred to the plaintiff quallifyed as aforesaid tho' often thereunto requested but the Same doth still refuse to render to the plaintiffs Damage Twelve pounds Tenn Shillings Sterling and thereupon he brings his Suite and prays Judgement for the Same with Costs of Suite and Shall pray etc.

T. Knight Secretary

[*Endorsed:*]
Narratio
Peterson Attorney versus Meads
In Debt £6:5:0
Entered March 11th 1705/6

[*CCR 192*]

No. Carolina Ss. To the honorable the Generall Court etc.

Thomas Peterson Attorney to Micajah Perry and New pensilvania Company is plaintiff against John Meads Defendant in a plea of Debt and Sayes that the Defendant by one writeing obligatory under his proper hand beareing Date the December the Twenty Seccond 1704 Stand Justly Indebted to the plaintiff quallifyed as aforesaid in the full and Just Summe of Twenty three Shillings and Six pence to be paid in good fresh porke at Mr. Glovers Landing which Said Sume is an Account of Thos. Armor in Virginia as in and by the said writeing obligatory here into Court brought and ready to be produced relation being thereunto had doth and may more fully and at large appeare which said Summe of Twenty three Shillings and Six pence the defendant hath not rendred to the plaintiff tho' often thereunto requested but the Same doth still refuse to render to the plaintiffs Damage two pounds Seaven Shillings and thereupon he brings his Suite and prayes Judgement for the Same with Costs of Suite and shall pray etc.

T. Knight Secretary

[*Endorsed:*]
Narratio
Peterson Attorney etc. versus Meads
In Debt
Entered March 11th 1705/6

[*CCR 148*]

No. Carolina Ss. To the provost Marshall or his Deputy

These are in her Matyes name to will and require you to Arrest the body of Jno. Meads and him Safely hold Soe that he may be and appeare at the next Generall Court to be holden at the house of Captain Jno. Hecklefield in Litle river on the last Tuesday in this Instant March then and there to Answer the plaint of Tho. Peterson Attorney of Micaja Perry and New Pensilvania Company in a Plea of Debt and have there this writt Dated at the Secretarys Office this 11th day of March Anno Domini 1705/6.

Testis T. Knight Secretary

[*Endorsed:*]
Breve
Peterson versus Meads
In Debt
Executed by leaving Copy of the writt and Declaration

[*CCR 188*]

This Bill Bindeth me John Meads of Passcotank precinct In No. Carrolina my heirs, Executors administraters and assignes To pay To Thomas Peterson on the account of the new Pensilvania Company his ortherd Assigns the full Summe of Six pounds five Shillings, In good fresh pork and Deliver it at the Landing of mr. Wm. Glover In Litle River as Wittness my hand and Seal This 22d December 1704.

W. Glover
Robert White

John Meaids

[*Peterson, attorney of Perry and Company* v. *Peggs*]

[*CCR 148*]

North Carolina Ss. To the Honorable Generall Court etc.

Thomas Peterson Attorney to Micajah Perry and New Pensilvania Company is plaintiff against Joseph Peggs Defendant in a Plea of Debt and Sayes that the Defendant by one writeing Obligatory and in his proper hand beareing Date the 6th December also Stands Justly Indebted to the plaintiff Quallifyed as aforesaid in the full and Just Sume of four pounds in good fresh porke to be Delivered at the Landing of Mr. John Jenings in the precinct of Pascotanke on or before the first day of febry. next as in and by the Said writeing here into Court brought and ready to be produced relation being thereunto had doth and may more fully and at large appeare which said Sume of four pounds the Defendant hath not rendred to the plaintiff [*illegible*] maner as aforesaid tho' often thereunto requested [*illegible*] to the plaintiffs Damage Eight [*torn*] Sterling and thereupon he brings his Suite and prays Judgment for the Same with Costs of Suite and Shall pray etc.

T. Knight Secretary

[*Endorsed:*]
Narratio
Peterson Attorney versus Peggs
In Debt
Entred Feb. 12th: 1705/6

[*CCR 148*]

North Carolina Ss. To the provost Marshall or his Deputy

These are in her Matyes name to will and require you to Arrest the body of Joseph Peggs and him Safely hold Soe that he may be and appeare at the next Generall Court to be holden at the house of Captain Jno. Hecklefield in Litle river on the last Tuesday in March next then and there to Answer the plaint of Thos. Peterson Attorney to Micajah Perry and New pensilvania Company in a plea of Debt and have there this writt Dated the 24th day of Janry. Anno Domini 1705/6.

Testis T. Knight Secretary

[*Endorsed:*]
Breve
Peterson Attorney etc. versus Peggs
Executed

[*Peterson, attorney of Perry and Company* v. *Rice*]

[*CCR 192*]

North Carolina Ss. To the honorable Generall Court etc.

Thomas Peterson Attorney to Micajah Perry and New Pensilvania Company is Plaintiff against Daniell Rice Defendant in a plea of Debt and Sayes that the Defendant by one writeing obligatory under his proper hand beareing Date the Eighth of December 1704 Stands Justly Indebted to the plaintiff Quallifyed as aforesaid in the full and Just Summe of Eight pounds Six Shillings and two pence In good fresh Merchantable porke and to deliver it at the Landing of Mr. Jno. Jenings in Pascotank on or before the first of february next Ensueing the Date thereof as in and by the Said writeing Obligatory here into Court brought and ready to be produced relation being there unto had doth and may more fully and at large appeare which Said Sume of Eight pounds Six Shillings and two pence the Defendant hath not rendred to the plaintiff tho' often thereunto requested but the Same doth Still refuse to render to the plaintiffs Damage Sixteen pounds twelve Shillings and four pence Sterling and thereupon he brings his Suite and prays Judgement for the Same with Costs of Suite and Shall pray etc.

T. Knight Secretary

[*Endorsed:*]
Narratio
Peterson Attorney versus Rice
In Debt
Entred Feb. 12th 1705/6

[*CCR 148*]

No. Carolina Ss. To the Provost Marshall or his Deputy

These are in her Matyes name to will and require you to Arrest the body of Daniell Rice and him Safely hold Soe that he may be and appeare at the next Generall Court to be holden at the house of Capt. John Hecklefield in Litle river on the last Tuesday in March next then and there to Answer the plaint of Tho. Peterson Attorney to Micajah Perry and New Pensilvania Company in a plea of Debt and have there this writt Dated at the Secretarys Office this 11th day of February anno Domini 1705/6.

Testis T. Knight Secretary

[*Endorsed:*]
Breve
Peterson versus Rice
In Debt
This ritt Executted by me George Harris deputy mashall

[*CCR 188*]

This Bill Bindeth me Daniel Rice of Passcotank In the Province of North Carrolina Planter me my heirs Executors Administrators and Assigns to pay To Thomas Peterson for the proper Use of the new Pensilvania Company his or there Assigns the full Summe of Eight pounds Six Shillings and two pence In good fresh Merchantable pork and to Deliver it at the Landing of Mr. John Jennings, In the L. River, on or before the first of Febry. next as Wittness my hand and Seal This Eighth of Decembr. 1704.

Testis W. Glover — Daniel Rise <*Signum*>

[*Endorsed:*]
Daniel Rice
£8:6:2

[*Peterson, attorney of Perry and Company* v. *Smith*]

[*CCR 148*]

No. Carolina Ss. To the provost Marshall or Deputy

These are in her Matyes name to will and require you to Sumons Jno. Fulford personally to be and appeare at the next Generall Court to be holden at the house of Captain Jno. Hecklefield in Litle river on The last Tuesday in March then and there to Give Evidence in a Cause there depending between Tho. Peterson Attorney of Michajah Perry and New pensilvania Company plaintiff and Richd. Smyth defendant on behalfe of the defendant an have there this Sumons Dated At the Secretarys Office this 20th day of Novr. Anno Domini 1705.

Testis Tobias Knight Secretary

[*Endorsed:*]
Sumons for Jno. Fulford
Executed per me Edward pitts Deputy Marshall

[*CCR 191*]

<*Smith ad sectam Peterson attorney of Perry etc.*>

And the Defendant in proper person Comes and Defends the force and Injury when etc. And for Plea Saith That att the Signing of the Obligation Exprest in the plaintiffs Declaration he the Defendant made this reservation videlicet That if he this Defendant could produce Receipts for the Summe Exprest in the aforesaid obligation That the Said obligation Should then be null and void and Saith That he this Defendant is ready to produce Reciepts for the aforesaid Sume And this he is ready to averr And of this he putts himselfe upon the Country.

Richd. Smith

[*CCR 192*]

North Carolina Ss. To the Provost Marshall or his Deputy

These are in her Majestyes name to will and require you to Attach Soe much of the Estate of Richd. Smyth wherever to be found in this Government as will pay and Satisfy Thomas Peterson Attorney to Micajah Perry and New pensilvania Company the Sume of Ninety four pounds one Shilling and three pence and the Same in Safe Custody keep untill otherwise ordered by due Course of Law and make returne of your proceedings herein to the next Generall Court Dated at the Secretarys Office this 8th day of Janry. Anno Domini 1705.

Tobs. Knight Secretary

[*Endorsed:*]
Attachment versus Smyth ad sectam Peterson
Executd per me Edward pitts Deputy marshall

[*CCR 190*]

Recd. of Mr. Smith February the 19th 1700/1

		£ s. *d.*
Imp.	61 Raccoons att 4*d.* per pr.	1: 0: 4
	2 Woolves att 2*s.*	0: 4: 0
	70 Fox and Catt att 9*d.*	1:12: 6
	2 Minks att	0: 1: 3
	5 Otters att 3*s.*	0:15: 0
	40 pounds of Beaver att 3*s.* per £	6: 0: 0
	18 Matts att 2*s.* per Matt	1:16: 0
	5 Bares att	0: 9: 0
		11:18: 1

Account of dearskins drest

	£ s. *d.*
460 does att 1*s.*:6*d.*	34:10: 0
40 does att 1:6	03: 0: 0
300 Bucks att 2:	30: 0: 0
the furrs	11:18: 1
	79: 8: 1

	£ s. *d.*	
37 prickett	1: 7: 9	
6 Bucks	0:12: 0	
20 does	1:10: 0	
	3: 9: 9	3: 9: 9
		82:17:10

12 does more 0:18: 0

Total 83:15:10

[*Endorsed:*]
Capt. Richard Smith Septbr. 15th 1704
Joseph Ming
Mr. Nicholas Tyler [*illegible*] Tho. Peterson [*illegible*]

[*Peterson, attorney of Zachary* v. *Pettiver*]

[*CCR 148*]

No. Carolina Ss. To the honorable the Generall Court etc.

Thomas Peterson Attorney to Daniell Zachary is plaintiff against John Pettiver Defendant in a plea of the Case and Complaines that Whereas the said Daniell Zachary did Sometyme in the Month of November 1699 Consigne Sundry Goods Wares and Merchandizes from Boston to the Defendant to the vallue of Twenty Seaven pounds Twelve Shillings and Tenn pence Prime Cost as by Copy of the Invoice of the Said Goods here into Court brought and ready to be produced relation being thereunto [*torn*] doth and may more fully and at large appeare Nevertheless the Defendant hath not rendred any Account of the Same goods as aforesaid to the Said Daniell Zachary nor is the plaintiff Quallifyed as aforesaid tho' often tymes thereunto requested but the Same doth Still refuse to render to the plaintiffs Damage the Sume of one hundred fifty pounds Sterling and thereupon he brings his Suite and prayes Judgement for the Same with Costs of Suite and Shall pray etc.

T. Knight Secretary

[*Endorsed:*]
Narratio
Peterson Attorney etc. versus Pettiver
In Case
Entered March 11th 1705/6

[*CCR 148*]

No. Carolina Ss. To the Provost Marshall or his Deputy

These are in her Matyes name to will and require you to Arrest the body of Jno. Pettiver and him Safely hold so that he may be and appeare at the next Generall Court to be holden at the house of Captain Jno. Hecklefield in Litle river on the last Tuesday in this Instant March then and there to Answer the plaint of Tho. Peterson Attorney to Daniell Zachary in a plea of the Case and have there this writt Dated at the Secretarys Office this 11th day of March Anno Domini 1705/6.

Testis T. Knight Secretary

[*Endorsed:*]
Breve
Peterson versus Pettiver
In Case

To Tho. Penrice To execute per order of John Hecklefield Provost Marshall
Executed March the 14th 1705/6 per Tho. Penrice

[*Porter* v. *Dereham*]

[*CCR 148*]

North Carolina Ss. To the honorable Generall Court

John Porter Esqr. is plaintiff against Thomas Dereham Defendant in a plea of Debt and Sayes that the Defendant Stands Justly Indebted to the Plaintiff in the full and Just Summe of fourteen pounds and Eight pence halfe penny Money to be paid in Merchantable drest Buck Skins at two Shillings per Skin and drest Doe Skinns at Eighteen pence per Skin fox and Wild Cat at Nine pence Each and good Matts at Eighteen pence Each and Raccoone at three pence Each and Dry Neates hide and tallow at the Current Country price with fifty per Cent abasement as in and by one Certaine writeing Obligatory here into Court brought and ready to be produced under the proper hand and Seale of the Defendant beareing Date the 10th day of Aprill Anno 1705 relation being thereunto had doth and may more fully and at Large appeare which Said Sume of fourteen pounds and Eight pence halfe peny the said Defendant hath not rendred to the plaintiff tho' often thereunto requested but the Same doth Still refuse to render to the plaintiffs Damage Twenty Eight pounds one Shilling and five pence and thereupon he brings his Suite and prays Judgement for the Same with Costs of Suite and Shall pray etc.

T. Knight Secretary

[*Endorsed:*]
Porter versus Dereham
In Debt

[*CCR 148*]

North Carolina Ss. To the Provost Marshall or his Deputy

These are in her Majestyes name to will and require you to Arrest the body of Thomas Dereham and him Safely Keep Soe that he be and appeare at the next Generall Court to be holden at the house of Captain John Hecklefield in Litle river on the last Tuesday in March next then and there to Answer the plaint of Jno. Porter Esqr. in a plea of Debt and have there this Writt Dated at the Secretarys Office this 24th day of Janry. Anno Domini 1705/6.

Testis T. Knight Secretary

[*Endorsed:*]
Breve
Porter versus Dereham
Executed per me Edward Pitts Deputy marshall

[*CCR 148*]

North Carolina Ss. To the provost Marshall or his Deputy

These are in her Majestyes name to will and require you to Sumons Levy

Trewhitt and Mary Trewhitt personally to be and appeare at the next Generall Court to be holden at the house of Captain John Hecklefield in Litle river on the last Tusday in March next then and there to Give Evidence in a Cause there depending between John Porter Esqr. plaintiff and Tho. Dereham defendant on behalfe of the plaintiff and have there this Sumons Dated at the Secretarys Office this 16th day of Febry. Anno Domini 1705/6.

Testis T. Knight Secretary

[*Endorsed:*]
Sumons for Levy Trewhitt and Mary Trewhitt
Executed per me Edwd. Pitts Deputy marshall

[*CCR 188*]

These presents oblidgeth me Thomas Dearham my heirs etc. to pay unto John Portr. order the Just quantity of fourteen pounds and Eight pence halfe penny mony to be paid in Merchantable Drest buck Skins at two Shillings per Skin and Drest Doe Skins at Eighteen pence per Skin fox and wild catt at nine pence Each and good matts at Eighteen pence Each and rackoon at thre pence Each: and Dry neates hide and tallow at the Currant Country prise with fifty per Cent a batement to the performance whereof I binde my Selfe my heirs etc. as witnes my hand and Seale this 18th day Aprll. Anno: 1705.

Testes Tho. Dereham
Levi Truewhitt
Mary Truewhitt <*her mark*>

[*Endorsed:*]
Mr. Dearham for £14: 0: 8½
Recd. one within bill fourteen drest doe Skins weight Sixteen pounds Sept. 21st: 1705 per John Porter [Senior] and one Matt
Received one account of the within bill from mr. Tho. Dereham fifty fower matts at the rate of Eighteen pence Each fower pounds one Shilling

per John Porter

Aprll 24: 1706
14: 0:8½
6:12:0
———
7: 8:8½

Received the day a bove written twenty tew Skins one this bill being recd. per John Porter

[*Porter* v. *Grills*]

[*CCR 148*]

North Carolina Ss. To the Provost Marshall or his Deputy

These are in her Majestyes name to will and require you to Attach Soe

much of the Estate of Richd. Grills as will pay and Satisfy Jno. Porter Esqr. the Sume of Twenty Six pounds with Costs and the Same in Safe Custody keep untill otherwise ordered by due Course of Law and make returne of your proceedings herein to the next Generall Court Dated at the Secretarys office this 8th day of Janry. Anno Domini 1705.

Tobs. Knight Secretary

[*Endorsed:*]
Attachment
Grills ads. Porter
Nulla bona

[*CCR 191*]

And Captain John Hecklefield Comes and Defends the force and Injury when etc. and Saith That Judgment against the Defendant for the Summe Exprest in the plaintiffs Declaration ought not to be Confirmd for he Saith That after A writt obtain'd against Richd. Grills for the aforesaid Summe he the plaintiff discoursing with the Defendant Concerning the Estate of the Said Richd. Grills did declare and utter to the plaintiff these words videlicet he (meaning the Said Richd. Grills) has enough Ile take all and pay all And this the Said John Hecklefield is ready to averr And of this he putts him selfe upon the Country.

John Hecklefield

[*Porter* v. *Smith and Hancock*]

[*CCR 148*]

North Carolina Ss. To the honorable Generall Court

John Porter Esqr. is plaintiff against Richard Smyth and Wm. Hancock both of the County of Bath Defendants in a plea of Debt and Sayes that the Defendants or either of them Joyntly and Severally Stands Justly Indebted unto the plaintiff in the full and Just Sume of One hundred and forty pounds Seaven Shillings and Eleven pence Money to be paid in Merchantable Drest Buck Skinns at two Shillings per Skin and Merchantable Drest Doe Skins at Eighteen pence per Skinn and fox and Wild Catt Skinns at Nine pence Each and to pay the Same by the last Day of July in the yeare 1704 as in and by One Certaine writeing Obligatory here into Court brought and ready to be produced under the proper hands and Seales of the Defendants beareing Date the 20th day of february Anno 1703/4 relation being thereunto had doth and may more fully and at large appeare which Said Summe of One hundred and forty pounds Seaven Shillings and Eleven pence the Defendants not either of them hath not rendred to the plaintiff tho' often thereunto requested but the Same Doe Still refuse to render to the plaintiffs Damage two hundred and Eighty pounds fifteen Shillings and ten pence and thereupon he brings his Suite and prays Judgement for the Same with Costs of Suit and Shall pray etc.

T. Knight Secretary

[*Endorsed:*]
Narratio
Porter versus Smyth etc.
In Debt
Entered Janry. 24th: 1705/6

[*CCR 148*]

North Carolina Ss. To the Provost Marshall or his Deputy

These are in her Matyes name to will and require you to Arrest the body of Richd. Smyth and Willm. Hancock and them Safely hold Soe that they may be and appeare at the next Generall Court to be holden at the house of Captain Jno. Hecklefield in Litle river on the last Tuesday in March next then and there to Answer the plaint of John Porter Esqr. in a plea of Debt and have there this Writt Dated at the Secretarys Office this 24th day of Janry. Anno Domini 1705/6.

Testis T. Knight Secretary

[*Endorsed:*]
Breve
Porter versus Smyth and Hancock
Executed

[*CCR 148*]

North Carolina Ss. To the Provost Marshall or his Deputy

These are in her Majestyes name to will and require you to Sumons Wm. Brice Geo. Birkenhead and Eliz. Birkenhead personally to be and appeare at the next Generall Court to be holden at the house of Captain Jno. Heckle-field in Litle river on the Last Tuesday in March next then and there to Give Evidence in a Cause there depending between John Porter Esqr. plaintiff and Richard Smyth and Wm. Hancock defendants on behalfe of the plaintiff and have there this Sumons Dated at the Secretarys Office this 16th day of Febry. Anno Domini 1705/6.

Testis T. Knight Secretary

[*Endorsed:*]
Sumons for Wm. Brice, Geo. Birkenhead, Eliz. Birkenhead.
Executed

[*Porter* v. *Truewhitt and Dereham*]

[*CCR 148*]

North Carolina Ss. To the honorable Generall Court

John Porter Esqr. is plaintiff against Levy Trewhitt and Thoms. Derham Defendants in a plea of Debt and Sayes that the Defendants or either of them Stands Justly Indebted unto the plaintiff in the full and Just Sume of Eleven pounds Eleven Shillings and three pence to be paid in Merchantable Drest

Deere Skinns Hides Tallow and Small Furrs at County price as in and by one Certaine writeing Obligatory under the proper hands and Seales of the Defendant beareing Date the Eighteenth day of Aprill 1705 Relation being thereunto had Doth and may more fully and at Large appeare which Said Sume of Eleven pounds Eleven Shillings and three pence the Defendant nor either of them hath not rendred unto the plaintiff tho' often thereunto requested but the Same doe Still refuse to render to the plaintiffs Damage Twenty three pounds two Shillings and Six pence and thereupon he brings his Suite and prayes Judgement for the Same with Costs of Suite and Shall pray etc.

T. Knight Secretary

[*Endorsed:*]
Narratio
Porter versus Trewhitt et al.
In Debt
Entered Janry. 24th: 1705/6

[*Swann* v. *Spruill*]

[*CCR 148*]

No. Carolina Ss. To the Provost Marshall or his Deputy

These are in her Majestyes name to will and require you to Attach Soe much of the Estate of Godfrey Spruell wherever to be found in this Government as will pay and Satisfy the Honorable Samll. Swann Esqr. the Summe of Seaven pounds Nineteen Shillings and Eleven pence with Costs and the Same in Safe Custody Keep untill otherwise ordered by due Course of Law and make returne of your proceedings herein to the next Generall Court Dated at the Secretarys office this 8th day of Janry. Anno Domini 1705/6.

Tobs. Knight Secretary

[*Endorsed:*]
Attachment
Spruell ads. Swann
Made up

[*Swann* v. *Blackwell*]

[*CCR 148*]

No. Carolina Ss. To the provost Marshall or his Deputy

These are in her Majestyes name to will and require you to Arrest the body of Charles Blakwell and him Safely hold Soe that he may be and appeare at the next Generall Court to be holden at the house of Captain John Hecklefield in Litle river on the last Tuseday in March next then and there to Answer the plaint of Wm. Swann Esqr. in a plea of Debt and have there this writt Dated at the Secretarys Office this [8] th day of Febry. Anno Domini 1705.

Testis T. Knight Secretary

[*Endorsed:*]
Swann versus Blackwell
Executed the 8th of Feb. 1704/6 [*sic*] Per John Heckliefield
Deputy Marshal

[*Tooke, executor* v. *Bell*]

[*CCR 180*]

No. Carolina Ss. To the honorable the Generall Court etc.

James Tooke Executor of the last will and Testament of Joseph M. Comander deceased is plaintiff against Wm. Bell defendant in a plea of Debt and Sayes that whereas the Defendant by one writeing obligatory under his proper hand beareing Date the 20th of March 1698 became Indebted to the Said Joseph M. Comander in the full and Just Sume of thirty two Shillings in and by the Said writeing obligatory here into Court brought and ready to be produced relation being thereunto had doth and may more fully and at large apeare Nevertheless the Defendant the Said Sume of thirty two Shillings to the Said Joseph M. Comander in his life time did not render nor to the plaintiff quallifyed as aforesaid Since his Decease tho' often thereunto requested but the Same doth Still refuse to render to the plantiffs Damage quallifyed as aforesaid three pounds foure Shillings Sterling and thereupon he brings his Suite and prayes Judgement for the Same with Costs of Suite and Shall pray etc.

T. Knight Secretary

[*Endorsed:*]
Tooke Executor etc. versus Bell
In Debt
Entered Feb. 26th: 1705/6

MISCELLANEOUS FILE PAPERS

[*Hatch, Anthony and Porter, John, bond*]

[*CCR 183*]

North Carolina Ss.

Know all Men by these presents That wee Anthony Hatch of this province gentleman and Jno. Porter Esqr. are held and firmely bound unto the true and absolute Lords and proprietors of this province of North Carolina in the full and Just Sume of Five hundred pounds to paid to them the Said proprietors their Successors to which payment well and truly to be made we bind our Selves our heyres Executors Administrators and Assignes Jointly and Severally and every of them firmely by these presents Sealed with our Seales and Dated this 25th day of Janury. Anno Domini 1705/6.

The Condition of this obligation is Such that Whereas Letters of Administration of the Goods and Chattles of Mr. Richard plater deceased have bin Granted to the above bounden Antho. Hatch If therefore the Said Antho.

Hatch doe and Shall well and truely Administer in and upon the Goods and Chatles rights and Credits of the aforesaid Richard Plater and true Inventory thereof returned in to the Secretarys Office within Six Monthes after the Date thereof All the Just Debts of the deceased Shall pay Soe farr as the Said Estate Shall Extend to and all other thing Shall doe according to the true Intent and meaneing of the Said Letters of Administration Then this obligation to be void and of none Effect or else to Stand remaine and be in full force power and virtue.

Sealed and Delivered
In the presence of
T. Knight Secretary

Anthony Hatch
John Porter

[*Endorsed:*]
Bond of Administrator
Anto. Hatch and Mr. Porter

[*Norcom, Jno., summons*]

[*CCR 148*]

No. Carolina Ss. To the Provost Marshall or his Deputy

These are in her Majestyes name to will and require you to Summons Jno. Norcom personally to be and appeare at the next Generall Court to be holden at the house of Captain Jno. Hecklefield in Litle river on the last Tuesday in this Instant March then and there to prove a power of Attorney from Arthur Lunn to Tho. Snoden and have there this Summons Dated at the Secretarys office this 4th day of March Anno Domini 1705/6.

Testis T. Knight Secretary

[*Endorsed:*]
Sumons for Jno. Norcom
Execute by me Richd. Leary Dubuty marshall

[*CCR 189*]

North Carolina Doquett of Actions to July Court 1706

Referrences etc. Attachments from March Court last

Peterson Attorney etc. versus petiver in Case. Referred.

Idem versus Smith in Debt. Referred.

Keel versus Scarbro. Referred.

Porter versus Trewhitt and Dereham. Attachment Executed.

Idem versus Dereham. Attachment Executed.

Idem versus Hancock and Smith. Attachment Executed.

Duckenfeild versus Monteague. Attachment Executed.

Idem versus Farrow. Attachment Executed.

Peterson versus Holmes. Attachment Executed.

Feilett versus Tull. Attachment.

Writts and Returnes to July Court

Keel versus Draper Case. Return Executed.

Galc Esqr. vcrsus Harris in Debt. Executed.

Idem versus Harris in Debt. Executed.

Idem versus Eundem in Case. Executed.

Idem versus Cartwrite in Case. Executed.

Hendricks versus Lewis in Case. Non est inventus.

Lowe versus Wilson in Trespass. Non est inventus.

Minge versus Leary in Detinue. Cepi Corpus.

Jones versus Symons in Case. Executed.

Swann Assignee etc. versus Fulford in Debt. Executed.

Idem versus Fulford in Debt. Executed.

Daniel Esqr. versus Cole in Case. Executed.

<*Referred.*> Pollock Esqr. versus Hecklefeild in Case. Cepi Corpus.

Rooks versus Tanner in Case. Executed.

Idem versus Collings in Case. Executed.

Sanders attorney versus Hecklefield. Non pros.

Hecklefield versus Collins. Non pros.

Hecklefeild versus powell in Case. Non est inventus.

Idem versus Kingsley. Attachment. Executed.

Peterson versus Kingsley. Attachment. Nulla Bona.

Pritchard versus Lamb. Scire Facias. Nihill.

Glover versus Steel. Scire Facias. Non pros.

Collings versus Abington Case. Executed.

Jeffiris versus Saunders Case. [*Illegible*]

John Wade versus James Dennis. Attachment.

Mr. Knight

Pray send me an account of the persons against whom Mr. Peterson had, either actions at common law or bills in chancery with the evidences last March Court.

Your servant

John Hecklefield

[*CCR 104*]

<347> North Carolina ss.

Att a General Court held for the Goverment aforesaid the 27th Day of August Anno Domini 1706 att the house of Captain John Hecklefield in Little River being adjourned by proclemation beareing Date the [*blank*] Day of [*blank*] last past from the 30th Day of July likewise past. Present the Honorable Christo. Gale Esqr.

This Court adjourned till the Morrow Morning 8 of the Clock.

Wednesday 8 of the Clock the Court mett and Sitt. Present The Honorable Christo. Gale, John Blount, Fra. DeLaMare, Wm. Bartlett Esqrs. Justices.

Upon petition of Tobias Knight Esqr. that Thomas Abington may be Clerk of this Court dureing this Session of the Court. His petition is granted and the Said Abington is accepted and accordingly he's taken the Oaths Usually taken and appointed by Law togeather with the oath of a Clarke for his farther Qualification.

Mr. John Blount tooke the Oaths appointed by Law togeather with the Oath of a Justice of the peace.

Mr. Thomas Snoden Tooke the Oaths appointed by Law togeather with the Oath of Attorney Generall.

Robert Keel comes to prosecute his Sute against Augustine Scarbro planter on a Refference from the last Court in a plea of Trespass upon the Case and Complaines that the Defendant in the precinct of pascotank and within the Jurisdiction of this Court with Force and Armes etc. into and upon a Certaine plantation the proper Estate and Rightfull Inheritance of the plaintiff hath wrongfully Entred etc. And the Said Augustine Scarbro by James Melvin his Attorney comes and Defends the force and injury when etc. and Desireth Judgment of the Declaration of him the said Robert plaintiff and Saith that the same ought to abate for that he the said Robert in the preface of his Declaration Setteth forth Robert Keel is plaintiff against Augustine Scarbro planter Defendant in a plea of Trespas upon the Case and in Soe <348> Declareing the Said plaintiff hath mistaken his Action and further he the Said Robert Saith with force and Armes etc. into and upon a certaine plantation and Tract of Land Scituate lying and being in the aforesaid precinct but Does not Sett forth the Day Month year when this Entry was made by the Defendant as by Law he ought to have Done nor doth he the Said plaintiff Sett forth how he doth Entitle himself to the Said plantation and all this the Said Augustine is ready to Verify whereupon he Demands Judgment of the Declaration that the Same may abate with Costs. And the plaintiff by Thomas Snoden and Edward Bonwick his Attorneys prayes time to answer the Defendants plea and Demurrer and the plaintiffs has halfe an Houers time allowed them And then the plaintiff by Thomas Snoden and Edward Bonwick his Attorney for Answer Demurr in Law to the insufficient Demurrer exhibited by the Defendant to the Action forementioned against him by this plaintiff and Say that the aforesaid pretended Demurrer of the Defendant is not Sufficient or Valid in Law to Debarr the plaintiffs Action for that the Same is Uncertaine void of Substance and forme and that in the Same is Conteyned Double plea and this he is ready to averr and pray judgment ut prius as in the plaintiffs Declaration. And the Said Defendant by James Melvin his Attorney joynes and Saith that the plea of the Defendant and the Matter therein conteyned is certaine and not double and thereof he Demands judgment And upon Motion of the plaintiffs Attorneys Liberty is granted with the Consent of the Defendant 'till Too Morrow Morneing Eight of the Clock.

Thomas peterson attorney of Daniell Zachary against Jno. pettiver in a plea of the Case Ordered that the Sute be Dismissed for want of the plaintiffs appearance with Costs.

A Letter of Attorney from Wm. Swann Esqr. to Mr. Thomas Snoden proved by the oath of Mr. John Wicker and that he Saw Richd. Thorp the other person named Signe the Same as an Evidence thereto.

And then this Court adjourned for half an Hour.

Att half an Hour the Court mett and Sitt.

Francis penrise came and in open Court accknowledged a Bill of Four pounds Six Shillings and four pence due from him unto the Honorable Landgrave Robert Daniell Esqr. Dated the Eighth Day of September 1705 and amongst other Bills assigned over to Colonel Wm. Wilkison in his life <349> time and Confesses Judgment for the Same to Ester Wilkison widdow and Executrix of the Said Colonel Wm. Wilkison for the Same.

Ordered that Francis penrise pay unto the Said Ester Wilkison qualifyed as aforesaid Four pounds Six Shillings and four pence in fresh porke with Costs alias Execution.

Francis penrice came and in open Court acknowledged a Bill for Twenty Eight pounds Tenn Shillings and Three pence in good Sound Merchantable porke Dated the 15th Day of Janry. 1704/5 due from him to Captain John Hecklefield and assigned to Colonel Wm. Wilkison in his life time and Confesses Judgment for the Same to Ester the widdow and Executrix of the Said Colonel Wm. Wilkison. Ordered that Francis penrice pay unto the Said Ester Wilkison qualifyed as aforesaid Twenty Eight pounds Tenn Shillings and Three pence according to Specialty with Costs alias Execution.

A Will of Dennis McLendans exhibited by John Bird one of the Executors proved by the Severall Oaths of Francis Foster Esqr. and Gilbert Smith. Upon petition of Jno. Bird one of the Executors of the will of Dennis McLenden Ordered that Such of the Estate of the Said Dennis McLendan is in the precinct of Chowan be inventoryed and apprised by Lewis Williams James Farloe Wm. Hooker and Thomas Man or any Three of Them And alsoe his Estate in pequimons be Inventoryed and apprised by Andrew Read Captain James Cole Mr. John pettiver and Francis Beasley or any Three of them which apprissers are to be Sworne before Some Majestrate.

A Letter of Attorney from Samuell Norton to John Jones proved by the Honorable Wm. Glover Esqr.

A Letter of Attorney from Mr. Thomas peterson to the Honorable William Glover Esqr. proved by the Subscription of Cornelius Ratcliffe.

Thomas peterson Attorney of Micajah perry and New pensilvania Company comes by the Honorable Wm. Glover Esqr. his Attorney to prosecute his Sute against Richard Smith of Bath County in a plea of Debt by a Refference from the last Court and Complaines that the Defendant Stands justly indebted to the plaintiff Qualifyed as aforesaid in the full and just Summ of Ninety four pounds One Shilling and Three pence to be paid in good Merchantable Fresh porke as in and by one Writeing Obligatory bearing Date the 16th Day of September 1704 and now ready to be produced in Court relation being thereunto had it doth and may appear etc. And the Defendant in <350> proper person comes and Defends the force and Injury when etc. And for plea Saith That att the Signeing of the Obligation Exprest in the plaintiffs Declaration he the Defendant made this Reservation videlicet That if hee this Defendant could produce Receipts for the Sum exprest in the aforesaid Obligation That the Said Obligation Should then be Null and Voyd and Saith that hee this Defendant is ready to produce Receipts for the aforesaid Summ And this he is ready to averr and of this he putts himself upon the Country And the plaintiff replys that what the Defendant in his plea Setts forth cann be noe Barr to the plaintiffs Bond any thing alleadged not being of Equall Dignity to the Said Bond and the Court haveing Maturely considered the whole Matter. Ordered that Richard Smith pay unto Thomas peterson Qualified as aforesaid The just Summ of Ninety four pounds One Shilling and Three pence in Fresh porke alias Execution. And the Defendant prays an Injunction to Stopp all further proceedings untill the whole matter be heard in the Honorable Court of Chancery which is granted the Defendant giveing Bond with Security to prosecute his Sute with Effect.

An Assignment of a patent of a Tract of Land from Walter Turnor and Elizabeth his wife acknowledged to Thomas Collings.

Mr. Thomas Boyd Attorney of Ralph Chapman acknowledges the Sale of a Tract of Land to Bryant Fitz-patrick.

Bryant Fitz-patrick accknowledges a Conveyance of a Tract of Land to Wm. Johnson.

Thomas peterson Attorney of Micajah perry and New pensilvania Company comes to prosecute his Sute on an Attachment the last Court against Thomas Holmes Defendant in a plea of Debt and Sayes that the Defendant by one Obligation under his proper hand and Seal bearing Date the Third Day Janry. 1704 Stands justly indebted to the plaintiff qualified as aforesaid in the full and <351> just Summ of Three pounds Tenn Shillings and four pence Sterling to be paid in Good Sound Merchantable porke or Corne upon Demand etc. and the Defendant comes and Confesses.

Ordered that the Said Thomas Holmes pay unto the Said Thomas peterson qualifyed as aforesaid Three pounds Tenn Shillings and four pence according to Specialty with Costs alias Execution.

Thomas Houghton Senior bound over the last Court to be of the good behavior and to appear this Court upon his appearance and noething comeing against him is Dismissed paying his Fees.

Whereas great Hinderance in the proceedings of this Court often happens by reason of persons negligence in their appearance Ordered that from henceforth it be a Rule of this Court that noe Action be posponed on the Doquett upon non appearance but that in Such Cases all Actions Shalbe Discharged as they are Entred on the Doquett and all Issues Shalbe made up the Court Day in the Morning before the Court Sitts and that there Shalbe Twelve Actions for Each Day of the Court and all Writts Shalbe returnable att a Day certaine and notice given to the Defendant in the Copy of the Declaration of the Day.

Robert Keel by Edward Bonwick his Attorney comes to prosecute his Sute against Charles Draper Defendant in a plea of the Case and Complaines that the Defendant Stands justly Indebted to the plaintiff in the Summe of one pound Thirteen Shillings and four pence by Account etc. And the Defendant in proper person comes and Defends the force and injury when etc. and for plea Saith that he owes noe Such Money as in the plaintiffs Declaration is Sett forth and for Tryall putts himself upon the Country and the plaintiff likewise Wherefore the Marshall is required to cause to come Twelve etc. who etc. by whom etc. and there came Mr. John pettiver Mr. Jos. Wicker Mr. Francis penrice Mr. John Sawyer Junior Mr. Wm. Williams Mr. Geo. Harris Mr. Robert White Mr. Henry Lysle Mr. Walter Tanner Mr. James Thickpen Mr. Thomas Norcomb Mr. James Clarke who impannelled and Sworne Say—We of the Jury find for the Defendant with Costs.

Ordered that the Sute be dismist and that the plaintiff pay Costs alias Execution.

And then this Court Adjourned 'till too Morrow Morneing Eight of the Clock.

<352> Thursday 29th This Court mett att 8 of the Clock and Sitt. Present the Honorable Christo. Gale Fra. Delamare Wm. Barcliff Esqrs. Justices.

Upon Complaint of Mr. Thomas Boyd provost Marshall that Nathaniel Nichols has refused to Execute a Warrant for the Queenes Service being pressed for that Service Ordered that the provost Marshall take into his Custody the said Nathaniel Nichols and him Safely hold untill he Shall Enter into Bond with good Security before the next Generall Court to answer all Such Matters and things as Shalbe then and there on her Majesties Behalfe Shalbe objected against him.

Mr. Thomas Boyd provost Marshall returnes the persons following to be Gentlemen of the Grandjury Videlicet Mr. John Bird Mr. Richd. Sewell Mr. Henry Lysle Mr. John Sawyer Mr. James Farlow Mr. Robert palmer Mr. Lewis Williams Mr. John Jones Mr. James Fewox Mr. John Relfe Mr. Robert Harrison Mr. Daniel Hall Mr. John Willoughby Mr. William Charleton and Mr. Wm. Tillett and they were accordingly Sworne.

The Honorable Jno. Blount Esqr. present.

Matthew pritchard and Sarah his wife formerly Sarah the wife of patrick Henley and Executrix of John Culpeper late of this province Deceased her late husband comes to prosecute their Writt of Scire facias against Joshua Lamb Junior Sole Heyr of Joshua Lamb late of This province Deceased The Marshall being Comanded to make Known to the Said Joshua Lamb Junior (by good etc.) that he be and appear att this Generall Court to shew Cause if any he hath why a Writt of Elegit should not goe Out against the Estate of the Said Joshua Lamb Deceased Upon an Attachment obteyned by the Said patrick Henly and Sarah his Wife Executrix etc. att a Court held for the province aforesaid the 24th Day of Febry. 1695 before the Honorable Thomas Harvey Esqr. then Deputy Governor of the Said province and the Honorable Daniel Akehurst and his Assotiates then Justices of the Said Court for Twenty Seven pounds with Costs. And the provost Marshall haveing made returne on the Said Writt—Nihil—Whereupon the Said Matthew pritchard and Sarah his wife Humbly pray that a Writt of Elegitt may be issued out against the Estate of the Said Joshua Lamb decease for the Said Sume of Twenty Seaven pounds with Costs and all other Costs accrewing Since according to the Laws and Statutes in the Case <353> mad and provided which is granted accordingly.

Upon petition of Mary West widdow and relict of Samuel West deceased praying that Letters of Administration may be granted to her of her Deceased husbands Estate (he haveing made noe will) and it appearing to this Court that she is nearest of Kinn to the Deceased this Court is of the Opinion that Letters of Administration may be granted to the said Mary West.

An then this Court adjourned for an Hour.

Att an Hours time the Court mett and Sitt present ut Supra.

An Indictment was found and presented by the Grand jury against George White in the following Words videlicet The Jurors for our Soveraigne Lady the Queen doe present upon their Oaths that George White by the name of George White now or late of the precinct of Chowan in the aforesaid province planter not haveing the Fear of God before his Eyes but being led away by the Instigation of the Devill on or about the 18th Day of June last past one Steer of the vallue of Twenty five Shillings the proper Goods and Chattles of John Harward with force and Armes did Felloniously Kill Steal and bear away against the peace of our Soveraigne Lady the Queen her Crowne and Dignity and Contrary to the forme of the Statute in that Case made and provided. Upon which Indictment the said George White was arreigned and upon his arraignement pleaded not Guilty and for tryall put himself upon his Country And Mr. Thomas Snoden the Queenes Attorney Generall On the behalf of the Queene joynes in the Issue Therefore its Comanded the Marshall that he cause to come twelve etc. And there came Mr. John pettiver Mr. Joseph Wicker Mr. Fra. penrise Mr. John Sawyer Mr.

Wm. Williams Mr. George Harris Mr. Robert White Mr. Wm. Reed Mr. James Thickpen Mr. Thomas Norcomb Mr. Wm. Jennings and Mr. George Clark who Empanelled and Sworne Say We of the Jury find the prisoner att the Barr not Guilty. Ordered that the said George White be discharged Sine Diem paying his Fees.

A Sale of a Tract of Land from the Honorable Thomas pollock Esqr. acknowledged to Samuel Bond.

Emanuel Lowe Esqr. Attorney of John Archdale Esqr. comes by Edward Bonwick his Attorney to prosecute his sute against George Wilson <354> in a plea of Trespass and Declares that Whereas the Said Geo. Wilson in the Month of December Anno Domini 1705 with force and Armes did come into and upon a Certaine Tract of Land of the Said Archdales called Colleton Island in the precinct of Coratuck within the Jurisdiction of this Court and then and there Cutt Down and carryed away the Cedar Trees of the said Archdale there lately Growing to the vallue of Twenty pounds Sterling and other etc. And the Marshall haveing returned a Non Est Inventus att the prayer of the plaintiff Ordered that Attachment issue out against the Defendants Estate.

William Swann Assignee of Edward Taylor comes by Thomas Snoden his Attorney to prosecute his Sute against John Fulford Defendant in a plea of Debt and Sayes that the Defendant Stands justly indebted to the plaintiff Qualifyed as aforesaid in the full and just Summ of Two pounds Fifteen Shillings as in and by a Certaine Writeing under his hand bearing Date the 25th Day of Janry. 1704/5 and here into Court etc. and the Defendant came not and upon Motion of the plaintiff Ordered that the Marshall have here the Body of the Said John Fulford the next Court alias Judgment against the Marshall.

William Swann by Thomas Snoden his Attorney comes to prosecute his Sute against John Fulford Defendant in a plea of Debt and Sayes that the Defendant Stands justly indebted to the plaintiff in the full and just Summ of Twenty Three pounds Four Shillings and Eleaven pence as in and by a Certaine Writeing under his proper hand bearing Date the 8th Day of September 1705 and here into Court etc. and the Defendant came not and upon Motion of the plaintiff Ordered that the Marshall have here the Body of the Said John Fulford the next Court alias Judgment against the Marshall.

John porter by Edward Bonwick his Attorney comes to prosecute his Sute against Thomas Derham in a plea of Debt and Sayes that the Defendant Stands justly indebted to the plaintiff in the full and Just Summ of Fourteen pounds and Eight pence half penny money to be paid in Merchantable Drest Buck Skins att

Two Shillings per Skin and Drest Doe Skins att Eighteen pence per Skin Foxes and Wild-Catts att Nine pence Each and good Matts att Eighteen pence Each and Raccoone att Three pence Each and Dry neat Hydes and Tallow att the Country Current price with Fifty per Cent abatement as in and by one Certaine Writeing Obligatory here into Court brought and ready to be produced under the known hand and Seal of the Defendant bearing Date the 18th Day of Aprill <355> Anno Domini 1705 Relation etc. And the Defendant by Levi Trewhitt his Attorney comes and produces an Account on which the Said obligation passed and Shows an Error of Twenty Shillings in makeing up the said Account which is owned by the plaintiff and the Defendant likewise makes appear Severall payments since the passing the Said Bill Soe that the just Ballance appeares to be Six pounds Eight Shillings and Eight pence half penny and for which he Confesses. Ordered that the said Thomas Derham pay unto the Said John porter Six pounds Eight Shillings and Eight pence half penny in Drest Buckskins att Two Shillings per Skin Drest Doe Skins att Eighteen pence per Skinn Fox and Wild Catt att Nine pence Each Good Matts att Eighteen pence Each Rackoones at Three pence Each, Dry Neates Hydes and Tallow att Country price with Fifty per Cent abatement; with Costs alias Execution.

John porter Esqr. comes by Edward Bonwick his Attorney to prosecute his Sute against Levi Trewhitt and Thomas Derham Defendants in a plea of Debt and Sayes that the Defendants or Either of them Stands justly indebted to the plaintiff in the full and just Summ of Eleaven pounds Eleven Shillings and Three pence to be paid in Merchantable Drest Deer Skins Hydes Tallow and Small Furrs att County price as in and by a Certaine Writeing Obligatory under the proper hands and Seales of the Defendants bearing Date the 18th Day of Aprill 1705 relation etc. And the Defendants by Thomas Snoden their Attorney comes and Defends the force and injury when etc. and for plea Say that the plaintiff his Account against the Defendants ought not to have but that the Same ought to abate being uncertaine and altogeather insufficient in Law to obleidge the Defendant Either of them to make answer for these Reasons Videlicet for want of an alias Dictus the Defendants might be Supposed to be Vexatiously Molested and for that in the plaintiffs Declaration is not Conteyned the Defendants Art Mistery Degree or Quality And this the Defendants are ready to Averr And pray an abatement in the Accounts etc. And the Court haveing Maturely considered the whole Matter are of the Opinion that this Account does not abate and the Defendant has liberty to make further plea And the Defendant Levi Trewhitt in his proper person for further plea Saith that he has paid One pound Thirteen Shillings part of the aforesaid Bill and makes the Same appear by his Oath and the plaintiff allowes off the Discount and the Defendant Trewhitt comes and Confesses Judgment for the Ballances being Nine pounds Eighteen Shillings <356> and Three pence.

Ordered that Levi Trewhitt and Thomas Derham or either of them pay unto the Said John Porter Nine pounds Eighteen Shillings and Three pence in Merchantable Drest Deer Skins Hydes Tallow and Small Furrs att County price with Costs alias Execution.

A Letter of Attorney from John porter Esqr. to the Honorable Wm. Glover Esqr. and Mr. Nath. Chevin proved by the Oath of Mr. Edward Bonwick.

The Honorable Saml. Swann Esqr. accknowledges the Assignement of A patent of a Tract of Land att New begun Creeke to John Archdale Esqr. conteyning 1000 Acres.

The Honorable Saml. Swann Esqr. accknowledges the assignement of a patent for an Island called Colleton Island to John Archdale Esqr.

A Letter of Attorney from Edward Felps to Francis phelps proved by the Oath of Dr. Godfrey Spruell.

A Scire facias on behalf of the Honorable Wm. Glover Esqr. versus Wm. Steel continued for want of Certainty of its being Executed.

Robert Keel haveing obteyned leave from the Court Yesterday to amend his Declaration and against Augustine Scarbro Defendant in a plea of Trespas upon the Case haveing amended his Declaration Complaines that the Defendant in the precinct of pascotanke and within the Jurisdiction of this Court with Force and Armes etc. into and upon a Certaine plantation and Tract of Land Scituate lying and being in the aforesaid precinct the proper Estate and Rightfull Inheritance of the plaintiff and whereon the Defendant now resides hath wrongfully Entred and the Same from the plaintiff doth Wrongfully hold and Deteyne etc. and the Defendant comes and by James Melvin his Attorney Stands to his former plea and Demurrer And the Court haveing heard and maturely considered what both parties have to Say are of the Opinion that this Action ought not to abate for anything in the Defendants plea alleadged. And the Defendant hath Liberty further to plead And the said Augustine Scarbro by James Melvin his Attorney comes and Defends the Force and Wrong when etc. and Saith that he is not Guilty in Manner and Forme and for Tryall putts himself upon the Country and the plaintiff likewise Therefore it is Comanded the Marshall that he cause to come Twelve etc. who etc. by whom etc. and there came Mr. John pettiver Mr. Joseph Wicker Mr. Francis penrice Mr. Geo. Harris Mr. Robt. White Mr. James Thickpen Mr. Thomas Norcomb Mr. Geo. Clarke Mr. John Relf Mr. Edward Bradshaw Mr. Tho. McKeel Mr. John McKeel who Impannelled and Sworne Say We of the Jury find for the Defendant with Costs. <357> Ordered that the Sute be Dismissed and the plaintiff pay Costs alias Execution.

Upon Motion of Thomas Snoden Attorney Generall Ordered that the provost Marshall take into his Custody Thomas Burroughs and him in Safe Custody hold Soe that he appear the Secon Day of the next Generall Court to answer what Shall in her Majesties Name behalf Shalbe objected against him. And Captain Thomas Luten informing that the Said Burroughs is a person Scarce Compos Mentis are willing to Suspend the Execution of the above Order for the present.

Upon petition of Wm. Read Ordered that William Reed be allowed for Two Dayes comeing and Two Dayes goeing and Three Dayes Attendance being Sumoned by Wm. Collings in his Sute against Thomas Abington.

Upon petition of Wm. Read Ordered that William Read be allowed for Two Dayes comeing and Two Dayes goeing and Two Dayes attendance being Sumoned by Charles Daper att the Sute of Robert Keel and that James Williams his man be allowed for one Dayes Attendance on the same Account.

And then this Court adjourned 'till Too Morrow Morning 8 of the Clock.

Fryday att 8 of the Clock the Court mett and Sitt.

Present the Honorable Christopher Gale, John Blount, Fra. DelaMare Willm. Barcliff Esqrs. Justices.

Joseph Wicker appeared att this Court and upon his Oath proved a Bill of John Fulfords due to William Swann for Twenty Three pounds four shilling and Eleven pence in porke Hydes and Tobacco dated the 18th Day of September 1705 and further Declares that he saw Ruth Wicker Signe the Same as an Evidence.

Mary Rookes comes to prosecute her Sute against Thomas Collings Defendant in a plea of the Case and Declares that the Defendant the Seaventh Day of January last past att the Dwelling house of Wm. White in the precinct of pequimons and within the jurisdiction of this Court designeing and Evilly intending to take away the Good name etc. of the plaintiff Did then and there in the hearing of Divers of her Majesties Leidge people pronounce <358> utter and Declare these falce Malitcous and Scandalous Words videlicet you meaning the plaintiff are a Dammed Witch and have bewitched my wife and Divers other falce etc. And the defendant in his proper person comes and Defends the force and Injury when etc. and for plea Saith that he is not Guilty in manner and fame as in the plaintiffs Declaration is Sett forth and for Tryall putts himself upon the Country and the plaintiff Likewise Therefore the Marshall is required to cause to come Twelve etc. who etc. by whom etc. and there came Mr. John Bird Mr. John Willoughby Mr. Wm. Johnson Mr. Thomas Barcliff Mr. John Holdbrooke Mr. William Fryley Mr. Henry Lysle Mr. Gilbert Smith Mr. Jonathan Jacocks Mr. James Fewox Mr. John Arnold Mr. Henry Sawyer who Empannelled and Sworne Say We of the Jury find for the plaintiff One Shilling with Costs And the Defendant Moves that they may be dismised from more Costs then Damages according to Law Upon which the Jury being asked (by conserd of the Defendant) their reason for finding Costs answered that it was Designed to make up the Deficcencies of the Damages.

Ordered that Thomas Collings pay unto Mary Rookes One Shilling Damages with Costs alias Execution.

And then this Court adjourned for an hour and then mett againe and Sitt. Present ut Supra.

Capt. John Hecklefield comes by Thomas Snoden his Attorney to prosecute his Attachment against George Kingersley and the Marshall returnes attached Three Dishes Six plates One Tankerd and One little Bason And the Honorable Wm. Glover Esqr. appeares as Attorney of Mr. Thomas peterson etc. and informes this Court that there is a Deed of Sale of the goods attached made to the Said peterson by Kingsley. It's therefore by consent referred to the next Court.

Upon a non est Inventus returned by the Marshall against Wm. powell att the sute of Captain John Hecklefield upon Motion of Thomas Snoden Attorney for the plaintiff Ordered that attachment issue against the Estate of the said powell.

And then this Court adjourned for half an Hour and then mett and Sitt. Present ut Supra.

<359> Mary Rookes by James Melvin her Attorney comes to prosecute her sute against Walter Tanner Defendant in a plea of the Case and Declares that the Defendant on the Thirty first Day of December last past att the Now Dwelling house of James Layton in the precinct of pequimons and within the Jurisdiction of this Court Designeing and Evely intending to take away the Good name etc. of the plaintiff did then and there in the heareing of Divers of her Majesties Leidge people these false Malitious and Scandalous Words (videlicit) Thou meaneing the plaintiff art a Witch and hast

bewitched me this Day and I will prove you a Witch and divers etc. And the Defendant by Thomas Snoden his Attorney comes and Defends the Force and injury when etc. And for plea Saith That the Defendant is not Guilty in manner and forme as in the plaintiffs Declaration is Exprest and of this he putts himselfe upon the Country and the plaintiff likewise Wherefore its Comanded the Marshall that he cause to come Twelve etc. who etc. by whom etc. and there came Mr. John Bird Mr. John Willoughby Mr. Willm. Johnson Mr. Thomas Barcliff Mr. John Holdbrooke Mr. Wm. Fryley Mr. Henry Lysle Mr. Gilbert Smith Mr. John Wheatley Mr. James Fewox Mr. John Arnold Mr. William Hall who Empannelled and Sworne Say we of the Jury find for the plaintiff Five shillings with Costs to make up the Diffiriencies of the Damages.

Ordered that Walter Tanner pay unto Mary Rookes Five Shillings with Costs alias Execution.

Upon petition of Ann Trumball Ordered that She be paid for Two Dayes attendance being Summoned by Mary Rookes in her Sute against Thomas Collings.

The honorable Colonel Thomas pollock Esqr. comes and by Edward Bonwick is Attorney to prosecute his Sute against Captain John Hecklefield Defendant in a plea of Trespass upon the Case and Complaines for that whereas the aforesaid plaintiff att a Generall Court held for the province aforesaid att the house of the Said Hecklefield on Tuesday the 31st Day of October Anno Domini 1704 had obteyned a Judgment the same Court against Henry Mountfort Master of a Brigantine of the said plaintiffs for the summ of Four Hundred pounds and thereupon had out an Execution <360> directed and Delivered to the said Hecklefield then provost Marshall of the province aforesaid By virtue whereof he tooke the Body of the said Mountfort to Satisfy to the said plaintiff the aforesaid Summ of Four Hundred pounds Yett Nevertheless the said John Hecklefield in Defraud of the said plaintiff and by his Negligent Keeping of the Said Henry Mountfort Sometime about September or October last past att Little River in the province aforesaid him the Said Henry Mountfort att large whether he would to goe and Escape without the Lycence and Consent of the said plaintiff did permitt and suffer the aforesaid the aforesaid [*sic*] Four Hundred pounds or any part thereof to the said plaintiff not being paid And the said Mountford Eversince hitherto did and yett Doth absent and Eloyne himself soe that he the Said Mountfort cannott be taken by any process of Law Since and thereby the Said plaintiff hath Utterly lost the benefitt and Advantage of the Recovery of the Said £400 whereby etc. And the Defendant by Thomas Snoden his Attorney comes and prayes a Refference to the next Generall Court which by the Consent of the plaintiffs Attorney is granted And the Defendants Attorney is Content that it be a Rule of Court that att the Said next Generall Court he plead to the plaintiffs Declaration.

Captain Thomas Luten accknowledges a power to Thomas Abington for the Recovery of Severall Debts of his in pascotank.

Mr. Joseph Wicker comes and by his Oath proves a Coppy of an Account by his Oath against Richd. Burtenshall for Two pounds Nine Shillings and four pence taken out of the Bookes of Edward Musson Deceased whose widdow he Married and further Declares that he finds noe Creditt given.

Mr. Joseph Wicker came and in open Court appointed Mr. Thomas Snoden to be his Attorney.

<361> [*Signed:*]
Francis DeLaMare, Christopher Gale, William Barcliff.

FILE PAPERS IN SUITS AND PROSECUTIONS

[*Collins* v. *Abington*]

[*CCR* 139]

No. Carolina Ss. To the provost Marshall or his Deputy

These are in her Matyes name to will and require you to Arrest the body of Thomas Abington and him Safely hold Soe that he be and appeare at the next Generall Court to be holden at the house of Captain John Hecklefield in Litle river on the last Tuseday in July next then and there to Answer the Suite of Thomas Collins in a plea of the Case and have there this writt Dated at the Secretarys Office this 4th day of June Anno Domini 1706.

Testis T. Knight Secretary

[*Endorsed:*]
Breve
Collins versus Abington
In Case
Executed John Meaids

[*Crown* v. *White*]

[*CCR* 188]

North Carolina ss.

The Jurors for our Soveraigne Lady the Queen doe present upon their Oaths That George White by the name of George White now or later of the precinct of Chowan in the Aforesaid Province Planter not having the fear of God before his Eyes but being led Away by the Instigation of the Devill on or about the 18th Day of June last past one Steer of the Value of Twenty five

Shillings the proper Goods and Chattells of John Harwood with force and Armes did feloniously kill Steal and bear away against the peace of our Soveraigne Lady the Queen her Crown and Dignity and Contrary to the forme of the Statute in that Case made and Provided etc.

Snoden per Domina Regina

[*Endorsed:*]
We of the Jury finde Bill of Vera
We of the Jury find the prisioner at the bar not Gilty

[*Daniell* v. *Coles*]

[*CCR 148*]

North Carolina Ss. To the honorable Generall Court etc.

The Honorable Landgrave Robert Daniell Esqr. is plaintiff against Captain James Cole Defendant in a plea of the Case and Complaines that the Defendant Stands Indebted to the plaintiff in the full and Just Sume of thirty three pounds Seaventeen Shillings by Account as by wayes and meanes Convenient the plaintiff is ready to make appeare which Said Summe of thirty Three pounds Seaven Shillings the Defendant hath not rendred to the plaintiff tho' often thereunto requested but the Same doth Still refuse to render to the plaintiffs Damage Sixty Seaven pounds Fourteen Shillings Sterling and thereupon he brings his Suite and prayes Judgement for the Same with Costs of Suit and Shall pray etc.

T. Knight Secretary

[*Endorsed:*]
Narratio
Daniell Ar. versus Cole
In Case
Filed July 6th 1706
Retraxit

[*Duckenfield* v. *Farrow*]

[*CCR 148*]

No. Carolina Ss. To the provost Marshall of the County of Bath or his Deputy

These are in her Majestyes name to will and require you to Attach Soe much of the Estate of Francis Farrow wherever to be found in this Government as will pay and Satisfy Wm. Duckenfield Esqr. the Summe of Fifteen pounds five Shillings and Six pence with Costs and the Same in Safe Custody Keep untill otherwise ordered by due Course of Law and make returne of your proceedings herein to the next Generall Court Dated at the Secretarys office this 17th day of May Anno Domini 1706.

Testis T. Knight Secretary

[*Endorsed:*]
Attachment
Farrow ads. Duckenfield
Non [*illegible*] debuty mashell James Cross

[*Duckenfield* v. *Monteague*]

[*CCR 148*]

No. Carolina Ss. To the provost Marshall of the County of Bath or his Deputy

These are in her Matyes name to will and require you to Attach Soe much of the Estate of Roger Monteague wherever to be found in your County as will pay and Satisfy Wm. Duckenfield Esqr. the Summe of thirty Seaven Shillings and Six pence with Costs and the Same in Safe Custody Keep untill otherwise ordered by due Course of Law and make returne of your proceedings therein to the next Generall Court Dated at the Secretarys Office this 17th day of May Anno Domini 1706.

Testis T. Knight Secretary

[*Endorsed:*]
Attachment
Montegue ads. Duckenfield
Payed to Mr. Edman pearce W. Barrow

[*Gale* v. *Cartwright*]

[*CCR 148*]

No. Carolina Ss. To the honorable Generall Court etc.

Christo. Gale Esquire is plaintiff against Wm. Cartwright Junior Defendant in a plea of the Case and Complaines that the Defendant Stands Indebted to the plaintiff in the full Summe of Two pounds Tenn Shillings due to the plaintiff by Account as being Attorney Generall and prosecuting an Information against the Defendant in her Majestyes behalfe as by wayes and meanes Convenient the plaintiff is ready to make appeare which Said Summe of Two pounds tenn Shillings the defendant hath not rendered to the plaintiff tho' often thereunto requested but the Same doth Still refuse to render to the plaintiffs Damage Five pounds Sterling and thereupon he brings his Suite and prayes Judgement for the Same with Costs of Suite and shall pray etc.

T. Knight Secretary

[*Endorsed:*]
Narratio
Gale Esqr. versus Cartright
In Case
Entered May 23d: 1706

[CCR 148]

No. Carolina Ss. To the provost Marshall or his Deputy

These are in her Majestyes name to will and require you to Arrest the body of Wm. Cartwright Junior and him Safely hold Soe that he may be and appeare at the next Generall Court to be holden at the house of Captain Jno. Hecklefield in Litle river on the last Tuseday in July next then and there to Answer the plaint of Christo. Gale Esqr. in a plea of the Case and have there this writt Dated at the Secretarys Office this 23d day of May Anno Domini 1706.

Testis T. Knight Secretary

[*Endorsed:*]
Breve
Gale Esqr. vesus Cartwright
In Case
Executed John Meaids

[*Gale* v. *Harris*]

[CCR 148]

No. Carolina Ss. To the honorable the Generall Court etc.

Christo. Gale Esqr. is plaintiff against David Harris Defendant in a Plea of the Case and Complaines that the Defendant stands Indebted to the plaintiff in the Sume of two pounds five shillings and Eleven pence by Account as by ways and meanes Convenient the plaintiff is ready to make appeare which Said Sume of two pounds five shillings and Eleven pence the defendant hath not rendred to the plaintiff tho often thereunto requested but the same doth Still refuse to render to the plaintiffs Damage five pounds And thereupon he brings his Suite and prays Judgement for the Same with Costs of Suite and shall pray etc.

T. Knight Secretary

[*Endorsed:*]
Narratio
Gale Esqr. versus Harris
In Case
Entered May 22d: 1706

[CCR 148]

No. Carolina Ss. To the Provost Marshall or his Deputy

These are in her Matyes name to will and require you to Arrest the body of David Harris and him Safely hold soe that he be and appeare at the next Generall Court to be holden at the house of Captain Jno. Hecklefield in Litle river on the last Tuesday in July next then and there to Answer the Plaint of

Christo. Gale Esqr. in a plea of the Case and have there this writt Dated at the Secretarys Office this 22d day of May Anno Domini 1706.

Testis T. Knight Secretary

[*Endorsed:*]
Breve
Gale Esqr. v. Harris
In Case
Executed John Mead

[*Gale* v. *Harris*]

[*CCR 148*]

No. Carolina Ss. To the honorable the Generall Court etc.

Christopher Gale Esqr. is plaintiff against David Harris Defendant in a plea of Debt and Sayes that the Defendant Stands Justly Indebted to the plaintiff in the full and Just Summe of a quantyty of Seaven good Barrells of Merchantable Tarr to be paid and Delivered at the Plaintiffs owne Landing as in and by one writeing obligatory under the proper hand and Seale of the Defendant beareing Date the third day of October Anno Domini 1705 and here into Court brought relation being thereunto had doth and may more fully and att large appeare Nevertheless the Defendant the said Seaven Barrells of Tarr to the Defendant hath not rendered tho often thereunto requested but the Same doth Still refuse to render to the plaintiffs Damage Seaven pounds Sterling and there upon he brings his Suite and prayes Judgement for the Same with Costs of Suite and shall pray etc.

T. Knight Secretary

[*Endorsed:*]
Narratio
Gale Esqr. versus Harris
In Debt
Entered May 22d: 1706

[*CCR 148*]

No. Carolina Ss. To the provost Marshall or his Deputy

These are in her Majestyes name to will and require you to Arrest the body of David Harris and him safely hold soe that he may be and appeare at the next Generall Court to be holden at the house of Captain Jno. Hecklefield in Litle river on the last Tuseday in July next then and there to Answer the plaint of Christopher Gale Esqr. in a plea of Debt and have there this writt Dated at the Secretarys Office this 22d day of May Anno Domini 1706.

Testis T. Knight Secretary

[*Endorsed:*]
Breve

Gale Esqr. versus Harris
In Debt
Executed John Meaid

[*Gale* v. *Harris*]

[*CCR 148*]

No. Carolina Ss. To the honorable the Generall Court etc.

Christo. Gale Esqr. is plaintiff against George Harris Defendant in a plea of Debt and Sayes that the Defendant Stands Justly Indebted to the plaintiff in the full and Just Summe of Four pounds Eight Shillings as in and by one writeing obligatory under the defendants proper hand and here in to Court brought relation being thereunto had doth and may more fully and at large appeare which said Sume of Four pounds Eight Shillings the Defendant hath not rendered to the plaintiff tho' often thereunto requested but the Same doth Still refuse to render to the plaintiffs Damage Eight pounds Sixteen Shillings Sterling and thereupon he brings his Suite and prayes Judgement for the Same with Costs of Suite and shall pray etc.

T. Knight Secretary

[*Endorsed:*]
Narratio
Gale Esqr. versus Harris
In Debt
Entered May 22d: 1706

[*CCR 148*]

No. Carolina Ss. To the provost Marshall or Deputy

These are in her Majestyes name to will and require you to Arrest the body of Geo. Harris and him Safely hold Soe that he may be and appeare at the next Generall Court to be holden at the house of Captain John Hecklefield in Litle river on the last Tuseday in July next then and there to Answer the plaint of Christo. Gale Esqr. in a plea of Debt and have there this writt Dated at the Secretarys office this 2d day of May Anno Domini 1706.

Testis T. Knight Secretary

[*Endorsed:*]
Breve
Gale Esqr. versus Harris
In Debt
Executed John Meaid

[*Hecklefield* v. *Kingsly*]

[*CCR 148*]

No. Carolina Ss.

Whereas George Kingsley is departed out of this Government and have not Left any Attorney to Answer for him according to Law being Indebted to Captain Jno. Hecklefield in the Sume of four pounds

To the provost Marshall or his Deputy

These are therefore in her Majestyes name to will and require you to Attach Soe much of the Estate of the said George Kingsly wherever to be found in this Government as will pay and Satisfy the Said John Hecklefield the said Sum of four pounds with Costs and the same in Safe Custody Keep untill other wise ordered by due Course of Law and make returne of your proceedings herein to the next Generall Court Dated at the Secretarys office this 17th day of Aprill Anno Domini 1706.

Testis T. Knight Secretary

[*Endorsed:*]
Attachment versus
Kingsly ads. Hecklefield
Executed John Meaid
3 dishes 6 plattes 1 tankerd 1 littell bassoon atteh John Meaids

[*Hendricks* v. *Lewis*]

[*CR 2.001*]

No. Carolina Ss. To the honorable the Generall Court etc.

John Hendricks is plaintiff against Tho. Lewis Defendant in a plea of the Case and Complaines that the Defendant Stands Indebted to the plaintiff in the full Sume of One pound Eleven Shillings and Six pence by Account as by wayes and meanes Convenient the plaintiff is ready to make appeare which said Sume of One pound Eleven Shillings and Six pence the Defendant hath not rendered to the plaintiff tho' often thereunto requested but the Same doth Still refuse to render to the plaintiffs Damage Four pounds Sterling and thereupon he brings his Suite and prayes Judgement for the Same with Costs of Suite and shall pray etc.

T. Knight Secretary

[*Endorsed:*]
Narratio
Hendricks versus Lewis
In Case
Entered May 29th: 1706

[*Henley, executrix* v. *Lamb, executrix*]

[*CR 2.001*]

North Carolina ss.

Anne by the grace of God Queen of England etc. To the Provost Marshall of the Province aforesaid Greeting

Whereas at a Court held for the Province aforesaid the 24th day of Febry. Anno Domini 1695 before the honorable Thomas Harvey Esqr. then Deputy Governour of our Said Province and the honorable Danll. Akehurst and his Associates then Justices of our said Court Patrick Henley and Sarah his Wife Executrix of the Last Will and Testament of John Culpeper late of Pascotanck Gentleman deceased obtained an Attachment against the Estate of Joshua Lamb late of this Province Deceased for the summe of twenty and Seven pounds with Cost which Said Attachment was returned by Thomas Relph then Marshall of the Said Province In these words following (Videlicet) I the subscriber being then Marshall could not find so much of the Estate of Joshua Lamb in this Goverment And Whereas the said Patrick Henly is Since Deceased and the said Sarah his Wife is now the Executrix of the last Will and Testament of the said Patrick and thereof hath taken Letters Testamentary and hath intermarried with Mathew Pritchet of the Precinct of Pascotank aforesaid You are therefore to make knowne to the said Mary Lamb Executrix of the said Joshua Lamb by good and lawfull men of Your Bailiwick that she be and appear at the next Genall Court to be held for our Said Province at the house of Capt. John Hacklefield in Little River in the said Province to shew cause if any she have why an Elegit should not go against the Estate of the said Joshua Lamb according to the Act of Assembly in that Case made and have you there this Writ and the Names of the Persons before whome you Execute the Same Dated At the Secretarys Office the 20th day of February Anno Domini 1705.

Testis T. Knight Secretary

[*Endorsed:*]
Nihill
Thos. Boyd provost Marshall

[*Jones* v. *Symons*]

[*CCR 148*]

No. Carolina Ss. To the honorable the Generall Court

John Jones is plaintiff against Edwd. Symons Defendant in a plea of the Case and Complaines that the Defendant Stand indebted to the plaintiff in the full Sume or Quantyty of Six Barrells of Tarr by Account as by wayes and meanes Convenient the plaintiff is ready to make appeare which said Quantyty of Six Barrells of Tarr the Defendant hath not paid or Delivered to the plaintiff tho' often thereunto requested but the same doth still refuse to pay or deliver to the plaintiffs Damage Six pound Sterling and thereupon he brings his Suite and prayes Judgement for the Same with Costs of Suite and shall pray.

T. Knight Secretary

[*Endorsed:*]
Narratio
Jones versus Symons

In Case
Entered June 3d: 1706

[*CCR 148*]

No. Carolina Ss. To the provost Marshall or his Deputy

These are in her Majestyes name to will and require you to Arrest the body of Edwd. Symons and him Safely hold Soe that he be and appeare att the next Generall Court to be holden at the house of Captain Jno. Hecklefield in Litle river on the last Tuesday in July next then and there to Answer the plaint of John Jones in a plea of the Case and have there this writt Dated at the Secretarys Office this 3d day of June Anno Domini 1706.

Testis T. Knight Secretary

[*Endorsed:*]
Breve
Jones versus Symons
In Case
Executed Tho. Boyd provost Marshall

[*Keele* v. *Draper*]

[*CCR 148*]

No. Carolina Ss. To the Honorable the Generall Court etc.

Rob. Keele is plaintiff against Charles Draper defendant in a plea of the Case and Complains that the Defendant Stands Indebted to the plaintiff in the Sume of One pound thirteen Shillings and four pence by Account as by wayes and meanes Convenient the plaintiff is ready to make appeare which said Summe of One pound thirteen Shillings and four pence the defendant hath not rendred to the plaintiff tho' often thereunto requested but the Same doth Still refuse to render to the plaintiffs Damage four pounds Sterling and thereupon he brings his Suite and prayes Judgement for the Same with Costs of Suite and Shall pray etc.

T. Knight Secretary

[*Endorsed:*]
Narratio
Keele versus Draper
In Case
Entered May 21st: 1706

[*CCR 148*]

No. Carolina Ss. To the provost Marshall or his Deputy

These are in her Matyes name to will and require you to Arrest the body of Charles Draper and him Safely hold Soe that he be and appeare at the next Generall Court to be holden at the house of Captain John Hecklefield in Litle river on the last Tuesday in July next then and there to Answer the plaint of Robert Keele in a plea of the Case and have there this writt Dated at the Secretarys Office this 21st day of May Anno Domini 1706.

Testis T. Knight Secretary

[*Endorsed:*]
Breve
Keele versus Draper
In Case
July the 10: 1706 Executed and Returned by me Wm. Bray

[*Keele* v. *Scarbrough*]

[*CCR 148*]

North Carolina Ss. To the provost Marshall or his Deputy

These are in her Majestyes name to will and require you to Sumons the Bodyes of Hana Conn personally to be and appeare at the next Generall Court to be holden at the house of Captain John Hecklefield in Litle river on the last Tuseday in July next then and there to Give Evidence in a Cause there Depending between Robert Keele plaintiff and Austin Scarbro' Defendant on behalfe of the plaintiff and have there this Sumons Dated at the Secretarys Office this 10th day of June Anno Domini 1706.

Testis T. Knight Secretary

No. Carolina Ss. To the provost Marshall or his Deputy

These are in her Majestyes name to will and require you to Sumons the Body of John Jening personally to be and apeare at the next Generall Court to be holden at the house of Captain John Hecklefield in Litle river on the last Tuseday in July next then and there to give Evidence in a Cause there Depending between Robert Keele plaintiff and Austin Scarbro' Defendant on behalfe of the plaintiff and have there this Sumons Dated at the Secretarys Office this 10th day of June Anno Domini 1706.

Testis T. Knight Secretary

[*Endorsed:*]
Keel and Scarbro Sumons
For Mr. R. Keele
Executed John Meaids

[*CCR 148*]

No. Carolina Ss. To the provost Marshall or his Deputy

These are in her Matyes name to will and require you to Sumons Tho. Barcock personally to be and appeare at the next Generall Court to be holden at the house of Captain John Hecklefield in Litle river on the last Tuesday in July next then and there to give Evidence in a Cause there Depending between

Robert Keel plaintiff and Augustine Scarbro Defendant on behalfe of the Defendant and have there this Sumons Dated at the Secretarys Office this 11th day of June Anno Domini 1706.

Testis T. Knight Secretary

[*Endorsed:*]
Sumons for Tho. Barcock
Executed John Mead

[*CCR 148*]

No. Carolina Ss. To the provost Marshall or his Deputy

These are in her Matyes name to will and require you to Sumons John Sawyer John Humfries and Tho. Frinch personally to be and appeare at the next Generall Court to be holden at the house of Captain John Hecklefield in Litle river the last Tuesday in July next then and there to Give Evidence in a Certaine Cause there depending between Robert Keele plaintiff and Augustin Scarbro' Defendant on Behalfe of the plaintiff and have there this Summons Dated at the Secretarys Office this 11th day of June Anno Domini 1706.

Testis T. Knight Secretary

[*Endorsed:*]
Sumons for J. Sawyer, J. Humfries, T. Frinch
Jno. Relfe sumoned
John Meaids

[*Minge* v. *Leary*]

[*CCR 191*]

North Carolina General Court Ss.

Richard Leary was Summoned to answer James Minge of a Plea that he render him One Mare one Sadle one Bridle one pair of Bootes and one Riding-Coat which from him he unjustly detaines

And whereupon the Said James Minge by Edward Bonwicke his Attorney saies That he the 26th day of March Anno Domini 1706 delivered to the aforesaid Richard Leary One Mare on Saddle one Bridle one pair of Bootes and one Riding-Coat to the value of Ten pounds Sterling to be safe kept and to him the said James to be redelivered when he should be thereunto required Yet the aforesaid Richard although often required the said Mare Sadle Bridle Boots and Riding-Coat to him the said James he hath not redelivered but the same to him hitherto to redeliver hath denyed and as yet doth deny and unjustly detain whereupon he saith that he is Damnified and hath damage to the value of £20 Sterling and thereupon produceth this Suit.

Bonwicke per Querens

[*CCR 148*]

No. Carolina Ss. To the Provost Marshall or his Deputy

These are in her Majestyes name to will and require you to Arrest the body of Richd. Leary and him Safely hold Soe that he be and appeare at the next Generall Court to be holden at the house of Capt. John Hecklefield in Litle river on the last Tuseday in July next then and there to Answer the plaint of James Minge of a plea that he render him one Mare one Sadle one bridle one pair of boots and one rideing Coate which from him he unjustly deteynes and have there this writt Dated at the Secretary's Office this 17th day of June Anno Domini 1706.

Testis T. Knight Secretary

[*Endorsed*]
Breve
Minge versus Leary
In Detinue
Executed John Meaid

[*Peterson, attorney of Perry and Company* v. *Daw*]

[*CCR 192*]

North Carolina Ss. To the honorable the Generall Court etc.

Thomas Peterson Attorney of Micajah Perry and New Pensilvania Company is plaintiff against Nicholas Daw Hatter of Matslepunngo in the County of Bath Defendant in a plea of Debt and Sayes that the Defendant Stands Justly Indebted to the plaintiff quallifyed as aforesaid in the full and Just Sume of forty pounds Sixteen Shillings and Tenn pence to be paid upon Demand Convenient in the aforesaid County in good and Sufficient Merchantable Comodityes of the Country as in and by on Certaine writeing under the proper hand of the Defendant bearing Date October the 2d 1705 here into Court brought relation being thereunto had doth and may more fully and at large appeare which Said Summe of Forty pounds Sixteen Shillings and ten pence the Defendant hath not rendred to the plaintiff tho' Often thereunto requested but the Same doth Still refuse to render to the plaintiffs Damage Eighty one pounds thirteen Shillings and Eight pence and thereupon he brings his Suite and prayes Judgement for the Same with Costs of Suite and Shall pray etc.

T. Knight Secretary

[*Endorsed:*]
Narratio
Peterson versus Daw
In Debt
Entered Augt. 17th 1706

[*Pollock* v. *Hecklefield*]

[*CCR 148*]

North Carolina Generall Court Ss.

John Hacklefeild Gentleman late Provost Marshall of the Province aforesaid was Attached to answer Collonell Thomas Pollock of a Plea of Trespass upon the Case

And whereupon the said Collonell Thomas Pollock by Edward Bonwicke his Attorney complaines for that whereas the aforesaid Plaintiff at a Generall Court held for the Province aforesaid at the house of the said Hacklefeild on Tuesday the 31th day of October Anno Domini 1704 had obtained a Judgment in the same Court against one Henry Mountfort Master of a Briggantine of the said Plaintiff for the summe of Four hundred pounds And thereupon had entered [an action] directed and delivered to the said Hacklefeild then Provost Marshall of the Province aforesaid By vertue whereof he took the body of the said Mountfort to satisfy to the said Plaintiff the aforesaid Summe of Four hundred pounds Yet nevertheless the said John Hacklefeild in defraud of the said Plaintiff and by his negligent keeping of the said Henry Mountfort some time about September or October last past At Little River in the Province aforesaid him the said Henry Mountfort at large whether he would to go and escape [without] the License and [consent] of the said Plaintiff did permit and suffer [*illegible*] aforesaid Four hundred pounds or any part thereof to the said Plaintiff not being paid And the said Mounfort ever [since] hitherto Did and yet doth absent and eloyne himselfe so that he the said Mounfort cannot be taken by any process of Law [since] And thereby the said Plaintiff hath utterly lost the benefit and advantage of the recovery of the said £400 whereby he saith that he is worsted and hath damage to the value of Eight hundred pounds and thereupon produceth this Suite.

Bonwicke per querens Pledges etc.
Jno. Doe
Ri. Roe

[*Endorsed:*]
Collonell Pollock Versus Hacklefeilde
Declaration
Filed July 8: 1706

[*Porter* v. *Dereham*]

[*CCR 148*]

No. Carolina Ss. To the Provost Marshall of the County of Bath or his Deputy

These are in her Majestyes name to will and require you to Attach Soe much of the Estate of Tho. Dereham wherever to be found in your County as will pay and Satisfy John Porter Esqr. Fourteen pounds and Eight pence halfe peny with Costs and the Same in Safe Custody Keep untill otherwise ordered by due Course of Law and make returne of your proceedings herein to the next Generall Court Dated at the Secretarys Office this 17th day of May Anno Domini 1706.

Testis T. Knight Secretary

[*Endorsed:*]
Attachment
Dereham ads. Porter
Atached 27 Shepe per me W. Barrow provest marshal

[*CCR 192*]

Know all men by these presents that I Thomas Dereham of Pamticoe in the County of Bath have and do by these presents putt, Constitute, and ordaine Levi Truewhitt of the said County my true and Lawfull atturny for me and in my name to answer to one action depending betwinn me and John Porter Senior in the honorable generall Court next ensueing for this province, and the Judgment of the said Court to abide, Wittness my hand and Seale this 17th of August 1706.

Signed Sealed and Delivered in the Presents of
Allen Robinett
John Brett

Tho. Dereham

[*Endorsed:*]
Derehams Letter of attorney
Hoc procuratio facta decimo Nono die Augusti Anno Domini 1706
coram me C. Gale [*illegible*] Justis, Curia provincia

[*Porter* v. *Smith*]

[*CCR 148*]

No. Carolina Ss.

Att a Generall Court holden the 8th day of May 1706

Ordered that Richd. Smyth pay unto John Porter Esqr. the Sume of one hundred and forty pounds Seaven Shillings and Eleven pence in Merchantable Drest Buck Skinns at two Shillings per Skin and Merchantable Drest Doe Skinns at Eighteen pence per Skinn and fox and Wild Catt Skinns at Nine pence Each with Costs alias Execution.

Wherein haveing fayled

To the provost Marshall or his Deputy of the County of Bath

These are therefore in her Matyes name to will and require you to Arrest the body of the said Richard Smyth and him in Safe Custody hold untill he shall well and truely pay and Satisfy the said John Porter the Said Sume of One hundred and forty pounds Seaven Shillings and Eleven pence in Merchantable Drest Buck Skinns at two Shillings per Skin and Merchantable Drest Doe Skins at Eighteen pence per Skinn and fox and wild Cat Skins at Nine pence

Each with Costs of Suite and make returne of your proceedings herein to the next Generall Court Dated at the Secretarys Office this 25th day of June Anno Domini 1706.

Testis T. Knight Secretary

Clerks Fee 01:03:06

[Per] T. Knight Secretary

[*Endorsed:*]
Executed per me W. Barrow Provost Marshall
And agreed by Bond and Security

[*Porter* v. *Truewhitt and Dereham*]

[*CCR 148*]

No. Carolina Ss. To the provost Marshall of the County of Bath or his Deputy

These are in her Majestyes name to will and require you to Attach Soe much of the Estate of Levy Trewhitt and Tho. Dereham or either of them as will pay and Satisfy John Porter Esqr. the Summe of Eleaven pounds Eleaven Shillings and three pence with Costs and the Same in Safe Custody Keep untill otherwise ordered by due Course of Law and make returne of your proceedings herein to the next Generall Court Dated at the Secretarys Office this 17th day of May Anno Domini 1706.

Testis T. Knight Secretary

[*Endorsed:*]
Attachment
Trewhitt and Dereham ads. Porter
Atach 27 Shepe per me W. Barrow provest Marshal

[*Rooks* v. *Collins*]

[*CCR 148*]

No. Carolina Ss. To the honorable Generall Court

Mary Rookes is plaintiff against Thomas Collins defendant in a plea of the Case and Complaines that the Defendant on the Seaventh day of Janry. last past at the Dwelling house of Willm. White in the precinct of pequimons and within the Jurisdiction of this Court designeing and Evely Intending to take away the Good name Fame Credit and reputation of the plaintiff did then and there in the heareing of divers of her Matyes Leidge people pronounce utter and declare these false Malitious and Scandelous words (viz.) You (meaneing the plaintiff) are a Damned witch and have bewitched my wife and divers other false Scandelous and Malitious words to and off the plaintiff did utter and declare to the plaintiffs Damage One hundred pounds Sterling and thereupon Shee brings this Suite and prayes Judgement for the Same with Costs of Suite and shall pray etc.

T. Knight Secretary

[*Endorsed:*]
Narratio
Rooks versus Collins
In Case
Filed July [9] th 1706
Wee of the Jury finde for the Plaintiff one shilling with Cost

[*CCR 148*]

No. Carolina Ss. To the Provost Marshall or Deputy

These are in her Majestyes name to will and require you to Arrest the body of Thomas Collins and him Safely hold soe that he may be and appeare at the next Generall Court to be holden at the house of Capt. Jno. Hecklefild in Litle river on the last Tuseday in July next then and there to Answer the plaint of Mary Rooks widdow in a plea of the Case and have there this writt Dated at the Secretary's office this 17th day of June Anno Domini 1706.

Testis T. Knight Secretary

[*Endorsed:*]
Breve
Rookes versus Collins
In Case
Executted John Meaid

[*Rooks* v. *Tanner*]

[*CCR 148*]

No. Carolina Ss. To the provost Marshall or his Deputy

These are in her Majestyes name to will and require you to Arrest the body of Walter Tanner and him Safely hold Soe that he may be and appeare at the next Generall Court to be holden at the house of Captain Jno. Hecklefield in Litle river on the last Tuseday in July next then and there to Answer the plaint of Mary Rookes in a plea of the Case and have there this writt Dated at the Secretarys Office this 17th day of June Anno Domini 1706.

Testis T. Knight Secretary

[*Endorsed:*]
Breve
Rookes versus Tanner
In Case
Executed John Meaid

[*Swann* v. *Fulford*]

[*CCR 191*]

No. Carolina Ss. To the honorable the Generall Court etc.

Wm. Swann Esqr. is plaintiff against John Fulford defendant in a ple of

Debt and Says that the Defendant Stands Justly Indebted to the plaintiff in the full and Just Sume of twenty three pounds four Shillings and Eleven pence as in and by one Certaine writeing under his proper hand beareing Date the Eighth day of September 1705 and here into Court brought relation being thereunto had doth and may more fully and at Large appeare which said Sume of twenty three pounds four Shillings and Eleven pence the Defendant hath not rendered to the plaintiff tho often thereunto requested but the Same doth Still refuse to render to the plaintiffs Damage forty Six pounds Nine Shillings and tenn pence Sterling and there upon he brings his Suite and prays Judgement for the Same with Costs of Suite and shall pray etc.

T. Knight Secretary

[*Endorsed:*]
Narratio
Swann versus Fulford
In Debt
Filed 15th June 1706

[*CCR 189*]

Docquett of Acctions to October Court 1706

Refferences and Attachments from July Court

1. Pollock Esqr. versus Hecklefield trespass Super Casu. Referred.

2. Low versus Wilson trespass. Attachment nulla bona.

3. Swann versus Fulford.

4. Idem versus Eundem.

5. Peterson Attorney etc. versus Hewett in Debt. Attachment Executed.

6. Hecklefield versus Powell in Case. Attachment returned att 17:10: in the hands of Bryant Lee.

Writts and Returnes to October Court

7. Peterson Attorney etc. versus Daw in Debt. Executed.

8. Idem versus Towers in Debt.

9. Idem versus Armour in Debt. Cepi Corpus.

10. Idem versus Wayman in Debt. Executed.

11. Idem versus White in Debt. Cepi Corpus.

12. Idem versus Collins Administrator etc. in Debt. Cepi Corpus.

13. Daniell Esqr. versus Moseley Esqr. in Case.

14. Idem versus Eundem in Debt.
15. Hawkins versus Cross in Debt. Cepi Corpus.
16. Idem versus Neale in Debt.
17. Houghton versus Warren in Case.
18. Coles versus Norton in Case.
19. Deeds versus Duckenfield in Debt.
20. Wicker versus Smyth in Debt. Cepi Corpus.
21. Porter and Company versus Paine in Detinue.
22. Parker versus Lane in Case.
23. Idem versus Sparrow in Debt. Executed.
24. Foster versus Chambers in Debt. Non est Inventus.
25. Waide versus Meads. Attachment Executed.
26. Blount versus Benington. Non est Inventus.

Finis

[*Endorsed:*]

Docquett October Court 1706

[*CCR 104*]

<361> No. Carolina Ss.

Att a Generall Court holden at the house of Captain Jno. Hecklefield in Litle river on Tuseday the 29th day of October Anno Domini 1706 and adjourned till the Morrow Morne 8 of Clock.

Wednesday morne 8 of Clock this Court met. Present the honorable Christo. Gale, Franc. Delamare, Wm. Bartlett Esqrs. Justices.

The Honorable Colonel Thoms. Pollock Esquire Comes by Edwd. Bonwick his Attorney by a referrence from the last Court to prosecute his suite against Jno. Hecklefield gentleman late provost Marshall of the province aforesaid defendant of a plea of Trespass on the Case and Complaines for that whereas the aforesaid plaintiff at a Generall Court held for the province aforesaid at the house of the said Hecklefield on Tuseday the thirty first day of October Anno Domini 1704 had obteyned a Judgement in the Same Court against one Henry Mountfort (Master of a Brigganteen of the said plaintiffs) for the Sume of Four hundred pounds and thereupon had out an Execution directed and delivered to the Said Hecklefield then provost Marshall of the province aforesaid by virtue whereof he tooke the body of the Said Mountfort to Satisfy to the Said plaintiff the aforesaid Summe of Four hundred pounds Yet nevertheless the said Jno. Hecklefield in defraud of the Said plaintiff and by his negligent Keeping of the said Henry Mountfort Sometyme about September or octob. last past at Litle river in the province aforesaid him the said Henry Mountfort at large whether he would to goe and Escape without the Lycence and Consent of the said plaintiff did permitt and Suffer the aforesaid Four hundred pounds or any part thereof to the said plaintiff not being paid and the said Mountfort ever since hitherto did and yet Doth absent and Eloyne him Selfe soe that he the said Mountfort cannot be taken by any process of Law Since and there by the said plaintiff <362> hath utterly lost the benefitt and advantage of the recovery of the said Four hundred pounds whereby he sayth that he is worsted and hath Damage to the vallue of Eight hundred pound and thereupon etc. And the defendant Comes by Thos. Snoden his Attorney and Confesses.

Ordered that the said Jno. Hecklefield pay unto the Said Thos. Pollock the said Summe of Four hundred pounds with Costs alias Execution.

Emanuell Lowe Comes by Edwd. Bonwick his Attorney to prosecute his Attachment from the last Court against Geo. Wilson for £20 and a Nulla Bona being returned thereon the plaintiff prayes the former Judgement may be Continued which is Granted.

Wm. Swann Esqr. Comes to prosecute his Suite against Jno. Fulford upon an order passed against the Marshall the last Court and sayes that the Defendant Stands Justly Indebted to the plaintiff by Bill under hand in the Full Sume of Twenty three pounds four Shillings and Eleven pence And the defendant Came not and the plaintiff prayes Judgement upon the aforesaid order against the Marshall and the Court haveing Considered the Matter duely Ordered that Captain Wm. Barrow provost Marshall of the County of Bath pay unto the said Wm. Swann the aforesaid Summe of Twenty three pounds four Shilling and Eleven pence with Costs alias Execution. And Capt. Wm. Barrow Comes and prayes an Attachment against the said Fulfords Estate which is Granted.

Wm. Swann Esqr. Assignee of Edwd. Taylor Comes to prosecute his Suite against Jno. Fulford in a plea of debt upon an order obteyned against the Marshall the last Court and declares for two pounds Fifteen Shilling by Bill under hand, and the defendant Came not and the plaintiff prayes Judgement upon the aforesaid order against the Marshall and the Court haveing duely Considered the whole matter

Ordered that Captain Wm. Barrow provost Marshall of the County of Bath pay unto the said Wm. Swann Assignee of Edwd. Taylor the aforesaid Summe of two pounds Fifteen Shillings with Costs alias Execution. And the said Wm. Barrow Comes and prayes an Attachment against the said Fulfords Estate which is Granted.

Capt. Jno. Hecklefield Comes and prayes a power of Attorney from Nicho. Daw to said Hecklefield may be recorded which is Granted.

<363> Capt. Jno. Hecklefield Comes by Thos. Snoden his Attorney to prosecute his Attachment from the last Court against Wm. Powell for fourteen pounds and four pence with Costs and the Marshall haveing returned Attached Seaventeen pounds ten Shillings in the hands of Bryant Lee. It is ordered that the said Attachment be Continued and that a Scire Facias Issue out against the said Lee to Shew Cause why he shall not pay the aforesaid Money to the said Hecklefield as Assetts of the Said Powells.

Thomas Peterson Attorney to Micajah Perry and New pensilvania Company Comes to prosecute his Suite against Nicho. Daw in a plea Debt and Declares for Forty pounds Sixteen Shillings and ten pence, And the defendant Comes by Capt. Jno. Hecklefield his Attorney upon record and Confesses.

Ordered that the Said Nicho. Daw pay unto the Said Thos. Peterson the said Summe of Forty pounds Sixteen Shillings and Tenn pence with Costs alias Execution.

Upon petition of Mr. Nicho. Tyler being Sumoned as an Evidence for Mr. Tho. Peterson against Nicho. Daw It is ordered That the said Tho. Peterson pay unto the said Tyler for Six dayes Comeing and Goeing and one dayes Attendance according to Act of Assembly in that behalfe made.

Thom. Peterson Attorney to Micajah Perry and New pensilvania Company Comes to prosecute his Suite against Christo. Wayman in a plea of Debt and Declares for two pounds Eight Shilling and one peny and the Defendant Comes and Confesses.

Ordered that the said Christo. Wayman pay unto said peterson the aforesaid Summe of two pounds Eight shillings and a penny with Costs alias Execution.

Thom. Peterson Attorney to Micajah Perry and New Pensilvania Company Comes to prosecute his Suite against Robt. White in a plea of Debt and declares for two pounds Sixteen Shillings and Five pence and the defendant Comes and Confesses.

Ordered that the said Robt. White pay unto the said Peterson the aforesaid Summe of two pounds Sixteen Shillings and Five pence with Costs alias Execution.

Thom. Peterson Attorney to Micajah Perry and New pensilvania Company Comes to prosecute his Suite against Thomas Collins Administrator of the Goods and Chattells of Alice Collins deceased and declares for Eighteen pound twelve Shillings in fresh porke and the defendant Comes by Thos. Snoden his Attorney <364> and for plea Saith that he hath not Assetts in his hands whereby to Satisfy the Debt aforesaid and farther sayth that he is Incapable of giveing a true Inventory of the said widdows Estate and prayes days may be Essoyned him for the Same.

Ordered that the said Action be Continued till the next Court and that the said Collins doe then returne a full Inventory of the Said Estate.

Richd. Stamp Comes and proves a power of Attorney from Jno. West to the Said Stamp by the Oath of Robert Wayman and prayes the Same may be recorded which is Granted.

The Honorable Landgrave Robt. Daniell Esqr. Attorney to Colonel Geo. Logan of Charles Towne in So. Carolina Comes to prosecute his Suite against the honorable Edwd. Moseley Esqr. in a plea of Debt and Sayes that the Defendant Stands Justly Indebted to the plaintiff quallifyed as aforesaid in the full and Just Sume of Nine pounds Currant Money of Carolina by bill under the defendants owne hand beareing date the 3d day of Aprill 1705 And the defendant by Edwd. Bonwick his Attorney Comes and defends the force and Injury when etc. and Sayth that for the manifold Imperfections in Sufficiences and uncertaintyes in the plaintiffs Declaration and the matter therein Conteyned he the said Defendant Cannott neither by the Law of the land is he bound to make Answer thereunto (and this he is ready to Averr etc.) And for these Causes the plaintiff brings his Action in his owne name as Attorney to Colonel Geo. Logan whereas his power of Attorney is Only to Sue in the name of Colonel Geo. Logan For if a private Attorney doe any thing he must doe it in the name of his master for whome he doth it and not in his owne name also such Attorney must take Care to pursue the Authority given them expressed by the Deed and Implyed by the Law. 2d Choses in Actions Cannot be assigned etc. And the plaintiff Joynes in the Demurrer and the Court haveing duely Considered the whole matter It is their oppinion that the said Demurrer be overruled and it is hereby overruled.

Ordered that the Said Edwd. Moseley pay unto the said Robt. Daniell Attorney to the said Geo. Logan the aforesaid Summe of

Nine pounds with Costs alias Execution.

The Honorable Landgrave Robert Daniell Esqr. Attorney to Geo. Logan of Charles Towne in So. Carolina Comes to prosecute his Suite against The Honorable Edwd. Moseley Esqr. in a plea of the Case and Complaines that Whereas the Said Defendant on the third day of Aprill 1705 was Indebted to the Said <365> Geo. Logan in the full Summe of Twenty two pounds Currant Money did draw and deliver to the said Logan a Certaine Noate under his hand beareing date the said third day of Aprill 1705 directed to the Honorable Colonel James Moore thereby requesting him the said Moore to pay unto the Said Logan the Said Summe of twenty two pounds which said Summe or any part thereof the Said Moore hath and Still doth refuse to pay as by the Said Noate here into Court brought relation being thereunto had doth and may appeare Nevertheless etc. And the defendant by Edwd. Bonwick his Attorney Comes and defends the force and Injury when etc. and sayth for the Manifold Imperfections In Sufficiences and uncertaintyes in the plaintiffs declaration and matter therein Conteyned he the said Defendant Cannot neither by the Law of the Land is he bound to make Answer thereunto and this he is ready to Averr Wherefore etc. And for these Causes (1st) The plaintiff brings his Action in his owne name as Attorney of Colonel Geo. Logan Whereas his power of Attorney is only to Sue in the name of Colonel Geo. Logan (2dly) Choses in Action Cannot be Assigned (3d) The plaintiff in his declaration Sets forth that the defendant did draw and deliver unto the Said Logan a Certaine Noate under his hand beareing Date the 3d day of Aprill 1705 directed to the Honorable Colonel James Moore thereby requesting him the said Moore to pay unto the Said Logan the Said Summe of Twenty two pounds which said Summe or any part thereof the said Moore hath and still doth refuse to pay as by the said noate here into Court brought relation being thereunto had doth and may appeare which is Nonsence and absurd for it Cannot possibley appeare by that noate that Colonel Moore refused to pay the Summe mentioned in the Same Noate. (4th) The plaintiff in his declaration dos not Say before what Notary publique or for what reason the said Noate was protested and that he brings into Court a protest etc. as by the Law and according to the Custome of Merchants he ought in an Action brought upon a Noate drawne in a Forraigne Country (5) verrity is the most Effectuall part of a Declaration and the plaintiff in his Declaration Sayes to the plaintiffs damage Forty pounds which is a false averment And the Colonel Comes and Joynes in the demurrer and the Court haveing heard and Considered the whole matter It is their oppinion that the said demurrer be overruled and it is hereby overruled.

Ordered that the said Edwd. Moseley pay unto the said Robt. Daniell Attorney of Geo. Logan the aforesaid Sume of Twenty two pounds with Costs alias Execution.

<366> The Honorable Landgrave Robt. Daniell Esqr. Comes and prayes that a power of Attorney from Geo. Logan Esqr. may be recorded which is Granted.

Then this Court adjourned till tomorrow morne 8 of Clock.

Thursday morne 8 of Clock this Court mett present ut Supra.

A Power of Attorney from Edwd. Jaquelin to the Honorable Samll. Swann Esqr. was proved by the Subscription of Franc. Jones and the Oath of Rebin Welsh and ordered to be Recorded.

A Power of Attorney from John Meads to Anne Meads was proved by the Oath of Wm. Armour and ordered to be recorded.

A Deed of Sale from Thos. Boyd Attorney to Jno. West was acknowledged by Richd. Stamp Attorney to said West to Wm. Voss.

Thoms. Norcom Comes and appeares being bound by Recognizance to Answer Jenkin Williams and prayes to be dismissed. Ordered that he be dismissed accordingly paying Costs.

Then this Court adjourned for an hour and met again.

Wm. Barrow Came and upon his Corporall Oath proved a Noate from Mr. Jno. Porter to Franc. Foster Esqr.

David Harris and his wife personally Came and acknowledged a Deed of Sale for two hundred Acres of Land unto Jno. Flowers.

Robert White Comes by Thomas Snoden Esqr. her Majestyes Attorney Generall and desires this Court to understand and be Informed that Robert Keel of this province not haveing the feare of God before his Eyes but being lead away by the Instigation of the Devill on or about the Month of September last past in this province with force and Armes in and upon the body of the said Robert White being then in the peace of our Soveraigne Lady the Queen an Assault did make and him the said Robert White Sorely beate and abuse and other Injuryes to him done against the peace of our Said Soveraigne Lady the Queen etc. <367> And the Defendant Comes and pleades not Guilty and puts himselfe upon his Country and the Marshall was Comanded to Cause to Come twelve etc. to whome etc. who neither etc. by whome etc. and there Came John Falconer Thoms. Palmer Richd. Neet Geo. Clarke Geo. Elcott Richd. Sttamp Thos. Colins Wm. Wayman Jno. Smyth Christo. Wayman Jno. Willoby and Geo. Goreing who being Swoarne and Impannelled Say wee of the Jury Find for the Queen And the Court haveing duely weighed the matter

Ordered that the Said Robert Keel doe Find good and Sufficient Suretyes for his appearance the next Court and that he be in the meane tyme of his good behaviour towards all his Majestyes Leidge people and pay all Costs alias Execution.

Robert Keel acknowledges towards our Soveraigne Lady the Queen the Sume of £40 and Thomas Boyd the Sume of 20 [*sic*] to be Levyed on their Severall Lands and Tenements Goods and Chattles by way of Recognizance. The Condition of the above recognizance is Such that if the above Robert Keele shall make his appearance at the next Generall Court and in the meane tyme shall be of his Good abeareance towards all her Matyes Leidge people and shall not depart the Court without Leave then the same to be void otherwise to be of full force.

Mr. Edwd. Bonwick Comes and prayes a Warrant of Attorney from Jno. Wade to said Bonwick might be recorded which was granted.

Jno. Wade by Edwd. Bonwick his Attorney Comes to prosecute his Attachment against John Meads for one pound Tenn Shillings and Wm. Reed Comes and Assumes the payment of the Said Sume with Costs.

Ordered that the said Reed pay unto the said Wade the said Sume of one pound tenn Shillings with Costs alias Execution.

Upon Information of Wm. Voss by Thos. Snoden her Majestyes Attorney Generall Ordered that the provost Marshall take into his Custody Franc Farrow and him Safely hold soe that he be and appeare at the next Generall Court to answer Such things as shall be objected against him on her Majestyes behalfe and that Nicho. Crisp be Sumoned as Evidence.

<368> Julius Deeds Comes by Fred. Jones his Attorney to prosecute his Suite against Wm. Duckenfield otherwise Called Wm. Duckenfield Esqr. of North Carolina of a plea that he render unto the Said Julius Eight hundred pounds of Lawfull Money of England which to the Said Julius the said Wm. oweth and unjustly deteyneth and Sayth that the Said Wm. the Seaventeenth day of December in the yeare of our Lord One thousand Six hundred Ninety Six in the County of Albemarle by his Certaine writeing obligatory with the Seale of the Said Wm. Sealed and here in Court produced whose Date is the Same day and yeare accknowledged himselfe to be firmely bound and holden unto the said Julius in the aforesaid Sume of Eight hundred pounds to be paid unto the Said Julius when he the Said Wm. Shod be thereunto required the Said Wm. tho' offten thereto required the said Eight hundred pounds to the said Julius hath not yet paid but him to pay hath altogether Gainsayd and does

Still Gainsay to the Damage of the Said Julius Eight hundred pounds Sterling etc. And the Defendant Comes by Thomas Snoden his Attorney and prayes Oyer of the said Jones's Power which was read unto him. And then the Defendant by the said Snoden his Attorney Comes and prayes Oyer of the Specialty and the Condition thereunder written which was read unto him in these following words (videlicet) Know all Men by these presents that I Willm. Duckenfield Esqr. of North Carolina doe owe and Stand Justly Indebted unto Messrs. Roger Jones and Julius Deeds of London Merchants the full and Just Summe of Eight hundred pounds Sterling to be paid to the said Roger Jones and Julius Deeds or either of them their Certaine Attorney Executors Administrators or Assignes to which payment well and truely to be made I bind my Selfe my Heyres Executors And Administrators firmely by these presents as Witness my hand and Seale this Seaventeenth day of December 1696. The Condition of this Obligation is Such that if the above bounden Wm. Duckenfield Esqr. his Heyres Executors or Administrators Shall and doe well and truely pay or Cause to be paid unto the above named Roger Jones and Julius Deeds or either of them their Certaine Attorney Executors Administrators or Assignes the full and Just Sume of three hundred Eighty two pounds fourteen Shillings and Seaven pence Sterling in Beaver at three Shillings per pound Otter at four Shillings per Skinn old Buck at two Shillings per Skinn Does at Eighteen pence per Skinn (that is to Say Drest Buck and Doe) fox at twelfe pence per Skinn Catt at twelve pence per Skinn all to be in prime and the likeing of the said Jones and Deeds their Certaine Attorney or Assignes and haveing signed two of the same Tenour and Date the one of which being accomplished the other to be null void and of none Effect. Then the said Defendant by the said Snoden his Attorney Comes and prayes Oyer of the Originall which was read unto him. And then the said Defendant by the Said Tho. Snoden his Attorney Comes and Sayes that the aforesaid Julius Deeds to the Specialty and Declaration aforesaid Ought not to be Answared because he Sayes that there is manifest variance betwixt the Specialty and Declaration aforesaid <369> And divers Incertaintys therein and this he is ready to Averr Wherefore he prayes Judgement etc. And for these Causes that the plaintiff has not in his Declaration Set forth as well Jones as Deeds according to the obligation. And by Consent of both partyes the matter is referred to the next Court and the Defendants Attorney doe Agree that it be a rule of this Court that if the aforesaid plea be overruled the next Court they shall plead either in Barr or to Issue. Ordered that it be a rule of this Court that if the aforesaid plea be overruled the next Court the said defendants doe plead either in Barr or to Issue.

Wm. Voss acknowledges towards our Soveraigne Lady the Queen the Summe of Five pounds upon Condition that he doe appeare at the next Court to prosecute his Information against Franc Farrow on behalfe of our Soveraigne Lady the Queen.

Franc Foster Esqr. Comes by Edwd. Bonwick his Attorney to prosecute his Suite against Wm. Chambers in a plea of Debt and Declares for Sixty Eight pounds and the Marshall haveing returned a Non est Inventus the plaintiff prayes an Attachment against the said defendants Estate which is Granted.

Joseph Wicker Assignee of James Cross Comes by Thos. Snoden his Attorney to prosecute his Suite against Jno. Smyth in a plea of Debt and Sayes that the Defendant Standes Justly indebted to the plaintiff quallifyed as aforesaid in the Full and Just Summe of thirty one pounds Sterling payable in porke Tobeacco Hides or Tallow at the Markett price of Corratuck as in and by a Certaine writeing obligatory under the proper hand and Seale of the defendant beareing date the 30th of Augt. 1705: hereinto Court brought doth and may appeare Nevertheless etc. and the defendant by Edwd. Bonwick his Attorney Comes and pleads non est factum and the plaintiff for want of his Evidences prayes a referrence to the next Court which is Granted And then the defendant Comes and Craves Leave to recall his former plea and Confesses Judgement for three pounds Fourteen Shillings and four pence being the ballance of said Bond according to Specialty.

Ordered that the said Smyth pay unto the said Wycker the aforesaid Summe of three pounds Fourteen Shillings and four pence according to Specialty with Costs alias Execution.

<370> Rubin Welch personally Came and upon his Corporall Oath proved a power of Attorney from Jno. Bilingsly to Fred Jones and prayd the same migh be recorded. Ordered that the said power of Attorney be recorded accordingly.

Bryan McDaniell personally Came and upon his Corporall oath proves a power of Attorney from Geo. Parker to Richard Sanderson Junior and prayd it may be recorded. Ordered that the said power of Attorney be recorded accordingly.

George Parker Executor of the last Will and Testament of Gabriell Parrot Comes by Richd. Sanderson Junior his Attorney to prosecute his Suite against Thos. Sparrow in a plea of Debt and Sayes for that whereas the said Thos. the fourth day of Augt. 1705 by his Certaine writeing obligatory under his proper hand and Seale and here into Court brought whose date is the same day and yeare acknowledged him Selfe to be Justly Indebted to the said Geo. Executor etc. in the full Summe of two hundred fifty four pounds Sixteen Shillings Sterling Money of England to be paid unto the said Geo. Whenever he the said Thos. should be thereunto requested Yet Nevertheless etc. And the defendant Comes by Edwd. Bonwick his Attorney and defends the force and Injury when etc. and Sayth that for the Manifold Imperfections uncertaintyes and In Sufficiences in the plaintiffs declaration and the matter therein Conteyned he the said defendant Cannot neither by the Law of the Land is he bound to make Answer thereunto and this he is ready to averr etc. wherefore etc. and for these Causes (1st) the plaintiff hath not said in his declaration what place the debt in the Same declaration mentioned was Contracted or where the said writeing obligatory was made. (2d) The plaintiff Sues as Executor of the last will and Testament of Gabriell Parrot but dos not averr in his Declaration aforesaid that he brings into Court Letters Testamentary by which it may sufficiently appeare to the Court that he is Executor etc. And this Honorable Court has thought fit to Suspend any farther Judgement in this Case till tomorrow Morne and then the plaintiff Came and Joynd in the Demurrer and the Court haveing duely heard and Considered the whole matter it is their oppinion that the said Demurrer be over ruled and then the defendant Comes and pleads non est factum and the plaintiff prayes a referrence till the next Court which is Granted. And ordered that the said plaintiff be and Continue in Custody of the Marshall till the said Court.

<371> Whereas by neglect of the order of the precinct Court of pequimons the road that leads from Christo. Gales Esqr. up the Sound Side being a verry Ancient Road is verry much out of repair to the great detriment of that Neighbourhood.

Ordered that the Said Road be Cleared and kept in good repaire as a Bridle stay as formerly.

Then this Court adjourned till tomorro Morne 8 of Clock.

Fryday Morne 8 of Clock this Court met present ut Supra.

Mr. Fredrick Jones personally Came and in open Court acknowledged Mr. Thos. Snoden his Attorney to prosecute a Suite in this Court at the next Generall Court against Jno. Pettiver ad sectam of Colonel Jenings to whome he is Attorney.

John Arnold and his wife personally Came and in open Court acknowledged an Assignement of a deed of Sale of a Tract of Land to Richd. Burtenshall.

Upon Motion of the Queens Attorney Generall ordered that

Jos. Simpson of Nuse be Sumoned as an Evidence for the Queen against Franc Farrow.

It is ordered by this Court that all petty Jurymen that was Sumoned to this Court and did not appeare be fined 10*s*. a peice.

Ordered that it be a rule of this Court for the future that all Grand Jurymen that shall be Sumoned to any Succeeding Court and doe not appeare shall be fined 20*s*. a peice and the petty Jurymen 10 shillings a peice.

Richard Burtenshall Comes and proves an Account of three pounds Fourteen Shillings and four pence against the Estate of John Anderson deceased.

Ordered that James Morgan who marryed the widdow and relict of said Anderson pay the same to the said Richd. Burtenshall with Costs alias Execution and the said Morgan is therewith Content.

Jno. Porter and Company Comes by Edwd. Bonwick his Attorney to prosecute his Suite against Samll. Paine in a plea of Detinue And the defendant Comes and is Content that it be a rule of this Court that he plead to Issue the next Court upon which the matter is referred to the next Court accordingly.

<372> Rubin Welch Comes and on his Corporall Oath proves a power of Attorney from Edmd. Jenings Esqr. to Mr. Fred. Jones and prays the same may be recorded.

Ordered that the said power of Attorney be recorded accordingly.

Jno. Heckleffield Comes by Thomas Snoden his Attorney to prosecute his Attachment against the Estate of Geo. Kingsly and the Marshall haveing returned Attachment

Ordered that the Said Goods be appraised for the use of said Heckleffield according to Law.

[*Signed:*]
C. Gale, francis DeLaMare, William Barclif.

RECORDED BY ORDER OF COURT

[*CCR 104*]

<371> S. Carolina Ss.

Know all Men by these presents That I Geo. Logan of Charles Towne in the Province aforesaid Esqr. Herewith do ordeyned Constituted and appointed and by these presents doe make ordeyne Constitute and appoint the Honorable Landgrave Robert Daniell Esqr. my true and Lawfull Attorney for me and in my name and for my use to aske demand and receive of all person and persons whatsoever all Such Sume and Summes of Money debts due and demands whatsoever as are now or shall hereafter grow due to me the said Geo. Logan from any person or persons whatsoever and more especially from Edwd. Moseley of No. Carolina and upon non payment thereof the Said person or persons or any of them their Executors or Administrators for me and in my name to Sue arrest Implead Imprison and prosecute for the Same and upon Such Suite to proceed to Judgement and Execution and thereupon the said person or persons or any of them their Executors and Administrators in Prison to hold and keep untill the payment thereof be made with all Costs and damages Susteyned and to be Susteyned by Occasion of the deteyneing of the Same and upon payment thereof the Said person or persons or any of them their Executors or Administrators forth of prison to discharge and accquittances for the Same or any part thereof for me and in my name to make Seale and deliver and also to doe performe and Execute all and every other Lawfull and reasonable Acts and things Whatsoever both for the obteyneing and dischargeing of the Same as shall be needfull to be done in Giveing and by these presents Granting unto my Said Attorney my full and absolute power in the premisses ratifyeing and holding for me all and whatsoever my said Attorney shall Lawfully doe or Cause to be done in and about the premisses by virtue of these presents In witness whereof I have hereunto Set my hand and Seale the 8th day of May and in the Fifth year of the raigne of our Soveraigne Lady Queen Anne of England Scotland and France and Ireland etc. Annoque Domini 1706.

Sealed and Delivered Geo. Logan
In the presence of
John Shaw his mark
Nathl. Wyresdale

Recorded the 6th day of December Anno Domini 1706 by order.

Testis T. Knight Secretary

<372> Know all Men by these presents that I John West of Bath County in pamptico for divers Good Causes and Considerations me thereunto moveing doe make Constitute and ordeyne my loveing freind Richard Stamp to be my true and lawfull Attorney for me and in my name to aske demand Sue for levy recover and receive of and from all and every person or persons all and every Such Sume and Summes of Money or any other thing or things properly belonging to me the Constituant in Albemarle County Giveing and by these presents Granting to my forsaid Attorney full power to Sell Allienate

Enfeafe and [Confiring] what Land belongeth unto me unto any person or persons that he my said Attorney shall See Convenient and if need be to appeare and the person of me the Constituant to represent before any Judges Justices or other Ministers of the Law in any Court of Judicature in the aforesaid County of Albemarle in my behalfe to answer defend and reply to all Actions matters and things relateing to the premisses to Account agree Compound and on receipt of the part or whole acquitances or other discharges to grant and deliver and generaly to doe all and every thing needfull relateing to me in the abovesaid County of Albemarle in all respects as fully and amply as I my Selfe might or Could doe if personally present rectifyeing and hold firme and vallid all and whatsoever my said Attorney shall Doe or Cause to be done by virtue of these presents In witness whereof I have hereto Set my hand and Seale this May 17th 1706.

Testis

John West

Thomas Stamp his mark
Robt. Warnon his mark

Recorded the 1st day of Decem. Anno Domini 1706 by order.

Testis T. Knight

<373> Know All Men by these presents That I Thos. Jones of James City County in Virginia Merchant have made ordeyned and Constituted and by these presents doe make ordaine and Constitute Mr. Fredrick Jones of the County aforesaid Merchant to be my true and Lawfull Attorney Giveing unto him full power Authority and Speciall Charge for me and in my name to aske demand Sue for Levy recover and receive of and From Christo. Gale and Thos. Dereham both of the province of No. Carolina and of and from all and every such other person or persons of the province aforesaid whome it may Concerne of and from their Heyres Executors Administrators Goods and Estate all and Singuler Such Summe and Summes of Money Goods Wares Merchandizes Effects Estate and things whatsoever as are due oweing and belonging or apperteyneing to me either by Bill Bond account bill or bill [*illegible*] Consignement or Consignements of goods or otherwise nothing Executed was received with the Costs Damages and Interests also to demand receive Examine and adjust accounts and any matter or thing in Difference to submitt unto and determine the arbitration or any other amicable meanes and upon the Recovery due receipts to make and pass due and [*illegible*] accquittance and discharge and

generally to transact doe and accomplish what I my Selfe could doe if personally present I hereby promissing to Satisfy and Confirme formally what my said Attorney or his Substitutes shall doe by virtue hereof In Witness whereof I have hereunto set my hand and Seale this Seccond day of September 1706.

Sealed and Delivered
In the presence of
T. Peterson
Rob. Fendall
Reubn. Welch

Tho. Jones

Recorded the 1st day of December Anno Domini 1706 by order.

Testis T. Knight Secretary

<374> Know All Men by these presents that I Jno. Billingsly of King Willm. County planter have made ordained Constituted and appointed and by these presents doe make ordeine Constitute and appoint my Loveing Freind Fredrick Jones of James City County Merchant my true and Lawfull Attorney for me and in my name and for my use to Aske demand and receive of all such person or persons in North Carolina or else where all Such Summe or Summes of Money Goods wares or other things as shall or may be due or any wayes appertenieing or belonging to mee From all or any Such person or persons in any wise and upon non payment or default in the delivery thereof I doe hereby Impower the Said Fred. Jones for me and in my name to Sue Arrest Implead Imprison and prosecute the Said person or persons for the Same and upon Such Suite to proceed to Judgement and Execution and thereupon the said person or persons their Heyres Executors Administrators and Assignes in prison to hold and keep untill payment and delivery thereof be made with all Costs and Damages Susteyned and to be Susteyned by occasion of the deteyneing of the Same and upon payment and delivery thereof the said person or persons their Heyres Executors Administrators or Assignes forth of prison to discharge and accquittances for the Same or any part thereof for me and in my name to make Seale and deliver Also for me and in my name if my Said Attorney Shall think fitt and Convenient to Nominate and appoint one or more Attorney or Attorneys under him and the Same againe at pleasure to revoke and also to doe performe and Execute all and every other Lawfull and reasonable Act as if I my Selfe were personally present ratifying and Confirmeing all and whatsoever my said Attorney shall Lawfully doe or Cause to be done in or about the premisses by virtue of these presents In Witness whereof I have

hereunto put my hand and Seale this 17th day of Augt. in the Second yeare of the raigne of our Soveraigne Lady Anne Queene of England etc. Annoque Domini 1703.

Signed Sealed and delivered In presence of Reubn. Welch Willm. Phillipps — John Billingsly

Recorded the 1st day of December Anno Domini 1706 by order

Testis T. Knight Secretary

<375> To all Christian people to whome these presents shall Come I Edmd. Jenings Esqr. of Yorke County in Virginia Send Greeting Know Yee that I the said Edmd. Jenings for Sufficient Causes and valluable Considerations me hereunto Especially moveing have made ordeyned Constituted and in my Stead and place put and deputed and by these presents doe make ordeyne Constitute and in my Stead and place put and depute Fredrick Jones of James City County of Virginia gentleman my true and Lawfull Attorney irrevocable for me and in my name and to my use to Aske demand Sue for recover and receive of John Pettiver of No. Carolina Gentleman all Such Summe and Summes of Money debts and demands whatsoever which now are due and belonging unto me the Said Edmd. Jennings by and from the said John pettiver and to have use and take all Lawfull wayes and meanes in my name or otherwise for recovery thereof by Attachment arrest distress reentry or otherwise and to Compound and agree for the Same and accquittances or other Sufficient discharges for the Same for me and in my name to make Seale and deliver and to doe all other Acts and things whatsoever Concerneing the premisses as fully in every respect as I my Selfe might or Could doe If I were personally present and Attorneys one or more under him for the purposes aforesaid to make and againe at his pleasure to revoke And I the said Edmd. Jennings doe hereby satisfy and Confirme whatsoever my Attorney shall Lawfully doe or Cause to be done in my name or otherwise by force of these presents In Witness whereof I have hereunto Set my hand and Seale this 21st day of october 1706.

Signed Sealed and delivered In the presence of John Smyth Reubn. Welch — E. Jennings

Recorded the 1st day of Xber Anno Domini 1706 by order.

Testis T. Knight Secretary

<376> Know all Men by these presents that I Edwd. Jaquelin of James City in Virginia doe hereby Constitute and appoint the honorable Samll. Swann Esqr. of North Carolina my true and Lawfull Attorney giveing and hereby granting him full power and authority for and in my name and to my use to aske demand Sue for recover and receive of and from all and every Such person or persons whom it may Concerne in No. Carolina aforesaid all and Singular Such Sume and Summes of Money as shall be due and apperteyneing unto me with power to Substitute one or more Attorneys under him and the Same at pleasure to revoke and to doe Such further and other matter and thing whatsoever as I the Said Edwd. Jaquelin might or Could doe if personally present In Witness whereof I have hereunto Set my hand and Seale this 23d day of October 1706.

Signed Sealed and delivered Edward Jaquelin
In the presence of
Reubn. Welch
Fra. Jones mark

Recorded the 1st day of Xber 1706 By order

Testis T. Knight Secretary

<377> Maryland SS.

Know all men by these presents that I George parker of Calvert County have for Sundry good Causes and weighty Considerations nominated Constituted Ordeyned and appointed and by these presents Doe Nominate, Constitute Ordeyne and appoint and in my Stead and place putt my Trusty and welbeloved friend Richard Saunders Junior of North Carolina gentleman my true and lawfull Attorney to ask Demand Levy Recover and receive for me and in my name and to my use and behooffe of all and all manner of persons whatsoever being indebted to me the said George parker either by Bond, Bill Judgments, Bills of Exchange or Accounts or any wayes whatsoever Either on my own proper Account or by virtue of my being Executor of Gabriel parrott etc. all Summ and Summs of Money and Tobacco as Shalbe due to me from any person or persons whatsoever liveing being or resideing in North or South Carolina Giveing and by these presents granting to my Said Attorney my Sole and full power and Authority in the premises to Sue arrest implead imprison and Condemn all and all manner of persons whatsoever being indebted to me them and Every of them and their and Every of their Heyers Executors and Administrators for me and in my name in any Court Spirituall or Temporall before any Judge or Justices whatsoever in North and South Carolina and them and Every of them their and Every and any of their Heyers Executors and Administrators againe out of prison to Deliver att his discretion and upon any receit of any Summ or Summs of money or Tobacco of them receved one or more accquittance or Acquittances Discharge or Discharges for me and in my name to make Signe Seal and Deliver as alsoe one or more Attorney or Attorneys under him to Substitute or appoint and againe att his pleasure to Revoake And further to doe Execute and performe and finish for me and in my name all and Singular thing or things which Shall or may be necessary to asking and concerneing the premises as fully throughly and Entirely as I the said George parker in my own person might or could doe in or about the Same Ratifying confirmeing and allowing whatsoever my said Attorney Shall Soe doe or cause to be done in the premises by these presents In Wittness whereof I the Said George parker have hereunto Sett my hand and Seal this Twenty fifth Day of June in the fifth year of the Reigne of our Soveraigne Lady Ann Queen of England Scottland france and Ireland etc. And in the Year of our Lord Anno Domini One Thousand Seven Hundred and Six.

Wittness present — Geo. parker
Bryan MacDaniel his mark
John parker
John Buxton

FILE PAPERS IN SUITS AND PROSECUTIONS

[*Blount* v. *Benington and wife*]

[*CCR 148*]

No. Carolina Ss. To the provost Marshall or his Deputy

These are in her Majestyes name to will and require you to Arrest the body of Cornelius Bennington [and] Eliz. his wife and them Safely hold Soe that they be and personally appeare at the next Generall Court to be holden at the house of Captain Jno. Hecklefield in Litle river on the last Tuseday in October next then and there to Answer the plaint of Jno. Blount Esqr. of a plea that they hold to him Covenant between them made according to the same forme and Effect of a Certaine Deed of Sale between them made etc. and have You there this writt Dated at the Secretarys Office this 17th day of September Anno Domini 1706.

Testis T. Knight Secretary

Take Good Bayle
[*Endorsed:*]
Breve

Blount versus Bennington
This is not don

[*Boyd* v. *Phelps*]

[*CCR 148*]

No. Carolina Ss. To the Provost Marshall or his Deputy

These are in her Majestyes name to will and require you to Arrest the body of Seth Phelps and him Safeley hold Soe that he be and appeare at the next Generall Court to be holden at the house of Captain Jno. Hecklefield in Litle river on the last Tuesday in October next then and there to Answer the plaint of Thos. Boyd in a plea of Debt and have there this writt Dated at the Secretarys Office this 4th day of September Anno Domini 1706.

Testis T. Knight Secretary

[*Endorsed:*]
Breve
Boyd versus Phelps
In Debt

[*Crown* v. *Norcom*]

[*CCR 148*]

No. Carolina

I Jenkin Wm. doe in the presence off God and under the penalty of perjury declare, That Tho. Norcome hath given such Threatning speeches to me and my family That I am in my Concience afraid that He the said Norcam will kill or maime me or some off my Family. Subscribed 8ber 14 1706.

The above subscription taken before me C. Gale — per me Jenkin Williams

In her Majestys name.

These are (in the name off the above subscription) to will and require you to take into your Custody the body off the said Norcom and him to hold soe that he be and appeare before me this Evening or Tomorrow morning by seaven of the Clock to enter into bond with sufficient suertys for his appearance att the next Generall Court and in the mean time to be of good abbearance and to keep the peace etc. and for soe doeing this shall be your Warrant. Given under my hand and Seale the 14th day off 8ber Anno Domini 1706.

To Miles Ramsbottam
to execute and return — C. Gale

No. Carolina

Memorandum That the day and Yeare above written Came before me Thos. Norcome and acknowledg'd himselfe to be Indebted to our Soveraigne

Lady the Queen her Heires and Successors in the Summe off Twenty pounds and allsoe to Mr. Norman in the Summe off Ten pounds to be leavy'd on their goods and Chattells Lands and Teniments.

The Condition of which Recognizance is such That iff the above bounden Tho. Norcam doe make his personall appearance before the Next Generall Court and doe keep the peace etc. (in the mean time) towards her Majesty and all her Leidge People and especially towards Jenkin Wms. and his Family Then the above Recognizance to be void and off noe Effect or else to remaine in Full force and virtue.

The above Recognizance taken the 14th day off 8ber Anno Domini 1706.

Coram me C. Gale

[*Endorsed:*]
Tho. Norcam's Recognizance for the peace
1706

[*Daniell, attorney of Logan* v. *Moseley*]

[*CCR 148*]

North Carolina Ss. To the honorable the Generall Court

The Honorable Landgrave Robert Daniell Esqr. Attorney to Colonel George Logan of Charles Towne in South Carolina is plaintiff against The Honorable Edwd. Moseley Esqr. Defendant in a plea of the Case and Complaines That Whereas the said Defendant on the third day of Aprill 1705 was Indebted to the Said George Logan in the full Sume of Twenty two pounds Current Money Did Draw and deliver unto the said Logan a Certaine Noate under his hand beareing Date the said third day of Aprill 1705: Directed to the Honorable Colonel James Moore thereby requesting him the Said Moore to pay unto the Said Logan the Said Summe of twenty two pounds which Said Sume or any part there of the Said Moore hath and Still doth refuse to pay as by the Said Noate here into Court brought and ready to be produced relation being thereunto had doth and may more fully and at large appeare Never the less the Said Defendant the Said Sume of twenty two pounds to the plaintiff hath not rendred but the Same doth refuse to render tho' offten thereunto requested to the plaintiffs Damage Quallifyed as afforesaid the Summe of Forty Four pounds Sterling and thereupon he brings his Suite and prays Judgement For the Same with Costs of Suite and shall pray etc.

T. Knight Secretary

[*Endorsed:*]
Narratio
Daniell Esqr. versus Moseley Esqr.
In Case

[*CCR 148*]

The honorable Edwd. Moseley Esqr. ads. The honorable Landgrave Robt. Daniell Esqr. Attorney of Collonell George Logan

And the said Defendant by Edwd. Bonwicke his Attorney comes and defends the force and injury when etc.

And saith that for the manifold imperfections insufficiences and uncertainties in the Plaintiffs Declaration and the matter therein contained he the said Defendant cannot neither by the Law of the Land is he bound to make answer thereunto (And this he is ready to aver) wherefore for want of a good and sufficient Declaration and good and sufficient matter therein to be contained he the said Defendant prayes Judgment if the Plaintiff aforesaid his Acction aforesaid against him the said Defendant by the Law ought to have and maintaine.

Bonwicke per Defendant

Et per Causis

1st The Plaintiff brings his Acction in his owne name as Attorney of Collonell George Logan Whereas his power of Attorney is only to sue in the name of Collonell George Logan.

2d Choses in Acction cannot be assigned.

3d The Plaintiff in his Declaration setts forth That the Defendant did draw and deliver unto the said Logan a certaine Noate under his hand bearing Date the third day of Aprill 1705 Directed to the honorable Collonell James Moore thereby requesting him the said Moore to pay unto the said Logan the said Summe of Twenty two pounds which said Summe or any part thereof the said Moore hath and Still doth refuse to pay as by the said Noate here into Court brought and ready to be produced relation being thereunto had doth and may more fully and at Large appear Which is nonsense and absurd for it cannot possibly appear by that noate that Collonell Moore refused to pay the Summe mentioned in the same Noate.

4th The Plaintiff in his Declaration does not say before what Notary Publique or for what reason the said Noate was protested and that he brings into Court a protest etc. as by the Law and according to the Custome of Merchants he ought in an Acction brought upon a Noate drawne in a Forraigne Colony.

Verity is the most essentiall part of a Declaration and the Plaintiff in his said Declaration saies to the Plaintiffs Damage Fourty pounds which is a false Averment.

[*Endorsed:*]

The honorable Edwd. Moseley Esqr. ads. The honorable Landgrave Daniell Demurrer of Narratio and non Causis

[*CCR 188*]

Charles Towne Aprill the 3rd 1705

Be pleased to pay to Colonel George Logan the Sum of twenty two pounds and place the Same to the Account of Sir Your most humble Servant

Tesstess
Wm. Hackett

Edwd. Moseley

To the honorable Colonel James Moore These

Memorandum this 8th day of May 1706

There appeared before me William Hasket the above Witness etc. being Sworne On the holy Evangelists did Say the above Edward Mosley Signe the above Noat.

Sworne before me the day and Year above John Buckley

Recorded in the Secretarys office in South Carolina May the 9th 1706 per Jno. Barnwell Secretary

[*Endorsed:*]
Mosley order
Colonel Moors
£22: -: -

[*Daniell, attorney of Logan* v. *Moseley*]

[*CCR 191*]

No. Carolina Ss. To the honorable the Generall Court etc.

The Honorable Landgrave Robert Daniell Esqr. Attorney to Colonel Geo. Logan of Charles Towne in South Carolina is plaintiff against the Honorable Edwd. Moseley Esqr. Defendant in a plea of Debt and Sayes that the Defendant Stands Justly Indebted to the plaintiff Quallifyed as aforesaid in the full and Just Sume of Nine pounds Current Money of Carolina as in and by one Certaine writeing under the proper hand of the Defendant beareing Date the third of Aprill 1705 here into Court brought and ready to be produced relation being thereunto had doth and may more fully and at large appeare Nevertheless the said Defendant the Said Summe of Nine pounds unto the plaintiff hath not rendred but the Same doth Still refuse to render to the plaintiffs Damage Quallifyed as aforesaid the Summe of Eighteen pounds Sterling and thereupon he brings his Suite and prayes Judgment for the Same with Costs of Suite and Shall pray etc.

T. Knight Secretary

[*Endorsed:*]
Narratio
Daniell Esqr. versus Moseley Esqr.
Debt

[*CCR 188*]

I promise to pay to the honorable Colonel George Logan the Sum of nine pounds Currant money of Carolina Witness my hand the 3rd of Aprill 1705.

Testis
Wm. Hackett

Edwd. Moseley

<Recorded in the Secretarys office in South Carolina May the 9th 1706 per Jno. Barnwell Secretary>

Memoranduen this 8th day of May 1706

There appeared before me William Hacket, the above Witness, and Made Oath On the holy Evangelists, that he did See the above Edward Moseley Signe, the above noat.

Sworn before me the day and Year above Said

John Buckley

[*Endorsed:*]
Moseleys Noat
£9
Geo. Logan

[*Deeds* v. *Duckenfield*]

[*CCR 148*]

North Carolina
Albermarle County

Julius Deeds Complains of William Duckenfeild otherwise called Wm. Duckenfeild Esqr. of North Carolina of a Plea that he render unto the said Julius eight hundred pounds of lawfull money of England which to the said Julius the said William oweth and unjustly deteineth for that to witt Whereas the said William the seventeenth Day of December in the Year of our Lord One thousand six hundred ninety six in the County of Albermarle aforesaid by his Certain Writing obligatory with the seal of the said William sealed and here in Court produced whose Date is the same Day and Year acknowledged himself to be firmly bound and holden unto the said Julius in the aforesaid summe of eight hundred pounds to be paid unto the said Julius when he the said William should be thereunto required Yett the said William tho' often thereto required the said eight hundred pounds to the said Julius hath not yett paid But him to pay hath altogether gainsay'd and does still gainsay To the Damage of the said Julius eight hundred pounds Sterling And thereof he brings suit etc.

[*Endorsed:*]
Declaration versus Duckenfeild
Julius Deeds versus William Duckenfeild otherwise called Wm. Duckenfeild Esqr. of North Carolina Debt £800

[*CCR 148*]

No. Carolina Ss. To the provost Marshall or his Deputy

These are in her Matyes name to will and require you to Arrest the body of William Duckenfield otherwise Called William Duckenfield Esqr. of North Carolina and him Safely hold Soe that he be and appeare at the next Generall Court to be holden at the house of Captain Jno. Hecklefield in Litle river on the last Tuesday in this Instant October then and there to Answer Julius Deeds of a plea that he render unto the Said Julius Eight hundred pounds of lawfull Money of England which to the said Julius the said William oweth and unjustly deteyneth and have you there this writt Dated at the Secretarys Office this 12th day of Octob. Ano Domini 1706.

Testis T. Knight Secretary

Excequeted by me Daniel Hallsey

Mr. Boyd I wold Have wated one you this Cort but my hors is Lame that I Can not Coum so having no other mienes Coum to my hands but this I have sent it by Cornl Pollock so with my Respeckes to youer selef and Capt. Duckenfeld and his wife I Rest youer oumbell sarvant to Comand. Daniel Hallsey ocktober 24 day 1706

[*Endorsed:*]

Deeds versus Duckenfield in debt

For Mr. Thomas Boyd Provis Marshall

[*Foster* v. *Chambers*]

[*CCR 102*]

[*Torn*] [*illegible*] for and in Consideration of the Summe of [*illegible*] [*torn*] pounds to me in hand payd by Francis Foster of Pequimins precinct in North Carolina doe oblidge my Selfe my Heires Executers and Administrators firmely by these presents unto the Said Francis Foster his Heires Executers Administraters and Assignes to pay and Deliver unto the Said Francis Foster his Executers and assignes one Negro Man between fiveteen and Twenty five yeares ole free and clear from any outward and visible Defect or knowne Distemper to Serve during the Naturall life of him the Said Negro which Said Slave I doe further oblidge my Selfe my Heires Executers and Administraters to Deliver unto the Said Francis Foster [*illegible*] or before the Twenty Fifth Day of December next Immediately [ensuinge] the Date of these presents upon penelty of paying unto the Said Francis Foster his Executers and assignes the Summe of Sixty Eight pounds in Porke att prise corrent the Danger of the Seas only Excepted And the Said Francis Foster himselfe [*illegible*] Executers and Administraters doth by these presents promise [that] if he his Executers or assignes Shall receive the Said Slave on or before the first Day of September next to pay unto the Said William Chambers the Summe of Forty Shillings in good merchantable wheat att the prise curant or if he Shall receive him att the time first above mentioned then to pay but one hundred and Sixty pounds of good fresh porke In witnesse whereof I have hereunto putt my hand and Seal this 22d Day of February 1702/3.

Witness present William Chambers Sigillum

Joseph Luten

Christopher Sutton his marke

[*Hawkins* v. *Crosse*]

[*CCR 148*]

No. Carolina Ss. To the honorable the Generall Court

John Hawkins is plaintiff against James Cross Defendant in a plea of Debt and Says that the Defendant by one writeing obligatory under his proper hand beareing Date the 29th of October 1703 Stand Justly Indebted to the plaintiff in the full and Just Summe of two pounds Seaven Shillings and Nine pence in Good Sound Merchantable Porke at his owne Landing in Pascotancke river at or upon the tenth day of December next Ensueing the date thereof as in and by the Said writeing here into Court brought and ready to be produced relation being thereunto had doth and may more fully and at large appeare which Said Sume of two pounds Seaven Shillings and Nine pence the Defendant hath not rendred to the plaintiff tho' often thereunto requested but the Same doth Still refuse to render to the plaintiffs Damage Four pounds Fifteen Shillings and Six pence and thereupon he brings his Suite and prays Judgement for the Same with Costs of Suite and Shall pray etc.

T. Knight Secretary

[*Endorsed:*]
Hawkins versus Cross
In Debt
Entered Sept. [*illegible*] 1706

[*Low, attorney of Archdale* v. *Wilson*]

[*CCR 191*]

North Carolina Generall Court Ss.

George Wilson was attached to answer Emanuell Low Esqr. Attorney of the Honorable J. Archdale Esqr. of a Plea of Trespass

And whereupon the said Emanuell by Edward Bonwicke his Attorney complaines That whereas the said George Wilson in the Month of December Anno Domini 1705 with force and armes Did come into and upon a certain Tract of Land of the said Archdale called Colleton Island in the Precinct of Corratuck with in the Jurisdiction of this Court and then and there cutt downe and carried away The Cedar trees of the said Archdale[15] well there lately growing to the value of Twenty pounds Sterling and other harmes to the said Emanuell he did to the great damage of the said Emanuell and against the peace of our Lady the Queen that now is Whereupon he saith he is damnified and hath damage to the value of £40 Sterling and thereupon he brings his Suite and prays Judgement for the Same with Costs of Suite and Shall pray etc.

Bonwicke per querens

[*Endorsed:*]
Low versus Wilson
Declaration

[*CCR 148*]

North Carolina Ss. To the provost Marshall or his Deputy.

---

[15] *Emanuell* written and lined out.

These are in her Majestyes name to will and require you to Attach Soe much of the Estate of George Wilson wherever to be found in this Government as will pay and Satisfy Emanuell Lowe Esqr. Attorney of the honorable Jno. Archdale Esqr. the full Sume of Twenty Pounds Sterling with Costs and the Same in Safe Custody keep untill otherwise ordered by due Course of Law and make returne of your proceedings herein to the next Generall Court Dated at the Secretarys Office this 17th day of September Anno Domini 1706.

Testis T. Knight Secretary

[*Endorsed:*]
Attachment
Lowe Attorney etc. versus Willson per £20
It tis not don

[*Parker* v. *Lane*]

[*CCR 148*]

No. Carolina Ss. To the honorable the Generall Court.

Geo. Parker is plaintiff against Dutton Lane Defendant in a plea of the Case and Complaines For that Whereas the said Dutton the Nineth day of May Seaventeen hundred and four was Indebted to the Said Geo. in the Summe of Fifty Seaven pounds three Shillings and nine pence Sterling Currant Money of England Did Draw and deliver to the Said Geo. Three Severale Bills of Exchange with the proper hand of the Said Dutton Subscribed and Dated the said Nineth day of May Seaventeen hundred and four and directed to one David Dennis Merchant in London requireing thereby the said David at Twenty dayes Sight of his the said Duttons first Bill of Exchange his Seccond nor third acct. paid to [*illegible*] the Said Geo. Parker or order the Said Summe of fifty Seaven pounds three Shillings and Nine pence Sterling Currant Money of England and he the Said Dutton the Day and yeare aforesaid upon himselfe assumed unto the Said Geo. that in Case the Said David Dennis Should refuse to pay or accept of one of the Said three Bills of Exchange according to the tenour of the Same to the said Geo. or to such other person as he should Indorse Consigne or order the Same that there the said Dutton would faithfully pay or Cause to be paid the Same to the said Geo. or order with Lawfully Charg and Interest [for] the same and the Said Geo. in fact Says that one Deane Cooke his Factor by order and direction of the Said Geo. did present the Said first bill of Exchange unto the Said David Dennis To whome the Same was directed as aforesaid and demanded acceptance and payment of the Said Bill according to the Tenour of the Same who did utterly refuse to accept or make payment of the Same whereupon the Said Geo. by the said Deane Cooke his Factor as aforesaid upon the Twenty Eigth day of September Anno 1704 according to the use and Custome of Merchants did promise Jeremiah Jenkins Notary Public in London by Lawfull authority and Admitted and Swoarne to make due and Legale protest of the said first Bill of Exchange the seccond nor third nor either of them being paid said first bill of Exchange being one and not paid together with the said protest herein to Court brought and ready to produced relation being thereunto had doth and may appeare Nevertheless the said Dutton the Said Summe of Fifty Seaven pounds three Shillings and Nine pence to the Said Geo. hath not rendred tho' often thereunto requested but the Same doth Still refuse to render to the Damage of the said Geo. One hundred and fourteen pounds Seaven Shillings and Six pence Sterling and thereupon he brings this Suite and prays Judgement for the Same with Costs of Sute and Shall pray etc.

T. Knight Secretary

[*Endorsed:*]
Narratio
Parker versus Lane in Case
Entered Octo. 14th: 1706

[*Peterson, attorney of Perry and Company* v. *Armour*]

[*CCR 192*]

No. Carolina Ss. To the honorable the Generall Court etc.

Thoms. Peterson Attorney to Micajah Perry and New pensilvania Company is plaintiff against Wm. Armour Defendant in a plea of Debt and Sayes that the Defendant Stands Justly Indebted to the plaintiff quallifyed as aforesaid in the full and Just Summe of Twenty Nine Shillings and ten pence in good fresh porke to be paid at the Landing of the honorable Wm. Glover Esqr. in Litle river as in and by one Certaine writeing under the hand of the Said Wm. Armour beareing Date the 21st december Anno Domini 1704 and here into Court brought and ready to be produced relation being thereunto had doth and may appeare Nevertheless the said Defendant the said Sume of Twenty Nine Shillings and Tenn pence in maner aforesaid to the plaintiff hath not rendred tho often thereunto requested but the Same doth Still refuse to render to the plaintiffs Damage two pounds Nineteen Shillings and Eight pence [*illegible*] and thereupon he brings his Suite and prays Judgment for the Same with Costs of Sute and shall pray etc.

T. Knight Secretary

[*Endorsed:*]
Peterson Atty. versus Armour
In Debt
[*Illegible*] 1706

[*CCR 192*]

North Carolina Ss. To the provost Marshall or his Deputy.

These are in her Majestyes name to will and require you to Arrest the body of Willm. Armour and him Safely hold Soe that he be and appeare at the next Generall Court to be holden at the house of Captain Jno. Hecklefield in Litle river on the Last tuseday in this Instant October then and there to Answer the plaint of Thoms. Peterson Attorney to Micajah Perry and New pensilvania

Company in a plea of Debt and have you there this writt Dated at the Secretarys Office this 8th day of October Anno Domini 1706.

Testis T. Knight Secretary

[*Endorsed:*]
Breve
Peterson versus Armour
In Debt
Cepi Corpus

[*Peterson, attorney of Perry and Company* v. *Collins*]

[*CCR 192*]

This Bill beindeth me Thomas Collings and my Heires to pay to mr. Thomas Peterson and pencelvaney Compenney the Summ of five pound ten Shilings in fresh pork at Willaim Glover's Landing as wittness my hand and Seal This 24th Day of December 1705.

Antho. Hatch — Thomas Collings his mark
Jno. Palin

[*Endorsed:*]
Tho. Collins
5:10*s*.

	5-10-
In payment of this bill	0-13-7½
Due To baleance	4-16-4½
Credit by a [*illegible*]	1-05-00
	3-11-4½

[*CCR 140*]

No. Carolina Ss. To the Honorable Generall Court etc.

The Humble petition of Antho. Hatch and John palin Sheweing that they being Sumons as Evidences att the Suit of Thos. peterson Esqr. against Capt. Thos. Collins that they may be allowed fore Their Travell and attendance and your petitioners Shall pray etc.

J. Palin

[*Peterson, attorney of Perry and Company* v. *Daw*]

[*CCR 192*]

North Carolina Ss. To the provost Marshall of the County of Bath or Deputy

These are in her Majestyes name to will and require you to Arrest the body of Nicholas Daw Hatter of Matchepungo and him Safely hold Soe that he be and appeare at the next Generall Court to be holden at the house of Captain

Jno. Hecklefield in Litle river on the last Tuesday in October next then and there to Answer the plaintiff Thomas Peterson Attorney of Micajah Perry and New Pensilvania Company in a plea of Debt and have there this writt Dated at the Secretarys office this 7th day of Augt. Anno Domini 1706.

Testis T. Knight Secretary

[*Endorsed:*]
Breve
Peterson versus Daw
In Debt
Executed per me W. Barrow Marshall

[*CCR 192*]

This Bill bindeth mee Nicholas Daw Hatter of Matshapungo in the County of Bath in North Carolina my heirs Executors or Administrators to pay or cause to bee paid unto Mr. Thomas peterson [*torn*] lawfull Attorney for the new pensylvania Company the sum of Fourty pounds sixteen shillings and ten pence to be paid uppon demand Convenient in the Aforesaid County in good sufficcient Merchantable Comodities of Countrey or to his or their Assignes or Order Witness my hand October the 2d 1705.

Testes
Georg Birkenhead
Nicholas Tylor

Nicholas Daw

[*CCR 192*]

Whereas Mr. Thomas Peterson Attorny of Macajah Perry and New Pensilvania Company hath Sued out of the Court of Common Pleas a Writt of Debt for Forty pounds Sixteen Shillings and ten pence (mony of this province) against Mr. Nicholas Daw of Bath County Returnable the next Generall Court holden for this province These are therefore to Request you or Either of you to Appear for me and to make Declaration for me the Said Nicolas Daw att the Sute of the Said Thomas Peterson, and thereupon to Confess Judgment either by Non Cum Informatus, Nihil Dicit, or Otherwise, as you Shall think fitting, and this Shall be your Sufficient Warrant in that behalf. In Witnes whereof I have hereunto Set my hand and Seall this Twenty Seventh day of Septemb. Anno Domini 1706.

To Captain John Hecklesfield
or Mr. Francis Penryse.

Nicholas Daw

[*Endorsed:*]
Daws Warrant of Attorney

[*Peterson, attorney of Perry and Company* v. *Hewett*]

[*CCR 192*]

No. Carolina Ss. To the Provost Marshall or his Deputy.

These are in her Majestyes name to will and require you to Attach Soe

much of the Estate of Bartho. Hewett as will pay and Satisfy Thomas Peterson Attorney to Micajah Perry and New Pensilvania Company the Summe of Nine pounds Seaventeen Shillings and Seaven pence Halfe penny with Costs and the Same in Safe Custody Keep untill otherwise ordered by due Course of Law and make returne of your proceedings herein to the next Generall Court together with this writt Dated at the Secretarys Office this 14th day of october Anno Domini 1706.

Testis T. Knight Secretary

[*Endorsed:*]
Attachment versus Hewett ad sectam Peterson Attorney etc.
Atteched by me bartholomew huwet body

[*Peterson, attorney of Perry and Company* v. *Wayman*]

[*CCR 192*]

No. Carolina Ss. To the honorable the Generall Court etc.

Thomas Peterson Attorney to Micajah Perry and New pensilvania Company is plaintiff against Christopher Wayman of Pascotanke in said province planter defendant in a plea of Debt and Sayes that the Defendant Stands Justly Indebted to the plaintiff quallifyed as aforesaid in the full and Just Sume of two pounds Eight Shillings and one peny halfepeny to be paid and delivered at the Landing of the Honorable Wm. Glover Esqr. in Litle river as in and by one Certaine writeing under the proper hand and Seale of the Defendant beareing Date the fifth day of Janry. Anno Domini 1704 and hereunto Court brought and ready to be produced relation bing thereunto had doth and may more fully and at Large appear Nevertheless the Defendant the Said Sume of two pounds Eight Shillings [*torn*] penny halfpenny in maner aforesaid hath not rendred tho' often thereunto requested but the Same doth Still refuse to render to the plaintiffs Damage four pound Sixteen Shilling and three pence Sterling and thereupon he brings this Suite and prayes Judgement for the Same with Costs of Suite and Shall pray etc.

T. Knight Secretary

[*Endorsed:*]
Narratio
Peterson Attorney etc. versus Wayman
In Debt
Entered Octo. 8th: 1706

[*CCR 188*]

This bill bindeth me Christopher Wayman of passcotank In the province of North Carrolina, planter and my hiers, Executors administrators and Assigns To pay To Thomas Peterson or order on account of the New Penslvania Company his or there assigns the Summ of Two pounds Eight Shillings and 1*d.* ½ In good fresh Merchantable pork and Deliver it at the Landing of Mr. Willm. Glover In Litle River as Witness my hand and Seal this fifth Day of Janry. 1704/5.

Wittnesse present Christopher Wayman Signum
John Hecklefield

[*Endorsed:*]
Chris. Wayman
2.8. 1½

JH 2/6 paid of it

[*Peterson, attorney of Perry and Company* v. *White*]

[*CCR 192*]

No. Carolina Ss. To the honorable the Generall Court etc.

Thoms. Peterson Attorney to Micajah Perry and New Pensilvania Company is plaintiff against Robert White Junior defendant in a plea of Debt and Sayes that the Defendant Stands Justly Indebted to the plaintiff in the full and Just Summe of Two pounds Sixteen Shillings and five pence in Good fresh porke to be paid at Wm. Glovers Landing in Litle river as in and by one Certaine writeing under the hand of the said Robert White beareing Date the 22d of December 1704 and here unto Court brought and ready to be produced relation being thereunto had doth and may appeare Nevertheless the said Defendant the Said Sume of two pounds Sixteen Shillings and five pence in maner aforesaid to the plaintiff hath not rendred tho' often thereunto requested but the Same doth Still refuse to render to the plaintiffs Damage five pounds Twelve Shillings and ten pence Sterling and thereupon he brings his Suite and prayes Judgement for the Same with Costs of Suite and Shall pray etc.

T. Knight Secretary

[*Endorsed:*]
Narratio
Peterson Attorney etc. versus White
In Debt
Entered Octo. 8th: 1706

[*CCR 148*]

North Carolina Ss. To the provost Marshall or his Deputy.

These are in her Matyes name to will and require you to Arrest the body of Robert White Junior and him Safely hold soe that he be and appeare at the next Generall Court to be holden at the house of Captain Jno. Hecklefield in Litle river on the last Tuesday in this Instant October then and there to Answer the plaint of Thos. Peterson Attorney to Micajah Perry and New Pensilvania Company in a Plea of Debt and have you there this writt Dated at the Secretary Office this 8th day of October Anno Domini 1706.

Testis T. Knight Secretary

[*Endorsed:*]
Breve

Peterson Attorney etc. versus White
Cepi Corpus
19th 8br

[*CCR 188*]

This bill bindeth me Robert White jr. of N. Carolina my heires Executors and administrators to pay unto mr. Thomas Peterson for the use of the new pensilvania Company the Summ of two pound Sixteen Shillings and five pence in good fresh porke at W. Glover's landing in little River Witnesse my hand and Seal the 22 of 10br 1704.

John Meaids
W. Glover

Robert White

[*Endorsed:*]
Rob. White
2:16:5

[*Rayfield* v. *Johnson*]

[*CCR 139*]

No. Carolina Ss. To the provost Marshall or Deputy

These are in her Majestyes name to will and require you to Arrest the body of Richd. Johnson and him Safeley hold Soe that he be and appeare at the next Generall Court to be holden at the house of Captain Jno. Hecklefield in Litle river on the last Tuesday in October next then and there to Answer the plaint of Willm. Rayfield in a plea of Debt and have there this writt Dated at the Secretarys Office this 4th day of Sept. Anno Domini 1706.

Testis T. Knight Secretary

[*Endorsed:*]
Breve
Rayfield versus Johnson
In Debt

[*Wade* v. *Meads*]

[*CCR 148*]

No. Carolina Ss. To the provost Marshall or his Deputy.

These are in her Majestyes name to will and require you to Sumons Wm. Barnsfield and Willm. Powers personally to be and appeare at the next Generall Court to be holden at the house of Captain Jno. Hecklefield in Litle river on the last Tuseday in this Instant October then and there to give Evidence between Jno. Wade and Jno. Meads Defendant on behalfe of the plaintiff and have you there this writt Dated at the Secretarys Office this 12th day of Octob. Anno Domini 1706.

Testis T. Knight Secretary

[*Endorsed:*]
Sumons for Barnesfield and Powers
Served by mee George Harris

[*Wicker, assignee* v. *Smith*]

[*CCR 148*]

No. Carolina Ss. To the honorable the Generall Court etc.

Joseph Wicker Assignee of James Cross is plaintiff against Jno. Smyth late of the precinct of pascotanke Defendant in a plea of Debt and Sayes that the Defendant Stands Justly Indebted to the plaintiff quallified as aforesaid in the full and Just Summe of Thirty one pounds Sterling payable in porke Tobacco Hides or Tallow at the Markett price of Corratuck to be paid and Delivered at the Landing or Storehouse of Mr. Joseph Chase and Company in the precinct of Corratuck as in and by one Certaine writeing obligatory under the proper hand and Seale of the Defendant beareing Date the 30th of Augt. 1705 and here into Court brought relation being thereunto had doth and may more fully and at large appeare Nevertheless the Said Defendant the Said Summe of Thirty one pounds in manner aforesaid to the plaintiff hath not rendred tho' often there unto requested but the same doth Still refuse to render to the plaintiffs Damage Sixty two pounds Sterling and thereupon he brings this Suite and prayes Judgement for the Same with Costs of Suite and Shall pray etc.

T. Knight Secretary

[*Endorsed:*]
Narratio
Wicker Assignee versus Smyth in Debt
Entered Oct. 10th: 1706

[*CCR 148*]

No. Carolina Ss. To the provost Marshall or his Deputy.

These are in her Matyes name to will and require you to Arrest the body of Jno. Smyth late of the precinct of pascotanke and him Safely hold Soe that he be and appeare at the next Generall Court to be holden at the house of Capt. Jno. Hecklefield in Litle river on the last Tuesday in this Instant octob. then and there to Answer the plaint of Joseph Wicker Assignee of James Cross in a plea of Debt and have you there this writt Dated at the Secretarys Office the 15th day of Octo. Anno Domini 1706.

Testis T. Knight Secretary

[*Endorsed:*]
Executed by me George Harris
Breve
Wicker Assigne versus Smyth in Debt

[*CCR 188*]

Know all men per these presents that I John Smith Late of the precinct of pascotank my heirs Executors administrators are heild and firmly Bound unto James Cross his heirs Executors or assigns the full and Just Sume of thirty one pound Sterling payable in porke tobacco hids or tallow at the Markitt price of Corrotuck to be paide and delivered at the Landing or Store house of Mr. Joseph Chace and Company in the precinct of Corrotuck [*torn*] well and truly to be made at or before the 10th of [*torn*] Insewing the date hereof as wittness my hand [*torn*] 30th of august 1705.

John Smith his Mark

In presence of us
Wm. Swann
Jose. Wicker

[*Endorsed:*]
September the 4 day 1705
Receved of this within menshoned bill twenty seaven pounds five Shillen and Eyght pence I Say Receved by me James Cross
Testeus
Wm. Bray
Thomas Vandermulen
I the Subscriber do assigne my Right of the Ballance of the within bill unto Mr. Joseph Wicker as Wittness by hand this 8th: of 7br 1705.

Wm. Swann James Cross

MISCELLANEOUS FILE PAPERS

[*Thomas, Morgan, petition*]

[*CCR 186*]

To the honourable Court;

The humble petition of Morgan Thomas doth in most humble manner present thus my humble petition to your honours to crave the admittance of Chuseing my Guardian my parents being lately deceased which causess me to make my humble address to your honours hopeing your honours will grant me that liberty to let me chuse one to manage that Small estate which my parents hath left me I being under age and not Capable of manageing of it my selfe which makes me apply my selfe to your Honours mercy and your humble petitioner Shall in duty pray.

[*CCR 104*]

<380> No. Carolina ss.

Att a Generall Cort held att the house of Captain John Hecklefield in Little River on Tuesday the 25th of March 1707.

Present the Honorable Christo. Gale Esqr.

The Acts of Assembly made att the last Session were openly read And then this Cort adjourned 'till the Morrow Morneing Eight of the Clock.

Wednesday Att 8 of the Clock in the Morning the Cort mett and Sitt. Present The Honorable Major Christo. Gale, Fra. DeLaMare, Wm. Barcliffe Esqrs. Justices.

Thomas Abington is upon Motion of the Secretary admitted Clerke of this Cort per Tempore and he's taken the Oaths appointed by Law togeather with the Oath of Clerke.

The Gentlemen of the Grand jury were Sworne and are as followeth Captain Richd. Saunderson Mr. Wm. Reed Mr. Francis penrice Mr. John Clarke Mr. phillip Torkesey Senior Mr. John Norton Mr. Isaac Guilford Mr. Tho. Gregory Mr. Matthew Winn Mr. Henry Creech Mr. Wm. Raymond Mr. Jno. Relf Mr. Robt. Morgan Mr. Henry pendleton Mr. Cornelius Jones.

Captain John Hecklefield comes to prosecute his Scire facias against Bryant Leigh for Money in his hands as assetts of Wm. powells and Bryant Leigh by his petition to this Honorable Cort Confesses for Seventeen pounds Tenn Shillings and prayes that the Same may be ordered to whom this Honorable Cort shall think fitt. Ordered that Bryant Leigh pay unto Captain John Hecklefield Seventeen pounds Tenn Shillings alias Execution.

Mr. Thomas peterson Attorney to Micajah perry and new pensilvania Company comes to prosecute his Sute against Thomas Collins Administrator of Allice Collings widdow deceased in a plea of Debt and Declares that the Defendant Qualifyed as aforesaid Stands justly indebted to the plaintiff in the Qualification aforesaid in the full and just Sume of Eighteen pounds Twelve Shillings in fresh porke etc. as in and by one Certaine Writeing Obligatory under the proper hand of the Said Alice bearing Date the 21st of Febry. 1704/5 and here into Cort brought relation etc. And the Defendant by Thomas Snoden his Attorney appeares and for plea Saith that he this Defendant att the time of the plaintiffs issueing out the Writt nor att any time Since hath not any Assetts <381> in his hands of the Deceased to Sattisfy the aforesaid Debt and this he is ready to averr. And the aforesaid plaintiff comes in proper person and Sayes the aforesaid Defendant hath not legally fulfilled the Administration aforesaid as the Said Defendant falsely Suggests in his plea And further Saith that his the Said plaintiffs Debt is of the Greatest Dignity of any that is against the Estate of the Said Alice Collings and therefore ought to be first paid and Sattisfyed and this he is ready to averr etc. And the Cort will advise 'till the next Morneing.

Thomas Collings Exhibites an Inventory of the Estate of Alice Collins widdow deceased upon his Oath amounting to £ 22=16=7.

Thomas Towers and Catherine his wife accknowledges the assignement of a Survey of a Tract of Land in pascotank to Cornelius Ratcliffe.

John porter Esqr. and Company comes by Edward Bonwick his Attorney comes to prosecute his Sute against Saml. painc by a Refferrence from the last Cort in a plea of Detinue and both parties are Content that it be refferred to the next Cort and there the Defendant plead to Isue.

Wm. Barnsfield comes by Edward Bonwick his Attorney to prosecute his Sute against Michael Conier in a plea of the Case and Declares that the Defendant Stands justly indebted to the plaintiff in the full Two pounds Twelve Shillings and Seven pence and the Marshall haveing Ruturned a Non Est inventus the plaintiff prayes an Attachment which is against the Defendants Goods which is granted.

William Houghton comes by Thomas Snoden his Attorney to prosecute his Sute against Henry Warren in a plea of the Case and Declares that the Defendant Stands indebted to the plaintiff in the full and just Summ of Seven pounds by account etc. and the Defendant by Thomas Norcomb his Attorney Saith the Defendant oweth not the Money and for tryall putts himself upon the Country and the plaintiff likewise. Therefore its comanded the Marshall that he cause to come Twelve etc. who etc. by whom etc. and there came to witt Mr. John Willoughby Mr. Wm. Wilson Mr. Edward Bagshaw Mr. John Cory Mr. Soloman Horner Mr. Tho. Snoden Mr. James Fewox Mr. John Jones Mr. Tho. Towers Mr. Saml. paine Mr. Richard Stamp and Mr. Anthony Wherry who Sworne Say We of the jury find for the plaintiff five pounds.

Ordered that Henry Warren pay unto Wm. Houghton Five pounds with Costs alias Execution.

Mary Cecow by Thomas Snoden her Majesties Attorney Generall comes by Thomas Snoden her Majesties Attorney Generall and Desires this Court to be informed and understand that Argyle Simons not haveing <382> the fear of God before his Eyes but being wholy moved by and thro the Instigation of the Devill did on or about the Month of November last past Sorely beat and abuse the Said Mary Cecow Soe that She Despaired of her life etc. And the Said Argyle Symons comes and Confesses the Fact and leaves himself to the Mercy of this Honorable Cort.

Ordered that the Said Argyle Symons pay all Charges that is

accrued by meanes thereof and that he give Bond with Good Security for his appearance att the next Cort and in the Mean time to be of the Good behavior.

The Grand Jury presented Winifrid Morris for haveing a Basterd Child borne of her Body. Thomas Snoden her Majesties Attorney Generall pray Judgment against Winifrid Morris upon breach of the Act Entituled an Act against Fornication and Adultery And the Said Winifrid Morris att the Barr accknowledges her Self to be Guilty of haveing a Basterd Child borne of her Body and throws her Self upon the Mercy of this Honorable Cort.

Ordered that the Said Winifrid Morris be punished by receiving Twenty one Stripes on her bare Back or pay fifty Shillings with Costs.

Jno. Jones accknowledges in the Sume of Twenty pounds Sterling by way of Recognizance With Condition that the Said Winifrid Morris appear att the next Cort and in the Mean time to be of good behavior towards all her Majesties Leige people.

Wm. Jackson bound over by Recognizance by pascotanck Cort apeared and upon his petition is Discharged paying Costs.

Wm. Armure bound over by Recognizance by pascotank Cort appearing upon his petition is discharged paying Costs.

John Thornton bound over by Recognizance by pascotank Cort haveing fayled to make his appeareance And Jacob Overman his Bayle being called haveing made faylure in bringing forth the Body of the Said John Thornton. Ordered that the provost Marshall or Deputy Estreat the Twenty pounds mentioned in the Recognizance for the Said Thorneton And 10 pounds for the Said Overman upon their Lands and Tenements Goods and Chattles and that a Warrant Issue out for that purpose.

<383> Ann Trumball Administratrix of Symon Trumball deceased proves an Account of her disbursements against her Husband Symon Trumballs Estate amounting to £22:18*s*.1*d*.½.

Argyle Symons in the Sume of £20, Captain Wm. Barrow in the Sume of £10, Mr. Robert Fendall in the sume of £10 Assume upon themselves by way of Recognizance Upon Condition that the Said Argyle Symons Shall appear att the next Generall Cort to be held for this province and in the mean time to be of the Good behavior towards all her Majesties Leige people and Especially towards Mary Cecow.

Upon petition of John Day Ordered that John Day be paid by Saml. paine Tenn Shillings and Six pence for his travell and Attendance being Sumoned by the Said paine att the Sute of [*blank*] with Costs alias Execution.

Thomas Collings and pernvana his Wife accknowledged an

Assignment of a patent of a Tract of Land to Jeremiah Barnes.

And then this Cort adjourned 'till too morrow Morn 8 of the Clock.

Thursday 27th Att 8 of the [*blank*] Cort mett and Sitt present ut Supra.

James Fuox Attorney of Edward phelps accknowledged the Sale of a Tract of Land to William Stephens.

Thomas peterson Attorney of Micajah perry and Company comes to prosecute his Sute against Thomas Collins Administrator etc. of Alice Collings Deceased upon a Curia advisare volamus yesterday and the Cort haveing heard and Maturely considered the whole Matter.

Ordered that Thomas Collings qualifyed as aforesaid pay unto Mr. Thomas peterson in the Qualification aforesaid Eighteen pounds Twelve Shillings with Costs alias Execution.

Upon petition of Sarah Ming Widdow and relict of Joseph Ming Deceased This Court are of opinion that Letters of Administration may be Comitted to her She giveing Security for the Same.

Upon petition of Sarah Ming Widdow ordered that Mr. Thomas Boyd Mr. Thomas Abington Thomas McKeel and Anthony Markeham Find Inventory and apprise the Estate of Joseph Ming deceased being first Sworne before a Majestrate.

Francis Foster Esqr. by Edward Bonwick his Attorney comes to prosecute his Attachment against the Estate of Wm. Chambers and Declares in a plea that he render to the Said plaintiff the Sume of Sixty <384> Eight pounds which to him he oweth and unjustly Deteyneth etc. for that whereas the Said William the 22th Day of Feabry. 1702/3 by his Certaine Bill Obligatory under the proper hand and Seale of the Said Wm. and here into Cort brought whose Date is the Same Day and year obleidge himself his heyrs Executors Administrators and Assignes to pay and Deliver unto the Said Francis his Executors or Assignes One Negro Man between Fifteen and five and Twenty yeares old free and Clear from any outward and visible Defect or Known Distemper att or before the Twenty fifth Day of December next Ensueing the Date of the Said Obligation or otherwise to pay unto the Said Francis the Said Sume of Sixty Eight pounds in porke att price Currant the Danger of the Seas only Excepted And the Said Francis in fact Sayes etc. And the Marshall haveing returned Severall Bills Attached in the hands the Honorable Wm. Glover Esqr. videlicet A Bill of Cornelius Learys for £2:11*s.*:0*d.*: A Bill of Danl. phillipps for £1:13*s.*=8*d.* A Bill of Daniel Russells for £1 16*s.*:9*d.* Mr. Tho. Abington £1=00*s.*=00*d.* Mr. pritchards Bond for £7=19*s.*=4*d.* Robert Temples Bill for £12:00*s.*=00*d.* Jos. King 6*s.*:3*d.* Timothy Clare £7:14*s.*:7*d.* phillipp Torkesey £16=3*s.*=00*d.* Danl. Rice £3:7*s.*:0*d.*

Ordered that the Said Bills be Delivered to the Said Francis Foster who is hereby impowered to put any of them in Sute in case of Refusall or Non payment.

George parker Executor of Gabriel parratt comes by Captain Richard Saunderson his Attorney to prosecute his Sute against Thomas Sparrow upon a Refferrence from the last Court in a plea of Debt and Sayes for that whereas the Said Thomas the fourth Day of August 1705 by his Certaine Writeing Obligatory under his proper hand and Seal hereinto Cort brought and ready to be produced whose Date is the Same Day and year accknowledged himself to be justly indebted to the Said George Executor etc. in the full Sume of Two Hundred fifty four pounds Sixteen Shillings Sterling Money of England to be paid unto the Geo. whenever he the Said Thomas Should be thereunto requested Yett nevertheless etc. And the Defendant by Edward Bonwick his Attorney moves for Security for what Costs and Damages Shalbe awarded by the Court in Case the plaintiff Shall lose his Account and Captain Richd. Saunderson and Mr. John Hawkins assume upon themselves on behalf of the plaintiff to pay all Costs and Damages in Case the plaintiff Shalbe Cast that Shalbe awarded by the Cort And the Defendant by Edward Bonwick his Attorney comes and Defends the force when etc. and for plea Saith Non est factum and for tryall putts himself upon the Country and the plaintiff likewise Therefore its Comanded the Marshall that he cause to come twelve etc. who etc. by whom etc. and there came videlicet Mr. Saml. Norton Mr. John Willowby Mr. Saml. paine Mr. Nicho. Tyler <385> Mr. James Morgan Mr. John Cory Mr. Tho. Snoden Mr. John Jones Mr. Thomas Towers Mr. Zachary Keaton Mr. Richd. Mardron and Mr. John Falkener who Sworne Say we of the Jury find for the plaintiff And by Edward Bonwick his Attorney moves in Stay and arrest of Judgment for this Reason videlicet There is a Generall Rule in the Law if the Defendant doth first plead a plea that doth tend to the Destruction of the Action forever he Shall not be admitted after to plead in abatement of the Writt And yett if there appear Matter Apparent in the Record for which the Writt ought to be abated then the Defendant may Shew it the Court in arrest of Judgment Corpus Libro 2d Justitut Regula plitoards[16] page 275. Now the Defendant by the Said Edward Bonwick his Attorney humbly Shews to the Honor-

[16] This word may be the surname of the plaintiff in the case being referred to.

able Cort that the Originall Writt of the aforesaid plaintiff against the said Defendant is made out in the Debet whereas it Should be in the Detinet Tautum only for which the Writt ought to be abated and prayes Judgment may be Stayed and arrested and the Court haveing heard and duely considered the aforesaid Reasons it is their opinion that the reasons are not Sufficient to abate the Writt and therefore are overuled And in Barr to Judgment Captain Richd. Saunders in behalf of the plaintiff is Content with the following assumption And Thomas Sparrow George Berkenhead and Captain Richd. Smith assume upon themselves their Joyntly and Severally to pay to the Said Captain Richd. Saunders att his Dwelling house in Coratuck the Sume of One Hundred Twenty Nine pounds Three Shillings and Tenn pence in the Country Comodities of this Country (Corne Excepted) Sometime within Three yeares now next insueing or Bring Sufficient Discharges from the Said parker for the Same.

Colonel Thomas pollock comes by Thomas Boyd his attorney to prosecute his Writt of Scire facias against Wm. Brice and the Defendant by Wm. Barrow his Attorney appears and Shews noe Cause why etc.

Ordered that the judgment be affirmed on which the Scire facias was granted.

The Honorable Wm. Glover Esqr. accknowledges a Conveyance of a Tract of Land to Jonathan Stanley and Catherine his wife acknowledges the assignement of her Right of Dower.

Thomas Snoden, Esqr. assignee of Edward Norrington comes to prosecute his Sute against Edward Norrington in a plea of Debt and Sayes that the Defendant Stands justly indebted to the plaintiff qualifyed as aforesaid in the full and just Sume of Eleaven pounds as in and by one Certaine Writeing. [17]

[*CCR 189*]

The Honorable Landgrave Robert Danl. Esqr. comes to prosecute his Sute against Levi Truitt and Declares as per Declaration and the Defendant appeares and Confesses as the Bill is Signed by him for Tho. Derham.

Ordered that Levi Truitt pay the Honorable Robt. Daniel Esqr. 3=19 in porke by Bill and Six Shillings per Account with Costs alias Execution.

The Honorable Landgrave Robert Daniel Esqr. comes to prosecute his Sute against Wm. Reed and Declares as per Declaration

[17] The text of the finished minutes in CCR 104 breaks off at this point. The material which follows is comprised of scratch minutes taken from two separate folders in CCR 189.

and the Defendant appears and Confesses.

Ordered that the said Wm. Read pay £50 to the Honorable Robert Daniel Esqr. according to Specialty with Costs alias Execution.

The Honorable Landgrave Robert Daniel Esqr. comes to prosecute his Sute against Eliz. Executrix of Derham and the Defendant by Edwd. Bonwick her Attorney comes and pleads as per plea.

Ordered that the Sute be Dismissed and the plaintiff pay Costs.

The Honorable Landgrave Robert Daniel Esqr. comes to prosecute his Sute against Captain Jno. Hecklefield and Declares as per Declaration and for want of the Defendants apearance Attachment is ordered to issue att the prayer of the plaintiff.

The Honorable Landgrave Robert Daniel Esqr. comes to prosecute his Sute against Boaz Bell and Declares as per Declaration and the Defendant by Edward Bonwick his attorney pleads as per plea for Tryall and putts himself upon the Country and the plaintiff likewise Therefore its Comanded the Marshall that he cause to come Twelve etc. who etc. by whom etc. and there came to witt Mr. Willoughby Mr. Saml. paine Mr. Nicho. Tyler Mr. James Morgan Mr. John Cory, Mr. Thomas Snoden Mr. John Jones Mr. Tho. Fewox Mr. Zachary Keton Mr. Richd. Mardron Mr. Wm. Scarbro Mr. Wm. Wilson who Sworne Say Wee of the Jury find for the plaintiff.

Ordered that the Said Boaz Bell pay unto the Honorable Robert Daniell Three pound Nineteen Shillings according to Speciallty with Costs alias Execution.

John Redwood by Thomas Snoden Esqr. his Attorney comes to prosecute his Sute against John pettiver and Declares as per Declaration and the Defendant came not and Attachment Granted upon prayer of the plaintiffs Attorney.

[*CCR 189*][18]

<1> Hogg or Hoggs Shalbe fined Two Thousand pounds Weight of porke for Every Such Hogg which Shalbe Stolen or Mismarked one half pd. the Informer and the other Half to him or them that Shall Sue for the Same to be recovered By Acction of Debt in any Cort of Record in this Country Yett Nevertheless the Defendant the aforesaid Act not att all minding or Regarding but the Same and the Authority thereof altogeather contemning and dispiseing did on or about the 22d Day of November last past in the precinct of pascotank in this Government Steal take and carry away Two Hoggs

[18] Scratch minutes from the second folder of CCR 189 begin here.

[the] proper Goods and Chattles of the plaintiff then and there being Contrary to the tenet Content and meaneing of the Said Act by which the Said plaintiff in fact Saith that Acction accrued unto him to have and receive of the aforesaid Defendants the Summ or Quantity of Four Thousand pound Weight of porke Yett Nevertheless the Defendants the aforesaid Summ or Quantity of Four Thousand Weight of porke to the plaintiff have not paid but the Same doth Still refuse to pay to the plaintiffs Damage Twenty five pounds and thereupon he brings this Sute etc. And the Defendants by Edward Bonwicke their Attorney come and Defend the force and injury when etc. and Say that for the manifold insufficienceyes [imper]fections and incertaintyes in the plaintiffs Decleration and the Matter therein Conteyned they the Said Defendants can nott neither by the Law of the Land are they bound to make answer thereunto and this they are ready to averr wherefore for want of a Sufficient Declaration and Sufficient Matter therein to be conteyned they the Said Defendants pray Judgment if the plaintiff aforesaid his Acction aforesaid against them by the Law ought to have and Mainteyne Bonwicke per Defendant versus [*blank*] Et per Causis The plaintiff in his Declaration aforesaid Setts forth That Robert Morgan is plaintiff against Henry Hayman and George Griffin Defendants in a plea of [*illegible*] Saith that whereas in and by one Act Intituled an Act against Killing of Cattle of Hoggs amongst Divers other Things therein Conteyned It is Enacted that what person or persons Shalbe Lawfully Convict in any Court of Record in this Country for Stealing or Mismarkeing any Hogg or Hoggs Shalbe fined Two Thousand Weight of porke [for] Every Such Hogg etc. But does not Say what Act it is [*illegible*] of parliament or by any other Authority made <2> or where the Said Act was made which are Grand Incertanitys and insufficiencies And the Court have heard and maturely considered the whole Matter are of Opinion that the Action is not well layd and therefore Ordered that the Sute be dismissed and that the plaintiff pay Costs alias Execution.

Upon petition of John Hawkins Ordered that the Said Hawkins be paid by Henry Haymond and Geo. Griffin Eight Shillings and [*torn*] pence for his travell and Attendance being Sumoned as an Evidence for them att the Sute of Robert Morgan with Costs alias Execution.

Upon petition of Henry Creech Ordered that the Said Creech be paid by Henry Hamond and George Griffin Eight Shillings and four pence for his travell and Attendance being Sumoned as an Evidence for them att the Sute of Robert Morgan with Costs alias

Execution.

Upon petition of Thomas Gregory Ordered that the Said Gregory be paid by Henry Haymon and George Griffin Eight Shillings and four pence for his travell and Attendance being Sumoned as an Evidence for them att the Sute of Robert Morgan with Costs alias Execution.

Upon petition of John Relf Ordered that the Said Relf be paid by Henry Hayman and George Griffin Eight Shillings and four pence for his Travell and Attendance being Sumoned as an Evidence for them att the Sute of Robert Morgan with Costs alias Execution.

Upon petition of John Norton Ordered that the Said Norton be paid by Henry Hayman and George Griffin Eight Shillings and four pence for his travell and Attendance being Sumoned as an Evidence for them att the Sute of Robert Morgan with Costs alias Execution.

And then this Court adjourned till too morrow Morneing Eight of the Clock.

<3> Fryday The Court Mett and Sitt att 8 of the Clock present ut Supra.

Julius Deeds comes to prosecute his Sute against Wm. Duckenfield Esqr. in a plea of Debt upon a Referrence from the last Court and by Consent of both parties referred to the next Cort.

Upon petition of Captain James Cole praying etc. Ordered that Letter of Administration may be granted to the Said Cole as principall Creditor to the Estate of Evan Thomas deceased and that Mr. John pettiver Isaac Wilson [*torn*] pearse and Francis Beasely Inventory and apprise the Said Estate and returne an Inventory thereof to the next Generall Cort.

John Hodgson by Thomas Snoden his Attorney comes to prosecute his Sute against John Bennett in a plea of the Case and Complains that the Defendant Stands indebted to the plaintiff in the full and just Sume of Fourty pounds which Said Sume of Fourty pounds the Defendant did faithfully promise and assume to pay unto the plaintiff in Consideration of a Marriage which was had and Solemnized betwixt the plaintiff and the Defendants Daughter Mary Sometime in October in the year 1705 etc. And the Defendant in his proper person comes and Defends the force and Injury when etc. and Saith that whereof the Said plaintiff Declareth that this Defendant Stands justly indebted to the Same plaintiff in the full and just Sume of Fourty pounds upon Consideration of a Marriage had and Solemnized between the Said plaintiff and the

Said Defendants Daughter Mary Sometime in October in the year 1705 which the Said Defendant sweireth that the Said plaintiff never was Married in October of the year 1705 to any Daughter of the Said Defendants neither hath the Said plaintiff any wife that is a Daughter of the Said Defendants neither Did this Defendant in October in the year 1705 nor att any other time faithfully promise and assume to pay unto the Said plaintiff fourty pounds upon the Consideration of any Marriage whatsoever neither did the Said plaintiff Ever Demand the aforesaid Sume nor any other Sume upon any Such Account as is aforementioned etc. and for tryall putts himselfe upon the Country and the plaintiff by Thomas Snoden his Attorney likewise. Wherefore it's Commanded the Marshall that he cause to come Twelve etc. who etc. by whom etc. and there came to witt Mr. Robert Lowry Mr. John Willoughby Mr. Saml. paine Mr. James Morgan Mr. Thomas Snoden Mr. <4> Thomas Towers Mr. John Clarke Mr. Matthew Winn Mr. Henry Bonner Mr. Robert Morgan Mr. John Clarke Mr. Robert Keel who Sworne Say we of the jury find for the Defendant.

Ordered that the Sute be dismissed and that the plaintiff pay Costs alias Execution.

Robert Keel bound over the last Cort appeares and upon his petition and Submission is Discharged.

Robert Keel assumes in open Court to pay Hannah Keon Thirty Shillings in full for her Attendance in the Sute between himselfe and Augustine Scarbro.

[*Signed:*]

C. Gale, francis De La Mare, William Barclift.

RECORDED BY ORDER OF COURT

[*CCR 189*]

<19> North Carolina ss.

[Know all men] by these presents that I John Wilkins Marriner have made Ordeyned constituted and appointed and by these presents doe make Ordeyne Constitute and appoint James Tooke of this province Marchant my true and lawfull Attorney for me and in my name and to my Use to ask Demand and Receive of and from all persons whatsoever all Such Sums of Money or other Things which doe or may any wayes belong unto me and likewise to appear in any Cort of Record in this Government and there to Defend any Action that Shalbe brought against me and to proceed therein in all Respects as if my Self was personally present And one or more Attorney or Attorneys under him to make and the Same againe to [*torn*] and Generally to act and doe in all Respects as if my Self might or could doe if personally present In Wittness whereof I have hereunto Sett my hand and Seal this 9th Day of May Anno Domini 1707.

Sealed and Delivered in the presence of Jno. Falconer T. Knight — John Wilkins Seal

To all People unto Whome These Presents shall Come Joshua Lamb of Roxbury in the Court of Suffolk in New England Gentleman Son of Joshua Lamb late of Roxbury afforesaid merchant Deceased sendeth Greeting Know Yee that that I the said Joshua Lamb for and In Consideration of the sume of forty pounds Currant Money of New England to me in hand paid at and before the Ensealing and Delivery of these presents well and truely paid or secured to be paid by Robert Sanders of Boston in the County of Suffolk aforesaid Mariner the Receipts whereof to full Content and Satisfaction I doe hereby acknowledge have given granted Bargain'd and sold Aliend Enfeafed Conveyd and Confirm'd And by these presents do full freely And absolutely give grant Bargain Sell alien Enfeafe Convey and Confirm unto the Said Rober Sanders one full quarter [or] fourth part of the Whole Island of Ronoake scituate and being in the County of Albemarle In the Province of Carolina togeather with one quarter or fourth part of what is thereon standing growing or being with all houseing out houses Edifices and Buildings and fences there unto belonging as allso one fourth part or quarter of all Catle hoggs And stock upon the Said [Island] And to me belonging or Appertaining and all Rights profits previleges Advantages [*torn*] And Appurtences whatsoever to the [quarter] or [fourth] parts of the said Island [of Ronoake] <20> belonging in any wise appurtaining [*torn*] the Reversion or Reversions [*torn*] and remaynd There of and allso all the [*torn*] Right title Interests Inheritance use [possession] propertie Clame And Demand whatsoever of [which] the same Joshua Lamb of in and to the same to have and to hold the said Quarter or fourth parts of the said Island and premisses with the Appurtences unto the said Robert Sanders his heirs And Assignes to his land their owne sole And proper use and Benufitt and behoofe for ever And I the Said Joshua Lamb do [*illegible*] [*torn*]uch my selfe at the time of [*torn*] Deliver of these presents to be the onely true Sole And Lawful owner of all the above granted and bargained premises and that I am Lawfully seised thereof in my owne proper rights of a good perfect absolute Indefeasable

Estate of Inheritance in fee simple Haveing in my selfe full power good Right and Lawfull Authority to grant Bargain Sell and assure the same unto the said Robert Sanders his heirs and assignes in Manner and form as afforesaid and That the said Robert Sanders his heirs or assignes shall and may by force and vertue of these present at all times for ever hereafter enter into and upon hold [*torn*] to occuppy [*illegible*] and Enjoy all and singular the above granted and Bargained premises with the appurtences free and Clear and Clearly acquit Exonerated and discharged of and from all and all manner of former and other gifts grants Bargains sailes Mortgages Joyntures Dowers Entailes wills Judgments Executions Claims Damages and Demands Whatsoever In Wittness whereof I have here unto set my hand and seale the nineteenth day of November Anno Domini 1706 Annoqe Regina [Regia] Anne mine [*sic*] Anglia Quinte.

Sealed and Delivered Joshua Lamb Seal
In presence of us
Joseph Comings
Jacob Cornwell
Edwd. Weaver Secretary

March 6th 1706/7 Then the above within writen deed was proved before the Honorable William Glover President of the Councell etc. by the above [Joseph] Cominge and Jacob Cornwell Witness [*torn*] who being sworne on the holy [Evangelist] [*torn*] Severall sayth that they did [*torn*] The [*torn*] <21> [*torn*] Seale and as his Act and deed deliver [*torn*] me to the within named Robert [*torn*]

Testis Tob. Knight Secretary

FILE PAPERS IN SUITS AND PROSECUTIONS

[*Alexander* v. *Symons*]

[*CCR 148*]

No. Carolina Ss. To the Honorable the Generall Court

Antho. Alexander is plaintiff against Edwd. Simons defendant in a plea of debt and Sayes that the Defendant Stands justly Indebted [*illegible*] plaintiff in the full and Just Summe or quantity of three barrels of [*torn*] to be paid at Bartho. Phelps's Landing as in and [*torn*] one Cetaine writeing obligatory under his proper [*torn*] beareing Date the 5th day of Augt. 1706 and here into Court brought doth and may appeare which [*torn*] the quantity of three barrels of tarr and the Said Defendant to the [*torn*] hath not paid tho' often thereunto requested but the [*torn*] doth Still refuse to pay to the plaintiffs

Damage [*illegible*] pounds fifteen Shillings Sterling and thereupon he brings this Suite etc.

T. Knight Secretary

[*Endorsed:*]
Narratio
Alexander versus Simons
In Debt

[*CCR 192*]

North Carolina Generall Court Ss. To Edward Bonwicke

These are to impower you to appear for me in the Same Court ad sectum Anthony Alexander in two Actions of Debt Brought against me Edwd. Simmons and confess Judgments for the same by Non sum informatus nihil dicit or otherwise howsoever as to you Shall seem meet and convenient Witness my hand and Seale the Four and Twentieth day of March Anno Domini 1707.

Testes
William Duckenfeild
Archiball Holmes

Edwd. Simmons his Marke

[*Barnsfield* v. *Conyer*]

[*CCR 148*]

No. Carolina Ss. To the Honorable the Generall Court etc.

William Barnesfield is plaintiff against Michael Conyer defendant in a plea of the [*torn*] and Complaines that the Defendant Stands Justly Indebted to the plaintiff in the [*torn*] Summe of two pounds Twelve Shillings and Seaven pence by Account as [*torn*] wayes and meanes Convenient the plaintiff is ready to make appeare [*torn*] Said Summe of two pounds tenn Shillings and Seaven pence the [defendant] [*torn*] not rendred to the plaintiff tho' often thereunto requested but the Same doth still refuse to render to the plaintiffs Damage Six pounds Sterling and thereupon he brings this Suite etc.

T. Knight Secretary

[*Endorsed:*]
[*Illegible*] versus Conyer
In Case
Entred Janry. 2d 1706/7

[*CCR 190*]

1706 Michael Conyer Debtor

	s.	*d.*
To: Wheat Linen etc. by account made up	19=	10
To: 2 Bushels Salt	12=	..
To: 2 pr. Shoes	10=	..
To: Earthen Ware	7=	..

To: 1: barrell		3=	9
	2=	12=	7
Per Contra Credit By 81 pounds Raw Hyde		6=	9
Ballance Due	2	5	10

Errors Excepted this 18th of December 1706 by me
<*The Marke of*> Wm. Barnsfeild.

This account proved by the oath of Wm. Barnesfeild

Testis Tho. Abington Clericus Curiae Tempore

[*Daniell* v. *Hecklefield*]

[*CCR 148*]

No. Carolina Ss. To the Honorable the Generall Court etc.

The Honorable Landgrave Robert Daniell Esqr. is Plaintiff against Jno. Hecklefield gentleman defendant in a plea of the Case and Complaines that the defendant Stands Indebted to the plaintiff in the full Summe of Twenty Eight pounds Eight pence by Account as by wayes and meanes Convenient the plaintiff is ready to make appeare which Said Sume of twenty Eight pounds Eight Shillings the defendant hath not rendred to the plaintiff tho' often thereunto requested but the Same doth Still refuse to render to the plaintiffs Damage Sixty pounds Sterling and thereupon he brings this Suite etc.

T. Knight Secretary

[*Endorsed:*]
Daniell versus Hecklefield
In Case
Entered Mar. 6th: 1706/7

[*CCR 139*]

No. Carolina Ss. To the provost Marshall or his Deputy

These are in her Majestyes name to will and require you to Arrest the body of Jno. Hecklefield gentleman and him Safely hold Soe that he be and appeare at the next Generall Court to be holden at the house of Captain Jno. Hecklefield in Litle river on the last Tuseday in this Instant March then and there to Answer the plaint of the Honorable Landgrave Robert Daniell Esqr. in a plea of the Case and have there this writt Dated at the Secretarys Office this 6th day of March Anno Domini 1706/7.

Testis T. Knight Secretary

[*Endorsed:*]
Daniell versus Hecklefield
In Case

Cepi Corpus per Wm. Boyd provost Marshall this 11th March 1706/7

[*Low, attorney of Archdale v. Jordan*]

[*CCR 191*]

No. Carolina Ss. To the Honorable the Generall Court etc.

Emanuell Lowe Esqr. [*torn*] Attorney to the honorable Jno. Archdale Esqr. is plaintiff against Joseph Jordan defendant in a plea of the Case and Complaines that whereas the Said Defendant did take to Farme hold occupy possess and Enjoy a Certaine plantation and Lands thereunto belonging of and from the said Archdale Scituate lyeing and being on New begun Creeke in the precinct of pascotank and being that whereon the said Defendant now lives from Sometyme in the Yeare 1699 till Sometyme in yeare 1704 att and under such a Certaine Yearely rent as the Said Archdale should reasonably deserve for the Same and the plaintiff (quallifyed as aforesaid) in fact Sayth that he doth reasonably deserve the Sume or quantity of three hundred weight of Fresh porke per Anno whereupon Account Accrews to the plaintiff quallifyed as aforesaid to have and receive of the defendant the full Sume or Quantity of fifteen hundred weight of Fresh porke Nevertheless the Said Defendant the said Sume or quantity of Fifteen hundred weight of Fresh porke to the plaintiff hath not rendred tho' often thereunto requested but the Same Doth Still refuse to render to the plaintiffs Damage Twenty pounds Sterling and thereupon he brings his Suite etc.

T. Knight Secretary

[*Endorsed:*]
Narratio
Lowe Attorney versus Jordan
In Case
Entred Mar. 6th 1706/7

[*CCR 148*]

No. Carolina Ss. To the provost Marshall or his Deputy

These are in her Majestyes name to will and require you to Arrest the body of Joseph Jordan and him Safely hold soe that he be and appeare at the next Generall Court to be holden at the house of Captain Jno. Hecklefield in Litle river on the last Tuseday in this Instant March then and there to Answer the plaint of Emanuell Lowe Esqr. Attorney to the Honorable Jno. Archdale Esqr. in a plea of the Case and have there this writt Dated at the Secretarys Office this 6th day of March Anno Domini 1706/7.

Testis T. Knight Secretary

[*Endorsed:*]
Breve
Lowe Attorney etc. versus Jordan
In Case
Cepi Corpus George Hariss

[*Low, attorney of Archdale* v. *Jordan and wife, administrators*]

[*CCR 179*]

No. Carolina Ss.   To the honorable the Generall Court etc.

Emanuell Lowe Esqr. Attorney to the Honorable Jno. Archdale Esqr. is plaintiff against Joseph Jordan and Filia his wife Administrators of the Goods and Chatles of Daniell Akehurst Esqr. deceased Defendants in a plea of the Case and Complaines that Whereas the Said Akehurst did in his life tyme hold occupy and posess a Certaine plantation and land thereunto belonging to the aforesaid Archdale Scituate lyeing and being on Newbegun Creeke in the precinct of Pascotanke and that whereon the aforesaid defendants now live from Some tyme in the yeare 1694 to Some tyme in the year 1699 at and under Such a Certaine Yearely Rent as the Said Archdale Should reasonably deserve for the Same And the plaintiff (qualifyed as aforesaid) in fact sayth that he doth reasonably deserve the Sume or quantyty of three hundred weight of Fresh porke per Anno Whereupon Account Accrews to the plaintiff quallifyed as aforesaid to have and receive of the Defendants (quallifyed as aforesaid) the full Sume or quantity of Fifteen hundred weight of Fresh porke Yet nevertheless the said Defendant the said Sume or Quantity of Fifteen hundred weight of Fresh porke to the plaintiff hath not paid tho' often thereunto requested but the Same doth Still refuse to pay to the plaintiffs Damage Twenty pounds Sterling and thereupon he brings his Suite etc.

T. Knight   Secretary

[*Endorsed:*]
Narratio
Lowe Attorney versus Jordan and uxor
In Case
Entered Mar. 6th 1706/7

[*CCR 148*]

No. Carolina Ss.   To the Provost Marshall or his Deputy.

These are in her Majestyes name to will and require you to Arrest the body of Joseph Jordan and Filia his wife administrators of the Goods and Chattles of Dan. Akehurst deceased and them Safely hold soe that they be and appeare at the next Generall Court to be holden at the house of Captain Jno. Hecklefield in Litle river on the last Tuesday in this Instant March then and there to Answer the plaint of Emanuell Lowe Esqr. Attorney to the honorable Jno. Archdale Esqr. in a plea of the Case and have there this writt dated at the Secretarys Office this 6th day of March Anno Domini 1706/7.

Testis   T. Knight   Secretary

[*Endorsed:*]
Breve
Lowe Attorney versus Jordan and uxor
In Case
Cepi Corpus   George Harris

[*Porter and Company* v. *Paine*]

[*CCR 148*]

No. Carolina Ss. To the honorable the Generall Court etc.

John Porter Esqr. and Company Complaines of Samuell paine of a plea that he render unto him one Cable and an Anchor which from them he unjustly deteynes for that whereas The Said Complainants the 27th day of March Anno Domini 1705 delivered to the aforesaid Samll. One Cable and an Anchor to the vallue of Twenty pounds Sterling to be Safely Kept and to the plaintiffs to be delivered when he the said Samll. should be thereunto requested Yet the aforesaid Samll. tho' often thereunto requested the said Cable and Anchor to the plaintiffs hath not redelivered but the Same to him hitherto to redeliver hath denyed and as yett doth deney and unjustly deteyne to the damage of the plaintiffs Forty pounds Sterling and thereupon they bring this Suite etc.

T. Knight Secretary

[*Endorsed:*]
Narratio
Porter and Company versus Paine
We of the Jurrery finde for the defendant

[*Redwood* v. *Pettiver*]

[*CCR 148*]

No. Carolina Ss. To the honorable the Generall Court etc.

John Redwood is Plaintiff against Jno. Pettiver defendant in a Plea of the Case and Complaines for that whereas the said John Pettiver the [*illegible*] of December 1703 was Indebted to the Said Jno. Redwood in the Summe of Eight pounds Sterling did draw and deliver unto the said Jno. Redwood three Severall Bills of Exchange with the proper hand of the said Jno. Pettiver Signed and dated the aforesaid Eighteenth day of December 1703 and directed to one Jno. Newton Merchant in Lawrence Lane London requireing thereby the said Jno. Newton Thirty dayes after Sight of his the Said Jno. Pettiver's first Bill of Exchange his Seccond nor third not paid to pay or cause to be paid to the Said Jno. Redwood or his order the Said Sume of Eight pounds Sterling And he the Said Jno. Pettiver the day and yeare aforesaid upon himselfe Assumed unto the Said John Redwood that in Case the Said Jno. Newton should refuse to pay or accept of one of the said three Bills of Exchange according to the Tenour of the Same to the Said Jno. Redwood or to Such other person as he Should Indorse Consigne or order the Same that then the Said Jno. Pettiver would faithfully pay or Cause to be paid the Same to the said Jno. Redwood or order with Lawfull Charges and Interest on the Same And the aforesaid Jno. Redwood in fact Says that Messrs. Perry and Lane of London Merchants by order and direction of the Said Jno. Redwood did present the Said First Bill of Exchange unto the said Jno. Newton to whome the Same was directed as aforesaid and demanded acceptance and payment of the Said Bill according to the tenour of the Same who did utterly refuse to accept or make payment of the Same whereupon the Said Jno. Redwood by the Said Messrs. Perry and Lane upon the thirty first day of Augt. Anno Domini 1704 according to the use and Custome of Merchants did procure James Puckle Notary and Tabellion Publick in London by Royall authority duly admitted and Sworne to make due and Legall protest of the Said first Bill of Exchange the Seccond nor third nor either of them being paid which Said first Bill of Exchange being due and not paid together with the Said protest here into Court brought and ready to be produced relation being thereunto had doth and may appeare Nevertheless the Said Jno. Pettiver the Said Sume of Eight pounds with the Lawfull Interest and Charges thereon paid to the Said Jno. Redwood hath not paid tho' often thereunto requested but the Same doth Still refuse to pay to the Damage of the Said Jno. Redwood Sixteene pounds Sterling and thereupon hee brings this Suite etc.

T. Knight Secretary

[*Endorsed:*]
Narratio
Redwood versus Pettiver
In Case
Entered Mar. 6th: 1706

[*CCR 148*]

S E Virginia December 18th 1703

<*Copia*> Thirty Days after Sight of this my first bill of Exchange my Second and third not paid Pay or Cause to be paid to Mr. John Redwood or his order Eight Pounds Sterling for the like vallue here Received and place to Account of Sir Your humble Servant=John Pettiver=To John Newton Merchant in Lawrance Lane London=Signed in Blanck=John Redwood=Timothy Metcalfe=Pay the Contents to Messrs. Mica. Perry and Company for the use of Phillip Ludwill Junior.

By This Publick Instrument of Protest be it knowne and Manifest unto all those who Shall See these Presents or hear the Same Read That on the Thirty First Day of the Month of August Anno Domini 1704 and in the Third year of the Reigne of our Sovereigne Lady Anne by the Grace of God of England Scotland France and Ireland Queen Defender of the Faith etc. At the Instance and Request of Messrs. Perry and Lane of London Merchants I James Puckle Notary and Tabellion Publick Dwelling in London by Royall Authority duly admitted and Sworne Exhibited the originall bill of Exchange whereof the Coppy is here before written Word for Word to John Newton to whome the Same is Directed and Demanded Payment thereof Whereupon he Answered that he would not pay the Said bill for Want of Effects Upon which answer I the Said Notary at the Request aforesaid have Protested and by these Presents doe Solemnly Protest as well against John Pettiver Drawer of the Said bill as against all others whome it doth or May Concerne for Change and Rechange together with all Costs Dammages and Interests allready Suffered and Sustained and to be Suffered and Sustained for Want of Payment of the Said bill of Exchange Thus Done and Protested in London aforesaid in the presence of James Dunnidge and John Eaton Wittnesses hereunto Required.

In promissorum fidem
Ja. Puckle Notary Publick

[*CCR 191*]

Jno. Pettiver ad sectam Jno. Redwood

And the said Jno. Pettiver by Edwd. Bonwicke his Attorney comes and Saies That he was not Served with any process as the Law of this Country directs and that the Copy of the Writ that was Served upon the said Defendant is Nonsence and uninteligible And prayes Judgment of that Service etc.

Bonwicke per Defendant

[*Snoden, assignee* v. *Dawson*]

[*CCR 148*]

[*Torn*] Carolina Ss. To the honorable the Generall Court etc.

Thomas Snoden Assignee of Edwd. Norrington is plaintiff against Antho. Dawson [*torn*] in a plea of Debt and Sayes that the Defendant Stands Justly Indebted to the [*torn*] quallifyed as aforesaid in the full and Just Summe [*torn*]ven pounds as in and by one Certaine writeing obligatory [*torn*] hand of the Defendant beareing Date the Nineth day of Janry. [*torn*] 1697 and here into Court brought doth and may appeare Nevertheless the Said Defendant the Said Summe of Seaven pounds [*torn*] plaintiff hath not rendred tho' often thereunto requested but the Same doth Still refuse to render to the plaintiffs Damage Fourteen pounds Sterling [*torn*] thereupon he brings his Suite etc. and prayes Judgment for the aforesaid Debt and damages with Costs etc.

MISCELLANEOUS FILE PAPERS

[*Gale, Sarah, letter of attorney*]

[*CCR 181*]

Know all men by these presents that I Sarah Gale widow and Relict of the late Honorable Thomas Harvey Deceased doe hereby Nominate Constitute and appoint Thomas Abington my True and Lawfull Attorney for me and in my name to appear in any Court of Record in this Goverment and accknowledge my Right of Dower in all the Lands of my Said late Husband Thomas Harvey but Especially my Estate for life given me by the Will of my Deceased Husband in one plantation and Tract of Land conteyning five Hundred Acres Scituate lying and being in the precinct of pequimons and whereon I now Live to my Son Thomas Harvey his heyers and Assignes forever Wittness my hand and Seal this 28th Day of November 1706.

Signed Sealed and Delivered
in the presence of

Sarah Gale

James Blount
John Crabhum

[*CCR 189*][19]

<7> North Carolina ss.

Att a Generall Court held for this Government aforesaid the 29th Day of July 1707 att the house of Captain John Heckleffeld at Little Riveres. Present The Honorable Major Christopher Gale, Mr. John Blount Esqrs. Justices.

James Ming Esqr. tooke the Oathes appointed togeather with the Oath of a Justice of the peace.

And then this Court adjourned till too Morrow Morning Eight of the Clock.

[*Torn*] Att 8 of the Clock [*torn*].

Present the Honorable Christopher Gale, Mr. John Blount, Mr. Francis Delamare, Mr. James Ming Justices.

A Letter of Attorney from John Wilkins to James Tookes proved by the Oath of Mr. Tobias Knight and Declares that [*illegible*] John Falkner Signed the Same as an Evidence.

Thomas Snoden Esqr. her Majesties Attorney Generall and prosecutor for [*illegible*] Desires this Cort to understand and be informed that whereas in and by an Act of Assembly Entituled private Burialls prohibited as is Enacted on these Words videlicet Whereas the private Burialls of Servants and other persons may give [*illegible*] of [Much Scandall] [*torn*] of being guilty of their Deaths from which of the persons be in Recent which are Suspected there [*illegible*] and if guilty noe punishment by reason they are the most part Buried without the Knowledge [or venire] of any other than Such of the Family as by [*illegible*] of Relation husband Wife or Child are [*illegible*] or Servants are Fearfull to make Discovery if Murder were Comitted for prevention whereof as alsoe for takeing away of that barbarous Custom of Burying the Bodys of the Dead in Comon and Unfenced places to the prey of Hoggs or other Vermine Be it Enacted by the palatine and Lords proprietors by and with the advice of this present Grand Assembly and the Authority thereof and its hereby Enacted that there be in Every plantation a place Sett [*torn*] for Burral of Such as Dye upon the plantation and before the Corps be buried there be att least Three or four of the Neigh-

[19] The initial pages of these minutes are highly deteriorated. Although written on a poor quality of paper, they appear to be finished minutes and are signed by the justices of the General Court.

bourhood called who may in Case of Suspicion veiw the Corps and have Suspicon yett according to the Decent Custom of [*illegible*] they may accompany the Corps to the Grave nevertheless Gabriell Newby of the [*illegible*] aforesaid the premises all Knowing yett the aforesaid All and [*illegible*] on or about the 23rd Day of Aprell last past One John Deal <8> an Orphant Boy to the said Gabriel properly belonging and apperteyning did privately Bury or cause to be buried in Contempt of the aforesaid Act the Lords proprietors Laws and [*illegible*] appeares and Confesses to the private Buriall and throws himself on the Mercy of the Court And the Court haveing duely weighed and Considered the Whole Matter Ordered that the said Gabriel Newby pay Six Shillings and Eight pence for Such his offence with Costs and that he be dismissed without Day.

[George] Goarding and Frances his Wife by Thomas Snoden Esqr. her [*torn*] informed that [*torn*] this [*torn*] haveing the Fear of God before his Eyes but being led away by the Instigation of the Devill on the Eighth Day of this Instant at Little River within the Jurisdiction of this Court in and upon the Said George and Frances then and there being in the pease of our Said Soveraigne Lady the Queen an [Assault] make and them the said George Goarding and Frances his wife did sorely Beat and use and other injuries to them Done against the peace of our Said Soveraigne Lady the Queen her Crown and Dignity etc. Contrary to the forme of the Statute in such Cases made and provided And the Said Defendant comes and pleads not Guilty in Manner and forme as is Sett forth and Declared and of this throws himself upon the Country And Thomas Snoden on behalf of the Queen Likewise And the Marshall is Comanded to cause to come Twelve etc. to whome etc. who neither etc. by whome etc. and there came Richd. Mardren Matthew Raysons Robert Sawyer John Relf James Morgan Robert Morgan Wm. Fryly Henry Barnett Anthony Wherry Richard Lewis Wm. Ward and James Ward who being impannelled and Sworne Say We of the Jury find for the plaintiff.

Ordered that the said Robert Cole be fined Thirteen Shillings and four pence for Such his Offence with Costs alias Execution And that he find Sureties for his appearance at the next Generall Cort and that in the mean time he be upon his good behaviour.

George [Conner] comes and accknowledges an Assignment of a patent [*torn*] Three Hundred and Twenty Acres of Land in pequimons to Cha. Draper.

Winifrid Merrells comes being bound by recognizance from the last Cort and pleads to be dismist and upon her Subscription and humble prayer as aforesaid It is ordered that She be dismissed accordingly.

John Redwood by Thomas Snoden Esqr. his Attorney comes to prosecute his [Suite] by Attachment from the Last Cort against John pettiver in a plea of the Case and Declares that whereas the Said John pettiver [*torn*] Eighteenth Day of December 1703 was indebted <9> to the Said John Redwood in the Sume of Eight pounds Sterling did draw and Deliver unto the Said John Redwood Three [Severell] Bills of Exchange with proper hand of the Said John pettiver Signed and Dated the aforesaid Eighteenth Day of December 1703 and directed to me John Newton Merchant in Lawrence Lane London requireing thereby the said John Newton Thirty Dayes after his the said for pettivers First Bill of Exchange his Second nor Third not paid to pay unto or cause to be paid to the Said John Redwood or his order the Said Sume of Eight pounds Sterling And herto the Said Jno. pettiver the Day and year aforesaid upon himself assumed unto the Said John Redwood that for Case the Said John therefor should refuse to pay or accept of one of the Said Three Bills of Exchange according to the [*torn*] pettiver would pay faithfully pay or cause to be paid the value to the Said John Redwood on Order with Lawfull Charges and Interrest on the Same And the aforesaid John Redwood in fact Sayes that Messrs. perry and Lane of London Merchants by Order and Directions of the Said John Redwood did present the Said first Bill of Exchange unto the said John Newton to whom the Same was directed as aforesaid and Demanded acceptance and payment of the Said Bill according to the Tenor of the Same who did Utterly refuse to accept or make payment of the Same Whereupon the Said John Redwood by the Said Messrs. perry and Lane upon the Thirty first Day of [*illegible*] August Anno Domini 1704 according to the Use and Custome of Merchants did procure James [*illegible*] Notary and Tabellion public in London by Royall Authority [*torn*] of the Said first Bill of Exchange [*torn*] second nor third nor Either of them notbeing paid with Said [*torn*] of Exchange being due and not paid togeather with the Said protest here into Cort brought and read and to be produced relation being thereunto [*illegible*] doth and may appear Nontheless the Said John pettiver the Said Sume of Eight pounds with the lawfull Interest and Charges thereunto the Said John Redwood hath not paid tho' often thereunto requested but still doth refuse to pay to the Damage of the Said Jno. Redwood Sixteen pounds etc. And the Defendant by Edward Bonwick his Attorney comes and prayes Oyer of the Said Snodens power which was read unto him Then the Defendant comes by the

Said Bonwick his Attorney and Demurrs and Sayes that he was not Served with any process as the Law of this Country directs and that the [*torn*] as served upon the Said Defendant is Nonsense and [*illegible*] [*torn*] of that Service And the plaintiff Joynes in the Demurrer and the Cort haveing heard and Considered the whole Matter It is their opinion that the Said Demurrer be Sealed And then the Said Defendant comes by the Said Bonwick his Attorney and Defends the Force and Injury when etc. And Saith that he did not assume and of this he putts himself upon the Country and the plaintiff likewise And the Marshall was Comanded that he cause to come Twelve etc. to whom etc. who neither etc. by whom etc. And there came Mr. Richd. Madren Matthew Raysons Robert Sawyer John Relfe James Morgan Robert Morgan Wm. Fryly Henry Bonner Anthony Wherry <10> Richard Lewis Wm. Hardy and John Walker who being Sworn and impannelled Say We of the Jury find for the plaintiff.

Ordered that the Said John pettiver pay unto the Said John Redwood the aforesaid Eight pounds the principall And One pound Seven Shillings and Six pence Charge of the protest with Costs alias Execution. And the Said petiver prays and Injunction to stopp all further proceedings And that he may have a hearing in the high and honorable Cort of Chancery which is granted give-ing Security.

[*Torn*]

Argyle Simons appeares being bound by recognizance from the last Cort And on his humbel petition is Dismissed paying his Fees.

Upon petition of Walter Tanner praying to be allowed for his Attendance being Sumoned by [*blank*] Norcom widdow

Ordered that the Said Walter Tanner be paid by the Said Norcom for his goeing Comeing and Attendance half a Crowne by the Said Norcom with Costs alias Execution.

Thomas Snoden Assignee of Edward Norrington comes to prosecute his Sute against an Attachment from the last Cort [*torn*] Defendant Stands justly indebted to the [*torn*] of England in the full and just Sume of Seven pounds [*torn*] and by One Certaine Writeing obligatory Under the proper hand of [*illegible*] beareing Date the Ninth Day of January Anno Domini 169[*illegible*] and here into Cort brought doth and may appeare Nevertheless the Defendant the Said Sume of Seven pounds to the plaintiff hath not rendered etc. To the plaintiffs Damage Fourteen pounds etc. And the Defendant came not and a Nulla bona being returned on the Said Attachment the plaintiff prayes A Writt of Elegit according to the Directions and appointment of a Certaine Act of Assembly

Entituled (Where a Writ of Elegit Shalbe granted).

Ordered that a Writt of Elegit be granted according to the [*torn*] for the payment of the Debt and Damages aforesaid And that Captain James Cole Francis Beasely John Barrow Senior peter Jones Joseph Smith John Wyett Captain John Stepney or any Six of them Thomas Long or any Six of them appraise the Lands of the said Dawson being first Sworne before Some Majestrate.

Edmund Jennings Esqr. by Thomas Snoden his Attorney comes to prosecute his Sute against John pettiver in a plea of Debt that he unto the Said Edmund the Sum of Fourty pounds Eight Shillings and Tenn pence Currant Money of England which to the Said <11> Edmund he oweth and unjustly deteyneth etc. for that to witt whereas the Said John the 10th Day of Janry. 1705/6 by his certaine Writeing Obligatory under his proper hand and Seal and here into Cort brought whose date is the Same Day and year accknowledged himself to be held and firmely bound unto the Said Edmund in the full Sume of Fourty pounds Eight Shillings and Tenn pence Currant Money of England to be paid to the Said Edmund when he the Said John Should be thereunto requested Nevertheless the Said John the Said Sume of Fourty pounds Eight Shillings and Tenn pence to the Said Edmund hath not paid etc. to the Damage of the Said Edmund £40=8*s*.=10*d*. And the Defendant comes and Confesses to the Sume of Twenty pounds and [*torn*] pence.

Ordered that John pettiver pay unto Edmund [*torn*] Esqr. of England Twenty pounds Four Shillings and five pence with Costs alias Execution.

John porter Esqr. and Company comes by a Refference from the last Cort by Edward Bonwick his Attorney to prosecute his Sute against Samuell paine in a plea that he render unto him one Cable and Anchor which from them he unjustly Deteynes for that whereas the Said plaintiffs the 27th Day of March Anno Domini 1706 Delivered to the aforesaid Samuel One Cable and Anchor of the vallue of Twenty pounds Sterling to be Safely Kept and to be Delivered to the plaintiffs when he the Said Samuel Should be thereunto requested Yett the aforesaid Samuell tho often thereunto requested the Said Cable and Anchor to the plaintiffs hath not redelivered but the Same to him hitherto to [*torn*] and as Yett doth Deny and unjustly Deteyne to the Damage of the plaintiffs Fourty pounds Sterling etc. And the Defendant by Thomas Snoden his Attorney Defends the force and Injury when etc. and for plea Saith That the Anchor and Cable Claimed by the plaintiff in his Declaration he this Defendant by Order of the plaintiff Delivered to John Anderson late of this province and doth not Deteyne the same in manner and forme as the plaintiff hath alleaged in his Declaration And this he is ready to averr Et de hoc ponit Se Super patriam And the plaintiff by Edward Bonwick his Attorney for Replication Saies that the Defendant doth Deteyn the Anchor and Cable as before in his Declaration he the Said plaintiff hath affirmed and in like Manner he putts himself upon the Country And the Marshall was Comanded that he cause to come Twelve etc. to whom etc. who neither etc. by whom etc. And there came Mr. Richard Madren Matthew Raysins Robert Sawyer John Relfe James Morgan Robt. Morgan Wm. Fryly Henry Bonner Anthony Wherry Richard Lewis Wm. Hardy and John Walker who being Sworne and impannelled Say We of the Jury find for the Defendant.

Ordered that the Sute be Dismissed and the plaintiff pay Costs alias Execution.

<12> Mrs. Mary Clarke Widdow Executrix of the last Will and Testament of Mr. Arthur Workeman deceased comes and produces an Account of the Debts and Creditts of the Estate of the Said Workeman and prayes that shee may be admitted to prove the Same.

Ordered that patrick Gormack Francis Delamare Robt. Wallis Esqrs. and Thomas Abington gentleman or any Three of them doe audett the aforesaid Account and that the Same be attested before Some Majestrate and Returned to the next Generall Court.

Then this Cort adjourned till too morrow Morne Six of the Clock.

[*Illegible*] att 6 of the Clock in the Morne the Cort Mett and Sett.

[*Torn*] Wm. Duckenfeild Esqr. [*torn*] plea of [*torn*] Refference from the last Court and the plaintiff came not.

Ordered that the Sute be dismissed and the plaintiff pay Costs alias Execution.

Robert Sherreiffe comes by Mr. John Lawson his Attorney to prosecute his Sute against Richard Farrell in a plea of Debt and Sayes that the Defendant Stands justly indebted to the plaintiff in the full Sume of Seaventeen pounds and Tenn Head of Hoggs being Two Sows and Eight Shoates as in and by one certaine Obligatory under the proper hand of the Defendant beareing Date the 17th Day of October 1706 and here into Cort brought doth and may appear Nevertheless the Said Defendant the aforesaid Sum of Seventeen pounds and Tenn head of Hoggs unto the plaintiff hath not paid and Delivered tho: often etc. to the plaintiffs Damage

Fourty pounds etc. And the Defendant comes and Confesses.

Ordered that Richd. Farrell pay unto Robert Shrive Seventeen pounds and Tenn Head of Hoggs with Costs alias Execution.

The Honorable Colonel Thomas pollock and Ester his Wife Executors etc. of Colonel Wm. Wilkison against James Fuox in a plea of Debt by Consent of both parties refferred to the next Cort.

Bryant Fittzpatrick accknowledges the assignement of a Tract of Land to William Ludford.

Margrett McBride widdow by Thomas Snoden Esqr. her Majesties Attorney Generall desires this honorable Court to Understand and be informed that William Read and William Bray of this province not haveing the Fear of God before their Eyes but being ledd by the Instigation of the Devill On or about the 22th Day of May Anno Domini 1707 att the now Dwelling House of Cornelius Jones in the precinct of pascotanck in this Government did make an Assault on the said Complainant and Severall Injuries Insolences and abuses upon her did committ to her Grevious Damage against the peace of our Soveraigne Lady thc Queene her Crowne and Dignity and contrary to the force of Severall Statutes in Such Cases made and provided And the Defendants Wm. Bray and Wm. Read appear and plead not Guilty and for Tryall putt themselves upon the Country and the Complainant by the Said Snoden her Majesties Attorney generall likewise Therefore its Comanded the Marshall that he cause to come twelve etc. by whom etc. who etc. And there came to witt Messrs. Richd. Mardron Mr. Matthew Raysons Mr. Robert Sawyer Mr. John Relf <13> Mr. James Morgan Mr. Robert Morgan Mr. Wm. Fryly Mr. Henry Bonner Mr. Anthony Wherry Mr. John Walker Mr. Wm. Hardy and Mr. Richd. Lewis who Sworne and Impannelled Say We of the Jury find for the Defendants.

Ordered that the Sute be Dismissed.

A Deed of Sale of a Mill in the precinct of Chowan from James Blount to Mrs. Mary Blount proved by the Oaths of Mr. Nath. Chevin and Mr. Edward Bonwick.

A Sale of a Tract of Land from Mr. James Blount to Mrs. Mary Blount proved by the Oaths of the Honorable John Arderne Esqr. and Major Christopher Gale Esqr.

The honorable Landgrave Robert Daniel Esqr. comes to prosecute his Sute against Frederick Jones Esqr. Administrator of the Goods and Chattles of Thomas Dereham in a plea of Debt and Sayes that the Defendant in the Qualification aforesaid Stands justly indebted to the plaintiff in the full and just Sume of Fifteen pounds and Eighteen Shillings in porke att fourty Shillings per

Barrell as in and by one Certaine Writeing Obligatory under the proper hand of the Said Thomas Dereham beareing Date the Fifth Day of October Anno 1704 and hereinto Court brought relation being thereunto had doth and may appear Nevertheless etc. And the Defendant comes not and the plaintiff prayes an Attachment against the Goods of the Said Dereham in the Hands of the Said Jones and it is granted accordingly etc.

Ordered that Attachment Isue out against the Goods and Chattles of the Said Thomas Dereham in the hands of Frederick Jones the Administrator.

An Inventory of the Estate of Evan Thomas deceased was returned upon the Oath of Captain James Cole the Administrator.

Captain James Cole proves by [*illegible*] his Oath an Account against the Estate of Evan Thomas Deceased amounting to Thirty Six pounds Six Shillings and four pence with Creditt for [*blank*] as per Account.

Wm. Fryly and Grace his Wife accknowledges a Sale of a Tract of Land lying in pequimons precinct [*torn*].

The Honorable Landgrave Robert Daniel Esqr. comes to prosecute his Sute by attachment from the last Court against John Hecklefield gentleman in a plea of the Case and Complaines that the Defendant Stands indebted to the plaintiff in the full Sume of Twenty Eight pounds and Eight pence by Account as by wayes and meanes Convenient the plaintiff is ready to make appear which Said Sume of Twenty Eight pounds and Eight pence the Defendant hath not rendred to the plaintiff tho' often thereunto requested but Still doth refuse to render to the plaintiffs Damage Sixty pounds Sterling etc. And the Defendant by Edward Bonwick his Attorney comes and Defends the force and <14> Injury when etc. and Saith that he doth not Stand indebted to the plaintiff in the Sume of Twenty Eight pounds and Eight pence by account as the plaintiff in his Declaration hath falsely Suggested and of this he putts himself upon the Country And the plaintiff likewise Therefore its Comanded the Marshall that he cause to come Twelve etc. to whom etc. who neither etc. by whom etc. And there came Mr. Richd. Mardren Mr. Matthew Raysons Robert Sawyer John Relf James Morgan Robert Morgan Wm. Fryly Henry Bonner Anthony Wherry John Walker Wm. Hardy and Richd. Lewis who Sworne and Impannelled Say we find for the plaintiff Fifteen pounds Two Shillings and Eight pence half penny.

Ordered that John Hecklefield pay unto the Honorable Landgrave Robert Daniel Esqr. Fifteen pounds Two Shillings and Eight pence half penny with Costs alias Execution.

Upon petition of Thomas Johnson praying to be allowed for one Dayes goeing and comeing and one Dayes Goeing [*illegible*] and Two Dayes Attendance being Sumoned as an Evidence by Saml. paine att the Sute of Jno. porter Esqr. and Company.

Ordered that the said Thomas Johnson be paid by Saml. paine Eight Shillings and four pence for Such travell and Attendance with Costs alias Execution.

John Blount Esqr. comes to prosecute his Sute against Jno. Wilkins Marriner late Master of the Sloop Non Such in a plea of Trespass [*torn*] and Complaines that whereas the Said plaintiff att the Island of Bermuda Sometime in the Month of March last past did by Charles-worth Glover his Factor and after the Manner and Custome of Merchants putt on Board the aforesaid Sloope Nonsuch (whereof the Said Defendant was then Master) a Negro Boy named Jack which Said Negro Boy was by the Said Defendant to be brought as a passenger in the Said Sloop for a certain Hyre Unto this province of North Carolina the Danger of the Sea Excepted thereto be Delivered to the Said plaintiff his Factor or Assignes Yett Nevertheless the Said Defendant after his Safe arriveall into the port of pascotank River in this province the aforesaid Negro Boy did not Deliver to the plaintiff his Factor or Assignes But the Said Negro Boy did imploy in his Service and under his Comand Soe that the Said Negro Boy in the Service and under the Comand of the defendant as aforesaid was there Drowned Soe that the Said [*torn*] Defendant neither the said Negro Boy nor any Sattisfaction for the Same hath rendred or Delivered unto the plaintiff his Factor or Assignes tho often thereunto requested but the Same doth Still refuse to render to the plaintiffs Damage Fifty pounds Sterling etc. And the Said Defendant comes with out Writt by Edward Bonwick his Attorney and Defends the force and Injury when etc. and Saith that he hath not Assumed and of this he putts himself upon the Country And the plaintiff likewise Therefore its Comanded the Marshall that he cause [to] come Twelve etc. to whom etc. who neither etc. by whom etc. and there came Mr. Thomas peterson Mr. Thomas Boyd Mr. John pettiver <15> Mr. Joseph Redding Mr. William Vaughan Captain Thomas Luten Mr. William Wilson Mr. John Relf Mr. Robert Sawyer Mr. John Walker Mr. Nath. Chevin Mr. Richard Mardron who Sworne and impannelled Say We of the Jury find for the plaintiff Four pounds Tenn Shillings.

Ordered that John Wilkins pay unto John Blount Esqr. Four pounds Tenn Shillings with Costs alias Execution.

Then this Cort adjourned 'till 8 of the Clock too morrow Morne.

Augt. 3d The Cort Mett att 8 of the Clock and Sitt present ut

Supra and Mr. Barcliff.

Mr. Ming absent and then adjourned for half an hour.

Att half an hour the Cort Mett and Sitt.

Mr. Barcliff and Mr. Mings absent.

Richard Odum comes by Thomas Snoden Esqr. his Attorney to prosecute his Sute against Richard Burke and Thomas Everett of a plea that they render unto the said plaintiff One hundred pounds Currant Money of this Country which to him they oweth and from him unjustly Deteynes for that whereas the aforesaid Defendants the Sixth Day of October 1706 by their Certaine Bill or writeing Obligatory under their proper hands and here into Cort brought whose date is the Same Day and year obleidged themselves their heires and assignes to Deliver up a Bond past by the Said George White and John White to the Said plaintiff for the accknowledgment of a Tract of Land and plantation and all Moveables when they should be thereunto requested to the true performance of which the Defendants by the Said Bill did bind themselves their heyers and Assignes in the penalty of one Hundred pounds Currant Money of this Country to be paid on Demand and the aforesaid plaintiff in fact Saith that the aforesaid Defendants nor Either of them hath not Delivered Unto the plaintiff the aforesaid Bond past by the aforesaid John White and George White to the aforesaid plaintiff tho' often thereunto requested by which Account Accrews to the said plaintiff to have of the aforesaid Defendants the aforesaid Sume of One hundred pounds Currant Money of this Country Yett nevertheless the Said Defendants nor either of them the Said One hundred pounds to the plaintiff hath not paid tho' often thereunto requested to the plaintiffs Damage One hundred pounds etc. And the Defendant Richard Burke comes and Confesses And makeing Sufficient Matter appear that this Case Should be disputed in the Honorable Cort of Chancery prayes that an Injunction may be granted to Stopp all further proceedings att Comon Law 'till the Case be there heard the next Cort of Chancery which is granted accordingly upon his giveing Security.

John porter Esqr. comes by Edward Bonwick his Attorney to prosecute his Scire facias against Frederick Jones Administrator of the Goods and Chattles of Thomas Dereham deceased and the Marshall haveing made returne Scire feci and the Defendant came not.

Ordered that a Judgment obteyned against the Said Thomas Dereham by the Said Porter for Six pounds Eight Shillings and Eight pence half penny with Costs att a Generall Cort held the 27th Day of Augt. Anno Domini 1706 be affirmed with Costs.

Thomas Twiddy bound over by Recognizance by pascotank Cort [*torn*] the penalty of Tenn pounds haveing made faylure in his appeareance And <16> John Cartwrite his Security in the penalty of Five pounds haveing fayled to bring forth the Body of the Said Twiddy whom he undertook to have here this Day

Ordered that Certificate of their Faylure be made into the Honorable Cort of Chancery.

And then this Cort adjourned for an hour.

Att an hour the Cort mett and Sitt.

A Letter of Attorney from John Clarke to Thomas Snoden Esqr. proved by the Oath of Charles-worth Glover.

Wm. Houghton comes to prosecute his appeall from the precinct Cort of perquimans against John Norcom and the Question there in Debate was whether the Declaration was valid and good in Law and that Court was of opinion that it was good and valid in Law And the Defendant Houghton prayed that all further proceedings might be stopt 'till a further hearing be had of the premises in this Honorable Generall Cort And this Court haveing Seriously Considered the whole Matter and duely weighed the whole proceedings are of opinion that the Said Declaration is good and valid in Law and Ordered that the Judgment of the precinct Cort of pequimons is hereby Confirmed and that the appeal be dismissed with Costs alias Execution.

Upon petition of Anthony Wherry praying to be allowed for one Dayes Comeing One Dayes goeing and Two dayes attendance being Sumoned by John Norcom and Wm. Houghton

Ordered that Anthony Wherry be paid by John Norcom Eight Shillings and four Pence for Shuch his Travell and Attendance with Costs alias Execution.

Upon petition of Mary Stanton praying to be allowed for One Dayes comeing and One Dayes goeing and One Dayes Attendance being Sumoned by John Blount Esqr. in his Sute against Jno. Willkins

Ordered that Mary Stanton be allowed Five Shillings Tenn pence for Such her Travell and Attendance with Costs alias Execution.

Upon petition of Mary Keaton praying to be allowed for one Dayes comeing and one Day goeing and one Dayes attendance being Sumoned by John Blount Esqr. in his Sute against Jno. Wilkins

Ordered that the Said Mary Keaton be paid by the Said John Blount Five Shillings and Tenn pence for Such her Travell and

Attendance with Costs alias Execution.

Mr. Mings and Mr. Barcliffe present.

Elizabeth Tomlin Spinster comes by David pritchard her Attorney to presente her Sute against George Goarding and Frances his wife in a plea of the Case and Complaines that whereas the aforesaid Frances on or about the Month of August last past att the now Dwelling house of the Said George with Evill inten to take away the Good name [*torn*] and reputation of the plaintiff did then and there in the hearing of Divers of her Majesties Leige people pronounce utter and Declare <17> these falce Scandalous and Malicious Words videlicet that Shee meaning the plaintiff was as Surely with Child as Ever of Frances Goarding was and by John Simson and divers other Falce Scandalous and Malicious Words to and of the plaintiff did then and there Declare and Utter whereby the plaintiff being then sole a Spinster and unmarried is Damynifyed and hath Damage to the Vallue of One Hundred pounds etc. And the Defendant Georg in his proper person comes and Defend the force and Injury when etc. and for plea Saith they are not Guilty and for tryall puts themselves upon the Country And the plaintiff likewise Therefore its comanded the Marshall that he cause to come twelve etc. who etc. by whom etc. and there came to witt Mr. Robert Harrison Mr. David Jackson Mr. Henry Warren Mr. Richd. Farrell Mr. John Jones Mr. Matthew Raysins Mr. Henry Bonner Mr. Wm. [*Torn*] Mr. Bartho. Hewitt Mr. Tho. Collins Mr. Tho. Barcliff Who Sworne and impannelled Say we of the Jury find for the plaintiff Seven pounds And the Defendant by Edward Bonwick their Attorney moves in arrest of Judgment and Sayes that the Words in the plaintiffs Declaration mentioned are not Actionable and this he does averr and prayes Day to make good the Same.

Ordered that Judgment be Suspended 'till the next Court and that the Defendant doe then make good his Averement otherwise Judgment to pass on the Verdict.

A Sale for a Tract of Land was by Bryan Fitzpatrick to Thomas Holloway.

Thomas Holloway accknowledges the Sale of a Tract of Land to Obadiah Fair.

John Doe comes by Thomas Snoden her Majesties Attorney Generall Desires this Honorable Cort to Understand and be informed that Hester the Wife of John Walker of this province not haveing the Fear of God before her Eyes but being ledd away by the Instigation of the Devill on or about the Six and Twenteth Day of March last past in the precinct of Chowan within this province Mary the wife of James Smith then and there in the peace of our Soveraigne Lady the Queen did Assault and her the Said Mary Sorely beat and abuse and other Injuries to her Done to her Griveous Damage against the peace of our Soveraign Lady the Queen and Contrary to the forme of the Statute in Such Cases made and provided And the Defendants by Edward Bonwick their Attorney come and plead not Guilty and for Tryall putt themselves upon the Country And Thomas Snoden Attorney Generall likewise Therefore its Comanded the Marshall that he cause to come Twelve etc. and whom etc. who neither etc. by whom etc. and there came Mr. Robert Harrison David Jackson Henry Warren Richd. Farrell John Jones Matthew Raysons Henry Bonner Wm. Hardy James Morgan Bartholomew Hewitt Thomas Collins Thomas Barcliff who Sworne and Empannelled Say Not Guilty.

Ordered that the plaint be Dismissed.

<18> Upon the petition of Wm. Griffin praying to be allowed for One Dayes comeing and One Dayes goeing And Two Dayes Attendance being Sumoned as an Evidence for John Blount Esqr. in his Sute against John Wilkins

Ordered that the Said Wm. Griffin be paid Eight Shillings and four pence by the Said John Blount for Such his Travell and Attendance with Costs alias Execution.

Robert Cox in the Sume of £20 Sterling
David Pritchard in the Sume of £10 Sterling } by way of Recognizance
Wm. D[*torn*]son in the Sume of £10 Sterling

[Which Sum] to be leavyed upon their Lands and Tenemants goods and Chattles to the use of our Soveraigne Lady the Queen Upon Condition that the Said Robert Cox Shall appear att the next Generall Court to be held for this Government and in the mean time to be of the Good behavior towards all her Majesties Leige people.

[*Signed:*]

C. Gale, James Minge, William Barclift.

FILE PAPERS IN SUITS AND PROSECUTIONS

[*Blount* v. *Wilkins*]

[*CCR 148*]

No. Carolina Ss. To the provost Marshall or his Deputy

These are in her Majestyes name to will and require you to Arrest the body of Jno. Wilkins and him Safely hold Soe that he be and appeare at the next Generall Court to be holden at the house of Captain Jno. Hecklefield in Litle river on the last Tuseday in July next then and there to Answer the plaint of John Blount Esqr. in a plea of Trespass on the Case and have there this writt Dated at the Secretarys Office this 18th day of Aprill Anno Domini 1707.

Testis T. Knight

[*Endorsed:*]
Non es adventes

[*CCR 148*]

No. Carolina Ss. To the provost Marshall or his Deputy.

These are in her Majestyes name to will and require you to Sumons Thos. Danforth personally to be and appeare at the next Generall Court to be holden at the house of Captain Jno. Hecklefield in Litle river on the last Tuseday in July next then and there to Give Evidence in a Cause there depending between Jno. Blount Esqr. plaintiff and Jno. Wilkins defendant on behalfe of the plaintiff and have there this Sumons Dated at the Secretarys Office this 25th day of Aprill Anno Domini 1707.

Testis T. Knight Secretary

[*Endorsed:*]
Sumons for Thos. Danforth
Non es adventes

[*CCR 148*]

<*Wilkins ads. Blount*>

And the said Defendant by Edwd. Bonwicke his Attorney comes and Defends the force and injury when etc. And saith that he hath not assumed and of this he puts himselfe upon the Country.

Bonwicke per Defendante

And the plaintiff likewise Boush [etc.]
[*Endorsed:*]
Wilkins ads. Blount
Wee of the Jury find for the plaintiffe four pounds Ten shillings[20]

[*CCR 148*]

The Deposition of Thomas Danforth of full Age Testifyeth and Saith That being at the house of mr. Joseph Jordan in Pascotank river in No. Carrolina sometime about the beginning of April Tho. Kempton Sailor on bord the Sloop Nonesuch John Wilkins master (lately arriv'd from Bermuda) came on Shore to said Jordans and inform'd me in presence of Mr. Jordan, his wife, Mrs. Keyton and Mrs. Stanton and others, that the negro Boy Jack (who belonged to Mr. Jno. Blount) was Drowned, and I bid him tell me the Manner and Circumstance's of the accident whereupon he gave me the following answer videlicet That being on bord with the Master John Wilkins, Enos Talmag the mate and Jno. Arnold a Sailor Wm. Griffin a hired man two negro Slaves, and all Buissy Stowing Barrils and other goods the said Kempton Leaned over the Side and Looked at the Negro Boy who was play-

[20] *With Costs of Suitt in Consideration of the Negro boy* written and lined out.

ing in the Canoe the Master called to said Kempton to do some buissness and not Stand Idle looking on the Boy, whereupon said Kempton went to perform the Same and in a Small time after the Buissness being don, the master and one of the hands put of from the Side in order to come to me for another Load, And had not gott quite out of call before he heard the men on bord hail him, and return'd to the Vessell, where the men told him the negro was not in the Vessell, after Strict Serch within and without bord, and no sign of him they returnd on Shore, the Said Kempton further said (and so did all that were on bord) that they were so full of buissness they never thought of the boy 'til they were going to Shore neither (tho' most of 'em were constant on the Deck) did they here any Noise, and this was about four or five days after the Lawfull entry of said vessell, and after they began to Load. The foregoing is the true account of what I heard from Thomas Kempton concerning the Negro Boy Jack.

Thos. Danforth

Suffolk Ss. Boston July 4th 1707

The above Thomas Danforth made Oath to the trouth of the foregoing narative of the Negro Boy Jack.

Jurat Coram Jer. Dummer Tabellion Public

[*CCR 148*]

North Carolina ss.

The Deposition of Charles=Worth Glover aged: Eighteen yeares or thereabouts Examined and Sworne Saith as Followeth That Sometime in the latter End of Feabry. last this Deponent went out of this Government in the Sloop Non Such John Wilkins Master bound for the Island of Bermudoes and being Factor to Jno. Blount Esqr. did according to his Order and Instructions purchass one Negro Boy att the said Island of Bermudoes and putt him on Board the Said Sloop Non Such in Order to his being Delivered to the Said Blount in North Carolina who told this Deponent that he had agreed with one Mr. Dantford (who had the Said Sloop upon hire) for Twenty five Shillings per head for the passage of a Negro or Negroes from thence to North Carolina which this Deponent accquainted the Said Wilkins of who replyed that it was well Enough or used Words to that Effect and upon which this Deponent did putt on Board the Said Sloop Non-Such One Negro Boy named Jack and for whom the Said Wilkins Master of the Said Sloop tooke out a Pass and on his Account charged this Deponent with it and att the arriveall in Pascotanke River in North Carolina this Deponent left the Said Negro on Board the Said Sloop the Said Wilkins telling him that he would be in Little River in Some Short time and further Saith not but what he has Declared upon his Oath before the honorable the Generall Court about Bread for the Said Boy.

Charles worth Glover

[*CCR 148*]

I the Subscriber doe as in the presence of God the wittness of the truth and under the penalty of perjury declare that what I Shall Say in the action between John Blount Esqr. plaintiff and John Wilkins Defendant Shalbe the truth the whole truth and nothing but the truth.

The marke of Mary Keytones

[*Coles and wife* v. *Frayly*]

[*CCR 148*]

No. Carolina Ss. To the honorable the Generall Court

Captain James Coles of precinct of pequimans and Mary his wife Complaines of Wm. [*illegible*] of the precinct of Chowan of a plea that he render unto the said plaintiffs the full Sume of Fifty pounds sterling which to the said plaintiffs he owes and unjustly deteyneth for that to witt whereas the said defendant on the 18th Day of December 1704 by his Certainie writeing obligatory with the Seale of the said Wm. Sealed and here in to Court brought whose date is the Same day and yeare acknowledged himselfe [*illegible*] Stand Justly Indebted to the plaintiffs in the full and Just Summe of Fifty pounds Sterling to be paid to the said plaintiffs when he the said Wm. sho'd be thereunto requested Yet nevertheless the said Defendant the said Summe of fifty pounds to the plaintiffs hath not paid tho' often thereunto requested but the same doth Still refuse to pay to the plaintiffs Damage Fifty pound Sterling and thereupon they bring their Suite etc.

T. Knight Secretary

[*Endorsed:*]
Narratio
Coles versus Fryly
In Debt
Entered June 30th: 1707

[*CCR 148*]

No. Carolina Ss. To the provost Marshall or his Deputy.

These are in her Majestyes name to will and require you to Arrest the body of Wm. Fryly and him Safeley hold soe that he be and appeare at the next Generall Court to be holden at the house of Captain Jno. Hecklefield in Litle river on the last Tusday in July next then and there to Answer to Captain James Cole of the precinct of pequimons and Mary his wife of a plea that he render unto the said plaintiffs the Sume of Fifty pounds Sterling which to the said plaintiffs he oweth and unjustly deteyneth etc. and have you there this writt Dated at the Secretarys Office this 30th day of June Anno Domini 1707.

Testis T. Knight Secretary

[*Endorsed:*]

Breve
Coles versus Fryly
In Debt
Exequted by Robt. Fendall Provost Marshall

[*Crown* v. *Cox*]

[*CCR 148*]

N. Carolina

Wheras Geo. Gordon maketh complaint that upon the 8 of this Instant Robert Cox of peqamons precinct made an assault upon the complainant and his wife at his the said Complainants dwelling house in little River and them did beat and strike and alsoe published a Scandalous Libell of the Complainants Wife against the peace of our Sovereigne Lady the Queen.

These are in her Majesties name to require you to cause the said Robert Cox to come before me on Munday next to answer the said complaint and summons James Foster and Mary his wife and Eliz. Buckney as evidence on behalfe of her Majesties Given under my hand the 9 of July 1707.

To Jno. Raper or W. Glover
Esaue Albertson Constables

[*CCR 191*]

And James Foster ut supra that he and Mary his wife shall appear ut supra to give Evidence etc.

And the said Robert Cox ut supra in the summ of twenty pounds and Wm. Jackson in the summ of ten pounds on condition that the said Cox appear ut supra to answer the said Complaint.

Given under my hand and seal the day and year above written.

W. Glover

[*Endorsed:*]
Information versus Cox

[*CCR 148*]

N. Carolina Ss. July 14 1707

And the said Robert Cox came before me and to the assault upon the said Geo. Gorden he confesseth as alsoe to the libel but the assault upon Frances the wife of the said Gordan he denyeth.

Mary Foster aged 39 years or therabout examined and sworne deposeth that about the 8 day of this Instant the depont was at the house of Geo. Gorden in Pequimons precinct and some dispute arising about some sider which the said Frances Gorden said should not be drunk there Robert Cox struck the said Frances with a staf and called her salt whore and when Geo. Gorden came to rescue his wife he the said Cox struck the said Geo. Gorden over the head soe that the staff broke and again often repeated that the said

Frances was a whore and he would prove it and called witnesse and further saith not.

Sworne before me W. Glover — Frances Foster <*Sign*>

[*Illegible*] that the above named Geo. Gorden came before me and acknowledged himselfe to be indebted to his Excellency the Palatine and Lords proprietors the summ of five pound on condition that he the said Gorden shall appear second day of the next Generall court to be holden at the house of Capt. Jno. Hecklefield to prosecute his complaint on behalfe of our Soveraigne lady the Queen against the above named Robt. Cox.

[*Crown* v. *Jennings and Davis*]

[*CCR 139*]

No. Carolina Ss. To the provost Marshall or his Deputy

These are in her Matyes name to will and require you to Sumons Jno. Jenings and Samll. Davis personally to be and appeare at the next Generall Court to be holden at the house of Captain Jno. Hecklefield in Litle river on the last Tuseday in July next then and there to Answer to all Such [*illegible*] and things as shall be objected against them by her Majestyes Attorney Generall Concerneing the packing of a Certaine Barrell of porke at Austin Scarbro's Contrary to Certaine Lawes in that Case made and provided and have there this Sumons Dated at the Secretarys Office this 30th day of June Anno Domini 1707.

Testis T. Knight Secretary

[*Endorsed:*]
Sumons for Jno. Jennings, Samll. Davis ad sectam Domina Regina

[*CCR 139*]

No. Carolina Ss. To the provost Marshall or his Deputy

These are in her Majestyes name to will and require you to Sumons Tho. Abington Jno. Hawkins Jno. Relfe Geo. Harris Cornelius Jones personally to be and appeare at the next Generall Court then and there to give Evidence against Jno. Jennings and Samll. Davis on behalfe of our Soveraigne Lady the queene and have there this Sumons Dated at the Secretarys Office this 30th: day of June Anno Domini 1707.

Testis T. Knight Secretary

[*Endorsed:*]
Sumons for Thos. Abington, Jno. Hawkeins, Jno. Relfe, Corn. Jones, Geo. Harris

[*Crown* v. *Nuby*]

[*CCR 140*]

No. Carolina ss. To the Honorable the Generall Court

John Doe by Thomas Snoden Esqr. her Majestyes Attorney Generall and procurator for the Lords proprietors of this Goverment desires this Honorable Court to understand and be informed that whereas in and by an Act of Assembly intituled private Burialls prohibited it is Enacted in these words videlicet Whereas the private Burialls of Servants and other persons may give occasion of much Scandal to divers persons tho' Some times undeserrvd of being Guilty of their Deaths from which if the persons be innocent which are Suspected there cann be noe vindication and if Guilty noe punishment by reason they are the most part buried without the Knowledge or [Desire] of any other then Such of the Family as by nearness of Relation as husband wife or Child are unwilling or Servants are fearfull to make discovery if Murder were Comitted for prevention whereof as alsoe for takeing away that barbarous Custome of burying the Corps of the Dead in Comon or unfenced places to the pray of Hoggs of other Vermine Be it Enacted by the palatine and Lords proprietors by and with the advice and Consent of this present Generall assembly and the Authority thereof and it's hereby Enacted that there bee in Every plantation a place Sett apart and fenced for a Buriall of Such as dye upon the plantation and before the Corps be buried there be att least three or four of the Neighbours called who may in Case of Suspicion veiwe the Corps and if noe Suspicion yett according to the decent Custome of all Christendom they may accompany the Corps to the Ground. Nevertheless Gabriell Newby of the aforesaid province the premises well Knowing yett the aforesaid Act and the Authority thereof altogeather comtemning and dispiseing on or about the 23d Day of Aprill last past One John Deal an Orphant Boy to the Said Gabriell properly belonging and apperteyning did privately bury or cause to be buried in Contempt of the aforesaid Act the Lords proprietors [*torn*] Laws etc.

Snoden per Domini proprietors

[*Endorsed:*]
Information against Newby

[*Crown* v. *Reed and Bray*]

[*CCR 148*]

North Carolina ss. To the Honorable the Generall Court.

Margrett McBride widdow by Thomas Snoden Esqr. her Majesties Attorney Generall desires this honorable Court to understand and be informed that Wm. Reed and Wm. Bray of this Province not haveing the fear of God before their Eyes but being led away by the Instigation of the Devill On or about the 22th Day of May anno Domini 1707 att the now Dwelling house of Cornelais Jones in the precinct of pascotanke in this Goverment did make an Assault on the said Complainant and Severall Injuryes insolencies and abuses upon her did Comitt to her Griveous Damage against the peace of our Soveraigne Lady the Queene her Crowne and Dignity and Contrary to the force of Severall Statutes in Such Cases made and provided.

Snoden per Domina Regina

[*Endorsed:*]
McBride against Reed and allius
Information
We of the Jurrey findth for the defindent

[*CCR 148*]

No. Carolina Ss. Wm. Glover Esqr. President of the Councell and Commander in Cheif etc. To the Worshipfull the Justices of the peace of the precinct of Corratuck or to any of them Greeting

Whereas Mrs. Margaret McBride hath made Grevious Complaint before me that Wm. Reed Wm. Bray Wm. Russell on or about the 22d day of May Anno 1707 at the now dwelling house of Corneilus Jones in the precinct of pascotanke did make an Assault upon the Complainant and Severall Injuryes Insolencyes [*torn*] abuses upon her did Comitt against the peace of our Soveraigne Lady the Queene that now is and for which Shee hath [*torn*] earnestly prayed releife.

Thesese are therefore in her Majestyes name to require you or any of you to whome these presents shall Come that Imeadiatly upon Sight or recipt thereof you Compell the aforesaid Wm. Reed Wm. Bray and Wm. Russell to appeare before you without delay then and there Severally to Enter into Recognizance with two Sufficient Securityes in the Sume of Twenty pounds and the Securityes in the Sume of tenn pounds apeice with Condition that they Severally make their appeareance at the next Generall Court then and there to Answer the said Complaint and that in the meane tyme they be of their good abearance towards her Majestye and all her Leidge people especially towards the aforesaid Margarett McBride And if in Case they or either of them shall refuse soe to doe that then you forthwith Cause them soe refuseing to be Conveyed to her Majestyes Goale there to remaine without Baile or Mainprise untill thence delivered by due Course of Law And you shall Certify your proceedings herein under your hands and Seales to the next Generall Court together with this writt Dated the 10th day of July Anno Domini 1707 And in the Sixth yeare of the raigne of our Soveraigne Lady Anne by the Grace of God Queen of Great Britaine etc.

W. Glover

[*CCR 148*]

Wheras a Writt of suplicavit Granted by the Honorable the president dated the 10th Instant July directed for Execution to the Justices of the peace of the precient of Corrotuck or any of them, the same Coming to my hand the 18th said month, did in obedience therto forthwith Issue warrant Requiring the Constable to attatch the bodies of Mr. William Reed Mr. William Bray and Mr. William Russell and them to Cause to appear before me, by virtue and force of which the Constable on the day of the date herof Caused Mr. William Reed and Mr. William Bray personall to appear before me, whome I have Caused seaverally to Enter Into Recognizences with two sufficient surties in the sume of twenty pound Each and the surties in the sume of ten pounds apeice with Condition that said Reed and Bray make their appearence at next Generall Court to answer such Complaints as shall be by Mrs. Margrett mcbride Exhibitted against them and also to be of good behaviour and abeareance towards hur Majestie and all hur good subjects and Leedge people, as by Recognizence herwith sent will more at Large appear Given under my hand and seall this 23d day of July 1707.

Wm. Swann

[*Endorsed:*]
Mack=bride versus Reed and Allius

[*CCR 148*]

Know all men by these presents that we William Reed Thomas Tayler and Benjamine Tulle are heild and firmly bound unto our Soveraigne Lady the Queen Ann by the Grace of god of England etc. Queen in the full and Just sume of forty pound sterling and William Reed being bound in twenty pound of the aforsaid sume and Thomas Tayler and Benjamine Tulle Each of them ten pounds apeace to which payment of the afforsaid sumes of money we the parties above named do bind us our heirs Executors administrators firmly by these presents in witness wherof we the parties above named have herunto putt our hands and seals this 23d day of July 1707.

The Condition of this obligation is such that if the above bound William Reed shall appear at the next Generall Court and there to answer such Complaines as shall by Mrs. Margrett Mackbride be Exhibitted against him and also be of good behaviour and good abaring toward hur Majestie and all other hur Majesties good subjects and Leedge people but more especially towards the person of Mrs. Margt. Mackbride then this obligation to be voyd Else to Remaine in full force and virtue.

Testes
Jos. Wicker
Peter Poyner Senior

William Reed
Thomas Tayler
Ben. Tulle

[*Endorsed:*]
Wm. Reeds Recognizance

[*CCR 192*]

I the Subscriber doe as in the presence of God the Wittness of the truth and under the penalty of perjury declare that what I Shall Say in the Matter now att Issue between our Soveraigne Lady the Queene plaintiff and Wm. Reed and Wm. Bray Shall bee the truth The whole Truth and nothing but the truth.

Elisabeth Stone

[*Crown* v. *Sawyer*]

[*CCR 148*]

No. Carolina Ss. To the provost Marshall or his Deputy

These are in her Matyes name to will and require you to Summons Thos. Sawyer personally to be and appeare at the next Generall Court to be holden at the house of Captain John Hecklefield in Litle river on the last Tuseday in July next then and there to Answer to all Such matters and things as shall be objected against him by the Queens Attorney Generall Concerning the makeing and putting up of tarr in Severall Barrells Contrary to the Severall Lawes in these Cases made and provided and have you there this Sumons Dated at the Secretarys Office this 30th day of June Anno Domini 1707.

Testis T. Knight Secretary

[*Endorsed:*]
Sumons for Thomas Sawyer ads. Domina Regina

[*CCR 148*]

No. Carolina Ss. To the provost Marshall or his Deputy

These are in her Majestyes name to will and require you to Sumons Captain Jno. Robinson and Mr. Wm. Reed personally to be and appeare at the next Generall Court to be holden at the house of Captain Jno. Hecklefield in Litle river on the last Tuseday in July next then and there to give Evidence against Thos. Sawyer on behalfe of the Queen and have there this Sumons Dated at the Secretarys Office this 30th day of June Anno Domini 1707.

Testis T. Knight Secretary

[*Endorsed:*]
Sumons for Captain Robinson and Wm. Reed

[*Crown* v. *Walker and wife*]

[*CCR 191*]

North Carolina ss. To the Honorable Generall Court

John Doe by Thomas Snoden her Majesties Attorney Generall desires this Honorable Court to understand and be inform'd That Hesther the wife of John Walker of this Province not having the fear of God before her Eyes but being led away by the Instigation of the Devill on or about the Six and Twentyeth Day of March last past in the precinct of Chowan within this Province Mary the wife of James Smith there and then in the peace of our Soveraigne Lady the Queen did assault and her the Said Mary Sorely beat and abuse and other Injuryes to her done to her grievous Dammage against the peace of our Said Soveraigne Lady the Queen and Contrary to the forme of the Statute in Such Cases made and provided.

Snoden per Domina Regina

[*Endorsed:*]
Domina Regina versus Walker and uxor
Information Sur pacis
Mary Smith: Jurat

Martha Smith Jurat
Eliz. Morris—Jurat for the Defendant
Wee of the Jewery fines for the defendandat

[*Daniell* v. *Hecklefield*]

[*CCR 140*]

No. Carolina Ss. To the honorable the Generall Court etc.

The Honorable Landgrave Robert Daniell is plaintiff against Jno. Hecklefield gentleman defendant in a plea of the Case and Complaines that the defendant Stands Indebted to the plaintiff in the full Summe of Twenty Eight pounds and Eight pence by account as by wayes and meanes Convenient the plaintiff is ready to make appeare which Said Summe of Twenty Eight pounds and Eight pence the defendant hath not rendred to the plaintiff tho' often thereunto requested but the Same doth Still refuse to render to the plaintiffs Damage Sixty pounds Sterling and thereupon he brings this Suite etc.

Vera Copia Testis T. Knight Secretary

[*CCR 139*]

No. Carolina Ss. To the provost Marshall or his Deputy

These are in her Majestyes name to will and require you to Attach Soe much of the Estate of Captain [*torn*] Hecklefield where ever to be found in this Government as will pay and Satisfy The Honorable Landgrave Robert Daniell Esqr. the Sume of Twenty Eight pounds and Eight pence and in Safe Custody keep untill otherwise ordered by due Course of Law and make returne of your proceedings herein to the next Generall Court Dated at the Secretarys Office this 17th day of June Anno Domini 1707.

Testis T. Knight Secretary

[*Endorsed:*]
Attachment versus Hecklefield ad sectam Daniell
Exequted one Negro woman Caled Jeane

[*CR 24.901.1*]

Capt. John Hackelfield is Dr.

	£ *s.* *d.*
To: 8 Glasses Nott Accounted when wee last Setteled Accounts to bee payed in Kind per the [*illegible*]	01:00:00
Noer. 16 To your Bill when Setteld all Accounts	19:32:09½
To: 19 Feett: ¾ of Glases att 18*d.*	01:09:07½
To: John Shaw att Ashly River	00:05:00
To: Guys work and Lead	00:03:09
To: my Chaigine	05:02:00
To: 500 Nayles	00:07:06
Totall is	28:00:08

payed	12:17:11½
Rest Dew	15:02:08½

Per the Contra is Cr.	£ s. d.
By 23 Tythables att: 9*s*: per head	10:07:00
By my Noate pd. Mr. Nortton	02:08:07½
By 2 Thimbles	00:01:04
By Expense att last Court ½ pt. Burnd Rum	00:01:00
	12:17:11½

March the 5th 1706/7 per Robt. Daniell

North Carolina ss. July 31th 1707

Att a Court held for the Goverment aforesaid the above account was proved by the Oath of the Honorable Landgrave Robt. Daniell Esqr. and that he has received noe part or parcell thereof but what he has given Creditt for att the time of Comenceing the Action.

Testis Tho. Abington Clericus Curiae

[*Jennings* v. *Pettiver*]

[*CCR 148*]

No. Carolina
Albemarle County Ss. To the honorable the Generall Court etc.

The Honorable Edmund Jenings Esquire Complaines [*torn*] John Pettiver of the County and Collony aforesaid Merchant [*torn*] that he render unto the said Edmund the Summe of Forty pounds Eight Shillings and Tenn pence Current Money of England which to the Said Edmund he oweth and unjustly deteyneth etc. for that [*torn*] whereas the said John the Sixteenth day of Janry. 1705/6 by his Certaine writeing obligatory under [*torn*] proper hand and Seale and here into Court brought whose date [*torn*] the Same day and yeare acknowledged himselfe to be held and firmly bounden unto the Said Edmd. in the full Summe of Forty pounds [*torn*] Shillings and Tenn pence Current Money of England [*torn*] said Edmund when he the Said John should be there[*torn*] Nevertheless the said John the Said Sume of Forty pounds Eigh[*torn*] and tenn pence to the Said Edmund hath not paid tho' often there [*torn*] requested but the Same doth Still refuse to pay to the Damage [*torn*] the Said Edmund Forty pounds Eight Shillings and ten pence Sterling [*torn*] thereupon he brings this Suite etc.

T. Knight Secretary

[*Endorsed:*]
Narratio
Jenings versus Pettiver

In Debt
Entered June 30th: 1707

[*CCR 148*]

[N.] Carolina Ss. To the Provost Marshall or his Deputy

These are in her Majestyes name to will and require you to Arrest the body of Jno. Pettiver and him Safely hold soe that he be and appeare at the next Generall Court to be holden at the house of Captain Jno. Hecklefield in Litle river on the last tuseday in July next then and there to Answer to Edmd. Jennings of a plea that he render unto the said Edmund the Summe of [forty] pounds Eight shillings and tennpence Current Money of England which to the said Edmd. he oweth and unjustly deteyneth etc. and have you there this writt Dated at the Secretarys Office this 30th day of June Anno Domini 1707.

Testis T. Knight Secretary

[*Endorsed:*]
Breve
Jennings versus Pettiver
In Debt
Cepi Corpus

[*CCR 188*]

No. Carolina Comm. Albermarle

[Novst.] universi per presentes me Johen Pettiver de Comm. et Colonia predicta mercatorem teneri et [sumitur] Obligari Honorabili Edmundo Jennings in Colonia Virginia armigero in quadragenta Libris, Octo Solidis, et decem denari bona et Current, anglia moneta Solvenda ad Edmond. Jennings aut Suo Certo in hacparte atturnato [*illegible*] admine, vel assign: Suis ad quam quidem Solutionem tene et fidelit: Cauendum obliga me Heredis Executors et Administrators meus [*illegible*] per presentes, Segillo meo Sigillat dat quarto anno [Regnum] Regina Anna nunc Anglia etc. annoque Domini 1705/6 et die decimo [Seato] Jan. in anno predicta.

The Condition of this Obligation is such that of the above bounden Jno. Pettiver his Heirs Executors administrators do well and truly pay or cause to be paid unto the Said Ed. Jennings his heirs Executors administrators or Assigns the full and Just Sume of Twenty pounds four Shillings five pence in Sterling Mony at the Said Ed. Jennings house in Virginia on or before the last day of July next ensuing as Date hereof then this Obligation to be void and of no Effect or else to remain in full force and Virtue.

Sigillat et deliverat John Pettiver
in presentia
James Minge, Robt. Fendall, Robt. Burbidge Copia

[*Jones, attorney of Deeds* v. *Duckenfield*]

[*CCR 148*]

No. Carolina Ss. To the provost Marshall or his Deputy

These are in her Matyes name to will and require you to Summons Henry Lile personally to be and appeare at the next Generall Court to be holden at the house of Captain Jno. Hecklefield in Litle river on the last Tuseday in July next then and there to give Evidence in a Cause between Fred. Jones Attorney of Julius Deeds and Wm. Duckenfield Esqr. defendant on behalfe of the plaintiff and have there this Sumons Dated at the Secretarys Office this 26th day of June Anno Domini 1707.

Testis T. Knight Secretary

[*Endorsed:*]
Sumons for Hen. Lile
Exequted by me Robt. Fendall Provost Marshall

[*Pollock and wife, executrix* v. *Fewox*]

[*CCR 186*]

North Carolina Generall Court Ss.

James Fewoxe of Chowan precinct in the Province aforesaid Planter alias [dictus] James Fewoxe was Summoned to answer unto the honorable Collonell Thomas Pollock and Esther his Wife Executrix of the last Will and Testament of William Wilkinson Late of Chowan aforesaid Esqr. deceased of a Plea that he render them the Summe of Two hundred pounds Sterling which from them he unjustly detaines.

And whereupon the said Collonell Thomas Pollock and Esther his Wife by Edwd. Bonwicke their Attorney Say that whereas the said James Fewoxe at Chowan aforesaid the Tenth day of February Anno Domini 1700 By his certaine Bill or writeing obligatory Sealed with his Seale as his Act and Deed delivered and here into Court brought whose Date is the day and yeare aforesaid did acknowledge himself to be indebted unto the said William Wilkinson in his life time or his just order the just Summe of One hundred and Seven pounds and Four Shillings Sterling money of England to be paid in these Species following (that is to Saie) Fourty pound in good well burned Tarr at eight Shillings each Barrell and each Barrell not to hold less than Twenty eight Gallons and Thirty pounds of the abovesaid Summe in good Fresh neat merchantable Pork and the other thirty Seven pound Four shillings in Corne hides Tallow and Skins one Third of the Said Sume to be paid on Demand and another third part in the yeare Seventeen hundred and one and the last third part by the Last of December Seventeen hundred and Two to the true performance of the which said Payments the said James Fewoxe (by the aforesaid Bill) did bind himselfe his heires executors and administrators in the Penalty of Two hundred pounds Sterling to be paid on Demand and the said Collonell Thomas Pollock and Esther his Wife in fact Say that the said James Fewoxe the aforesaid Summe of £107:4*s*. Sterling at the times in the said Bill and according to the forme and effect thereof hath not paid So that there by Account accrued to the Said William Wilkinson in his life time and to the said Collonell Pollock and Esther his Wife in their said Capacity Since the Death of the said William Wilkinson to require and have of the said James Fewoxe the aforesaid Summe of Two hundred pounds Sterling Yet neverthe-less the said James Fewoxe the aforesaid Summe of £200 Sterling unto the said William Wilkinson in his life time hath not paid nor to the said Esther while Sole Since the Death of the said William Wilkinson nor to the said Collonell Thomas Pollock and Esther his Wife Since Especially between them had and celebrated hath he paid the same But the same to pay altho often thereunto required hath denyed and refused and Still doth deny and refuse and unjustly detaine to the Damage of the said Collonell Thomas Pollock and Esther his Wife in their Said Capacity the Summe of Two hundred pounds Sterling and thereupon they bring their Suite and into Court they bring their Lettres Testamentary where by etc.

Bonwicke per querens pledg etc. Jno Doe
Ri. Roe

[*Endorsed:*]
Executors Wilkinson versus Fewoxe
Narratio
Make out Capias according to Declaration and Send a Coppy hereof
Subpoena Godfrey Spruell
Refferred by consent to the next Court

[*CCR 186*]

No. Carolina Ss. To the provost Marshall or his Deputy

These are in her Majestyes name to will and require you to Arrest the body of James Fewoxe of Chowan precinct in the province aforesaid planter alias [dictus] James Fewoxe and him Safely hold Soe that he be and appeare at the next Generall Court to be holden at the house of Captain Jno. Hecklefield in Litle river on the last Tuseday in July next then and there to Answer to the Honorable Colonel Thos. Pollock and Esther his wife Executrix of the last will and Testament of Wm. Wilkison late of Chowan aforesaid Esqr. deceased of a plea that he render them the Sume of two hundred pounds Sterling which from them he unjustly deteynes and have you there this writt Dated at the Secretarys Office the 26th day of June Anno Domini 1707.

Testis T. Knight Secretary

[*Endorsed:*]
Breve
Executors of Wilkison versus Fewoxe in Debt
Cepi Corpis

[*CCR 186*]

No. Carolina Ss. To the Provost Marshall or his Deputy etc.

These are in her Majestyes name to will and require you to Summons Godfry Spruell personally to be and appeare at the next Generall Court to be holden at the home of Captain Jno. Hecklefield in Litle river on the last Tuseday in July next then and there to give Evidence in a Cause there depending between The Honorable Colonel Thomas pollock and Ester his wife Executors etc. of Colonel Wm. Wilkison deceased plaintiffs and James Fewox defendant on behalfe of the plaintiffs and have there this Summons Dated the 26th day of June Anno Domini 1707.

Testis T. Knight Secretary

[*Endorsed:*]
Sumons for Godfr. Spruell
Exected

[*CCR 181*]

Know all men by these presents that wee Colonel Thomas Pollock and James Fewox both of the County of Albemarle do binde our selves unto each other in the full and Just Summ of one hundred pounds Currant mony of this goverment to which payment well and truely to be made unto each other wee binde our selves our heires Executors administrators and assignes firmly by these presents as Wittness our hands and Seales this 31st of July 1707.

The Condition of the aforesaid obligation is Such that whereas the aforesaid Colonel Thomas Pollock hath an action depending at this generall Court against the said James Fewox and hath agreed with each other to Stand to the ward and Judgment of Mr. Thomas Peterson and Mr. Nathyniell Chevin arbretraton Indefirently Chosen as well on the one part as on the other to arbretrate award order and Judge of and upon all manner of Actions Sutes Debts and accounts and Controversyes Depending betwinn the said Colonel Thomas Pollock and the said James fewox, that then this obligation to be voyd otherwise to Stand in full force power and vertue (etc.) against the non performer.

Signed Sealed and
Delivered in the Presents
of us
Testes
Levi Truewhitt
francis DeLaMare

Thomas Pollock
James fewox his Mark

[*Endorsed:*]
Arbitration bond
Pollock and fewox

[*Porter* v. *Jones, administrator*]

[*CCR 148*]

No. Carolina Ss.

Whereas at a Generall Court holden at the house of Captain Jno. Hecklefield in Litle river on the 27th day of Augt. Anno Domini 17[*torn*] Christo. Gale Esqr. and his [Associate] Justices of the Said Court Jno. Porter Esqr. obteyned a Judgement against Thomas Dereham in the following words (videlicet) Ordered that the Said Thos. Dereham pay unto the Said Jno. Porter Six Pounds Eight Shillings and Eight pence halfe in Drest Buck Skins at two Shillings per Skin Drest Doe Skins at Eighteen pence per Skin Fox and Wild Catt at Nine pence Each Good Matts at Eighteen pence Each Rackoons at three pence each Dry Neat [Hides] and tallow Country price with Fifty per Cent abate[*torn*] with Costs alias Execution And Whereas the Said Thos. Dereham is Since Deceased and hath not Satisfied the aforesaid Judgment and Fred. [*torn*] is Administrator of the Good and Chatles of the [said] Dereham.

You [*torn*] fore to make knowne to the Said Fred. Jones by Good and Lawfull Men of your Baylywick that he be and appear at the next Generall Court [to] be holden at the [house] of Captain Jno. Hecklefield in Litle river on the [*torn*] Tuseday in July next [*torn*] and there to [*illegible*] have why [*torn*] Execution Shall not [*torn*] against him in the qualyite aforsaid for the Debt and Damages aforsaid and make returne of your proceedings therein to the next Generall Court Dated at the Secretarys Office this 21th day of June [*torn*] 1707.

Testis T. Knight Secretary

[*Endorsed:*]
Porter against Jones Administrator of Deham

[*Porter* v. *Paine*]

[*CCR 148*]

No. Carolina Ss. To the provost Marshall or Deputy

These are in her Majestyes name to will and require you to Sumons Thos. Johnson personally to be and appeare at the next Generall Court to be holden at the house of Captain Jno. Hecklefields in Litle river on the last Tuseday in July next then and there to give Evidence in a Cause there depending betweene Jno. porter plaintiff and Samuell paine Defendant on behalfe of the defendant and have there this Sumons Dated at the Secretarys Office this 30th day of Janry. Anno Domini 1707.

Testis T. Knight Secretary

[*Endorsed:*]
Sumons for Thos. Johnson

[*Rayman* v. *Hassell*]

[*CCR 148*]

No. Carolina Ss. To the Honorable the Generall Court etc.

Willm. Rayman is plaintiff against John Hassell defendant in a plea of

Debt and Sayes that the Defendant Stands Justly Indebted unto the plaintiff in the Full and Just Summe of three pounds Sterling to be paid in Tarr at tenn shillings per Barrell and delivered at the same Raymons Landing as in and by one Certaine writeing Obligatory under the proper hand and seale of the defendant beareing date the first day of June 1705 and here unto Court brought and ready to be produced doth and may more fully and at large appeare Nevertheless the said Defendant the said Sume of three pounds in maner aforesaid to the plaintiff hath not rendred tho' often thereunto requested but the Same doth Still refuse to render to the plaintiffs Damage Six pounds Sterling and thereupon he brings his Suite etc.

T. Knight Secretary

[*Endorsed:*]
Narratio
Rayman versus Hassell
In Debt
Entered June 30th 1707

[*Redwood* v. *Pettiver*]

[*CCR 148*]

No. Carolina Ss. To the Provost Marshall or his Deputy

These are in her Majestyes name to will and require you to Attach Soe much of the Estate of Jno. Pettiver wherever to be found in this Government as will pay and Satisfy Jno. Redwood the full Summe of Eight pounds Sterling with Costs and the Same in Safe Custody hold untill otherwise ordered by due Course of Law and make returne of your proceedings herein to the next Generall Court Dated at the Secretarys Office in this 30th day of June Anno Domini 1707.

Testis T. Knight Secretary

[*Endorsed:*]
Attachment versus
Pettiver ads. Redwood
Exequted
Two beds and furniture of one bed viz. Curtines and valins and Shets and blanket and Rug

[*Shrieve* v. *Farrell*]

[*CCR 148*]

[*Torn*] Carolina Ss. To the honorable the Generall Court etc.

Robert Shrieve is plaintiff against Richd. Farrell of the County of Albemarle defendant in a plea of Debt and sayes that the Defendant stands Justly Indebted to the plaintiff in the full Sume of Seaventeen pounds [*torn*] Ten head of Hoggs being two sowes and Eight shoates as in and by one

Certaine writeing obligatory under the proper hand of the Defendant beareing Date of Seaventeenth day of October 1706 here in to Court Brought [*illegible*] appeare Nevertheless the said Defendant the [*torn*] Seaventeen pounds and the [*illegible*] head of Hoggs [*illegible*] hath not paid and delivered tho' often thereunto requested but the same doth Still refuse to pay and deliver to the plaintiffs Damage Forty pounds Sterling and thereupon he brings his Suite etc.

T. Knight Secretary

[*Endorsed:*]
Narratio
Shrieve versus [*illegible*]
In Debt
Entered June 30th: 1707

[*CCR 148*]

No. Carolina Ss. To the provost Marshall or his Deputy

These are in her Majestyes name to will and require you to Arrest the body of Richd. Farrell and him Safely hold soe that he be and appeare at the next Generall Court to be holden at the house of Captain Jno. Hecklefield in Litle river on the last Tuseday in July next then and there to Answer the plaint of Robert Shrieve in a plea of Debt and have there this writt Dated at the Secretarys Office this 30th day of June Anno Domini 1707.

Testis T. Knight Secretary

[*Endorsed:*]
Breve
Shrieve versus Farrell
In Debt

[*CR 2.001*]

North Carralina

This bill bindeth me Richard farrell of the County of Albamarle in the precinct of Paspatanck me my heirs Executors or administrators to pay or cause to be payed unto Robert Shreve of the County of Bath in the precinct of pamplico to him his heirs Executors administrators or assigns the full and Just Summ or quantity of Seventeene pound bing Uppon the account of the Half the track of Land that I now I live Uppon and ten Head of Hogs being two sowes and eight Shoets Which Sum of Money I oblidge Me My Heires administrators assignes to be Paid at or uppon the tenth Day of March Next insuing in Witness thereof I have hereunto Set my hand this Sevententh Day of october 1706.

Testes
Maurice Shultess

Richard Farell his Mark

[*Endorsed:*]

Farrels bill to Robt. Shrieve

MISCELLANEOUS FILE PAPERS

[*Wilkins, John, letter of attorney*]

[*CCR 192*]

No. Carolina Ss.

Know all Men by these presents that I Jno. Wilkins marriner have made Ordeyned Constituted and appointed and by thes presents doe make ordeyne Constitute and appoint James Tooke of this province merchant my true and Lawfull Attorney for me and in my name and to my use to aske demand and receive of and from all persons whatsoever all Such Sumes of Money or other things which doe or may any wayes belong unto me and like wise to appeare in any Court of record in this Government and there to defend any Action or Actions that shall be brought against me and to proceed therein in all respects as if I my Selfe was personally present and one or more Attorney or Attorneys under him to make and the Same againe to revoke and generally to Act and doe in all respects as if I my Selfe might or Could doe if personally present In Witness whereof I have hereunto Sett my hand and Seale this 5th day of May Anno Domini 1707.

Sealed and delivered John Wilkins
In the presence of
Jno. Falconar
T. Knight

[*Endorsed:*]
July 30th 1707
There appeared the within Tobias Knight one of the within Evidences and on his Oath proved the within power of Attorney.

[*CCR 189*] [21]

<1> Journall of the Generall Court October Anno Domini 1707

<2> [*Blank*]

<3> North Carolina Ss. Att a Generall Court holden at the house of Capt. Jno. Hecklefield in Litle river on the 28th day of Octob. Anno Domini 1707. Present The Honorable Christo. Gale, Wm. Barcliff, James Minge Justices.

Robert Cox appeard and pray'd to be dismiss'd from being bound over by Recognizance the last Court and on his humble Submission was dismissed accordingly.

Then this Court adjourned till tomorrow Morn 8 of Clock.

Wednesday Morne 8 of Clock this Court met. Present ut Supra.

[21] These minutes are signed by the justices of the General Court and appear to be finished minutes.

Ordered that it be a rule of this Court for the future that if any person in pleading shall Interupt another whilst he is pleading shall pay ten Shillings to the use of the Lords proprietors.

Eliz. Tomlin Comes by Thos. Snoden her Attorney and prays Judgment upon a verdict the last Court obteyned against Geo. Gording and Frances his wife it being on Stay in Arrest of Judgment and the Defendants Produceing noe Laws or reason why the said Judgment should be dismissed

Ordered that the said Judgement be passed and Confirmed on the verdict and that the said Geo. etc. pay etc.

James Minge Esqr. Comes and [*torn*] on his oath on the holy Evangelist proved the last will and Testament of Thos. Norcom.

Ordered that Allen Robbinnett Edwd. Wilson Richd. Davenport Jno. Davenport and Thos. Everett or any three of them being first Sworne before the next Magestrate doe appraise the said Estate of the said Norcom [*illegible*] and Inventory thereof into the Secretarys Office according to Lawe.

<4> Upon petition of Hannah Foster Shewing as per petition and the Court haveing heard and Considered the whole matter Ordered that the said James Foster be in Safe Custody of the Marshall until he shall Give Bond with Good Security in the Sum of Ten pounds that he shall at the next Generall Court produce Certification [*illegible*] lawfull Testimony of his [marriage] with Mary his now pretended wife and that in the meane tyme they be of the Good behavior.

Jno. Hopkins Comes by Thos. Snoden his Attorney and produces Copy for Reccord from the precinct Court of perquimond as followes etc. [*blank*] and by petition Shewes that the aforesaid Jno. Lewis is Since removed out of the Jurisdiction of that Court and prayes that a Scire facias may Issue out of this Court that the said Lewis may Shew Cause why Execution shall not goe against him out of this Court for the Debt and Damages aforesaid.

A Generall Power of Attorney was produced by The Honorable Jno. Porter Esqr. from John Gamball to the said Porter Attested under the hand and Seale of Thos. Laurence Notary Public and prays the Same may be recorded which is Granted.

Upon petition of Dariass Neale shewing etc. as per petition Ordered that the said Sanderson be Sumoned to the next Court to Answer the said petition.

<5> In pursuance of an order of the last Court Mrs. Mary Clark presents to this Court an Account of the Debts and Credits of the Estate of Arthure Workman Deceased Examined and Attested by Pat Gorman franc. De La Mare and Thos. Abington and the Re-

pleavin appears to be due from the said Mary Clark is Eight pounds Eight Shillings and two pence.

Jno. Arderne Esqr. Comes and on his Oath on the holy Evangelist taken proved a power of Attorney from Robert West to Thos. Boyd.

Thos. West and Thos. Boyd Attorney of Robt. West Came and acknowledged a Deed of Sale of a tract of Land to Richd. Stamp.

Upon petition of Grace [Meltone] Shewing that her husband is Dead without will and prayes Letters of Administration accordingly. It is the oppinion of this Court that she may have Letters of Administration accordingly.

A power of Attorney from Landgrave Daniell to Tho. Boyd ordered to be recorded.

Landgrave Robert Daniell comes by Thos. Boyd to prosecute his Attachment from the Last Court and a Nulla Bona being returned thereon by Consent of both partys it is Continued to the next Court.

Thos. Peterson Attorney etc. Comes to prosecute his Suite against Jno. Bishop and Declares as per Narratio and the Defendant Comes and Confessed.

Ordered that the said Bishop pay unto the said Peterson the aforesaid Sume of Eight pounds Twelve Shillings and Eight pence in Good fresh pork with Costs alias Execution.

Upon non appearance of Colonel Thos. Cary against Fred. Jones ordered that the suite be Dismissed and the plaintiff pay Costs alias Execution.

<6> Jonathan Joyner Sr. Comes to prosecute his Suite against Jno. Pettiver and Complaines as per Narratio and the Defendant appeared not and the plaintiff prays Attachment against his Estate which is Granted.

Upon petition of Wm. Jackson and Sarah Jackson advised that the said Eliz. Tomlin pay unto the said Jackson and his wife for three dayes Attendance according to Act.

John Clark Assigne Comes to prosecute his Suite against George Kinzerly and a non est Inventus being returned the plaintiff prays an Attachment against his Estate which is Granted.

Colonel Thos. Pollock Comes by Edwd. Bonwick his Attorney to prosecute his Attachment against Wm. Powell. Ordered that the said Attachment be Continued till the next Court.

Jno. Whorly appeares being bound by Recognizance to Answer the Complaint of Mrs. Mary Blount and the said Mary Blount not appearing ordered that the Recognizance be Dismissed.

Capt. Jno. Hecklefield Comes and proves an Account against

the Estate of Jno. McKeel for 02:05:02 James Tooke Executor etc. being present allowed of the same.

Ordered that James Tooke Executor of the last will and Testament of said McKeel pay unto the Said Hecklefield the said Summe of 02:05:02 alias Execution.

Thos. Peterson Attorney etc. Comes to prosecute his Scire facias against Thos. Houghton and a Nihill being Returned thereon Ordered that the former Judgment be Confirmed and that the said Houghton pay etc. alias Execution.

<7> David Harris appeared being in Custody for haveing threatned to burne Colonel Daniells Shipp and of other most Gross and abusive Language and haveing humbly Submitted himself to the Mercy of the Court.

Ordered that the said David Harris doe find Good Suretys for his appearance [*torn*] next Court and that he be in the meanwhile on his Good behaviour with Costs alias Execution.

[*Signed:*]
C. Gale, James Minge, William Barcliff.

FILE PAPERS IN SUITS AND PROSECUTIONS

[*Blount* v. *Whorly*]

[*CCR 148*]

No. Carolina Ss.

On this Twilfth day of Septr. Anno 1707 personally came and appeared before me John Whorly And Acknowledged himself to be indebted unto our soveraign Lady Queen Ann in the Sum of ten pounds Allso Thomas Cooper appeared, and did then Acknowledge himself to be likewise indebted to our said soveraign Lady the Queen in the Sum of ten pounds to be Levied on their goods and Chattles.

With This Condition, That if the said John Whorly Do make his personall appearance att the next generall Court to be holden att Little river on the Last Tuesday in Octobr. next ensuing to answer the Complaint of [*torn*] Mary Blount for a certain breach of the peace made by said Worly on her said Blount, and in the mean time Do keep her Majesties peace, as well towards all her Majesties Liege people, as towards the said Mary in perticular. Then this recognizance to be void, or Else to be of full force.

Acknowledged before me this Day and year above written.

Edwd. Moseley

North Carolina Ss.

On this 12th Day of Septr. Anno Domini 1707 personally came and appeared before me Mrs. Mary Blount and acknowledged herself to be indebted unto our soveraign Lady Queen Ann in the Sum of ten pounds to be Levied on her goods and Chattles.

With this Condition that if she the said Mary Do appear att the next generall Court and there prosecute John Whorly for a certain breach of the peace made by said Worly on her Then this recognizance to be void or Else to remain in full force.

Acknowledged before me.

Edwd. Moseley

[*Endorsed:*]
To M. T. Knight Secretary
[*Illegible*]

[*Cary* v. *Jones*]

[*CCR 148*]

No. Carolina Ss. To the provost Marshall of the County of Bath or his Deputy

These are in her Majestyes name to will and require you to Arrest the body of Fred. Jones and him Safely hold soe that he be and appeare at the next Generall Court to be holden at the house of Capt. Jno. Hecklefeild in Litle river on the last Tuseday in Octobr. next then and there to Answer the plaint of the Honorable Thos. Cary Esqr. in a plea of trespass on the Case and have there this writt Dated at the Secretarys Office this 13th day of Septr. Anno Domini 1707.

Testis T. Knight Secretary

[*Endorsed:*]
By virtue of the within mentioned I Attached the Body of Mr. Rubin Welch the Attorney of Mr. Fraderick Jones per Me

W. Barrow Provost Marshall

[*Clarke, assignee* v. *Kingsly*]

[*CCR 148*]

No. Carolina Ss. To the honorable the Generall Court etc.

John Clark Assignee of John Porter Esqr. is plaintiff against Geo. Kingerly defendant in a plea of Debt and Sayes that the Defendant Stands Justly Indebted to the plaintiff quallifyed as aforesaid in the full and Just Summe of Four pounds Nine Shillings and Eleven pence in fresh neat drest porke as in and by one Certaine writeing obligatory under his proper hand beareing Date the 22d of feb. 1703 and here into Court brought doth and may appeare Nevertheless the said Defendant the aforesaid Summe of four pounds Nine Shillings and Eleaven pence hath not paid to the plaintiff tho' often thereunto requested but the Same Doth Still refuse to pay to the plaintiffs Damage Eight pounds nineteen shillings and tenn pence Sterling and thereupon he brings this Suite etc.

T. Knight Secretary

[*Endorsed:*]
Narratio
Clark versus Kingerly
In Debt

[*CCR 188*]

North Carolyna

This bill bindeth me Geo. Kinzerlye my heirs or Aignes to pay unto John Porter him his heirs or Assignes the Full Sum of foure pounds nine Shillings 11*d*. to be pd. in fresh neat drest pork at the dwelling house of John Anderson in pequimens River on demand as Witnes my hand the 22th of february Anno 1703/4.

Testes
John Anderson
Walter tanner his marke

Geo. Kinzerlye Signum

[*Endorsed:*]
Geo. Kinzerlyes bill for 4:09:11*d*.
I the Subscribr assigne unto John Clark this within bill warrunting the Same Shall appear Justly dew witnes my hand in Chowan in North Carolina this 25th May 1706.
Testes
John Arderne

John Porter

[*Daniell* v. *Harris*]

[*CCR 148*]

Wheras complaint hath been made to me by the Honorable Collonel Rott. Daniell Esqr. aganst David Harries thatt he hath threatned to burne his Shipe and of other most gross and abusive languadge Thes are therfor in her majestyes Name to Will and requyer your mr. John Jones to take the forsaid David Harries in your custody and him convey to the marshals untill he Shall give good Security for his keeping the Peace to all her matyes Subjects And espetially to the Honorable Rott. Daniell esqr. aforsaid and to appear att the nixt generall court and answer what shall ther be objected against him. Heerof faill nott att your perill as you will answer the contrary. Given under my hand and Seall this 8 day of Agust. 1707.

Thos. Pollock

[*Daniell* v. *Jones, administrator*]

[*CCR 140*]

North Carolina ss. To the provost Marshall or Deputy

These are in her Maties name to require you to attach Soe much of the

Estate of Thomas Derham Deceased in the hands of Mr. Fredrick Jones Administrator as will Satisfy the Honorable Landgrave Robt. Daniel Esqr. the Summe of Fifteen pounds and Eighteen Shillings with Costs and the Same in your Custody Deteyne untill thence Delivered by due Course of Law and your proceedings therein returne to the next Generall Court togeather with this Writt Dated at the Secretarys Office the 4th Day of Augt. 1707.

Testis T. Knight Secretary

[*Endorsed:*]
Nulla Bona per me W. Barrow Provost Marshall

[*Jeycocks* v. *Pettiver*]

[*CCR 148*]

No. Carolina Ss. To the Honorable the Generall Court etc.

Jonathan Jeycocks is plaintiff against Jno. Pettiver Defendant in a plea of Debt and Sayes that the Defendant Stands Justly Indebted to the plaintiff in the Full and Just Summe of Seaven pounds Five Shillings in good Merchantable Wheate to be pd. on demand as in and by one Certaine writeing Obligatory under the proper hand of the said Defendant beareing Date the 22d day of May Anno Domini 1707 and hereinto Court brought and ready to be produced doth and may appear Nevertheless the Said Defendant the aforesaid Summ of Seaven pounds Five Shillings in maner aforsaid to the plaintiff hath not paid tho' often thereunto requested but the Same doth Still refuse to pay to the plaintiffs Damage Fourteen pounds tenn Shillings Sterling and thereupon he brings his Suite etc.

T. Knight Secretary

[*Endorsed:*]
Narratio
Jeycocks versus Pettiver
In Debt
Entered Octob. [11th] 1707

[*CCR 148*]

No. Carolina Ss. To the Provost Marshall of the County of Albemarle or to his Deputy.

These are in her Majestyes name to will and require you to Arrest the body of Jno. pettiver and him Safely hold Soe that he be and appeare at the next Generall Court to be holden at the house of Captain Jno. Hecklefield in Litle river on the last Tuesday in this Instant Octor. then and there to Answer to the plaint of Jonathan Jeycocks in a plea of Debt and have you there this Writt Dated at the Secretarys Office this 11th day of Octor. Anno Domini 1707.

Testis T. Knight Secretary

[*Endorsed:*]
Breve

Jeycocks versus Pettiver
In Debt
Cepi corpus by me Robt. Fendall Provost marshall

[*Peterson, attorney of Perry and Company* v. *Bishop*]

[*CCR 148*]

No. Carolina Ss. To the Honorable the Generall Court

Thos. Peterson Attorney to Micajah Perry and New Pensilvania Company is plaintiff against Jno. Bishopp of pasquotanke river in the province of No. Carolina defendant in a plea of Debt and Sayes that the Defendant Stands Justly Indebted to the plaintiff quallifyed as aforesaid in the full and Just Summe of Eight Pounds Twelve Shillings and Eight pence in Good fresh porke to be delivered at the landing of Mr. Jas. Jennings in the said River as in and by one Certaine writeing obligatory under the Defendants proper hand beareing Date 12th December 1704 hereinto Court brought and ready to be produced doth and may appeare Nevertheless the Said Defendant the aforesaid Sume of Eight pounds twelve Shillings and Eight pence in maner aforesaid to the plaintiff hath not rendred tho' often thereunto requested but the Same doth Still refuse to render to the plaintiffs Damage Seaventeen pounds five Shillings and four pence Sterling and thereupon he brings this Suite etc.

T. Knight Secretary

[*Endorsed:*]
Narratio
Peterson Attorney versus Bishopp
In Debt
Entered September 10th: 1707

[*CCR 188*]

This Bill Bindeth me John Bishop of pascotank River In the province of North Carrolina planter me my heirs Executors administrators and Assignes to pay to Thomas Peterson for Accounts and Use of the New Pensilvania Company his or there Assigns, the full Summe of Eight pounds twelve Shillings and Eight pence, In good fresh pork and Deliver it at the Landing of Mr. Jno. Jennings In the Said River on or before the first of Febry. next as wittness my hand and Seal This 12th of Decembry 1704.

John Bishop

John Billitt
W. Glover

[*Peterson, attorney of Perry and Company* v. *Houghton*]

[*CCR 192*]

No. Carolina Ss. To the Provost Marshall of the County of Albemarle or to his Deputy

Whereas at a Generall Court holden for this Province at the house of Captain Jno. Hecklefield in Litle river on the 27th day of March 1705 Before The Honorable Wm. Glover Esqr. and his Associates Justices of the Said Court The pensilvania Company by Thos. Peterson their Attorney Obteyned a Judgement against Thos. Houghton for the Summe of Tenn pounds One Shilling and three pence with Costs alias Execution.

These are therefore in her Majestyes name to will and require you that you Cause to be made knowne unto the Said Thos. Houghton by twelve Good and Lawfull Men of your County that he be and appeare at the next Generall Court to be holden at the house of Captain Jno. Hecklefield in Litle River on the last tuseday in this Instant Octor. then and there to Shew Cause if any he have why [*illegible*] shall not Goe out against him for the Debt and Damages aforesaid and have you there this Writt together with the persons names before whome you Execute the Same Dated at the Secretarys Office this 1st day of Octobr. Anno Domini 1707.

Testis T. Knight Secretary

[*Endorsed:*]
Scire facias against Thos. Houghton ad sectam Tho. Peterson Attorney etc.
John Stepney, Jams Coles, Thomas Long <*his mark*>, Jno. Norcom <*his mark*>, Jno. Hopkins <*his mark*>, Richard Devenport <*his mark*>, peter Jones <*his mark*>, Jno. Bennit <*his mark*>, Richd. Devenport <*his mark*>, Edward Perrey <*his mark*>, John Wiatt, John Barrow
Executed By Leving a Coppey of this writ per me Anthony Wherry
Deputy marshall

MISCELLANEOUS FILE PAPERS

[*Knight, Tobias, petition*]

[*CCR 191*]

North Carolina Ss. To the Honorable the Generall Court etc.

The Humble petition of Tobias Knight Sheweth That by reason of his late Great Indisposition of body he is wholy uncapable of Attending this honorable Court without Indangering his health doe therefore pray

That this honorable Court will accept of Mr. Abington in his roome as Clerke of the Said Court dureing this Session and your petitioner as in Duty bound Shall pray etc.

T. Knight

[*West, Robert, letter of attorney*]

[*CR 2.001*]

I Robert West of choan Precinct doe hereby make and appoint Thomas Boyd my true and lawfull atturney for me to deliver and acknouledge a Bill of Sale of land att Flatty creek Sold by me and my Brother Thomas to Ritchd.

Stamp att the Generall courtt for this province or any other proper court as witness my hand this 24 of octor. 1707.

Testes
John Arderne
Thomas Pollock

Robert West

[*Endorsed:*]
Att a Generall Court October 29th 1707 proved by the Oath of Mr. Jno. Arderne. T. Knight Secretary

FILE PAPERS IN SUITS AND PROSECUTIONS[22]

[*Clarke, assignee* v. *Kingsly*]

[*CCR 148*]

No. Carolina Ss. To the provost Marshall or Deputy.

These are in her Matyes Name to will and require you Attach Soe much of the Estate of Geo. Kingerly wherever to be found in this Government and will pay and Satisfy Jno. Clarke Assignee of Jno. porter the Sume of four pounds Nine shillings and Eleven pence with Costs and the Same in safe Custody hold untill otherwise ordered by due Course of Law and make returne of your proceedings herein to the next Generall Court Dated at the Secretarys Office this 13th day of March Anno Domini 1707/8.

Testis T. Knight Secretary

[*Endorsed:*]
Attachment versus Kingerly ad sectam Clarke
Attached the hogs mark'd with a cropp in the right ear an under
Keel in the left the above hogs running in the woods. Per Tho. Collins
Deputy Marshall

[*Hatch, administrator* v. *Swann*]

[*CCR 139*]

No. Carolina Ss. To the Provost Marshall of the County of Albemarle or his Deputy

These are in her Majestyes name to will and require you to Attach Soe much of the Estate of Thos. Swan wherever to be found in this Government as will pay and Satisfy Antho. Hatch' the Administrator with the will Annext of Richd. Plato deceased the full sume of Seven pounds Twelve Shillings and the Same in Safe Custody keep untill other wise ordered by due Course of

[22] Although minutes are extant for a session of the General Court beginning March 30, 1708, they are badly mutilated. Fourteen small fragments exist, and they show signs of having been burned. It is possible to read on one fragment that Francis Delamare and William Barcliff were present as justices. A certain *Boyd* is referred to as the attorney general. In all likelihood, this is Thomas Boyd, who had been appointed provost marshal by Thomas Cary in May, 1706, and who served as a justice of the General Court in July, 1708. Remaining fragments do not contain any substantive information.

Law and make returne of your proceedings herein to the next Generall Court Dated at the Secretarys Office this 11th day of Feb. Anno Domini 1707/8.

Testis T. Knight Secretary

In Captain Coles hands 2:1:8

[*Endorsed:*]
Attachment versus Swann ad sectam Hatch
Attach'd one bed per Tho. Collins Deputy Marshall

[*Peterson, attorney of Perry and Company* v. *Keele*]

[*CCR 148*]

No. Carolina Ss. To the honorable the Generall Court etc.

Thos. Peterson Attorney to Micajah Perry and New [Pensilvania] Company is plaintiff against Robert Keele defendant in a plea of Debt Sayes that the defendant Stands Justly indebted unto the plaintiff [*torn*] the quallifications aforesaid the full and Just Summe of [*torn*] fourteen Shillings and a halfepenny to be [paid in] good Sound Marchantable neat fresh porke [*torn*] the use of Mr. Jno. Jenings in pascotanck as by one Certaine writeing Obligatory under [his] proper hand beareing Date the twenty[*torn*] day of March 1705 and here into [*torn*] doth and may appeare Nevertheless the said [*torn*] aforesaid Summe of two pounds fourteen Shillings and halfepeny to the said plaintiff hath not [*torn*] often thereunto requested but the Same doth refuse to pay to the plaintiffs Damage five pounds Eight shillings and one penny Sterling and thereupon [*torn*] brings this Suite etc.

T. Knight Secretary

[*Endorsed:*]
Narratio
Peterson [*illegible*]
In Debt

[*CCR 148*]

No. Carolina Ss. To the Provost Marshall or his Deputy

These are in her Majestyes name to will and require you to Arrest the body of Robt. Keele and him Safely hold soe that he be and appeare at the next Generall Court to be holden at the house of Captain Jno. Hecklefield in Litle river on the last Tuseday in March next then and there to Answer the plaint of Thos. Peterson Attorney to Micajah Perry and New pensilvania Company in a plea of Debt and have there this writt Dated at the Secretarys Office this 1st day of December Anno Domini 1707.

Testis T. Knight Secretary

[*Endorsed:*]
Breve

Peterson versus Keele
In Debt

[*CCR 188*]

No. Carolina

This bill bindeth me Robt. Keel of Pasquetank my Heirs executors or Assignes to pay or Cause to be pd. unto Mr. Thomas Peterson in behalfe of New Pensylvania Company his or their Assignes or Order the full and Just Sume of two Pounds fourteen Shillings and Halfe penny To [*illegible*] good Sound merchandable neet fresh Porke to be brought to Mr. Jno. Jennings house in Pasquotank upon demand Ass Wittnesse my Hand this twenty Eight day of March 1705.

Testes
Jno. Falconar

Robt. Keel

[*Endorsed:*]
Robt. Keel
£2 14*s*.

[*Peterson, attorney of Perry and Company* v. *Lawson*]

[*CCR 148*]

No. Carolina Ss. To the honorable the Generall Court etc.

Thos. Peterson Attorney to Micajah Perry and New Pensilvania Company is plaintiff against Jno. Lawson Defendant in a plea of Debt and Sayes that the Defendant stands Justly Indebted to the plaintiff in the Quallification aforesaid in the full and Just Summe of Twelve pounds Nine Shillings and Nine pence in Merchantable Skins and furrs at a price agreed upon as in and by one Certaine writeing Obligatory under the proper hand of the said Defendant beareing Date September the 30th 1704 and here into Court brought relation being thereunto had doth and may appeare Nevertheless the Said Defendant the aforesaid Summe of Twelve pounds Nine Shillings and Nine pence in maner aforesaid to the plaintiff hath not paid tho' often thereunto requested but the Same doth Still refuse to pay to the plaintiffs Damage (in the aforesaid Qualification) Twenty four pounds Nineteen Shillings and Six pence Sterling and thereupon he brings this Suite etc.

T. Knight Secretary

[*Endorsed:*]
Narratio
Peterson versus Lawson
In Debt

[*CCR 148*]

No. Carolina Ss. To the provost Marshall of the County of Bath or his Deputy

These are in her Majestyes name to will and require you to Arrest the body of Jno. Lawson and him Safely hold Soe that he be and appeare at the next Generall Court to be holden at the house of Captain Jno. Hecklefield in Litle river on the last Tuseday in March next then and there to Answer the plaint of Thos. Peterson Attorney to Micajah Perry and New Pensilvania Company in a plea of Debt and have there this writt Dated at the Secretarys Office this 27th day of Janry. Anno Domini 1707/8.

[*Endorsed:*]
Breve
Peterson versus Lawson
In Debt
Executed per Me W. Barrow provost Marshall

[*Peterson, attorney of Perry and Company* v. *Peggs*]

[*CCR 148*]

No. Carolina Ss. To the Provost Marshall or his Deputy

These are in her Majestyes name to will and require you to Arrest the body of Joseph Peggs and him Safely hold Soe that he be and appeare at the next Generall Court to be holden at the house of Captain Jno. Hecklefield in Litle river on the last Tuseday in March next then and there to Answer to Thos. Peterson Attorney to Micajah Perry and New pensilvania Company of a plea that he render unto him the Said Thos. the Summe of Twenty one pounds Eleven Shillings and Six pence Current Money of Said province which to him he oweth and unjustly Deteyneth and have there this writt Dated at the Secretarys Office this 1st day of Xber Anno Domini 1707.

Testis T. Knight Secretary

[*Endorsed:*]
Peterson versus Peggs
Debt

[*CCR 188*]

Know all Men by These presents that I Joseph Pegge of pascotank In North Carrolina planter do bind my Self my heirs Executors and administrators to pay to Thomas Peterson (On account of the New Pensilvania Company) his administrators and assigns the Just Sum of Twenty One pounds Eleven Shillings and Six pence Currant money of the province as Wittness my hand and Seal This 12th day of March Anno 1705/6.

The Condition of this Obligation is such That if the Above bound Joseph Peggs, his Executors and Asigns do well and truly pay Unto the abovesaid Thomas Peterson his administrators Or Assigns the full Sum of Ten pounds Fifteen Shillings and Six pence, In good fresh pork and Deliver it at the Landing of Mr. Jno. Jenings In pascotank on or before the 10th of December next then this Obligation to be void and of none Effect or Else to Remain In

full force and vertue Sign'd Seald and Delivered
In presence of Us
Cornelius Ratclyff

Joseph pegg

[*Endorsed:*]
Jo. Peggs Obligation

	£ 8:10:6
Interest	:17:
Account	£ 1: 8:
	10:15:6

[*CCR 148*]

This Bill Bindeth me Joseph Pegg of the Precinct of passcotank In the province of North Carrolina Planter me my heirs Executors Administrators or Assigns to pay To Thomas Peterson for the proper use of the New Pensilvania Company his or there Assigns the full Summe of four pounds In good fresh pork and Deliver it at the Landing of mr. John Jennings In the Said precinct on or before the first day of Febry. Next as wittness my hand and Seal This 6th Decembr 1707.

Testis
W. Glover

Joseph pegs

[*Endorsed:*]
Jos. Pegg
4.0.0

[*Pettiver* v. *Napier*]

[*CCR 148*]

No. Carolina Ss. To the Provost Marshall of the County of Albemarle or to his Deputy.

These are in her Majestyes name to will and require you to Arrest the body of Robert Napier alias Drew Robert Napier late of New Kent County in the Collony of Virginia Gentleman and him safely hold soe that he be and appeare at the next Generall Court to be holden at the house of Captain Jno. Hecklefield in Litle river on the last Tuseday in March next then and there to Answer the plaint of Jno. Pettiver of a plea of the Case and have there this Writt Dated at the Secretarys Office this 19th day of 9ber Anno Domini 1707.

Testis T. Knight Secretary

The damage is [*illegible*] 03:00½
Take good Baile

[*Endorsed:*]
Breve
Pettiver versus Napier
In Case

[*Snoden* v. *Gash*]

[*CCR 148*]

No. Carolina Ss. To the Provost Marshall or his Deputy

These are in her Matyes name and will require you to Arrest the body of Richd. Gash and him Safeley hold soe that he be and appeare at the next Generall Court to be holden at the house of Captain Jno. Hecklefield in Litle river on the last Tuseday in this Instant March then and there to Answer the plaint of Thos. Snoden Senior in a plea of the Case and have there this writt Dated at the Secretarys Office this 13th day of March Anno Domini 1707/8.

Testis T. Knight Secretary

[*Endorsed:*]
Breve
Snoden versus Gash
In Case
Executed per John Hecklefield Provost Marshall

[*Tiner* v. *Harkill*]

[*CCR 191*]

North Carolina ss. To the Honorable the Generall Court

Nicholas Tyner is plaintiff and George Harkill Defendant in a plea of Detinue and Complaines that the Defendant Deteynes from the plaintiff Two Feather Bedds and furniture Two Chests Two pewter Dishes, One pewter Tankerd two pewter porringers One iron pott, One Brass Kettle three Earthen plates One Cow and Calf and one Fourteen foot Boat as by wayes and meanes Convenient the plaintiff is ready to make appear Which Said Goods the Defendant unjustly Deteynes from the plaintiff and the Same refuses to render tho' often thereunto requested to the plaintiffs great Damage and Injury and prays Judgement of this Honorable Court that the Same may be returned with Costs and shall pray etc.

Nicho. Tiner his Mark

[*Endorsed:*]
[*Illegible*]
Entered 30th Octob. 1707

[*CCR 148*]

North Carolina Ss. To the provost Marshall for the County of Bath

These are in her Majesties Name to require you to arrest the Body of George Harkill and him in safe Custody hold soe that he may appear att the next Generall Court to be held for this Goverment att the house of Captain

John Hecklefield in Little River the last Tuesday in March next to answer the plaint of Nicho. Tyner in a plea of Detinue and have there this Writt Dated att the Secretarys Office this 30th Day of October 1707.

Tho. Abington Clericus Curiae Pro Tempore

[*Endorsed:*]

Executed per me W. Barrow Provost marshall

[*CCR 192*]

North Carolina Ss.

Know all men by these presents that I Geo. Harkill have bargained and sold and Do by these presents Sell alien make over and Confirme unto Mr. Nicholas Tiner these goods and Chattells Following Videlicet two Feather beds and furniture two Chests two pewter Dishes one Pewter Tankard two pewter poringers one Iron pott one Brass Kettle three Earthen plates one Cow and Calfe and one fourteen foot boat The Same to have and to hold to the abovesaid Mr. Nich. Tiner his heirs etc. for Ever free and Clear of all Claimes of any Person or persons whatsoever Seald with My Seale this 2d of Aprill 1705.

The Condition of the above Saile is Such that whereas att the [Juast] and Speciall Request of the above bounden George Harkill the abovesaid Mr. Nich. Tiner is become bound Jountly and Severally with the Said Harkill for the payment of Sixteen pounds two shillings and two pence ¾ If therefore the Said Harkill Shall well and truly pay the Said Sum of money and Same Harmless and Indemnify the Said Tiner off and From the Same That then the above Said be voyd and of None Effect or else to Stand in Force and power.

Seald and Delivred
In Presence of
Nath. Chevin
Daniel Hallsey

gorg harkell

[*Endorsed:*]
Harkills Bond

[*Wright, attorney of Foster* v. *Knowles*]

[*CCR 191*]

North Carolins Ss. To the Honorable Generall Court

Hannah Wright Attorney of James Foster is plaintiff against Mary Knowles Defendant in an action of Detinue and Complaines that the Defendant detaines and unjustly witholds from the plaintiff (Qualifyed as aforesiad) One Feather bed Two Quilts Two blanketts Two Ruggs and Severall other goods and Chattells Comprised in A certaine Schedule hereunto annex'd the plaintiffs proper Estate Qualifyed as aforesaid and the Same to the plaintiff (Qualifyed as aforesaid) refuses to deliver tho' by the plaintiff thereunto requested

Wherefore the plaintiff (Qualifyed as aforesaid) prayes Judgment for the aforesaid Feather bed Quilts Blanketts Ruggs and the rest of the goods and Chattells Comprised in the Schedule hereunto annex't with Costs of Suite And Shall pray etc.

Snoden per Querens

[*CCR 148*]

No. Carolina Ss. To the provost Marshall or his Deputy

These are in her Majestyes name to will and require you to Arrest the body of Mary Knowles and her Safely hold Soe that she be and appeare at the next Generall Court to be holden at the house of Capt. Jno. Hecklefield in Litle river on the last Tuseday in this Instant March then and there to Answer the plaint of Hanah Wright Attorney of James Foster in a plea of Detinue and have there this writt Dated at the Secretarys Office this 13th day of March Anno Domini 1707/8.

Testis T. Knight Secretary

[*Endorsed:*]
Breve
Wright versus Knowles
In Detinue
Executed On the person order'd by precept per John Hecklefield
Provost Marshall

[*CCR 191*]

To 1 Catt Tayle bed 1 bolster 4 pillows

To 2 pewter dishes 1 pewter bason 4 pewter plates

To 1 Earthen holland ware dish

To 4 East indy potts painted and guilded

To 1 qt. pott 1 pint pott and ½ pt. pott all pewter

To 2 pewter dram bottles 1 flint glass dram bottle 2 Spining wheeles 1 woolen and 1 linen

To 1 Iron pott between 5 and 6 gallons and hookes

To 1: bell mettle pott 2 Gallons and hookes

To frying panns Old

To 1: warming pann and grid Iron 1 hackle

To: 1: pr. toe Cards 1 pr. wooll Cards to 20: qt. bottles and 1 pottle bottle to 1 looking glass to 1 pewter Chamber pott to 1 gallon rumlett to 1:13 gallon beer Cask to 2 Chests 2: boxes and 1 trunk: 3 falling axes one broad ax 4 Iron wedges 4 Carpenters Chissells 1 gouge 1 drawing knige 2 handsaws 3 Augers 7 [grin] tetts severall sizes two doz. of spoones 3 pt. potts 1 qt. pott 1½ pt. pott tinn 1 pr. Stiliards and pee 1: new weeding hoe 1 new hilling hoe new 4 hilling hoes old 3 old weeding hoes 1 grubbing hoe 3 tinn panns 3 tinn funnels 1 pr. fire tongs large.

[*Endorsed:*]

Wright Attorney etc. versus Knowles

MISCELLANEOUS FILE PAPERS

[*Justices' commission*]

[*CCR 192*]

No. Carolina Ss. The Honorable William Glover Esqr. President of the Councell and Comander in Cheif And the rest of our Trusty and well beloved Councellors of State Greeting.

To our Trusty and well beloved John Blount Francis DeLaMare James Minge Wm. Barcliffe

Wee being well assured of your prudence Loyalty and Integrity doe hereby Comissionate and appoint you Jointly and Severally during our pleasure Justices for the Government of North Carolina to Keep or Cause to be Kept her Majestyes peace as also all Lawes and ordinances made for the well Government of this province And wee doe hereby Authorize and Impower You or any three of you (whereof wee will that one of you Jno. Blount and Franc. DeLaMare shall be one) to hold a Generall Court for this Government at the tymes hereafter Expres't (that is to Say) on the last Tuseday in the Monthes of July, October and March and the Same to adjourne from tyme to tyme and from place to place as you or any three of you (whereof wee will that one of you the Said Jno. Blount and Francis DeLaMare shall be one) shall thinke Meet and in the Said Court to hold pleas heare and determine all and all manner of Actions Suites and Causes whatsoever as well Criminall and Civill Reall Mixt Personall or any other Kind or Nature whatsoever and in all Such Causes to award Judgement and to Issue out all Such Writts and process as to the [*torn*][23] the Lawes and Ordinances of this Government and as neare as Conveniently may be to the Lawes And Customes of England And forasmuch as by reason of the difficulty of Passages and the Extremity of weather it may happen that three or more of you Cannot appeare at the tyme above Exprest wee doe hereby further Authorize and Impower you or any of you in Such Case being present to adjourne the Court for any tyme not Exceeding tenn dayes to the Same place and wee doe hereby Comand the provost Marshall to Cause to Come before you at the times Exprest above or any other tymes by you appointed Soe many Good and Lawfull Men of this Government as shall be necessary for the tryall of all Such Causes as Shall be brought before you.

Given under our hands and the Seale of the Collony this 2d day of Aprill the Seaventh yeare of the Raigne of our Soveraign Lady Anne Queene of England etc. Annoque Domini 1708.

[23] One entire line is torn out here.

[*Endorsed:*]
Comission of the Peace for the Generall Court

[*CCR 189*][24]

<1> Att a Generale Court of Our soveraigne Lady Anne Queen of Great Brittaine etc. held for the Province of North Carolina at the house of Captain John Hacklefields in Litle River the twenty Seaventh Day of July And in the Seaventh Yeare of Her Said Majestys Reigne Annoque Domini 1708. Present The Honorable Francis Delamar, Thomas Boyde, Nathaniell Chevin Esqrs. Justices.

Geo. Lumley Clerk

Captain John Hacklefield Presented a Commission of the Peace from the Honorable Councell etc. And Recorded as follows videlicet.

North Carolina Ss.

William Glover Esqr. President of the Councell and Commander in Cheife And the Rest of Our Trusty and well beloved Councellors of State Greeting,

To Our Trusty and Well beloved Edward Mosely John Blunt Francis Delamare, James Minge, Thomas Boyde and Nathel. Chevin Esqrs.

Wee being Well assured of your prudence Loyallty and Integrity Do hereby Commisionate And Appoint You Joyntly And Severally dureing Our Pleasure Justices for the Government of North Carolina to Keep and Cause to be Kept Her Majestys peace as allso all Laws and Ordinances made for the well Government of this Province And Wee do here by Authorize And Impower you or Any thre of you whereof Wee will that one of you Edwd. Mosely, John Blunt, and Francis Delamare shall be one to hold a Generale Court at the time hereafter Expressed on the last Tuesday in the month of July [*illegible*] and March [*illegible*] (that is to Say Adjourne from time to time And from place to place as you or Any three of You) Whereof Wee will that one of You Edward Mosely, John Blunt, Francis Delamare shall be one, shall think and Meet And In the said Courts to hold pleas hear And determine all And All Manner of actions

[24] These are finished minutes. The inclusion of various commissions and proclamations as well as the frequent repetition of Lumley's signature indicates the inexperience of the new clerk of court. The docket is included within the text of the minutes starting on page 11 of the manuscript.

Suites And Causes Whatsoever As well Criminall and Civill, Reall mixt personall or Any other Kind or Nature Whatsoever and In all such Causes to Award Judgment And to Issue Out all Such writts and process as to <2> the due Administration of Juistice doe belong in all things proceeding to the Laws And Ordinances of this Government And as Neer as Conveniently May be to the Laws And Customes of England And for as much as by Reason of the difficullty of Passages and the Extremity of the Weather it May happen that three or More of You Cannot Appear at the time above Expresd Wee Doe hereby further Authorize And Impower you or Any of You in Such Case being present to adjourne for any time not Exceeding Tenn days to the same place And Wee Doe hereby Command the Provost Marshall to Cause to Come before You at the time above Expressed or Any other time by you appointed So Many good And Lawfull Men of this Government as shall be Necessary for the Tryall of All such Causes as shall be brought before You,

Given Under Our hands and the seale of the Collony this 14th day of May in the seaventh Year of the Raigne of Our Soveraigne Lady Anne Queen of Great Brittaine etc. Anno Domini 1708.

[*Signed:*]
W. Glover, Thomas Cary, Thomas Pollock, John Porter, Francis Forster.

Allsoe the Dedimus Potestatem was presented, as Under Videlicet.

To The Honorable Edward Mosley John Blunt and Francis Delamare Esqrs. or to Either of them. These are to Impower And Authorize You or Either of You Joyntly And Severally to administer the Oaths Appointed by Law to the Rest of the Justices of the Peace for the Generall Court at the Next Court to be holden for this Government on the last Tuesday in July Next And that you allsoe take the Same Oaths at the same Time and In so doeing this shall be your Warrants Given under my hand and seale this 20th day of June Anno Domini 1708.

Wm. Glover President

The which Comission and Dedimus Potestatem being Duely published And Read, The Oaths by Act of Parliament with the Oath of abjuration as allso the Oath of Justice was duly administered unto Thomas Boyd and Nathel. Chivin Esqrs. by Francis Delamare Esqr. <3> Who also had the same oaths in due form administered to him And after they had all taken the same they tooke their places upon the Bench According to Custome.

George Lumley produces A Comission from Mr. Tobias Knight as Under Videlicet.

North Carolina Ss. To George Lumley Gentleman

By vertue of a Commission to me directed from the Honorable William Glover Esqr. President etc. thereby Appointing me to be secretary of this Province I out of the Confidence I have in the Prudence Wisdome And abillity of You the said Geo. Lumley Doe hereby Comissionate And Appoint you to be Clerk to the Honorable the Court of Chancery the Generall Court, And the Precinct Court of Paquimons and a true Record of all the Orders And Proceedings at the Afforesaid Courts you shall faith full keep or Cause to be kept and all other things, Power and Authority you shall Do And performe as to be Clerk of the Afforsaid Courts doe or may in Anywise belong or Appertaine And all the Just Fees perquisites And Profitts of the said Offices you shall have Receive And take Rendering to me or my Assignes A true And Just Account the one halfe of all such Fees as shall become due in the Afforesaid Court of Chancery and the Generale Court The Remainder to be And Remaine to your owne use And behoofe And this Comission to Continue dureing my pleasure Given under my hand and seale this 2d day of June Anno Domini 1708.

T. Knight Secretary

The Which Comission being Read the said Geo. Lumley takes the Aforementioned Oaths as allso that of Clerk and was admitted accordingly.

Mr. Tobias Knight secratary offers to this Court a Proclamtion from the Honorable the President and Councell And prays the Same may be published which Accordingly was Read openly in the Court house Yard and is as follows

<4> North Carolina Ss. By the Honorable the President and Councell

A Proclamation

Whereas His Excellency the Pallatine and Lords Proprietors by their Comissions under their Great Seale bearing Date the Eight day of March 1706/7 have Authorized And Impowerd us to take upon us And Administer the Government of this Province of North Carolina which Comission was on the 20th day of October last Past duely published And put in Execution Notwithstanding Which Information is Made unto us that as well in the County of Bath as In this County severall persons have Conspired to Raise Insurection against the peace of Our soveraigne Lady the Queen. Wee Duly This Our Proclamation Strictly on Her Majestys behalfe Charge And Comand all her Majestys Loveing subjects within this Province to Render due obedience to Our soveraigne Lady the Queen And the Government And as it is Established under her by Vertue of the said Comission.

Wee do further Comand All Officers both Millitary And Civill to use their utmost Endeavour in their Respective stations to prevent hinder And suppress All Riotts Mutenys And Insurections that shall or may be made or Raised And the Offenders to Apprehend so that they may be brought to Justice According to Her Majestys Laws in such Case provided Given under Our hands And the seale of the Collony this 13th day of May in the 7th year of the Raigne of Our Soveraigne Lady Queen Anne, Anno Domini 1708.
God save The Queen.

[*Signed:*]
Will. Glover, Thomas Cary, Thomas Pollock, John Porter, Francis Forster.

The afforesaid Mr. Tobias Knight brings allso into Open Court A Protest signed by the Honorable Collonel Thomas Pollock And Declared that twas the desire and Request of the Afforsaid Collonel Pollock that the said Protest might be Openly published and afterwards Reorded which was According done by the Clerk of said Court; and is as follows, Videlicet

<5> North Carolina Ss. July the 24th 1708

Whereas his Excellency John Lord Grandvill Palitine and Sixe more of the Lords Proprietors of North Carolina have Sent in A Commission here under their hands And the Great Seale of the Province Dated the Eight day of March 1706/7. By which Commission after haveing Revoked Anulled and Made Voyd all Power And Authority given by Sir Nathn. Johnson to Thomas Cary Esqr. to be Deputy Governor of this Province they for the Present good Government of this Province Did Grant full Power to the President and Deputies to take upon them the Administration of this Government in the absence of Sir Nathl. Johnson By vertue of Which Commission the Major part of the Deputys bein Mett at the house of Mr. John Hacklefield at Litle River at the time of the Generale Court in October last had the Afforesaid Comission Read And published And Chose William Glover Esqr. as president which Choyce was afterwards allowd of And Confirm'd by the Remaining Deputies Joyning with And Acting under the Afforesaid Wm. Glover Esqr.

as president Notwithstanding which full Choise of the said William Glover Esqr. president Some of the Deputies bein Evilly disposed And not Regarding the publick peace And tranquillity of this Government have by their Actings Manifestly shewed that they Intend not only to Turne out the Afforesaid Wm. Glover Esqr. from being president But in overthrowing the present Government to bring all into Confusion Wherefore I Dreading the Evill Consequences of such their Actings and Doeings Do as Well on the behalfe of Lords proprietors as of my Selfe and the Rest of the peaceable people of this Province publickly protest against all such unjust And illegall proceedings And that whatever Evil Consequences Confusion And Disorder does thereupon follow may lye at their Doors.

Thomas Pollock

A True Coppy from the originall [per] Lumley Clerk

The Court Adjournes for An hour.

Lumley Clerk

Mett againe and present as before The Honorable Francis Delamare, Tho. Boyd, and Nathl. Chevin, Esqrs.

Lumley Clerk

<6> A Deposition of William Williams betwixt James Cross And Samuell Paine taken on behalfe of said Paine. Vide Do. upon the file.

The Provost Marshall and Danl. Guthrey his Deputy Retorns part of their writts.

The Court Adjourns for an hour.

Met again and present as before.

The Grand Inquest for this Province as under videlicet William 1 Norris Foreman, 2 Wm. Symson 3 Wm. Cartright 4 James Mackdaniell 5 Robert Temple, 6 Richd. Ferrell, 7 Lewis Williams 8 James Pritchet, 9 Saml. Jackson, 10 John Bell 11 John Clarke, 12 Cornelius Fitzpatrick, 13 Ja. Thickpen, 14 Humphrey Edwids, 15 Anthony Allexandr, 16 Wm. Newton 17 Tho. Collins, 18 David Ellder, 19 Jno. Forde 20 Francis Kizell, 21 Thomas Blitchenden (Being all duely sworne had the Charge given them, And was then Orderd to withdrawe And Consider of their duty in such Cases according to Law etc. And they do withdraw etc.)

The Court Then Adjournes till tomorrow Morning at seaven of the Clok.

Met againe at the same place Wedsnday July 28th 1708 and Present the Honorable Francis Delamare, Tho. Boyd and Nathl. Chevin Esqrs.

James Laton of the Precinct of Paquimons brings before this Court A Pattent for Two hundred and nine Acres of Land Granted to John Anderson And Acknowled by said Anderson to him by way of Assignment as appears Recorded July 27th 1704.

Tho. Snowdon Clerk

And allso A Deed by way of Assignement from the said Anderson And his wife to the said Laton Relateing to and being [*illegible*] Land as Appear Recorded July 27th 1704.

Per Tho. Snowdon Clerk

Both which Pattent and Deed the above James Laton doth Acknowledge to have fully and Clearly sold as appears by Assignement upon the same in this Office unto Daniell Guthree of the Precinct of Paquimons.

Recorded per Lumley Clerk

<7> A Deed of Land Acknowledg'd here in Open Court from William Hartley to Anthony Allexandr for a Plantation in Allegator Near stump point as may appear at large by the Deed recorded in the Precinct for the same.

Lumley Clerk

An assignement of adeed of Land acknowledged and Indorsed per Thomas Twiddy to Sollamon Horner as Appears at large in the Precinct of Pascotanck And deliverd in Open Court to Mr. Paileing Clerk to be Enterd there.

Per Geo. Lumley Clerk

Mr. Wm. Barrow find for not appearing as A Pettit Juror when Called, five shillings.

Appearance Dockquet Called.

The Pettit Jury Calld And Setled as under Samuell Paine foreman 1 William Luffmon 2 Tho. Snodon Junior 3: Geo. Gordon 4: Tho. Penrice 5 Tho. Horton 6 Geo. Tailor 7 John Haswell 8 Robt. Hoseah 9 Wm. Williams 10 Edward Bradshaw 11 Ezaceariah Keeton 12.

The Court Adjournes for halfe an hour.

Mett againe and Present as before.

The Grand Inquest being Retornd is duely Called over and

appearing Exactly to the pannell. The Court orders the Clerk to aske if they have any Presentments or not, upon which they Retorne a paper presented to this Honorable Court by the Honorable Thomas Cary Esqr. And signed by him Mr. John Porter, Mr. Edwd. Mosely and Mr. Francis Forster as a Complaint against the Honorable Wm. Glover Esqr. Which Said paper the Grand Inquest as aforesaid has had in their Consideration And Retornd the same Endorsed in these Express Words Wee of the Grand Jury Do find the within premisses is a Libell to tend Rather to The disturbance then the tranquillity of the Countrey and that Wm. Glover Esqr. is President of <8> this Province July 28th 1708 William Norris Foreman of the aforsaid Inquest.

Upon Which this Honorable Court Enters into Judgment And Orders the afforesaid Libell to be burnt by the Common hangman, and; Execution thereupon Issued to the Provost Marshall who Retorned the said Execution Endorsed.

Executed per me Jno. Hacklefield Provost Marshall

William Jackson appears to his Reconizance upon the Honorable the Presidents Warrant And No Evidence appearing against him he is discharg'd from the same Paying his Fees.

The Court adjournes for An hour. Mett againe and present as before.

John Dixe prays the Liberty of this Honorable Court to Enter Three hundred Acrees of Land More or less at the Northwest side of Mashy Gatt which was Accordingly Granted.

Lumley Clerk

Humphrey Edwards makes Oath upon the holy Evangelist That Nicholas Daw at Pamplicoe sent for him to sett his hand to a paper Concerning the Government, but When he Came to his house he the said Daw was gone from home, however he the said Edwards gave Order And left word with Nicholas Daws Wife to Make her husband Put his Name to the Afforesaid sometime in May last and is Satisfied his hand is to it but say he knows not what was writt in the paper this virbatem from his owne mouth per Lumley Clerk.

The Court Adjournes till Tomorrow morning.

Met againe Thursday July 29th 1708 and present the Honorable Francis Delamare, Thomas Boyde, Nathiniell Chevin, Esqrs. Justices.

To the Honorable the Generale Court The Petition of Thomas and Henry Swan Humbly prays Liberty to choose their Guardian Henry Swan, Thomas Swan. And Appearing in their proper persons they declare in Open Court that they Make Choyce of their Brother Mr. William Swann to be their Guardian.

Lumley Clerk

<9> North Carolina Ss. To the Honorable Generale Court etc.

The Petition of Sosin Kembull most Humbly sheweth that Richard Stradford your petitioners Loyall servant hath absented himselfe from Your petitioners service the space of two years And as [*illegible*] as since May, And pray he May be adjudged to serve According as the Law Directs in such Cases And he as in duty bound shall pray.

The which petition being Read the Servants [appeared] And Could not gainsay to what was Offerd [*torn*] Therefor This Honorable Court upon due Consideration Gives Judgment that the said Richard Stradford servant Afforesaid do serve his said Master the full and Just Term of four Years from this time.

Lumley Clerk

A paper oferd to this Honorable Court in these words, videlicet Obidiah fair Enters all the waist Land between Andrew Wilson And Richard Burtenshaw att Allegator July 28th 1708.

Obidiah Faire his Marke

Mr. Thomas Snodon files A Warrant of Attorney to him from John Falconer Impowering him to Appear att this Generale Court at the suit of Wm. Jennings in An Action of Debt, vide file.

Lumley Clerk

Joseph Jordan appears to his Recognizance And acknowledges himselfe to stand justly indebted to Our Soveraigne Lady the Queen in the sume of four hundred pound sterling to be Leavi'd upon his goods and Chattells Lands And teniments if he doth not make his personall Appearance att the Next Generale Court to be held for this Province And in the meantime to be of good Abbearance and behaviour to all her Majestys subjects And therewith he is Content.

Lumley Clerk

Thomas Boyd Esqr. as the Afforesaid Joseph Jordan security Acknowledges himselfe bound in the same sume as Afforesaid for his Appearance.

Lumley Clerk

Charle Griffen Gentleman allso Enters into Recognizance in

the Afforesaid summe to prosecute the Afforesaid Joseph Jordan As An Evidence on the behalfe of Our Soveraigne Lady the Queen and is Therewith Content.

Lumley Clerk

<10> Mary Dennis being in Custody of the Provost Marshall At the Suite of Our Soveraigne Lady the Queen being Calld, Appears And for some Reasons Appearing to this Honorable Court is againe Comitt into the Custody of Captain Jno. Hacklefield Provost Marshall, who is Orderd to have her here att the Next Generale Court held for this Province.

Lumley Clerk

And then the Court Orderd all the Evidences against the said Mary Denniss to be Called as bound by Recognizance who appeard according and acknowledged the same, and Orderd to be Continued as upon the file which is Continued.

Lumley Clerk

Archbald Holms being bound to Our Soveraigne Lady the Queen in the Summe of fifty pounds Currant Money that he appear at this Generale Court, And George Berhenhead And Anthy. Allexander Bound allso in twenty five pound Each as security for his Appearance, the said Archbald Holmes being by the Court Solemnly Called appeareth not.

Lumley Clerk

Thomas Collins Appearing in the Custody of the Marshall [*illegible*] is Called And Acknowledges himselfe to stand Justly Indebted to Our Soveraigne Lady the Queen in the summe of fifty pounds sterling to be Leavid upon his good and Chattells Land And tenniments if he doth not make his personall Appearance at the Next Generale Court to be held for this Province and in the meantime bee of good abearance and behaviour to her majestys subjects, and therewith he is content.

Lumley Clerk

Orderd that Robert Coxe his Recognizance as Appears upon the file be Continued till next Court, and it is Continued.

Lumley Clerk

Orderd that Thomas Twiddy Recognizance as appears upon the file be Continued till next Court, and it is Continued.

Lumley Clerk

<11> Appearance Docquet

1 Jossiah Rolfe against James Coles. Trespass Case. Cepi.

2 Wm. White against Thomas Collins. Trespass Case. Cepi.

3 Eliza. Swann Executrix of Saml. Swann etc. against Thomas Snoden. Detinue. 40*s*. sur demise. Cepi.

4 Thomas Peterson and Company against Captain Jno. Hacklefield administrator of Geo. Fordage. Trespass Case. Cepi.

5 Wm. Glover Esqr. against Thomas Twiddy. Trespass Case. Cepi.

6 Saml. Jackson against Thomas Twiddy. Detinue. Cepi.

7 Mary Blunt against John Forde. No Declaration. Trespass Case. Cepi.

The seven Actions were all Retornd Cepi Corpus and Continued till next Court.

8 Hannah Manwaring against James Thickpen. Trespass Case. Cepi.

9 Wm. White and Ann his wife against The same. Trespass. Cepi.

10 Thomas Peterson and Company against Samuell Bundy. Trespass Case.

1 Thomas Peterson and Company against Thomas Boyde Esqr. Executor of Archbald Burnett. Trespass Case. No Returne.

2 Nathl. Chevin Esqr. against Henry Bonner. Trespass Case.

3 Wm. Read against Jno. Alldridge. Detinue.

These three Actions above Were deliverd but had noe Returne made upon them.

1 Thomas Blitchenden against Wm. Russell. In Trover. Non est inventus.

2 The same against John Neell. Detinue. Non est inventus.

3 The same against Thomas Litle. Detinue. Non est inventus.

4 The same against James Cafton. Detinue. Non est inventus.

5 The same against Lawrence [*illegible*]. Detinue. Non est inventus.

6 The same against Wm. Reed. In Trover. Non est inventus.

7 The same against Thomas Litle. Trespass Case. Non est

inventus.

The above seaven Actions were all Retornd Non Est Inventus.

<12> 1 Erasmas Harslif against Willm. Steelle. Detinue. Cepi.

2 Robert Coxe against thomas Twiddy. Trespass Case. Cepi.

The above two Actions were Enterd the first discontinued the Defendant paying Cost and the 2d discontinued per the plaintiff.

1 Captain Jno. Hacklefield against Wm. Swan. Detinue. Cepi. Entered agreed per plaintiff.

Impliances upon the Tryall Docquet from last Court.

The Honorable Landgrave Robert Daniell Esqr. against Fredrick Jones Esqr. Detinue.

The Honorable Thomas Cary Esqr. against Fredrick Jones, Esqr. Trespass Case.

Captain Jno. Hacklefield against Saml. Norton. Trespass Case.

These last three Actions were Continued by this Honorable Court.

Sollomon Horner against Samuell Jackson. Trespass.

Comand was Given to the Provost Marshall or his deputy of North Carolina to arrest the body of Saml. Jackson And him saife hold so that he be And appear at the Next Generale Court to be holden at the House of Captain John Hacklefields in Litle River on the last Tuesday in July next then And there to Answer the plaintiff Soled. Horner in a plea of Tresapass and have you there this writt dated at the Secretarys office this 29th day of June Anno Domini 1708.

Testis Tob. Knight Secretary

Att which said Court videlicet the 27th day of July Anno Domini 1708 the day of The Return of the said Writt Came George Harris Deputy Marshall for the Province Afforesaid And Made Returne thereof Executed by me George Harris Deputy Marshall.

The Declaration being sent with writt follow in these Words videlicet

No. Carolina Ss. To The Honorable the Generale Court etc.

Sollamon Horner is plaintiff against Saml. Jackson defendant in a plea of Trespass And Complains that the defendant sometime in March last with force And Arms etc. in the Precinct of Pascotancke within the Jurisdiction of this Court malitiously Intending to

Damnise And hurt the plaintiff then and there did shoot and Kill the horse of the value of Eight pounds the <13> Proper goods and Chattells of the plaintiff for which said horse the defendant to the plaintiff hath not pd. nor any satisfaction for the Same hath made, Whereby the plaintiff saith he is damnified And hath Damage to the summe of sixteen pounds sterling And thereupon he brings this suite.

T. Knight Secretary

<*Jackson* versus *Horner Plea*>

And the Defendant non Culpabilis modo et forma and for Tryall puts himselfe upon the Countrey.

Snoden per [*torn*]

And the Plentiff in like manner in etc. per Soll. Horner. Thereupon Comand was given to Provost Marshall for this Province that he Imediately Cause to Come Twelve etc. By whome etc. Who Neither etc. to Recognize because etc. and now here this day to witt the same day Comes the Provost Marshall And Says he has Ready Twelve etc. as he was Comanded And Returns the Pannell thereof to witt Samuell Paine Foreman, Wm. Lufman, Thomas Snoden Junior, George Gordane, Thomas Penrice, Thomas Horton, Geo. Taylor, John Haswell, Robert Hosech, Wm. Williams, Edward Bradshaw, Ezacciriah Keeton, 12: Who being seated, cryed, And sworne to say the truth in the premisses do say upon their Oaths Wee of the Jury find for the Defendant Which being by the honorable Court heard And fully understood, it is Considered by the said Honorable Court that the said Solled. As Afforesaid Take nothing by his writt or declaration as Afforesaid, but be in Mercy for his false clameing and that the said Samuell Goe thereof without Day etc.

And it is Likewise Considered by the Honors the Justices here the same day And Year that the said Samuell Jackson Recover againe the said Sollomon Horner the summe of Eight shillings and four pence for a non suite and allso the sume of one pound sixteen shillings and ten pence For his Cost and Charges in this behalfe laid out and Expended According to the form of the Act of Assembly etc.

Lumley Clerk

<*Wm. Jennings* against *John Falconer*>

And the said Plentiffs brought Her Majestys writt of Capias ad Respondendum against the said Defendant, And the same writ being Returnd on the 27th day of July being the Day of the Returne thereof Anno Domini 1708; was Endorsed Cepi Corpus per me Daniell Guthree Deputy marshall. And A Declaration being sent along with the writ follows in these Words,

No. Carolina Ss. To The Honorable the Gerale Court

Wm. Jennings is plaintiff against John Falconer defendant in a plea of Debt And says That the Defendant stands Justly Indebted to the plentif in the full And Just summe of Two pounds Tenn Shillings to be paid as followeth (videlicet) Two barrells of Pitch att Twenty shillings per barrell And the other Tenn <14> Shillings in Countrey Comodite as in and by one Certaine writeing obligatory under his proper hand bearing Date the Fifteenth day of May 1707 And hereinto Court brought doth and May Appear Nevertheless the said Defendant the Afforesaid sume of Two pounds Tenn shillings in Manner aforesaid to the plaintiff hath not paid tho often thereunto required but the Same doth still Refuse to pay to the plaintiffs damage five pounds sterling And thereupon he brings this Suite etc.

T. Knight Secretary

Whereupon John Falconer Defendant by Thomas Snoden his Attorney Appears att the said Court to witt the twenty seaventh day of July Annoqe Domi 1708 And say he Cannot gainesay the plaintiff his Action So as Afforesaid against him brought nor but that he stands Justly Indebted unto the plentiff in the sums afforesaid Expressed And is therefore willing that Judgement be Enterd against him for the same with the Fees Accrueing to the Clerk, And noe more Fees or Charges, and further the said Judgement is Confessed as afforesaid with stay of Execution untill next Generalle Court.

Which being by the Honorable Court heard it is by them Considerd the 27th day of July 1708 that the said William Jennings Recover against the said John Falconer as well the Summes afforesaid mentioned in the plaintiffs declaration the Debt Afforesaid as the sume of [*blank*] being the Cost of Suite for Clerks Fees And the defendant in Mercy etc.

Lumley Clerk

Then this Honorable Court Orders Geo. Harris Deputy Marshall to Adjourne the Same till A Court in Course, According to Act of Assembly which he has done by publicke Proclamation as Customary in this Province, etc.

Geo. Lumley Clerk etc.

RECORDED BY ORDER OF COURT

[*CCR 189*]

<15> Know all men by these presents that I Thomas Arnold of North Carolina planter Am holden And forever bound unto John Lewis of North Carolina in the full and just sume of fifty pounds Sterling Money of England Which payments well and truely to be made and I the Said Thomas Arnold do bind my Selfe my heirs and [*torn*] firmly by These presents unto John Lewis heirs or Assignes or Lawfull Attorney in the [*torn*] summe as Wittness my hand And Seale. [*Torn*].

The Condition of the above Obligation is such that the abovesaid John Lewis his heirs or assignes or Lawfull Attorney shall not be Molested nor disposessed from A Tract of Land Containing Ninety Acres Lyeing on the Mouth of Scupper Long River with houseing And All other things Thereunto belonging then the above obligation to be Voyd and of None Effect otherways to Stand And Remain in full force power and Vertue in Law as Wittness My hand and seale this Three And twenty day of July Anno Domini 1708.

Signed Sealed and Deliverd Thomas Arnold
in Presence of Us
Wallter Bounsill
Wm. Collins his marke

FILE PAPERS IN SUITS AND PROSECUTIONS

[*Horner* v. *Jackson*]

[*CCR 148*]

No. Carolina Ss. To the Provost Marshall or his Deputy

These are in her Majestyes name to will and require you to Arrest the body of Samll. Jackson and him Safely hold Soe that he be and appeare at the next Generall Court to be holden at the house of Captain Jno. Hecklefeild in Litle river on the last Tuseday in July next then and there to Answer the plaint of Solomon Horner in a plea of Trespass and have you there this Writt Dated at the Secretarys Office this 29th day of June Anno Domini 1708.

Testis T. Knight Secretary

[*Endorsed:*]
Breve
Horner versus Jackson
In Trespass
Executed by me George Harris deputy marshall

MISCELLANEOUS FILE PAPERS

[*Justices' commission*]

[*CCR 139*]

No. Carolina Ss. William Glover Esqr. President of the Councell and Comander in Cheife and the rest of our Trusty and well beloved Councellors of State Greeting

To our trusty and well beloved Edwd. Moseley John Blount Francis Delamare James Minge Thos. Boyd and Nathaniell Chevin Esqrs.

Wee being well Assured of your prudence Loyalty and Integrity doe hereby Comissionate and appoint you Jointly and Severally dureing our pleasure Justices for the Government of North Carolina to Keep or Cause to be Kept her Majestyes peace as also all Lawes and ordinances made for the well Government of this province and wee doe hereby Authorize and Impower you or any three of you (whereof wee will that one of you Edwd. Moseley Jno. Blount and Fra. Delamare shall be one) to hold a Generall Court at the tymes hereafter Expres't (that is to Say) on the last Tuesday in the Monthes of July Octobr. and March and the Same to adjourne from tyme to tyme and from place to place as you or any three of you (whereof wee will that one of you Edwd. Moseley Jno. Blount and Fra. Delamare shall be one) shall thinke meet and in the said Court to hold pleas heare and Determine all and all manner of Actions Suites and Causes what soever as well Criminall and Civill reall Mixt personall or any other Kind or Nature whatsoever and in all Such Causes to award Judgement and to Issue out all Such writts and process as to the due administration of Justice Doe belong in all things proceeding to the Lawes and ordinances of this Government and as neare as Conveniently may be to the Lawes and Customes of England and for as much as by reason of the difficulty of passages and the Extreamity of the weather it may happen that three or more of you Cannot appeare at the tyme above Exprest wee doe hereby further Authorize you and Impower you or any of You in Such Case being present to adjourne the Court for any tyme not Exceeding tenn Dayes [*illegible*] doe hereby [*illegible*] provost Marshall to Cause to Come before you at the tyme above Exprest or any other tyme by you appointed Soe many Good and Lawfull Men of this Government as shall be necessary for the tryall of all Such Causes as shall be brought before you.

Given under our hands and the Seale of the Collony this 14th day of May in the 7th yeare of the raigne of our Soveraigne Lady Anne Queen of greate Britanie etc. Annoque Domini 1708.

[*Signed:*]
W. Glover, Thomas Cary, Thomas Pollock, John Porter, Fran. Foster.

[*Endorsed:*]
Jurat Thomas Boyd Esqr., Nathll. Chevin Esqr., Francis Delamare Esqr.
Commission of the peace for the Generall Court
Entered upon Record per G. Lumley Clerk

[*Justices' authorization*]

GENERAL COURT, DATE UNDETERMINED

[*CCR 139*]

To the Honorable Edwd. Moseley Jno. Blount and Francis Delamare Esqrs. or to either of them

These are to Impower and authorize You or either of you Jointly and Severally to administer the Oathes appointed by Law to the rest of the Justices of the peace for the Generall Court at the next Court to be holden for this Goverment on the last Tuseday in July next and that you also take the Same oathes at the Same tyme and in So doeing this Shall be your Warrant Given under my hand and Seale this 20th day of June Anno Domini 1708.

W. Glover President

[*Endorsed:*]
Dedimus Potestatem

FILE PAPERS IN SUITS AND PROSECUTIONS

[*Crown* v. *Swaine*]

[*CCR 140*]

No. Carolina Ss.

The Honorable Henderson Walker Esqr. President of the Councill and Comander in Cheife Came here the 3d Day of the Generall Cort and givs the Court here to understand and be informed That Whereas By an Act of Assembly made for preventing Sabbath Breaking Yett By Information of Robt. Murrey made to the Honorable president Mr. Stephen Swaine the said Act not Regarding and the Penallty thereof not Fearing Did unlawfull Brand a hors on the Sabbath Day and Bring horses out of the woods in order thereon to [*torn*] therefore the Honorable president prays the Penallty of the said act may be Inflicted upon the said Swaine.

[*Fewox* v. *Bray*]

[*CCR 179*]

North Carolina Ss. To the Honorable the Generall Court

The Humble petition of James Fewox humbly Complaining Sheweth unto your Honors That whereas your petitioner in July Court Anno 1704 by petition to this Honorable Court Shewing that by an order of Court past the 25th day of October 1703 the provost Marshall was ordered to take the Estate of Thomas Boucheir deceased into his possession till otherwise ordered by due Course of Law And likewise Shewes that the Said Boucheirs Estate was Indebted to him in the Summe of Seaventeen pounds Six Shillings and that by virtue of the aforsaid order Willm. Bray Marshall of Coratuck Seized the Said Boucheirs Estate and the Same hath Confiscated and disposed of Contrary to Law And it was ordered that the Said Bray Should make his Appeareance at the next Generall Coart to be held for this province to Answare the Said [*torn*] Fewox's Complaint Nevertheless the Said [*torn*] not appeared nor made Answare thereunto Since the Said order.

Wherefore your petitioner humbly prayes that he may be admitted to prove his Account before your honors and that your honors will grant him an order against the Said Bray for the Same and Shall pray etc.

James Fewox

[*Endorsed:*]
Petition to the Generall Court
Fewox's Petition

[*Frayly* v. *Long*]

[*CCR 140*]

To the Honorable Generall Court

The Humble Petition of Wm. Fryly in Humbly manner shewing to your Honors that in Augst. last past Mr. James Long did assault Beat and abuse your humble petitioner upon her Majestys Road and upon which your humble petitioner made his Complaint to the Honorable Henderson Walker and his Honor Isued his warrant for the said James Long and the said Long appeard before his Honor and his Honor Bound the said Long to this Honorable Court and your petitioner finding no process appearing to this Court and your petitioner having his Evidence here desire that your honors will be pleasd to have and to take their Deposition and your petitioner in Duty Bound will pray.

[*Peterson, attorney of Perry and Company* v. *Brothers and wife*]

[*CCR 192*]

[*Torn*] the honorable the Generall Court

Thos. Peterson Attorney to Micajah Perry and New Pensilvania Company is Plaintiff against Wm. Brothers and Sarah his wife defendants in a plea of Debt and sayes that the Defendants Stands Justly Indebted to the plaintiff Quallifyed as aforesaid in the full and Just Summe of three pounds Six Shilling and Nine pence in Good Merchantable fresh porke to be delivered at Mr. Jno. Jenings's Landing in pascotanke river as in and by one Certaine writeing obligatory and the proper hand of the Said Sarah by name of Sarah and beareing date the [*torn*] december 1704 and here into Court [*torn*] and may appeare Nevertheless the said Defendants nor either of them the aforesaid Summe of three pounds Six Shillings and Nine pence in manner aforesaid to the Defendant hat not paid tho' often thereunto requested but the Same doth Still refuse to pay to the plaintiffs Damage Six pounds thirteen Shillings and Six pence Sterling and thereupon he brings this Suite etc.

T. Knight Secretary

[*Endorsed:*]
Narratio

GENERAL COURT, DATE UNDETERMINED

Peterson versus Brothers
In Debt

[*Peterson, attorney of Perry and Company* v. *Willoughby*]

[*CCR 192*]

No. Carolina Ss. To the Honorable the Generall Court etc.

Thos. Peterson Attorney to Micajah Perry and New Pensilvania Company plaintiff against Jno. Willoughby of the precinct of pequimens in the Said province planter Defendant in a plea of Debt and Sayes [*torn*] the Defendant Stands Justly Indebted to the plaintiff Quallifyed as aforesaid in the full and Just Summe of Nine pounds four Shillings and tenn pence in the Staple Comodityes of the province as [*torn*] and by one Certaine writeing Obligatory under [*torn*] hand beareing Date the 31st Augt. 1704 and hereinto [*torn*] brought doth and may appeare Nevertheless the said Defendant the Said Summe of Nine pounds four Shillings and tenn pence to the plaintiff hath not paid tho' often thereunto requested but the Same doth Still refuse to pay to the plaintiffs Damage Eighteen pounds thirteen Shilling and Eight pence Sterling and thereupon he brings this Suite etc.

T. Knight Secretary

[*Endorsed:*]
Narratio
Peterson versus Willoughby
In Debt

MISCELLANEOUS FILE PAPERS

[*McKeel, John, petition*]

[*CCR 186*]

To the Honorable Generall Court

The Humble Petition of John McKeel Humbly Shewing that Benjamin West being orderd by the Precinct Court to Live with your Petitioner till he Come of age; Yett Nevertheless by the Fals Information of mr. Thos. Boyd who hath Informd the Court that the Said boy of age he the Said Benj. West has absented himselfe and Chosen mr. Thos. Boyd his Guardian Contrary to Equity and Justice Intending to turn your Petitioner off the Plantation Therefore your Petitioner humbly Prays Releife in the Premisses and that your Petitioner may have the Liberty of the Plantation and shall Pray etc.

John McKeel

[*Perry and Company, letter of attorney*]

[*SS 310*]

By this publick Instrument of procuration or [*torn*] it knowne and

Manifest unto all those who shall See these [*torn*] heare the Same read that on the fifteenth day of the Month of [*torn*] Anno Domini 1702 and in the Seccond Yeare of the Raigne of our [*torn*] Lady Anne by the Grace of God Queen of England Scotland and Ireland Defender of the faith etc. before me James [*torn*] Notary and Tabellion publick Dwelling in London by [*torn*] Authority Duely admitted and Sworne and in the presence of Witnesses here after named Personally appeared [*torn*] Micajah perry Thos. Byefield Joseph Marshall [*torn*] Cooper Jno. Frecune Silvanus Grove Henry Gould Jno. Hodgekins and Samll. Waldensfield of London [*torn*] being as they declare the Majority of the Directors and Managers of the Comerce of the New pensilvania Traders of London which Said Apeares for and on the part and be halfe of themselves and the rest of the Said New pensi[*torn*] Traders Declared to have made ordained and Constituted by these presents Doe make ordaine and Constitute Mr. [*torn*] Peterson of Virginia Merchant their true and Lawfull Attorney Giveing and by these presents Granting to [*torn*] said Attorney full power and Lawfull Authority for [*torn*] the Said Constituants and the rest of the Said Traders and to name and to their use to Aske Demand Levy Sue by all Lawfull ways and meanes Recover and receive from Colonel Robert Quarry his Executors and Administrators and [*torn*] from all other person or persons whome it shall [*torn*] Concerne all and Singuler. Such Summe and Summes of Goods Wares Merchanizes Effects Estate and things whatsoever nothing excepted nor reserved which [*torn*] or any of them (Inhabiting in North Carolina) [*torn*] or Shall hereafter owe and Stand indebted or have in hands Custody or possession (in North Carolina [*torn*] to the Said New pensilvania Traders in what name or names Soever or by what reason or meanes Due or belonging or in any wise Apperteyneing And to th[*torn*] with all and every person or persons whome it doth Concerne to Account and to veiw Setle and adjust all [*torn*] the Ballance of all, Such Accounts and all Goods and Money to them the Said New pensilvania Traders whe[*torn*] Bond Bill Booke note or other wise how Soever in North Carolina aforesaid to receive Upon Recoverys or receipt [*torn*] give one or more accquitances or other Sufficient [*torn*] Due forme of Law But in Case of refusal or delay [*torn*] Debtor or Debtors or any other person or persons whom [*torn*] all or may Concerne to make and rendr Just and true [*torn*] and payment and Satisfacction in the premisses him her them thereunto to Compell by all Lawfull wayes and meanes Soever And to that end if need bee to appeare before all Lords Judges and Justices in any Court or Courts [*torn*] to doe Say pursue Implead Seize Sequester Attach Imprison and to Condemne and out of prison againe [*torn*] deliver And generally in and Concerneing the premisses and all matters and things thereunto relateing to doe performe and execute all and whatsoever shall be requisite and necessary as fully Amply and effectually to all Intents and Constructions and purposses as they the Said Constituants might or Could doe if personally present And that altho' the Cause sho'd require more especiall or ample power then is herein before express'd they the Said Constituants hereby promiseing to Ratify Confirme and hold for good and vallid all and whatsoever their Said Attorney shall lawfully Doe or Cause to be done in or a bout the premisses by virtue of these presents Thus done and pass'd in London aforesaid [*torn*] the presence of James Dunidge and Edwd. Travers.

[*Signed:*]
Micajah Perry, Thos. Byfield, Jos. Marshall, Thos. Cooper, John Frecune, Silvan Grove, Henry Gouldney, John Hodgkins, Samll. Waldenfield.

Witnesses hereunto requir'cd [*torn*]
and Delivered
In presence of
[*Torn*] Dunnidge
[*Torn*] Travers

In premissorium Fidem
Jabus. Puckle Nots. publius.

To all to Whome these presents shall Come wee Sir Samll. Dashwood Knight Lord Mayor and the Aldermen of the City of London Doe hereby make knowne and Certify that Mr. James Puckle who hath Signed and attested the procuration [*torn*] Letter of Attorney here before written is a Notary and Tabellion publick Legally by Royall Authority admitted.

[*Torn*]

[*Plater, Richard, account*]

[*CCR 190*]

Mr. Richd. Plater Dr.

To Calling Tooks action and plea 00:01:06
To order and Justices 00:03:06

N. Chevin Clerk

[*Endorsed:*]
Mr. Plater

[*Smith, Richard, account*]

[*CCR 190*]

Mr. Rich. Smith is Debtor [*torn*] Per Contra Credit January the [*torn*] 1701

	£	*s.*	*d.*
To 44 pounds of Shott att 2*d.*½	0	9	2
1 doz. of small Knives:	0	1	3
1 doz. of bottles:	0	6	0
6 brass Kettles: wt. 16 pounds att 20*d.* per pound:	1	6	8
Ditto 1 doz. of bottles:	0	6	0
2 pounds of Flints: att 2*s.*:	0	4	0
118 pounds of Shott: att 2*d.* ½:	0	17	6
2 barrells of powder:	5	5	0
2 pair of blew plains:	2	5	6
1 pair of Red plains:	1	3	7½
1 pair of Stript duffills:	3	15	0

1 pair of blew plains:	1	2	9
Ditto 1 pair:	4	16	4
66 pounds of Tobacco:	0	6	6
200 Gallons of Rum: att 3*s.* 6*d.*	35	0	0
5 brass Kettles wt. 19 pounds: att 20*d.*:	1	11	8
1 pounds of virmillion and 1 pound of red lead	0	12	9
6 doz. of fish hookes at 6*d.*:	0	3	0
700 Flints: att 2*s.* per pound:	0	14	0
2 hhds. of Tobacco wt. grose 892:	5	0	0
Your bill given up:	66	16	9½
238 Gallons of Rum att 3*s.* 6:	41	13	0
118 pounds of Shott: and 22 bottles:	1	7	3
25: Gallons of Rum att 3*s.* 6:	4	7	6
116 pounds of Shott att 2*d.* ½ per pound:	1	4	2
4 doz. of fish hookes att 6*d.*:	0	2	0
[*Torn*] of Shott att 2*d.* ½	2	10	0
By Shott returned:	0	8	9
Aug. the 2d: 1700: 80 bucks: 119 does 9 roccoones 14 fox and Catt: 3 Muskratts 2 Otters 5 pounds 6 ounces of beaver all Amounting to:	18	14	1½
Feb. the 19th: 1700: 49 does 29 bucks 8 pricketts 4 roccoons: 1 Catt and 1 bare to the Sum of	7	3	10
Febr. the 21th: 1700 furr and skins Amounting to:	83	15	10
May the 15th: 1701: 26 pounds of beaver 34 fox and Catt: 29 roccoons: 2 Woolves 2 bares 3 otters 21 pounds of beaver 41 pricketts: 194 does 140 bucks: Amounting to	40	07	11
10 Guns returnd	9	7	4
21 buckles	0	7	6
3½ doz. of Spring tongs	0	2	4
Books Janr. the 3d. 1701/2	160:	7:	7½
46 Roccoons att 4*d.*	0	11	2
9 fox and Catt: att 9*d.*	0	7	7
5 bares skins att 2*s.*	0	10	0
3 Woolves att 18*d.*	0	4	6
1 Otter and 1 Catt	0	3	9
1 Ratt 4*d.*: 20 does att 18*d.*	1	10	4
22 Pricketts att 1*s.* and 2 fawns: 18*d.*	1	3	6
7 pounds of Beaver att 3*s.* per pound	1	1	0
70 fox and ratt:	2	12	6
136 roccoons	2	5	4
2 Woolves and 4 bares:	0	11	0
5 Otters: and 1 panther	0	17	0
	172	5:	3

GENERAL COURT, DATE UNDETERMINED

[*Endorsed:*]
Mr. Rich. Smith Account Indian pay
Colonel Robt. Quary a Cont

[*Symons, Thomas, oath*]

[*CCR* 192]

No. Carolina SS.

I Thomas Simons doe in the presence of God and Penalty of Perjury Promise to bear faith and true allegiance to his Majesty king William and Will be faithfull to his Excellency the Palatine and Lords proprietors of Carolina.

And doe from my heart detest and abhor as Impious the heriticall this damnable Doctrine and position that Princes Excomunicatd or deprivd by the pope or any Authority of the See of Rome may be deposed or Murdered by their Subjects or any other whatsoever and I doe declare that noe forreigne prince person prelate State or potentate hath or ought to have any Jurisdiction power Superiority Preleminery or Authority Ecclesiasticall or Spirituall in these Realms. And I doe Ingage as a Justice within this Goverment of N. Carolina in all Articls of the Comission to me directed to doe equal right to the poor and to the king after my Cuning Witt and power and after the Laws and Customes of this Goverment And Statutes therof made and as near as may be after the Laws of England I will not Lett for Gift or other Cause but well and truely Shall doe my office of Justice And I Will not be of Councill of any Quarrell hanging before yo.

thomas Symons

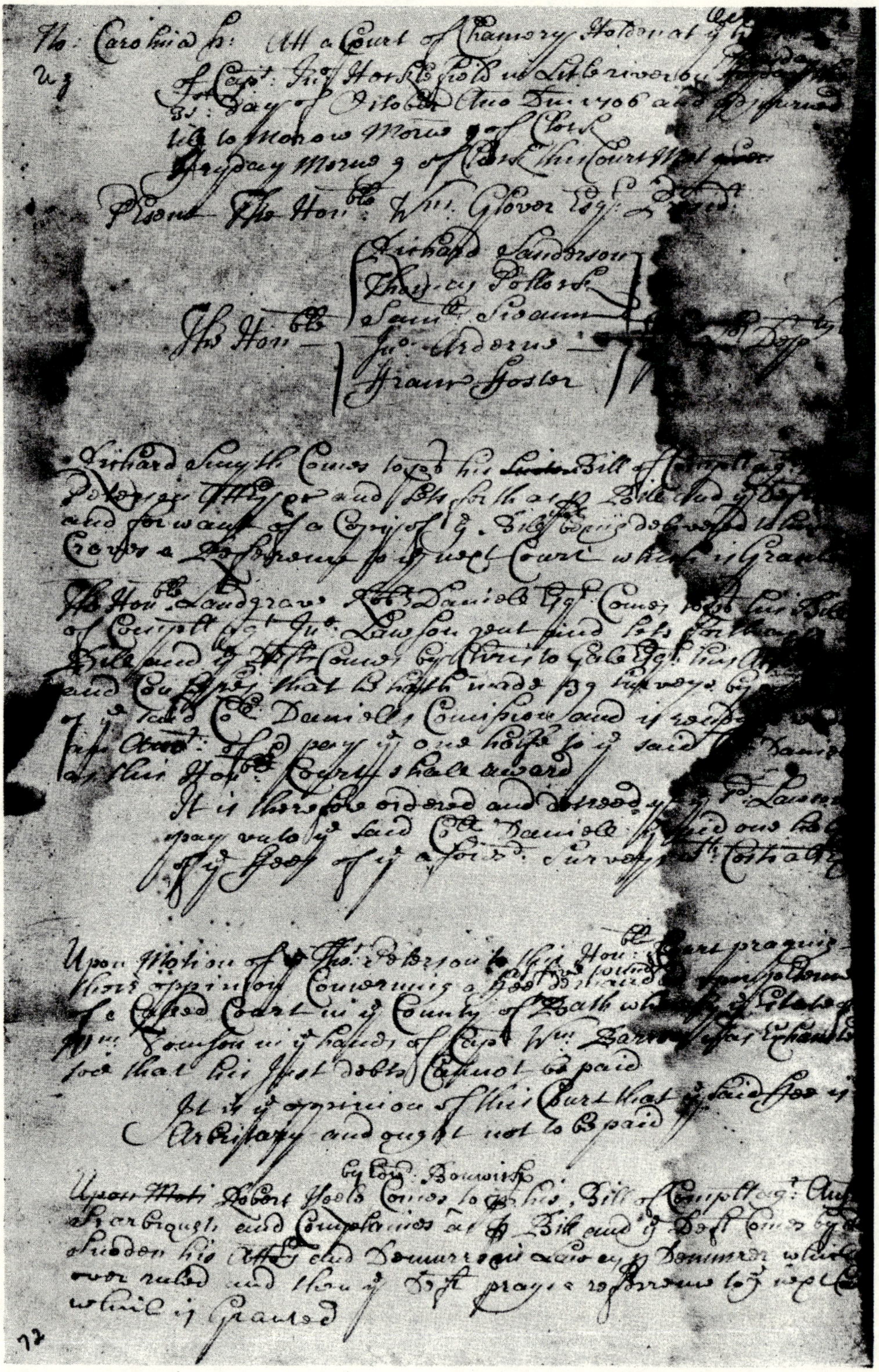

First Page of Minutes, Court of Chancery, October 1706
In the Hand of Tobias Knight

Records of the Court of Chancery

Records of the Court of Chancery

FILE PAPERS

[*Walker, attorney of Gambell* v. *Pollock and Hunt, executors*]

[*CCR 181*]

North Carolina Ss. To the provost Marshall or Depty

These are in his Majesties Name to Will and require you to Subpena Colonel Tho. Pollock and Capt. Jno. Hunt Executors of the Last Will and Testament of Mr. Adam Gambell Deceased to Apeare the 3d Day of the Next Generall Court to Answer to a Bill filed against them in Chancery by the Honourable Henderson Walker Esqr. President etc. Attorney of Jno. Gambell Attorney of James Gambell Hereof fayl not Dated March the 17th 1701/2.

N. Chevin Clk. Cancellariae

[*Endorsed:*]
This presept was Executed marh the 24 1701/2 by me Thos. Luten provost marshall

[*CCR 181*]

The Estate of adam gemble deceased

To the writting over and Ballancing of his accountts and cost of [*blank*].
To fees in Proving the will and recording
the inventoryes etc. .... 01=14=06
To my trouble in comming to court to answer
Suits a ganst Gembels estate 3 tyms [*blank*]

Per Contra Cr.

By Mr. Nicholas Crisp
By Mr. Chevin
By Hendersin Walker Esqr.
By [*blank*] yds. of muslin from Mr. Chevin
By 5 Barrels Salt

[*Endorsed:*]
Chancery file

[*CCR 181*]

North Carolina Ss.

Att A Court of Chancery holden att the House of Doctor Jno. Hecklefeild in Little River the 11th Day of June 1702 Present the Honorable President and Rest of Comissioners.

Decreed that Capt. Jno. Hunt Executor of the Last Will and Testament of Adam Gambell Deceased pay Unto Mr. Jno. Smith Attorney of Mr. Robt. Hambleton Mr. James Fogo Mr. Alexander Paterson the Sum of forty Nine pounds Six Shillings and two pence halfepeny being the Whole and Remaines Due in his hands to be pd. in Fresh pork as allso 30 good Pork Barrills Acording to Law and 30 Bushells of Salt alias Execution.

Copia Vera N. Chevin, Clk. Cancillariae

[*Endorsed:*]
Received of Capt. John Huntt the net quantity of five thoussand two Hundred and Sixtie Nine pounds of fresh pork in Value thertie two pounds Eighteen Shillings and Seaven pence halfe penie one accountt of this within writen decree this 30th of 9ber 1703 by me Hugh Campbell Attorney of John Smith
Received of the Said John Hunt twentie Six porke barrells twentie Six bushells of Sallt one account of the within mentioned decree this 10th of xber 1703 by me Hugh: Campbell

[***Macclendon and wife, administrators*** v. ***Foster and Sutton, guardians***]

[*CCR 186*]

Albemarle County

These are in the Names of his Excellency the Lord palatine And the Lords proprietors to order you to Suppena Francis Foster and Joseph Sutton Senior Guardians to Richard Whitbey and Deborah Whitbey in their minority personally to appeare att the Next Court of Chancery the Third Day of the Said Court there to make answer to the Bill of Complaint Exhibited by Dennis MacClendon and Deborah his wife Administrators etc. against them the Said Francis Foster and Joseph Sutton Senior And hereof faile not att your perill Given under my hand this 30th Day of September Anno Domini 1702.
To Peter Bray Deputy Marshall

Nath. Chevin Clericus Cancellariae

[*Chapman* v. *Powell*]

[*CCR 191*]

North Carolina Ss.

Mr. Ralph Chapin Greiviously Complaineing that he the Complainant Coming a stranger in to this Government through Ignorance Did pass anto Wm. powell a Certaine Bill or Bond for a tract of Land which the Said powell pretended Right too Alltho Indeed he had no Right to Sell or Dispose of the Same and therefore the Complainant Saith that By any Purchase of or from the Said Powell he hath no Benefitt And further the Said Chapman Complains that the Said Powell has brought against him 2 Actions in the County of Bath (for the aforsaid Bill and an account thereunto Relateing) where this Complainant is wholy a Stranger and therefore Most Humbly pray for a Writt of Injunction to Remove the Said Actions Brought by the Said Powell against him into theire Lordships Court of Chancery.

These are therefore in her Majesties Name to Will and require And Strictly to Charge you that you Disist from any further proceedings Upon the Said Actions brought by the Said Powell against the aforsaid Chapman that a heareing thereof may be had in theire Lordships Court of Chancery the 3d Day of the Next Generall Court.

Given under my hand this 29th May 1703.

To Mr. Levie Truwhitt Hen. Walker
Clk. County Bath or any other
officer or Minister Concernd

[*Gillam, executrix* v. *Duckenfield*]

[*CCR 181*]

To the Honorable Henderson Walker Esqr. president of the Councill and the Rest of the Honorable Members of this Court of Chancery

The Humble Petition of Sarah Gillam Executrix of [*torn*] Last Will and Testament of Thomas Gillam Deceased Humbly Sheweth That Whereas the Said Gillam was Executor of the Last Will and Testament of Wm. Stevens who was Assignee [*torn*] Legatee of Wm. Rigg Deceased of the Bill of thirty pounds Sterling Due from Mr. William Duckenfield and Since the Death of the Said Rigg the Said Mr. Duckenfeild hath obteind Comission of Administration on the Estate of the Said Rigg by what ways and meanes your petitioner Knows Not but Refuses the Said thirty pounds to pay unto Your petitioner Aledging that he hath not Assetts in his hands So that Your petitioner is wholy Kept out of her Right without Releived by Your Honors Wherupon your petitioner Humbly prayes that the abovesaid Mr. Wm. Duckenfeild may be brought before this Honorable Court by A Sumons or such other wayes as to your Honors Shall Seem Meet To give Answer to Your Honors By what wayes and means he obteined administration on the Said Riggs Estate. And Likewise An Account how he hath Disposed of the Same By which means your Petitioner shall Know whither there be any of Riggs Estate [*torn*] Hands to make good the Said Bill Acon[*torn*] by the Said Rigg And your Petitioner [*torn*] Duty Bound Pray etc.

July 7th 1703
To the Court of Chancery Copia Vera Nath[*torn*]

[*Endorsed:*]
Gillam Versus Duckenfeild
Bill Cancillaria

[*Chevin* v. *Phillips*]

[*CCR 139*]

North Carolina ss. To the Provost Marshall or Depty

These are in her Majtis Name to will and require you to subponea Daniel

Phillips to make his Personall Appearance att the Next Court of Chancery which shall be held the third Day of the Next Generall Court which begins the Last Tuseday in Oct. Next att the House of Capt. Jno. Hecklefeild in Little River To make Answer to a Bill of Complaint Exhibitted against Him By Nathanel Chevin And have there this Writt.

Dated the 30th of 7ber 1703 Thos. Snoden Clericus Cancellariae

[*Endorsed:*]
Draw a Warrant for John Bishopp to Survey 290 acres for Bishopp and to Sell 4 rights for the Same.
A Subpoena For Phillipps ad sectam Chevin

[*Phillips* v. *Bishop*]

[*CCR 191*]

North Carolina ss. To the Honorable Court of Chancery

In humble wise Complaining Sheweth unto your Honors your Honors Daily Orator Daniell Phillipps That your Orator was arrested to the precinct Court of Pascotank held the Third Tuesday in October last by John Bishopp of this Government in an action of the Case upon account and by him there Impleaded for the Summe of Eight pounds and Eleven Shillings and then and there prov'd an account for the Same by his Oath And your Orator pleaded nothing Due to the Said John Bishopp by account And put himselfe upon the Country And by A verdict of twelve true and lawfull men etc. your Orator was orderd to pay the Summe of Three pounds Nyne Shillings and Six pence of the aforesaid account proved by the Said John Bishopp in manner aforesaid Nevertheless Soe itt is may itt please your Honors That by the Depositions of two lawfull persons within this Government and ready to be produc'd before your Honors your humble Orator is ready to Averr that Certaine Articles in the Said John Bishopp's account and prov'd by the Said Bishopps Oath are false and whereas by the Strict rules of the Common Law your humble Orator is remedilesse your humbly Orator prayes her Majesties most Gracious writt of Subpoena may be directed to the Said John Bishopp him Commanding to make his personall appearence before your Honors on Wednesday the Twelfth Day of this Instant Aprill to make answer to the premisses and that your Orator may be relieved therein and he as in Duty bound Shall pray etc.

[*Endorsed:*]
Phillipps versus Bishopp
Bill in Cancellaria
3d of Aprill [*1704*]

[*CCR 139*]

In Cancellaria [*July 1704*]

Martin versus Platt.

Smethwick and Uxor versus Duckenfield Esqr.

COURT OF CHANCERY, JULY 1704

Hecklefield and Uxor versus Godfrey.

Jordan versus Pritchard.

Rookes versus Albertson.

FILE PAPERS

[*Hecklefield and wife, administratrix* v. *Godfrey*]

[*CCR 181*]

North Carolina Scilicet To the Honourable Court of Chancery

The plaint of Jno. Hacklfield and Elizabeth his wife Administratrix of the goods and Chattells of John Godfry deceased in most humble manner Sheweth That Francis Godfry late of this Province being Seized of certaine land and tenaments in free and common Socage died haveing issue William and John and by the Said Francis Godfry's last will and testament devised to his Son John certaine lands and tenements for ever And the Said John Godfrey and Elizabeth one of your Honours Orators had issue Elizabeth Godfrey who died intestate without issue and William Godfry Brother of the aforesaid John Godfrey being heir to the reall estate of the aforesaid John Godfrey Neverthe-less So it is may it please your Honors that the aforesaid Elizabeth Godfry Stood indebted in her life time to your Orators in the Sum of Sixty and five pounds of current money of England to wit for meat drink washing lodging apparell and education for the Space of three yeares your Orator Elizabeth being lyable thereunto as gardian and Prochin amie of the aforesaid Elizabeth dureing her minority Expecting honest Satisfaction when of age or marryed which aforesaid three yeares being from the death of her father John Godfry and the time of the Said Elizabeths decease at the rate of fiveteen pounds per annum And likewise for your Orators trouble attendance and charge upon the Said Elizabeth in her Sickness your Orators bona fide Say they reasonably deserve ten pounds And further your Orators Say they are reddy to make appeare that the funerall expenses of the aforesaid Elizabeth, paid and dis-bursed by your orators amounted to ten pounds all which aforesaid Summe amount in the whole to Sixty and five pounds And whereas by the Strict rules of the Common Law not being obleiged by bill or bond to pay the Just debts of the aforesaid Elizabeth your orators are remediless yet in equity and good Conscience your orators humbly conceive that Willm. Godfry heir at law to the aforesaid Elizabeth is lyable to pay her Just debts becoming due to your Orators as aforesaid the whole of Eliz. estate now resting in the Said William Wherfore your Orators humbly pray that her Majesties most gracious writ of Subpoena may be issued to the Said William Godfrey him Commanding to make answer to the premises And that your Orators may be releived therin And they as in duty bound Shall Pray etc.

Andrew Rosse per plaintiff

[*CCR 181*]

North Carolina Ss. To the Honorable Court of Chancery

Jno. Hacklfield and Elizabeth his wife etc. Complainants
William Godfry defendant

The Plantifs in demurer to the incertainty and altogether insufficiency of the Defendants Answer to the bill exhibited against him Ought not to be received nor allowed by this Honourable Court.

Imprimis For in that The defendant in two answer utterly denyes the Summ of Sixty five pounds to be due and that in Christianity the Complainants ought not to demand anything.

2ly That the Complainants in the answer is charged with an unreasonable charge for the meat drink washing Lodging education attendance in Sickness and funerall expenses [*torn*] Elizth. Godfrey after they have demed any thing to be due to the Complainants for the Same which answer for its uncertainty and Sufficiency ought not to be received But that this Honourable Court may grant a decree for the Just debt exhibited Lawfully becomeing due to the Complainants as they can by Law make appeare that Willm. Godfry heir of the Said Elizabeth Godfry is obledged to pay the charges of her maintainance attendance education and funerall expenses etc.

Andrew Roses attorney per plaintiff

I the Subscriber Attorney for the Defendant doe Joyn in this Demurrer.

Tho. Boyd attorney Defendant

[*Jordan* v. *Pritchard, executor*]

[*CCR 179*]

North Carolina ss. To the Honorable Landgrave Robt. Daniell Esqr.

Lieutenant Generall Vice Admirall and Deputy Governor and the Rest of the Honorable Councill of State of North Carolina aforesaid

The Bill of Complaint of Joseph Jordan Complaynant against David pritchard Executor of the last Will and Testament of John Bornitt deceased Defendant Humbly Sheweth unto your Honors That att a Court held for the precinct of pascotanke the 18th Day of Aprill 1704 the Defendant Comenced his Sute against the Complaynant for fourty Shillings due to the Said Bornitt and upon a Tryall had a Verdict past for the plaintiff whereupon the Complainant appealed to this Honorable Court Now Soe it is may it please your Honors that if any thing was really due it must be part of the Consideration Money mentioned in a Deed of Sale made by the Said Bornitt To the Complainant for One Hundred Acres of Land and Upon due Search made the Complainant can find but Fifty and therefore humbly Conceives that he is noe way obleidged to pay the full Consideration and the Complainant being tyed up from any Releife by the Strict Rules of the Comon Law is noe where Releiveable but before this Honorable Court.

May it therefore please your Honors to grant unto the Complainant a Writt of Subpoena to be directed to the Said David prittchard Comanding him att a Day certaine to appear before your honors and that you will take the premises into your grave Serious Considerations and releive the Complainant according to Your Honors wonted Equity and Justice and the Complainant Shall pray etc.

Joseph Jordan

[*Endorsed:*]
Jordan versus Pritchard Bill in Cancellaria
Enterd the 15th July 1704
Referrd

[*Martin* v. *Platt*]

[*CCR 191*]

No. Caralina ss. To the Honorable Court of Chancery

The Bill of Complaint of Joel Martin against Thomas platt Humbly Sheweth That the Complainant was arrested by Thomas Platt the Defendant to the Generall Court held for this Province in the last Tuesday in July in the year of our Lord 1703 for the Sume of four pounds for the transportation of the Said Joell Martin and family from Virginia to the County of Bath in this Government And att A Generall Court held in October afterwards obtained Judgment against the Complainant for the Same Default of the Complainants appearance Now Soe it is may it please your Honors the Complaynant doth averr that he hath paid all the freight that was due to the Owner of the Said Sloop who liveth in Virginia and therefore Humbly prayes that the Said Order may be reversed and your Orator Shall pray etc.

[*Rooks* v. *Albertson*]

[*CCR 187*]

North Carolina ss. To the Honorable Court of Chancery

[*Illegible*] humble wise Complaining Sheweth unto your Honors your Daily Orator Mary Rookes That att A Councell held for this Province the Third Day of the Generall Court held in March in the year of our Lord 1701 Esau Albertson of this Province by false Information Suggested unto your Honors That A certaine Tract of Land Scituate lying and being in this Province and belonging and of right appertaining [*torn*] your Orator was laps'd for want of Seating And the Said Esau Albertson Exhibiting A petition to your Honors for the [*torn*] Obtaind an Order to be Granted of the Same paying unto your Orator five pounds And your humble Orator in facte Sayth that the aforesaid Tract of Land was not laps'd for want of Seating as the Defendant falsly Suggested unto your Honors as by Especiall wayes and meanes your Orator [*torn*] ready to make appear Nevertheless Soe itt is may itt please [*torn*] Honors That your Orator and the Defendant being att variance [*torn*] time after the Defendants obtaining the aforesaid order for the aforesaid Tract of Land Chose two Arbitrators to make a full finall End of all Suites Debates and

Controversyes pending between your Orator and the Defendant which Said Arbitrators Awarded that your Orator Should pay or passe a Bill to [*torn*] Defendant for the Summe of Nyne pounds And the Defendant Should for that Consideration repossesse your Orator with the aforesaid Tract of Land which Award your Orator [*torn*] time performed And the Defendant hath not by [*torn*] manner of Instrument or writing repossess'd your Orator [*torn*] the aforesaid Tract of Land but the Defendant is Still in possession of the Same and remaines recorded laps'd for the Defendant Contrary to Equity and good Conscience And whereas by the Strict rules of the Common Law your Orator is unrelieveable in the premisses by reason the Defendant has Inhans'd into his possession the Arbitration bond wherein your Orator and the Defendant were Severally bound to Stand to the Award of the Said Arbitrators or else the aforesaid bond unknown to your Orator is by Some meanes or other lost or Imbeze'ld your Orator humbly prayes That her Majesties most Gracious writt of Subpoena may be Directed to the Said Esau Albertson him Commanding to make his personall appearence before your Honors the Third Day of the next Generall Court to make answer to the premisses that your orator may be relieved in the premisses And She [*torn*] pray.

Tho. Snoden Clericus [*illegible*]

[*Endorsed:*]
Rookes versus Albertson
Bill in Cancellaria
Entred 7th February

[*CCR 191*]

This bill bindeth me mery roocks me my aieres or asines to pay or Cas to be paid unto Aasa allbord his aieres or asines the full and just sun of twenty poun storling of ingland as witnes my hand and sell.

This bill bindeth me Aasa Allbrd me my aieres or asines to pay or Cas to be paid unto mery roockes hur aiers or asines the full sum of twenty poundes storling mony of Ingland as witnes by hand and sele.

The Condison of this obligation is such that if the abve bound mery roocks and Asea Allbord his heirs Execters and Administraturs and every of them, do and shall for his and thair partes and be halfe stand, to abide observe and in and by all thinges, well and truly performe and acomplis the award Arbitrament, order determination, Finall end and judgment of William bartly of Litle river in the prescint of pequimines and Samuall Charles of the seme precinck adbertreteres indifierantly Chosen elected and nemed as well on the part and behalf of the said mary roockes as on the part and behalph of the above nemed asa Allbordson aword arbitrete order judge determine finell end to meck, Consorning the Land that Lise in debete betwen mery roockes and Aseu Allbordson and to vallu the lebr and mery roockes to pay Asu Allbordson for his laber and she tacke the Land againe then this abeve obligation to be vaid or eles to Stand in full force and vertu as witnes our handes and seles tis fift of the 11 month 1702.

Testis
Francis Tomes
Samuel Charles

The marcke of Mary roock
Asa Allbordson his marcke

[*Endorsed:*]
Chancery
A Bond
This the 19 da of [*illegible*] then the arbetraters hath conclude upon eight pound to be pay un [*blank*].

[*Hunt* v. *Blount and wife*]

[*CCR 148*]

North Carolina ss. To the Provost Marshall or Deputy

These are in the Name of his Excellency the Palatine and the rest of the true and absolute Lords and Proprietors to will and require you to Summons Lyonel Reading Soe that he make his personall appearance att the Third Day of the next Generall Court to be held for this Province the last Tuesday of March next att the House of Captain John Hecklefield in Little River to give Evidence in A Matter Depending between Mister John Hunt Complainant and John Blunt and his wife Defendants in the Honorable Court of Chancery And have there this Summons Dated the 4th day of November 1704.

Tho. Snoden Clericus Curiae

[*Mercer and wife* v. *Swann*]

[*CCR 191*]

North Carolina ss. By the Honorable Landgrave Robert Daniell Esqr. Lieutenant Generall Vice Admirall and Deputy Governor

Thomas Mercer Complaining that he was Arrested by the Honorable Samuel Swann to the Generall Court held for the Province aforesaid the last Tuesday in October last past and there was Impleaded by the Said Samuel Swann Esqr. for that he the Said Thomas Mercer in to A Certaine Plantation the proper Estate and rightfull Inheritance of the Said Samuel Swann Esqr. with force and Armes had wrongfully Entred And the Same from the Said Samuel Swann Esqr. did wrongfully detaine and withhold And humbly praying an Injunction in Chancery

These are in the Name of his Excellency the Palatine and the rest of the true and absolute Lords and Proprietors to will and require you to Desist from all further proceedings in the aforesaid Matter untill A hearing be of the premisses in the Honorable Court of Chancery to be held for this Province the Third Day of the next Generall Court att the House of Captain John Hecklefield in Little River Given under my hand and Seal att Armes this 6th Day of November Anno Domini 1704.

To Willm. Glover Esqr.
and the rest of the
Members of the Generall Court

Robt. Daniell

[*CCR 187*]

North Carolina ss. To the Honorable Court of Chancery

In humble wise Complaining Sheweth unto your Honors your Daily Orators Thomas Mercer and Dianah his wife That your Orator Thomas Mercer was arrested to the Generall Court held for this Province the last Tuesday in October last past and there Impleaded by Saml. Swann Esqr. for That he your Orator had Entred upon A Tract of Land the rightfull Inheritance of him the Said Samll. Swann Esqr. and the Same from him the Said Saml. Swann Esqr. did withhold and Detaine Neverthelesse Soe itt is may itt please your Honors That one Tho. Harris and your Orator Dianah his wife one of the Complainants upwards of Thirty Yeares Agoe purchased of George Catchmaide of this Government the aforesaid Tract of Land And that the Said Thomas Harris and Dianah his wife one of the Complainants honestly and bona fide payd and made Satisfaction unto the Said George Catchmaide for the Same And your Orator Dianah one of the Complainants further Sayth That the Said Thomas Harris in his life time and your Orator Dianah his then wife were putt in quiett and peaceable possession of the Tract of Land aforesaid by the Said George Catchmaide and Confirm'd in the Same by Delivery of Turf and Twigg from the Said Tho. Catchmaide (who was then accounted the present possessor and rightfull owner of the aforesaid Tract of Land) unto the Said Thomas Harris and Dianah his wife one of your Honors Complainants And that the aforesaid Tract of Land Imediately after possession given by the Said Catchmaide to the Said Tho. Harris and Dianah his wife one of your Orators and was Surveyd by Mr. George Durant in Tho. Harris's Name whose wife Dianah one of your humble Orators att that time was. And your Orators are informd That the Said Saml. Swann Esqr. by Some Subtill or indirect meanes to your Orators unknown hath obtain'd A Pattent for the Same Neverthelesse your Orators have been in peaceable possession of the premisses upwards of thirty yeares and have duely payd the Quittrents of right belonging to the Lords Proprietors of this Government for the Same Wherefore Your humble Orators pray That A writt of Subpoena may be directed to the Said Saml. Swann Esqr. him requiring to make his personall appearance before your Honors on the Third Day of the next Generall Court to be held for this province the last Tuesday in March next to make answer to the premisses And that your humble Orators may be relieved therein And they as in Duty bound Shall pray etc.

Tho. Snoden Clericus Cancellariae

[*Endorsed:*]
Mercer and uxor versus Swann Esqr. etc.
Bill in Cancellaria
Entred 26th February 1704/5

[*CCR 191*]

North Carolina ss. To the Provost Marshall or Deputy

These are in the Name of his Excellency the Palatine and the rest of the

true and absolute Lords and Proprietors to will and require you to Subpoena Saml. Swann Esqr. to make his personall appearance on The Third Day of the next Generall Court to be held for this Province the last Tuesday in March next att the House of Captain John Hecklefield in Little River to make answer to A Bill of Complaint Exhibited against him by Thomas Mercer and Dianah his wife Complainants in the Honorable Court of Chancery And have there this Subpoena Dated 26th Day of February 1704/5.

Tho. Snoden Clericus Cancellariae

[*Endorsed:*]
Subpoena
Mercer and uxor versus Swann Esqr.
In Cancellaria
This Sumons Executed on major Swann

[*CCR 191*]

Novervit Universi per presentis Nos Thomas Mercer De precinct Pequimins in Provincia de North Carolina Planter and Johem Hecklefield de eadem Generosum teneri et firmit obligari Ju[*torn*]Cur General es Dem Province in Quadringont [*torn*] bone et leglis monete Anglie Solvened eisdem [*torn*] aut Suis cert Attorn Executoribis Administratoribis [*torn*] Successoribis Suis Ad quam quidem Solution bene et fidelit faciend [*illegible*] nos et utrum [*illegible*] et in solido [*torn*] Executor et Administrator urco et utrius [*torn*] firmit per presentes Sigillis urio Signat Dat Secundo Die Novembr. Anno regin Due Rue Anne Anglie etc. tertio Annogue Domini 1704.

The Condition of the above written obligation is Such That if the above bound Thomas Mercer [*torn*] Shall make his personall appearance att the next Court of Chancery to be held for the Province aforesaid and then and there prosecute his Appeal against the [*torn*] Samuel Swann Esqr. and in all Matters Save [*torn*] harmlesse and Indempnifyed the Justices of [*torn*] Generall Court their Heires and Successors for or by reason of granting the aforsaid Appeall That then the abovewritten obligation to be void and of none effecte or else to be and remaine in full force power and vertue.

Signed Sealed and Delivered in the presence of
Ben. tulle, Hum. Legge, Tho. Snoden, John Hecklefield

Thomas Mercer Signum

[*CCR 191*]

Att A Court of Chancery held att the house of Capt. John Hacklesfeild in Little River the 29th day of March 1705. The Honorable Deputy Governor etc. Present the Honorable Samll. Swann, Richd. Sanderson, Wm. Glover, John Arderne Esqrs. Lords Deputyes.

Thomas Mercer and Dianah his Wife Come to prosecute their Bill in Chancery Exhibited against the Honorable Samll. Swann Esqr. and Sett forth etc. per bill.

And in Answere to the Same Samll. Swann Esqr. Defendant to the aforesaid bill of Complaint Sayth that for the most part the Said bill is untrue Slanderous and insufficient etc.

The Complainants not being able to make any Title to the aforesaid Land and on the Contrary the Said haveing been found to Escheat to the Lords Proprietors and the Said Samll. Swann Esqr. having Obtained a Patten to the Same

Ordred and Decreed that the Suite be dismist and the Complainants pay Costs alias Execution.

A True Coppy per Geo. Lumley Clerk

[*Endorsed:*]
Chancery order att Swanns Land

[*Norton* v. *Low*]

[*CCR 191*]

North Carolina ss. To the Provost Marshall or Deputy

These are in the Name of his Excellency the Palatine and the rest of the true and absolute Lords and Proprietors to will and require you to Subpoena Anne Low Attorney of Emanuel Low to make her personall appearance on the Third Day of the next Generall Court to be held for this Province the last Tuesday in March next att the House of Captain John Hecklefield in Little River to make answer to the Bill of Complaint of Samuel Norton Complainant against Emanuel Low Defendant in the Honorable Court of Chancery And have there this Subpoena Dated the 19th Day of February Anno Domini 1704/5.

Tho. Snoden Clericus Cancellariae

[*Endorsed:*]
Subpoena the 5th March 1704/5

[*Hunt* v. *Bunting*]

[*CCR 191*]

North Carolina ss. To the Honorable Court of Chancery [*October 1705*]

The Petition of John Bunting Most humbly Sheweth That your Petitioner is Defendant to a Bill of Complaint Exhibited by Captain John Hunt and now Depending before your Honors and prayes to Come to Tryall not being [able] by reason of Old Age to attend another Court And that your Honors will be pleasd (your Petitioner being altogether unskill'd in the Method of pleading) to assigne your Petitioner of the Honorable Councill to plead for your petitioner on his behalfe And he as in Duty bound Shall pray etc.[1]

John Bunting

---

[1] Bunting had made a similar request when this suit was tried in the March, 1698/9, General Court. See volume III in this series, pp. 267 and 283.

[*Keele* v. *Wallis*]

[*CCR 191*]

North Carolina Ss. To the provost Marshall or his Deputy

These are in her Matyes name to will and require you to Sumons Thomas Barcock and John Billett Soe that they be and personally appeare at the next Court of Chancery to be holden at the house of Captain Jno. Hecklefield in Litle river on the third day of the next Generall Court then and there to Give Evidence in a Cause there depending between Robert Keel Complainant and Robert Wallis Defendant on the behalfe of the Defendant and have there this Sumons Dated at the Secretarys Office the 2d day of October Anno Domini 1705.

Testis Tobs. Knight Secretary

[*Endorsed:*]
Thas Somanes Executed by me George Harris debety mashall

[*CCR 139*]

No. Carolina Ss. To the provost Marshall or his Deputy

These are in her Majestyes name to will and require you to Sumons Jno. Jennings and Dorothy his wife personally to be and appeare before the honorable Court of Chancery at the house of Captain Jno. Hecklefield in Litle river on Tuesday the 6th day of this Instant November then and there to give Evidence in a Cause ther depending between Robt. Keel Complainant and Robt. Wallis defendant on behalfe of the Complainant and have there this Sumons Dated Nov. 3 1705.

Testis T. Knight Secretary

[*Endorsed:*]
Executed by me
George Harris debety mashall

[*Snoden and wife* v. *Brethett*]

[*CCR 139*]

North Carolina ss. To the Provost Marshall or Deputy

These are in her Majesties Name to will and require you to Subpoena Willm. Brethett to make his personall appearance on the Third Day of the next Generall Court to be held for this Province the last Tuesday of this Instant October att the House of Captain John Hecklefield in Little River to answer the Complaint of Thomas Snoden and Constance his wife Complainants And have there this Subpoena Dated the 12th Day of October Anno Domini 1705.

Tho. Snoden and Tobs. Knight Secretary

[*Endorsed:*]
To Tho. Houghton to execute

per order of John Hecklefield Provost Marshall
Executed

[*CCR 191*]

North Carolina Ss. To the provost Marshall or his Deputy

These are in her Matyes name to will and require you to Summon Stephen Swaine and James Ward personally to be and appeare at the next Court of Chancery to be holden at the house of Captain Jno. Hecklefield on the third day of the next Generall Court then and there to give Evidence in a Cause there depending between Thomas Snoden and Constance his wife Complainants and Wm. Breasted defendant on behalfe of the Complainants and have there this Summons Dated at the secretarys Office this 10th day of Octobr. Anno Domini 1705.

Testis Tobs. Knight Secretary

[*Endorsed:*]
Subpoena in Cancelleria for Steph. Swaine and James Ward
To Tho. Houghton to Execute per order of John Hecklefield Provost Marshall
Executed

[*Wilkison* v. *Oliver*]

[*CCR 191*]

North Carolina Ss.

The Deposition of John Blunt Aged Thirty four Years or therabouts Desposieth and Saith That Sometime In the first week In September Last was twelve months Your Deponent being at the house of Colonel William Wilkison with Thomas Luten I heard the Said Colonel Wilkison Say That Now he Thought it a very fitt time while the Deponant and Thomas Luten was There to Make a Reharsall of the Bargain Between Aron Oliver and himself, and the Said Aron being Call'd Into the parlor where the Company was, Colonel Wilkison Reharseth These words or To This purpose, That he had agreed with the Said Oliver to Live with [him] as a Server in the house, to waigh measure or any Thing he Should be put about (working In the ground being Excepted) In Concideration of the time as a Server, to have Twenty Shillings per Month and In Case the Said Colonel Wilkison Should Send him Abroad as a Recever Then to give him forty Shilling per month for the time of Receving and after These words the Colonel Asked Aron if this was not our bargain, who answered Yes, after which a Motion was made by Somebody In the Room wheather the agreement Should be put In writeing or nott, To which Colonel Wilkison made Answer twas Needless [*torn*] Reason Your Deponent and Thomas Luten being There it Could not be Douted but they Should Remember the Bargain. Some Short time after This Thomas Luten Sath that he haveing a very tretcherous memory he would take Some Small memorandum of the heads of the Agreement Which I Encorrag'd for the

Strengthning of my own memory. And Colonel Wilkison Said he might Draw what he pleased for his own Satisfaction upon which Captain Luten went to the table and wrote about two Lines and a halfe or Tharabouts, on a Small peice of paper, and further Your Deponant hath Some Thoughts of a Qustion put wheather it Should be Sign'd by the partys Concern'd or not but dos not Remember its being Sign'd or wittnessed by Either himself or any other, and further the Deponent Sayeth Not.

John Blount

Sworne Before the Court of Chancery 6 of 9ber 1705

Testis Tobs. Knight Secretary

[*Endorsed:*]
Mr. Jon. Blounts deposition

[*CCR 191*]

North Carolina Ss.

I William Wilkinson aged about sixty two years being sworn upon the holy evangelists do depose and say, that I the said deponent did never speake to Captain Thomas Newton, or any other person whatsoever, to make or draw up any writeing or writeings between me the deponent and Aaron Oliver, only as to the settling of accounts between me the deponent and the said Aaron Oliver, and that I the said deponent did never sign or subscribe any paper or papers, writeing or writeings between me the deponent and the said Aaron Oliver, nor yet did ever any person or persons whatsoever sign or subscribe any paper or papers, writeing or writeings by my order, consent or privity and further sayeth not.

Wm. Wilkison

The above Deposition was Swoarne
to in the honorable Court of Chancery
November 6th 1705

Testis Tobs. Knight Secretary

[*Newby and Stafford, summons*]

[*CCR 191*]

No. Carolina Ss. To the provost Marshall or his Deputy

These are in her Majestyes to will and require you to Summons James Newby and Amy Stafford personally to be and appeare before the honorable Court of Chancery at the house of Captain Jno. Hecklefield on Tuesday the 6th day of this Instant November then and there to give Evidence on behalfe of Martha Plater and have there this Sumons Dated at the Secretarys office this 3d day of November Anno Domini 1705.

Testis T. Knight Secretary

To Mr. Jno. Rapier per order of John Hecklefield Provost Marshall
[*Laker* v. *Alex., the Indian*]

[*CCR 191*]

No. Carolina Ss. To the provost Marshall or his Deputy

These are in her Majestyes name to will and require you to Sumons Alex. the Indian personally to be and appeare at the next Court of Chancery to be holden at the house of Captain Jno. Hecklefield in Litle river on the third day of the next Generall Court then and there to Answer the bill of Complaint of Juliana Laker widdow Complainant and have there this writt Dated at the Secretarys Office this 7th day of Novembr. Anno Domini 1705.

Testis Tobs. Knight Secretary

[*Endorsed:*]
Executed the 7th of Novber. 1705 per Tho. Houghton Deputy Marshall

[*Lunn* v. *Pettiver*]

[*CCR 191*]

North Carolina Ss. To the Provost Marshall or his Deputy

These are in her Majestyes name to will and require You to Sumons William Houghton personally to be and appeare at the next Court of Chancery to be holden at the house of Captain Jno. Hecklefield in Litle river on the third day of the next Generall Court then and there to give Evidence in a Cause there Depending between Arthur Lunn Complainant and Jno. Pettiver Defendant on behalfe of the Complainant and have there this Sumons Dated at the Secretarys office the 4th day of March Anno Domini 1705/6.

Testis T. Knight Secretary

[*Endorsed:*]
Summons in Cancellaria for Wm. Houghton
Exequted by me Richd. Leary Deputy marshall

[*CCR 191*]

North Carolina Ss. To the Provost Marshall or his Deputy

These are in her Majestyes name to will and require you to Sumons Richd. Leary personally to be and appear at the next Court of Chancery to be holden at the house of Captain Jno. Hecklefeild in Litle river on the third day of the next Generall Court then and there to give Evidence in a Cause there depending between Arthur Lunn Complainant and Jno. Pettiver Defendant on the behalfe of the Complainant and have there this Summons Dated at the Secretarys Office this 4th day of March Anno Domini 1705/6.

Testis T. Knight Secretary

[*Endorsed:*]
Summons in Cancellaria for Richd. Leary
Exequted by me Richd. Leary Deputy marshal

[*Feillett* v. *Sawyer and Jennings*]

[*CCR 191*]

No. Carolina Ss. To the Provost Marshall or his Deputy

These are in her Matyes name to will and require you to Sumons Eliz. Bolt personally to be and appeare at the next Court of Chancery to be holden at the house of Captain John Hecklefield in Litle river on the third day of the next Generall Court then and there to Give Evidence in two Cases there depending between Dr. James Feilett Complainant and Henry Sawyer and Wm. Jennings defendants on behalfe of the Complainant and have there this Sumons Dated at the Secretarys office this 17th day of July Anno Domini 1706.

Testis T. Knight Secretary

[*Endorsed:*]
Summons for Elizabeth Bolt
Executed John Meaids

[*Wilkison, executrix* v. *Oliver*]

[*CCR 186*]

North Carolina Ss.

Know All Men by these presents that Wee Aaron Oliver and John Falconer are held and firmely bound unto the true and absolute Lords and proprietors of this province in the full and Just Sume of Forty pounds Current Money of this province to be paid to them the Said Lords proprietors their Successors to which payment well and truely to be made wee bind our Selves and either of us our and either of our Heyrs Executors administrators Assignes and every of them Jointly and Severally firmely by these presents Sealed with our Selves and Dated this 21st day of June Anno Domini 1706.

The Condition of this obligation is such that Whereas the above bounden Aaron Oliver prayes that a Superseadias may be Granted in order to Stop all farther proceedings at the Comon Law against the said Aaron Oliver at the Suite of Esther Wilkison Executrix of the last Will and Testament Colonel Wm. Wilkinson Deceased pursuant to an order of the precinct Court of Chowan Dated [*blank*] until a farther hearein thereof be had in the honorable Court of Chancery Now if the said Aaron Oliver doe and Shall prosecute the said Appeale with Effect the next Court of Chancery to be holden the 31st day of July next and doe and Shall in all things Stand to and abide the Decree and order of the said Court Then this obligation to be void and of none Effect or also to be and remaine in full force.

Sealed and Delivered
In the presence of
T. Knight Secretary

Aron Oliver
Jno. Falconar

[*CCR 139*]

No. Carolina Ss. Att A Court of Chancery Holden at the house of Captain Jno. Hecklefield in Litle river on Thursday the 31st day of October Anno Domini 1706 and adjourned till to Morow Morne 9 of Clock.

Fryday Morne 9 of Clock this Court Met Present The Honorable Wm. Glover Esqr. President, The Honorable Richard Sanderson, Thomas Pollock, Samll. Swann, Jno. Arderne, Franc. Foster Esqrs. Lords Deputys.

Richard Smyth Comes to prosecute his Bill of Complaint against Thos. Peterson Attorney etc. and Sets forth as per Bill And the Defendant Comes and for want of a Copy of the Bill not being delivered to him Craves a Reference to the next Court which is Granted.

The Honorable Landgrave Robt. Daniell Esqr. Comes to prosecute his Bill of Complaint against Jno. Lawson gentleman and Sets forth as per Bill and the Defendant Comes by Christo. Gale Esqr. his Attorney and Confesses that he hath made 39 Surveys by [*illegible*] of the said Colonel Daniells Comission and is ready to render an Account of the pay the one halfe to the said Colonel Daniell as this Honorable Court shall award.

It is therefore ordered and desired that the Said Lawson pay unto the Said Colonel Daniell the said one halfe of the Fees of the aforesaid Survey with Costs alias Execution.

Upon Motion of Thos. Peterson to this Honorable Court praying their oppinion Concerning a Fee as five pounds demanded upon pretense of a Called Court in the County of Bath whereby the Estate of Wm. Tomson in the hands of Captain Wm. Barrow was Exhausted soe that his Just debts Cannot be paid.

It is the oppinion of this Court that the Said Fee is Arbritary and ought not to be paid.

Robert Keele by Edwd. Bonwick Comes to prosecute his Bill of Complaint against Austin Scarbrough and Complaines as per Bill and the Defendant Comes by Tho. Snoden his Attorney and Demurrs in Law as per Demmurer which is over ruled and then the Defendant prayes referrence to the next Court which is Granted.

Thos. Stanton Comes to prosecute his Bill of Complaint against Caleb Bundy defendant and Complaines as per Bill and the Defendant Comes and for plea and Answare Sayth as per Answer and this Court haveing heard and Considered the whole matter

It is Ordered and Decreed that the Suite be Dismissed and the plaintiff pay Costs alias Execution.

Upon petition of Geo. Harris Ordered that he be allowed for one days Attendance being Sumoned as an Evidence for Caleb Bundy at the Suite of Tho. Stanton.

Then this Court adjourned till tomorrow Morne: 9 of Clock.

Saturday Morne 9 of Clock this Court met present ut Supra Except The Honorable Samuell Swann.

Geo. Ellis Comes by Thos. Snoden his Attorney to prosecute his Suite against Samull. Pike and Complaines as per Bill and the Said Defendant Comes by Edwd. Bonwick his Attorney And Answers [*illegible*] and this Court haveing heard the whole matter

It is ordered and Decreed that the Suite be dissmised and the plaintiff pay Costs alias Execution.

Upon petition of the honorable Colonel Thomas Pollock Esqr. shewing that one Neale Mackinney late of this County deceased was Indebted to your Orator in a Considerable Sume and all his Estate being but about three pounds due to him by Bill which will not beare the Charge of administration and prays that this Honorable Court will Impower him to receive the Said Bills and what other debts he Can find due to him in this Goverment.

Orderd that the Said Thos. Pollock has power to receive all Such debts as he Can find due to the Said Meck[*torn*] in this Government and that he render an Account whea[*torn*] [*illegible*] shall be There Legally required.

Upon Petition of the honorable Colonel Thomas Pollock Administrator of Geo. Chambers Shewing that Whereas [*illegible*] Geo. Chambers etc. per petition and prays that this Honorable Court will make Such order in this Matter as to Equity belongs Soe that the Estate may be had to Satisfy the Debts.

And whereas it dos appeare to this Court that the Said woman is non Compos Mentis

It is therefore ordered that all persons that have had any of the Estate of the Said Geo. Chambers of her by [*illegible*] pretended Sales doe deliver up the Same to the Said Colonel Pollock he paying what Moneys they have disbursed for the Same whoe is Likewise to give an account thereof when he shall be thereto Lawfully required.

[*Signed:*]
W. Glover, Rich. Sanderson, Thomas Pollock, John Arderne, Francis Foster.

[*Endorsed:*]
October Court Chancery 1707 [*sic*]

FILE PAPERS

[*Daniell* v. *Lawson*]

[*CR 2.002*]

No. Carolina Ss. To the Honorable the Court of Chancery

The Bill of Complaint of the honorable Landgrave Robert Daniell Esqr. late Deputy Governor of this province Complainant against John Lawson of the County of Bath gentleman defendant In humble wise Complaineing Sheweth unto your Honors that your Orator did Sometyme in the yeare Seaventee hundred and four which was dureing the tyme your Orator was deputy Governor as aforesaid Comissionate the said Defendant to be Surveyor of the Said County of Bath In Consideration whereof the Said Defendant did faithfully promise and Assume to Account with and pay unto your Orator the one halfe part of all Such Fees as Sho'd become due unto him by virtue of the Said Comission as Surveyor as aforesaid whenever he Sho'd be thereunto requested And your orator farther Sheweth that in pursuance of and by virtue of the Said Comission the said Defendant did Survey divers tracts of Land whereby a Considerable Sume of Money is and ought to become due unto your Orator Nevertheless Soe it is may it please your Honors that the said Defendant not at all minding or regarding Such his Agreement and Assumption as aforesaid all the Fees that is become due unto him by virtue of the aforesaid Comission hath received and taken to his owne use and does refuse to Account with or pay unto your Orator any part thereof Contrary to all equity and Good Concience And your Orator being uncertaine how much there is due to him as aforesaid is thereby likely to be left remediless unless releived by your Honors Justice Equity and Good Conscience Doe therefore In all humble maner pray that a writt of Subpoena may be directed to the said John Lawson him Comanding to make his personall appeareance before your honors on the third day of the next Generall Court then and there to make Answer to all and Singuler the premisses And that he may Give an Account upon Oath how much he has received and is due to him by virtue of the aforesaid Comission and pay unto your Orator Such part thereof as is due unto your Orator as aforesaid And your Orator as in Duty bound shall pray etc.

T. Knight Secretary

[*Endorsed:*]
Bill in Cancellaria
Daniell Esqr. versus Lawson
Filed Septembr. 20th: 1706

[*CR 2.001*]

Mr. Norton has Mr. Hains Survey and grant with the 20 Surveys I Sent in

Messeurs. Mens Names.
1 Thos. Pierce

2 Jno. [*illegible*] Sen.
3 Captain Wm. Barrow
4 Tho. [*torn*]
5 Jno. Adams
6 Arch. Holms
7 Hen. Warren
8 Jeremia Goodridg
9 Jno. Barras
10 Jno. Sullivan
11 Jno. Bunting
12 Arch. Holms
13 Hen. Warren
14 Jam. Hains
15 Robt. Shrieve
16. Robt. Mellyne
17 Wm. Price
18 Nicholas Daw
19 Jam. Walch
20 Wm. Wynly
21 Lod. Martin
22 Maurice Lluellyn
23 Jno. Bright
24 Wm. Wynn
25 Jam. Walch
26 Robt. Shrieve
27 Robt. Mellyne
28 Ch. Smith
29 [*Illegible*]
30 Ben. Saunderson
31 Wm. Bell
32 Geo. Bell
33 Rich. Talpar
34 Fran. Lynfield
35 Sy. Fesgue
36 Jno. Bright
37 Hen. Slade
38 David Perkins
39 Captain Barrow

These may Certifie the Honorable the Deputy Governor and Councell that I Survey'd these 39 Surveys by a Commission from the Honorable Landgrave Robt. Daniell Esqr.

Your Honors most Obedient Humble Servant
John Lawson

[*Endorsed:*]
Oct. 1st. 1706
Came before me John Lawson and made oath to the within Acct. off

Surveys as per Certificate underwritten. C. Gale

I doe hereby Impowre you Chr. Gale Esqr. to Appear Answer and Confess to bill in Chancery Exhibited against me by the Honorable Landgrave Robt. Daniell Esqr. and this shall be the Sufficient Warrant.

Your Servant
John Lawson

[*Ellis* v. *Pike*]

[*CCR 181*]

No. Carolina Ss. To the honorable Court of Chancery etc.

The Bill of Complaint of George Ellis Sonne and Heyre at Law apparent to James Ellis late the precinct of Pascotanke deceased Complainant against Samll. Pike of the said Precinct planter defendant In humblewise Complaineing Sheweth unto your honors:

That your Orators Said Father James Ellis did in his life tyme purchase a Certaine plantation and Tract of Land Scituate lyeing and being in the said precinct of Pascotanke being that whereon the Defendant now lives and from one Jno. Nixon the said Defendants Father in Law and was possessed of the Same and dyed Soe possest thereof as aforesaid whereby the Same ought to decend and doth of right belong to your Orator Nevertheless Soe it is may it please your Honors That the Said Defendant hath entered into and upon the Said plantation and tract of Land the proper Inheritance of your Orator and the Same from your Orator doth wrongfully withold and Deteyne Contrary to Equity and Good Concience And your Orator Farther Sheweth that the said Defendant [*illegible*] said Nixon the said Defendants father in Law did in Your Orators Infancy by Some Cunning Crafty and Fraudulent Meanes gett into his or their Custody all Such Deeds of Sale Conveyances writeing Escripts and papers that did any wise belong to your Orator and that did Entitle your Orator to the premisses aforesaid and the Same the Defendant doe Still wrongfully withold and Deteyne from your Orator Contrary to all Equity and Good Concience by reason whereof your Orator in the Strict rules of Comon Law is become wholey remediless Doe therefore and in all humble maner pray that a writt of Subpoena may be directed to the said Samll. Pike him Comanding to make his personall appeareance before your honors on the third day of the next Generall Court then and there to make Answer to all and Singuler the premisses upon Oath and that he may likewise make knowne and produce upon Oath all Such Deed or Deeds of Sale Conveyances writeings Escripts or papers whatsoever which he hath in his Custody or doe any wayes know of or did ever See that doe any wayes touch or Conserve your Orators title to the premisses aforesaid and that your Honors will then take the Same into your Serious Consideration Soe that your Orator may be releived therein and your Orator as in Duty bound shall pray etc.

T. Knight Secretary

[*Endorsed:*]
Bill in Cancellaria
Ellis versus Pike
Filed Octo. 20th: 1706

[*CCR 191*]

North Carolina Ss. To the provost Marshall or his Deputy

These are in her Majestyes name to will and require you to Sumons Samll. Pike personally to be and appeare at the next Court of Chancery to be holden at the house of Captain Jno. Hecklefield in Litle river on the third day of next Generall Court then and there to make Answer to the Bill of Complaint of George Ellis Complainant and have you there this Subpoena Dated at the Secretarys office this 10th day of Octob. Anno Domini 1706.

Testis T. Knight Secretary

[*Endorsed:*]
Subpoena in Cancellaria for Pike ad sectam Ellis

[*CCR 191*]

No. Carolina Ss. To the provost Marshall or Deputy

These are in her Matyes name to will and require you to Sumons Stephen Scott personally to be and appeare at the next Court of Chancery to be holden at the house of Capt. Jno. Hecklefield in Litle river on the third day of the next Generall Court then and there to Give Evidence in a Cause there depending between Geo. Ellis Complainant against Samll. Pike Defendant on behalfe of the Complainant and have you there this Subpoena Dated at the Secretarys Office this 10th day of Octo. Anno Domini 1706.

Testis. T. Knight Secretary

[*Endorsed:*]
Sumons in Cancellaria for Ste. Scott

[*CCR 191*]

In Cancellaria The Answer of Samuell Pike Defendant to the Bill of Complaint of George Ellis Complainant

The said Defendant saving and reserving to himselfe now and at all times hereafter all benifit of exceptions to the uncertainties insufficiencies and imperfections in the Bill of the said Complainant contained For a full perfect and direct answer unto all and every the matters allegations and things which are in the said Bill of Complaint contained in any Sort or wise materiall or effectuall for the said Defendant (by the Law) to answer unto Saith That the Father of the said Complainant did not purchase the Tract of Land in the said Bill of Complaint mentioned neither doth the same of right belong to the said Complainant neither hath the said Defendant in his custodie and Deeds of Sale Conveyances writeings Scripts or papers that does in anywise belong to the said Complainant or hath had or knowes or now hath and this he is ready to aver and prove as this honorable Court shall award without that any other matter or thing in the said Bill of Complaint contained material to charge this Defendant with all or effectuall by him to be answered unto and not hereby Sufficiently answered confessed or avoided travers'd or denyed is true in such manner and forme as herein before is expressed And humbly prayes from hence to be dismissed with his reasonable Costs and charges in this behalfe wrongfully sustained.

Bonwicke per Pike

I doe Somnly and Sincerely in the presence of God (the witness of the truth of what I am to Say) declare that the above Answer is the truth the whole truth and nothing but the truth of what I know Concerning the Same.

Samuel Pike

[*Endorsed:*]
Pike ad sectam Ellis
Respond in Cancellaria

[*CCR 187*]

The deposition of Stephen Scott aged Forty yeares or thereabouts upon his Subscription Sayth That att A certaine time discoursing with Saml. Pike this Deponent heard Saml. Pike Say That his pattent was lost but Sayes the said Pike I have the Bill of Sale Sayes this Deponent what Bill of Sale the said Pike answered the Bill of Sale which was past from John Nixon to James Ellis which I look upon to be Substantialler then the pattent because the Courses of the Pattent were destroyed by A Decree in Chancery And further this Deponent Sayth not.

I doe Sincerely declare in the presence of God the witnesse of the truth of what I Say That the above Deposition is the truth according to the best of my knowledge.

Stephen Scott

[*Keele* v. *Scarbrough*]

[*CCR 191*]

North Carolina Ss. To the provost Marshall or his Deputy

These are in her Matyes name to will and require you to Sumons Augustine Scarbrough personally to be and appeare at the next Court of Chancery to be holden for this province at the house of Captain Jno. Hecklefield in Litle river on the third day of the next Generall Court then and there to make Answer to the bill of Complaint of Robert Keele Complainant and have you there this Subpoena Dated at the Secretarys Office this 25th day of September Anno Domini 1706.

Testis T. Knight Secretary

Subpoena for Scarbro' ad sectam Keel in Cancellaria
Sarved by mae George Harris

[*Smith* v. *Peterson, attorney of Perry and Company*]

[*CCR* 192]

No. Carolina Ss. To the Honorable the Court of Chancery etc.

The Bill of Complaint of Richd. Smyth, of the County of Bath in the said Province Complaines against Thomas Peterson Attorney to Micajah Perry and New Pensilvania Company Defendant

Your Honors Dayly Orator Richd. Smyth in humble wise Complaineing Sheweth unto your Honors that Whereas your Orator did purchase Divers Goods Wares and Merchandizes of and From one Nich[*torn*] Tyler of the County aforesaid but properly belonging to the said Pensilvania Company and did accordingly pay and Satisfy the Said Tyler and the Defendant or one of them for the Same Nevertheless the Said Defendant being Attorney to the Said Company did on or a bout the Sixteenth day of September 170[*torn*] Demand of your Orator to Account with the Defendant for the Goods Soe purchased as aforesaid which your Orator did Accordingly And for want of Some receipts and accounts formerly past and adjusted by the Said Tyler to your Orator which your Orator Could not then readily find the said Defendant did then bring your Orator in Debt to the Said Company the Summe of Ninety four pounds One Shilling and three pence for which Money your Orator at the request of the Defendant did pass his Bill or obligation there by oblidgeing himselfe to pay the Same to the said Defendant or his Assignes for the rest of the Company aforesaid but your Orator at the Same Tyme did make that reservation and the Defendant did then also faithfully promise and Assume that in Case your Orator at any tyme hereafter Should produce any receipts from the Said Tyler for the said Sume in the said Obligation Exprest or any part thereof the Said Defendant would allow of and discount the Same out of the Said Obligation And your Orator farther Sheweth that Since the passing the aforesaid obligation your Orator has found and produced receipts for the whole Summe with overpluss and demanded discount of the Same from the Defendant according to Such his Promised Assumption aforesaid which receipts your Orator is Still ready to produce and make appeare to be Just before your honors Nevertheless Soe it is may it please your honors that the Said Defendant Evely Intending and Fraudulently designeing to defraud and Cheat your Orator doth absolutely refuse to allow of the aforesaid receipts Contrary to his promise and Assumption aforesaid and has Sued and Impleaded your Orator in an Action of Debt in the Common Law upon the aforesaid Obligation And thereupon obteyned a Judgment by which meanes your Orator is become wholy remediless unless releived by your honors Justice Equity and Good Conscience Doe therefore in all Humble maner pray that a writt of Subpoena may be directed to the said Thos. Peterson him Comanding to make his personall appeareance before your honors on [*torn*] third of the next Generall Court then and there to make Answer to all and Singuler the premisses upon Oath And that your honors will there[*torn*] the Same into your Serious Consideration Soe that the Said peterson [*torn*] be obleidged to allow unto your Orator what shall appeare to be due by virtue of the said Defendants promise and Assumption aforesaid or be otherwise releived therein and your Orator as in Duty bound shall praye.

T. Knight Secretary

[*Endorsed:*]
Bill in Cancellaria
Smythe versus Peterson Attorney etc.

[*CCR 192*]

No. Carolina Ss. To the provost Marshall or his Deputy

These are in her Majestyes name to will and require you to Sumons Thoms. Peterson Attorney to Micajah Perry and New Pensilvania Company personally to be and appeare at the next Court of Chancery to be holden at the house of Captain Jno. Hecklefield in Litle river on the third day of the next Generall Court then and there to make Answer to the bill of Complaint of Robt. Smyth of the County of Bath Complainant and have you there this Subpoena Dated at the Secretarys Office this 9th day of October Anno Domini 1706.

Testis T. Knight Secretary

[*Endorsed:*]
Subpoena for Peterson Attorney etc. ad sectam Smyth

[*CCR 192*]

No. Carolina Ss. To the honorable Court of Chancery

The Answer of Thos. Peterson Attorney of Micajah Perry and New Pensilvania Company to the Bill of Complaint of Richd. Smyth Complainant And the Said Defendant Sayth that he is not bound to make Answer to the aforesaid Bill of Complaint for that he had not a Coppy of the aforesaid Bill delivered unto him within ten dayes afore the Court as by the Lawes and Customes of this Honorable Court he ought to have had and of this he prays Judgement etc.

[*CCR 148*]

Received of Mr. Richard Smith for the use of Colonel Robert Quary and Company in deare skins and furrs seaven pounds and Eight shillings Aprill the 17th 1700.

Per me Nicholas Tylor

[*Endorsed:*]
280=19= 8
023=13= 3
032=07= 0
———
366=19=11

[*CCR 148*]

August the 2: 1700

Then Received of Mr. Rich. Smith 80 buckskins 119 doeskins 9 Raccoons 14 Foxes 3 Muskratts 2 Otters Beaver: 3 pounds 6 ounces for the use of Colonel Robert Quary and Company.

By mee: Nicholas Tyler

8:--:--
8:18: 6
: 3:--
10: 6
6: 9
16: 1½

18:14:10½

[*CCR 148*]

August the 22th: 1701

Then Received of Mr. Rich. Smith sixty and one pounds two shillins and three pence for the use of Colonel Robert Quary and Company.

Per Me Nicholas Tylor

[*CCR 148*]

December the 31th 1701

Then Received of Mr. Rich. Smith in furr and skins six pounds ten shillings and four pence for the use of Colonel Robt. Quary and Company.

Per Me Nicholas Tylor

[*CCR 148*]

January the 13th 1702/3
Received of Mr. Richi. Smith

68: fox and Catt: 136 Raccons: 2 Woolves 4 Bares: 5 Otters One Panther 34½ pounds of Beaver: 80 does: drest: ditto: Fox: 2 Minks 6 dito to: 2: foxis

2—11—
2—05—4
— 2—
8—
15—
1—6
5— 3—6
6— —6

1
2
1–6

17–11–4

[*CCR 148*]

Received of Mr. Richd. Smith Fifty Six Matts Amounting to Seven pounds fifteen shillings and six pence English pay Pamplicoue the 18th Septr. 1704.

T. Peterson

31 Large at 3/ per	4:13: -
25 small 2/6 per	3: 2:6
	£7:15:6

[*Stanton* v. *Bundy*]

[*CCR 187*]

No. Carolina Ss. To the honorable the Court of Chancery

The Bill of Complaint of Thoms. Stanton Complainant against Caleb Bundy defendant In humblewise Complaineing Sheweth unto your Honors

That Whereas your Orator was formerly posessed of a Certaine Tract of Land Conteyneing One hundred Acres Sictuate Lyeing and being in the precinct of Pascotanke as by a Certaine pattent and divers other scripts and writteing now ready to be produced to your Honors doth and may appeare Nevertheless Soe it is may it please your Honors that the Said Defendant Evely Intending and Fraudulently designeing to defraud and Cheate your [*torn*] of his Just right and Inherritance into and upon the aforesaid [*torn*] of Land hath wrongfully Entered and the Same from your [*torn*] doth wrongfully withold and Deteyne Contrary to Equity and Good Concience And your Orator farther Sheweth that [*torn*] did apply himselfe to the Honorable Deputy Governor and Councell for relief at or upon the Second day of November 1703 who did then See fitt to order the Surveyor Generall or his Deputy should Survey and lay out [*torn*] said Tract of Land for your Orator in pursuance to which order the Surveyor did goe to Lay out the Same but was then Molested and hindred by the Defendant where upon your Orator did apply himselfe a Second tyme to the Honorable Deputy Governor and Councell aforesaid at or upon the 30th day of March [*torn*] who upon Consideration had of the whole matter did order that Mr. Thos. Boyd Mr. Francis DeLaMare Mr. James Tooke and Mr. Jno. Jones or any three of them with Jno. Anderson and Robt. Keele Surveyors Should lay out and Survey the aforesaid Tract of Land according to the old pattent for your Orator In pursuance to which order the Said Surveyors did goe to Lay out the Same Accordingly but the Surveyors did not begin the Survey according to the said old pattent Contrary to the said order of Councell Soe that they did then Survey and Lay out but Twenty Nine Acres part of the said one hundred and the said Defendant Doe still wrongfully withold and deteyne from your Orator Seaventy one Acres being the remainder of the Said one hundred Acres the proper Just right of your Orator as your Orator is ready to make appeare to this honorable Court Doe therefor in all humble maner pray that a Writt of Subpoena may be directed to the Said Caleb Bundy him Comanding to make his personall appeareance before your Honors on the third day of the next Generall Court then and there to make Answer to all and Singuler the premisses and that your Honors will be pleased to order the Surveyor Generall to Lay out the Said Land according to the old pattent and Survey for your Orator or that your orator may be otherwise releived therein and your Orator as in Duty bound shall pray etc.

T. Knight Secretary

[*Endorsed:*]
Bill in Cancellaria
Stanton versus Bundy
Fyled Octo. 10th 1706

[*CCR 191*]

No. Carolina Ss. To the Provost Marshall or his Deputy

These are in her Majestyes name to will and require you to Sumons Caleb Bundy personally to be and appeare at the next Court of Chancery to be holden at the house of Captain Jno. Hecklefield in Litle river on the third day of the next Generall Court then and there to make Answer to the bill of Complaint of Thomas Stanton Complainant and have you there this Subpoena Dated at the Secretarys office this 10th day of October Anno Domini 1706.

Testis T. Knight Secretary

[*Endorsed:*]
Subpoena in Cancellaria for Bundy ad sectam Stanton
Executed by me George Hariss

[*Low, attorney of Archdale* v. *Reed*]

[*CCR 191*]

No. Carolina Ss. To the provost Marshall or his Deputy

These are in her Matyes name to will and require you to Sumons Wm. Reed Esqr. personally to be and appeare at the next Court of Chancery to be holden at the house of Captain Jno. Hecklefield in Litle river on the third day of the next Generall Coart then and there to make Answer to the Bill of Complaint of Emanuell Lowe Esqr. Attorney for the honorable Jno. Archdale Esqr.

and have you there this Subpoena Dated at the Secretarys Office this 30th day of June Anno Domini 1707.

Testis T. Knight Secretary

[*Endorsed:*]
Subpoena in Cancellaria
Lowe versus Reed

[*Daniell* v. *Hecklefield*]

[*CCR 148*]

North Carolina Ss. By the Honorable the Deputy Governor etc.

To the provost Marshall or his Deputy

Whereas the Honorable Landgrave Robert Danielle hath obteyned a Judgement at a Generall Court held for this province on the 29th day of July last past for the Sume of Fifteen pounds two Shillings and Eight pence Halfe penny with Costs and the said Hecklefields Goods being taken or likely be taken in Execution for the Same

These are in her Matyes name to will and require you that you desist in Levying the Execution aforesaid or if you have executed the Same that you forthwith discharge it untill a heareing there of be had in the honorable Court of Chancery and make returne of your proceedings herein to the next Court of Chancery Given under my hand this [*illegible*] day of Sept. Anno Domini 1707.

Thomas Cary

[*Moseley* v. *Howard*]

[*CCR 191*]

North Carolina Curia Cancellariae

To the honorable Thos. Cary Esqr. Deputy Governor and to the rest of the true and absolute Lords and Proprietors Deputies being the high Court of Chancery for the Goverment

In most humble wise Complaining Sheweth unto your Honors your Orator Edward Moseley of the precinct of Chowan That sometime in the month of January last past One Jacob Howard Master of the Sloop New Speedwell being in this Goverment And Designed on a voyage to Bermuda, and Directly back again to this Government Your Orator Did in Consideration of his returning Directly to this Government Ship on board his said Vesell One hundred bushells of Indian Corne, four barrells pork, and one barrell of Lard And Consigned the Same to Mr. Thomas Brookes of Bermuda with Instructions (which the Said Howard was privy to) that the Neat proceeds of your Orators said Goods should be remitted in [pounds sterling] of [England] But now so it is May it please your Honnors That the said Howard pretending stress of weather went with his said Vessell to Antegua and there took upon him to Dispose of your Orators goods aforesaid and (not minding your Orators Instructions which he was privy to, and which the said Howard Acknowledged he saw in your Orators Letters to said Brooks of Bermuda) hath brought your Orator two hogsheads of Molasses and a small quantity of Sugar pretending that he sold your Orators goods for Molasses and Sugar, contrary to your Orators Instructions aforesaid And which as your Orator is informed cannot be any thing near to the vallue of what your Orators goods sold for. In tender Consideration of the premisses And forasmuch as your Orator is not releiveable in the premisses at Common Law for want of such sufficient proof as is required by the strict rules thereof, But is altogether remediless in the Same, unless by the aid of this honorable Court your Orator may have a perticular Discovery of the truth of all and Singular the premisses by the corporall Oath of said Howard Who when he Doth Answer thereto upon Oath must and will Discover the Same. To the end therefore that he may so Do, And in perticular sett forth and Discover What he the said Howard did Sell your Orators goods for and att what prices, That your Orator may have the neat proceeds thereof, paying the usual and accustomed freight for the Same when Delivered to your Orator. May it please Your Honnors to grant unto the aforesaid Orator the Writt or Writts of Subpoena, to be Directed to him the said Jacob Howard thereby Comanding him at a certain day and under a certain pain therein to be Limitted personally to be and appear before your Honnors in this honorable Court then and there to make Direct Answer upon Oath to all and Singular the premisses before sett forth, as fully and amply as if the same had been here again repeated and interrogated. And further to stand to and abide such Order and Decree therein as to your Honnors in your Wisdom, shall seem most agreable to Equity and good Conscience. And Your Orator as in Duty Bound shall ever pray etc.

August 28th 1707 Edwd. Moseley Complainant

[*Endorsed:*]
Edward Moseley against Jacob Howard Marriner
Bill in Chancery

[*CCR 191*]

No. Carolina Ss. To the Provost Marshall of the County of Albemarle or to his Deputy

These are in her Majestyes name to will and require you to Sumons Jacob Howard personally to be and appeare at the next Court of Chancery to be holden at the house of Captain Jno. Hecklefield in Litle river on the third day of the next Generall Court then and there to Answer the Bill of Complaint of Edwd. Moseley Esqr. and have there this Subpoena Dated at the Secretarys Office this 11th day of Octor. Anno Domini 1707.

Testis T. Knight Secretary

[*Endorsed:*]
Subpoena in Cancellaria
Moseley versus Howard

[*Houghton* v. *Davenport*]

[*CCR 191*]

No. Carolina Ss. To the provost Marshall or his Deputy

These are in her Majestyes name to will and require you to Sumons Richd. Davenport personally to be and appeare at the next Court of Chancery to be holden at the house of Captain John Hecklefield in Litle river on the third day of the next Generall Court then and there to Answer the bill of Complaint of Thos. Houghton Senior Complainant and have there this Subpoena Dated at the Secretarys Office this 13th day of March Anno Domini 1707/8.

Testis T. Knight Secretary

[*Endorsed:*]
Subpoena in Cancellaria
Houghton versus Davenport

[*Relfe* v. *Cary*]

[*CCR 139*]

No. Carolina Ss. To the honorable the Court of Chancery

The Bill of Complaint of Wm. Relfe Complainant against The Honorable Colonel Thos. Cary in this Honorable Court present Defendant In humblewise Complaineing Sheweth unto your Honors that in the yeare 1704 your Orator was Imployed by the honorable Colonel Rob. Daniell then Deputy Governor of this province to Collect the Quit Rents in pascotanke river by virtue of which power your Orator did Collect and receive one hundred and Sixty bushells of Indyan Corne but Soe it was may it please your Honors that before your Orator had rendred the Same or any Account thereof to the aforesaid Rob. Daniell The said Colonel Thos. Cary Arrived in this Government with Comission to be Deputy Governor of the Same and as Soone as the Said Defendant had published the Same he the said Defendant Sent a Certaine writeing under his hand as Dep. Governor to your Orator thereby requiring your Orator keep all Such Sume or Sumes of Money or other things as he had received for Quit rents in his hands untill further order from him as he (your Orator) wo'd answer the Contrary at his perill In obedience to which Command your Orator did reteyne the aforesaid one hundred and Sixty bushells of Corne and refused to deliver the Same to the aforesaid Colonel Daniell when demanded And your Orator Farther Sheweth that at Divers other tymes your Orator told the said Defendant by what Authority he received the aforesaid Corne and that Colonel Daniell had Sent to demand the Same and requested his honors orders what to doe with it for that he thought he ought to deliver it to him by whose power he received it and the Said Defendant then told him that he ought to observe his order (viz. to keep the Same till further order from him) which if he did he the said Defendant wo'd Save him harmeless and he sho'd Come to noe Damage thereby or words to that Effect In pursuance whereof your orator wholy relying upon the word and promise of the Defendant and in regard to the Authority he then had did keep the said Corne in his Custody untill the same [*torn*] utterly Spoiled And your Orator farther Sheweth that The aforesaid Colonel Daniell did Since that tyme Comence a Suite in this Honorable Court against your Orator for the aforesaid Corne per obligation by a Decree for the Same with Costs alias Execution as by the proceeding now ready to be produced doth appeare pursuant to which decree your Orators body was taken in Execution and thereby obleidged to pay the aforesaid quantity of 160 bushell Corne and the Costs of the aforesaid Suite to the aforesaid Colonel Daniell And the aforesaid Defendant doth now utterly refuse to pay the Same again unto your Orator or give your orator any redress therein tho' by your orator thereto often requested Notwithstanding his faithfull promises as aforesaid Contrary to all Equity and Good Concience Soe that your Orator is left wholy remediless in the premisses and is likely utterly to lose the aforesaid quantity of 160 bushells of Corn with the aforesaid Costs unless releived by your Honors Justice Equity and Good Concience Doe therefore in all humble maner pray that the said Colonel Thos. Cary may have Answer make to all and Singuler the premisses and that your Honors will then award that the said Colonel Cary may pay unto your Orator as well all the Costs and damages Susteyned by reason of the aforesaid Suite in this Honorable Court and by the Storehouse roome of the aforesaid Corne for neare twelve Months and all other the trouble and travell occasioned to your Orator there by as the aforesaid Quantity of one hundred and Sixty bushells of Corne and your Orator as in Duty bound shall pray.

T. Knight Secretary

[*Endorsed:*]
Bill in Cancellaria
Relfe versus Cary
Filed March 15th 1707/8

[*CCR 189*][2]

[*Torn*][3]llock pleads that this Court has [*torn*] Court of Chancery to heare and [*torn*] [*illegible*] the Reasons following No. 1.

[2] Although these fragmented minutes carry an endorsement dated March, 1701/2, internal evidence indicates that they are later than that—possibly June, 1702 or slightly later. The minutes are in Nathaniel Chevin's handwriting; the endorsement is in a later, unidentified hand.

[3] The entire upper portion of this page is torn off.

The Court haveing con[*torn*] Reasons and Afirme their Ju[*torn*] tion founded upon a statute of parliament maide in March 1701/2 Intile [*blank*]

And acordingly the Defendant is ordered to Answer the plaintiffs Bill. And the Defendant farther saith that the Letter of Attorney foresaid which is produced from James Gambell of Glascow and Jno. Gamle in London the plaintiff pleads that the said Letter of procreation [*torn*] is Signd and Seald under the hands of the provost and prays the Courts opinion therein And the Honorable Court is of opinion that the said Letter of attorney is of full force and power And Sufficiently provd.

And for further pleas Colonel pollock saith that Debts should be pd. before Legalies Further No. 2 [*torn*] and the Complainant Saith [*torn*] and that there is a [*illegible*] others and to Mr. Hambleton fogo and peterson and to others Unknown and allso finds [*illegible*] Given which ought to be pd.

To which the Complainant Replies that peterson and those presents Cannot Claime [above] one ½ of the Account the where [*torn*] from a Cargo of goods brought in by the said Gambell [*torn*] Copartner with the aforementioned Hambleton fogo and peterson one half be longing to the [*illegible*] Gambell.

[*Torn*].

[*Torn*] that if the said James Gambell [*illegible*] his Lawfull attorney or attorneys Shall have full power and Athority att all times to Defend [*illegible*] the said Estate as well against the said Hambleton as any other that shall Lay Claime there to And that the Defendant Shall not Enter into any Agreement or make any Composition for the Same without theire consent Which the Court have my Condition the [*illegible*] and being of opinion the General Legatee oaght not in Equity to be any Longer Deteined from his Just Due, the Defendants being Securd as [*torn*] from all Damage that may Acrue by said payment of Money to the Complainants And your Humble Complainant prays that the Defendant may give an Account of the Estate According to the Complainants Bill.

And the Account being Calld out Colonel pollock pleads as No. 3.

Plea to [*torn*] on oath. No. 4 and that the accounts are Examined by the Honorable Court and the [*illegible*] comes [*illegible*].

[*Torn*].

To which Reasons the Complainant Answers that when these accounts were Rendred by Colonel pollock etc. And Auditted there was no person that had any power to question the Justice thereof and so was never Justly Examind And therefore prays that the said accounts may be fairly stated and made up and that the Complainant may have his Just Dew.

Capt. Jno. Hunt upon oath Saith that he agreed with Adam Gambell for 15 per cent for Receiveing and packing etc. of all his pork.

[*Endorsed:*]
March 1701/2

FILE PAPERS

[*Bennet, John, petition*]

[*CCR 192*]

To the honnorable Court of chancery Apointed for the County of Albymarle In the Province of north Carrlina

Your honnors humble Orator John Bennet humbly Sheweth that uppon the 13th day of July In the yeare of our lord 1699 your honnors humble orator Sold unto Bengiman Tulle of the Precinck of Corrowtuck A Servant Girle named margret Barrit for eight years And foure month and the Saide Tulle haveing kept the Said Servant Girle withoute any molestation from mee your honnors humble petitioner or any belonging to mee [*illegible*] on the 27th day of Aprill Anno 1701 the Saide Tulle Sent a noate to mee your honors humble petitioner to Acquaint Your honnors that the Saide Servant Girle did Intend to Petition for her freedom which I your honnors humble petitioner knew by law Itt wass Impossable to bee obtained for att The expiration of the Saide Tearme afore Saide the Saide Tulle is obleged To deliver the Saide Servant Girle to your honnors humble Orator or to the heires of your honnors humble Orator to Serve the Remaining Part of her Time butt the Saide Servant Girle Presenting her Petition to the Court held for the precinck of corrowtuck the 28 and 29 dayes of Aprill Anno 1701 wherein which Saide Petition Itt wass falsely Aserted that the Saide Servant Girle wass Transported from Europe to Corrowtuck when ass the Truth is the Saide Servant Girle wass transported from Ireland Into Stafford County In virginia and therre Sold by the mate of the vessell unto mr. william Richardson to Serve the Saide Richardson or his assines According to the Judgment of Court and accordingly wass Ajudged at Princes ann Court but the aforesaide Court of corrowtuck not Considdering that According to law your honnors humble orator ought to have bene Summoned to Appeare the next ensuing Court to have made Appeare his Title to the afore Saide Servant Girle did Contrary to the Priviledg of a freeborne Subject of england Grant and Order uppon the 29th of Aprill Anno 1701 that the Saide Servant Girle Should bee free from her master bengiman tulle and that the Saide Tulle Should pay unto the Said Servant Girle the useall quantity of Corne and Cloathes uppon the 27th day of may Anno 1701 The afore Saide Bengiman Tulle Sent a noate unto your honnors humble Petitioner to demand a Servant or mone to which your honnors humble Orator Sent an Answer which had bene Sufficient to have Prevented any furder Truble if the Saide Tulle Could butt have understood Common Sence butt not withstanding uppon the last day of may 1701 the deputy marshall for the Precinck of Corrowtuck Came to your honnors humble Orator house and Clapped your honnors humble Orator on the Shoulder and Told your honnors humble Orator that hee did arest your honnors humble Petitioner whereuppon your honnors humble Petitioner did desire of the afore Saide marshall to Shew unto your honnors humble Petitioner the writt by vertue of which hee ought to bee empowered butt the Saide marshall told your honnors humble Petitioner that a Sworne officer neede not Shew his writt butt your honnors humble Petitioner Replied unto the Saide marshall that hee ought to Shew your honnors humble Petitioner the writt or otherwise your honnors humble Petitioner told the Saide marshall hee Should Take Itt for no arest whereuppon Your honnors humble Petitioner drew a Complaint against the Saide marshall butt by reason of Siknes was Prevented of Going to the next Court held for the Precinck of Corrowtuck whereuppon the afore Saide marshall afirmed to the Court that hee had arrested your honnors humble Petitioner uppon which Saide Informemation the Court Granted an order to the deputy marshall to take the boddy of your honnors humble Petitioner Into his Costody to See him att the next Court or otherwise to Pay unto bengiman tulle Seaventene Pound and not one Peny due hard measure and Please your honnors your honnors humble Petitioner being Informed by Sum of his neabours of the afore Saide Illegal proceedings did Promise a Coppy of the order of Court which when your honnors humble Petitioner had Considdered att the orphans Court next ensuing your honnors humble Petitioner did write unto the Court to acquaint theire worships how unconsadart and Repugnant to law theire late order Granted to the marshall was to take the boddy of your honnors humble into his Costody thinking theay would Considder and Countermand not withstanding uppon the 22d of October 1701 the depute marshall Came and Served the order afore Saide uppon your honnors humble petitioner whereuppon your honnors humble petitioner being a very aileing man to Lye inprison would bee very hard your honnors humble Petitioner wass forced to procur a keeper and the Saide keeper wass bound In a bond of an hundred Pounds Pennalty that your honnors humble Petitioner did make his personal appeareance according ass the afore Saide order did appoint And uppon the 28th day of October Anno 1701 the Court for the Precinck of Corrowtuck being then holden your honnors humble Petitioner being Called by the Court to Answar to A Pretended Action of bengeman tully of the afore Saide Precinck whereuppon your honnors humble Petitioner Presented a Complaint to the Court of A Presumtious misdemenour offered by the deputy marshal afore Saide unto your honnors humble Petitioner Pretending to arest your honnors humble Petitioner butt had no writt therefore no Power neither Any declareration delivered uppon which your honnors humble petitioner Declared unto the worshippfull Court that there was no way to Injone your honnors humble petitioner by law to Jone Issue butt iff theay Could Presribe any your honnors humble Petitioner wass Ready to Obey Immediatly affter your honnors humble

Petitioner was departed the Rome the Court except mr. edward Taylor did Consult to Grant an Order against your honnors humble Petitioner which when your honnors humble Petitioner understood your honnors humble Petitioner told the Court Rather then theay Should Grant an Order against your honnors humble Petitioner would Jone Issue That So your honnors humble Petitioner might have the Priviledg to Appeale to your honnors butt the jury wass empanneled and your honnors humble Petitioner declared unto them that your Saide honnors humble Petitioner was never arested in the afore Saide Pretended Action nor no declareration delivered nor no Petition Proved nor ever Could bee proved your honnors humble Petitioner Intending theire by to make the Jury Senceable that theire wass no Occasion for theire Going oute uppon the afore Saide Pretended Action ass Indeede the foreman thomas brunt Replyed to your honnors humble petitioner then Saide the afore Saide brunt theire is no Occasion for uss to Go oute not withstanding the afore Saide Jury went oute and brought A verdict against your honnors humble Petitioner for which Saide Illegall Proceedings your honnors humble Petitioner hath brought his petition of Complaint and Appealed to your honnors humblely Craveing of your honnors To Considder that first uppon the aforesaide Servant Girles Petition the aforesaide Court of Corrowtuck Ground theire Order uppon the Severall assertions In the Saide petition and other Informations and no Person Appeareing or makeing any Alligation to the Contrary ass to the Assertions theay are false and the Informations of no valliddity and for no Person Appeareing to defend and make theire Title appeare to the Saide Servant Girle how Could Itt be expected when never theireunto Required ass the Law Injoines In Such Cases for by the Act made In the Reigne of King Charles the first itt Saith Itt is asserted and Accorded for the Good Goverment of the Commons that no man bee putt to Answer without Presentment before Justises or matter of Record or by due Process and writt Originall according to the old law of the land and iff any thing bee hence forth done to the Contrary Itt Shall bee voide In the law and holden for error butt In this afore Saide Order theire wass no due Process therefore voide In the law and to bee holden for error [truly] by your honnors humble complanant humbly prayeth your honnors to Considder of the deputy marshalls Pretending to Arest your honnors humble petitioner and Refused to Shew any writ when theireunto Required by your honnors humble Petitioner Although the law Saith Positively that no freeman of ingland ought to bee Imprissoned nor otherwise Restrained withoute Cause Shewen for which by law hee ought to bee So Imprissoned butt your honnors humble Petitioner had no Cause Shewen butt only the deputy marshalls Say So tharefore a breach of the Law and very Pregidisiall to your honnors humble complanant.

3ly your honnors humble Complainenant humble Prayeth your honnors to Considder the Illegallity of the afore Cited order Granted by the afore Saide Court to the deputy marshall to Take the boddy of your honnors humble Complainenant Into his Costody or otherwise for Your honnors humble Complaineant to pay unto the afore Saide bengiman Tulle Seaventenne Pound ass for the Sum of mone mentioned your honnor humble Complaineant did not nor doeth not Give the Saide tulle one Pene and ass for your honnors humble Complaineant to bee Committed to prisson if your honnors humble Complaineant had bene Really arrested the afore Saide Could by law have only Granted an Attachment to the deputy marshall against your honnors humble Complaineant estate theirefore itt must nesesarily bee Concluded to bee false Imprisoment whereuppon your honnors humble Complaineant doeth humbly pray your honnors to Grant Ann order for makeing voide and erronious the aforesaide order Granted by the afore Saide Court of Corrowtuck to free the aforesaide Servant Girle according as is mentioned In the afore Cited act of Parliment and lastly your honnors humble Complaineant humbly prayth your honnors to Command a discharge from bengiman Tulle for A bill of Seaventene Pound with Cost which John hodgson wass forced to Give the Saide Tulle to keepe the Boddy of your honnors humble Complaineant from prison with Such Reasonable Sattisfaction ass your honnors Shall find to bee meete and Convenient for So Greate Truble and Charge Causelesly Sustained with Cost of all the Courts and your honnors humble Complaineant ass In duty Bound Shall ever Pray for your honnors Temporall and etternall felisity.

[*Jennings* v. *Bell*]

[*CCR 191*]

No. Carolina Ss. To The Honorable Court of Chancery

Wm. Jenins in most Humble maner Complaines That Jno. Bell of the precinct of Pascatank became Bound to your Humble Orator by two Bills the one Bearing Date July 22th 1699 for £4 payable by the 10th of Decmer. in the Yeare 1700 the other Bill bearing Equall Date with the former and of the Same Value payable Decembr. the 10th 1701 And the Evidences to the Said Bills being one Wm. Keen and Daniel Phillips the Said Keen being gone out of the Countrey and the Said Phillips upon Oath Saith that he Cannot tell wither it be his hand or not And the Said Jno. Bell Deniing the Said Debts tho Justly Dew Your Humble Orator is Left Alltogether without Remedy att Comon Law And therefore Humbly prays your Honorable Writt of Subpena that The Said Jno. Bell may be brought before this Honorable Court And may upon Oath be Examined whither he Did not Signe and Delivr the Said Bills unto your Humble Orator and that your Humble orator may Receive such Decree or order as to [*illegible*] William Shall Seem most meet And Your Humble Orator Shall Ever pray etc.

Copia Vera N. Chevin Clk. Cancellariae

[*Endorsed:*]
Chancery Bill
Jenins Versus Bell

[*Paine, Samuell, petition*]

COURT OF CHANCERY, DATE UNDETERMINED

[*CCR 191*]

North Carolina Ss. To The Honorable Court of Chancery

Samuell Paine deposeth upon The holy Evangilist That Wm. Reed Recd. of him The Summe of one pound seven shilling for Quitt Rents, as Appears by The said Paines obligation which he had discharged and taken in, This deponent further Declares That in discourseing with The said William Reed he The said paine told him That he heard Mr. John Porter say That he had never signed Any Comission to give The said Read power to Receive nine year Quitt Rents upon the sand bancks upon which This deponant further adds That The said Wm. Reed did declare to him That he had from under The hands of The Governor and Councill but Espetiall from under The hand of Mr. John Porter, And would make the Said Mr. Porter a Lyer to his face and further This Deponant saith not.

[*Endorsed:*]
Samll. Payen
Depossition

[*Pamtecough inhabitants, petition*]

[*CCR 187*]

No. Carolina ss. Curia Cancellariae

To the honorable Colonel Thomas Cary Esqr. Deputy Governor and to his honorable Councill being the high Court of Chancery for this Government

The Petition of William Barrow, Morris Lewellin on behalf of themselves and others Inhabitants of Pantogoe Humbly Sheweth That your Petitioners and Divers others the Inhabitants of this Government dureing the time of the honorable Robert Daniell his being Governour, obtained Pattents for their Land, and thereupon gave their Bills payable to said Daniell for the Fees, and they further Shew that the said Pattents have been declared void and of none effect.

Whereupon they pray that this your honorable Court will Order the said Daniell to appear and Deliver up their aforesaid Bills And your petitioners as in Duty bound shall ever pray etc.

[*Signed:*]
W. Barrow, Maurice Luellyn, Archibald Holmes, John Buntin, Warrin <*his mark*>

[*Endorsed:*]
Pamticoe Petition

Miscellaneous Court Documents

Fragments of Minutes, Court of Admiralty, October 1704
In the Hand of Thomas Snoden

Miscellaneous Court Documents

[*Court of Admiralty*]

[*CCR 189*][1]

North Carolina ss.

Att A Court of Admiralty held att the House of Captain John Hecklefield in Little River the 3d Day of October 1704 Present The Honorable Wm. Glover Esqr. Justice, John Porter Esqr., Tho. Symonds Esqr., Wm. Bartlett Esqr. Judges

The Court being Satt A new Court [*torn*] published and read and allowed for this [*torn*] of A Court of Admiralty and the [*torn*] tooke the Oaths appointed by Law [*torn*] Judges of the Same.

A Commission Constituting [*torn*] Register of the Court of [*torn*] and allowed and he tooke [*torn*] by the Law.

A Commission Const[*torn*] Marshall of the [*torn*] read and allowed [*torn*]. [*Torn*] Court of [*torn*] and he tooke [*torn*] appointed by Law.

An Information brought before this Court By [*torn*] Captain Wm. Barrow Informant in these Words [*torn*] Captain Wm. Barrow Deputy Collector of her [Majesties] Customes within the Port of Pamticoe in the [County] of Bath in this Province Informeth this Honorable Court by Chr. Gale Esqr. her Majesties Attorney Generall for this Province That Levi Truewhitt of this Province on or about the Month of August last past did arrive into the port of Pamticoe aforesaid in this Province with A Sloop called the Pamticoe Adventure Burthen about Six Tunns loaden with Sundry Goods and Merchandize the Perticulars unknown to your Informant and the Same hath unloaden and putt on Shoar and broke bulk without making any Entry of his Said Vessell and Goods in this Port Contrary to the lawes and Statutes in those Cases made and Provided Wherefore Seizure is made of the aforesaid Vessell and all her apparrell and furniture Goods and Merchandizes to her Majesties use as Justly forfeited to her Majestie and prayes the Judgment of this Court with Costs.

Gale per Domina [*torn*]

[*Torn*] for Plea the Defendant referrs the whole Matter [*torn*] Honorable Court.

[1] These minutes are badly torn and deteriorated. In some places, entire paragraphs are missing. The minutes are in the handwriting of Thomas Snoden, who was clerk of the General Court at the time.

[*Torn*] Opinion of this Honorable Court and to That [*torn*] Majestie be dismist And that Levi Truewhitt pay these following [*torn*] to Captain John Hecklefield Marshall the [*torn*] Shillings To Thomas Snoden [*torn*] the Summe of Three pounds [*torn*] to the Members of this Court.

[*Torn*] W. Glover

FILE PAPERS

[*CCR 142*]

Sept. 26: 1704

Honourable Sir

These Comes to Aquaint you that Levi Trewett Master of the Pamplico Adventure within This Government within sixteen houers after his Arivall att Pamlico att The house of Tho. Durum without Enterin the Said Slope Did Break bulk unload and Carrey on Shore to the house of the Said Durrum Sundry Goods and Martchandize Contrary to Law videlicet [*blank*].

Wharefore I humbly pray that a Court of Admaralty may be Called with all Convenent Speed for the Said Slope and Cargo and that in the mean time his honour please to take Care of the Said Slope and Goods which is the humble Desire of him Who is Yours to Command.

W. Barrow

To The honourable Landsgrave Robt. Danell Esqr. Leutenant Generall and Vice Admarall and Debety Governer of North Carrolinia

[*Endorsed:*]
Capt. Wm. Barrow his information Against the Sloop Pamlico Adventure

[*CCR 192*]

No. Carolina To Capt. John Hackelfeild Marshal of the Admiralty

You are hearby Commanded and Impowered to tak into your Custody and posesion the Sloop Pamlico Adventure Levi Trewhitt Commander Together with all her tackell Apparell goods and Merchandize whatsoever thatt is now on board the said Sloop And the Same In Saife Custodie Keep untill the said Sloop and all her Apparrel to gether with the said goods Shall bee delivered by Dew Course of Law and for your Soe Doing these Shall bee your Warrant Given under my hand and Seal this 26th Daye of Septer. Anno: 1704.

Robt. Daniell

[*Endorsed:*]
Writts
Attachment

[*Special Courts*] [2]

[2] Papers of the Grand Court and the Palatine's Court as well as Special Courts are grouped under this heading.

[*CCR 148*]

[N.] Carolina Ss.

Whearas Capt. John Hackelfield Complaines thatt att the Generall Courtt in the Precinct of Pequimons, Anthony Alexander obtained A Judgment Against him; for the Sume of Six pounds and Fifteen Shillings thee which Sume the said Hackelfield Doeth Aver hee hath tendered According to Contract; Before the said Judgment was obtained (Together with all the Cost).

These are theirfore in the name of the Palattine [Court] To Command you and Eveuari of you to Cease and forbeare to Iusue any [*torn*] Hackelfield Prosses on and Concerning the premises etc. Given under my hand and Seal this 15th Daye of Aprill 1704.

To Ralph Fletcher Esqr.
And all other officers
of the Precinct Courtt of
Piquimons — Robt. Daniell

[*CCR 148*]

N. Carolina Ss. By the Governor

This Day Mr. Cornelius Joanes by his Petition [*torn*] thatt Notwithstanding hee hath Cast George [*torn*] the Precinck Court of Pascotank by Verdickt of [*torn*] and that the Same was Confirmed in the Grand Court uppon Apeal of the said Griffine yitt hee the said Greiffine hath Again Arrested him the said Joanes in the Same Action for which the Tryals have binne in the Courts as aforesaid.

These are theirfore to Command you and Everri of you to Cease from and forbeare any [*illegible*]ings in the said Action And that hee the said George Griffin bee and Appeare before the Grand Council att their next Setting to Answer the premises. Given under my hand and Seal this 2d Day of July Anno 1704.

To Wm. Glover Esqr.
and the Rest of the Judges
and other officers of the Grand Courtt — Robert Daniell

[*CCR 148*]

N. Carolina Ss.

Whereas Complaint is Made unto me by Capt. Jno. Hackinfild Provest Marshal that pursuant to a Warrant under my hand and Seal Bareing date the Fowerth of this Instant, to apprehend the body of Jno. More, Alis Ralph Smith, Alis Sivestor Mathews, being Convickted of Forgrie and to be Guilty of Felionie That In pursuance ther of he the Said Hackenfeild Did Repeaier to the house of Jos. Jourdan where he Found the said Jno. More Alis Ralph Smith Alias Sivestor Mathews, In Companie with the Said Jos. Jordan, Cornilus Ratlifh, and Wm. Cartwright and that he the Said Hackinfield did in the Same roome Apperhend the Said Jno. More etc. who strugled and Indevred to make his Escape wherefore he the Said Hackefild Required and Commanded the Assistance of them the Said Jurdan Ratlife and Cartwright who Did refuse to assist or anyways to help him by Reason whereof his prisoner made his Escape which is Contrary to Law.

These are therefore In her Majesties Name to will and Require you to attach the Bodyes of them Joseph Jurdan Cornelis Ratlife and Wm. Cartwright and them In Safe Custody Keep Soe that they be and appere Att the Next grand Court holden for this part of this province then and there to Answer for This Their Contept, Where of Faile not as youl Answer the Contrey. Given under my hand and Seal This 12th February 1704/5.

To the Provost Marshall or his deputy — Robt. Daniell

[*CCR 104*]

<334> No. Carolina Ss.

Att a Councell holden at the house of Capt. Jno. Hecklefield in Litle river on Thursday 1st day of November Anno Domini 1705. Present The Honorable Colonel Thos. Cary Esqr. Deputy Governor etc. The Honorable Samll. Swann, Tho. Pollock, Wm. Glover, Edwd. Mosely Esquires Lords Deputies.

The Honorable Deputy Governor reporting to this Board that he has Seized a parcell of Goods belonging to Charles Gee for an unlawfull [Trade]. It is therefore ordered that a Court Shall be holden on the thirteenth day of this Instant November for the Tryall and Condemnation of the Said Goods by the Members of the Generall Court and that the Marshall Give notice to the said Members accordingly and Sumons an Able Jury for the Tryall of the Same.

Att a Speciall Court holden In pursuance to the above written order at the house of Capt. Jno. Hecklefield in Litle river on Tuesday the thirteenth day of November Anno Donini 1705/6 [*sic*]. Present The Honorable Wm. Glover, Jno. Porter, Christo. Gale, Wm. Collins Esquires Justices.

Jno. Doe Comes by Thomas Snoden Esqr. her Majestyes Attorney Generall and desires this Court to understand and be Informed that Charles Gee hath Imported Divers Goods and Comodityes into this Province (videlicet) Seaven Hatchetts: Four Yards of Blew Duffells: Twenty pounds of powder ten Yards ½ of red plaines: twelve Yards three quarters Blew Ditto: twenty two Yards three quarters Blew Ditto: Nineteen Yards quarter Blew Ditto: Nineteen Yards and three quarters Red Ditto: one Gun Lock two Doz. Flints two pr. Sizers Six Yards Blew Duffells six Yards Blew Ditto Ketles quart 10½ pounds Fourteen pound ½ of powder Four Yards ½ Dowles halfe a pound of Browne thred Fyfty five pounds and halfe of [Slortt] and hath not delivered to the Governor of this Province or to any person or Officer by <335> him Authorized or appointed his Name and Surname or a true Inventory or perticuler of the aforesaid Goods and Comoditys by him the Said Charles Gee Imported as aforesaid but hath Traded and purchased Skins in this province with other Goods Soe unlawfully Imported as aforesaid Contrary to the Tenour Intent and meaneing of one Act made in the fifteenth yeare of the Raigne of his Majestye King Charles 2d Intituled (an Act for Encouragement of Trade) and in Contempt of her Majestye her Lawes and Statutes Wherefore Seizure is made of the aforesaid Goods and Comoditys with a Certaine parcell of Skins quantity unknowne, and prayes Condemnation of the Same according to the Tenor of the aforesaid Act And the provost Marshall was required to Sumons the said Charles Gee to make his personall appeareance at this Court to Shew Cause why the Said Goods may not be Condemned according to Law and a Non est Inventus being returned on the aforesaid Sumons the Informant prayes an Attachment against all the Estate of the Said Gee wherever to be found in this Government which is Granted.

Then this Court adjourned till the next Generall Court.

[*Signed:*]
W. Glover, John Porter, C. Gale.

[*CCR 191*]

North Carilina Scilicet To the Honourable Grand Courte

John Pettiver Humbley Sheweth to Youre Honoures that John Hackilfield having Comenced Suite against Youre Pettishoner to this Courte upon ane Acounte and he being abroade when the saide Copey of the Ritt wass Left at his house and the time being soe Very short after he Came home that he Coulde nott send to the Shriefe in order to Sommons his Evidences to prove the full payment of his Saide Acounte Exehibted aganst him Thearefore he humbley Craves of Youre honoures an Imparlance to the next Grand Courte in order he May be Prepared to Come to a tryall with the Saide John Hackillfield and Youre Pettishoner Shall Pray.

John Pettiver

[*Endorsed:*]
John Pettiver Pettishon for an Imparlance

[*CCR 140*]

North Carolina Scilicet

To The Honourable Grand Courte
John Hackilfield Plantive
John Pettiver Defendant

The Defendant for Plea Sath the Acct. Speceiefyed and Signefyed in the plantive Declaration in Greate parte being falsley Charged against him the Said Defendant and for the Remaing parte theare ofe it being fulley Satisfyed Contented and over paid wich he is Readdy to Make apeare and thearefore he flings him Selfe to Youre honouers prudent Jugment and to his Country home he Craves of Your honoures May try the Ishue.

John Pettiver

[*Endorsed:*]
Pettivers Plea against Hackilfield Acct.

[*CCR 148*]

William Frayly of Chowan doth declare and Swear on the wholy Evangelist That he Saw Charle Gee trade with John Hawkins for the Value of ten pounds and paid him in powder shott Linnen and other goods which he brought from Virginia and then he [deligned] for Pamptico to sell the rest and further this deponent Saith not. No. 3. 1705.

Coram me
Thomas Cary

Will Frayley

[*CCR 148*]

Charles Smith of Machepungo doth declare and swear on the holy Evangelist that Charles Gee when he came to the house of Capt. Barrow that he did there declare that he Brought five horse Loads of Goods and had sold all the rest for skins and mony Except what he had there on horse back and was come there to dispose of the remainder part and Farther Declareing he had no clerance from Virginia nor had not any Leave of any in this Goverment to trade, but hoped it was no Crime and Farther this Deponent Saith not. November 3 1705.

Coram me
Thomas Cary

Charles Smith

[*CCR 192*]

No. Carolina

By the Honorable the president and Councill A proclamation

Whereas Some of the Members of the Grand Courte are Imploy'd in her Majesties Service and thereby hindred from attending att the next Court to be held att the house of Capt. John Hecklefeild on the last Tuesday of this Instant July; order'd that the Said Court be adjourn'd till the laste Tuesday in Augt. next being the 27th of the Said Month and itt is hereby adjourn'd. Given under theire hands and the Seale of the collony the 13th day of July Anno Domini 1706.
God Save the Queen

[*Signed:*]
W. Glover, Thomas Pollock, John Arderne, Edwd. Moseley

[*CCR 191*]

North Carolina Scilicet To the honourable Grand Courte

Tho. Boyde Plantive

James Crose Defendant

The Defendant for Plea Saith the bill Specefyed and Sigenefyed in the plantives Declarashion and Exehibeted against him the Saide Defendant is uterley Voide and of Noe afeckt in it Selfe by Reason it being fulley Satisfyed Contented and maide acckording to the true tennor and Meaning of the Saide bill wich he is Readey to make proofe of the Same upon his Corparell Oath theare for he humbley Craves an Nonsuite.

James Crose

[*CCR 187*]

To the Honarable the grand Court of north carolina:

The pition of william Maund Senior Sheweth that hee having Imported himsilf four times in this province and having brought in Sundry porsangers and Sirvants request rites for the Same whose names are under written

Wm. Maund Sinior	4
Emanuel Clienet	1
Philip Bayly	1
Joseph breiding	1
Samuel wilson	1
Henry Smith	1
Thomas [*illegible*]	1
Jno. Bryan	1
	11

Wm. Maund Junior	1
Thomas [*blank*]	1
Samfri a nigro	1
Thomas Youngblood	1
Onicald Francis	1
Thomas Lake	1
	6

in all 17

Robt. Humble 1

[*Endorsed:*]
The within rights Sworn to by Wm. Maund

[*Council in Judicial Capacity*][3]

[3] Some of the documents under this heading probably were intended for the Court of Chancery, which was composed of the governor and council.

[*CCR 148*]

Know all men by these presents That we Daniell Dean and Jane his wife both of this County Stand held and firmely [bound to his] Excellency the Palatine and Lords proprietors [*illegible*] Bound to the true payment whereof wee bind us and either of us our heirs Executors and Administrators Joyntly and severally firmely by These presents Sealed with our Seales Dated the 24th october 1702.

The Condition of this obligation is Such that if the above bounden Jane Dean doe personally appear before the Councill holden the 30 day of october next and there to answear all Such matters and things as on his Magestes behalf shall be objected against her then this obligation to be voyd or else to stand in full force and vertue.

Sealed in the
presents of us
John Walker
Nath. Chevin

Daniell Dean Signum
Jane Dean Signum

[*Endorsed:*]
James Deane
Dean and his Wifes Bond to apear att Councill 30th Instant

[*CCR 180*]

North Carolina ss.

These are in the Name of his Excellency the Palatine and the rest of the true and absolute Lords and Proprietors to will and require you to Inquire by the Oaths of twelve true and lawfull men Freeholders of the province aforesaid what Lands and Tenements Edwd. Catchmaide dyed Seized of and whether in his life time either by his last will or otherwise he dispos'd of the Same Given under the Seale of the Colony this 27th Day of July Anno Domini 1704.

To the Escheator to
Execute and make returne.

Robt. Daniell
Francis Tomes
Samuel Swann
John Arderne

[*CCR 179*]

No. Carolina Ss. To the Provost Marshall or his Deputy

These are in her Majestyes name to will and require you to Cite Mrs. Mary

Blount widdow and relict of Mr. Thomas Blount deceased personally to be and appeare before the Honorable the Governor and Councell at the house of Captain John Hecklefield in Litle river on the third day of the next Generall Court then there to Shew Cause why Letters Testamentary may not be Granted to Mr. James Blount pursuant to the last Will and Testament of the Said Thomas Blount and have you there this Citation Dated at the Secretarys Office this 21st day of May Anno Domini 1706.

Testis T. Knight Secretary

[*Endorsed:*]
Citation for Mrs. Mary Blount
Sarved by me Daniel Hallsey Deputy Marshall

[*CCR 148*]

No. Carolina Ss. By the Honorable Thomas Pollock Esqr.

To the Provost Marshall or his Deputy

Whereas Complaint has bin made unto me by Christopher Gale Esqr. that Jno. Norcome has uttered divers verry Scandelous words and Expresions against the Honorable the president and Cuniselle

These are therefore in her Matyes name to require you that you forthwith apprehend the Said Norcome and him into Custody take and keep untill he shall give good security personally to be and appeare before the Honorable the president and Counsell on the third day of the next Generall Court to Answer the said Complaint and have there this warrant. Given under my hand and Seale this 29th day of August Anno Domini 1706.

Sumons James Ward and his wife — Thomas Pollock

[*Endorsed:*]
Exequted by me Richard Leary Debuty marshall

[*CCR 139*]

[*Torn*] Ss. To the Provost Marshall of the County of Albemarle or to his Deputy

These are in her Majestyes name to will and require you to Summons Richd. Davenport personally to be and appeare at the Councell to be holden at the house of Captain Jno. Hecklefield in Litle river on the third day of the next Generall Court then and there to Answer the Complaint of Thos. Snoden and have there this Sumons Dated at the Secretarys Office this 19th day of Octor. Anno Domini 1707.

Testis T. Knight Secretary

[*Endorsed:*]
Cepi corpus by me Robt. Fendall

[*CCR 181*]

No. Carolina Ss. To The Honorable The President And Councill, Now Juditially Sitting

The Petition of Nathl. Nickholson Humbly Sheweth That whereas Thomas Harris late of This Province of North Carolina Deceased Dyed posessed of An Estate of Land And Allso personall which will appear by his Last will, and Testament And Inventory thereto Annexed (on which will) he left his Relect or widdow Named Diana Foster his Sole Executrix who had by The Deceased Husband one Son by Name John Harris who had Severall Children now but one alive whome yor Humble Petitioner Maried and has Now Issue by her, being The Grand Child of The Afforesaid Thomas Harris Deceased, And Lives Now upon a Plantation formerly Lawfull possessed by The Afforesaid Thomas Harris, as Your Petitioner is now Ready And willing to Make Appear to this Honorable Councill Board when permitted, by Such Evidence Now Ready to Declare The truth of their Knowledge.

And Your Humble Petitioner being daily Threatend to be disposessed by Henry and Thomas Swann pretending a Right by way of Escheat Which your Humble Petitioner Earnestly Craves Your Honors will for Releife in so Just a Matter take into your Serious Consideration The premises There being An Apparent heiris att The time of That Pretended Escheating Tho In her Minority And without friend, to protest such proceedings, I Do hope for Advice from This Honorable Board where to flye to for Remedy, att Common Law, or Equity upon such great Disturbance, The aforesaid Henry and Thomas pretending to a Decree in Chancery That gives them title to The Said Land or Plantation Which I humbly pray may be Inspected into and The Great hardship That attends yor Petitioner if so Illeagally Prosecuted and Debard from his Just Right And yor Humble petitioner as in Duty bound shall ever pray etc.

[*Endorsed:*]
The Petition of Nathaniel Nicholson
Post pond

[*CCR 148*]

North Carolina Ss. November 27th 1708

Whereas Richard Devenporte was Lawfully summoned to Appear Att a Councill Board now held att The house of James Thickpens as An Evidence for Nathl. Nickholson And being aged about sixty sixe years and very unable and Incapable of Travelling Do begg leave to give my Deposition And I do now swear upon The holy Evalgelist That I never did know That Thomas Harris of this Province Deceased was ever a Tennant so far as I Know but Enjoyed his Land That Nathl. Nickholson now Lives upon peaceably and quietly dureing his life, And further This Deponant saith Not.

Richard Devenport his marke

[*Endorsed:*]
The Deposition of Richd. Devenport
Jurat Coram me The day within mentioned Fran. Foster

[*CCR 148*]

No. Carolina Novber. 25th 1708

The deposition of Wm. Godfrey aged about 50 years or thereabouts sworne upon the holy Evanglesist saith That Thomas Harris the first settler on the land where now Nathaniell Nichollson liveth near Muddy Creek, did never know any person laying claim to the said land and so with out molestation did possesse the same dureing his life, and further saith not.

Sworne before me Wm. Godfreys marke
William Barclift
Wittnesse present
Thomas Blitchenden
John Hecklefield

The above deposition Elizabeth Hecklefield doth swear to and knoweth no more as by her oath she doth affirme the date abovesaid.

Sworne to before me the above date Elizabeth Hecklefields marke
William Barclift
Thomas Blitchenden
John Hecklefield

[*Endorsed:*]
The Deposition Wm. Godfrey and Elizabeth Hecklefield

[*CCR 148*]

North Carolina ss. To the Honorable Governor and Councill etc.

The humble Petition of John Evans Most humbly Sheweth that your Petitioner is an Inhabitant of Coratuck in this Government And that Sometime in October last being upon the Road in the Same precinct and in the Peace of our Soveraigne Lady the Queen was forcibly Sett upon by Phillip Stone of the Said precinct and was then and there Robbed by the said Stone of A Bill of Eighteen pounds payable from the said Stone to your Petitioner who prayes to be relieved by your Honors (the premisses Consider'd) And he Shall pray etc.

John Evans

[*Endorsed:*]

Sworne to by John Evans the 2d Day of November before the Grand Councell

Per Tho. Snoden Clericus Curiae

[*Notes to Clerks of Court*]

[*CCR 188*]

Bro. Chevin

Inclosed is a Declaration fyled with me about 11 dayes Since and A Letter to Mr. Phillipps [*illegible*] please to Deliver assoon as it comes to Hand. I have Sent it open if you Should not See him you may discharge the Action between Gregory and Mayo I hope to See you Sometime too [*illegible*] and bring those Chancery papers as Ordered and [*illegible*].

March the last 1702

Your Bro. and ready Servant
Tho. Abington

[*Endorsed:*]
To Mr. Nath. Chevin
Clerk of the Generall Cort
With Care and Speed I pray

[*CCR 188*]

July the 7th 1702

Bro. Nat.

By Order of John Slocumb I have here sent you A Bills of sale, and desires you to send me word when Receved all at present in greatt hast from who is yours to Command.

Levi Truewhitt Court Clk.

I have mist a bond of one Walter Cradock which I beleave I Sealed up in the last returne to you under a mistake if I have pray lett me know of it.

[*Endorsed:*]
Capt. Goodridgs Letter of Atturny [*sic*]

[*CR 2.001*]

Agust 16: 1704

Sir

Having had very greatt loss and dammadge in whatt I had aboard the Briganteen by Henry Montfortt the masterrs carlessness and negligence would ther for desyer you to enter ane actione of the case aganst him for me for four hundered Pound damages and another actione in myne and mr. David Hendersons nam for three hundered Pound dammages and send up writt by the bearer also I have sentt down the copyes of the declarations which [*illegible*] the soe necessary or convenient to alter them being drawne in hast doe itt and dispatch mr. Henderson as soon as possible Sir.

Your friend
Tho. Pollock

[*CR 2.001*]

Mr. Snoden Xbr the 18th 1704

Sir

Have here inclosed to you five declarations for which desire you will enter Actions accordingly and allso issue out Summons for the Evidences which are incerted on the back side of each declaration, desire you would be as expeditious as possibly you can because Some of the persons live att Pamplicoe however desire they may be arrested to the next generall court which is what offers at present from your friend and Servant

Wm. Freyley

[*Endorsed:*]
To Mr. Thoms. Snoden In Pequimins These

[*CCR 187*]

Mr. Tho. Snoden I have Bargained with the honorable Governor for all the Land I hold in Scopernung River being 1136 Acers bought of Colonel Polocke as apeares Upon Record with Rights and Surveys in his name, and 640 Acers Surveyd by Jon. Anderson with Rights in the office, Please to Gett Patents of purchase and Gett them Reddy against the next meeting of the Governor and Councell is the nedfull from Your Servant.

8th Janry. 1704 Godfre. Spruill

Mr. Tho. Snoden I desyre you to Enter the wast Land between Edwd. Batcheler Edwd. Phelps Jon. Hassall and Godfrey Spruill and Isue a warrent to the Surveyor; to Survey it for me this Spring is the Request of your Servant.

8th Janry. 1704 Wm. Wilkison

Doctor Spruel Noat to Mr. Snoden
Joseph Jordan Dr.

To Drawing Information	00=16=08
To Entring plea	00=01=00
To Recording venire	00=00=04
To 12 Jury Oaths	00=04=00
To Recording Jury Oath and verdict	00=02=00
To Order	00=01=00
To Summons 4 Evidences	00=04=00
To 4 Evidences Oaths	00=01=04
To Recording Gale Queens Attorney	00=01=00
	01=11=04
	2= 8

1=	8=	8
1=	11=	4
1=	6=	8
1=	8=	8
4—	6—	8

[*CCR 191*]

Brother Snoden

These are to Request you to apeare for me this Generall Court to prosecute my action as I am attorney of Jno. Redwood Versus Jno. Pettiver in a Refferrence from Last Court for so doing this shall be your warrant from per

Your Brother and Servant
Nath. Chevin

[*Endorsed:*]
Mr. Redwoods Letter of Attourney to Mr. Chivins

INDEX

Index

Cases, proper names, and subjects are entered in this index. Each case is entered under the names of plaintiff and defendant. Ordinarily it is entered under all other names appearing in the heading, but in some instances cross-references are given instead. Lengthy headings are abbreviated in all entries except those for plaintiffs. In actions nominally brought by attorneys, the attorneys are regarded as plaintiffs for indexing purposes, and headings are abbreviated in entries under the names of the real plaintiffs in such actions. Garnishees are not named in the headings for actions initiated by attachment, nor are such actions entered under their names. Garnishees, however, may be named as plaintiffs or defendants in certain proceedings related to attachment actions which for indexing purposes are treated as separate cases. Criminal actions and contempt proceedings are entered in the name of the crown, although some of these may have been brought in the name of the proprietors.

Multiple cases bearing the same heading are distinguished by numerals enclosed in square brackets following the caption. A series of numerals indicating the number of such cases is enclosed in a single set of brackets if the actions have identical page references. Otherwise, each case is identified by a numeral set off in brackets and followed by the references pertinent to that case. For indexing purposes, appeals are treated the same way as multiple cases. References which may pertain to any of the actions in such a group are cited for all.

For indexing purposes, one spelling of each person's name has been selected from the most prevalent spelling occurring in the documents. Variant spellings are given in parentheses in the first entry under the name but not in subsequent entries. A cross-reference to the selected spelling is given under most variants of the surname. Cross-references are given between names known to refer to the same person, such as the maiden and married names of a woman, and between those thought, but with a degree of uncertainty, to be variants of the same name. Separate entries are made for individuals bearing the same name; an additional entry is made for references which may pertain to any of those individuals.

Modern spelling is used for place-names unless the editor has been unable to identify the place, in which case the spelling is one occurring in the documents. Variant spellings, in parentheses, are given for North Carolina place names and a few others. Cross-references to the spelling used in the entry are given under some variants of local place-names but not those closely resembling the modern spelling. Subject entries are in modern spelling.

INDEX

INDEX

INDEX

INDEX